SAMIZDAT, TAMIZDAT, AND BEYOND

Studies in Contemporary European History

Editors:

Konrad Jarausch, Lurcy Professor of European Civilization, University of North Carolina, Chapel Hill, and a Director of the Zentrum für Zeithistorische Studien, Potsdam, Germany

Henry Rousso, Senior Fellow at the Institut d'historie du temps present (Centre national de la recherché scientifique, Paris) and co-founder of the European network "EURHISTXX"

Volume 1
Between Utopia and Disillusionment: A Narrative of the Political Transformation in Eastern Europe
   Henri Vogt

Volume 2
The Inverted Mirror: Mythologizing the Enemy in France and Germany, 1898–1914
   Michael E. Nolan

Volume 3
Conflicted Memories: Europeanizing Contemporary Histories
   Edited by Konrad H. Jarausch and Thomas Lindenberger with the Collaboration of Annelie Ramsbrock

Volume 4
Playing Politics with History: The Bundestag Inquiries into East Germany
   Andrew H. Beattie

Volume 5
Alsace to the Alsatians? Visions and Divisions of Alsatian Regionalism, 1870–1939
   Christopher J. Fischer

Volume 6
A European Memory? Contested Histories and Politics of Remembrance
   Edited by Małgorzata Pakier and Bo Stråth

Volume 7
Experience and Memory: The Second World War in Europe
   Edited by Jörg Echternkamp and Stefan Martens

Volume 8
Children, Families, and States: Time Policies of Childcare, Preschool, and Primary Education in Europe
   Edited by Karen Hagemann, Konrad H. Jarausch, and Cristina Allemann-Ghionda

Volume 9
Social Policy in the Smaller European Union States
   Edited by Gary B. Cohen, Ben W. Ansell, Robert Henry Cox, and Jane Gingrich

Volume 10
A State of Peace in Europe: West Germany and the CSCE, 1966–1975
   Petri Hakkarainen

Volume 11
Visions of the End of the Cold War
   Edited by Frederic Bozo, Marie-Pierre Rey, N. Piers Ludlow, and Bernd Rother

Volume 12
Investigating Srebrenica: Institutions, Facts, Responsibilities
   Edited by Isabelle Delpla, Xavier Bougarel, and Jean-Louis Fournel

Volume 13
Samizdat, Tamizdat, and Beyond: Transnational Media During and After Socialism
   Edited by Friederike Kind-Kovács and Jessie Labov

Volume 14
Shaping the Transnational Sphere: Experts, Networks, and Issues from the 1840s to the 1930s
   Edited by Davide Rodogno, Bernhard Struck, and Jakob Vogel

Volume 15
Tailoring Truth: Politicizing the Past and Negotiating Memory in East Germany, 1945–1990
   Jon Berndt Olsen

SAMIZDAT, TAMIZDAT, AND BEYOND

Transnational Media During and After Socialism

Edited by
Friederike Kind-Kovács
and Jessie Labov

Published in 2013 by
Berghahn Books
www.berghahnbooks.com

© 2013, 2015 Friederike Kind-Kovács and Jessie Labov
First paperback edition published in 2015.

All rights reserved.
Except for the quotation of short passages
for the purposes of criticism and review, no part of this book
may be reproduced in any form or by any means, electronic or
mechanical, including photocopying, recording, or any information
storage and retrieval system now known or to be invented,
without written permission of the publisher.

Library of Congress Cataloging-in-Publication Data

Samizdat, tamizdat, and beyond : transnational media during and after socialism / edited by Friederike Kind-Kovács and Jessie Labov.
  p. cm. — (Studies in contemporary European history ; 13)
  Includes bibliographical references and index.
  ISBN 978-0-85745-585-7 (hardback : alk. paper) — ISBN 978-1-78238-918-7 (paperback : alk. paper) — ISBN 978-0-85745-586-4 (ebook)
  1. Mass media—Political aspects—Europe, Eastern—History—20th century. 2. Underground literature—Europe, Eastern—History and criticism. 3. Mass media and culture—Europe, Eastern. 4. Post-communism—Europe, Eastern. I. Kind-Kovács, Friederike, 1978– II. Labov, Jessie.
P95.82.E852S36 2012
302.230947′0904—dc23

2012001692

British Library Cataloguing in Publication Data

A catalogue record for this book is available from the British Library.

Printed on acid-free paper

ISBN: 978-0-85745-585-7 hardback
ISBN: 978-1-78238-918-7 paperback
ISBN: 978-0-85745-586-4 ebook

CONTENTS

List of Illustrations   viii

Acknowledgments   ix

Foreword   xi
    Thomas Lindenberger

Introduction
    Samizdat and Tamizdat   1
        Friederike Kind-Kovács and Jessie Labov

Section I: Producing and Circulating Samizdat/Tamizdat Before 1989

Chapter 1
    Ardis Facsimile and Reprint Editions: Giving Back Russian Literature   27
        Ann Komaromi

Chapter 2
    The Baltic Connection: Transnational Samizdat Networks between Émigrés in Sweden and the Democratic Opposition in Poland   51
        Lars Fredrik Stöcker

Chapter 3
    Radio Free Europe and Radio Liberty as the "Echo Chamber" of Tamizdat   70
        Friederike Kind-Kovács

Chapter 4
    Contact Beyond Borders and Historical Problems: *Kultura,* Russian Emigration, and the Polish Opposition   92
        Karolina Zioło-Pużuk

Section II: Diffusing Nonconformist Ideas Through Samizdat/Tamizdat Before 1989

Chapter 5
"Free Conversations in an Occupied Country": Cultural Transfer, Social Networking, and Political Dissent in Romanian Tamizdat 107
Cristina Petrescu

Chapter 6
The Danger of Over-Interpreting Dissident Writing in the West: Communist Terror in Czechoslovakia, 1948–1968 137
Muriel Blaive

Chapter 7
Renaissance or Reconstruction? Intellectual Transfer of Civil Society Discourses Between Eastern and Western Europe 156
Agnes Arndt

Section III: Transforming Modes and Practices of Alternative Culture

Chapter 8
The Bards of Magnitizdat: An Aesthetic Political History of Russian Underground Recordings 175
Brian A. Horne

Chapter 9
Writing about Apparently Nonexistent Art: The Tamizdat Journal *A-Ja* and Russian Unofficial Arts in the 1970s and 1980s 190
Valentina Parisi

Chapter 10
"Video Knows No Borders": Samizdat Television and the Unofficial Public Sphere in "Normalized" Czechoslovakia 206
Alice Lovejoy

Section IV: Moving From Samizdat/Tamizdat To Alternative Media Today

Chapter 11
Postprintium? Digital Literary Samizdat on the Russian Internet 221
Henrike Schmidt

Chapter 12
    Independent Media, Transnational Borders, and Networks of Resistance: Collaborative Art Radio between Belgrade (Radio B92) and Vienna (ORF)   245
        Daniel Gilfillan

Chapter 13
    "From Wallpapers to Blogs": Samizdat and Internet in China   263
        Martin Hala

Chapter 14
    Reflections on the Revolutions in Europe: Lessons for the Middle East and the Arab Spring   281
        Barbara J. Falk

Afterword
    The Legacies of Dissent: Charter 77, the Helsinki Effect, and the Emergence of a European Public Space   316
        Jacques Rupnik

Appendix   333

Selected Bibliography   339

Notes on Contributors   346

Index   351

Illustrations

1.1. Ardis facsimile reprint editions   28

1.2. Carl and Ellendea Proffer in the Ardis office, ca. 1977   29

1.3. Title page from the facsimile reprint of Osip Mandel'shtam, *Egipetskaia marka* (Ardis 1976)   30

1.4. Ardis carriage logo from the facsimile reprint of Osip Mandel'shtam, *Egipetskaia marka* (Ardis 1976)   30

1.5. Title page of Vladimir Nabokov's *Lolita,* Russian edition (Ardis, 1976)   37

1.6. Vladimir Nabokov's *Lolita* (Ardis, 1976), page 23   42

Acknowledgments

The very concepts behind this volume would never have found light without a generous grant from the German Volkswagen Foundation's funding initiative "Unity amidst Variety? Intellectual Foundations and Requirements for an Enlarged Europe," which helped to establish a vital and productive transatlantic community of scholars working in this area. The Zentrum für Zeithistorische Forschung (ZZF) in Potsdam provided the intellectual setting to initiate and elaborate the project, and has offered continual support since then. The Institut für die Wissenschaften vom Menschen (Institute for Human Sciences, IWM) in Vienna made it possible for this newly formed community to meet for the first time at an international conference. Without the intellectual contribution and practical assistance of the IWM, in particular of Susanne Fröschl, Luise Wascher, Jana Matischok, and above all the guidance of IWM fellows János Kovács and Klaus Nellen, this very important face-to-face meeting of samizdat/tamizdat researchers, archivists, and former practitioners would have not been realized.

Olga Zaslavskaya and Camelia Crăciun were two of the key figures in forming this community, along with Ann Komaromi and Barbara Falk, and we remain grateful to them as friends and colleagues for all of their help. It was thanks to Olga Zaslavskaya in particular that the International Samizdat [Research] Association was established at the Open Society Archivum in Budapest. IS[R]A is closely concerned with building links between archives, libraries, and researchers of samizdat/tamizdat; the present volume represents the scholarly side of this project, and is clearly the result of the momentum behind IS[R]A as it begins to make its mark in the larger field of Cold War Studies.

This volume has achieved its present shape due to the efforts of multiple editors, reviewers, and massagers of text, who provided valuable suggestions about the scope, vision, and intention of the collection. Among many, we would like to single out Mike Levine, Paulina Bren, Ema Vyroubálova, Kevin Rothrock, and Sinziana Paltineanu. Without their contribution this book would be a bulkier and bumpier journey for its readers, and much less of a labor of love for its editors.

Along the long road from Vienna there have been three scholars who have kept this project alive through their advice and counsel to its editors: Marsha Siefert, Irena Grudzińska Gross, and Thomas Lindenberger. They are the ghosts in this machine, absolutely tireless in providing intellectual feedback, and always willing to share valuable insight from their years of publishing.

Our friends and colleagues at our respective academic homes, the Department for Southeast and East European History at the University of Regensburg and the Department of Slavic and East European Languages and Literatures at the Ohio State University, have also been very important in providing us with the intellectual space and temporal flexibility that have allowed us to finalize this book project.

It was thanks to the interest and enthusiasm of our series editors at Berghahn Books, Konrad Jarausch and Henry Rousso, that we have had the pleasure of working with Ann Przyzycki DeVita and Marion Berghahn to bring this book to the public we have been seeking. We thank them—as well as the contributors to this volume—for their patience and faith in us throughout their process.

Last but most important has been the support of those nearest and dearest to the two editors: Gyuri, Dani, Gyula, and Laura, as well as our closest families and friends. Throughout the entire project, they have contributed enormously to this volume by accepting it into our daily lives, and for this they deserve our deepest appreciation.

Foreword

Thomas Lindenberger

Does Europe have—or *is* it—a public sphere of its own? In the times of the endless euro crisis this question seems to become more and more of a purely academic nature. Financial entanglements force Europeans to discuss shared interests and values among themselves to a degree and with an intensity unthinkable only some years ago. At the same time a new bifurcated structure of the continent is taking shape: it's no longer East vs. West, it is rather a North-South partition that is demarcating zones of stability and sustainable prosperity from those of chronic underemployment, economic stagnation, and receding standards of living. Before we begin to take the enforced and accelerated Europeanization of public spheres as yet another price to pay for the mixed blessings of capitalist globalization, it is worthwhile to look back on its prehistory: from this we could learn that transnational open communication among Europeans was promoted from below as much as enforced from above; it was—and can always be—an instance of critique and challenge of the powers that be. Far from ever constituting a supranational public replacing existing national public spheres, an ongoing stream of transnational exchanges of ideas and their means of representation has always accompanied the ruptures and transitions Europeans have had to go through.

Reflecting on the "Europeanness" of the continent's societies and their shared institutions, policies, and communication has now become popular among historians as well. This book testifies to one rather recent example of such critical debates reaching across borders of states and material constraints. While most accounts addressing this issue refer to century-old shared traditions and practices such as the Renaissance, the Enlightenment, and the rise of modernity in general, much less attention has been paid so far to the question of the imminent prehistory of today's Europe, namely to the era of the Cold War. Twenty years after the unexpected dissolution of the Soviet Empire and the swift political and economic integration of its satellites into the EU it is high time to assess what the project of European integration might owe to the prior experience of exchanging ideas and sharing projects for a joint future.

This is where the collection of essays in this book takes off: it offers rich material for reconstructing the historical existence of a transnational and transsystemic space of communication during the continent's four-decade-long division. This precarious exchange of ideas, sounds, and images relied on practicing one of the core enlightenment principles, namely the human right to free expression of opinion independent of any national or other spatial restrictions imposed by political rule. Contrary to the conventional notion of a continent neatly partitioned by the Iron Curtain whose parts were supposedly isolated from each other, these contributions document the myriad of partly official, partly unofficial and clandestine communication lines between nonconformist writers, publishers, and human rights activists that were upheld and intensified during the Cold War and would eventually contribute to its ending.

The point of departure is the twin phenomenon of samizdat and tamizdat. "Samizdat" ("publishing on one's own" under communist rule) was the necessary consequence of the communist regimes' monopolistic control of all publishing in the countries of the Soviet bloc and gained particular importance with the partial reduction of totalitarian pressure on the "captive nations" following Stalin's death. Much less familiar to Western audiences was samizdat's derivative "tamizdat" ("publishing there"). It stands for the attempts and practices to publish Eastern bloc authors in the West, entailing an intricate network of actors such as smugglers, translators, émigrés, writers, and publishers as well as diplomats. The complex political, social, and discursive texture of this literary practice led to the emergence of a distinct transnational literary community across the politically divided continent. It was marked by bidirectionality: against the stereotypes of "the West" informing and instructing "the East," it was eventually the impact of the "Other Europe" in the East, sought out by Western publishers for a Western public, which made a difference during the last decade of the Cold War.

These intellectuals' endeavours to create an international "community of letters" that would confront and overcome authoritarian restrictions on publishing in single states stand in the long tradition of the *République des lettres,* which found its first apogee in prerevolutionary, late absolutist France. Censorship, secret police surveillance, and arbitrary persecution of critical minds were already the hallmark of the earliest modern state authorities in Europe. Since they were intrinsically based on the principle of territoriality of rule, borders were highly significant, and shuttling between different territories in order to circumvent silencing and persecution became a standard procedure. But the Cold War chapter of this long story cannot—not yet, helas!—be regarded as a mere epilogue to a final overcoming of authoritarian "regulation" of the circulation of thoughts, sounds, and images. The highly precarious status of journalism in ex-Soviet countries such as Russia, Belarus, and Ukraine, and more recently even in an EU member state such as Hungary, disabuses us of any comforting security.

Undoubtedly, samizdat-tamizdat is of more than purely academic relevance, it conveys an important lesson for the future of European intellectual and cultural life. And since the worldwide access to information technology allows us nowadays to communicate with similar intensity around the globe, the same can be said for European exchanges with intellectuals, artists, and human right activists in China, North Africa, the Middle East, and both Americas. Although writers, journalists, and artists devoted to the values of free expression may sometimes seem idealistic and, more often than not, isolated, if not outright marginalized, one thing remains obvious: their intransigence and indefatigability will remain a fundamental prerequisite for any improvement of the human condition, everywhere on the globe, and therefore also in Europe, its latest province.

Vienna, September 2011

Introduction

SAMIZDAT AND TAMIZDAT
Entangled Phenomena?

Friederike Kind-Kovács and Jessie Labov

When we try to characterize the post-Soviet societies that emerged in Central and Eastern Europe after 1989, we often remark on the free flow of people, goods, information, and ideas across borders that were formerly closed. In fact, our current attempts to define the time we live in as one of global, open access have only strengthened the image of Cold War–era Eastern Europe as a collection of isolated and closed societies. This volume attempts to provide a very different picture of pre-1989 Eastern Europe, marking the pathways and networks along which information and ideas *did* circulate across the Iron Curtain, and across the internal borders of the USSR and its satellite states. The parallel phenomena of samizdat ("do-it-yourself" underground publishing) and tamizdat (publishing abroad),[1] as well as the much broader circulation of cultural products that was instigated and sustained by these practices, in many ways anticipates what we identify as "cultural globalization" in Eastern Europe today.[2] Since tamizdat was dependent on the existence of a transnational system of literary production, diffusion, and reception, we hope to approach tamizdat not only from its textual side but also to portray it as a transnational social activity with its own rules and practices. Without diminishing the experience of the vast majority of people who never touched a single piece of underground literature (and certainly were not free to travel outside of the fixed boundaries of their state), we feel there is a need to chronicle how cultural expressions did cross borders in different forms, how and why there were opportunities for this exchange, and where we can see the legacy of this system in the post-Soviet sphere. This volume additionally aims to cross the borders within the study of anticommunist dissent that have constrained our understanding of samizdat and alternative culture

---

Notes for this chapter begin on page 19.

in Eastern Europe, broadening the field to include many new approaches, disciplines, and directions for future research.[3]

In addition to providing a short overview of the history of samizdat studies, an outline of our conceptual ideas, and a brief resume of the individual articles in the volume, we would like to use this space to introduce some of the concepts that have emerged from this debate, including some that challenge the very approaches laid out in this volume. We need to take into account both the materiality of the texts that were being published and distributed during the Cold War, and the intellectual discourse that resulted from their movement. In fact, we are only just beginning to develop these and other critical approaches to samizdat/tamizdat and related phenomena in alternative culture. Rather than promote another celebratory, anniversary-style series of memoirs recounting the experience of former dissidents, we hope instead to encourage a dialogue with young scholars that raises difficult questions and conflicting perspectives on literary and cultural phenomena before 1989. A critical approach is all the more needed, because since the collapse of Soviet-type state socialism, samizdat has typically been considered simply a relic of the heroic epoch of political opposition and protest movements. Before the phenomenon is entirely fossilized as a museum piece of Cold War politics, this volume hopes to revive the complex character of samizdat and tamizdat, unearthing its cultural and social components, and showing a space in nonconformist culture where visual art, text, and sound meet. In this context, we would like to address another major misconception about samizdat: that it was an exclusively Polish, Russian, Czechoslovak, Hungarian, or even Eastern European phenomenon. This volume offers a new perspective on the Cold War era, telling the story of the cross-border transmission of a pan-European and transatlantic uncensored culture.

While the essays collected in this volume by no means cover every possible avenue into the study of samizdat/tamizdat, they do represent a wide range of possibilities, based on a broad understanding of the terms. Most articles concerning samizdat begin with a short history of the term and then arrive at some type of definition, yet there are a seemingly endless number of possible definitions. Is it a publishing or a reading practice? A proscribed set of texts? A state of mind? There is even less of a consensus on the lesser-known term *tamizdat:* what determines whether a text is tamizdat or not? Its content? Its producer? Its conditions of publication? Or its eventual audience? By asking each of the authors to address the particular question "what makes us consider a text samizdat/tamizdat?" we present a diverse discussion on the possible definitions of these phenomena. While we are aware that our understanding of samizdat and tamizdat might be subject to debate, we nevertheless want to propose some working definitions beforehand. As the goal of this volume is to mark out the widest possible area for study of these two, interrelated phenomena without losing coherence, we would like to include all of these possibilities in what *can* be samizdat/tamizdat, and construct a negative definition of the term, identifying specifically what is *not* samizdat/tamizdat, in order to determine what *is*. Simply speaking: any text (written or visual) endorsed by an official organ of the state that reaches its audience without any change in meaning cannot be understood as samizdat. That same text might be transformed into samizdat, or, as Maya Nadkarni suggests, take on a "samizdat function," under the right circumstances.[4] Thus, one way of recognizing a samizdat text might be by its distinctive aesthetic or material quality (for example, its typewritten style). With the word *tamizdat*, on the other hand, we denote all those texts that mirror the samizdat world in the West. The negative definition of tamizdat concerns geography as well as hegemony: a text not originating outside of the country or region of origin that does not in some way define itself in reference to the existing political and/or aesthetic conventions of the state of origin cannot be understood as tamizdat. Tamizdat, thus, refers to texts published abroad, either officially reprinted samizdat, or texts first appearing in the West. The audience for both kinds of texts ranges from the samizdat readership in the former Soviet bloc to émigré communities, to Western intellectuals concerned with developments in the East. The fact that samizdat/tamizdat were written symbols of the human suffering in the Eastern bloc encouraged a less critical and often even naive reading of the texts both then and now. Thus, we hope here to critically view some of the inherent dangers of samizdat/tamizdat publication, without diminishing its relevance as visualizations of human experiences. They represented a compendium of knowledge that was—to a large extent—untouched by censorship. One could even argue that taken together, samizdat and tamizdat represent a collective memoir of uncensored literary activity during the Cold War.

Furthermore, as there are countless examples of cultural expressions that do not seem to qualify as samizdat or tamizdat, our suggestion for future study of the field is to explore exactly those semantic borders. Samizdat itself quite often crossed the line between official and unofficial culture, in spheres of communication sometimes referred to as the "grey zone," meaning cultural products "on the borders of legality and illegality."[5] Looking at both the shared patterns of samizdat/tamizdat publishing activity, and at the thin line between official and unofficial cultures,[6] we can see the advantages of expanding the conceptual field. Indeed, we should also look for examples of the phenomenon that seem to challenge our understanding of what *can* or *cannot* be samizdat/tamizdat, to the sometimes unstable distinction between samizdat and tamizdat, or perhaps to those texts whose meaning shifts depending on the conditions of production or dissemination. At times, this inclusive approach to samizdat/tamizdat leads directly to a the wider field of underground or alternative culture; we feel that further integration between the study of samizdat/tamizdat and the much wider field of alternative cultural studies can only strengthen our grasp of the concept, not diminish it.

Reassessing Trajectories of Samizdat/Tamizdat Research

The scholarly treatment of samizdat began with the treatment of its political dimension—mostly within the USSR—in the 1970s.[7] Since that point, the dominant narrative surrounding the study of samizdat and tamizdat has consisted of a political history of how internal nonconformism[8] contributed to the end of state socialism. In fact, during the last stages of the Cold War, this narrative was joined to the political project itself, as human rights groups (and Sovietologists alike) drew international attention to the work of underground writers and publishers, at times to protect them from persecution, and at times to magnify their political impact. Even in other contexts, these terms are invoked in a political way to describe *any* clandestine production and circulation of texts. Collections such as *Political, Social, and Religious Thought of Russian Samizdat* in 1977 attempted to place samizdat firmly in one or another ideological camp, with the main interest presumed to be its content, without regard for its material form.[9]

It was not until H. Gordon Skilling and Stanisław Barańczak's work beginning in the early 1980s that attention focused on the *practice* of underground publishing as a phenomenon, and shifted much of the theater of operation to Central Europe. Skilling's 1982 article "Return to the Pre-Gutenberg Era?" offers a cross-cultural and transnational view of the samizdat phenomenon, with separate sections devoted to Russian, Czech, Polish, and Chinese forms.[10] He argues for some historical continuity with earlier types of censored writing (such as that which led to Dostoevsky's imprisonment for circulating an anti-clerical letter from Belinsky to Gogol), but declares modern samizdat "a new medium of communication."[11] Barańczak's 1982 article also stresses the social practices that had arisen around samizdat, extending samizdat's domain from a completely clandestine underground operation to a much wider phenomenon of independent publishing. In the 1980s, the political force of the samizdat phenomenon was understood less through its explicit political content, and more through the way it began to penetrate other aspects of life, including the "grey zone" of existence that was neither official nor unofficial.[12] In the late 1970s, Dimitry S. Pospielovsky published the first and only study of the interrelationship between the sphere of samizdat and of tamizdat before the transition era.[13] He suggested viewing these two spheres of textual production and circulation not as isolated phenomena but as two interconnected forms of literary expression of one and the same Russian culture.[14]

In the early 1990s, as the need for samizdat and tamizdat itself suddenly evaporated, there were volumes published in almost every national context "commemorating" the existence of these unofficial literary spheres.[15] We might see this as an attempt to mark the end of an era or as an effort to preserve the cultural memory of the literary underground.[16] There is some historical irony here—a negative side-effect of the tamizdat system itself— as the majority of materials collected during the Cold War in the West remained there after 1989, beyond easy access for its original producers and other scholars from the former East.[17] Another major feature of early transition-era treatments of samizdat is the concern for the ex-samizdat writers in the post-1989 literary marketplace. Particularly in regards to Central European countries, articles emphasize what Jakub Karpiński calls "The Difficult Return to Normality": the culture shock that many writers and artists felt after 1989 when they lost an audience for artistic expressions that had previously *mattered* because of the limitations imposed upon them.[18]

More recently since the late 1990s, the emphasis in scholarship about samizdat and tamizdat has shifted again, this time with more focus on the graphic and textual character of the samizdat/tamizdat text, the visual culture embedded in this practice, and the complex relationship between underground and "aboveground" culture in the former Soviet states. Serguei Oushakine's 2001 article "The Terrifying Mimicry of Samizdat"[19] insists that samizdat was simply an inverted reflection of the same dominant discourse that kept the authorities in power. Using a Foucauldian understanding of mimetic resistance as his reference point, Oushakine argues that samizdat created a closed circle of discourse between the powerful and the powerless, that "the dissidents' discursive dependence on the regime reflects a fundamental fact of the dissidents' ontological—that is, discursive—proximity to the regime they chose to mirror."[20] This view could not be further from the heroizing narrative of effective resistance to authority told about samizdat in the 1970s and 1980s, and perhaps could only have surfaced *after* 1989, when the discussion of samizdat had been in some respects depoliticized. The exhibition catalog emanating from the Forschungsstelle Osteuropa in Bremen, *Samizdat: alternative Kultur in Zentral- und Osteuropa, die 60er bis 80er Jahre,* includes several articles that focus on the visual aspects of samizdat as well as the history of how such materials were transferred across borders. This represents a growing interest in the material history of samizdat, also seen in articles about the historical legacy of underground publishing, and in Ann Komaromi's 2004 essay "The Material Existence of Soviet Samizdat."[21] Unlike Oushakine, Komaromi upholds the subversive nature of samizdat, but works through a poststructuralist frame to locate its most potent symbolic register in the aesthetics of the samizdat text: "The wretched material character of the samizdat text evokes the deep abyss between the material and the ideal and between the desire for culture and the fear of its destruction. A sense of the width of this great gulf marks samizdat culture."[22] She sees the difference between the samizdat text and the official text as parodic, rather than mimetic, and effectively decouples the political content of samizdat from its meaning as a Baudrillardian object-sign, pointing our attention to its physicality, and the importance of that physicality in the consumptive practice of reading samizdat. The implications of Komaromi's views reach far into the present collection,[23] as we attempt to link the circulation of samizdat and tamizdat, and further explore its aesthetic resonances in other media.

Another major implication of the focus on the material is an attention to the aesthetics of the samizdat/tamizdat text, an approach following Komaromi's 2004 essay as well as her work since. Komaromi has suggested that we turn to the growing field of book history and print culture for inspiration in attending to the aesthetics of the samizdat/tamizdat text.[24] In this approach to samizdat/tamizdat, the effect of repeated transmission across borders of a single text via different media, through the hands of professional and amateur redaction, leads to an accumulation of "noise" that becomes a mark of distinction. These typographic, graphic, material, or aural traces allow us to read, for example, one iteration of a samizdat text separately from that same text reproduced in tamizdat. Among other modes of interpretation, this approach involves identifying and decoding the noise generated by transmission, as well as taking into account the phenomenological effect of that noise on those consuming samizdat/tamizdat. It allows us to travel across medium with the text (e.g., from print to radio broadcast and back), and to extend the inquiry to other genres and forms of art. Despite their differences in approach, both Oushakine and Komaromi manage to steer the academic conversation about samizdat and, by implication, tamizdat away from the heavily politicized view of the 1970s, of the emphasis on socially engaged praxis of the 1980s, and the early 1990s narrative of crisis.[25]

In addition to new forms of reading and perceiving samizdat, new research has begun to expose the simultaneously productive and biased interdependence of literary underground movements and public/publishing spheres in the West and its cross-border impact. The new attention to cultural transfer across the Iron Curtain represents an innovative alternative to the Cold War narrative about a strict division of Europe. A small number of studies have emerged which delve deeper into deciphering the cultural and literary entanglements that went beyond the ideological contest between the socialist East and the capitalist West.[26] In particular, approaches proposed by Padraic Kenney and Patrick Major/Rana Mitter provide challenging tools with which to elaborate the manifold layers and forms of "diffusion" between East and West.[27] Ioana Popa has shown how translation channels actually enabled the transnational reception of samizdat texts outside their place of origin.[28]

The study of samizdat, however, has often ignored those forms of samizdat that did not contribute to the cause of developing civil society along the democratic model endorsed by leading dissidents. Despite being filtered before reaching the West, tamizdat texts reflect not only heroic views but also mirror the political and cultural complexity of the samizdat world. Instances of ultraconservative, nationalist, and anti-Semitic samizdat in Russia,[29] for example, remain underrepresented and underexplored in the critical literature about samizdat.[30] Apart from the questionable political opinions represented in the texts, the scholars have often failed to assess the reliability of samizdat and tamizdat as sources of information. As early as 1985, Thomas Oleszczuk had addressed the question of possible bias in samizdat,[31] setting out possible biases and distortions in samizdat content.[32] The possibility of bias involved in tamizdat was even greater. A recent study on tamizdat by Joseph Benatov proposes to critically evaluate the inherent danger of reading tamizdat as a representation of samizdat, as "a mental shorthand for interpreting the larger Eastern European socialist experience."[33] Benatov addresses the possibly negative consequences of that "cultural translation" of a samizdat text into a tamizdat text could have on the original text. While samizdat texts were produced in illegal spheres, their exposure to a Western public often resulted in the exclusive reading of tamizdat texts for their political subtexts. Peter Steiner's recent theoretical introduction to a special issue of *Poetics Today*, "Publish and Perish: *Samizdat* and Underground Cultural Practices in the Soviet Bloc II," encourages breaking altogether with this Cold War reading and interpretation of uncensored texts: "The concept of 'totalitarianism' that usually provides a convenient backdrop for any discussion of uncensored publishing in the Soviet Union and Eastern Europe exemplifies the perils of homogenizing some seventy years of Communism into an ahistoric sameness."[34] One can also see evidence of this emerging field in a number of recent historical studies, which have uncovered the limits of state socialism in the cultural sphere, as well revealed the transnational interconnectedness of Cold War societies.[35] The 2010 Aleksanteri volume *Winter Kept Us Warm: Cold War Interactions Reconsidered* breaks with the traditional pattern of Cold War studies, by exemplifying "interaction and connections between East and West"[36] as well as presenting "various actors engaged in mutually-beneficial cooperation,"[37] which ran counter to official politics. In many ways our volume mirrors this challenge, and instead of offering another "ahistorical" perspective on samizdat/tamizdat—as if it were always already a product of the Cold War—it elaborates the many unusual and also problematic facets of samizdat/tamizdat as a joint historical endeavor.

Mapping Out New Approaches to Transnational Diffusion

This volume crosses its first and perhaps most important border by going beyond the political sphere into the cultural one, presenting a new understanding of the history of samizdat/tamizdat as a history of parallel and of shared cultural developments that are not typically considered "samizdat." By bringing into focus its cultural significance, the current understanding of samizdat as a solely "dissident" medium with an overtly political message can be broadened. Uniting a range of cultural phenomena under the heading of alternative culture is based on the conviction that the term designates a community of deviance in relation to the cultural system of the state. Related areas of nonconformist activity beyond the explicitly political print publication embrace a much wider cultural sphere of alternative and semiofficial texts, including other forms and genres of literature, broadcast media, reproductions of visual art, and music.

While many different spheres of culture were bound together in resistance through nonconformist artistic expression, we also need to ask about the epistemological differences between these forms of art. How can we distinguish the cultural meaning of a samizdat text from a theatrical event, a film, or a magnitizdat recording? Martin Daughtry draws our attention to "the extraordinary value of performance, a value that both encompasses and exceeds the written text."[38] There *can* be a performative element involved in the transmission of samizdat/tamizdat texts we usually consider to be written: in radio broadcasts, at poetry readings, or text transformed through a musical rendition, as with so-called guitar poetry. But the social dimension of performance was most important for theater or for certain conceptual art exhibitions, which included a distribution of texts after the event. The challenge for this approach is to use the dimension of the performative to bridge the concept of samizdat as defining a *community* with more strictly aesthetic concerns, while still demonstrating how event-based forms were able to serve as a means of communication despite leaving no material trace of dissemination.

Another consequence of the interactive character of samizdat/tamizdat is the generation of social relationships through practice. As the critical positions of nonconformist authors inside the Soviet sphere and their Western counterparts were translated into literary exchanges, the circulating texts can be perceived both as visible ties as well as products of this social activity.[39] In particular, women were essential in running the machinery of samizdat publications in the East, smuggling texts, and supporting tamizdat publications in the West, while being almost completely eclipsed by their better-known male colleagues and husbands. Regardless of gender roles, the practice of samizdat/tamizdat was a fundamentally collaborative and cumulative phenomenon.[40] Thus, even a microhistorical study can reveal particular, critical junctions in the social network, and help us to comprehensively map how these underground and émigré networks of publishing and broadcasting fit together.[41]

We propose to read the system of samizdat/tamizdat circulation as much more than a single flow of material smuggled from East to West, or from West to East; it was a network of transfer and dissemination, translation and retranslation, amplification and distortion, and ultimately collecting and archiving, which we can still easily trace today. The philosophy of samizdat/tamizdat has always been to promote a free flow of information and culture independent of any political or cultural border. However, literary circulation across borders raises questions about the reception of texts outside their place of origination. Within these patterns of diffusion, the transfer of literature across borders also resulted in an aesthetic cross-fertilization between two cultural spheres that had become visible in the broad aesthetic variety of tamizdat text. When reaching a Western audience, samizdat not only represented an "aesthetic revolt against socialist realism"[42] inside the Soviet bloc, but also often induced changes in the Western reception of the text. The aesthetic form of a typewritten poem made visual the difficulties of its physical production and in this way the daily life of the existing uncensored literary world. On the other hand, when being reprinted in a Western "official" literary or cultural journal, tamizdat publications often lost their original aesthetic form. After all, samizdat authors had originally crossed aesthetic boundaries of the professional text understanding when relying on the "pre-Gutenberg" practice of publishing. The inability of the literary underground to come up to the official publishing standards had developed into a resistance to the official norms of publishing. With the exception of a range of samizdat art journals, samizdat texts were often not printed on high-quality paper, and were rarely well-formatted or illustrated. But it was exactly in this poverty that they propagated a new aesthetic of the text, namely one of deformation. And when deciding to rely again on official publishers (this time Western), underground authors had to leave behind the long dominant image of their texts as the product of "do-it-yourself" activity.[43]

The translation of samizdat into Western languages and of Western literature into Eastern European languages also served to give these writers an international literary existence across the Iron Curtain. In this case, official Western publications found their way into the literary underground inside the Soviet sphere, overcoming the geographic, political and literary divisions between the East and West. Here the relevant questions are about the function of samizdat literature as a nexus between cultures of different political histories, different media practices, as well as different literary traditions. Even if the transnational community was divided into a "Free Europe" and a "Captured Europe," tamizdat makes the case against the existence of merely one-sided cultural transfers from the West to the East during the Cultural Cold War. Thus, the articles collected in this volume challenge the thesis that there had only existed "a one-sided transfer of the political ideologies, models and life forms of the Western social order to the east, to the socialist countries."[44] Even further, the idea of "self-publication" originated in the USSR, and spread among nonconformist authors and activists across national borders, inspiring like-minded people in other state-socialist countries like Hungary and Poland to follow their examples. Thus, the spread of knowledge about similar materials outside one's own nation raised the interest in foreign samizdat material. As a response, a great deal of samizdat materials circulated secretly across the borders of the Soviet bloc.

Looking simultaneously at the history of the underground and transfer media offers a way to think past the predominant interpretation of the history of samizdat/tamizdat in national terms, since the entire phenomenon was dependent on the existence of transnational networks. Only a transnational approach can account for the emergence of these uncensored media in various countries at different times. This allows us to consider the possibility of samizdat in countries outside of the typical boundaries of Russia and the Visegrad countries. (Radio Free Europe/Radio Liberty, for example, operated in twenty-six languages across all of East-Central Europe and the former Soviet Republics.[45]) Articles on countries such as Romania and the former Yugoslavia—areas often overlooked in general treatments of this subject—enlarge our picture of samizdat in Southeastern Europe; we also cover the very particular case of FRG–GDR communication as both a site of and a gateway for the transfer of materials. Most importantly, in order to understand how both European literary movements and political thought developed during the late twentieth century, we need to know how writing from and about Central and Eastern Europe was disseminated across political borders, how it was read in widely different contexts in both East and West, and we need to especially reconsider émigré movements as a transnational phenomenon.

Additionally, while samizdat has historically shown no hesitation in crossing boundaries to reach all available media, we might ask whether the Internet is really just another "medium" or rather a different mode of communication. By including post-1989 independent media in this volume, we propose a new trajectory of the field of samizdat/tamizdat research. While an argument for historical continuity between the events of the 1970s and 1980s and the transition era cannot account for all the developments in independent media, certain cultural practices of transnational communication from the pre-1989 era continue in today's media environment. We can compare the underground circulation of uncensored texts in the Cold War era with recent examples of censorship and forms of independent media that continue to evolve today, looking, for example, at new media and underground communication in countries like China, Iran, and the former Yugoslavia. Combining research studies of pre-1989 and post-1989 phenomena that bypass official censorship and containment serves to foster discussion on the historical applicability of the terms to recent developments and to (re)evaluate the historical relevance of alternative and cross-border media throughout the twentieth century. As discussed above, samizdat/tamizdat is by definition a translatable and transferable practice, but it remains a question how far it can travel outside of its original context before it becomes unrecognizable. Some scholars, including contributors to this volume, point to the blog and participatory media (e.g., LiveJournal) as the natural successor to self-published formats such as zines and perhaps samizdat. While this might be the case, it would also be useful to remain open to other types of online communities and communication as possible inheritors of the samizdat/tamizdat legacy.

We feel that our commitment to bridging discussions about the Cold War era with discussions about challenges to freedom of the press today in the former USSR offers a valuable contribution to this field of research.[46] By focusing on the theme of freedom of the press today, this section discusses (dis)continuities of media before and after 1989 and considers the legacy of this system on the circulation of ideas after 1989, discussing both recent instances of samizdat/tamizdat (e.g., in resistance movements in the former Yugoslavia and Ukraine) and the vast and uncharted impact of the Internet on transnational communication. Current strategies of underground media and alternative culture are evaluated in light of recent political conditions. This should contribute to a better understanding of the relationship between democracy, censorship, and underground media throughout the twentieth and early twenty-first century. While people, texts, and goods now circulate much more freely, some of the same linguistic and cultural barriers (and prejudices) between Central and Eastern Europeans, their diasporas, and the rest of the world remain.

Contents of This Volume

The first section, "Producing and Circulating Samizdat/Tamizdat before 1989," traces the path of material objects in samizdat/tamizdat circulation. The four chapters discuss the dissemination of texts between the East and West and the role social networks played in the transfer of literature. In her essay on Ardis, "Ardis Facsimile and Reprint Editions: Giving Back Russian Literature," Ann Komaromi explores the idea of the tamizdat text as a *gift* in the structuralist and poststructuralist sense of the term. Komaromi shows how specific tamizdat editions circulated between the Ardis publishers (Carl and Ellendea Proffer), authors, and collectors representing a spiritual link to Russian culture, "the secret and treasured values of a moral and spiritual character that transcended divisions between Soviet and émigré Russians."[47]

In the second chapter, "The Baltic Connection: Transnational Networks of Resistance between Poland and Sweden after 1976," Fredrik Stöcker investigates the transfer channels between Polish dissidents and Scandinavia and their contribution to the production and dissemination of samizdat from 1976 onward. Stöcker approaches the transnational connection as an informal space that served to produce—what he calls—a kind of "open source intelligence." With this phrase Stöcker is referring to both the material and the knowledge collected by Polish émigrés in Sweden through various channels (such as the regime's official press, Western radio, the "interrogation" of tourists, sailors, or newly arrived political refugees). These materials were collected in Sweden and were then smuggled back into Poland, where they served as a substitute for domestic samizdat activity.

In the third chapter, "Radio Free Europe and Radio Liberty as the 'Echo Chamber' of tamizdat," Friederike Kind-Kovács examines the special role of foreign radio broadcasting in the dissemination of literary texts across the Iron Curtain. Departing from the traditional treatment of RFE/RL as a politically divisive weapon of Cold War soft diplomacy, Kind-Kovács instead shows how these institutions functioned as "the tools of intellectuals bent on spreading uncensored literature"[48] and, subsequently, how the radio stations contributed to the slow reemergence of dialogue across the Iron Curtain. Kind-Kovács concludes by noting that in reconnecting the literary spheres separated by Cold War politics, radio broadcasting anticipated some of the fundamental goals of Web-based cultural activism today (for example, the e-zine *Tamizdat*). In this way, Kind-Kovács's essay unearths a philosophy of cultural transmission that has remained in place despite political changes and the transformation of the global media—as we see more clearly in the last section of this volume.

In the fourth chapter, "Contact Beyond Borders and Historical Problems," Karolina Zioło-Pużuk uses a comparative framework to examine a different network: the links between Polish and Russian émigré journals and the impact of this interaction on the Polish opposition underground. Zioło-Pużuk presents the different levels of contact between the journals *Kultura* and *Kontinent*, both in material terms about the transfer and translation of texts and in philosophical terms about the shared vision and political perspectives of Jerzy Giedroyc and Vladimir Maksimov. Zioło-Pużuk is able to add a clear trajectory of *Kultura*'s engagement with Russian dissidents and exiles, and the reverberations of this engagement in *Kultura*'s Polish audience. In keeping with the theme of this section (uncovering those figures who would not be visible in a purely text-based account of samizdat and tamizdat), Zioło-Pużuk demonstrates the key role played by Natalya Gorbanevskaya as a mediator, translator, and friend of both Giedroyc and Maksimov.

In addition to offering a wider and more comparative view of the entangled history of samizdat and tamizdat, the second section, "Diffusing Non-Conformist Ideas through Samizdat/Tamizdat before 1989," gives some insight into the content of these circulating media. The three different contributions analyze in different ways how historical and social discourses, narratives, and policies were shaped by the exchange of ideas across the Iron Curtain, and the shared intellectual history between the East and West. By examining how particular texts and diverse media of dissemination contributed to the rise of relevant intellectual debates across the Iron Curtain, each of the essays demonstrates the impact of cross-border transfer on the rise of a transnational public sphere.

Cristina Petrescu's essay on political dissent in Romania, "Free Conversations in an Occupied Country," offers a rare glimpse of an understudied phenomenon whose very existence is contested: Romanian tamizdat. Petrescu notes that the apparent lack of Romanian samizdat, along with the relatively small amount of Romanian tamizdat, might lead to the conclusion that there was no significant dissent in Romania. However, by using a comparative analysis to first describe the specificity of the Romanian communist system on a macro level, and then by providing a detailed account of a particular critical intellectual circle (which did in fact produce noncirculated samizdat), Petrescu shows that there is more to Romanian dissidence than the "exceptionalism thesis." Petrescu compares the nonconformist journal *Dialog* published by the University of Iași and the first ever Western-produced Romanian publication *Agora*. In daring to call her case study a "unique example of a failed tamizdat," she challenges a fundamental tenet of Cold War studies, noting that "the transnational flow of ideas reached even the autarchic Romania."[49]

Muriel Blaive's essay on "The Danger of Over-Interpreting Dissident Writing in the West," shows how the Western academic community adopted and legitimized a particular historical narrative produced in post-1968 Czechoslovakia about the Stalinist terror. The Western attempts to broadcast news about the "captive nations" in the 1950s and early 1960s resulted in a perfect storm of a strongly anticommunist, downright apocalyptic view of the East. Blaive shows how this development gave rise to the widespread conviction that life in Stalinist-era Czechoslovakia was harder and more brutal than in any other Soviet republic or satellite state. Blaive presents the larger implications of the wholesale adoption of this "ideological heritage"[50]: first, the implications for the wider circulation of ideas in samizdat and tamizdat during the Cold War, and, second, for scholarship in Czechoslovak studies, which continues to this day to leave this thesis uncontested and unexamined.

We see a parallel example of the development of ideas *between* East and West—that is, in the dialectic produced by their circulation—in Agnes Arndt's treatment of the term *civil society*. Arndt is able to show how Michnik's ideas about "the New Evolutionism" were formed in dialogue with a generation of Poles in emigration in Paris and London, and then taken up by Western intellectuals such as Andrew Arato and John Keane to proscribe the term *civil society*. In the later 1980s and in the transition era, this term "enabled Polish intellectuals to get in touch with a transnational discourse, to establish a common linguistic ground between East and West."[51] Arndt is interested in the overlap between intellectual histories on either side of the Iron Curtain, demonstrating how one line of thought accumulated more and more uses and currency until it crystallized into a term that transformed politics itself.

Different forms of independent and alternative culture are represented in the third section, entitled "Transforming Modes and Practices of Alternative Culture." With these three essays, we broaden the current understanding of samizdat as a solely political phenomenon and bring into focus its cultural significance. The new possibilities for research presented in this section highlight the intersections between samizdat/tamizdat in the spheres of music, art, video, and alternative lifestyles—in other words, on the borders of semiofficial and popular culture. Brian Horne's article on the phenomenon of *magnitizdat*, "The Bards of Magnitizdat: An Aesthetic Political History of Russian Underground Recordings" illustrates the reproductive pathway of a new musical genre in the 1960s, the Russian bards' song or *avtorskaya pesnya*, which has typically been analyzed for its textual and antiauthoritarian content. In a gesture reminiscent of Komaromi's treatment of the materiality of the samizdat/tamizdat text, Horne insists that the nonverbal components that make up magnitizdat—the bards' voice, the roughness of the recording, and the informal settings in which it was both recorded and replayed—are just as important to its reception as the content of the lyrics. Using this approach, Horne is able to account for the range of official and unofficial reactions to bards' songs, from censorship to acceptance, developing an aesthetic political history of unofficial media that challenges some of the simplest assumptions about oppositional culture and its democratizing effects.

Valentina Parisi's contribution, "Writing about Apparently Nonexistent Art: the *Tamizdat* Journal *A-Ja* and Russian Unofficial Art in the 1970s and 1980s," takes the example of an art review published by sculptor Igor' Shelkovskij in France that did more than just record developments in the Soviet underground art scene. Parisi convincingly demonstrates that *A-Ja* functioned as a screen on which events and conversations held by both the underground and émigré artists and art critics could be projected, and then processed and absorbed in a way that would be impossible in the USSR itself. In its limited run of seven issues, *A-Ja* combined elements of samizdat and tamizdat, visual culture, and the private oral history of "kitchen talks" in the Soviet sphere, and new formulations in art history and aesthetics theory that could not have taken place in any other space.

In the last chapter in this section, "'Video Knows No Borders': Samizdat Television and the Unofficial Public Sphere in 'Normalized' Czechoslovakia," Alice Lovejoy chronicles the flow of samizdat documentary video in and out of the country in the mid to late 1980s, when consumer video technology first became commercially available. She focuses on two productions: *Original Videojournal* (1987–1989), closely associated with Charter 77 underground; and *Videomagazine* (1986–1989), a tamizdat video periodical produced in London by Czech émigré and journalist Karel Kyncl. She positions these unofficial audiovisual productions in relationship to "official" films of the Czech Army and Ministry of the Interior, as well as unofficial news circulating in corresponding print media underground. Ultimately, Lovejoy addresses a series of questions that could well be applied to all of the articles in this section, about whether the exchange of unofficial media catalyzed the creation of alternative public spheres in communist Czechoslovakia, and to what degree this effect coincides with dissident views of a "parallel polis" or "second culture."

The major goal of the fourth section, "Moving from Samizdat/Tamizdat to Press Freedom and Alternative Media Today," is to create a bridge from the concept of samizdat and tamizdat during the Cold War to today's forms of underground media. We continue with the question raised by

Jacques Rupnik in the preface to this volume: How could samizdat practices be used as an example for nonconformist movements elsewhere in the world? The very notion of ideas crossing borders comes into question in the Internet age, as the World Wide Web has generated its own cartography that does not always align with our historical or geographic borders. We are particularly interested in the role of the Internet in countries where "classic" mass media are still or again under state control. How can we compare samizdat to present-day oppositional or resistance writing on the Internet? Why do some blogs today refer to themselves as a form of samizdat?

The five essays that close the volume take very different approaches to this topic. In "Postprintium: Digital Literary Samizdat on the Russian Internet?" Henrike Schmidt looks at the development of materials resembling (or self-identifying as) samizdat between 1990 and 2006 on the Russian Internet. She takes into account many possible contexts for this comparison: the modes of production, the ideological content, changes in media infrastructure, as well as increasing state control of the media after 1998 and 1999. Inverting the concept of samizdat as *prä-printium*,[52] a phenomenon reaching back to pre-Gutenberg techniques, Schmidt coins the term *postprintium* to chart the relationship between these texts and the media platforms that support them. She ultimately concludes that, from a theoretical point of view, it would be more productive to restrict the term *samizdat* to the period spanning from 1956 to 1985, though it is practically very useful to recognize the self-referential circulation of the term in the post-1989 online environment on the level of discourse analysis.

From the possibility of post-1989 samizdat in print form, we move to an instance of post-1989 radio broadcasting that echoes the Cold War samizdat/tamizdat paradigm. Daniel Gilfillan's essay, "Independent Media, Transnational Borders, and Networks of Resistance: Collaborative Art Radio between Belgrade (Radio B92) and Vienna (ORF)," uses the work of sound artist Gordan Paunović during the NATO bombing of Belgrade to show how community-based radio and underground artistic practices in the Milošević era interacted with the global media at this critical point in April of 1999. Gilfillan is sensitive to two layers of censorship active in this media environment: on the one hand, political pressures from an increasingly isolated nationalist regime, and, on the other, the silencing of local voices throughout Serbia as a result of the increased availability of global media. It is Paunović's amplification of local voices through the medium of radio, and the subsequent cross-border broadcast via Austrian *Kunstradio*, that reproduces the structure, affect, and effect of the samizdat/tamizdat phenomenon.

The following contribution is situated the farthest away geographically from Eastern Europe (although no farther than Skilling's landmark article, which also includes a section on samizdat in China). From the beginning of his essay "'From Wallpapers to Blogs': Samizdat and Internet in China," Martin Hala takes on the utopic presuppositions about both samizdat, and the use of the Internet as a democratizing agent. After retracing the history of samizdat practices in China (specifically by analyzing the *dazibao*, or "big character posters" of the late 1970s), Hala chronicles the changes in information access that have accompanied the recent shifts in Chinese economic policy. While recognizing the breadth and scope of the Chinese blogosphere, Hala draws a sharp distinction between practitioners of *dazibao* (samizdat), who took a conscious step "outside of the officially sanctioned discourse"[53] and Chinese bloggers, who have been in many ways co-opted by the system in which they are entrenched. Ultimately, Hala sees self-expression on the Internet transforming the Chinese social sphere in a similar way that samizdat/tamizdat transformed Eastern European society, while having a much more muted effect on the political sphere.

The chapter in this volume that most courageously pushes the definition of samizdat/tamizdat beyond both temporal *and* geographic boundaries is undoubtedly "Reflections on the Revolutions in Europe: Lessons for the Middle East and the Arab Spring" by Barbara Falk. If Schmidt's and Gilfillan's articles correspond to the treatment of pre-1989 samizdat/tamizdat in section II, Falk's article is very much a post-1989 corollary to section III on the circulation of ideas. She explores the theoretical and practical innovations that developed out of the dissident movements in Eastern Europe and asks whether they might be relevant to debates about democratization in North Africa and the Middle East today. Falk also addresses the utopic claims that arose about the role of social media in revolution in the wake of the Arab Spring: "Internet freedom does not produce human freedom any more than free market economics does liberal polities—as Russia and China both ably demonstrate."[54] This is an essay in its truest sense: a rigorous "trying out" of ideas in a new light, moving through the history of civil society and nonviolence, Michnik's "new evolutionism," the realities of civil society on the ground in the Middle East today, and, finally, a new series of "Theses on Hope and Hopelessness" after Leszek Kołakowski's 1971 essay of the same name. After carrying out this rigorous thought experiment, Falk offers some recommendations for how such a translation might occur.

Projection of Future Research Trends

The most visible intervention in the study of samizdat/tamizdat offered here is its liberation from textual, geographic, and temporal boundaries.[55] This strategy allows us to work with the symbolic resonance of samizdat/tamizdat in other fields of culture and societal discourses. With this approach we propose to move away from content-based studies of these materials to an analysis of a media system, the effects of it on subjective experiences, and the metatextual concerns it raises. The book proposes four possible interpretive frameworks, including the circulation of texts and the ideas inherent in them, the theoretical expansion of samizdat to other cultural practices, and contemporary media environments. Given the changing landscape of the field, including the very conditions under which samizdat/tamizdat texts might be treated, we suggest a few major trajectories for future academic study that extend beyond the possible scope of this book.

One major aim of this volume is to show that the realization of the tamizdat project was based on the assumption of the reciprocity of exchanges. For a coherent picture of this transnational system, there is an obvious need for collaborative studies that bring together research conducted in many different language environments, as the phenomenon itself was multilingual. It is not simply a question of parallel universes that could be compared or contrasted, but interdependent flows of texts and ideas between languages that are mutually constitutive. Anticipated changes in the infrastructure of archives containing samizdat and tamizdat open new doors: with digitization projects and interoperable searching platforms under development, it is easy to imagine macrolevel studies that would trace the migration of text corpora. By using search tools that access data from multiple archives, together with geographical information system (GIS) software, previously unrecognized patterns of dissemination and marginalized texts can emerge that would give us a more detailed image of the larger system.

In order to balance this macrolevel view, researchers need to simultaneously develop strategies for closely reading the narrative structure of samizdat/tamizdat at the microhistorical level. There will be blank spots on this systemic map, and studies closer to the ground can help to explain *why* certain samizdat/tamizdat materials have survived, circulated, and been canonized while others have not. Given the hierarchies within both official publishing institutions and the canon of dissident literature, some authors have been justly/unjustly marginalized from one or the other sphere; others fall through the cracks completely. Meanwhile, nationalistic, anti-Semitic, or discriminatory aspects of underground and émigré texts have been largely overlooked; more attentive readings would present a more nuanced picture of their ambiguous character.

Furthermore, the spatial and temporal mapping of the migration of texts should be grounded through an integrated perspective on individual experiences. Here, biographical narratives can reveal the layers of personal meanings embedded in and surrounding samizdat/tamizdat production. Instead of focusing on oral history as a simple, descriptive collection of memories and anecdotes, encouraging in-depth narration of single experiences within the samizdat/tamizdat field brings us as researchers closer to lived lives in this conflicted period. This leads us to question whether the predominant narrative in Eastern or Western context was indeed the Cold War as an isolationist experience. At both the macro and the micro level of samizdat/tamizdat research, we can see that real and imagined contact imprinted itself on lived experiences across the divide.

Notes

1. The term *tamizdat* was first used in connection with the publication of Boris Pasternak's *Dr. Zhivago* in Russian by the Italian publishing house Feltrinelli Editore in Milan in 1957. See Carlo Feltrinelli, *Senior Service. Das Leben meines Vaters Giangiacomo Feltrinelli* (Munich, 2003). Although the term *tamizdat* is connected to the appearance of *Dr. Zhivago*, the phenomenon was more often referred to as "Western publication" or exile publication, not distinguishing between the publication of the text by Western or by émigré publishers. For further definitions, see Wolfgang Kasack, "Tamizdat," in *Dictionary of Russian Literature Since 1917* (New York, 1988), 407–8; or Wolfgang Kasack, "Tamizdat," in *Lexikon der Russischen Literatur des 20. Jahrhunderts. Vom Beginn des Jahrhunderts bis zum Ende der Sowjetaera* (Munich, 1992), 1270–74. Alternatively, see the comparative article on both alternative publishing phenomena: Emmanuel Waegemans, "*Samizdat* and *Tamizdat* (1956–1985) 12.1. Die 'andere Stimme' Russlands in Zeitschriften," in *Geschichte der russischen Literatur. Von Peter dem Grossen bis zur Gegenwart (1700–1995)* (Konstanz, 1993), 409–10.
2. It is worth pointing out some of the differences, as well, in that: (1) formally, "cultural globalization" today takes advantage of mobile communications devices; (2) structurally, access to information was a much larger issue, and for every instance of cross-border communication that did occur, the majority of people lived in a more restricted information environment; (3) experientially, the real and imagined (or feared) consequences of consuming information were much more significant and strongly affected people's reading, listening, and viewing practices.
3. For an excellent overview of current historiography of the field of dissent, political resistance, and uncensored media in the region, see Barbara Falk, "Resistance and Dissent in Central and Eastern Europe," *East European Politics and Society* 25, no. 2 (May 2011): 318–60.
4. Maya Nadkarni, "Samizdat as Film" (presentation), *From Samizdat to Tamizdat* conference, Institut für die Wissenschaften vom Menschen, Vienna, 2006.
5. H. Gordon Skilling, "Independent Communications in Communist East Europe," *Cross Currents* 5 (1986), 63.
6. As Skilling comments: "the line between the two cultures or two forms of communication is not always sharp and distinct." Skilling, "Independent Communications," 69.
7. The following survey is mostly concerned with scholarly treatments of the subject of samizdat in the Western academic press; there were also, certainly, self-representations

of the phenomenon within samizdat texts themselves, and the beginnings of a critical literature in the countries which has emerged in the last decade (e.g., for a useful review of Russian sources on samizdat, see Ann Komaromi, "The Material Existence of Soviet Samizdat," *Slavic Review* 63, no. 3 [2004]: 597–618). The articles in this volume are among the first to try to effectively integrate these different streams of critical sources, and it is the hope of the editors that future studies will continue to do so.

8. We will employ the idea of "nonconformity," referring to the writers' refusal to conform to the literary conventions of the Soviet regime, instead of applying the overly loaded terms of *dissent* or *dissidence*. Ann Komaromi has recently proposed a new approach to the field of *dissidence* as part of a "mixed private-public sphere." See Ann Komaromi, "Samizdat and Soviet Dissident Publics," *Slavic Review* 71, no. 1 (2012): 70–90, 72.

9. For samizdat as a source of information that was covered inadequately by the official press, see F. J. M. Feldbrugge, "New Sources of Information on the Soviet Union and their Impact on East-West Relations," *Co-Existence* 13, no. 2 (1976): 209–20; Rudolf L. Tökés, *Dissent in the USSR: Politics, Ideology and People* (Baltimore, 1975); Alexander Meerson-Aksenov and Boris Shragin, *The Political, Social and Religious Thought of Russian "Samizdat": An Anthology*, trans. Nicholas Lupinin (Belmont, 1977).

10. H. Gordon Skilling, "Samizdat: A Return to the Pre-Gutenberg Era?" *Cross Currents* 1 (1982): 64–80.

11. Skilling, "Samizdat," 64. Skilling divided the phases of samizdat into three distinct periods: "literary *samizdat*," "social *samizdat*" with more political content, and a third phase of samizdat that extended to social programs and expositions of independent social and political thought. See for this, ibid., 67.

12. See also Tomasz Mianowicz, "Unofficial Publishing Lives on," *Index on Censorship* 12, no. 2 (1983): 24–25; Kestutis K. Girnius, "The Opposition Movement in Postwar Lithuania," *Journal of Baltic Studies* 13, no. 1 (1982): 66–73; Dietrich Beyrau and Ivo Bock, "Samisdat in Osteuropa Und Tschechische Schreibmaschinen-Kultur," *Bohemia* 29, no. 2 (1988): 280–99; and H. Gordon Skilling, "Independent Currents in Czechoslovakia," *Problems of Communism* 34, no. 1 (1985): 32–49; H. Gordon Skilling, "Samizdat and an Independent Society in Central and Eastern Europe," (Columbus, 1989).

13. Dimitry S. Pospielovsky, "From Gosizdat to *samizdat* and *tamizdat*," *Canadian Slavonic Papers* 20 (1978): 44–62, available at http://www.bookrags.com/criticism/samizdat-literature_04/ (accessed 20 August 2011), 1–26, 5. Another study has been provided by Mary Lewallen Nichols, "Soviet Literature as a Tool of Education, Gosizdat and *tamizdat* Writers: 1974–1984," vols. 1–4, dissertation (Arizona State University, 1986). A study in Russian L. Donatov, "*Tamizdat*–literatura v izgnanii," *Posev* 28 (February 1972): 47–51.

14. See Pospielovsky, "From Gosizdat to *samizdat* and *tamizdat*."

15. See Aleksander Smolar, "The Polish Opposition," in *Crisis and Reform in Eastern Europe*, ed. Ferenc Fehér and Andrew Arato (New Brunswick, 1991), 175–252; Taras Kuzio, "Unofficial Groups and Semi-Official Groups and Samizdat Publications in Ukraine," in *Echoes of Glasnost in Soviet Ukraine*, ed. Romana M. Bahry (North York, 1990); Stefani Hoffman, "Jewish Samizdat and the Rise of Jewish National Consciousness," in *Jewish Culture and Identity in the Soviet Union*, ed. Yaacov Roi and Avi Beker (New York, 1991), 88–111; James P. Scanlan, "From Samizdat to Perestroika: The Soviet Marxist Critique of Soviet Society," in *The Road to Disillusion: from critical Marxism to post-communism in Eastern Europe*, ed. Raymond Taras, (New York, 1992), 19–40.

16. Visible in titles such as Stanisław Barańczak, "Goodbye, Samizdat," *Wilson Quarterly* 14, no. 2 (1990): 59–66; Marketa Goetz-Stankiewicz and Timothy Garton Ash, *Good-Bye, Samizdat: Twenty Years of Czechoslovak Underground Writing* (Evanston, 1992); G. M.

Tamás, "Farewell to the Left," *East European Politics and Societies* 5, no. 1 (1991): 92–112; or Johnston M. Mitchell, "The Evolution of a Free Press in Hungary: 1986–1990," in *Revolutions for Freedom: The Mass Media in Eastern and Central Europe*, ed. Al Hester and L. Earle Reybold (Athens, GA, 1991).
17. Olga Zaslavskaya, "From Dispersed to Distributed Archives: The Past and the Present of Samizdat Material," *Poetics Today* 29, no. 4 (2008): 669–712.
18. Jakub Karpiński, "The Difficult Return to Normality," *Uncaptive Minds* 3, no. 5 (1990): 24–26; Ivan Klima, "The Unexpected Merits of Oppression," *Nation* 250, no. 22 (1990): 769–73; Gayle Feldman, "Poland's Underground Publishing Surfaces, Seeks International Help," *Publishers Weekly* 237, no. 2 (1990): 28–29; Philip Roth, "A Conversation in Prague," *New York Review of Books* 37, no. 6 (1990): 14.
19. Serguei Alex. Oushakine, "The Terrifying Mimicry of Samizdat," *Public Culture* 13, no. 2, (2001): 191–214.
20. Ibid., 207.
21. Gordon Johnston, "What is the History of Samizdat?" *Social History* 24, no. 2 (1999): 115–33; Komaromi, "The Material Existence of Soviet Samizdat."
22. Komaromi, "The Material Existence of Soviet Samizdat," 616.
23. It should be noted that the present collection also contains her essay on the tamizdat publisher Ardis.
24. In particular, she invoked Jerome McGann's "bibliographic" and "paratextual" codes of the text: once decoded, these embedded meanings reveal the "life cycle" of the text. Ann Komaromi, "Samizdat as Extra-Gutenberg Phenomenon," *Poetics Today* 29, no. 4 (2009): 659.
25. Most recently a project started to look at the interrelationship between Samizdat as a core element of European memory. See "Between Memory and Utopia: Samizdat as a Symbol of European Culture, History, Boundaries, Perspectives," available at http://www.maldura.unipd.it/samizdat/english/index.htm (accessed 20 August 2011).
26. Yale Richmond, *Cultural Exchanges and the Cold War* (University Park, 2003). For very inspiring theoretical reflections on transnational approaches, see Michael Werner, Bénédicte Zimmermann, "Penser l'histoire croisée: entre empirie et réflexivité," in *Annales HSS* 1 (2003): 7–36; and Michael Werner and Bénédicte Zimmermann, "Vergleich, Transfer, Verflechtung. Der Ansatz der *Histoire Croisée* und die Herausforderung des Transnationalen," *Geschichte und Gesellschaft* 28 (2002), 607–36.
27. Padraic Kenney, "Opposition Networks and Transnational Diffusion in the Revolutions of 1989," in *cc*, ed. Gerd-Rainer Horn and Padraic Kenney (Lanham, 2004), 207–23. Patrick Major and Rana Mitter, "East is East and West is West? Towards a Comparative Socio-Cultural History of the Cold War," in *Across the Blocs: Cold War Cultural and Social History*, ed. Patrick Major and Rana Mitter (London, 2004), 1–22.
28. Ioana Popa, "Translation channels. A Primer on politicized literary transfer," *Target* 18, no. 2 (2006): 205–28. Ioana Popa, "Un transfert littéraire politisé. Circuits de traduction des littératures d'Europe de l'Est en France, 1947–1989," *Actes de la recherche en sciences sociales* 2, 144 (2002): 55–69.
29. A very interesting study on possibly *bad samizdat* was presented by Julie Draskoczy, "Imagining the Nation: Anti-Semitism in Soviet Samizdat," at the conference on Underground Publishing and the Public Sphere: Comparative and Transnational Perspectives, Berlin, WZB, 27–29 July 2006.
30. For two rare examples of this type of study, see Hammer 1984 on the case of the Russian "Slavophile" journal *Veche*; and chapter 9, "Samizdat Russkikh Natsionalistov 1970–1982 Godakh," in Nikolai Mitrokhin, *Russkaia partiia: Dvizhenie russkikh natsionalistov v SSSR. 1953–1985* (Moscow, 2003): 430–88.

31. Thomas Oleszczuk, "An Analysis of Bias in Samizdat Sources: A Lithuanian Case Study," *Soviet Studies* 37, no. 1 (January 1985): 131–7.
32. These included: (1) the "varying coverage over time due to the vulnerability of the ... underground 'correspondent' of samizdat to arrest and trial," (2) the "social ... 'maturation' of samizdat communication networks," (3) "incorrect information or noise, especially typographical errors," and, lastly (4), "the probable 'audience' of samizdat ... (meaning a false) perception of what interest[ed] their readers." Oleszczuk, 132–34.
33. Joseph Benatov, "Demystifying the Logic of Tamizdat: Philip Roth's Anti-Spectacular Literary Politics," *Poetics Today* 30, no. 1 (Spring 2009): 107–32. Peter Steiner, "Introduction: On Samizdat, Tamizdat, Magnitizdat, and Other Strange Words That Are Difficult to Pronounce," *Poetics Today* 29, no. 4 (Winter 2008): 613–28.
34. Steiner, "Introduction: On Samizdat," 614.
35. Poul Villaume and Odd Arne Westad, eds., *Perforating the Iron Curtain: European Détente, Transatlantic Relations and the Cold War, 1965–1985* (Copenhagen, 2010). Sari Autio-Sarasmo and Brendan Humphreys, eds., *Winter Kept Us Warm: Cold War Interactions Reconsidered* (Helsinki, 2010). See here, in particular, the article by Bent Boel, "French Support for Eastern European Dissidence, 1968–1989: Approaches and Controversies," 215–42.
36. Autio-Sarasmo and Humphreys, "Introduction," in *Winter Kept Us Warm*, 17.
37. Ibid., 18.
38. Martin Daughtry, "Magnitizdat as Cultural Practice," a paper prepared for the conference "Samizdat and Underground Culture in the Soviet Block Countries," University of Pennsylvania, 6–7 April 2006, 5.
39. See for the case of the Ancien regime, Dena Goodman, *The Republic of Letters: A Cultural History of the French Enlightenment* (Ithaca, 1994), 17. She writes, "another sort of regular movement was necessary for its functioning as well: the circulation of letters."
40. At the time, this social practice involved underground or émigré publishing houses such as Petlice, Ardis, Kultura, Kontinent, Magyar Füzetek, or collection points such as RFE/RL in Munich.
41. Particularly important to this cumulative project will be both the Samizdat Text Corpora based at the Open Society Archives in Budapest (http://www.samizdatportal.org/index.php/about-stc, accessed 20 August 2011) and the database of "Soviet Samizdat Periodicals" launched at the University of Toronto in summer 2011.
42. Gleb Struve, "The Aesthetic Function in Russian Literature," *Slavic Review* 21, no. 3 (September 1962): 424.
43. On the patterns and ways of miscommunication between the literary underground and its Western counterpart, see Friederike Kind-Kovács, "Life Stories Reconnected: Publishing Tamizdat as a Symbolic Act of Recreating Biographical Coherence?" in Autio-Sarasmo and Humphreys, *Winter Kept Us Warm*, 181ff.
44. Translation by the author. Peter Niedermüller, "Kultur, Transfer und Politik im ostmitteleuropäischen Sozialismus," in *Transnationale Öffentlichkeiten und Identitäten im 20. Jahrhundert*, ed. Hartmut Kaelble, Martin Kirsch, and Alexander Schmidt-Gernig (Frankfurt, 2002), 161.
45. A. Ross Johnson, *Cold War Broadcasting: Impact on the Soviet Union and Eastern Europe* (Budapest/New York, 2010); Richard Cummings, *Crusade for Freedom: Rallying Americans Behind Cold War Broadcasting, 1950–1960* (Jefferson, 2010).
46. One step in this direction can be seen by the recent issue of the German journal *Osteuropa*, entitled "Blick zurück nach vorn: Samizdat, Internet und die Freiheit des Wortes," Osteuropa 11 (2010).
47. Komaromi, chapter 1.

48. Kind-Kovács, chapter 3.
49. Petrescu, chapter 5.
50. Blaive, chapter 6.
51. Arndt, chapter 7.
52. Günter Hirt, Sascha Wonders, and Sabine Hänsgen, *Präprintium. Moskauer Bücher aus dem Samizdat* (Bremen, 1998).
53. Hala, chapter 13.
54. Falk, chapter 14.
55. While the articles in this volume project forward past the temporal boundary of 1989, one could also potentially turn the lens of analysis toward the past; see Kind-Kovács and Labov, "Independent Media Crossing Borders in L'Ancien Régime France and Cold War Europe," in *Underground Publishing and the Public Sphere: 1790–Present,* ed. Thomas Lindenberger and Jan Behrends (Vienna, forthcoming).

Section I
Producing and Circulating Samizdat/Tamizdat Before 1989

Chapter 1

ARDIS FACSIMILE AND REPRINT EDITIONS
Giving Back Russian Literature

Ann Komaromi

> Good God, in this eerie, alien world, / letters of life, and whole lines, / have been transposed by the / typesetters. Let's fold / our wings, my lofty angel.
>
> —Vladimir Nabokov[1]

Recent approaches to samizdat and tamizdat have challenged accustomed Cold War narratives and an exclusive focus on socially or politically themed content.[2] We can alternatively define samizdat and tamizdat materially, i.e., on the basis of their production and circulation outside of official Soviet print institutions. Working with such a definition, we find that texts presented as apolitical literature comprise an important part of the body of texts we may consider to be samizdat/tamizdat.[3] We may of course interpret aspects of such purportedly apolitical texts in terms of their political significance, but we will seek to do so in terms other than those of outmoded political binaries or fixed Cold War narratives.

In the search for an alternative perspective on samizdat/tamizdat, Ardis Publishing provides a particularly interesting case for study. Ardis, a small publishing house in Michigan begun by scholars Carl and Ellendea Proffer, published mainly modernist and neomodernist Russian literature. The Proffers claimed this was an absolutely apolitical enterprise, though not all of the publications and activities associated with Ardis bear this out. However, such a claim was not simple dissimulation, as we shall see. The aim of this chapter is to interrogate the complexity of cross-border textual exchanges that are not obviously political. We shall explore in the case of Ardis the rich social aspects of samizdat/tamizdat transfers, including

---

Notes for this chapter begin on page 47.

FIGURE 1.1. Ardis facsimile reprint editions

interpersonal relationships, and the establishment of individual identities and alternative communities through textual exchange.

This essay takes as its particular focus Ardis's facsimile reprints of early twentieth-century Russian editions.

These editions illustrate in a striking way the materiality of the tamizdat text. They are remarkable book-objects evoking a modernist literary spirit that would transcend or master social and historical contingency, while underscoring the ambiguous role of that spirit in the late Soviet period.

An Introduction to Ardis Publishers

As stated, Ardis Publishers (1971–2002) was founded in Ann Arbor, Michigan, by Slavists Carl and Ellendea Proffer.

FIGURE 1.2. Carl and Ellendea Proffer in the Ardis office, ca. 1977

The Proffers understood the needs of Slavic scholars whom they felt were poorly served by the politicized approaches to Russian literature championed by Soviet officialdom and the Western mainstream. Ardis published a number of little-known Russian modernist texts in translation along with scholarly works. Over the course of the 1970s, Ardis also became a significant producer of tamizdat, that is, texts in Russian that could not be obtained in the USSR and were of special interest to a Soviet audience. In particular, Ardis published Russian translations of Nabokov's works originally written in English, including reprints of the previously published translations of *Lolita* (1976), and new editions in Russian of *Pnin* (1983) and *Blednyi Ogon'* (translation of *Pale Fire*, 1983). They also published poet Joseph Brodsky before he became a Nobel Prize winner and Poet Laureate of the United States. Indeed, Carl Proffer helped bring Brodsky to the United States. Brodsky called Ardis the most important thing to happen to the Russian alphabet since the invention of the printing press.[4] Both Nabokov and Brodsky embody the kind of border crossing Ardis publications exemplify.

The Ardis carriage, the publisher's mark that appears on all Ardis editions, is one of Vladimir Favorsky's engravings, according to Ellendea who found a book of Favorsky's work in Moscow.

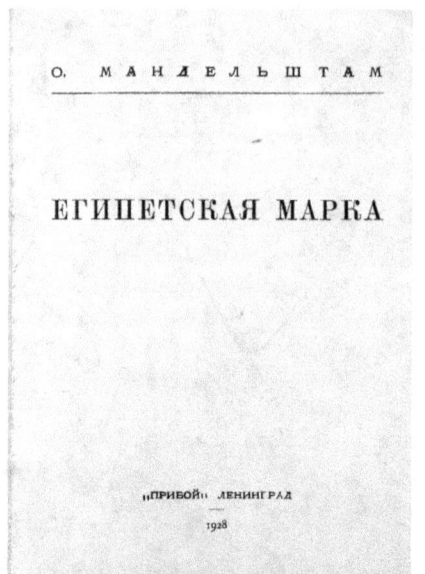 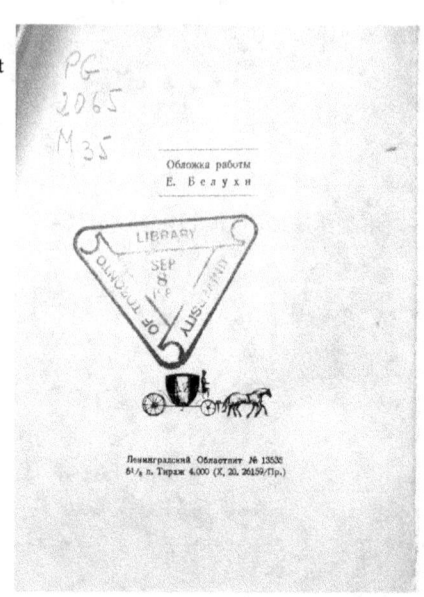

FIGURE 1.3. Title page from the facsimile reprint of Osip Mandel'shtam, *Egipetskaia marka* (Ardis, 1976)

FIGURE 1.4. Ardis carriage logo from facsimile reprint of Osip Mandel'shtam, *Egipetskaia marka* (Ardis, 1976)

The carriage symbolized the Ardis mission to fulfill Pushkin's maxim that "translation is the post-horse of enlightenment."[5] Ardis published a number of English translations of relatively obscure, high-quality Russian works, including little-known poetry and essays from the early part of the twentieth century in the journal *Russian Literature Triquarterly*. Ardis also put out volumes on *The Silver Age of Russian Culture* (1975) and *The Ardis Anthology of Russian Futurism* (1979). This was part of one of Ardis's major projects, to reproduce unpublished (or out-of-print) Russian modernist texts. Existing copies of such works came from bookshops in Europe or they were smuggled out of the Soviet Union, before Ardis reprinted them and sent copies back across the border to the Russian readership in the Soviet Union. These facsimile and reprint editions were unusual. All of them preserved the textual content and graphical layout of original editions from the 1910s to 1930. The ones marked "facsimile" also reproduced the remarkable formats, illustrations, and cover designs of the original editions, which few had ever seen.

Giving Back Russian Literature

Ellendea Proffer would later speak about "giving back" Russian literature through Ardis editions,[6] an ethos most clearly illustrated by these reprint editions. It is worth exploring this aspect of gift giving in Ardis publishing. Gift giving reveals much about Ardis's establishment and evolution, which is a story that does not fit traditional Cold War political narratives about censorship and subversion. Crucial to gift giving is the temporary suspension of the logic of economic and/or symbolic exchange (including transactions of political significance). The Proffers and those with whom they worked did not set out seeking profit or political impact with Ardis. More important to them were the personal relationships and extension of personal identity their activity supported. Giving rare books as gifts had great significance.

A short digression into gift theory might help us appreciate the role of a gift-giving ethos in Ardis activity. According to anthropological studies, gift giving occurs in the absence of economic relations. Marcel Mauss's influential study *The Gift* (*Essai sur le Don,* 1950) treated gift exchange in the rituals of traditional Melanesian cultures, where gift giving created and supported social ties between groups.[7] Structuralist scholar Claude Lévi-Strauss expanded the reach of Mauss's theories about premodern societies and ritual circumstances to the realm of the profane and everyday relations of contemporary societies.[8] In both cases, a significant deferral of material or symbolic interest occurs. In the course of this exchange, the identities of giver and receiver are created and enhanced by the social relationship established.

The gestation of the idea of the Ardis venture can be spied in some early book exchanges in which the Proffers participated. In 1969, when the Proffers first visited the USSR as part of an academic exchange program, they shared their observations in letters to the Nabokovs. Carl had been writing to Vladimir and Vera Nabokov since 1966 regarding his work on *Keys to Lolita,* a study Carl published with Indiana University Press in 1968. After his visit to the Soviet Union, he started writing to them about Vladimir Nabokov's Soviet readers. In the postscript to the initial Russian language edition of *Lolita* in 1967, Nabokov professed scarcely to believe in the possibility of his contemporary Soviet readers:

> Issuing *Lolita* in Russian I pursue a very simple goal: I want my best book in English—or to say it more modestly, one of my best books in English—to be translated correctly into my native tongue. This is the whim of a bibliophile, nothing more. As a writer I have become accustomed to the fact that for almost a half a century a blind spot darkens the east side of my consciousness—what sort of Soviet edition of *Lolita* could there be![9]

Nabokov is here being tricky, or disingenuous. In fact, although there could undoubtedly be no official Soviet edition of *Lolita,* there were unauthorized copies of Nabokov's works in circulation, and Nabokov knew it.[10] To the Proffers, however, evidence of Nabokov's Soviet readers was news.

Carl Proffer wrote to the Nabokovs on 5 May 1969 about the popularity of Nabokov's books among members of the Soviet intelligentsia whom they had met. The Proffers wrote about Soviet readers who enthusiastically read *Lolita, Drugie berega* (*Other Shores*), *Priglashenie na kazn'* (*Invitation to a Beheading*), and *Dar* (*The Gift*). One acquaintance of the Proffers, Andrei Sergeev, a book collector, offered to provide Nabokov through the Proffers with a copy of Nabokov's first book, *Stikhi* (*Verses*), published in St. Petersburg in 1916.[11] The Proffers were happy to act as mediators for Sergeev and others. When a second copy of *Stikhi* was offered, Carl described it as a "gift." While the donor wanted nothing in return, Carl explained, he would surely be pleased to receive an autographed copy of the Russian *Lolita*. Another acquaintance of the Proffers offered to send a copy of Vladimir Nabokov's father's book (*Iz voiuiushchei Anglii*, by D.V. Nabokov, Petrograd, 1916). Vera wrote Carl that Vladimir would particularly like to have this book. The donor refused to say how much the book cost him, although Carl speculated that it must have been as expensive as ten or fifteen rubles, which was a significant sum. Of course, wrote Carl, for the donors, as for the Nabokovs, "feelings" meant more than money. In offering Nabokov's father's book, the donor wanted Nabokov to know that his Russian readers lived, as he put it, "in a less metaphysical realm" than Nabokov supposed: they existed in reality. Carl suggested that two or three autographed editions in return from Nabokov would be appreciated.[12]

There are two points to be made about these books considered from the point of view of gift theory: first, the books were explicitly not valued for their economic worth. They instead possessed spiritual value as gifts—value not unlike the transcendent spiritual character of objects traded in the Melanesian gift exchange as described by Mauss. These books represented "culture," the secret and treasured values of a moral and spiritual character that transcended divisions between Soviet and émigré Russians. Secondly, I would emphasize the way that these books traveled—*as gifts*—helped affirm and extend a shared identity across the political divide of the Iron Curtain.[13] The survival of copies of Nabokov's prerevolutionary *Stikhi* demonstrated the secret endurance of his name across the divisions of time and political borders. Exile of the family and assassination of Nabokov's father did not erase the family name from the Russian consciousness in the Soviet Union. Nabokov's father's book embodied this fact in a particularly poignant way. When the book returned to Vladimir, it might be thought to have functioned as a sign of his personal and cultural connection to a homeland left behind. For his part, the donor explicitly sought Nabokov's recognition of Soviet readers. In this way, the signed editions Nabokov sent back to his Soviet well-wishers acknowledged their identity as partners who shared a real and living Russian culture beyond borders. The Nabokovs may have known about their Soviet readers before, but they gained new ways of relating to their Soviet cultural compatriots through the Proffers. As a result, the Nabokovs became unexpectedly personally engaged with that readership: the Nabokovs sent gifts through the Proffers for dissidents and help for other authors, including jeans from Sears-Roebuck for Joseph Brodsky.[14]

Carl and Ellendea Proffer functioned as mediators in this exchange between Nabokov and his Soviet friends. They possessed the ability to travel across the border between the two worlds. This right, for as long as it lasted, seems fantastic, given the millions of Russians, including the dozens of personal friends and acquaintances of the Proffers, who could not cross over this way. The Proffers used their freedom to help others create or affirm identities and connections across formidable borders. That movement also helped the Proffers forge their own new identity.

The founding of Ardis Publishing had much to do with the affective experiences of alienation, loss, and longing produced by crossing borders. The Proffers' imaginations had been previously captured by Nabokovian fictional realms born of his life as an émigré. During their visit to Moscow, the Proffers felt their own sense of being lost in a foreign world, and they sought relief in literature. Ellendea described their first winter in Moscow in 1969:

> After a few months we were beginning to sink deeply into the Russian world, and we became desperate for something new to read in English.... [A] package arrived through the diplomatic pouch. Nabokov had instructed *Playboy* magazine to send Carl advance galleys of *Ada*, so that he could give a comment in the letters column when the magazine ran their much publicized excerpt of the new novel by the author of *Lolita*.
>
> This was passionate reading indeed.... We gulped the novel down, virtually memorizing certain parts, and forever after *Ada* had a special place in our memories, tied to that hotel, that winter, and our desperate desire to read something new in English to offset the power of the Russian world we were exploring. Something to remind us, perhaps, that we came from the English language.

Nabokov's novel would later inspire the name "Ardis":

> When it came time in 1971 for the restless Carl to name the publishing house which existed only in his mind, he thought of *Ada*, a novel which takes place in a mythical place blending features of both Russia and America, quite like our own life. The key scenes of the novel take place at Ardis Hall, a literary family estate straight out of Jane Austen by way of Lev Tolstoy, and filled with Nabokov's own love for the estates of his Russian childhood.[15]

The Proffers based the name of their new enterprise on a book that transcended cultural distinctions and came to them across political borders.

The name described Ardis as an operation committed to the literature that rose above such borders.

With Ardis, the Proffers acquired their own identity as gift givers. Significantly, their first reprint edition was Osip Mandel'shtam's 1913 collection *Kamen'* (*Stone*), which was originally printed for a very brief run and was nearly lost. Nadezhda Mandel'shtam told the Proffers about *Kamen'*, but she did not have a copy. When the Proffers obtained a copy of the collection from another friend, a Soviet book collector, they produced a new (facsimile) edition and gave a copy to Nadezhda. Nadezhda Mandel'shtam was one of the Proffers most beloved friends, as well as a crucial contact for them. She impressed the Proffers with her indomitable spirit and lively character. She herself had served as a bearer of culture across time, preserving many of her husband Osip Mandel'shtam's verses in memory. Her memoirs about Russian literary life in the early twentieth century were just about to come out when the Proffers met her in 1969 (*Vospominaniia*, and its English counterpart, *Hope against Hope*, were published in 1970). Recipient of the new "gift" edition of Mandel'shtam's *Kamen'*, Nadezhda helped the Proffers become significant mediators of Russian culture across time and political boundaries. In fact, if Vladimir Nabokov was the source of Ardis's name and in some way its conceptual "father," Nadezhda might be regarded as the "mother" who brought Ardis into the world. She provided practical help for the realization of the Proffers' project. Nadezhda introduced the Proffers to many of their most significant acquaintances inside the USSR, including artists Boris Birger, Andrei Sergeev, Lev Kopelev, and Raisa Orlova. She introduced them to Bulgakov's widow, Elena Sergeevna, and she gave them a letter of introduction to Joseph Brodsky in Leningrad.[16]

At first, the Proffers were unsure about trying to realize a full-fledged publishing venture. They thought they could broaden American readers' horizons when it came to twentieth-century Russian literature, but there was no outside support or clear mandate for that kind of publishing. The Proffers' editorial introduction in the first issue of their flagship journal *Russian Literature Triquarterly* explained their enterprise as something both independent and not yet entirely formed:

> We see the journal as a "post-horse of enlightenment." Whether it will be a thoroughbred or a nag remains to be seen.
>
> We will not publish articles on literary politics or similar cold-war criticism of either the American or Soviet variety. This is a literary journal, not a political one. It is unique for our field in that it is a private publication with no institutional backing or affiliation. The contents reflect the tastes of the editors, the needs of English-speaking readers, and chance.[17]

Ardis's audience was, from the beginning, relatively narrow and academic. The mission was avowedly apolitical, and sometimes even anti-political. The facsimile editions of Russian modernist poetry exemplify Ardis's "disinterest" in profit and politics. Those editions lost money. However, they provided something else, which Carl Proffer alluded to in his letter to Nabokov in 1973 about the pleasure with which he and his wife reprinted Russian poetry. These editions exemplified the taste and high-mindedness of the Proffers. They represented cultural prestige among their acquaintances in the Russian intelligentsia. At the same time, however, Carl told Nabokov that Ardis depended on English-language publications to help square accounts.[18] The Proffers's friends valued Ardis reprints of volumes by Anna Akhmatova, Marina Tsvetaeva, Nikolai Gumilev, Osip Mandelshtam, Konstantin Vaginov, and other giants of Russian modernist poetry. However, those friends were not paying customers. The Proffers produced these facsimile editions to return a piece of Russian culture to their friends, demonstrating at the same time their own taste and passion for this lost heritage.

Ardis's small-format poetic reprint editions look amazing; they have personality. These collections of poetry were originally released in small print runs and miniature formats, in order to save paper (economic constraints being paramount in the post–World War I and early Soviet periods—there had never been a large market for poetry). Ardis reprinted Mandel'shtam's *Kamen'* and Tsvetaeva's *Versty* (*Versts*) at 18 centimeters. Many facsimiles, including *Chetki* (*Rosary*), Vaginov's *Puteshestvie v khaos* (*Journey into Chaos*), Mandel'shtam's *Tristia*, Pasternak's *Temy i variatsii* (*Themes and Variations*), and Gumilev's *Ognennyi stolp* (*Pillar of Fire*) were smaller, at just 16 centimeters. Akhmatova's *Anno Domini MCMXXI* was fourteen centimeters, and her *Podorozhnik* (*Plantain*), with its beautiful cover design by M. V. Dobuzhinskii, was a mere 12 centimeters high. No one else produced reprints like these. In the 1960s, Bradda Books in Letchworth, England, did similar editions in its "Rarity Reprints" series, to be succeeded in the Ardis era by Prideaux Press, which printed a number of the same titles in its "Russian Titles for the Specialist" series (see copies out of Letchworth of *Tristia, Versty, Ognennyi stolp*, and others). These Letchworth academic publications appeared in drab standardized covers and formats. Possev in Munich—another tamizdat press—produced small-format editions, too, but of a different type and for other reasons. Run by the anti-Soviet émigré organization NTS (*Narodno-Trudovoi Soiuz*, the Popular Workers' Union), Possev did a whole series of pocket-size editions, including Solzhenitsyn's *Rakovyi korpus* (*The Cancer Ward*, 1968, 14.5 centimeters), and an edition of the six-volume collected works of Solzhenitsyn in Russian (*Sobranie sochinenii*, 2nd ed., 1971, 15 centimeters) as part of a targeted campaign to distribute prohibited literature clandestinely within the Soviet Union.[19] Ardis did not publish facsimiles and reprints in order to distribute its products in the USSR widely or clandestinely. They produced these editions of poetry for a few Soviet friends and a handful of Slavic specialists. Their work also served the purpose of preservation. Their editions were printed on acid-free paper as soon as the Proffers understood the need to do so. A sizeable portion of the small print runs (just five hundred copies for many of the poetic facsimiles) went to libraries. The Proffers alone of these tamizdat publishers appreciated the craft of the book objects as part of the legacy of modernist culture.

Over the course of the 1970s, Ardis produced more than sixty reprints of Russian-language editions (see the listing in this book's appendix), making up between a fourth and a third of the total number of titles released by Ardis in that decade. The list encompasses the overwhelming majority of Russian titles Ardis did at this time. Ardis advertised them as "facsimiles and reprints." "Facsimiles" meant editions that mimicked the original dimensions and cover designs. The "reprints" (which are technically "facsimiles," as well) also presented the original text, without additions or expurgation, in the original typographic layout. However, the reprints did not look like special book objects in the same way. In some cases, the covers of the original editions were damaged or missing and could not be reproduced. In other cases, the covers were relatively plain, as was the case with the titles Viktor Shklovskii and Boris Tomashevskii published in 1971. In many instances, the original publisher's advertising appears at the end, and the original marks of the publishers are reproduced—the Petropolis Bronze Horseman and the legendary Alkonost bird (see Aleksander Blok's *Dvenadtsat'* for a large and detailed reproduction of this distinctive publisher's mark). Ardis did editions of Silver Age Poetry, Acmeist and Futurist works, early Soviet titles and Formalist scholarship. They worked from originals they found in European booksellers or received from Soviet friends. They relied on the recommendations of Russian friends and their own cultivated taste for modernist literature selections.

Among these reproductions, the Nabokov reprints comprise a special subset. Beginning in 1974, Ardis started systematically reprinting all the extant Russian editions of Nabokov's works. Within the 1970s alone, Ardis reprinted *Mashen'ka* (*Mary*), *Podvig* (*Glory*), *Dar* (*The Gift*), *Vozvrashchenie Chorba* (*The Return of Chorb*), *Lolita*, *Vesna v Fial'te* (*Spring in Fialta*), *Drugie berega* (*Other Shores*), *Kamera obskura* (*Laughter in the Dark*), *Otchaianie* (*Despair*), *Sogliadatai* (*The Eye*), *Zashchita Luzhina* (*Luzhin's Defense*), *Korol', dama, valet* (*King, Queen, Knave*), and *Priglashenie na kazn'* (*Invitation to a Beheading*). Ardis did not have money to publish Nabokov in English, and Nabokov would never have considered publishing his English works with such a small house. Ardis could, however, reprint Nabokov's Russian titles, which were very important for the Soviet Russian audience, whose previous access to such works had been very limited.

Many Russian readers recall an Ardis edition as their first encounter with Nabokov's work.[20] The new and relatively uniform title pages Ardis did for this set of reprints, with a characteristic Nabokov-Ardis font and design, create a special visual identification of Ardis with Nabokov.

Nabokov's writing bridged the modernist and contemporary eras in time, and Russia and America in space. As Nabokov's Russian-language publisher in the United States, Ardis made the leap from being a small publishing house resurrecting modernist literature to a vital enterprise working with contemporary Russian readers and writers. Ardis's growth as a symbol and its grounding in a social network of members of the Russian intelligentsia gave the Proffers more confidence to assert their own alternative definition of Russian literature. At the "Third Wave" conference in Los Angeles in 1981, Carl Proffer denounced the idea of separate Soviet Russian and Russian émigré literatures (a division that had been fundamental for the authority claimed by ideologues over Soviet Russian letters, just as it was to the Russian émigré publishing houses like YMCA in Paris): "No, there is only one Russian literature that matters—and this is it, folks. It's all around the hemisphere, without any borders outside of grammar."[21] Ellendea claimed: "We were giving back Nabokov as much as Akhmatova."[22] The mention of émigré Nabokov together with the "lost" modernist Akhmatova illustrates the (re)unification of Russian literature beyond such distinctions.

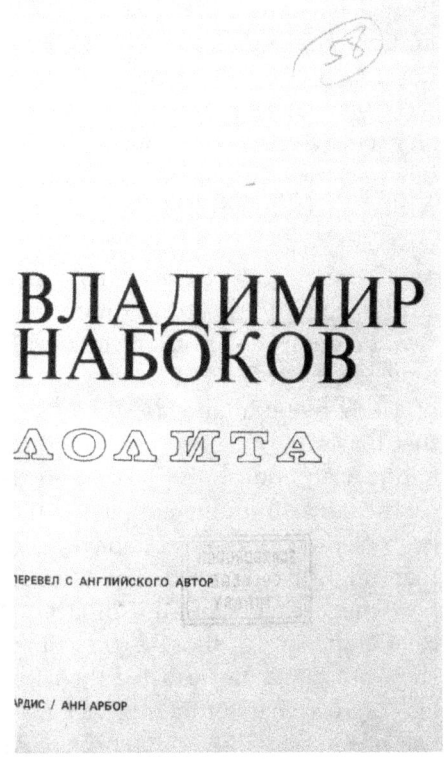

FIGURE 1.5. Title page of Vladimir Nabokov's *Lolita*, Russian edition (Ardis, 1976)

Political Subtexts? Reading the Material Texts

The Proffers gradually adopted this inclusive literary position in their publishing, including more and more contemporary Soviet Russian writers in their lists, along with classics of Russian modernism and Russian emigration. The engagement with contemporary Soviet writers and readers developed gradually. Evidence suggests that at first, at least, the Proffers were unaware that their audience in the Soviet Union extended beyond an exclusive circle of friends. The recollections of Soviet readers likewise demonstrate that a broad Soviet Russian audience learned only later about Ardis. As a student in Leningrad in the 1970s, Ivan Tolstoy first became aware of Ardis Publishing in 1976 through their Nabokov editions, and he never encountered any publications released in the first three years of Ardis's operations. Ardis editions in the late 1970s were useful, said Tolstoy, for a particular reason: one could look at the list of Russian titles on the back to know what was being published in the West. The publication of a title by Akhmatova, Mandel'shtam, or Gumilev in the West meant that that same title (in original editions) would now be available in the antiquarian bookstores.[23] Thus, Ardis helped break the de facto ban on certain books through tamizdat publication. Ardis's impact on the cultural process, therefore, seems to have been both narrower and farther-reaching than might be expected. The titles Ardis made available reached only a few Soviet readers, but the impact of those editions exceeded the numerical significance of those Ardis copies alone. A review of Ardis editions shows that they never listed their Russian titles before 1976, indicating a lack of awareness of their Soviet audience and its needs. The subsequent lists of Russian titles on the back of Ardis reprints in the late 1970s generally did not show prices, indicating that they were intended for informational rather than commercial purposes, i.e., for Soviet readers.

The title lists on the back of the Russian editions indicate recognition at Ardis of its relatively broad Soviet readership. By the end of the 1970s, Ardis became aware of the larger Soviet reading public as recipient of their "gifts." At the Moscow Book Fair in 1977, and again in 1987, Soviet visitors verbally expressed gratitude and surreptitiously stripped the Ardis exhibit of its stock, including display copies—an entirely understandable contingency, but not one Ardis staff had quite expected. Ellendea Proffer recalled the 1977 Book Fair as a special moment when they learned how surprisingly large and dispersed the Soviet audience for Ardis editions was. Many loved the Ardis edition on Esenin (Gordon McVay, *Esenin: A Life*, 1976) for its abundance of photographs. Others showed them Ardis editions of Nabokov that had clearly passed through many hands.[24]

By the late 1970s, Ardis was also publishing young writers who were unable to publish experimental works in the Soviet Union. These "neo-modernist" writers included Sasha Sokolov, whom Nabokov loved. Ardis published Sokolov's *Shkola dlia durakov* (*School for Fools*) in 1976. Ardis published Andrei Bitov's uncensored magnum opus *Pushkinskii dom* (*Pushkin*

House, 1978). Ardis also put out Vasilii Aksenov's uncensored *Ozhog* (*The Burn*) in 1980. Aksenov's inflammatory novel enraged Soviet authorities. However, the Proffers had already become personae non grata in the Soviet Union by the time it came out. The 1979 *Metropole* anthology, which Aksenov organized and Ardis published, turned Soviet authorities against Ardis along with the Soviet Union of Writers members who participated. *Metropole* embodied the same scandalously inclusive version of Russian literature that Carl Proffer articulated: the anthology provocatively and publicly trampled over distinctions between censored and uncensored Soviet literature, and between Soviet and Western "bourgeois" literature by bringing American author John Updike into the fold. As a result of publishing *Metropole*, the Proffers were prohibited from visiting the USSR and subsequently denied visas.

While Ardis Russian publishing was economically unviable, it was of interest to a Soviet Russian readership, and that was reason enough for Soviet authorities to treat the organization as a challenge to its cultural hegemony and a threat to its proper borders. Cultural subversion undoubtedly has political implications. To what degree was the CIA subsidizing Ardis as part of its cultural warfare? We know, for example, that the CIA Book Program subsidized the publishing and distribution of an enormous number of books for Eastern bloc and Soviet readers. Much of this was literary or "cultural" — that is, not specifically political — reading.[25] Emerging details about the extent of CIA involvement in the Russian publication of Boris Pasternak's *Doctor Zhivago* demonstrate that the Agency intervention in tamizdat was both fundamental and carefully concealed.[26] This involvement was not necessarily secretive, although it was in no one's interest to publicize it at the time — everyone who had dealings with the International Literary Center in New York, for instance, knew it was a CIA operation. Ardis filled orders from the Center. We might ask what percentage of Ardis editions was destined for such operations as an indication of indirect benefit from CIA operations to Ardis.

The extent of CIA support for a small publishing house like Ardis producing editions of Russian literature is not clear. What seems clear, however, is that the support could not have been direct or great. There appears to have been no Agency funding or planning behind the operation of Ardis. The quality of their reprints suggests that Ardis was exactly what it appeared to be: an amateur enterprise, undertaken on a shoestring budget by enthusiasts who loved Russian literature. The Proffers had to learn the publishing trade as they went along. They do not appear to have benefited from coordinated professional and financial support. For example, the appearance of the Ardis imprint is erratic. On some editions, the Ardis name, the carriage silhouette, address, and reprint information appear.

In other cases, there is an Ardis carriage but no name. In a few instances, reprints do not display the Ardis name at all. The Ardis copy of Mikhail Bulgakov's *D'iavoliada* (*The Diaboliad*) viewed for this study has only a carriage on the back and no Ardis name, while an Ardis reprint of Vladislav Khodasevich's *Tiazhelaia Lira* (*The Heavy Lyre*) examined bears absolutely no indication that it is a reprint or an Ardis product at all—the reprint was identifiable as Ardis through library records alone. This obscurity appears to be the result of Ardis's improvisational nature and irregular advertising. The unique two-in-one reprinted edition of Boris Pil'niak's and Mikhail Zoshchenko's *Stat'i i materialy,* released the first year Ardis began publishing, looks unprofessional. Ardis's own cover features the authors' names and title transliterated into Latin characters. The order of authors appears as Pil'niak and Zoshchenko on the cover and inside the edition, although the order of authors is reversed in Ardis advertising lists, probably because the alphabetical order differs depending on whether one renders it in Cyrillic or Latin characters. The title of Mikhail Kuzmin's *Zanaveshennye kartinki* (*Covered Pictures*) appears in Ardis advertising as *ZanaveshAnnye kartinki,* a nonstandard spelling taken from the stylized picture of old orthography on the front, rather than from the standard spelling on the title page. Ardis advertising at the back of *RLT* describes the ruse behind the edition's publication in Amsterdam: *Zanaveshennye kartinki* was in fact published by Petropolis in Petersburg, though this fact was concealed to protect the publisher from the consequences of distributing erotic pictures. This bibliographic information is lacking from the Ardis reprint edition itself, although one might expect a well-prepared reprint edition to include a note about such significant facts of the publication history.

In fact, Ardis facsimiles and reprints lack annotations and extra notes of any kind. This comes as no surprise, given that the chief advantage of reprints was that they were inexpensive and required relatively little labor. This is the real secret of the Ardis Russian facsimile and reprint editions: they were all produced by photo-offset lithography. This printing process involves an inked image from a photolithographic plate on a cylinder that is transferred (or "offset") to a blanket running over a second cylinder, which transfers the image to paper.[27] All the Proffers had to do was provide the camera-ready book to the printer. This method obviated labor-intensive typesetting and copyediting. In addition, the Proffers happened to enjoy the good fortune of an abundance of printers doing small print runs in the Ann Arbor area. Such fortunate circumstances of geography and history made Ardis possible. The Ann Arbor printers taught the Proffers some tricks of the trade along the way, including shooting down the image of the page and cutting out extra margin space, in order to save on paper. The Ardis edition of Fedor Sologub's *Melkii bes* (*The Petty*

Demon, 1979) illustrates this technique.[28] Ardis was not able to reproduce the paper of original editions, and, in the case of Akhmatova's *Podorozhnik* (*Plantain*), for example, with its black-white-yellow cover design on white matte paper, they reproduced it in simple black and white on shiny paper. The Proffers did the best they could with what means they had available.

The remarkable fact is that Ardis produced these facsimiles at all. The Ardis quirks and idiosyncrasies enhance the character of their editions, which are truly products of their time. As is the case with samizdat, the relatively amateurish quality of these and other tamizdat editions may be read as a significant indication of "authenticity" (real enthusiasm, rather than commercial or political interest) for us now.[29] It is doubtful, however, that Soviet readers interpreted the book objects in the same way. On the contrary, Soviet authors praised the beautiful professional Western editions from Ardis. Some authors, lacking knowledge of and experience in the Western book trade, suspected Ardis must have been making much more money than they revealed. That Ardis profited substantially from this work seems doubtful.

A particularly intriguing oddity among the Ardis reprints is the duplication of a mistake that Ardis did not make. The mistake occurred first in the 1967 Phaedra edition of *Lolita*, which looks to have been typeset on a Linotype machine, where whole lines were cast at once and arranged vertically for printing. On page twenty-three, a line is transposed from the bottom of the page to the middle, producing the "*gi- liarnaia lisa*" (the "cratic fox," as Jim Kates rendered it in English).

The arctic (*poliarnaia*) fox undergoes mutation thanks to the printer's mistake. The fantastic beast brings to life the fatal (*gi-bel'nyi*) mark of matter and circumstance on the printed literary work. Ardis's offset reprint extended the life of this mutant creature by reproducing it. Soviet readers, thrilled by the release of *Lolita* in Russian and closely attentive to the form of samizdat/tamizdat books, noticed the striking misprint. Poet Mikhail Aizenberg recalled the "cratic fox" as a symbol of his time:

> Who remembers now the "cratic fox"?
>
> Those were the days, my friend.
>
> We referred to that book often, kissing every page,
>
> We swore oaths not in words, but in quotations.[30]

We cannot know whether Aizenberg saw the mistake in a Phaedra or Ardis edition, a published book or a samizdat photographic copy—the spontaneous reproduction of uncensored texts is part of their relatively uncontrolled textual life, the kind of life that spontaneously generated the "cratic fox."

чалась главным образом в изобретении и редактировании парфюмерных объявлений. Я приветствовал ее поверхностный характер и псевдо-литературный налет и занимался ею кое-как, когда вздумается. С другой стороны, новый, военного времени, университет в Нью-Йорке уговаривал меня дописать мою сравнительную историю французской литературы. Первый том занял у меня года два работы, при чем я редкий день трудился меньше пятнадцати часов. Оглядываясь на этот период, я вижу его аккуратно разделенным на просторный свет и узкую тень: свет относится к радостям изысканий в чертогах библиотек; тень — к пытке желаний, к бессоннице — словом к тому, о чем я уже достаточно поговорил. Знакомый со мною читатель легко себе представит, как усердно, в пыльную жару, я высматривал — увы, всегда издали — нимфеток, играющих в Центральном Парке, и как мне были отвратительны декоративные, дезодоризованные секретарши и конторщицы, которыми один из шутников у нас в деле все старался меня прельстить. Опустим все это. Гилярной лисы.

бельный упадок душевных сил привел меня в санаторию на полтора года; я вернулся к работе — и вскоре опять занемог.

Выздоровление могла обещать бодрая жизнь на вольном воздухе. Любимый мой врач, очаровательный циник с короткой темной бородкой, познакомил меня со своим братом, который собирался вести экспедицию в приполярные области Канады. Я к ней был прикомандирован в качестве «наблюдателя за психическими реакциями». От времени до времени я делил (не очень, впрочем, успешно) с двумя молодыми ботаниками и старым плотником пухлявые прелести одной из наших специалисток по питанию, докторши Аниты Джонсон — которую вскоре услали на самолете во-свояси, о чем вспоминаю с удовольствием. Цель экспедиции не представлялась мне ясно. Судя по многочисленности метеорологов, участвовавших в ней, можно было подумать, что мы прослеживаем к его берлоге (где-то повидимому на Острове Принца Уэльского) блуждающий и шаткий северный магнитный полюс. Одна из групп основала с помощью канадцев метеорологическую станцию на Пьеровой Стрелке в Мельвильском Зунде. Другая, тоже заблуждавшаяся группа собирала планктон. Третья изучала связь между туберкулезом и тундрой. Берт, фильмовый фотограф, очень неуверенный в себе тип, вместе с которым меня заставляли одно время усиленно заниматься физическим трудом (у него, как и у меня, были психические нелады) уверял, что «большие люди» в нашей экспедиции, настоящие ее руководители, которых мы никогда не видали, имели целью проверить влияние климатического потепления на мех по-

23

FIGURE 1.6. Vladimir Nabokov's *Lolita* (Ardis, 1976), page twenty-three

Nabokov must have hated this typo.[31] Given his artistic commitment to an imaginative world carefully separated from history and shaped by the controlling hand of the author alone, such a mistake must have personally offended him as a mark of the "eerie and alien world" Nabokov mentioned in his verses about typesetters. Viewed from a greater distance, part of the interest of these facsimiles and reprints is their juxtaposition of an ideal poetic vision with the messy traces of history. Indeed, samizdat and tamizdat copies highlight precisely the palimpsest nature of the text, whose life is the work of many hands.

This misprint may direct our attention to the materialized life of the text, or, indeed, via the Ardis reprint, to its multiple "lives." The life Ardis gave to the texts it reprinted depended, as already noted, on photo-offset lithography—a technology disdained by many for producing "lifeless print."[32] Photolithograph prints have been criticized for their ghostly, flat character, as compared to the tactile feel of print press texts. These photolithographs lack depth when compared to print press pages, in much the way electronic texts lack substance as compared to books on paper. We might ask whether the psychological discomfort generated for some by newer media correspond to the unsettling of accustomed models of authorship and fixed significance.

Offset lithography represented the first real departure from typographical printing since Gutenberg. Bernard Newdigate, manager of the Shakespeare Head Press and an influential typographical journalist, believed in the value of the arts and crafts movement and private presses for democratizing the printing trade, and he displayed a prophetic enthusiasm for offset lithography and photocomposition as early as 1923. Newdigate thought these technologies, which many disparaged as cheap and nasty, were in fact just as good as the uses to which they were put. Sebastian Carter, writing in the 1980s, put Newdigate's views in historical perspective: "At the time when Newdigate was writing, the technology of typographical printing had been basically the same since Gutenberg: the surfaces of metal letters cast in relief were inked and pressed against paper. The way they were cast and assembled might have changed, and the way pressure was applied, but not the general principle." Lithography, a planographic process that was the basis of offset printing and photocomposition, differed fundamentally.[33]

Contemporary Western paradigms developed in the Gutenberg Era tend to idealize "the text" as created by the author, infinitely reproducible, and essentially fixed.[34] The individual writing subject, elaborated in modern Western literature, becomes the source of meaning and the locus of rights and responsibilities: the author owns the text.

Samizdat and tamizdat expose the inadequacy of these models in the context of twentieth-century developments, when the state undermined the rights of individual authors, and corrupted a cultural process supposed to be based on individual contributions. In 1973 the USSR accession to the Universal Copyright Convention provoked heated debates in the West. Samizdat had become hot material, and many publishers and academics were concerned that the Soviet Union, rather than protecting authors, intended to use the UCC to crack down on the flow of uncensored publications from the Soviet Union. The Proffers joined the debate with an open letter to Senator John McClellan, pointing out that the policies of *Mezhkniga* (the agency in charge of foreign sales and translations of works under Soviet copyright) returned less than half the copyright royalties to authors. There were other manipulations too, they explained, such as that concerning print runs advertised in Soviet editions: "Russians on the inside know that editions of '50,000' may be only 2,000 (a device which has been used in the past by the Soviets to show how enlightened they are with regard to certain Western titles). This technique can also be reversed, putting public figures like 2,000 on an edition of 50,000 or 100,000. This is a perfectly arbitrary matter, and there is little reason to expect honesty in the way it is handled."[35]

Joseph Brodsky, newly arrived to the United States, added his statement in support of the Proffers's view:

> Since I left the USSR only a few months ago after 32 years there, 14 of them as a writer, I think I know as much as anyone here about the censorship, writers' situation, and fears, and official Soviet attitudes to authors' rights.
>
> What is going to happen is quite simple. If Soviet government rights are upheld in the West, Russian culture will be destroyed on a global scale. The finest writers and artists will be further enslaved. Censorship will be enforced by international law.[36]

The Proffers' letter suggests that they had special insider knowledge, as a result of their acquaintances among Soviet authors and readers. Their concern, they argued, was not really the politically explosive samizdat, even if the high profile of the topic must have made it an exciting time to be in the business of publishing uncensored Russian material. The Proffers wrote, "More important than current *samizdat* manuscripts in quantity and in literary quality are the many works which are actually published in the USSR in very small editions or in provincial literary journals." They specifically mentioned poetry by Akhmatova, Pasternak, Tsvetaeva, and writing by Zoshchenko—works repressed or changed significantly by ideological censorship. In many cases Ardis reproduced these works based on the original text, as the authors first wrote them. One of the interesting tensions in Ardis was the political value of their avowedly "apolitical" publishing. On the one hand, we have the stated Ardis commitment to literary texts, valued as autonomous entities, independent of social context and political agendas. On the other hand, the worth of what the Proffers did at Ardis had to do with their support of texts threatened by the Soviet social context and political agenda. Seen in terms of the issues of textual culture being discussed here, the spirit of Ardis came from modern Gutenberg ideals, while the actual Ardis operation depended on technologies that exceeded those of the classic print era, in order to address the abuse of authors and texts by Soviet officials and institutions.

New Textual Culture

Knotty issues associated with "texts" and "authors" in contemporary times cannot be limited to the Soviet case or to similar. Problems with the classic Gutenberg values of a fixed text and individual author become more acute in the context of globalization and new media. Librarian Janice T. Pilch examined the contemporary emphasis on intellectual property as an economic phenomenon that negatively impacts the circulation and development of ideas and knowledge. Surveying the development of copyright laws, Pilch historically contextualized their paradigms and questioned the contemporary hegemony of the concept of "intellectual property" in international law: "In the discourse on globalization, this is critical for libraries and educational institutions. It is an understatement to say that the WTO weighs commercial aspects and uses of intellectual property at the expense of its noncommercial value." Pilch concluded that "one of the major challenges to copyright today is maintaining a balance between the private interests of creators of works and copyright holders and the public right to benefit from using those works."[37] Attempts to control textual reproduction and circulation often benefit corporations more than individuals. In the age of digital worldwide media and widely varying local copyright controls, how justified is the primacy given to intellectual property?

Bibliography expert D. F. McKenzie, writing on textual issues in the digital age, advocated more careful attention to media: "form effects meaning," he wrote.[38] The specific method used to copy texts contributes to the meaning of the reproduction, so that, for example, Ardis's reprint of Mandel'shtam's *Kamen'* has political and cultural significance different from that of a hypothetical late Soviet reprint of the book. For this reason, the sociology of the production and dissemination of texts raises crucial questions. McKenzie identified a significant shift in bibliography:

from questions of textual authority to those of dissemination and readership as matters of economic and political motive. Those relationships are difficult to pin down, but they are powerful in the ways they preclude certain forms of discourse and enable others; and because they determine the very conditions under which meanings are created, they lie at the heart of what has come to be known as *histoire du livre*, a form of inquiry relevant to the history of every text-dependent discipline.[39]

McKenzie's remarks are relevant to a critical history of tamizdat. We will need to pay attention to the forms of tamizdat texts, the methods of production and circulation, and the identity of financiers, producers, and distributors. Surely, it matters if the CIA funded the Russian publication of *Doctor Zhivago*, not because it limits Pasternak's achievement or the autonomy of form and themes in the novel, but because that literary work is inscribed into a network of cultural and political ramifications that involve the Nobel prize and the development of tamizdat as a system in the wake of the foreign publication of Pasternak's novel.

A caveat seems in order, however. If we treat the history of samizdat and tamizdat as a detective story that revolves around the machinations of the CIA (or the KGB), institutions become the sole agents determining the moral and meaning of our critical history. We risk falling prey to a grotesque version of the single author model we have problematized. This version that ascribes all authority to the secret State institution perpetuates the Soviet regime's betrayal of humane values and individual authors. The conclusions of a suspicious sociohistorical hermeneutics pursued along these lines would be predetermined and reductive. We might strive rather to resurrect traditional human concerns in a new way. We might ask, for example, about the unpredetermined roles of individuals who participated in unauthorized textual production and circulation. We might look to elucidate the new or evolving identities and social relationships formed through the independent production and circulation of texts. The story of tamizdat is more than a Cold War spy novel or a historical curiosity. Critical analysis of tamizdat might help effect its transfer as a topic of interest for our current post- (or extra-) Gutenberg age, an age of mobile texts and multiple agents involved in the creation of meaning and value.[40]

Conclusion

The Ardis facsimiles and reprints illustrate the sometimes unexpected conjunctions of an ideal poetic spirit and the social and historical body of the tamizdat text. They suggest something about the directions we might pursue in our investigations of tamizdat. Raisa Orlova said of the Proffers and their products:

> Thanks to those publishers who publish the books of my contemporaries and thanks first of all to Carl and Ellendea Proffer, who created "Ardis" in Ann Arbor, without which it would be impossible to imagine the recent history of Russian literature. They resurrected thousands of forgotten pages of our past.
>
> Mandel'shtam's *Stone* (*Kamen'*), Akhmatova's *Rosary* (*Chetki*) — with what trembling, with what agitated gentleness we and our friends took these first small thin "reprints" into our hands, carefully turning the pages. ... I do not belong to the tribe of bibliophiles, but I feel the charm of the first edition.[41]

Orlova evoked the spirit of the ideal text identified with its author and resurrected in these reprint editions. While even the facsimiles, produced by photolithography, are in fact *not* the same as the first edition, these slim volumes recall those original texts, and add something more: the emotion they evoke in Orlova's account suggests the extra value and meaning acquired by books of Russian poetry that have traveled so improbably to the present from the lost past, via Ann Arbor, Michigan. Orlova's gratitude to the Proffers obliquely introduces their agency in supporting the contemporary lives of these texts and underscores the status acquired by the American Proffers in the process of "giving back" this Russian heritage. The reaction to the resurrected texts and the appreciation of the role the Proffers played underscore the profoundly human nature of this textual exchange. Motivated largely by personal feeling, this exchange resembles at this point the moment of gift giving more than it does an espionage drama and certainly more than a capitalist success story: here and in other instances of tamizdat, we will do well to defer assumptions of political interest or profit until we have elucidated the largely unpredictable human relations involved. A more detailed and thoughtful apprehension of those social relations of tamizdat may shed light on the history of this era, and also give us insights into issues of our more mobile and varied textual condition today.

Notes

1. Translated and quoted by Dmitri Nabokov in his eulogy for Vera Nabokova, "Nabokov File. Letters on Russian," Ardis Press Materials.
2. See Ann Komaromi, "Samizdat and Soviet Dissident Publics," *Slavic Review* 71/2 (2012), 71.
3. See, for example, the literary editions in V. E. Dolinin et al., eds., *Samizdat Leningrada, 1950-e–1980-e. Literaturnaia entsiklopediia* (Moscow, 2003); and samizdat rock journals in

Aleksandr Kushnir, *Zolotoe podpol'e. Polnaia illiustrirovannaia entsiklopediia rok-samizdata. 1967–1994. Istoriia. Antologiia. Bibliograpfiia* (Nizhnii Novgorod, 1994).
4. In his eulogy for Carl Proffer in New York on 1 April 1985 at the PEN American Center, Brodsky said, "What Carl Proffer has done to Russian literature of this century amounts to Gutenberg's invention, for he reintroduced the press" (transcript among Ardis Press Papers). Cynthia Haven cited Brodsky on this point in "Letter from Dana Point," *Times Literary Supplement*, 31 May 2002: 15.
5. Cited in the first issue of Ardis's *Russian Literature Triquarterly*, preface.
6. Phone interview with Ellendea Proffer, 7 January 2007.
7. See Marcel Mauss, *The Gift: The Form and Reason for Exchange in Archaic Societies*, trans. W. D. Halls (New York, 1990).
8. Christopher Johnson concisely outlined Lévi-Strauss's extension of concepts from Mauss in *Claude Lévi-Strauss: The Formative Years* (Cambridge, 2003), 42–5.
9. See Vladimir Nabokov, *Lolita* (New York, 1967), 298.
10. According to the introduction to the publication of the Proffers' correspondence with the Nabokovs, letters from Soviet readers about Nabokov's works had been transmitted through Radio Liberty before Carl ever wrote about such readers. See "Perepiska Nabokovykh s Profferami," *Zvezda 7* (July 2005): 123–71. Radio Liberty had secretly arranged the publication of *Zashchita Luzhina* (*Luzhin's Defense*) and *Priglashenie na kazn'* (*Invitation to a Beheading*) under French publishing house imprints made up for the purpose—*Éditions Victor* and *Éditions de la Seine*, respectively. In accordance with the CIA cultural mission, these editions were meant expressly for Soviet readers. Nabokov had probably heard about a samizdat translation of *Lolita* and we might understand his postscript to be a coy hint about making sure it was *his* version Russian readers would get.
11. Carl Proffer's letter to the Nabokovs, 17 March 1969, "Perepiska," 135–37.
12. Carl Proffer's letter to the Nabokovs, 14 May 1969, "Perepiska," 137.
13. Mauss referred to the *kula* exchange in the Trobriand Islands in Melanesia. The exchange "has its mythical, religious, and magical aspect. The *vaygu'a* are not unimportant things, mere pieces of money. Each one, at least the dearest and most sought after— ... has its name, a personality, a history and even a tale attached to it. So much is this so that certain individuals can even take their own name from them" (Mauss, *The Gift*, 24). Jacques Derrida attempted to rehabilitate the magical and affective aspects of gift giving (visible in Mauss's account) from a structuralist reduction to a material or symbolic exchange (in Lévi-Strauss's theory). Derrida stressed the gift's role in constituting identity, and he underscored the necessary break in the cycle of exchange on which the gift depends: "for there to be a gift, it is necessary [*il faut*] that the donee not give back, amortize, reimburse, acquit himself, enter into a contract, and that he never have contracted a debt." See Jacque Derrida, *Given Time: I. Counterfeit Money*, trans. Peggy Kamuf, (Chicago, 1992), 13.
14. Carl Proffer spoke about these jeans for Brodsky in a letter to the Nabokovs of 3 October 1969, and the mention appeared again in Vera Proffer's reply of 13 October 1969, "Perepiska," 140–41.
15. Ellendea Proffer Teasley, "Ardis. 25 Years of Russian Literature. Library of Foreign Literature, Moscow, Russia, May 28, 1996–June 18, 1996" (brochure, "Ardis"), 9.
16. Carl Proffer wrote about their friendship with Nadezhda Mandel'shtam in *The Widows of Russia and Other Writings* (Ann Arbor, 1987).
17. *Russian Literature Triquarterly*, no. 1 (1971).
18. Carl Proffer explained the balance of prestige and profit from editions in a letter to Nabokov, 31 October 1973, "Perepiska," 150.

19. V. D. Poremskii had in fact developed the idea for the small book project already in the 1950s. See the discussion in NTS. *Mysl' i delo. 1930–2000* (Moscow, 2000), 54. The book includes a list of titles offered by Possev.
20. Nabokov scholar D. Barton Johnson shared his anecdotal information on the significance of Ardis Nabokov editions for Soviet readers in correspondence with the author, January 2007.
21. Carl Proffer's speech, "The Remarkable Decade That Destroyed Russian Émigré Literature," was published in Carl R. Proffer, *The Widows of Russia* (Ann Arbor, 1987), 129.
22. Interview with Ellendea Proffer, January 2007.
23. Correspondence with Ivan Tolstoy, October 2006.
24. From my interview with Ellendea Proffer, April 2006.
25. See John P. C. Matthews, "The West's Secret Marshall Plan for the Mind," *International Journal of Intelligence and Counter Intelligence* 16 (2003): 409–27, as well as the obituary of George C. Minden from the *New York Times*, 23 April 2006.
26. See Ivan Tolstoi, *Otmytyi roman Pasternaka. "Doktor Zhivago" mezhdu KGB i TsRU* [The Laundered Novel. Doctor Zhivago between the KGB and the CIA] (Moscow, 2009). The book was previewed in English in an article by Peter Finn, "The Plot Thickens," *Washington Post*, 27 January 2007, http://www.washingtonpost.com/wp-dyn/content/article/2007/01/26/AR2007012601758.html (accessed 19 August 2011).
27. The process and terminology is concisely defined in the Glossary of William Proctor Williams and Craig S. Abbott, *An Introduction to Bibliographical and Textual Studies*, 3rd ed. (New York, 1999).
28. Ellendea Proffer shared information about the techniques they used in an interview, April 2006.
29. This does not preclude the fact that the CIA may have been glad to see tamizdat operations whose products it utilized look like such independent enterprises. The Bedford Publishing company established directly by the CIA began on a shoestring budget. See Isaac Patch, *Closing the Circle: A Buckalino Journey Around Our Time* (Wellesley, 1996), 257–9.
30. Кто помнит, что за зверь «гилярная лиса»? / Была такая в жизни полоса./ В настольной книге расцелован каждый лист,/ и не словами, а цитатами клялись. The poem appeared in Mikhail Aizenberg, *Ukazatel' imen* (Moscow, 1993), 99. I am indebted to Jim Kates for sharing his unpublished English version of the poem, which I borrow and modify slightly here. His translation into "cratic fox" shows the deformation of the expected "arctic fox" and is as phonetically possible (if semantically nonsensical) as the Russian *giliarnaia lisa*. I am indebted also to Vera Krimnus, who first quoted these lines in her excellent thesis, "Breaking the Mold: American Slavists & Russian Writers in the Late Soviet Era," Wesleyan University, 2005.
31. There is no evidence of reaction to this specific mistake. Carl Proffer wrote about correcting another two misprints in *Podvig* ("I xeroxed pages, cut out words from elsewhere in the text, and pasted them over the original errors — though a careful eye will detect the slight enlargement caused by xeroxing"), and he apologized for uncorrected mistakes in *Mashen'ka*. Letter of 4 November 1974, Ardis Press Papers, New Acquisition, Box 13, "Copies of Nabokov Correspondence."
32. See Philip Gaskell, *A New Introduction to Bibliography: The Classic Manual of Bibliography* (New Castle, 1972), 320. Gaskell devoted very little space to printing processes after 1950. The offset lithography is mentioned only in the context of facsimiles, which are themselves treated only as a special problem of dating and identification, raising suspicions that they are possible fakes.
33. Sebastian Carter, *Twentieth Century Type Designers* (London, 1995), 137.

34. See Elizabeth Eisenstein's influential study, *The Printing Press as an Agent of Change: Communication and Cultural Transformations in Early–Modern Europe* (Cambridge, 1979). For Eisenstein, print culture represents standardization, dissemination, and fixity, and it wrought a cultural revolution in Europe, providing the basis for the paradigm shifts of the Scientific Revolution and the Reformation.
35. See the letter of 10 April 1973, from the Proffers to Sen. McClellan, in Stefan Congrat-Butlar, ed., "The USSR Accession to the Universal Copyright Convention" (brochure, P.E.N. American Center, New York, 1973), 15.
36. Joseph Brodsky's statement, "The USSR Accession," 15.
37. Janice T. Pilch, "U.S. Copyright Relations with Central, East European, and Eurasian Nations in Historical Perspective," *Slavic Review* 65, no. 2 (Summer 2006): 325–48.
38. D. F. McKenzie, *Bibliography and the Sociology of Texts* (Cambridge, 1999), 9.
39. McKenzie, *Bibliography*, 1.
40. This analogy is pursued also in Ann Komaromi, "Samizdat as Extra-Gutenberg Phenomenon," *Poetics Today* 29, no. 4 (2009).
41. R. D. Orlova-Kopeleva, *Dveri otkryvaiutsia medlenno* (Moscow, 1994), http://lib.ru/MEMUARY/KOPELEW/orlova.txt (my translation) (accessed 26 August 2011).

Chapter 2

THE BALTIC CONNECTION
Transnational Samizdat Networks between Émigrés in Sweden and the Democratic Opposition in Poland

Lars Fredrik Stöcker

Toward the end of the 1960s, Cold War Europe entered a phase of transition that revolutionized the premises of postwar international politics. After years of confrontation between Moscow and Washington, which had brought the world to the brink of a nuclear conflict, coexistence and cooperation across the Iron Curtain became the catchphrases that determined the foreign policy of the superpowers and their allies. Consequently, the period that followed the peak of the Cold War conflict of the early 1960s has been designated as the "long peace"[1] of the postwar era, characterized by the joint ambition of both camps to consolidate the international political system after decades of ideological warfare.

From the Kremlin's perspective, détente constituted a much-welcomed turn in international politics. The West's willingness to establish a peaceful dialogue was interpreted as a confirmation of the political status quo in Central and Eastern Europe, which was expected to contribute to the internal stabilization of the crisis-torn communist regimes.[2] Yet, paradoxically, the essentially conservative and restorative turn of détente paved the way for a development that eventually led to the erosion of communism from within. The Helsinki process and the human rights discourse that derived from it turned into political ammunition that legitimized social resistance behind the Iron Curtain and triggered the formation of a transnational network of oppositional organizations within the Soviet orbit.[3] Already by the mid 1970s, a veritable culture of opposition had emerged within most of the authoritarian communist societies, which led

---

Notes for this chapter begin on page 65.

to the establishment of a parallel public sphere. Samizdat, the illegal mass reproduction of texts that were incompatible with the guidelines of the communist regimes' censorship policies, has become the synonym for the dissident strategies of creating a public and yet underground platform, on which oppositional discourses were generated and disseminated.

The notion of *samizdat* itself as the umbrella term for the "subterranean culture[s] beneath the enforced conformity"[4] of the communist regimes in Central and Eastern Europe has its origins in the post-Stalinist Soviet Union. It was the 1965 show trial against dissident writers Yuli Daniel and Andrei Sinyavsky that created the crucial incentive for the formation of an organized political opposition, which responded to the regime's repressive policy that stifled any kind of publicly expressed criticism by establishing a network of underground publishing.[5] During the following decade, this oppositional strategy spread throughout the Soviet bloc, which is why research on samizdat cannot be exclusively national in focus. Furthermore, the parallel term *tamizdat*, which describes both the reproduction of samizdat and other uncensored material from behind the Iron Curtain in the West, not only mirrored samizdat activities in the Soviet bloc, but extended them to a sphere beyond its national context. Thus, there were entanglements that even reached beyond the fault lines of the Cold War. In an attempt to challenge the traditional Cold War narrative and the topos of the communist societies in Central and Eastern Europe as hermetically closed and isolated entities, this essay highlights an under-researched aspect of samizdat as a phenomenon that not only profited from, but also subsisted on interaction and exchange across the Iron Curtain.

The benefits of this approach that stresses the transnational features of the underground publishing activities in the Soviet bloc will be illustrated with the example of Polish samizdat, usually referred to in its national context as *drugi obieg* (second circulation). Of special interest is the period between 1976, which marks the birth of a united opposition movement beyond class borders in communist Poland, and 1980, when the emergence of the Solidarity movement considerably changed the preconditions for and strategies of social resistance. This essay discusses the Polish opposition's contacts with the noncommunist countries and especially with neutral Sweden, as well as the repercussions of these connections for the production and dissemination of samizdat. On the basis of archival findings, contemporary publications and media, the networks that interconnected key agents on both sides of the Iron Curtain will be investigated. In this context, the role of the Polish émigrés, who practically supported the underground publishing activities in Poland from the opposite coast and at the same time established the necessary channels for the circulation of samizdat texts in the West, deserves closer attention.[6] With the focus on the interplay between the émigré community and domestic opposition, this essay addresses a neglected chapter of European postwar history and relates closely to the current innovative tendencies and discourses within Cold War historiography.

This so-called new Cold War history, which emerged after the fall of communism and the opening of the archives in the states within the former Soviet bloc, has emancipated itself from the traditionally prevailing dominance of political and diplomatic history. By integrating social and cultural history approaches into the research on the conflict,[7] the ideological level of the conflict as a "war of words"[8] has gained increased attention. Especially in view of the end of the bipolar world, which followed the erosion of communism in Central and Eastern Europe and the Soviet bloc as a whole due to a "collapse of legitimacy,"[9] Cold War historians increasingly take into account the "ideas, values and belief systems" that had actually been "at the heart of the struggle"[10] long before the revolutions of 1989 heralded its end. This shift in perspective has led to increased attention to ideas and concepts that migrated even across the Iron Curtain,[11] which challenges the topos of the impermeability of the fault line between the blocs as a self-evident and unquestionable paradigm for Cold War research. While international research on cross-boundary interaction beyond the Iron Curtain is still at an early stage and the theoretical guidelines for a new research framework are only nascent, first steps have been taken toward a programmatic turn within Cold War historiography. It is no coincidence that one of the most recent works was developed in Finland, which during the Cold War decades quite rightly perceived itself as a transition zone or bridge between the blocs. The editors of the recently published volume *Reassessing Cold War Europe* call for intensified attention to the nonconfrontational aspects of Cold War history and the "wide space of vivid interaction" that could blossom in spite of the Iron Curtain, which thus "failed to prevent dynamic and vivid contacts" between East and West.[12]

The question of agency is central to this reformulated approach to Europe's Cold War history. It constitutes a sharp contrast to traditional research on the bipolar world of the postwar decades, which considered sub-state actors to be irrelevant.[13] Taking inspiration from this actor-centered approach, it is useful to take a closer look at the Central and Eastern European exiles in the West, not only as the protagonists of an additional, parallel level of their nations' postwar history, but as mediators between the blocs with both the necessary potential and a lively interest in surmounting the Iron Curtain. What is true for the divided nations such as West and East Germany or communist China and nationalist Taiwan—namely that these constellations fostered a significant intensification of interaction on a nongovernmental level[14]—should also apply to the relationship between the communist-ruled parts of Europe and the diaspora communities, whose mediating function as "channels" between East and West has already been highlighted.[15] The prerequisites for such entanglements beyond the Iron Curtain were created by détente,[16] which led to the "intensification of peaceful interaction,"[17] not only between European states, but between actors on various levels. With the state-sanctioned lifting of the Iron Curtain and the "'people first' approach to détente,"[18] the stage for legal interaction in the form of social exchange and personal encounters was significantly enlarged, which definitely affected the relationship between exiles and their home countries. The question of whether the neutral states played an underestimated role in this context, not only as mediators in the process of détente on the level of high politics,[19] but also as a specific space between the blocs that shaped the development of the Cold War,[20] has been posed in the literature and plays a certain role in the present study.

In the case of the reconfiguration of the Polish People's Republic's relations with its northern neighbors, which was mainly determined by the Gierek regime's need for modern technologies and favorable credits, the Swedish and Finnish neutrality policies certainly played a crucial role for Warsaw's energetic efforts to strengthen its ties across the Baltic Sea from 1970 onward. The bilateral relations with Sweden as the leading Scandinavian country were prioritized and most probably considered as politically "safe," as the decision makers in Poland expected Stockholm to stick to a "neutrality at any price" approach, which seemed to exclude the possibility of any Swedish interference in Polish internal affairs.[21] One of the most tangible and immediate results of this process of détente in the Baltic Sea Region was the significant expansion of the infrastructure between the shores. Already in 1973, the ferry connections between the Polish coast and Scandinavia were expanded to Finland and the visa requirements for Finnish citizens were lifted. At that point, the negotiations between Warsaw and Stockholm about a similar agreement had already started as a further step toward a rapprochement policy that developed between the neutral Scandinavian states and the communist satellites in the early 1970s.[22] The promotion of tourism between Sweden and Poland was a direct result of a large-scale agreement that was supposed to intensify the bilateral relations on various levels. Separate treaties had already regulated the increased cooperation in the spheres of culture, science, and education on a grass root level,[23] when the abolishment of the visa requirements for Swedish citizens who intended to travel to Poland was announced in June 1974.[24]

The Swedish social democratic government's own *Ostpolitik* aimed at reducing the geopolitical tensions in the country's immediate neighborhood. At the peak of Swedish-Polish rapprochement in the early 1970s, Stockholm showed a lively interest in overcoming the sticking points that had strained the bilateral relations for the past decades, above all the question of the institutionally well-organized, anticommunist émigré circles in Sweden, who were loyal to the London-based Polish government-in-exile.[25] Although the Swedish *Polonia,* the community of Polish émigrés and their descendants, was predominantly apolitical and maintained close cultural contacts with the home country,[26] there was a small but lively circle of anticommunist exile activists. Among the leading protagonists were both the former employees of the Polish legation in Stockholm who had refused to return to Warsaw under the changed political conditions in 1945 and representatives of the later waves of both politically and economically motivated immigration to Sweden.

Seen from the perspective of the Swedish government, the most problematic part of the Swedish *Polonia* was the Polish staff of Radio Free Europe's Scandinavian bureau in Stockholm, whose members had systematically been collecting uncensored information on the political development in communist Poland from Polish refugees, tourists, and sailors in Sweden since the early 1950s.[27] Although Swedish legislation did not explicitly prohibit political activity on the part of foreigners, provided that it did not constitute a direct threat to the state,[28] the existence of a strident Polish opposition to the communist government in Warsaw on Swedish territory was perceived as a dilemma. Addressing this question was obviously seen as an essential signal in the spirit of détente, as was reflected by Prime Minister Olof Palme's statement during the visit of Wojciech Jaruzelski, the Polish minister of defense, to Stockholm in September 1972, in which he stated that RFE constituted an "anomalous" phenomenon that had to be buried as a remnant of the Cold War.[29] Yet, it soon turned out that the so-called new emigration, which in several waves reached Sweden throughout the 1970s, constituted a much more serious threat to the positive development of the bilateral relations across the Baltic Sea.

The first representatives of this new generation of Polish political refugees arrived in the aftermath of the Warsaw government's "anti-Zionist campaign" of 1968, which forced almost 13,000 Polish Jews to leave the country between 1969 and 1971.[30] Around 2000 of these political refugees, the majority being highly educated members of the Polish intelligentsia and former state officials, settled down in Sweden, following an official invitation of the Swedish state that was the result of a special parliamentary decision.[31] As a consequence of the Polish protests in 1970, a second wave of 2500 Polish political refugees reached Sweden, while the number of Poles that were granted political asylum between 1971 and 1974 amounted to an additional 1000 per annum.[32]

For the long-established community of Polish anticommunist activists, the size of the new wave of political refugees was perceived as a certain threat, not least due to the fear that the regime in Warsaw would take the opportunity to infiltrate the Polish refugee organizations in Sweden by smuggling its own agents into the rows of newcomers.[33] The *Rada Uchodźstwa Polskiego* (Polish Refugee Council), the central organization of the part of the Polish community that had remained loyal to the exile government, even added a clause to its statute to prevent the representatives of the "new emigration" from gaining influence within the "old emigration's" institutional network. However, it turned out that the political refugees that reached Sweden after 1969 were not interested in joining the organizational structures of the Swedish *Polonia*.[34] Their arrival heralded a new chapter of anticommunist activity on Swedish soil, whose aims and strategies greatly differed from those of the established exile circles. The established émigrés had perceived themselves as an exclave of "Polish London" and coordinated their political activities within the larger structures of the Polish diaspora's anticommunist struggle in the West. The new generation of political refugees, by contrast, was intimately familiar with the realities of communist Poland, which determined their perspective and scope of action. They provided networks in the home country, which they intended to use in their struggle against the repressive regime from their new place of residence on Poland's opposite coast. The gradual lifting of the Iron Curtain between Sweden and Poland, which had created an increasingly expanded infrastructure across the Baltic Sea, opened up an unforeseen sphere of oppositional activity, which developed into a vibrant Swedish-Polish network.

With the arrival of the Polish Jews from 1969 onward, new first-hand information from behind the Iron Curtain reached Sweden in the form of eyewitness reports and written documentation that some of the refugees had smuggled out of the country, which significantly revitalized the critical public discourse on the political development in Poland. This was reflected in the contemporary media coverage, whose tone formed a clear contrast to the government's rapprochement policy. At the same time, Polish-Jewish émigrés started a lively publishing activity in the West with their own regularly edited journals that continued the underground political discourse, which had developed in communist Poland during the late 1960s among the representatives of the young intelligentsia.[35] One of the most important journals, titled *Aneks*, was published in Uppsala, the new home to a network of Polish-Jewish sociologists, who prior to their forced emigration had been working in outstanding academic institutions in Warsaw. The ideological influence that the smuggling of the émigré journal *Kultura* to Poland had had on the younger generation of Polish intellectuals became evident in the Uppsala journal. In its form and content, *Aneks* was heavily based on the famous exile journal edited by Polish count Jerzy Giedroyć in Paris, the "capital of Eastern European dissent in the West"[36] and the heart of the intellectual discourse of the Polish diaspora since 1947. While it was indeed focused on developments in Poland, it was, its authors claimed, essentially dedicated to fighting the idea of socialism in general.[37]

The circles around the Uppsala journal were closely linked to a small outpost of Giedroyć's *Kultura* in Sweden, which had been established in 1971 as the *Towarzystwo Przyjaciół "Kultury"* (Society of the Friends of *Kultura*) under the auspices of its chairman Norbert Żaba, a former diplomat and journalist who had emigrated to Sweden during World War II. Beginning in the early 1970s, the connection between Giedroyć, Żaba, and the Polish-Jewish representatives of the "new emigration" resulted in the development of a clandestine smuggling network, which due to the specific conditions that arose under Polish-Swedish détente led to the establishment of a reliable connection between Poland and the West via Sweden.[38] Under the leadership of the journalist Józef Lebenbaum from Łódź a small activist circle in the strategically well-located town of Lund in southern Sweden secured the flow of uncensored information in the form of exile literature and other censored publications to Poland. Both Polish tourists and recruited Swedish couriers were used to smuggle books on the ferries that connected Poland to the harbors of Trelleborg and Ystad, while larger transports were organized on private boats. The handover of the smuggled goods was conducted on the open sea in cooperation with the crews of Polish yachts, which officially cruised around in Poland's territorial waters and thus were not subject to border controls.[39]

Thus, Sweden's neutrality and geographical proximity to Poland became significant assets that could be effectively used by the Polish émigré circles to support oppositional circles in the home country. Even before the decisive 1976 protests that led to the formation of an organized social opposition, Sweden had become an important hub in the anticommunist Polish diaspora's networks, whose main aim was to undermine the Warsaw regime's legitimacy. As the Swedish connection was much safer than the continental route, which had been used so far for the sporadic smuggling of exile publications, especially from Paris,[40] smuggling activities across the Baltic Sea were considerably expanded and soon provided even Czechoslovakia and the Soviet Union with censored books and journals. Ironically, the establishment of this reliable transnational network of contacts was a corollary of détente, which had opened up a much wider space of Polish-Swedish interaction on all levels. The channels that developed due to the vitalization of exchange across the Baltic Sea would play a pivotal role in supporting the social opposition that developed in Poland during the second half of the 1970s.[41]

In June 1976, the Warsaw suburb of Ursus and the provincial town of Radom were shook by a wave of mass protests, which had been triggered by a sudden increase of food prices that had caused thousands of workers to go on strike. The brutal suppression of the protests by police forces turned the events into one of the decisive watershed moments of Polish postwar history, whose most visible signal was the foundation of the *Komitet Obrony Robotników* (Workers' Defense Committee, KOR) in September 1976. Led by a group of intellectuals, among others Jacek Kuroń and Adam Michnik, who both had been involved into dissident activities during the student protests of March 1968, the Committee bridged the traditional gap between the intelligentsia and the working population,[42] which was a breakthrough in the history of social resistance in Poland. Due to the convergence of two seemingly incompatible traditions of anticommunist resistance within the framework of KOR—the oppositional camps of Catholics and the supporters of democratic socialism[43]—and the integration of the masses of workers and peasants, the way was paved for the emergence of the first organized opposition to the communist regime that united large segments of society in a common cause. KOR dedicated its activity to the protection of the workers' civic rights, as did a number of smaller organizations, such as the right-wing *Ruch Obrony Praw Człowieka i Obywatela* (Movement for Defense of Human and Civic Rights, ROPCiO), and thus became one of the most important social organizations in the Soviet bloc that legitimized its existence by referring to the Helsinki Final Act and the human rights discourse.[44]

This new "language of rights"[45] found its expression in an increasing number of samizdat publications, which initially focused on informing the domestic public of the brutality of the regime's police forces and the arbitrariness of the courts.[46] Soon, the Polish oppositional network's samizdat activities would expand considerably with the emergence of a series of underground publishing houses. The first and most important among them was the *Niezależna Oficyna Wydawnicza* (Independent Printing House, NOWa). This marked a decisive turning point in the history of Polish anticommunist opposition on both sides of the Iron Curtain, as the rapid development of a parallel public sphere in the country itself, which could emerge due to the expansion of the samizdat infrastructure, now constituted the most important source of uncensored information for the domestic population. The broadcasts of Western radio stations such as RFE and Voice of America, to a large degree a product of the open source intelligence activities and large-scale interrogation programs of the Polish exiles in the West, lost their significance as the largest threat to the communist regime's legitimacy and forced the Polish state's intelligence service to almost completely reformulate its defense strategies.[47] This led to an important shift in the interplay between exile and home country. Samizdat took over the role that the anticommunist radio broadcasts of the first generation of émigrés had previously played. An increasing number of the political refugees in the West, particularly the recently emigrated, acknowledged the changing conditions for the expression of divergent views and left the interpretation of political developments and the formulation of oppositional strategies to the domestic resistance structures. Instead of clinging to the already antiquated ideals and political visions of the circles around the London government-in-exile, a number of inter- and transnationally operating émigré activists established a far-reaching network of support for the home country that answered the immediate needs of the oppositional forces.

The efforts of the circles around Norbert Żaba and the members of the *Aneks*-group, who since the early 1970s had maintained close cooperation with Jerzy Giedroyć and his confidants in France, had resulted in a reliable infrastructure that ensured a regular transfer of Western publications behind the Iron Curtain. In view of the radical changes that followed the institutionalization of social resistance in Poland, these channels became increasingly significant, especially as the underground publishing houses were highly dependent on support from the West. Due to the development of political samizdat into a central means of mass communication in Poland from 1976 onward, the effectiveness of the samizdat apparatus presupposed to a larger degree than before a functioning regular supply of the required technical equipment, especially stencil duplicators, which enabled the oppositional activists to reproduce texts on a larger scale with relatively simple means. As the domestic market did not offer any of the needed devices, the mimeograph machines themselves, as well as all necessary spare parts and further equipment, had to be smuggled from the West.[48] The support program was planned and organized by a vast émigré network with nodes in Paris, London, and the United States, while the practical implementation of the plans was conducted by the exile circles in Sweden, which turned the neutral country into the central hub of the clandestine traffic.[49]

A number of political refugees who had arrived in Sweden in the early 1970s played the decisive key role in the smuggling of technical equipment for the underground publishing houses. Their own personal networks behind the Iron Curtain were indispensable for an effective transfer and the dissemination of the smuggled goods within the country itself. Jakub Święcicki and Ryszard Szulkin, both members of a small émigré circle that under the name of *Grupa Kontaktowa* (contact group) formed the official representation of KOR in Sweden,[50] were the central figures involved in these activities.[51] Among the most important contacts in Western Europe were Giedroyć in Paris as well as Eugeniusz Smolar in London. Before his emigration to London, Smolar belonged to the group of Polish-Jewish intellectuals who had founded a new home in Uppsala and was the coeditor of *Aneks*, the journal whose founders from the beginning onward had established close contacts to Paris in order to coordinate the smuggling of literature across the Baltic Sea. In London, one of Smolar's main tasks was to organize the required funds for the secret supply of the publishing houses in Poland.[52]

A significant part of the necessary financing came from the Polish communities in North America and Western Europe, then transferred into the hands of the émigré activists in Sweden, but there were also Swedish donations that helped to carry out the clandestine support project. Apart from the local *Polonia*, academics and students from universities and colleges in Stockholm contributed money, as did the *Östeuropeiska Solidaritetskommittén* (Eastern European Solidarity Committee, ÖESK),[53] an organization that had emerged from the youth league of the Swedish liberals, in which both Święcicki and Szulkin were active members. The largest part of the money was spent on the transport of smuggled goods, which was organized in different ways and often depended on the sudden opening up of opportunities. Typically, the émigrés recruited random couriers among Swedish citizens that traveled behind the Iron Curtain for other reasons, often journalists or representatives of Swedish student or youth clubs, which often cooperated with partner organizations in Poland. For larger transports, especially of stencil duplicators and other machines, the émigrés had to find special couriers, whose personal travel costs had to be fully covered, which considerably constrained the limited budget.[54] Therefore, volunteers among the Swedish tourists who traveled in their own cars and commercial truck drivers were attractive alternatives.[55]

It was not only the bigger underground publishing houses such as NOWa, but also smaller samizdat centers that profited from the *pomoc poligraficzna* (printing support), as the smuggling activities were referred to; among others, the *Studencki Komitet Solidarności* (Students' Solidarity Committee), established in Cracow after the alleged murder of student Stanisław Pyjas by security service agents in May 1977, and its branches that developed in different Polish cities. The Swedish couriers ensured that the written purchase orders of the underground printing houses, according to which the Polish émigrés composed the deliveries, reached their corresponding addressees so that the illegal transports could match the concrete needs.[56] An individual transport can be reconstructed from one of the few incidents that occurred during the second half of the 1970s, when a voluntary courier, the Swedish student Björn Gunnar Laquist, was stopped in his car after he left the ferry in the port of Gdańsk in December 1979. In his trunk, the custom officials found a mimeograph machine, which was designated for NOWa,[57] several ribbons for the rotating drum, two pressure rollers, and a quartz lamp.[58] However, the range of necessary materials was much broader. Among the items listed on the orders that reached the Polish émigrés from their home country, all kinds of products needed for the mass reproduction of texts could be found, from special chemicals, solvents for ink production, color ribbons for typewriters, bookbinding glue, paper cutting machines, and woven mesh for screen printing to simple staplers.[59]

The role of this very practical support supplied by the Swedish connection cannot be underestimated, especially considering the fact that NOWa—the biggest publishing house of the democratic opposition—worked almost exclusively with technical equipment and devices that had reached Poland via Sweden.[60] Moreover, the northern route was still one of the most important channels used to satisfy Polish society's interest in the literary production in the free world. Already in the beginning of the 1970s, the smuggling of forbidden literature was organized via close cooperation between Giedroyć in France and Żaba and Święcicki in Sweden, particularly to support the underground educational structures, or "flying universities," that offered university students additional courses independent of the official ideology.[61] The organized smuggling of literature, however, was a heterogeneous international enterprise that involved a huge variety of hidden corridors across the Iron Curtain both before and after 1976. The specificity of the connections across the Baltic Sea lay mainly in the niche that the activists in Stockholm and Lund filled. With their focus on the smuggling of technical items and equipment, they made a significant contribution to the development of a nationwide oppositional discourse, years before the trade union *Solidarność* provided the prerequisites for the emergence of a more public sphere.

The Swedish-Polish rapprochement policy of the 1970s thus led to the development of a very diverse web of entanglements across the sea, fostering exchange between the representatives of trade, science, and youth culture in both countries to the same degree as between exile activists and the democratic Polish opposition. At the same time, the interaction cannot be reduced to a one-sided West–East transfer. Both the relative permeability of the Iron Curtain between neutral Sweden and its southern neighbor and the well-organized clandestine courier routes made the Scandinavian country equally interesting for actors west of the bloc border. Due to its specific bridging function and the well-organized émigré networks in Stockholm and Lund, the country became a vibrant center of fresh, first-hand information on the developments in Poland.[62] The same routes that transferred equipment for the underground publishing houses were used for the clandestine smuggling of photographic documentation and huge amounts of samizdat publications out of the country.[63] Consequently, the Polish activists in Sweden, who maintained regular and very close contact with the informational bureau of KOR in Poland,[64] became a frequently consulted source of information for both international media and the representatives of the Polish diaspora in the West. Apart from fostering the production and circulation of texts that occurred within the framework of the *drugi obieg* behind the Iron Curtain, the Swedish connection thus led to their dissemination outside the Soviet bloc as well.[65]

Of specific importance, though, was the propagation of the Polish democratic opposition's aims and ideological background on the "home front" in Sweden itself, which developed into an additional field of activity for the small activist circles. In contrast to the sympathetic reactions to the formation of KOR among intellectuals throughout the Western hemisphere, the response of both the Swedish government and the public can best be characterized as restrained.[66] Thus, the organizers of the smuggling routes took on the parallel role of mediating between societies on both sides of the Iron Curtain, which turned out to be of crucial importance for further developments both in Sweden and in Poland itself. The first steps were taken by the activists of ÖESK, among them Szulkin and Święcicki, who initiated the appearance of Polish tamizdat in Sweden, which rapidly developed during the second half of the 1970s. In several special publications about the June protests and the emergence of KOR in autumn and winter 1976, the Committee circulated documents and eyewitness reports in Swedish. This was the first source of information for the Swedish public that took an interest in the changed realities across the sea, and it was intensified by comments and articles that severely criticized the lack of knowledge about the Polish opposition in Sweden.[67]

During the years that followed, the community of Polish refugees in Sweden proved that it was able to establish networks within their host society and to influence the public discourse to a much larger degree than the émigrés in, for example, Great Britain.[68] Their intimate relation with the leading protagonists of the democratic opposition in Poland and the relatively liberal travel regulations between Sweden and Poland enabled them to turn the textual encounter of the Swedes with the oppositional voices from Poland into a dynamic interpersonal interaction. It was particularly the engagement of the Polish émigrés with leading Swedish social democrats such as Sten Johansson, the editor of the Swedish Social Democratic Party's theoretical mouthpiece *Tiden*, that led to the durable intellectual connections across the bloc border;[69] this allowed a considerable number of prominent representatives of Poland's oppositional culture to visit Sweden during the late 1970s, among them Kuroń, Michnik, and Jan Józef Lipski.[70] By convincing key Swedish politicians, intellectuals, and journalists to join the cause of the Polish democratic opposition, the representatives of KOR in Sweden managed to create the groundwork for successful lobbying.

For example, due to the financial support of *Tiden*, Maria Borowska and Jakub Święcicki were finally able to publish a representative selection of Polish samizdat texts translated into Swedish in a volume titled *Kamp för demokrati* (Fight for democracy), which to a large degree changed the public's perception of the Polish opposition.[71] The presentation of the liberal and social democratic circles around KOR helped to diminish the power of popular stereotypes in Sweden about anticommunist groups in Poland, whose supposedly Catholic-chauvinistic, fanatically anti-Russian and, most of all, anti-Semitic reflexes had cemented a negative image in Swedish society.[72] It was, therefore, not only the dissemination of Polish samizdat texts in the West that had an impact, but the cultural translation process conducted by the exiles, who filtered the huge amount of samizdat publications that leaked out from communist Poland into a distillate that was likely to gain support from Western societies. Although this—ironically enough—implied a censorship policy on the part of the émigré activists and presupposed a certain distortion of the Polish opposition into a mirror of Western ideals, the efforts finally succeeded in breaking down mental barriers. The level of support for the Polish democratic opposition rose considerably and increased the gap between Swedish government and society in their respective attitude toward the Polish democratic opposition. The active support of leading members of Swedish society for the émigrés' propagation efforts was indispensable, such as the articles of the journalist Gunnar Fredriksson, which revolutionized the previously impersonal news coverage on Polish issues,[73] or the analyses of Sten Johansson. His comparisons between the Polish opposition and the tradition of popular movements and social self-organization in Swedish history[74] certainly helped to raise the level of understanding among the Swedes, as did his fine distinction between the Catholic appearance of the Polish democratic opposition and the secular contents of its ideological program.[75]

Samizdat and tamizdat were thus an essential part of an entangled web of transnational interaction and a transborder dialogue that could develop in spite of the Iron Curtain, not only between exiles and representatives of the domestic opposition, but also between societies, which had important repercussions for events both in Poland and Sweden. At the moment of consolidation of the Solidarity movement in summer 1980, the characteristics and aims of the Polish democratic opposition were already well known in Sweden thanks to the lobbying activities of the émigrés. This contributed to the unusual social support for Solidarity in Sweden and led to the rapid development of effective organizational structures to assist the young trade union. Sweden's own traditionally strong trade union movement played an outstanding role within the larger framework of Solidarity's cooperation with the West; this cannot only be ascribed to Sweden's neutrality and geographical proximity, but also to the fact that there already existed stable transnational networks established by the Polish émigrés.[76] Due to their intervention and mediating efforts, foreign support for the emergence of an uncensored publishing culture was elevated to a higher level, especially during the period between summer 1980 and the declaration of Martial Law in December 1981, when the borders between samizdat and open publishing were blurred due to the openly legal status of Solidarity. The clandestine support of the underground publishing houses, which the Polish émigrés had established during the second half of the 1970s, turned into open, mass support on the part of the Swedish trade unions, which supplied Solidarity's publishing houses with the necessary expertise and technical equipment. When the social movement was forced to go underground again with the imposition of Martial Law, it was the Swedish trade union movement that continued the clandestine support of Solidarity's publishing houses in close cooperation with the already experienced émigré circles in Sweden.[77] Thus, the large-scale emergence of Solidarity's free, underground press in the 1980s was a process that mirrored the beginnings of the interplay across the Iron Curtain, although the network of actors involved was much more diverse than during the late 1970s.

As this short overview of the various Polish-Swedish contacts during a decisive period of European postwar history has illustrated, the interconnection of events and developments in East and West is a factor that cannot be underestimated, especially during the latter decades of the Cold War in Europe, characterized by uncountable exchanges across the Iron Curtain under the influence of détente. The development of the Polish samizdat activities from the mid 1970s onward reflects the need to find a methodology that can take these interactions into account, as the result of causalities and interrelations that can only be detected and interpreted through a widening of the perspective on the Cold War world. While a purely national framework might still be relevant in, for example, the research on the roots of samizdat in closed societies such as the Soviet Union of the 1960s, the increasing permeability of the Iron Curtain between the satellites and the West from the late 1960s onward calls for attention to this transnational dimension. Although the origins of the Polish samizdat activities are definitely grounded in events that occurred on the domestic stage, the effectiveness of the underground publishing houses was highly dependent on the foreign connections that ensured a regular supply of the necessary technical equipment, provided by the smuggling activities across the Baltic Sea that made an important contribution to underground publishing behind the Iron Curtain.

The tamizdat activities in Sweden, on the other hand, have to be seen within the same context. It was primarily the same network of actors on both sides of the bloc border that was responsible for the dissemination of samizdat in Sweden and other Western countries, and even in Poland itself, as the same channels that provided the needed equipment for the production of texts also were used to foster their circulation. The inseparability of the two phenomena led to a certain continuity between the publications of the domestic opposition and the émigré communities, as the authors of a common Polish-Swedish tamizdat project, a journal entitled *Hotel Örnsköld*, were claiming already in the mid 1980s.[78] As a result, cooperations such as those between the Independent Polish Agency in Lund[79] and the liberal underground journal *Miesięcznik Polityczny "Niepodległość"* (Political monthly "Independence"), which transferred the copyright of its texts, as well as their distribution rights outside the country, to the émigré circles in Sweden,[80] could be achieved despite the Iron Curtain. This illustrates the specificity of Polish samizdat and tamizdat as elements of a "pan-European" uncensored culture of Polish political thought, which could develop and spread on both sides of the Iron Curtain due to the mediating efforts of the Polish exiles, bridging the gaps between the two Europes long before they were about to reunite.

Notes

1. John Lewis Gaddis, *We Now Know: Rethinking Cold War History* (Oxford, 1997), 261.
2. John Lewis Gaddis, *The Cold War: A New History* (New York, 2005), 181, 187.
3. Sarah B. Snyder, "'A Sort of Lifeline' for Eastern Europe," in *Perforating the Iron Curtain: European Détente, Transatlantic Relations, and the Cold War, 1965–1985*, ed. Poul Villaume and Odd-Arne Westad (Copenhagen, 2010), 180.
4. Jeremi Suri, *Power and Protest: Global Revolution and the Rise of Détente* (Cambridge, MA, 2003), 108.
5. Tony Judt, *Die Geschichte Europas seit dem Zweiten Weltkrieg* (Munich, 2006), 477–78.
6. The period between 1976 and 1980, which marks the beginnings of clandestine interaction between oppositional key agents in Sweden and Poland on a larger scale, is virtually uninvestigated, although some information can be found in an article that reproduces fragments of oral history interviews with Polish émigrés in Sweden. See Katarzyna Pu-

chalska, "Szwecja Polsce—Droga przez Bałtyk," *KARTA* 47 (2006), 110–49. The vivid networks between Swedish social organizations and members of Poland's Solidarity movement, on the other hand, which developed mainly due to the mediating efforts of the Polish émigrés throughout the 1980s, have been addressed in several articles. See Maria Heino and Barbara Törnquist-Plewa, "Svenska stödkommittén för Solidaritet. The Swedish Solidarity Support Committee and Independent Polish Agency in Lund," in *Skandinavien och Polen. Möten, relationer och ömsesidig påverkan,* ed. Barbara Törnquist-Plewa (Lund, 2007), 25–61; Klaus Misgeld, "Chapter 2: Sweden. Focus on fundamental trade union rights," in *Solidarity with Solidarity. Western European Trade Unions and the Polish Crisis, 1980-1982,* ed. Idesbald Goddeeris (Lanham, 2010), 19–50. Apart from that, a special edition of a Swedish journal was dedicated to the solidarity of Swedish society with the Polish trade union and the practical support across the Baltic Sea, containing both eyewitness accounts as well as more scholarly essays; see *Arbetarhistoria* 4 (2006). For a similar approach to social networks between, in this case, France and Poland, see Bent Boel, "French Support for Eastern European Dissidence, 1968-1989," in Villaume and Westad, *Perforating the Iron Curtain,* 215–41, as well as the various case studies discussed in the abovementioned volume titled *Solidarity with Solidarity.*
7. Michael F. Hopkins, "Continuing debate and new approaches in Cold War History," *The Historical Journal* 50, no. 4 (2007), 933–34.
8. Patrick Major and Rana Mitter, "East is East and West is West? Towards a Comparative Socio-Cultural History of the Cold War," in *Across the Blocs: Cold War Cultural and Social History,* ed. Patrick Major and Rana Mitter (London, 2004), 4.
9. Gaddis, *We Now Know,* 283.
10. Jussi Hanhimäki and Odd Arne Westad, "Introduction: Studying the Cold War," in *The Cold War: A History in Documents and Eyewitness Accounts,* ed. Jussi Hanhimäki and Odd Arne Westad (New York, 2003), xii.
11. Major and Mitter, "East is East and West is West?" 14.
12. Sari Autio-Sarasmo and Katalin Miklóssy, "Introduction: The Cold War from a new perspective," in *Reassessing Cold War Europe,* ed. Sari Autio-Sarasmo and Katalin Miklóssy (London, 2011), 4, 6. The range of case studies presented in the volume is nonetheless limited to the fields of state-sanctioned exchange such as technology transfer and trade interaction.
13. Ibid., 8.
14. Major and Mitter, "East is East and West is West?" 12.
15. Boel, "French Support for Eastern European Dissidence," 228.
16. Nevertheless, a certain degree of successful one-way transfers across the Iron Curtain with concrete consequences for the political development has also been proven for the high tide of the Cold War. See, for example, Mark Pittaway, "The Education of Dissent: The Reception of the Voice of Free Hungary, 1951–56," in Major and Mitter, *Across the Blocs,* 97–116.
17. Poul Villaume and Odd Arne Westad, "Introduction: The Secrets of European Détente," in Villaume and Westad, *Perforating the Iron Curtain,* 7.
18. Angela Romano, "The Main Task of the European Political Cooperation," in Villaume and Westad, *Perforating the Iron Curtain,* 133.
19. Thomas Fischer, "Bridging the Gap between East and West. The N + N as Catalysts of the CSCE Process, 1972–1983," in Villaume and Westad, *Perforating the Iron Curtain,* 168.
20. Autio-Sarasmo and Miklóssy, "Introduction," 7.
21. Bernard Piotrowski, "Szwecja w polskiej polityce zagranicznej. Od odzyskanej niepodległości do wydarzeń sierpniowych 1980 roku," in *Polska—Szwecja 1919–1999,* ed. Jan Szymański (Gdańsk, 2002), 198, 211.

22. Urgent Note of the Polish United Workers' Party's Central Committee on the lifting of the visa requirements for the passenger traffic with Finland, 23 November 1973. Archiwum Akt Nowych (The Central Archive of Modern Records, AAN, Warsaw), KC PZPR, XIA/555, reproduced in *Polskie Dokumenty Diplomatyczne 1973*, ed. Piotr M. Majewski (Warsaw, 2006), 644–45.
23. Piotrowski, "Szwecja w polskiej polityce zagranicznej," 217.
24. Jan Szymański, "Polen och Sverige i skuggan av Europas 1800- och 1900-tals historia," in *Polen och Sverige: År av rivalitet och vänskap / Szwecja—Polska. Lata rywalizacji i przyjaźni*, ed. Joanna Nicklasson-Młynarska (Stockholm, 1999), 64.
25. The exact size of the Polish community in Sweden during the Cold War decades is difficult to estimate, especially due to the fact that a large and constantly increasing number of Poles obtained Swedish citizenship. A Polish report from the mid 1970s mentions a number of roughly thirty thousand Swedish citizens of Polish origin, mostly war refugees and their descendants. See an undated report of the Polish Ministry of the Interior on Polish citizens in Stockholm (secret), 1975. Instytut Pamięci Narodowej—Komisja Ścigania Zbrodni przeciwko Narodowi Polskiemu (Institute of National Remembrance—Commission for the Prosecution of Crimes against the Polish Nation, IPN, Warsaw), BU 1067/13.231. The number of Polish citizens in Sweden, on the other hand, was around eleven thousand in 1970. See Elżbieta Later Chodyłowa, "Szwecja," in *Polska Diaspora*, ed. Adam Walaszek (Cracow, 2001), 228.
26. Unsigned and undated report of the Polish Ministry of the Interior on the Swedish *Polonia* (confidential), 1970. IPN BU 418/17.274, 276.
27. Report on the activities of "subversive centers and groups" on Scandinavian territory of the Polish Ministry of the Interior, 26 February 1972. IPN BU 418/17.234.
28. Report on the Swedish *Polonia*. IPN BU 418/17.269.
29. Cryptograph No. 10267/3522 of the Polish embassy in Stockholm (urgent), 22 September 1972. Archiwum Ministerstwa Spraw Zagranicznych (Archive of the Foreign Ministry, AMSZ, Warsaw), Dep. IV 45/47, w. 7, Sz-O-220-7, reproduced in *Polskie Dokumenty Diplomatyczne 1972*, ed. Włodzimierz Borodziej (Warsaw, 2005), 516.
30. Dariusz Stola, *Emigracja Pomarcowa* (Warsaw, 2000), 9.
31. Ludomir Garczyński-Gąssowski, "Organizacje polskie w Szwecji 1971–1989," in *Polacy w Szwecji po II wojnie światowej* (Stockholm, 1992), 32.
32. Elżbieta Later Chodyłowa, "Polonia w krajach skandynawskich," in *Polonia w Europie*, ed. Barbara Szydłowska-Cegłowa (Poznań, 1992), 616.
33. Stefan Trzciński, "Polskie fale emigracyjne do Szwecji 1939–1986," in *Polacy w Szwecji*, 64.
34. Garczyński-Gąssowski, "Organizacje polskie w Szwecji," 32.
35. Report on the activities of "subversive centers and groups" on Scandinavian Territory. IPN BU 418/17.235, 236. The Polish Jews that arrived in Sweden around the turn of the decade were the key agents that considerably revitalized the Polish community's oppositional activities on Poland's opposite shore. Nevertheless, only a small number of them remained among the leading émigré actors supporting social resistance in Poland, who from the mid 1970s onward were mostly non-Jewish refugees who had left their country of origin after the 1970 protests. Among the Polish Jews in Sweden, only a minority considered themselves to be Poles after only a few years in Sweden and developed an increasingly strong Jewish identity, which the Polish historian Dariusz Stola ascribes to the policy of the Warsaw regime, which in the course of the "anti-Zionist campaign" excluded Poles of Jewish origin from the national community. See Stola, *Emigracja pomarcowa*, 24.
36. Boel, "French Support for Eastern European Dissidence," 229.
37. Report on Polish citizens in Stockholm. IPN 1067/13.243-244.

38. Ibid., IPN 1067/13.245.
39. Puchalska, "Szwecja Polsce," 124.
40. One of the routes that had been favored earlier by the circles around Giedroyć for the smuggling of émigré publications in private cars connected France to Poland via the German Democratic Republic and Czechoslovakia. See Małgorzata Ptasińska-Wójcik, "Inwigilacja Instytutu Literackiego przez Służbę Bezpieczeństwa w czasach Gomułki," in *Aparat bezpieczeństwa wobec emigracji politycznej i Polonii*, ed. Ryszard Terlecki (Warsaw, 2005), 181.
41. Undated report on the completed to date and planned activities of the Independent Polish Agency in Lund titled "IPA—Założenia oraz opis dotychczasowych i planowanych działań," after 1983. Archiwum Opozycji (Archive of the Opposition, Ośrodek KARTA, AO, Warsaw), IPA, dark blue folder No. 6 labeled "Mat. redakcyjne, varia," 1. The collections of the IPA, which were transferred to the archive in 2007 by Józef Lebenbaum, are still not officially accessible and thus lack even basic cataloging.
42. Judt, *Die Geschichte Europas*, 652.
43. Arista Maria Cirtautas, *The Polish Solidarity Movement: Revolution, Democracy and Natural Rights* (London, 1997), 165, 167.
44. *Od Solidarności do wolności* (Warsaw, 2005), 42.
45. Cirtautas, *The Polish Solidarity Movement*, 165.
46. Maria Borowska and Jakub Święcicki, "Inledning," in *Kamp för demokrati. Artiklar och ställningstaganden från den polska demokratiska rörelsen*, ed. Maria Borowska and Jakub Święcicki (Stockholm, 1979), 19.
47. Paweł Machcewicz, "Walka z Radiem Wolna Europa (1950–1975)," in *Aparat bezpieczeństwa*, ed. Terlecki, 101.
48. *FPU-Fakta* 5 (1978), regularly occurring publication of *Folkpartiets Ungdomsförbund* (Youth league of the Liberal People's Party). AO III/2450.4, 9.
49. "IPA—Założenia oraz opis dotychczasowych i planowanych działań." AO, IPA, f. 6, 2.
50. Informational note of the *Grupa Kontaktowa*, most probably May or June 1978. AO III/2450.5. The group had been established in Stockholm on 15 May 1978 in the presence of prominent KOR-member Leszek Kołakowski and formed thus an authorized representation of the oppositional movement in the West.
51. Puchalska, "Szwecja Polsce," 118.
52. Undated letter to Jakub Święcicki. AO III/2450.9.
53. Account on the incoming funds and expenses for the technical support of the Polish opposition during the period between October 1978 and April 1979, compiled by Jakub Święcicki (confidential). AO III/2450.9.
54. Letter from Jakub Święcicki to an unidentified Polish émigré, 23 April 1979. AO III/2450.18.
55. Letter from Eugeniusz Smolar to Jakub Święcicki and his wife Elżbieta, 12 May 1977. AO III/2450.11.
56. Smuggled letter from a female contact in Warsaw to Jakub Święcicki, 10 March 1977. AO III/2450.9.
57. Copy of a magazine article titled "När svensk greps för smuggling hamnade han mitt i helvetet: Så knacks Björn, 29, i ett polskt skräckfängelse," *Lektyr*, most probably December 1979 or January 1980. AO III/2450.6, folder 2, 29.
58. Protocol of the Customs Office in Gdańsk, issued in its German translation, titled "Abschrift—Strafentscheidung," 29 January 1980. AO III/2450.6, folder 1.
59. Letter from Jakub Święcicki to an unidentified Polish émigré, 23 April 1979. AO III/2450.18.
60. "När svensk greps för smuggling hamnade han mitt i helvetet," *Lektyr*, 46.

61. Letters from Jerzy Giedroyć to Jakub Święcicki, 30 December 1977, 16 May 1978, 7 December 1978. AO III/2450.10.
62. Garczyński-Gąssowski, "Organizacje polskie w Szwecji," 36.
63. Undated letter from an unidentified contact in Poland to Jakub Święcicki. AO III/2450.9; Letter from Eugeniusz Smolar to Jakub Święcicki and his wife Elżbieta, 3 August 1977. AO III/2450.11; Letter from Jerzy Giedroyć to Jakub Święcicki, 1 December 1977. AO III/2450.10.
64. Garczyński-Gąssowski, "Organizacje polskie w Szwecji," 36–37.
65. As Serguei Oushakine points out, tamizdat does not designate a one-sided transfer, but depicts the dual function of migrating samizdat texts, which equally were reflected back to the Soviet bloc from the West. See Serguei Alex Oushakine, "The Terrifying Mimicry of Samizdat," *Public Culture* 13, no. 2 (2001): 109. In the case of Sweden as well, the texts that reached Poland's opposite coasts were reprinted and smuggled back to their country of origin. A number of Swedish representatives of KOR, for example, organized the systematic dissemination of brochures among the Polish tourists that entered the ferries to the home country in Swedish ports; these contained a selection of essays and documents published both in the émigré journal *Kultura* and domestic samizdat. See the undated letter from one of the members of the *Grupa Kontaktowa* to a contact in Poland, most probably 1978. AO III/2450.5.
66. Leaflet of the ÖESK, autumn 1976. AO III/2450.4.
67. Two publications of the ÖESK titled *Dokument från oroligheterna i Polen sommaren 1976*, September and December 1976. AO III/2450.4.
68. Later Chodyłowa, "Polonia w krajach skandynawskich," 627.
69. Puchalska, "Szwecja Polsce," 113.
70. Maria Borowska, "Poparcie Szwedów dla polskiej walki o demokrację 1976–1989," unpublished essay, May 2003. AO III/2450.20.
71. Ibid.
72. "Opposition," *Svenska Dagbladet*, 10 March 1980.
73. Puchalska, "Szwecja Polsce," 116.
74. Sten Johansson, "Förord," in Borowska and Święcicki, *Kamp för demokrati*, 9.
75. Sten Johansson and Maria Borowska, *Polens sak är vår. Om övergången till demokrati under kommunismen* (Stockholm, 1981), 56–57.
76. Klaus Misgeld, "Solidaritet med Solidaritet. Den svenska arbetarrörelsen och demokratirörelsen i Polen kring 1980," *Arbetarhistoria* 4 (2006), 26–27.
77. Göran Jacobsson, "De hittade lönnfacket. För Solidarnosc i polskt fängelse," *Arbetarhistoria* 4 (2006), 18.
78. "Inledning," *Hotel Örnsköld—polsk dikt och debatt* 2 (1985), 4. The journal was modeled on the Paris journal *Kultura* and presented a regularly edited selection of translated documents, essays, and literary production in Poland as well as texts written by Polish émigrés from 1984 onward. The editors were both Poles from the circles around KOR in Sweden and a number of Swedish intellectuals, translators, and writers, which can be seen as another product of the effective networking activities of the Polish émigré circles both across the Iron Curtain and within their host society.
79. The Independent Polish Agency was an informational center led by Lebenbaum, who had founded the agency in April 1983 together with, among others, Jerzy Giedroyć in Paris and NOWa's main editor Mirosław Chojecki, who had emigrated to the West in 1981. See an undated report written by Józef Lebenbaum on the IPA. AO, IPA, dark blue folder No. 6 labeled "Mat. redakcyjne, varia," 2.
80. Undated information sheet of the IPA titled "Niepodległość—Miesięcznik Polityczny," most probably 1984. AO, IPA, dark blue folder No. 4 labeled "IPA ≈ 80."

Chapter 3

RADIO FREE EUROPE AND RADIO LIBERTY AS THE "ECHO CHAMBER" OF TAMIZDAT

Friederike Kind-Kovács

The Cold War image of a "divided world, divided sky"[1] is slowly but consistently fading in contemporary history research. It is indeed true that from the perspective of the ideological incompatibility of the two world powers during the Cold War, the idea of a "dichotomy of the northern hemisphere"[2] and its representation in the sphere of audiovisual media holds. At the same time, and this is the line of argumentation of the present chapter, radio during the Cold War equally provided an influential link between the two—ideologically separated—worlds. The dissatisfaction with the irreversible seeming disconnectedness of Europe and with the official impermeability of the "information curtain"[3] was since the early 1950s translated into the practice of cross-border broadcasting as well as of cross-border circulation of literature. Among the radio stations that targeted the Soviet sphere during the Cold War were the *Voice of America* (VOA), the BBC, and in particular the two American-sponsored radio stations in Munich, *Radio Free Europe* (RFE) and *Radio Liberty* (RL). Although the Soviet Union and its satellite states were successful in jamming Western broadcasting, in particular RFE and RL succeeded in reaching its target audiences in the Soviet orbit, where they promoted their vision of democracy, culture, and human rights. Although both radio stations were installed in the early Cold War period to broadcast first-hand sources into the Eastern bloc[4] and to win in this way the self-declared battle for the hearts and the minds of the people behind the Iron Curtain, the radios also contributed to a transsystemic rapprochement. Despite its ideological load, this broadcast undertaking was not just a plaything of so-called Cold Warriors in the *Cultural Cold War*,[5] but it equally served to invent and

---

Notes for this chapter begin on page 87.

materialize a nonofficial contact zone across the Iron Curtain. In doing so, the air became rather divided by, what György Péteri termed a "Nylon Curtain" instead of an Iron Curtain. This Nylon Curtain was not only "transparent but it also yielded to strong osmotic tendencies that were globalizing knowledge across the systemic divide about culture, goods, and services."[6] Against this background, exemplifying the role of RFE and RL as transnational products of the Cold War provides a means to test this herein unfolding notion of a more entangled than divided Cold War Europe.

It was since the early 1950s, namely in 1951, that RFE streamed its first broadcast to Czechoslovakia. It was later divided into five national broadcast services (Czechoslovakia, Bulgaria, Hungary, Romania, and Poland), which featured programs in the target language. RL followed in 1953 with its first broadcast into the Soviet. While RFE and RL operated separately throughout the 1950s and 1960s, they merged in October 1976 into a joint venture, which became known as RFE/RL. From very early on, RFE and RL reported both on international news and internal affairs of the targeted countries. In addition to this, notably since the 1960s uncensored documents and texts from the state socialist countries were perceived as most powerful in mirroring the real life and thoughts of the people from "behind the Iron Curtain."[7] These materials from inside the Soviet Union and its satellites countries, which had become known as samizdat (self-published) and tamizdat (published-over-there), provided the staff of RFE and RL with a large body of valuable sources to be employed both as reliable background information as well as written materials that would be reproduced for the actual broadcasts. By also broadcasting programs about "painting, sculpture, and music," RFE "stress[ed] that which is not permitted in the Soviet lands (and was forbidden by Hitler): modernism, 'formalism.'"[8] These forms of art should be presented by RFE "not for their own sake but as evidence of freedom of expression and experimentation, as contemporary continuation of the evolutionary nature of art."[9] Programs on literature needed to especially "be of uncompromisingly high quality and should deal with the writers of the free world, whose work is being most widely discussed."[10] An alternative invasive means were the readings of samizdat texts, which had been smuggled out from the Soviet Union as representations of literary nonconformism. Streaming these texts back across the Iron Curtain via radio broadcast proved to be a powerful means of overcoming the literary division of Cold War Europe. While radio and literature are often seen as two separate spheres of Cold War activity, the present chapter analyzes RFE and RL as a framework for close cooperation between literary circulation and broadcasting in the period of the Cold War.

Already since the late 1950s and early 1960s had the publication of samizdat in Western Europe and the United States developed into a serious alternative to underground publishing inside the Soviet Union and its satellite countries. In an article in *The Times* in 1977, Leopold Labedz observes the intensifying flow of literature across the Iron Curtain: "Things are better controlled now but the problem still exists. Ever since the denunciation of Stalin by Khrushchev Soviet and East European writers began publishing their works abroad (*Tamizdat*). The outgoing flow is obviously on the increase and so is the incoming flow, in spite of all the efforts to check it."[11] Apart from the physical transfer of literary goods across the various physical borders, the transferred literature would then—once in the West—be either printed and published or simply read in the radios. As outlined in a mission statement in 1982, RFE and RL—in contrast to the VOA—were neither meant to concentrate on "presenting U.S. Government policy and projecting American society," nor were they employed to create "American radio in the sense of organized political opposition."[12] Instead, Washington created these stations in order to "project a diverse international awareness."[13] Based on this mission, these two radio stations played a particularly central role in the oral dissemination of tamizdat inside and outside the Soviet space. Their main driving force was their special awareness of the literary underground press's great potential for the rapprochement between the intellectual communities in a divided Europe. The fact that RFE and RL established one of the biggest samizdat archives proves their belief in the high value of samizdat literature for confronting the public in the East and the West with first-hand sources from inside the Soviet Union and its satellites. Well-known Hungarian broadcaster for RFE, George Urban, even claimed that "outside Poland, we [RFE] were *the* natural outlet for samizdat."[14] Despite their exceptional significance to history, research on the role of radio stations during the Cold War has almost only produced monographs[15] and autobiographies[16] that focused on the struggle over the moral dilemma and the inherent danger of financial dependence of media and other cultural products of the Cold War on governmental funding. In 1971, this dilemma spilled into the open, when the public learned that the CIA was a primary sponsor of RFE and RL.[17] Consequently, RFE's and RL's problematic entanglements with governmental politics produced large moral and ethical debates among historians and sociologists. Sparing the reader the details, I will simply follow Hugh Wilford's evaluation of the relationship between the CIA and its cultural and literary operations in 2008, which stated that "the CIA could not always predict or control the actions of the musicians, writers, and artists it secretly patronized."[18] Keeping this image of RFE and RL in mind, I will offer an alternative approach to analyzing RFE and RL, namely treating these stations as the tools of intellectuals bent on spreading uncensored literature. My approach will allow us to look beyond the political layer of RFE's and RL's history. Thus, instead of reproducing another extensive examination of the radio's relationship to the CIA, this chapter aims at reviewing the contributions of RFE and RL to increasing the circulation and publicity of samizdat and tamizdat across the Iron Curtain. I argue that these two radio stations—apart from their natural aim as news broadcasters to reach a broader public than their colleagues in print—offer us today a rich opportunity to understand the possible effects of media that crossed geographical, cultural, and ideological borders during the Cold War. This will allow an insight into the slow process of the reemergence of trans–Iron Curtain communication.

The chapter will first outline the implementation of various projects to increase the physical flow of uncensored manuscripts, focusing in particular on the practical realization of the early "person-to-person" projects of the Free Europe organizations. It then will analyze the function of RFE and RL in orally broadcasting written materials into the Soviet sphere and in thus serving as an "echo chamber" of tamizdat.

Producing and Distribution Books across the Iron Curtain

The *National Committee for a Free Europe* (NCFE), later the *Free Europe Committee* (FEC) was established in 1949 by the Truman Administration and served as the head organization of various *Free Europe* programs. Its main mission was to employ refugees and exiles from Eastern Europe, let their voices be streamed on the air and to transmit their experiences back into the Soviet Orbit.[19] Mostly through its publishing division, the *Free Europe Press* (FEP), and its broadcasting division, *Radio Free Europe,* could the NCFE realize these objectives. Until 1971, the NCFE was funded through the US Congress via the CIA. While RFE and RL aimed at broadcasting written material back into the Soviet Union and its satellite states, the FEP division produced reports, analyses, and a journal. It was initially headed by Samuel Walker, and from 1957 on by George Minden. Originally, FEP aimed to increase the movement of literature between the blocs,[20] often through person-to-person contacts. Most of the services of *Free Europe Press* existed at a national level (meaning there were national programs for Poland or Hungary, for instance).[21] One of the major initiatives was the British exile publishing house *Polonia Book Fund,* which was very engaged in publishing books from Poland, later trying to bring them back into the country in order to provide the "captive nations" with uncensored literature. *Free Europe Press*, on the other hand, took up the job of translating books into other East European languages, so authors from one country could read the literature from the other bloc countries. "FEP (Free Europe Publications) arranges for the translation and printing of books and booklets ... for mailing into the captive countries. The outstanding example is the translation of Djilas' *New Class* into Polish, Czech, Hungarian, Romanian and Bulgarian. Another is the Polish translation of Orwell's *Animal Farm*."[22] In the late 1950s and early 1960s, the *Polonia Book Fund* established a "Person-to-Person Program," which consisted of a social network for the distribution of books. "The principal vehicles for FEP's exploitation of East-West contact are East Europe Institute and its person-to-person distribution project. Through a network of distribution points in London, Brussels, Paris, Rome, Stockholm and Munich, Person-To-Person presently distributes over 1,000 books per month to East European travelers in the West."[23] East-West personal contacts shaped this network. The various publishing initiatives relied greatly on the possibility to act through a "network of cultural institutions ... that come into contact with visitors in the context of libraries, book shops, publishing houses, clubs and cultural associations."[24] Activists in the West, often émigrés, and their contacts inside the "captive nations" worked together closely to increase the flow of literature. "A climate of mutual trust exists between our stringers and unpaid representatives, book suppliers and distributors, and—most important—between our Program personnel and our recipients, who have come to expect from us friendly help, guidance and information as well as political literature."[25] As the institutionalization of this literary transfer was still in its infancy, individuals played an important part in keeping the contacts alive and helping the books reach their destinations. A monthly report of the *Polonia Book Fund* in 1959 argued: "The enthusiasm of an average recipient towards the Program and his willingness to take the risks of illegal transportation of anti-Communist literature, provides the best proof of the effectiveness of the activity."[26] In this program, East European travelers smuggled unavailable or forbidden books into the Eastern bloc. One example for these exchanges was the circulation of the most famous tamizdat novel. In 1959, it was reported to the *Polonia Book Fund* that "'the greatest interest among visitors,' writes our Brussels representative, 'is still caused by *Doctor Zhivago*. It is a hit.'"[27] In another thank you letter from Poland: "Above all many thanks for your consignment of '*Dr. Zhivago*' which is still our best-seller and is likely to remain such for many a month."[28] A similar note came from their Rome representative: "The younger visitors ask for the strongest political literature (Anders, Djilas, Pasternak). The elderly people are more cautious."[29] Another note from Paris confirmed the far-reaching fame of Pasternak's book, even in the Soviet Union, where the book was not yet officially published:

> From Paris we have received the following comments: About 1/3 of the books distributed this month are copies of *"Dr. Zhivago."* This figure confirms once again the demand, which this novel enjoys among visitors from Poland. Most of this month's visitors approached us (at their own initiative) with a request to obtain a free copy of *Dr. Zhivago*, about which they have all heard or read before. It is considered a "bore" in Poland—as one visitor put it—but everybody reads it for the mere fact that it was banned and that it was published in exile, which makes it even more definitely interesting: Of course this rather cynical comment is perhaps a little exaggerated, but generally speaking Polish readers expected more of a political load in this book.[30]

In addition to Russian bestsellers like *Dr. Zhivago*, many books in the original language that were unavailable inside Poland were produced by the *Polonia Book Fund* and distributed to visitors that dared to smuggle literature back home.

> The wide selection of publications of political, historical and cultural value available in Polish (many of them translations of leading western authors) enables us to offer suitable literature to all kind of visitors, depending on their intellectual or professional interests. The primary objective of the program has been to provide books, which under no circumstances would be published or obtainable from normal sources in Poland. Such books now constitute 95 percent of the total output of the Program.[31]

Visitors were largely intellectuals and professionals,[32] or groups of tourists, into whose hands the *Book Fund* could entrust its literature. From Britain, the *Book Fund* learned that, apart from conventional agents like students and doctors, other less conventional groups of travelers were employing new methods of literary transfer. Large groups of sailors and fisherman from the *Other Europe* reached the Scottish ports and happily received book shipments to return to their home countries: "Britain: The largest group of recipients this month were the sailors and fishermen visiting Scottish ports where our local representative has an efficient network of distributors. The second largest group were the students, and the third a rather unusual quantity of doctors."[33] Besides the opportunity to obtain literature during travels to the West, *Polonia Book Fund* also provided the interested reader with ways to get hold of uncensored literature inside the Soviet Bloc, as well. Literature that had been published abroad and smuggled back into its country of origin was obtained particularly successfully through second-hand bookshops and mobile libraries that traveled between the bloc countries. Even by the mid 1980s, Eastern Europeans could obtain those Western bestsellers that were censored for anticommunist messages only in diplomatic libraries or for instance in second-hand bookshops. Richard Swartz, a Swedish correspondent to Central Europe, described the situation in a Budapest bookshop in a 1985 article:

On the shelf of a Budapest second-hand bookshop I found by accident George Orwell's *1984*. ... Around me there are other costumers hunting for books: it seems almost impossible that they have not discovered the book which is on the *Index* in Eastern Europe and which is perceived as ideological contraband. They must have seen it, but left it in the shelf. After a moment of hesitation I left it standing there. I had read it, and whom in present day Eastern Europe could I give it as a present, who could be interested in it in a different way than just as a kind of political pornography?[34]

Torn between his excitement about finding a critical Western novel in a second-hand bookshop and his disbelief that no other costumer had tried before him to get hold of the book, Swartz leaves the shop empty-handed. However, upon arriving at his Hungarian friends' home, he is greeted with disbelief that he did not buy the book: "'You are a stupid idiot,' say my Hungarian friends to me, when I tell them, that I saw Orwell's *1984* in a second-hand bookshop in the Vaci utca. 'How can one have so little brain and leave such a book there?' Full of regret I returned to the shop that same afternoon with the idea to buy Orwell's novel, but I can't find it anymore. *1984* has vanished."[35] This anecdote demonstrates the continuity of hunting for censored Western books, showing that it lasted until the even late period of state socialism. However, going back to the origins of the semilegal search for censored books, *Polonia Book Fund* was aware of the circulation of their own published books in such second-hand bookshops. Its members recalled in 1959: "The most popular sources are the antique and second-hand book stores and 'bric-a-brac' shops where copies of Djilas, Anders, Miłosz ... can be obtained. ... *Dr. Zhivago* was the title of the most sought after book in these shops a month ago. Of course the transactions are made illegally 'under the counter.'"[36]

As we can see from written reactions to the projects of *Polonia Book Fund*, their activity was well acknowledged by readers inside Poland. One university lecturer wrote in a letter of 1959: "It is important that you should keep up and develop your activity. I want to confirm what I told you about the 'mobile libraries' with your literature, which are privately organized in the country. I know about two such libraries in Warsaw and one in Cracow and one in Łódź. The books are in motion. Your address is circulated among trusted people going to Paris as a source for obtaining more and new exile editions."[37]

Getting access to certain books through the *Book Fund* was often a person's first encounter with literature that had been produced at home in the underground but published abroad. Some readers expressed their excitement about the range and the quality of books published in exile: "I am so grateful to you for the opportunity of making full acquaintance with the publications, which otherwise I would never have a chance to read. I am amazed by the astonishing publication effort in exile and 'quality' of certain books. Those, which I have obtained from you, will be treasured not only by myself, but by a wide circle of my trusted friends as well."[38]

After it became clear to readers inside the Soviet sphere that they could receive through this mailing project otherwise unavailable literature, RFE and RL received more and more requests for Western books. A report dedicated entirely to this phenomenon entitled "Poland looks to U.S. for books" reached the *Polish Institute* in the United States:[39] "Enormous demand for books ... coming from Polish scholars, scientists, writers and librarians far exceed the Institute's limited means for filling requests. ... The eagerness for books arises in part from the great destruction of Polish libraries during the war. Isolation from the West and shortage of foreign funds are also factors."[40]

Inspired by such requests from the "captive people," FEP established a mailing program that utilized its East-West contacts. This program served not to only circulate East European literature unavailable in the Soviet bloc, but also to transfer Western knowledge, expressed in writing, to intellectuals there. This strategy was meant to be successfully implemented not only by streaming broadcasts and sending underground literature back into their countries of origin, but also by simultaneously flooding the East with Western literature in their original languages and in local translations. The literature sent over had great variety, including "good literature, reference books, art books, science books, and textbooks." The selection depended on the most likely "maximum political impact with a minimum of provocation."[41] RFE and RL wanted to keep their new audiences and readers in touch with the intellectual achievements of the Free World, and, according to their reports from 1962, they had reached their original aim: "The mailing project has now reached a stage where it provided practically all the intellectuals and institutions in Hungary and Poland, and important sections of the reading public in the other East European countries, with the latest relevant works published in the Free World (some of them by us in cooperation with Polish and Hungarian exile publishers)."[42]

In order to conceal the identity of RFE and RL, individuals from the "Free World" privately sent packages of books to certain residences and institutions in the "captive nations." "FEP has mailed into the three Baltic States and the five Satellite States ... (books, journals, pamphlets, features) on every phase of free world life and thought. Most of these titles are mailed in the original English, French, or German ... [as] such operation cannot be identified with Free Europe Committee, it has been necessary to persuade either the publishers of the matter mailed, or others to lend their names as the senders of this material."[43]

A functioning network of mail senders in the West slowly developed and successfully implemented the new mailing project.

> In order to circumvent censorship which would never have admitted printed matter sent by Free Europe Committee, we asked several publishers, universities, libraries, and cultural associations in Austria, Switzerland, Germany, Sweden, France, England, Canada, and this country to act as intermediaries in sending books selected by us. Some twenty publishers and libraries accepted our suggestion, and we started sending out books to the twenty thousand-odd names we had been able to gather out of telephone directories and newspapers. … We are now addressing an audience of roughly 100000 intellectuals, professionals, newspapermen, artists and even government and party officials.[44]

By 1962, roughly three hundred European and two hundred American publishers had become part of the publishing project, helping to distribute large amounts of books to institutions and individuals in the East.[45]

One side effect of sending books that were either written by émigré Poles or just published abroad was to inform underground writers about their counterparts in the West. To know that there existed a large group of émigrés that were engaged in fighting suppression by the Polish government from abroad inspired underground activists to continue their resistance and further contributed to mutual understanding. A personal report from 1959 described the transfer of books in the following way: "*The Yearbook of Poles Abroad* created a sensation here. People in Poland had no idea that so many Polish Institutions, firms, clubs, etc. exist[ed] in the West."[46] After the books had been handed over to visitors, the next question was how to take the books across the border, through customs. Based on a series of sources from 1959, it appears that there were varying assessments of the situation. One monthly report explained that Polish customs officers were surprisingly unproblematic: "I have recently received 4 written confirmations from … recipients that all the books were transported safely to Poland. The customs examination is, generally speaking, quite superficial and there is no need to declare the possession of books."[47] Other reports again revealed that the officials inside Poland had become aware of the great amount of uncensored literature circulating in their country that had not been produced domestically. "A group of intellectuals from Poland … told him (the representative in Scotland) that the regime authorities are very concerned about the large quantity of anti-communist literature circulating in Poland … which entered the country through unknown channels. There are rumors that the customs officers have received instructions to confiscate all literature from the luggage of persons traveling to Poland. The same applies to sailors of the ships returning to homeports."[48] Despite the disagreement between these observations, it is clear that they are two sides of the same coin: while custom officers were initially unaware of the relevance of books, their circulation in large amounts raised the authorities' interest, from which followed increased control of book packages at the borders.

(Orally) Transmitting Tamizdat via RFE and RL

Although Soviet officials tried to block any form of independent radio news through jamming, RFE and RL largely succeeded in reaching their target audience in the *Other Europe*. The radio's ability to present samizdat material in an oral format particularly increased its impact on the listener. The oral transmission of the texts, namely the loud readings of samizdat and tamizdat texts in the mother tongue, reached the listening people in a far more immediate way than any written text did. It was the personal tone and the personal story, which was best captured when read aloud.[49] Eugeniusz Smolar, then a BBC veteran of many years, perceived the activity of the radio stations as highly relevant in three ways, because they (1) informed the target country of the developments inside its own society; (2) kept the people informed of important events in the other Soviet Bloc countries; and (3) presented news from the West. A circle of hope and cooperation slowly rose as the transfer of knowledge and information from other countries increased. Smolar stated in 2006: "The whole activity was an interlink between what happened in Poland, in Czechoslovakia, in Hungary. Because those were the countries with which we kept in close touch, with our own activity in the West, including—very important—Radio Free Europe, Radio Liberty, the BBC, VOA, even Radio Vatican to some extent. This is very important, it was a circle of hope."[50]

RFE and RL were the two main radio stations that reported on and broadcast readings of samizdat literature into countries behind the Iron Curtain. They also started receiving letters and manuscripts from the Soviet bloc (transmitted through all sorts of channels). Defining the radios' role vis-à-vis samizdat and tamizdat materials requires measuring the degree of priority given to samizdat in their broadcasting efforts, the fairness with which they handled this material, and also the possible results of their networking activities. RFE and RL (as the prototypical Western media that relied on the back-and-forth transmission of texts from a pool of samizdat) served as an important mediator for the flow of news and literature between the divided spheres. However, at times, serious competition emerged between Western tamizdat publishers and the radios regarding the question as to who had priority access to samizdat and tamizdat materials. In a letter to Don Graves at the Department of State in Washington in 1976, Albert Boiter, the director of the research section at RFE and RL, complained about the attempt of *Khronika Press* in New York to deconstruct "the role of Radio Liberty as the prime medium of 'redistributing' samizdat texts to Soviet listeners."[51] *Khronika Press* had become known for its English-language translation and publication of the Russian samizdat journal *Chronicle of Current Events,* representing an important Western tamizdat outlet. When contacting Graves at the Department of State, Boiter had decided to "go through interagency channels … to find out who is denying Radio Liberty its legitimate role to be a primary recipient of human rights samizdat delivered to the West."[52] The main problem he saw in the fact that "documents dispatched from Moscow have to go first to the U.S. then to New York and London before becoming available (if at all) to RL"[53] in Munich. The timely transmission of materials was a key aspect for keeping the radio broadcast of RFE/RL up to date on the basis of information that was only available in samizdat, for which reason a delay of several months was highly problematic to the radios. Beyond such competitive struggles over physical access and appropriate use of the materials, the radios were central in transmitting information gained from samizdat. Gayle Durham Hollander described Western reporters and foreign radio as "a 'transmission belt' to the larger world," which had turned into an "extension of the domestic alternative network … 'amplifying' the activities and writings of the democratic movement."[54] In a telex in 1971, Gene Sosin similarly argued that "foreign radio broadcasts [are] … a major factor in amplifying voices of dissent, encouraging this or that group to emulate others more bold and acting as a partial restraint on regime repression."[55] Even if Soviet officials hoped to "curb widespread distribution of samizdat," RL's staff was convinced that the transmission of uncensored materials could not be stopped "unless they (the Soviet officials) can cut off the flow of such documents to the West."[56] Otherwise, the body of literature that reached the West would only increase in amount. RFE and RL had at their disposal many ways of obtaining information and material, especially through "contacts with citizens from the socialist countries, who travel to the West as tourists, to attend congresses and scientific conferences, symposia, or to take part in sports events. There is a group of people among the employees of the Czechoslovak department of Radio Free Europe, who have been assigned the task by the American intelligence agency to contact these visitors from the socialist countries and to obtain information from them."[57]

Radio provided a truly influential link between the literary underground and the world of Western ideas, problems, outlooks, and even events. Poles widely listened to RFE, RL, VOA, and the Polish Section of

BBC, despite continuous jamming. These stations had a tremendous impact on millions of listeners throughout the whole country. The role of these institutions in linking the two worlds can hardly be overestimated. Just as RFE and RL helped to bounce tamizdat texts back into the Soviet sphere, they provided a means of communication (so-called intercommunication) for citizens inside the bloc. In 1971, Max Hayward labeled RFE and RL the "echo chamber"[58] and the "sounding board"[59] for samizdat material. In an article in the German *Süddeutsche Zeitung* in 1970, Claude Angeli estimated that radio stations played a vital role in broadcasting the underground's voice back into the "captive countries": "In fact, there is hardly a western medium of communication which finds such a great echo among the population of the eastern Bloc as the two radio stations."[60] However, when a 1970 article in *Le Nouvel Observateur* outlined the manifold functions of RFE and RL, it interpreted their impact as serving first and foremost the people inside the bloc.

> Decidedly, they work hard at "Free Europe." The impact is not only a question of watts and transmitter. ... Because "Free Europe" is unique in its kind. It is five radio stations with something more to them. It is not only a fabulous enterprise spending many dollars and earning not one cent. It is not only journalists, specialists on the East, technicians, producers, disc jockeys and bureaus in a dozen countries. It is not only programs for farmers, housewives, intellectuals or average citizens, and not only concerts and songs, the latest records on sale in Bucharest, Warsaw or Budapest, or the latest "Beatles." For the listener in the East, "Free Europe" is both American radio and national radio, ordinary radio and radio discreetly listened to, a radio-window toward the West, toward the USSR and the other socialist countries, and radio-window toward his own country. Doubtlessly, no other station in the world, American or other, exercises such influence, direct or indirect, on the public opinion of five countries. "Free Europe" is a radio of combat, a "second power" to be reckoned with in Eastern Europe.[61]

Andrei Sinyavsky summarized the double perspective on RFE and RL, first retrospectively as a one-time underground writer inside the Soviet Union, and second as a new émigré in France, reporting from time to time for RL:

> At the time of my arrest, during my confinement in a camp (from 1965 to 1971), and my subsequent release, right up to my departure to the West in 1973, I had numerous occasions of being convinced of the enormous and fundamental influence of Radio Liberty on the way of thinking and on the social and political climate in the Soviet Union. The Russians are practically deprived of any newspaper from the West. Under these conditions, Radio Liberty offers almost the only source of broad information—first and foremost on the internal life in Russia, about arrests and other forms of repression, the growth of noncon-

formist ideas, on the reaction of public opinion in the West about Russian affairs. In addition, this information becomes a form of pressure on government institutions in the Soviet Union, which reflects directly on the fate of so-called dissidents.[62]

Aside from its purely "informing" policy, Sinyavsky referred to the possible political effect of reportages on imprisoned activists, citing his own personal experiences in prison. In a letter in 1976, he wrote: "I noticed that each time the campaign in my defense in the West was intensified and the news of this was broadcasted by *Radio Liberty* to Russia, my situation was alleviated."[63] His personal experience with the possible positive effects of RL on writers inside the Soviet Union compelled him to speak through RL to his colleagues and friends "over-there" after his emigration. Sinyavsky evaluated RL's work as follows: "Recently, as a resident of the West, I have frequently had the proof from my friends still in Russia that 'our voices' reach them through 'Liberty' and that the activities of this radio station is becoming more and more necessary for the ideological liberation of the people living in the Soviet Union."[64] Such reportages understood samizdat texts smuggled out from the Soviet Union as representations of the various topics that animated nonconformist writers. Read in this way, the Western media considered it necessary to return the texts to the Eastern bloc for continued dissemination and information. Here Sinyavsky reiterated the general hope of RFE and RL to slowly break down the Soviet monopoly on ideas and values by using the languages and voices of the very people in those communist countries.

In order to perform this echo function, various types of radio shows were established that either used samizdat as a resource for reporting on developments inside the Soviet bloc or directly broadcasted samizdat documents by writers like Pasternak, Solzhenitsyn, Sinyavsky, and other uncensored authors. Émigrés often performed readings of the literary works of their unemigrated colleagues. The main broadcasting shows in 1971 were called *Letters and Documents*, which presented original samizdat documents, *Unpublished Works of Soviet Authors*, which broadcasted texts of literary samizdat works, and *Samizdat Review*, which covered nonconformist developments.[65] RFE and RL filled six out of thirty-six hours of programming with samizdat material.[66] Although the radio stations were primarily interested in the use of samizdat documents for broadcasting, they started as a byproduct to "to perform a service to scholars, specialists, journalists and the like outside the station by functioning as a repository and distribution point for samizdat documents."[67]

While, at its inception, streaming shows into the Soviet sphere was paramount, projects developed in the 1970s that were directed at the Western audience. Spreading information and documents in translation served to address not only the public in the East, but also the Western public, highly interested in uncensored news. RFE and RL helped to preserve this literature and to accumulate an important collection of otherwise lost literature. Apart from collections of documents in the form of a *biblioteke samizdata*[68] and the installation of archival repositories accessible to the academic community, the function of RFE and RL lay especially in providing commentaries about the samizdat texts (to make the material truly accessible to and understood by the Western public).[69] In a March 1971 letter, in the fateful year of the discovery of the CIA involvement with RFE and RL, Albert Boiter formulated his impression of a change in the Western interest in samizdat material: "It is my impression from recent travels in France, UK and Germany that the samizdat phenomenon is on the verge of more systematic and even large-scale exploitation by many European research institutions. We at RL are trying to keep abreast all these developments and to facilitate where we can the serious study of the Soviet dissident movement."[70] The new strategy was to pay more attention to the Western intellectual sphere, which needed more clarification and education about developments inside samizdat. "'Radio liberty samizdat service' is being inaugurated in order to provide an easily-accessible and systematic means by which Radio Liberty can share with interested scholars, journalists, libraries, research institutions, etc. the original-language texts of all new samizdat material which comes into its possession in return for the cost of duplication and postage."[71]

During a conference in 1971 entitled *Dissent in the Soviet Union*,[72] Karel van het Reve summarized the new interest of the Western scholarly community in the alternative voice of Russia: "Universities, libraries, newspapers all over the world are slowly awakening to the fact that besides and behind the official Russia there is another Russia, more interesting perhaps than the official Russia."[73] Especially Sovietologists started to "realize that it is more important and certainly more interesting to read the *Khronika* than to read *Pravda*."[74] Besides the new awakening of a scholarly approach to nonconformism in the Soviet sphere, van het Reve questioned his Western listeners by comparing the all-daring attitude of Soviet underground writers and activists to the little engagement of Western scholars:

> Most of you, when asked to bring a printed copy of one of his [Solzhenitsyn's] books to a certain address in Moscow or Kiev, or to bring the manuscript of another of his books from Leningrad to Toronto, would refuse to do this. … But the thought that a man should not be able to print a book in Paris if he chooses to do so awakens in them certain instincts that make them do both these things.[75]

In this comment, the underlying aim of such thematic conferences at that time is clear, namely, the hope to gain support from Western scholars for underground writers and their fight for the freedoms of speech and publication. A range of Sovietologists and experts on Eastern Europe additionally followed suit, hoping to establish a regular journal for the English-speaking, academic reader. The journal's main aim would be:

> to present quickly, but on a basis of high academic standards, the most important current samizdat documents to the English reader. The vehicle for this needs to be a journal, and the proposed title is simply Samizdat. ... The journal should have an international advisory board of mostly well-known academics, and should appear about six times a year. Three-quarters of the contents would be translated recent documents or excerpts from documents, and the remaining quarter would contain two or three analytical articles by western scholars. ... Obviously the journal would be a very useful focus for samizdat publishing generally.[76]

During a similar conference organized by RFE and RL in London in 1971, entitled *The Future of Samizdat: Significance and Prospects,* academics and employees of RFE and RL debated future approaches to samizdat materials (especially the new attention to samizdat circulation in the Western intellectual sphere). Among Western scholars above all the quality and intellectual sophistication of samizdat materials for a Western audience were debated. Once dragged out of its historical and cultural context, samizdat text, many argued, lost much of its original quality. In addition, most of the literature was, at least initially, not meant to appear abroad, and was not written with the Western reader in mind. Since much of the material dealt with the internal problems of Soviet society, and since it was shaped in the Soviet frame of reference (and meant for internal use), the transmission of the texts did not occur without creating communication gaps. The Western reader as the addressee became officially involved only when the material was specifically addressed to institutions and individuals abroad. Albert Boiter saw in this the other dimension of samizdat: "Only in the last few years has it occurred to many Soviet authors of samizdat that by sending copies of their work abroad, where it can be published and attract international attention, they can add an extra dimension which may be helpful to their particular causes."[77]

However, as Leopold Labedz remarked, the underground readership inside the Soviet sphere absorbed most of the materials that reached the West. Labetz was convinced that reading the material outside its place of origin caused miscommunications and misunderstandings. In 1971, he claimed in an opening statement concerning the future of samizdat publications that there existed a "juxtaposition of the problems involved in the presentation of samizdat in the West as compared to the echo chamber. An echo chamber is adequate because, after all, it bounces back in the same kind of milieu and to the audience which is producing it."⁷⁸ He argued that a great deal of the documents once transferred to the West to be spread in academia, had—in scholarly terms—little to offer the intellectual debates in the West: "There would be very few documents, only those Soviet samizdat documents which are able to stand up to a free and open discussion without looking primitive or unsophisticated. So, that is why these documents can have political significance—but not always intellectual significance outside their own historical context—that is, only in the Soviet Union."⁷⁹

Harshly criticizing Labedz, Leonard Schapiro was firmly convinced that it was exactly the unspoiled and unconventional character of the documents that transferred the unknown meaning and knowledge from a region of Europe otherwise represented only in the official Soviet press. "There is a tremendous force behind publishing the ordinary, naïve, unknown, unimportant chap. Why is he unimportant? He may be unimportant intellectually, but he is important because the strength of these things, the movement or whatever it is, is the strength of the hydra: if you cut of one head another one grows."⁸⁰ Although he did not discuss the intellectual value of the texts themselves, Schapiro convincingly turned attention to the importance of the physical appearance of samizdat materials in the West. As discussed above, the prospect of gaining an audience in the West seemed to offer enough emotional impact to the Western reader that he should not actually only judge the texts for the intellectual quality.

> Now that is something that emerges out of some kind of sense of confidence. Some kind of sense that you are not alone, that there are lots of people around you. ... You are not just going to be bumped off in a cellar ... but a feeling that "Well, all right, they've put him in" ... but there is still a voice somewhere which recognizes me. And even if I come out with something, which intellectually is not Solzhenitsyn, or Amalrik, nevertheless, what I write is something that people take account of.⁸¹

Max Hayward intimately recounted his experience in 1959 and 1960 when reading an early samizdat piece, *A Voice from Russia*, published in the *Sunday Times*: "It was enormously impressive because it was one of the first indications that there were people there, who had preserved the capacity to scream. One had a feeling at one time that perhaps the Soviet people had been somehow totally crippled, reduced to muteness, perhaps forever. How did we know that the contrary was the case except through these pathetic (as we now read them) voices?"⁸² Reading this specific piece, he gained a personal understanding of this literature's psychological function, which he warned others not to underestimate: "They started off by screaming, which was a therapeutic thing. A nightmare was coming to an end and you screamed as you startled yourself out of your sleep. This is what happened after Stalin's death. One heard these first anguished voices, which, if one reads them now, seem terribly lame. Yet at the time we were terribly impressed by them."[83]

Apart from informing Western readers about developments inside the bloc, samizdat also highlighted the emergence of a well-functioning and very reliable network of people.

> In the last three years a remarkable network obviously has grown up in the Soviet Union of samizdat correspondents. I would like to stress, in particular, that I think this network is a strong one because it is serviced, it is operated, by people, who have very little to lose, who have "sat" for long periods in the past and are therefore people, who are rather desperate, and who are willing to run great risks to operate the samizdat network.[84]

The West valued samizdat primarily for its social activism (for a long time relatively ignoring the actual content of samizdat texts). Not going into more detail about the discussion of the intellectual merits of the literature transferred and absorbed in the West, this literature introduced new communicative channels for the exchange of information during the period of détente. The double function of RFE and RL depended greatly on collaborators who could combine two qualities simultaneously: familiarity with the Soviet context and also familiarity with the Western intellectual scene. Without such key aid, Labedz argued, the two worlds would remain worlds apart.[85] Herein we can see the high value placed on the social activism of RFE and RL. It seems that, especially in the early 1970s, the new tendencies of détente (aiming in accordance with the Helsinki Accords at a "free flow of information" and *glasnost*—that is "openness" or "publicity") figured more and more in the debates inside RFE and RL. This leitmotif, however, laid the foundation for any samizdat activity.[86] In this respect, the plea for *glasnost*—which connotes the exact opposite of the pervading silence that censorship tried to impose—was already prevalent in the early 1970s (not the mid 1980s) in literary circles on both sides of the Iron Curtain. The overall aim of American cultural policy was to counteract the suppressed stream of information, which had become the most significant dividing line between the blocs. The *Council for a Free Czechoslovakia* was specifically engaged in improving cultural relations between the United States and Czechoslovakia. Its members were aware, however, that better contact between Czechoslovakia and the United States was only possible by pursuing the cultural reunification of Europe.

> The American long-term interest in Europe will be best served when the dividing line between the western and the eastern parts of the Continent is removed

or at least reduced to practical insignificance. The principal source of Europe's malady, which so profoundly affects the United States lies in the suppression of fundamental freedoms in the East. ... It is in the interest of the United States and the western democracies that Central and Eastern Europe should not remain buried under a twentieth-century version of the Peace of Westphalia.[87]

Better communication and an increased flow of information became more and more part of the Western understanding of their policy of détente starting to take shape in the early 1970s.

The belief in the connectedness of two, politically separated literary spheres seems to have sparked the idea that broadcast could serve as one, particularly effective means to deconstruct Europe's division in the sphere of literature. The idea to physically transfer literature between the East and West symbolized a first practical step to reconnect the literary communities. Only through the physical transfer of literature could the oral dissemination of uncensored contents via broadcast be guaranteed. By initiating person-to-person projects and engaging a wide variety of carrier pigeons for smuggling literature out of the Soviet bloc and back, RFE and RL contributed to the resulting intellectual exchange of ideas. Voicing the samizdat texts via broadcasting enabled authors to reach a far broader and far more varied (not to mention international) audience than the physical circulation of their texts allowed.[88] Thus, broadcasting brought in listeners that books, journals, and newspapers (though indeed very significant) could have never reached.[89] For this reason among others, RFE and RL played a crucial role in spreading the materials and contents of samizdat and tamizdat as well as in reconnecting the intellectual worlds on both sides of the Iron Curtain.

Notes

1. Thomas Lindenberger, "Geteilte Welt, geteilter Himmel? Der Kalte Krieg und die Massenmedien in gesellschaftsgeschichtlicher Perspektive," in *Zwischen Pop und Propaganda. Radio in der DDR*, ed. Klaus Arnold and Christoph Classen (Berlin, 2004), 27–46.
2. Ibid., 43.
3. A. Ross Johnson, *Radio Free Europe and Radio Liberty: The CIA Years and Beyond* (Stanford, 2010), 184. On the role and function of RFE/RL during the Cold War, see also A. Ross Johnson and R. Eugene Parta, *Cold War Broadcasting: Impact on the Soviet Union and Eastern Europe: A Collection of Studies and Documents* (Budapest, 2010).
4. "The Mission of Radio Free Europe and Radio Liberty Broadcast," reproduced from the Board for International Broadcasting, Eight Annual Report, 1982, reprinted in William

A. Buell, "Radio Free Europe/Radio Liberty in the Mid 1980s," in *Western Broadcasting Over the Iron Curtain*, ed. K. R. M. Short (London, 1986), 85.
5. Tony Shaw, "Politics of Cold War Culture," *Journal of Cold War Studies* 3, no. 3 (Fall 2001): 59–76. Robert Griffith, "The Cultural Turn in Cold War Studies," *Reviews in American History* 29 (2001): 150–57.
6. György Péteri, *Nylon Curtain-Transnational and Transsystemic Tendencies in the Cultural Life of State-Socialist Russia and East Central Europe* (Trondheim, 2006), 4.
7. "News from behind the Iron Curtain" was a well-known journal of the Free Europe Press that was published in New York from 1952 to 1956.
8. "Broadcasting to Youth," Radio Free Europe Policy Handbook, 30 November 1951, Hoover Institution Archives [HIA], RFE/RL Corporate Records, Sheet 13.
9. Ibid.
10. Ibid., Sheet 14.
11. Leopold Labedz, "How the blue pencil can be blunted," *The Times*, 27 September 1977, 16.
12. "The Mission of Radio Free Europe and Radio Liberty Broadcast," reproduced from the Board for International Broadcasting, Eight Annual Report, 1982, reprinted in Buell, "Radio Free Europe/Radio Liberty in the Mid 1980s," 85.
13. Ibid.
14. George R. Urban, *Radio Free Europe and the Pursuit of Democracy: My War Within the Cold War* (New Haven, 1997), 124.
15. Frances Stonor Saunders, *The Cultural Cold War: The CIA and the World of Arts and Letters* (New York, 1999); Giles Scott-Smith, *The Politics of Apolitical Culture: The Congress for Cultural Freedom, the CIA, and Post-War American Hegemony* (London, 2002); Michael L. Krenn, *Fall-Out Shelters for the Human Spirit: American Art and the Cold War* (Chapel Hill, 2005); Reinhold Wagenleitner, *American Cultural Diplomacy, the Cinema and the Cold War in Central Europe* (Minneapolis, 1992); Frank Ninkovich, *U.S. Information Policy and Cultural Diplomacy* (New York, 1996); Naima Prevots, *Dance for Export: Cultural Diplomacy and the Cold War* (Middletown, 1998); Penny M. Von Eschen, *Satchmo Blows Up the World: Jazz Ambassadors Play the Cold War* (Harvard, 2004).
16. See Urban, *Radio Free Europe and the Pursuit of Democracy*; Sig Mickelson, *America's Other Voice: the Story of Radio Free Europe and Radio Liberty* (New York, 1983).
17. A recent study on early RFE funding has been provided by Richard H. Cummings, *Radio Free Europe's Crusade for Freedom: Rallying Americans behind Cold War Broadcasting, 1950–1960* (North Carolina, 2010).
18. Hugh Wilford, *The Mighty Wurlitzer* (Cambridge, MA, 2008), 113.
19. See for this Cissie Dore Hill, "Voices of Hope: The Story of Radio Free Europe and Radio Liberty," *Hoover Digest* 4 (2001). Online at http://www.hoover.org/publications/digest/3475896.html (accessed 19 August 2011). See also Arch Puddington, *Broadcasting Freedom: The Cold War Triumph of Radio Free Europe and Radio Liberty* (Lexington, 2003), 12.
20. Rudolf L. Tőkés, "Human Rights and Political Change in eastern Europe," in *Opposition in Eastern Europe*, ed. Rudolf L. Tőkés (London, 1979), 1.
21. An extensive discussion of the various journals published through FEP and their mission to recreate a joint Europe as a concept will be published separately.
22. FEP Publications, 15 May 1958, Free Europe Organization 1951–59, HIA, RFE/RL Corporate Records, Box 197, Folder 6, Sheet 5.
23. "Memorandum: New Opportunities Arising from East-West Contacts and Additional Means of Reaching Persons in the Captive Countries," 1959 (?), Publications Develop-

ment Corporation Operations Reports 1959, HIA, RFE/RL Corporate Records, Box 262, Folder 5, Sheet 2.
24. FEP Operations, 16 May 1958, "East European Operations," Free Europe Organizations and Publications 1951–59, HIA, RFE/RL Corporate Records, Box 197, Folder 6, 1.
25. "Polonia Book Fund Ltd.," Person-to-Person Program, Monthly Report for December 1959, Publications Development Operations Reports 1959, HIA, RFE/RL Corporate Records, Box 262, Folder 5, Sheet 1.
26. Ibid.
27. "Polonia Book Fund Ltd.," Person-to-Person Program, Monthly Report for October 1959, HIA, RFE/RL Corporate Records, Publications Development Corporation, Operations Reports, 1959, Box. 262, Folder 5, Sheet 3. Also mentioned in a monthly report for November 1959 by *Polonia Book Fund,* HIA, RFE Corporate Records, Publications Development Corporation, Operations Reports 1959, Box. 262, Folder 5, Sheet 3.
28. "Polonia Book Fund Ltd.," Person-To-Person Program, Monthly Report for November 1959, Publications Development Corporation, Operations Report 1959, HIA, RFE/RL Corporate Records, Box No. 262, Folder 5, Sheet 3.
29. "Polonia Book Fund Ltd.," Person-to-Person Program, Monthly Report for October 1959, 8 December 1959, Publications Development Corporation, Operations Reports 1959, HIA, RFE/RL Corporate Records, Box 262, Folder 5, Sheet 3.
30. "Polonia Book Fund Ltd.," Person-to-Person Program, Monthly Report for December 1959, Publications Development Operations Reports 1959, HIA, RFE/RL Corporate Records, Box 262, Folder 5, Sheet 5.
31. Ibid., Sheet 1.
32. "Polonia Book Fund Ltd.," Person-To-Person Program, Monthly Report for November 1959, Publications Development Corporation, Operations Report 1959, HIA, RFE/RL Corporate Records, Box No. 262, Folder 5, Sheet 2.
33. Ibid.
34. Richard Swartz, "Organisierte Bequemlichkeit: Leben in der Repression. Eine Provokante Skizze," *Kursbuch 81. Die andere Hälfte Europas* (September 1985): 120.
35. Ibid.
36. "Polonia Book Fund Ltd.," Person-to-Person Program, Monthly Report for October 1959, 8 December 1959, Publications Development Corporation, Operations Reports 1959, HIA, RFE/RL Corporate Records, Box 262, Folder 5, Sheet 6.
37. Ibid., Sheet 4.
38. Ibid.
39. A. B. Czartoryski, "Poland Looks to U.S. for Books, Technical Knowledge," Polish Institute of Arts and Sciences in America received 13 May 1958, Books to Bela PIAS, HIA, RFE/RL Corporate Records, Box 255, Folder 9, Sheet 1.
40. Ibid.
41. Mailing Project: A summary, 26 July 1962, East West contacts, Publications and special projects. 1961–64, HIA, Corporate Records, Box 258, Folder 8, Sheet 1.
42. Ibid.
43. FEP Publications, 15 May 1958, Free Europe Organization 1951–59, HIA, RFE/RL Corporate Records, Box 197, Folder 6, Sheet 5.
44. Mailing Project: A summary, 26. July 1962, East West contacts, Publications and special projects, 1961–64, HIA, RFE/RL Corporate Records, Box 258, Folder 8, Sheet 1.
45. John P. C. Matthews, "The West's Secret Marshall Plan for the Mind," *The International Journal of Intelligence and CounterIntelligence* 16, no. 3 (2003). Republished online at http://cryptome.org/cia-minden.htm#matthews (accessed 19 August 2011), 13.

46. "Polonia Book Fund Ltd.," Person-To-Person Program, Monthly Report for November 1959, Publications Development Corporation, Operations Report 1959, HIA, RFE/RL Corporate Records, Box No. 262, Folder 5, Sheet 3.
47. Ibid.
48. Ibid.
49. See Michael Nelson, *War of the Black Heavens: The Battles of Western Broadcasting in the Cold War* (London, 1997).
50. Eugeniusz Smolar during a roundtable discussion. See "From Memories to Legacies," at the conference *From Samizdat to Tamizdat: Independent Media Crossing Borders Before and After 1989*, IWM, Vienna Tuesday, 12 September 2006.
51. Confidential Letters. HIA, RFE/RL Corporate Records, Samizdat General, 1975–1976. Box 295, File 1.
52. Confidential Letters. HIA, RFE/RL Corporate Records, Samizdat General, 1975–1976. Box 295, File 1.
53. Confidential Letters. HIA, RFE/RL Corporate Records, Samizdat General, 1975–1976. Box 295, File 1.
54. Hollander, "Political Communication and Dissent in the USSR," 259–60. See Gene Sosin, *Sparks of Liberty: An insider's memoir of Radio Liberty* (Pennsylvania, 1999), 154–55. See Urban, *Radio Free Europe and the Pursuit of Democracy*, 124–25. See also Allan Michie, *Voices Through the Iron Curtain: The Radio Free Europe Story* (New York, 1963).
55. Sosin telex to Boiter and Vad Der Rhoer, 28 October 1971, stated again at a conference on samizdat in North America 1972. See Sosin, *Sparks of Liberty*, 154–55.
56. See Edward van der Rhoer, "Radio Liberty's Present Uses of *Samizdat*," in *The Future of Samizdat: Significance and Prospects*, transcript of conference held in London, by Radio Liberty Committee, 23 April 1971, HIA, RFE/RL Corporate Records, 1–47, Sheet 5.
57. Cees Agent Minarik describes work for RFE. Statement to Press, 29 January 1976, HIA, Radomir Luza Papers, Box 134, Sheet 7.
58. See Leo Labedz, "Opening Statements by Panelists," in *The Future of Samizdat: Significance and Prospects*, transcript of conference, Sheet 9.
59. See Max Hayward, "Opening Statements by Panelists," in *The Future of Samizdat: Significance and Prospects*, transcript of conference, 15.
60. Article in *Süddeutsche Zeitung*, 22 February 1970, cited in "West European Press estimates of Radio Free Europe," HIA, RFE/RL Corporate Records, Stefan Karbonski Papers, Box 4, Sheet 3.
61. Article by Claude Angeli in *Le Nouvel Observateur* (12 January 1970,) cited in "West European Press estimates of Radio Free Europe," HIA, RFE/RL Corporate Records, Stefan Karbonski Papers, Box 4, Sheet 1–2.
62. Letter by Andrei Sinyavsky to Mr. Mickelson, Paris, 10 January 1976, Emigré testimonials, HIA, RFE/RL Corporate Records, Box 178, Folder 13.
63. Ibid.
64. Ibid.
65. See Albrecht Boiter "Radio Liberty's Present Uses of *Samizdat*," in *The Future of Samizdat: Significance and Prospects*, transcript of conference, 3.
66. Ibid., 4.
67. Criteria for Duplicating Original *Samizdat* Documents (Draft), 4 February 1972, Samizdat General 1972, HIA, RFE/RL Corporate Records, Box 294, Folder 8, Sheet 1.
68. Letter by Albert Boiter to Richard Pipes, 16 March 1971, Samizdat General 1972, HIA, RFE/RL Corporate Records, Box 294, Folder 7, Sheet 1. Apart from such institutional archives, individuals such as Gordon Skilling, for instance, "Assembled at the University of Toronto a large *samizdat* library containing several hundred volumes." See Ladislav

Matejka, *Introduction to the Electronic Version of Cross Currents: A Yearbook of Central European Culture*, 5, online available at: http://quod.lib.umich.edu/c/crossc/intro.html (accessed 19 August 2011).

69. Memorandum from Gene Sosin to Albert Boiter, Subject: My Reactions to London Panelists Viewpoints on RL's Future Approach to *Samizdat*, 28 May 1971, Samizdat 1972, HIA, RFE/RL Corporate Records, Box 294, Folder 8, Sheet 1.
70. Letter by Albert Boiter to Richard Pipes, 16 March 1971, Samizdat General 1972, HIA, RFE/RL Corporate Records, Box 294, Folder 7, Sheet 1.
71. Announcing the Inauguration of the Radio Liberty Samizdat Service (Draft), Samizdat General 1972, HIA, RFE/RL Corporate Records, Box 294, Folder 7, Sheet 1.
72. The Conference took place between 22 and 23 October and was organized by *The Interdepartmental Committee on Communist and East European Affairs*. See RFE/RL Corporate Records. Historical File, Provisional, Box 14, Folder Samizdat 1971.
73. Speech by K. Van Het Rev, in *London Panel Discussion on Samizdat and Dissent*, 22 and 23 October 1971, by Radio Liberty Committee, HIA, RFE/RL Corporate Records. Historical File, Provisional, Box 14, Folder Samizdat 1971, Sheet 4.
74. Ibid., Sheet 5.
75. Ibid., Sheet 14.
76. Peter Reddaway, "Approximate Plans for Future Publishing of *Samizdat*," 28 June 1971, Samizdat General 1972, HIA, RFE/RL Corporate Records, Box 294, Folder 7, Sheet 2.
77. Albert Boiter, "Samizdat: Primary Source Material in the Study of Current Soviet Affairs," written for a panel on "Varieties of Dissent in the USSR-An Interdisciplinary Approach at the Fifth National Convention American Association for the Advancement of Slavic Studies in Dallas, Texas, 15–18 March 1972, Samizdat General 1972, HIA, RFE/RL Corporate Records, Box 294, Folder 7, Sheet 6.
78. Leopold Labedz, "Opening Statements by Panelists," in *The Future of Samizdat: Significance and Prospects*, transcript of conference, 10.
79. Ibid.
80. Leonard Schapiro, "Opening Statements by Panelists," in *The Future of Samizdat: Significance and Prospects*, transcript of conference, Sheet 11.
81. Max Hayward, "Opening Statements by Panelists," in *The Future of Samizdat: Significance and Prospects*, transcript of conference, Sheet 11.
82. Labedz, "Opening Statements by Panelists," Sheet 10.
83. Ibid.
84. Extract of a Speech given by Peter Reddaway during the conference, *The Future of Samizdat: Significance and Prospects*, transcript of conference, Sheet 3–4.
85. Labedz, "Opening Statements by Panelists," 10.
86. Albert Boiter, "Samizdat: Primary Source Material in the Study of Current Soviet Affairs," written for a Panel on "Varieties of Dissent in the USSR—An Interdisciplinary Approach at the Fifth National Convention American Association for the Advancement of Slavic Studies in Dallas, Texas, 15–18 March 1972, Samizdat General 1972, HIA, *RFE* Corporate Records, Box 294, Folder 7, Sheet 7.
87. Council of Free Czechoslovakia, A Memorandum on the United States Policy towards Czechoslovakia, New York, 20 May 1981, HIA, Radomir Luza Papers, Box 134, Sheet 3.
88. Puddington, *Broadcasting Freedom*, 170 and 268.
89. In Support of H.R. 9637. Statement Presented before the Committee on Foreign Relations of the United States House of Representatives by John A. Grnouski, 10 a.m., Tuesday, 14 September 1971, HIA, RFE/RL Corporate Records, Stefan Karbonski Papers, Box 4, Sheet 1–9.

Chapter 4

CONTACT BEYOND BORDERS AND HISTORICAL PROBLEMS
Kultura, Russian Emigration, and the Polish Opposition

Karolina Zioło-Pużuk

Kultura was the most important Polish émigré journal, which influenced not only Polish émigré circles, but also most significantly, Polish opposition activists. From its establishment in 1946 until its last issue published in 2000, Kultura shaped the most vital aspects of Polish political thought, particularly the relations between Poland and its Eastern neighbors Ukraine and Russia. Therefore, current relations between East-Central European nations and Poland—i.e., the Polish support for the Orange Revolution in Ukraine in 2004 and 2005 and democratic movements in Belarus—can be seen as the outcome of a dialogue Jerzy Giedroyc, the editor of Kultura, started in the 1950s. As Timothy Garton-Ash and Timothy Snyder stated in the text on the Orange Revolution in Ukraine,

> the Polish presence in Kyiv was the latest evidence of a sustained strategy. In the 1970s, back when Poland was still a Soviet satellite, the influential émigré monthly Kultura, based in Paris, proposed a new policy for Poland after the end of communism. Poles should accept the new postwar eastern borders, even though Stalin had seized half of their country. If Poles accepted these borders in advance and did not demand the return of their former lands, they could better cooperate with the democratic opposition movements in the neighboring Lithuanian, Belarusian, and Ukrainian Soviet Republics, and establish friendly relations with them when the Soviet Union collapsed.[1]

Meanwhile, Kontinent, a Russian émigré journal established in 1974 and based in Paris along with Kultura, played an important role in developing a Polish-Russian multidimensional dialogue about history, politics, past conflicts, and future perspectives. This chapter will present how the coop-

---

Notes for this chapter begin on page 103.

eration between *Kultura* and *Kontinent,* as well as the ideas expressed on the pages of these journals, influenced the theory and practice of international relations in East and Central Europe after 1989.

Kultura's prominent position in émigré circles, however, started before it began its cooperation with the Russian journal *Kontinent.* The first publication of Andrei Sinyavsky and Yuli Daniel's work in the early 1960s shows not only that *Kultura,* The Literary Institute, and Jerzy Giedroyc (founder of both) were established, trustworthy, and prolific publishing institutions, but also illustrates the main aspects of *Kultura*'s policy, that is, the idea to establish and develop a dialogue between West and East and also among Eastern and Central European states.

It should be stated further that Jerzy Giedroyc's attitude toward democratic movements in Eastern Europe was not only sympathetic but also actively supportive and went beyond mere written declarations. Giedroyc was the first publisher who had the courage to publish Sinyavsky's and Daniel's works in the West.[2] Giedroyc received the manuscripts of Abram Tertz (real name, Andrei Sinyavsky, though Giedroyc did not know the actual name of the writer, who used this pseudonym to guarantee his own safety) from Helena Zamoyska, who traveled frequently from France to Russia and obtained these stories there from the author.[3] In 1956, Sinyavsky and Daniel sent their works abroad for the first time. Sinyavsky's *The Trial Begins* was first published in 1959 and broadcast over Radio Liberty. The story *Hands* by Yuli Daniel (Nikolai Arzhak) was published in the journal *Kultura,* number 19 in 1961. Tertz's *Fantastic Stories* was published both in Polish and Russian in 1961. Publishing books both in Russian and Polish can be regarded as evidence that Giedroyc not only concentrated his publishing policy on Polish readers but also tried to reach wider émigré circles. His policy was not simply profit orientated, and he was concerned foremost about the political and social impact of any book he decided to publish.

The letters written by Helena Zamoyska, her husband, August Zamoyski, and Jerzy Giedroyc preserved in The Literary Institute Archive in Paris provide an interesting insight into Giedroyc's involvement in the Sinyavsky-Daniel trial and demonstrate his interest in their fate and the fate of their works sent abroad. The fact that Helena Zamoyska decided to hand over the manuscripts to Giedroyc in the late 1950s suggests that by that time *Kultura* had gained a reputation as one of the leading émigré publishers. Furthermore, Giedroyc himself was seen as a publisher who could represent the interests of all East European writers, not only Polish writers. The archival correspondence between the Zamoyskis and Giedroyc about publishing Tertz's short stories describes in detail the publishing and editing process that, quite unusually, did not involve the writers. Hence, most of the responsibility for the final result of this process rested in the hands of the editor and the publisher. Furthermore, these letters reflect that Giedroyc was not only aware of the significance of this publication, but also aware of its possible political consequences.

Kultura and *Kontinent*: The Establishment of Both Journals and Beginnings of Cooperation

Although *Kultura* and *Kontinent* were established almost thirty years apart, the ideas behind establishing both journals seem to me similar and their position in émigré circles are also quite easily paralleled. Giedroyc's Literary Institute was established in Rome in 1946 and a year later the first issues of *Kultura* were published. Some of the founding members cooperated from a distance, while others maintained contact sporadically or devoted their lives to the Institute and *Kultura* from the beginning. Jerzy Giedroyc was the editor-in-chief of *Kultura* from its start until the end of his life, and, according to his will, the journal ended with him. *Kultura* was published monthly without interruption from 1947 until Jerzy Giedroyc's death in 2000 (totaling almost six hundred published issues). In 1953, the Literary Institute started publishing books in a series entitled *Biblioteka Kultury* (Kultura Library), putting out a total of 512 books over the next forty-eight years.

Giedroyc's work with the Russian émigré journal *Kontinent* was a result of his long-standing interest in Polish-Russian relations as well as the role of Poland in shaping the Central and East European region. It was also a consequence of Giedroyc's broad understanding of opposition with the political system that dominated the region after World War II. Giedroyc was aware of the importance of ties between émigré circles, and he pursued close cooperation between Polish, Russian, and Ukraine diasporas. In a text published on the twenty-fifth anniversary of *Kultura*, Józef Czapski emphasized the importance of relations between Poland and Ukraine, Lithuania, and, above all, Russia, based on the conviction that the political situation in those countries was directly connected with the internal situation in the USSR. He also put forward the idea of tightening relations with Russian liberal circles.[4]

The first issue of *Kontinent*, by contrast, was published in 1974, hence in a very different political and social situation in Europe. Solzhenitsyn inspired the establishment and the name of *Kontinent*; he was inspired in turn by *Kultura* and the way it had successfully operated for almost three decades. Vladimir Maksimov, who became the editor-in-chief of *Kontinent*, described how he found out about *Kultura* in an interview published in *Kultura* in 1974: "In Moscow, in 1960, an officer from the KGB came to me. He sat down and with menacing tone and said (in informal address) the following: 'Listen, Maksimov, an emissary will come to see you from *Kultura*, the Polish monthly in Paris. I advise you as father to son: don't get into it.' No 'emissary' came, but that's how I found out about *Kultura*'s existence."[5]

Recently uncovered *Kultura* archives have turned up the first letter of the Russian writer Natalya Gorbanevskaya's to Jerzy Giedroyc, dating from 1974.[6] In this letter, Gorbanevskaya mentioned her plans to write several texts on Polish culture for Russian readers and also expressed the hope of seeing Giedroyc as soon as she received permission to emigrate. Gorbanevskaya described the first meeting with *Kultura*'s emissary: "I came out of prison in 1972, and a year or two later the first—and last—emissary from *Kultura* came to me, and he brought me the second Russian issue of *Kultura*. ... I already had this issue!"[7] Gorbanevskaya finally reached Paris, where her cooperation with *Kultura* and *Kontinent* started, when she got the chance to emigrate from the Soviet Union in 1975. She soon became the most important link between the editors-in-chief and their journals. Gorbanevskaya admitted her exceptionally close relationship to *Kultura*: "*Kultura* was almost like a home to me. ... Giedroyc was the most intelligent person I have met in the emigration and the second most intelligent I have met in my life—just after Akhmatova."[8]

The people most responsible for *Kultura*—Giedroyc, Czapski, and Herling-Grudziński—were members of *Kontinent*'s editorial board from the first issue. At first, the cooperation between the two journals was not as successful as expected. Six months after the publication of the first issue of *Kontinent*, Giedroyc wrote a letter to Maksimov stating that he was willing to withdraw from the editorial board, as they were simply nominal members without any real ability to influence the creation of the journal. His decision also had an ideological basis:

> We thought that in the first issues of the journal there should be a clear declaration admitting with no qualifying statements the right to self-determination for Ukraine and the right for the independence of the Baltic States. We also counted on a gesture towards Poland, an unambiguous declaration of *Kontinent*'s attitude towards the Ribbentrop-Molotov Pact, which revealed the full responsibility of Soviet Russia in Hitler's aggression towards Poland, an attitude towards sending one million and half Polish citizens to exile in Siberia in 1940, to the genocide in Katyń and to the actions taken by the Soviet army in 1944 in the face of the dying Warsaw Uprising. I assure you that such declarations could become a turning point in Polish-Russian relations.[9]

At the same time, Giedroyc expressed his willingness to help Maksimov in the difficult everyday editorial work, based on his experience creating and leading *Kultura*. Although Gorbanevskaya belittles the importance of this letter and puts it down to initial editorial difficulties, she confirms that she did not witness those difficulties herself as this took place before she started her cooperation with *Kontinent* and *Kultura*.[10] A letter from 25 March 1981 sent to Maksimov by Józef Czapski, Jerzy Giedroyc, and Gustaw Herling-Grudziński confirms her opinion. This was a response to a letter from Maksimov, who had asked if they were satisfied with the role they played on the editorial board of his journal. The response from *Kultura* counterparts was very reassuring. They expressed contentedness about their mutual relations. Furthermore, they understood that by remaining as members of the editorial board they not only had a chance to influence the content of the journal, but they also would be offering a declaration of their full support for Maksimov's initiative.

Kultura and *Kontinent*: The Cooperation

The three Russian issues of *Kultura* aimed to establish a dialogue between Poland and Russia (a dialogue that would include not only émigré circles, but also Russians who had never left Russia). The publication of the first Russian edition of *Kultura* in May 1960 was clear proof of the journal's broad focus. This issue reached readers in the Soviet Union, as did the second and third Russian issues of the journal published in 1971 and 1981, respectively. The main reason for starting this Polish-Russian dialogue by publishing Russian issues in a Polish émigré journal was the conviction that only full understanding could lead to a successful fight for freedom and that this understanding would be even more crucial once freedom was achieved. The dialogue had been initiated, but it was sporadic until 1974 in the absence of a reliable interlocutor on the Russian side that could maintain an uninterrupted conversation. In 1974, when Maksimov assumed editorship of *Kontinent*, the Russian émigré journal filled the role that had been missing in the dialogue and cooperation between *Kultura* and Russia. The fundamental idea behind *Kontinent* was similar to Giedroyc's ideas behind *Kultura*. Gorbanevskaya remembered receiving information about Maksimov's plans to establish a new émigré journal when she was still in Moscow: "And Maksimov told me: 'They asked me to publish a journal, but I do not want to publish yet another journal of the Russian emigration. I want it to be an organ of the East European emigrants.'"[11]

Although both *Kultura* and *Kontinent* were émigré journals that concentrated on widening the understanding between Central and Eastern European nations, they differed in many ways. The main difference was that *Kontinent* was more of a literary journal, whereas *Kultura* was more politically and socially orientated. The emphasis was also different in the respective journals, as described in the appeal for financial help *Kultura* published for *Kontinent* in 1989: "Fifteen years ago, a group of independent-thinking intellectuals from the West and the East, together with help from the well-known German publisher Axel Springer, created the literary-political-religious journal *Kontinent*."[12]

Gorbanevskaya was the most important link between *Kontinent* and *Kultura* thanks undoubtedly to her knowledge of Polish, interests in Poland, and understanding of Polish affairs, but also because of her remarkable journalistic and editorial abilities. The correspondence between Giedroyc and Gorbanevskaya from 1976 until the mid 1990s (according to the Literary Institute archives, their first letter is dated 15 March 1976, and the last one, 1997) describes the tightening cooperation between the two, a growing friendship, and the fact that soon after her arrival in Paris she was included in the circle of close friends at the Maisons-Laffitte house (according to a letter from 19 March 1976, with an invitation to Czapski's birthday party organized for close friends of *Kultura*). These letters were not only requests about everyday publishing activities, but they also demonstrated how both journals were important information centers for opposition activists in their home countries and abroad.[13]

Gorbanevskaya frequently worked as a Russian translator of Polish texts that were published in various Russian periodicals abroad or broadcast over the radio. In numerous letters, Giedroyc suggested texts to Gorbanevskaya that might potentially interest the Russian readers. She described her work as a liaison between journals: "My cooperation in the first place involved looking for texts that could be published in *Kontinent*, in Russian in the issues of *Kultura* and books that were published by *Kultura*; next I was translating texts suggested by Giedroyc. Aside from that I was often taking part in the meetings. I learned to speak Polish well in Paris."[14]

The first issue of *Kontinent* in 1974 featured a letter signed by the editorial board of *Kultura* that discussed some ideas expressed in Solzhenitsyn's *Letter to the Soviet Leaders*. The editorial board defended most, but not all, of Solzhenitsyn's ideas, adding an additional explanation to the argument presented in Solzhenitsyn's letter. The analysis of Solzhenitsyn's text was intended to have a certain impact on *Kontinent*'s readers. This was a way of presenting *Kultura* and the circle of people involved as open to discussions not only about Polish issues, but above all, about problems important in all Central and Eastern European nations. *Kultura* showed respect for the great Russian writer and thinker, but simultaneously proved its ability to engage in creative political discourse. The first issue of *Kontinent* also contained some information about *Kultura*, its achievements and its goals. It again underlined the idea of a common cause: "And finally the third feature of *'Kultura'* — a strong feeling that the fates of Poland, USSR and Eastern European nations are inseparable, the feeling of the brotherhood of all nations, struggling for freedom and independence."[15] Thus, *Kultura* presented itself to Russian readers as an ally that shared their views on many issues vital to both Russia and Poland.

In a time of important events in Poland, the editor-in-chief of *Kontinent* did not remain indifferent. On many occasions, *Kontinent* expressed its support for Poland and its democratic opposition. Maksimov marked turning points in Polish history in the pages of his journal. The year 1976 was a breakthrough for the Polish opposition and underground, and could not go unnoticed by émigré journals, including *Kontinent*. The tenth issue of *Kontinent* featured Jerzy Andrzejewski's letter to workers who started the protests and reprinted the first issue of *Biuletyn Infromacyjny KOR* (Information Bulletin KOR), an underground newspaper that published information about strikes, protests, and regulations and tried to help those who suffered repressions or arrests. The first issue of *Information Bulletin* was released in September 1976 and Gorbanevskaya introduced it in *Kontinent* as the first issue of a Polish equivalent of the Russian samizdat newspaper *Chronicle of Current Events*. Indeed, *Information Bulletin* (just like *Chronicle*) gave detailed accounts of the workers' protests and strikes, and of the intelligentsia's protests. The editor's final note described the content of the following two issues of *Information Bulletin*. They also published Jerzy Andrzejewski's correspondence addresses (in Warsaw), should any of the Russian readers like to provide help for those who suffered repressions as a consequence of strikes and supporting actions.[16]

The twenty-fourth issue of *Kontinent* published an even more significant document than their already-expressed support and previously confirmed willingness to help.[17] On the fortieth anniversary of the Katyń massacre, thirty-two Russian dissidents signed a proclamation admitting the Soviet state's responsibility for the murder of almost fifteen thousand prisoners of war (mostly Polish officers) in the spring of 1940.[18] This document can be seen as proof that the dialogue between Polish and Russian emigrants and opposition activists was not only well established and developed enough to address this painful subject, but it was also successful and open. Both sides struggled to act and react responsibly to current events as well as to carry on the discussion about their place in history. Although the aim of solving all or most of their historical problems and conflicts may seem utopian, it was a way to manifest goodwill and was the sine qua non for serious dialogue in the case of such complicated relations as those between neighboring states.

We should not forget the political situation in which this dialogue occurred. Most importantly, it involved leading activists and intellectuals of both nations outside and sometimes even against official channels. For many years, Poland and the USSR were indeed constantly declaring their never-ending friendship and ongoing brotherhood in the fight for the socialist future, but in reality they remained either indifferent or even hostile to one another, as prejudices and misunderstandings grew on both sides. For this reason, the dialogue Giedroyc initiated in the 1950s and which continued on the pages of *Kontinent* and *Kultura* cannot be overestimated. Both Polish and Russian émigré circles represented by *Kultura* and *Kontinent* had the courage to tackle even the most sensitive and painful memories and discuss historical and current issues openly. In an interview in 2004, Gorbanevskaya reaffirmed the importance of overcoming the existing preconceptions and prejudices that caused hostility between neighboring nationalities:

> Of course, we were all living in the same "labor-camp." But on the other hand, when I finished translating Orłoś's "Beautiful den" for *Kontinent* I was told by Tatiana Maksimovna Litvinova "Oh, Natashka I thought that it was much better in Poland." The rest of Poland, apart from two cities: Warsaw and Krakow, was almost just like Russia. But of course, when in 1981 there were strikes caused by the lowering of meat rations in Poland, at the same time in our country in the provinces there was no meat at all. ... It was very difficult to explain it to the Russian listener.[19]

Historical misconceptions about everyday life may belong to different categories and have differing degrees of importance, but they originate in the same basic miscommunication and mutual ignorance. Explaining economic differences in one country may be equally difficult in resolving historically motivated conflicts, because they are often accompanied by emotional distance. For that reason in 1981, the third Russian issue of *Kultura* was devoted to explaining current events in Poland and what motivated Poles striving for change.

Jerzy Giedroyc was personally interested in explaining and putting forward his ideas, as well as introducing Polish perceptions of Polish problems. A letter dated 24 April 1976 to Vladimir Maksimov is a good example of that policy. Giedroyc discussed Maksimov's idea of nationalism and separating the Russian nation from the Soviet political regime. Giedroyc tried to understand Maksimov's point and to some extent agreed with his conclusions, but he stressed his belief that the protests that took place in Moscow (as a reaction, for example, to the invasion of Czechoslovakia) involved only a limited group of intellectuals and did not represent the wider beliefs of society. At the same time, he admitted that these protests were heroic and deserved international recognition. Giedroyc also argued that the growth of nationalistic ideas was a response to the Soviet policy of Russification, finishing his letter reassuringly: "Please believe me that it is not easy for us to write about all the mistakes of Polish politics and patiently discuss sometimes painful grudges."[20] Understanding the difficulties of objectivity and sincerity when discussing one's own nation's history, Giedroyc was again able to cast himself as a considerate friend, not a stern judge or politician.

The ties between the two journals were not limited to contacts between Giedroyc, Maksimov, and Gorbanevskaya. There was cooperation on many levels, often unofficial and friendly. Therefore, ideas could circulate freely before they reached the pages of either *Kontinent* or *Kultura*. Undoubtedly, publishing policy was the domain of the powerful editors-in-chief, the most significant and influential of whom are mentioned above, but they were not the only ones. Most of all, both Giedroyc and Maksimov had an exceptional influence on anyone who had a chance to work, even briefly, in their milieu. Andrzej Mietkowski, a Polish translator and opposition activist who stayed in the West after 1981, had a chance to observe the *Kontinent-Kultura* cooperation in the early 1980s. He explained the differences between the two journals as follows:

> I was sent to the quarterly *Kontinent* by Jerzy Giedroyc when I started working for *Kultura*. I got in touch with its chief Vladimir Maksimov and also Ms. Irina Illovayskaya, the editor-in-chief of *Russkaya Mysl*. Gorbanevskaya was a natural consequence of the previous contacts, especially that she had been known for her interests in Poland. ... I was twenty-five back then so I wasn't a sophisticated analyst, but I must say, that I instantly felt that Giedroyc was right. This was a basis on which I built my outlook on life. Giedroyc was a member of the editorial board of *Kontinent,* he published Ukrainian texts in *Kultura,* respected Maksimov and they remained in a close contact, which meant for me that *Kontinent* was something like Russian *Kultura*. I saw it like that back then. Looking at it from this perspective I see that there are some qualifications needed in that statement. Jerzy Giedroyc was not only a great Editor, but also a statesman, with remarkable way of thinking about the state. Maksimov was undoubtedly a good writer, interesting and decent man, but constantly engaged in different, sometimes hard to understand, émigré tirades. Fortunately, in the editorial office there was also Natasha Gorbanevskaya.[21]

The exceptional position of Gorbanevskaya and her role as a link between Polish and Russian emigration can be illustrated by another little-known fact: Gorbanevskaya came up with the title of a Polish émigré journal, *Kontakt*, established by Mirosław Chojecki. Chojecki was a leader of the underground publishing house NOWA, but also stayed in exile in Paris after martial law was declared in 1981. Giedroyc put forward the idea of creating a new journal that would respond to the needs of the new, postmartial law émigrés (again demonstrating that this journal did not cater exclusively to Poles): "After all, the emigrants from the Soviet Union suffered the same oppressions. People who lived by Vistula river, by Veltava river, Lithuanians, Russians and Hungarians, they felt the oppression of the Soviet rule in the same way. We wanted to create a Polish editorial board, but in touch with other nation's journals."[22] Chojecki exchanged ideas with Gorbanevskaya and they reached an agreement:

> We agreed that the journal should have two main roles to play. To provide full information on the events in Poland to the Polish circles abroad and other people that remained in the West. And to inform fellow countryman in Poland about the events in the neighboring countries. This was the time when censorship filtered out details with any information about the Soviet Bloc countries so it was not possible to write anything about Czech or Russian opposition activists. We had an idea but we didn't have a title of a journal. ... So we sat there and discussed the idea of possible titles when suddenly Natasha suggested: why not call it *Kontakt*? We thought that the idea was brilliant, all the more so because this was an international word.[23]

By the 1980s, numerous émigré groups were pursuing Giedroyc's vision of cooperation between émigré circles for the common cause of mutual respect for each other's right to self-determination. Gorbanevskaya's friendship with Chojecki and her symbolic role in *Kontinent*'s history illustrate the improved understanding achieved between émigré circles. Giedroyc's *Kultura* played a crucial role in this process.

The "Polish Issue" of *Kontinent*

The key moment in the cooperation between the two journals came in 1977, with the publication of *Kontinent*'s twelfth issue, the so-called Polish issue. Throughout the beginning of 1977, Giedroyc, Gorbanevskaya, and Maksimov were in constant contact about preparations for the "Polish issue" of *Kontinent*.[24] Although it was called "Polish," it was published in Russian (the care that went into appropriately and accurately translating the texts was one of the issues that reappeared in later letters) and was not devoted only to Polish authors, but it featured many important texts previously published in Polish. A letter dated 24 April 1977 contained Giedroyc's suggestions about the texts that should be published in the next issue: a short story by Gustaw Herling-Grudziński, a reprint of the cover and editorial from a Polish underground journal, a fragment of a text by Juliusz Mieroszewski, an essay by M. Bronski, and a previously unpublished piece by Witold Gombrowicz titled "Sursum corda." The texts that ultimately appeared in the issue were different. There were published texts by Stanisław Barańczak, Kazimierz Orłoś, Józef Czapski, Jan Nowak and an interview with Adam Michnik, the leading Polish opposition activist, columnist, and historian. In a letter to Gorbanevskaya on 23 July 1977, Giedroyc expressed his satisfaction with the final result of their cooperation: "I have just received 12th issue of the *Kontinent,* which to be honest truly moved me a lot. Thank you very much for it and please send my gratitude and friendship to Maksimov."[25]

The twelfth issue featured not only the above-mentioned texts but also a reprint of a telegram sent by members of the editorial board to *Kultura* for the journal's thirtieth anniversary: "From the first day of its existence this journal has developed and has supported the glorious tradition of the spiritual connection and political solidarity with the best representatives of the Russian literature and social thought in our country as well as abroad. ... The existence of the journal *Kultura* is the most eloquent proof in the modern world that Poland and Polish culture did not perish and will never perish."[26] This issue also included Czapski's introduction to the journal's fundamental political and social ideas and an overview of its thirty years of activity.[27] *Kontinent* printed a letter signed by Vladimir Bukovsky, Gorbanevskaya, and Maksimov, in which the signatories expressed the belief that overcoming mutual harm was the only way to freedom. Furthermore, they supported the Polish opposition movement in this statement against the repressions of those who were members of KOR and workers on strike. The letter finished with the following statement: "We hope that the breath of freedom will become a normal atmosphere in Poland and in all of Eastern Europe and in our unhappy country."[28]

Conclusions

Undoubtedly, *Kultura* influenced Polish opposition activists in many ways. Frequent interactions between *Kultura* and those who visited the house in the Maisons-Laffitte enriched the exchange of ideas. For these reasons, *Kultura* (and Jerzy Giedroyc, especially) helped shape contemporary Polish political ideas and the mode of conducting political and social discourse. Furthermore, Giedroyc's idea of creating an environment for cooperation between all Eastern and Central European nations helped inspire Chojecki to establish *Kontakt*. Giedroyc's legacy was also a force when underground newspapers and journals in Poland discussed issues concerning the Soviet Union and Eastern Europe. Journalist and opposition activist Wojciech Maziarski described Giedroyc's and *Kultura*'s influence in the 1980s as follows:

I will say it that way—for me and my friends the ideas of Giedroyc was a real political ABC regarding our attitude towards our Eastern neighbors. I have never met Giedroyc personally, but I studied attentively his work and Mieroszewskis's texts. From those texts we have learned—by "we" I mean not only people involved in the journal [underground] "Obóz" or East European Information Agency, but the majority of the Polish opposition—the fundamental rule of supporting Ukrainian, Byelorussia, Lithuanian and Latvian and Estonian's aspiration to independence and to understand it as a Polish raison d'être. ... Yes, the ideas of *Kultura* were the rudiments of the geopolitics for me and all my milieu.[29]

Russian and Ukrainian problems were in the center of Giedroyc's political portfolio, and *Kultura* influenced the opposition program's treatment of Russian and Ukrainian issues. Indirectly, through the Maisons-Laffitte circle, Russian emigration and prominent Russian opposition activists also influenced the Polish opposition. The ideas first discussed on the pages of Polish and Russian émigré journals found their way to Polish underground publications through *Kultura* and those who remained in contact with Maisons-Laffitte. *Kultura* was the most influential Polish political journal for over fifty years. It can be said that, in an ideological and intellectual sense, many of the changes that began in 1989 were prepared by Giedroyc's activism.

Notes

1. Timothy Garton-Ash and Timothy Snyder, "The Orange Revolution," *The New York Review of Books,* 28 April 2005, http://www.nybooks.com/articles/archives/2005/apr/28/the-orange-revolution/?page=1 (accessed 20 August 2011).
2. Jozef Czapski, "Dwadzieścia pięć lat," *Kultura* 298–299, nos. 7–8 (1972): 7.
3. Jerzy Giedroyc, *Jerzy Giedroyc's Correspondence with Helena Zamoyska and August Zamoyski* (Paris: The Literary Institute Archives).
4. Czapski, "Dwadzieścia pięć lat," nos. 7–8 (1972): 7.
5. Gustaw Herling-Grudziński, "Z 'Archipelagu' na 'Kontynent,'" *Kultura* 325, no. 10 (1974): 84–88.
6. Jerzy Giedroyc, *Russian Correspondence* (Paris: The Literary Institute Archives).
7. Natalya Gorbanevskaya, "*Kultura* w Moskwie," 121.
8. Gorbanevskaya, interview with the author (Paris, 2004).
9. Giedroyc, *Correspondence with Helena Zamoyska and August Zamoyski.*
10. Gorbanevskaya, interview with the author (Paris, 2006).
11. Gorbanevskaya, interview with the author (Paris, 2004).
12. Jozef Brodskij, Milovan Dżilas et al., "Apel," *Kultura* (1989): 124.
13. Giedroyc, *Russian Correspondence.*

14. Gorbanevskaya, interview with the author (Paris, 2004).
15. *Kontinent* 1 (1974): 274.
16. *Kontinent* 10 (1976): 176–88.
17. *Kontinent* 24 (1980): 142.
18. The Russian Federation has never admitted the responsibility for the massacre in Katyń, but admitted the responsibility of the Stalinist government for it.
19. Gorbanevskaya, interview with the author (Paris, 2004).
20. Giedroyc, *Russian Correspondence*.
21. Andrzej Mietkowski, interview with the author (Warsaw, 2005).
22. Mirosław Chojecki, interview with the author (Warsaw, 2005).
23. Ibid.
24. There are six letters on that subject from Giedroyc to Gorbanevskaya preserved in the Archives of the Literary Institute. The first one is dated 7 March 1977 and the last one 23 July 1977. The letters contain rather skimpy information about the process of preparing an issue and are responses to telephone conversations; therefore, it is difficult to describe the editorial work in detail.
25. Giedroyc, *Russian Correspondence*.
26. *Kontinent* 12 (1977): 226.
27. Czapski, "Dwadzieścia pięć lat," nos. 7–8 (1972): 7.
28. *Kontinent* 12 (1977): 436.
29. Wojciech Maziarski, interview with the author (Warsaw, 2005).

Section II

DIFFUSING NONCONFORMIST IDEAS THROUGH SAMIZDAT/TAMIZDAT BEFORE 1989

Chapter 5

"FREE CONVERSATIONS IN AN OCCUPIED COUNTRY"
Cultural Transfer, Social Networking, and Political Dissent in Romanian Tamizdat

Cristina Petrescu

According to the logic of the Cold War, samizdat and tamizdat texts represented the main sources for the study of political dissent. One could even measure the intensity of criticism against the communist regime in a given country by measuring the quantity and quality of such publications. In Romania, the subject of this chapter, samizdat hardly existed (except for the work of some Hungarians living in Transylvania), while tamizdat (also fairly rare) consisted mostly of texts produced by diasporas and, to a much lesser degree, of writings from within the country. Such conditions immediately suggest that Romanian dissent must have been too weak to leave any durable traces. Indeed, it is common knowledge among students of the Eastern bloc that there were far fewer individuals who publicly criticized the regime in Romania, not to mention the ephemerality of any organized movements. This quasi-absence of critical political thinking in fixed, written form of either samizdat or tamizdat features prominently as an a posteriori argument to explain Romania's position among the six countries in which communism collapsed in 1989. After two decades of transition, is there something fresh to be learned from those few Romanian uncensored texts produced by the nonconformist individuals, once known as dissidents?

This chapter offers an answer to this question by combining macro- and microlevel analyses. The first section highlights the characteristics unique to Romanian communism (i.e., the political, social, and cultural conditions of the creation of uncensored texts in this country). Accordingly, it revisits

---

Notes for this chapter begin on page 127.

from a comparative perspective the main arguments emphasizing Romanian specificities, which have so far been formulated to explain what prevented the citizens of this country from expressing their discontent with a regime that, by the 1980s, was one of the least bearable in Europe. Then, it moves beyond this context to argue that all these conditions affected not only the extent of dissent and thus the very production of uncensored texts, but also the chances of diffusing these texts across borders. In short, one effect of Romanian communism was that nonconformist intellectuals and their texts were not only fewer than elsewhere in the Soviet bloc, but also less visible to those interested in evaluating underground activities behind the Iron Curtain. Thus, they have barely made their way into the canon.

The second part of this chapter focuses on the practices related to the transnational diffusion of nonconformist ideas and illustrates the shifting meanings of uncensored texts produced before 1989. Since cases of open dissent did exist in Romania, I raise the question of how dissidents overcame the challenges presented by the Romanian communist system and went public with their criticisms. Instead of making comparisons, this approach rather highlights entanglements. Furthermore, since macro perspectives seem to have exhausted their explanatory potential, I have adopted a smaller scale of analysis in order to deepen our knowledge on this subject. More precisely, this second part of this chapter is a microhistorical study focusing on a single nonconformist intellectual circle, which is unknown to non-Romanians, has been forgotten in the meantime by their compatriots, and has not been mentioned in histories of dissent. It was members of this group that under adverse conditions authored the book-length essay subtitled "Free Conversations in an Occupied Country" and managed to send it abroad to be published. In an atomized society, this circle functioned as a network that acted in solidarity to logistically support the open political dissent of a few members. Despite the very strict control exercised by Nicolae Ceaușescu's regime over influences from the "Free World," this group maintained clandestine communication channels that exposed them to Western culture and unofficial alternative cultures in other communist countries. In this way, this intellectual circle not only counteracted cultural isolation, but also succeeded in producing a coherent criticism of the communist regime. As such, the group played a significant role in a country too much at ease with an illegitimate regime before 1989. While most Romanians—although exasperated by the deep economic crisis—were unable to express even to themselves what was wrong with the regime, these few lone dissidents were distilling the essence of popular discontent, and implicitly preparing the "people from below" for the revolution that would come in 1989.

Therefore, this chapter draws attention not only to those critical texts made public before 1989, but also to the above-mentioned essay. This uncensored text could be published only after the collapse of communism, and therefore too late to contribute to this systemic change and too late to assure its authors an honorable place in the pantheon of dissidence in East-Central Europe. This text, however, was technically a form of tamizdat: the authors were known for their open critique of communism, the review that published it in the United States was dedicated to the promotion of Romanian alternative culture, to say nothing of the adverse conditions that needed to be overcome to transmit the essay across the borders. It is the joint effort to make such a text public that this author brings as an example of forbidden transnational activity. In a globalized world that takes for granted the free circulation of persons and ideas, such an example reminds one that nondemocratic regimes have always built real or imaginary walls. In response, freethinking individuals have found ways to surpass their isolation and create transnational communities of likeminded people even when more recent forms of media such as the Internet were not at their disposal.

The Context: Romanian Dissent in a Comparative Perspective

Treating Romania as the exception to the countries of the former Soviet bloc has become commonplace. Indeed, there is much to support this "exceptionalism thesis": (1) the weakness of the leftist intellectual traditions, the marginality of revisionism, and the nonexistence of a reformist wing in the party; (2) the strong nationalistic turn initiated in the 1960s and Romania's maverick, supposedly "independent," position in the communist camp and the Warsaw Treaty Organization, which made for many years Nicolae Ceaușescu, the Secretary General of the Romanian Communist Party (RCP) after 1965 and the president of the country after 1974, the greatest national "dissident"; (3) the extremeness of Ceaușescu's personality cult, which led to the gradual establishment of a regime of "dynastic socialism" in the 1980s; (4) the already-mentioned quasi nonexistence of critical voices during late communism, despite a noticeable decrease in the quality of life for almost everybody; (5) the bloodiness of the revolution that ended the communist regime in Romania; and (6) the massive support won in the first free elections by the second and the third echelons of the former RCP—at a time when alternative elites enjoyed electoral successes in other former communist countries. In short, major historical developments in postwar Romania made it so different that, at least since the late 1980s, authors writing about the Soviet bloc have always had to mention that Romania represented the exception to the general evolutionary trend. I do not challenge the conventional knowledge about Romania (as it is summarized above). However, instead of simply reiterating the tenets of the "exceptionalism thesis," I review them from a comparative perspective in order to go beyond an artificially isolated national framework.

Analyses by Western scholars have revealed a number of factors that partially explain Romanian society's incapacity to organize itself against the communist state. The most frequently cited reasons are: (1) political traditions specific to Orthodox countries,[1] which never encouraged the development of critical movements (the sort typical to countries where Western Christianity dominates); (2) officially promoted nationalism, through which the authorities not only legitimized the regime, but also monopolized the topic of anti-Sovietism;[2] and (3) an all-powerful repressive apparatus, which successfully prevented the emergence of an organized dissident movement.[3] Each of these reasons explains the weakness of dissent in Romania by making implicit or explicit comparisons to other states in the former Soviet bloc. In the following section, I explore these three factors across the entire communist period in order to elaborate why Romanian samizdat and tamizdat were quasi nonexistent. Here I combine in a comparative analysis my intimate knowledge of Romanian communism as a person who lived through this period with my expertise on Soviet-style regimes. I argue that the absence of uncensored texts in published form does not necessarily imply the absence of dissent. Such publications constituted only visible dissent, and, in order to understand their relationship to their invisible counterpart, one must take into account in what conditions the intellectual critics could produce and diffuse them.

Understanding the influence of Orthodox traditions of submissiveness requires exploring the *longue durée* of certain cultural practices that originated in the Middle Ages and were sustained over generations to shape the future political culture in Romania. Generally speaking, it is undeniable that political traditions in Romania differ not only from those of the West, where critical thinking and social disobedience have powerful historical roots, but also from the traditions of the Central European countries, where significant and active oppositions developed under communism. Synchronic regional comparisons suggest that dissent in Romania was only a small-scale phenomenon before the collapse of communism, consisting of isolated, unstructured groups. Thus, the opposition never emerged as a genuine threat to the regime, as happened in communist countries west of the cultural-religious fault line that divides the continent between Western and Eastern Christianity. What is more, post–Helsinki

Accords dissident activity in Romania presents a curious discrepancy between the behavior of the Orthodox majority and other groups. With the exception of a short-lived human rights movement in 1977, appeals to the Helsinki framework into the 1980s were made primarily by members of the Hungarian minority and members of religious denominations other than Greek Orthodox. In short, as seen from the West, one might indeed have concluded that only atypical citizens (people who were not ethnic Romanians of Greek Orthodox faith) were frustrated by the Ceaușescu regime's policies. In contrast, Romanians seemed to employ the Helsinki framework exclusively for a single purpose: assuring their right to emigrate. The preference for "exit" instead of "voice" dates back as far as the aborted 1977 human rights movement, which tried to mirror Charter 77 and succeeded in gathering roughly two hundred members during its brief activity.[4] Moreover, since the wide majority of the Romanians endured Ceaușescu's regime in silence, many analysts conclude that communism resonated with the paternalism of the Byzantine Orthodoxy after all.[5]

Contrary to this thesis, one can see that the opposition by Hungarians in Romania to assimilationist measures undertaken by Bucharest, while noticeable when measured against Romanian dissent of the late 1980s, was weak in comparison to the resistance offered by Hungarians living in the former Czechoslovakia. There, despite the regime having no better a reputation on the repression of dissidents, a Committee to Defend the Rights of the Hungarian Ethnic Minority functioned from the late 1970s until the fall of communism.[6] In Romania, though the treatment of the Hungarian minority was even worse than in Czechoslovakia, no such committee ever existed. Members of the Hungarian community in Transylvania spoke up publicly several times to protest discrimination against their ethnic group. Still, no organized Hungarian dissident movement emerged—with the exception of the tiny *Ellenpontok* group, which lasted just three years.[7] In short, the failure of even Romania's Hungarians to organize a protest movement draws into question explanations of Romanians' submissiveness exclusively based on religiously influenced political traditions.

Furthermore, while the Orthodoxy thesis might partially explain the weakness of dissent under Ceaușescu, the existence of a post-takeover phenomenon dubbed "resistance in the mountains" contradicts it.[8] In the early years of communism, some Romanians driven by the hope that the regime could be overthrown with the help of "the Americans" tried to live as outlaws, as Robin Hoods waiting in the forests and mountains for the return of their legitimate king, ready to fight in his name. This type of resistance was gradually repressed and abandoned after the 1956 Hungarian Revolution failed; Romanians, along with others in the Soviet bloc, understood then that communism was there to stay. Such developments occurred also elsewhere during the late 1940s and 1950s (such as in Poland or Ukraine), but they were hardly conducive to building an organized movement that would challenge the new regime. Yet, in the Romanian context, this limited expression of resistance amounted to a significant form of opposition, which was larger in participatory terms than any other developed in the post-Helsinki period. In light of the fact that Orthodox Romanians were not always obedient communist citizens, it is doubtful that premodern cultural influences on modern political behavior can alone explain society's silence under Ceaușescu. Far more useful would be the examination of those societal changes that took place under communism and diminished the potential of revolts in Romania. Such societal changes were closely linked to the other two factors that hampered the emergence of dissent: the secret police as instrument of social control, and the nationalistic policy instituted to win popular support.

It has been said of the secret police that the Romanian *Securitate* was the most efficient institution of its kind—except perhaps for *Stasi*—acting in the most brutal Stalinist style to destroy the real and imagined opponents to communism.[9] It is important to remember, however, that control methods in the 1970s and the 1980s differed fundamentally from those of earlier times. During Stalinism, the secret police in Romania, as in all Soviet-occupied countries, was the primary institution charged with applying terror randomly in order to reduce the potential of revolt. This goal was actually achieved in the early 1960s, with the destruction of the precommunist political, economic, and intellectual elite in the Romanian Gulag. The release of all political prisoners in 1964 illustrates that the regime was finally confident enough in its victory over the Romanian society. When suppression was no longer necessary to ensure stability, the use of random terror was gradually replaced with the tactic of prevention by widespread surveillance. This, of course, did not mean that no dissident was ever again jailed, but the extent of repression was far less significant than in the earlier period.[10] The secret police employed different methods ranging from the treatment of activism as an individual matter to expulsion. Softer forms of repression, such as detention in psychiatric hospitals, were still employed.[11] In many cases, however, troublesome individuals were singled out immediately, while their public criticisms were transformed into personal grievances and solved accordingly.[12] The state employed these methods with high efficiency at a time when the so-called new social contract[13] kept the regime in power by securing the compliance of large segments of the population through a skillfully orchestrated policy of co-optation.[14]

The societal transformations brought about by the dual policy of repression and co-optation only partially explain the scarcity of people willing to step up and express themselves publicly against the regime. Oral testimonies indicate that what counted more than the activity of the secret police itself was the general perception of its efficiency. It was images from the 1950s of the omnipotent and merciless *Securitate* that haunted many Romanians until the end of the regime and even afterwards.[15] This, of course, is not to downplay the crucial role the secret police apparatus did play in containing the emergence of dissident networks.[16] Indeed, authorities successfully prevented revolts in Romania as long as the standard of living was increasing. When endemic shortages ultimately threatened this co-optation strategy, the state brutally repressed workers' revolts, but it could not unrestrictedly persecute the freethinking intellectuals protected by international human rights organizations. Among the Romanian dissidents known in the West, none were actually suppressed. Scholars are still without a thorough institutional study of the former secret police, but the very increase in the number of dissidents in the late 1980s demonstrates the ultimate failure of the *Securitate* and calls into question the widely perceived perfection of the Romanian repressive machine.

Turning to the influence of the regime's nationalist turn, it is true that it effectively restrained many from expressing criticism. If communism was far from the best of all worlds, Romanian communists at least made the best of a bad situation, succeeding where neighbors failed to restore, at least partially, their independence from Moscow, so many in Romania believed. After the withdrawal of the Soviet troops in 1958, the state undertook other political steps over the next decade to assert its autonomy from the Soviet Union, while Romania reoriented itself once again to the West.[17] This apparently "liberal" policy also attracted many intellectuals, who seemed keen on defending national interests under the banner of the communist party.[18] This trend's peak came at the August 1968 moment, when Nicolae Ceaușescu, firebrand leader of an already "maverick" member of the Warsaw Treaty Organization, condemned the invasion of Czechoslovakia. In this action, Ceaușescu gained almost full support from the country's population, including even former political prisoners, despite the fact that his domestic policy bore little resemblance to the policies of the Prague Spring's leaders.[19] This tactic was extremely successful at the international level as well, as Romania was increasingly perceived by the West to be the strongest dissenter in the Soviet bloc.[20]

The support the national-communist regime enjoyed in the 1960s, however, vanished by the early 1980s. First in intellectual circles, Ceaușescu's nationalist policies became less popular when the state began exclusively promoting cultural productions inspired by autochthonous values in place of Western-influenced works. The result was cultural autarchy and the deprofessionalization of all disciplines.[21] Romanian culture's crisis accompanied an economic crisis unparalleled elsewhere in the Soviet bloc that affected the daily lives of every citizen. This problem also originated in the regime's nationalism, namely the absurd policy of reclaiming Romanian financial independence by paying all external debts. By the mid 1980s, nationalist dogmatism transformed Romania into one of the most Stalinist countries in Europe (surpassed perhaps only by Albania). After Mikhail Gorbachev came to power and began to reform the Soviet Union, nationalism lost nearly all appeal (remaining popular only among those with anti-Hungarian prejudices). In short, nationalism during the Ceaușescu regime did more to isolate Romania than anything, setting it apart from both the East and the West and failing entirely to defend supposed national interests.

As for its influence in limiting the potential of revolt, it is ironical to note that it contributed indeed to the discouragement of dissent even after the collapse in living standards robbed the regime and its nationalism of all legitimacy, but in a more perverse way. It is well known that the Helsinki Final Act of 1975, which brought the issue of human rights to the center of the East-West relations, provided dissident movements in the Soviet bloc with a legal, mutually accepted agreement that ensured certain protections in confrontations with communist authorities. The degree to which a bloc country honored the Helsinki Accords in any certain case was highly dependent on the degree to which Western officials were aware of the case. In Romania, these agreements had minimal influence. Elsewhere, Western support and supervision was vital to shielding pockets of dissidents who would otherwise have found themselves at the mercy of the state (as was the case during the Stalinist years). Ceaușescu, however, only signed the Helsinki Final Act in hope of raising another international obstacle against Soviet tanks (consistent with his policy of guarding the country's independence, his most precious asset).[22] Since no legal levers to force the observance of these agreements existed, he rejected most Western attempts to intervene in the name of human rights. When diplomats raised concerns about human rights violations, Ceaușescu perceived them as attempts to interfere in Romania's internal affairs. This reaction was in part fuelled by the fact that, until the late 1980s, most Western criticisms involved abuses against ethnic and religious minorities (not against the Romanian majority). In short, even after nationalism gradually lost its legitimacy, the communist leadership continued to be driven by nationalism and, careless on the issue of human rights, abused dissidents, although this damaged Romania's international reputation. [23]

All of the above explain the weakness of dissent in communist Romania and implicitly the quasi nonexistence of samizdat and tamizdat publications in this country as compared to others in the Soviet bloc. However, one should also consider this issue not only from a purely comparative perspective, but also from one that focuses on entanglements. Considering the East-West streams of influence, it is worth remembering that our current knowledge of dissidents and their uncensored texts relies heavily (if not entirely) on their access to the Western media in that period. Freethinking citizens needed a broadcasting agency or a publisher in order to make their ideas known to the public at home and abroad. It was this transnational connection that assured not only the diffusion of uncensored texts to a wide audience, but also their very survival. At a time when the preservation of such materials by dissidents themselves was a risky enterprise, while no local institutions archived such documents (except for the secret police), the visibility of uncensored texts and their protection against obscurity was possible via this transnational circuit.

In Romania, a number of factors (such as the regime's success in preventing contacts between intellectuals and Westerners, or its posture of occupying a "dissident" position within the Soviet military bloc) heavily diminished the transnational visibility of Romanian uncensored thinking. In other words, Romanian intellectuals had less opportunity to become known in the West than their counterparts in Poland, Czechoslovakia, and Hungary, who—though not always freer to travel—had more chances to deliver their messages to Western journalists, academics, and diplomats. While talented Western scholars like Timothy Garton Ash advocated the cause of the Central Europeans, Romanians were left mostly on their own behind the Iron Curtain.[24] While Lech Wałęsa could be interviewed directly over the phone from the West, Romanian authorities strictly barred foreign press correspondents, journalists, and diplomats from contacting dissidents. Thus, Romanian dissidents' visibility depended almost entirely on their own ability to find channels of communication with those abroad who would make them known and offer some kind of protection. Of these channels abroad, most significant were the collaborators of the Romanian desks of Radio Free Europe (RFE) in Munich and Paris, and to a lesser degree those working for Voice of America (VOA) and BBC. Many freethinking intellectuals, figures too public to be repressed, still never sent their open letters abroad, dooming their criticism against the regime to obscurity.[25] Also, from among those who dared to speak up, many disappeared in prisons or psychiatric hospitals without a trace before information about them could reach the West. In short, most of these men and women who did not manage to transmit their uncensored thoughts across the borders will remain unknown even to those who try to reconstruct the past.

Regarding the intra-bloc transnational influences on Romanian dissent, another issue deserves attention. As mentioned, oppositional activities in

Central European countries had always been catalysts for Romanians. In late communism, however, this stream of influence had a perverse effect on the outside visibility of Romanian dissidents. The local event that catalyzed them was a workers' strike in November 1987—arguably the first genuine anti-Ceaușescu revolt. Nevertheless, this revolt followed events in Poland after the foundation of Solidarity, reverberations in Hungary, Czechoslovakia, the GDR, and especially the "revolution from above" initiated by Mikhail Gorbachev—all crucial to the emergence of what can be described in comparison to earlier years as a genuine mobilization against the regime.[26] Because Romania had always lagged behind, it always had more difficulty in attracting journalists who preferred to report on the Soviet Union (important for the twists imposed from above), Poland (exceptional for the evolution from below), or even the former Czechoslovakia, Hungary, or the GDR (for more visible activism). In a strange historical paradox, while documentary filmmakers coming to Romania searched desperately for intellectuals able to explain the situation of the country (in order to use them between scenes with empty shops or demolished neighborhoods in Bucharest), Romanian intellectuals who sent their dissident texts to the West found it very difficult to interest local media.[27] Their subject matter, however essential in the Romanian context, was all too familiar to Westerners, as the Poles, Czechs, Hungarians, and Russians had already expressed similar thoughts.[28] In this context, late "Ceaușescuism"—bizarre for its megalomania, its cult of personality, xenophobic nationalism, and delirious programs of complete urban and rural reconstruction[29]—was far more attention grabbing in the West than the work of its few critics echoing the dissidents from other communist countries.

In 1989, the floodgates opened across East-Central Europe and crowds spilled onto the streets to settle long-unfinished business. In Romania, where there were only a handful of active dissidents, communism collapsed the same year, following a popular revolt, combined—it could be argued—with a coup d'état. This clearly illustrates that dissent played only a very limited role, if any, in the Revolution of 1989. Thus, today's historian reconstructing this phenomenon should refrain from employing any teleological schemes that reverse history by reading successful resistance into Romanian history just because the century ended with a revolution against communism. The events of 1953 in East Germany, 1956 in Poland and Hungary, 1968 in Poland and Czechoslovakia, or even the 1971 and 1976 strikes in Poland are well enough studied to require no detailing here. These events are often regarded to be the preparatory steps for the post-Helsinki protest movements (the Hungarian threefold opposition, the Charter 77, the Polish KOR, and Solidarity), which are in turn considered to be the prelude to the Revolutions of 1989.

The Romanian population also resisted communism, often expressing its discontent publicly, well before the Helsinki process. However, it is clearer that little continuity existed between opposition from the early days of communism and the opposition that developed after the mid 1970s in this country. Moreover, the majority of dissidents did not consider, at least until the end of the 1980s, that they were contributing to the downfall of the regime. Most of these men and women merely sought instead to put an end to the dichotomy that split their public and private lives. If in the cases of Poland, the GDR, Czechoslovakia, or Hungary, the existence of dissident groups and large opposition movements might be counted among the causes of 1989, the same approach should cautiously be adopted for Romania. Instead of adopting a teleological perspective by reading the dissident phenomenon only as a series of steps toward the collapse of communism, I concentrate on a single and lesser-known dissident group and highlight the cultural influences and the social networks—both national and transnational—that catalyzed its activity. The level of analysis is narrowed in order to determine how it succeeded in articulating a coherent critique of the communist system in a country that was culturally isolated, socially atomized, and politically frozen by the obsolete dogma of Stalinism. What is more, I draw attention to a tamizdat text that "missed the deadline" due to its twisted travel across the borders in the pre-Internet era. The publication of this uncensored text only after December 1989 deprived it of its political significance. Thus, one can move beyond interpreting this nonconformist text from the classical perspective of dissent and illustrate its post-1989 shift in meaning.

The Text(s): Romanian Dissent Comparable to Central-European Dissent?

This microhistorical study focuses on a circle of critical intellectuals from the Romanian provincial city of Iași, the capital of historical Moldova, and a university center (known as the "Romanian Heidelberg"). The group's origin was linked to the journal *Dialog*, a publication addressed primarily to students. Although the journal did not have a long history stretching back before communism, it did enjoy a certain local prestige due to fact that it was published under the auspices of the University of Iași, which was the oldest institution of higher education in Romania. In general, *Dialog* promoted breaking the discursive monopoly of the party-state by publishing as many texts as possible that were in dissonance with the chorus of communist officialdom, which could be found in all publications—even *Dialog*. From their time as humanities students, all members of the group contributed articles to this provincial university journal and some even joined its editorial board.[30] It was actually due to their contributions that *Dialog* turned increasingly into a nonconformist publication.

In order to circumvent the system of censorship, their messages needed subtle and indirect expression. While broader Bucharest journals were strictly supervised, this provincial publication more narrowly targeted educated readers able to decode *Dialog*'s fine-spun critical thoughts on the regime. For instance, an author disguised his criticism of communist ideology referring to the founding fathers—Marx and Engels—as Hegel's shaggy epigones. Though far from explicit, the journal's messages were uniquely daring in a country where nearly every publication spoke only praise for the regime. In such a context, harsh reviews of books by "court poets," composers of poems celebrating the party and the supreme leader, though completely justified by journalistic professionalism, constituted serious dissent from an otherwise regime-obedient public discourse. The article series highlighting historical monuments menaced by demolition suggested an implicit criticism of the so-called program of urban systematization, which implied the razing of entire historical neighborhoods. Most amusingly, the front-page reproductions of ridiculous paintings glorifying Romania's dictator (usually the work of inept sycophants) represented exaggerations that discerning readers grasped as mockeries of the cult of personality.[31]

Simply put, members of this group prodded the boundaries of encoded language, testing time and again the limits of public discourse. Their articles would not have been published without the tacit complicity of the officials ideologically responsible for censoring such a small publication with a "limited public."[32] Thanks to this network, *Dialog* was able to print articles with political allusions that would not have been permitted elsewhere.[33] In some cases, risky articles were purposefully allowed into the public sphere in order to function as a kind of safety valve to placate the more restless members of the population (individuals, of course, able to understand the encrypted language of *Dialog*). This arrangement sustaining the existence of inactive, but dissident-minded citizens endured as long as tongue-in-cheek critical journalism remained basically harmless to the regime. This cat-and-mouse game came to an end, nevertheless, as soon as one member of the group crossed the line of tolerated criticism. In May 1983, following the accidental interception of a private letter, in which the author mocked the regime's mania for discovering the Tracian roots of the Romanians,[34] most members of the group were arrested, repeatedly interrogated and pressured by the secret police to confess to plotting against the regime.

The letter was no different in substance or style from articles published in *Dialog*, but it bore witness to the existence of transnational activity.[35]

The harsh reaction to the discovery of this international correspondence illustrated vividly where the freedom of speech ended. Expressions acceptable in a local journal with a limited audience were not acceptable at more visible levels, in Western broadcasting channels with far broader distribution, inside as well as outside Romania. With this crackdown, the collective novel authored by four members of the group, ready to circulate in samizdat, along with all the books in foreign languages that were found in individuals' residences (including, for example, even benign novels by Charles Dickens) were confiscated by the secret police.[36] None of those arrested was ever imprisoned. However, the direct consequence of this episode was the increase of state interference in publication policies, stifling a whole generation of writers to make their literary debut. In contrast, the regime had more toleration for their colleagues of generation, who only distanced themselves aesthetically, rather than politically, from official dogma in the field of culture. Practically banned from publication, the members of this group remained unknown to the Romanian public. Unable to overcome the difficulty of circulating samizdat in a country where every typewriter was annually registered at the police station,[37] they were effectively silenced.

Though the *Dialog* group disbanded after the arrests, their experiment, which challenged censorship with encoded language and provoked interrogations by the secret police, would in the end foster the cohesion among its members. This solidarity would rear its head later on, when some of them eventually decided to speak out against the regime. The expulsion from the communist-controlled public sphere, though, did not radicalize immediately the former *Dialog* group members into seeking out alternative modes of expression or entering into open dissent. After the short-lived experience of testing the limits of official toleration on taboo subjects, these journalists retreated into strictly professional pursuits in literary criticism, maintaining their work at international standards. This was the path traveled by Romania's writers, who neither willingly praised the regime nor dared to criticize it publicly, but attempted instead to "resist through culture," as they put it after 1989.[38] The increasingly nationalist Romanian communist regime regarded even this pursuit as a serious affront to Ceaușescu's 1971 cultural revolution, which had imposed complete autarky in the literary and artistic domains for the sake of creating a Romanian culture free of foreign influences. Nevertheless, "resistance through culture" as a deviation from the officially imposed cultural policy was tolerated.

Only years later did some members of this group decide to abandon this apolitical path. The routinization of silent resistance and the continued rareness of public criticism against the regime raise the question:

what pushed someone to become an open dissident in Romania? In other words, under what conditions did one decide to publicly express his or her criticism of the regime in a country where no dissident movement existed? The individual cases discussed below illustrate that this choice was triggered not only by individuals' private ruminations, but also by favorable circumstances, in particular by the very existence of a transnational connection. Of the members of *Dialog,* it was Dan Petrescu (born in 1949), the author of the above-mentioned letter, who first decided to become an open dissident.[39] This step was taken following two subsequent coincidences. The first experience involved a personal opportunity to build contacts in the "Free World." During a visit to Paris (his first visit ever to the other side of the Iron Curtain), members of the diaspora asked Petrescu to become a contact person for Western journalists in search of learning more about Ceaușescu's Romania than one could gain from official sources. The second, more widely known, event in Petrescu's story was a major strike in Brașov (Romania's second largest city), which caught the West's attention. The strike revealed the country's unbearable situation to an outside world that knew very little about life in Romania in the absence of a dissident movement able to offer alternative news. In effect, the Brașov strike in November 1987 reoriented the agenda of Western journalists, who had been covering Ceaușescu's aberrant policies, and refocused their attention on these policies' reverberations in Romanian society.[40] In short, Petrescu offered up to the Western media his own critical views on the regime exactly when his country for the first time started attracting real attention on the other side of the Iron Curtain. Without the strike, Romania would not likely have jumped to the front page. Without his visit to Paris, no journalist would have known to look for Petrescu, and he might have never realized the chance to break free from isolation in Iași.

When he "became a dissident," after granting his first interview to Gilles Schiller, journalist for the French newspaper *Libération,* Petrescu himself did not fully realize the importance of the moment.[41] The transcript of this interview was published under the title "Ceaușescu is not the only blameworthy person" on 27 January 1988, one day after the gaudy national celebration of his birthday.[42] Petrescu said nothing entirely original, but rather adapted to Romanian context ideas of Central European dissidents.[43] Such approach was not new; as mentioned, Romania's perpetually weak civil society forced its intellectuals to rely on the appropriation of Central European ideas and ideals (as was the case in 1956 and 1977), while Western broadcasting agencies played a tremendously vital role in this cultural and political transfer. More so than other Romanian dissidents, Petrescu's topics of discussion—the ubiquity of guilt, the imperative for moral regeneration, the necessity to create an alliance between workers and intellectuals—resembled the writings of established dissidents in Poland, Czechoslovakia, and Hungary. His most important idea is perhaps captured by the interview's title: the Secretary General of the party was not the only person responsible for Romania's disastrous situation. This view completely contradicted the belief held by most Romanians, including the workers of Brașov, that all problems would be solved only if Ceaușescu disappeared. No real change could occur, Petrescu argued, until the system that made a leader like Ceaușescu possible was destroyed. In short, previous criticism against the regime was self-limiting; it envisaged only reforms within communism, similar to *perestroika* and *glasnost'* in the Soviet Union.[44] This was the first time that a Romanian dissident endorsed the need to overthrow communism as a whole.

One dissident gesture always followed another. During the last two years of communism, Petrescu established himself as one of the most lucid and radical dissidents, in addition to being among the most prolific. His activity as dissident, unfortunately, cannot be fully evaluated today because much of his work was not preserved. As samizdat did not circulate in Romania, the public's only access to free information came via Western broadcasting agencies. For this reason, most of Petrescu's writings were sent to the Romanian desks of RFE and VOA, while only a few reached Western newspapers and magazines. Of those never published, some were lost forever with the destruction of the VOA archives and the transfer of the RFE documents from Munich to Prague and then to Budapest. In the surviving texts, few recurrent ideas are worth mentioning. In an essay entitled "Little study about the anatomy of evil," Petrescu expanded on ideas first expressed in an interview that was smuggled out of the country by the French lecturer living in Iași.[45] In the essay, he reiterated that the "main source of evil" was the communist system itself—not just the people who embodied it. Unlike those who believed that the regime (in spite of obvious unpopularity) survived thanks only to the *Securitate*'s successful suppression of any civil initiative, Petrescu argued that the party-state's existence was assured by the implicit collaboration of a silently obedient population. In other words, echoing Václav Havel, it came down to the complicity of the greengrocer, who unquestioningly accepted the "social contract" offered by the communist system.[46]

Warning the public about the ubiquity of guilt, Petrescu challenged conventional wisdom about the omnipresence and invincibility of the Romanian secret police. As already mentioned, Romanians have believed that communist citizens fell into two mutually exclusive categories: (1) employees and collaborators of the *Securitate,* and (2) innocent victims of the former. Being impossible to know the category one's neighbors occupied, 22 million people let themselves be controlled by the fear of a mythically powerful secret police. Moreover, the delay in the post-1989 legal process of disclosing informants and collaborators combined with the scarcity of in-depth studies on the *Securitate* heavily contributed to the perpetuation of the popular perception that the secret police still controls everything in post-1989 Romania.[47] Petrescu's idea about the functioning of the secret police challenged this commonly accepted view, and continues to upset people even today. His most original act of dissent remains a letter symbolically addressed to the *Securitate*. This text is an interesting testimony on the methods used by the secret police to intimidate those around Petrescu in an attempt to block the emergence of any coherent dissident movement. In the letter, he memorably observed that, in a country where nothing worked properly, there could never be a single institution that worked perfectly—not even the secret police.[48] One might even say that his own life as a dissident illustrated this thesis on the *Securitate*, as I will discuss below.

By the fall of communism, Petrescu had become the most prominent dissident in Romania, second only to the Cluj-based Doina Cornea, known for her appearance in the film "The Red Disaster," broadcast in late 1988 on televisions across Europe.[49] Of the texts that survived, it is worth examining a paper addressed to the international conference "Ein Traum von Europa," held in West Berlin in May 1988. Although Romanian authorities did not allow Petrescu to attend the event, the very invitation marked his symbolic entrance into the greater family of East-Central European dissidents. His perspective represented the worldview from what was then the most isolated country in Europe on what at that time seemed to be the hypothetical reunification of the continent. As with many others before him, Petrescu urged critics of communist regimes on both sides of the Iron Curtain to cooperate in the hope of accomplishing it against all odds.[50] From today's perspective, this message appears banal, but when regarded in context, it illustrates the widespread dissident conviction that only transnational solidarity would put an end to the nondemocratic experiments in the Soviet bloc.

Returning to the question of how was Dan Petrescu's dissent possible, one must also ask how such people physically survived in communist Romania? The moment Petrescu spoke out publicly against the regime, secret police began to monitor his every move. Some agents watched day and night over his house, while others were responsible for following him or his wife in case they went out. Microphones were installed inside his walls, accessed from the neighboring apartment, his phone line was cut, and his friends were warned to stay away. In short, a great deal was done to isolate him from all possible contacts with the outside world.[51] Petrescu was not imprisoned after openly criticizing the regime, however, in large part thanks to the Western media intensely publicizing his case. History proved that the only means of surviving as a dissident in Romania, where antiregime networks did not exist, was to maintain (at any cost) transnational contacts. Above all, support received from conationals abroad was instrumental to establishing visibility in the West, as well as the physical safety of dissidents at home. News about Petrescu and his encounters with the secret police were continuously broadcast by RFE thanks to the involvement of Paris-based Romanian expats, in particular Mihnea Berindei and the League for the Defense of Human Rights in Romania.[52] The Romanian community in the United States (especially Petrescu's brother-in-law, Ioan Petru Culianu, who was known as Mircea Eliade's closest academic collaborator, and former dissident Dorin Tudoran) also offered its support to Petrescu, mainly through VOA.

At the same time, Petrescu's dissidence would not have been possible without the support of local intellectuals, particularly those from the community of former *Dialog* contributors. Its members, though they avoided open dissidence, did nevertheless contribute to Petrescu's success. Most importantly, these men helped Petrescu send his work abroad—a nearly impossible task after the police set up 24-hour surveillance of his home. This network of friends maintained foreign contacts and assumed all the risks of engaging in a forbidden transnational activity. They risked their own safety less so than Petrescu did by speaking out against the regime, but their role as the "hidden part of the iceberg," whose task was to support the "tip," was instrumental. In other words, the open dissent of one person, the only thing that was visible in the West, was possible only because others, who remained unknown to the public at the time, acted in solidarity. As Petrescu put it, they were also prepared to replace him in the event that he was arrested and dragged to one of the basements of the secret police. However, only a handful of intellectuals from this circle actually followed in the footsteps of Dan Petrescu. The second Iași-based dissident was Liviu Cangeopol (born in 1956), who sent to *Libération* a piece in the form of an interview intriguingly entitled "Be Satisfied Mister Ceaușescu: You Will Make History!" Cangeopol observed ironically that the current era would remain a reference point in Romanian history—not for any glorious accomplishments, as the Secretary General believed, but because communism had transformed Romanians into a self-loathing people incapable of political opposition. Like Petrescu, Cangeopol also argued that it was not just the leadership, but also the population that silently accepted the hardships of the regime, that was responsible for Romania's situation in the late 1980s.[53]

These two Iași-based intellectuals, Dan Petrescu and Liviu Cangeopol, were among the very few Romanians who dared to publish tamizdat, despite being heavily watched by the secret police.[54] It was the magazine *Agora*—the first ever Western-produced Romanian publication dedicated exclusively to alternative culture—that published their full, book-length dialogue. Their enterprise also marked the first ever collaboration between two critical intellectuals on a common project, a vital step in ending the isolation that crippled Romanian dissent.[55] Moreover, this uncensored essay represented a singularly dissident text of such proportions ever produced in communist Romania, approaching other forms of Central European dissent in content. The exchange of ideas between Petrescu and Cangeopol was typewritten in the summer of 1988 at the former's residence. Addressing issues ranging from the poverty of daily life to the absurdity of party policies, the two authors captured the essence of everyday life in Romania in the last years under communism, and produced a sociological-political analysis of the country's situation based on first-hand information. More importantly, their book advocated openly and clearly changing the very foundation of society, not merely reforming the regime. Thus, in the history of anticommunist dissent in Romania, these dissidents' common work remains the most radical criticism of the system.

Beyond its political meaning, this uncensored text illustrates the perils of any transnational enterprise directed against a regime that aimed to isolate Romanian society from the rest of the world. At the time of its writing, both authors were under strict surveillance by *Securitate* agents, who had also installed electronic listening devices in the walls of Petrescu's house, as mentioned above. In the face of such challenges, Petrescu and Cangeopol scripted their dialogue on a typewriter alternatively and in complete silence. In other words, the dialogue that this uncensored text reflects never took actually place except on paper. The draft was transferred at another location to audiocassettes, at which point the tape was packaged and finally sent abroad via an Italian lecturer based in Iași, who was ultimately expelled from Romania for her encounters with Dan Petrescu and the rest of the group. Illustrating the seriousness of obstacles in any transnational activity, the tapes were hidden in jars of beauty cream in order to pass successfully through border control. The Italian lecturer then sent the tapes to the Romanian desk of RFE in Paris, where they were then sent to another member of this group, who had in the meantime succeeded in emigrating to Belgium. Transcribed to paper in Brussels, this text could finally find its way to a publisher in the United States.[56] These considerable efforts to export material to the West and the subsequent difficulties in transcription delayed the publication of this dissident text until after the fall of communism.[57] Consequently, it lost most of its prospective audience to the avalanche of events that unfolded in a now postcommunist Romania, and it never received the reception it deserved.

Nevertheless, with the success alone of writing and sending their manuscript abroad, Petrescu and Cangeopol proved the fallibility of the *Securitate*, demonstrating the police's true inability to repress every act of resistance.[58] They showed the world that, even in Romania, it was possible to fool the most ubiquitous and secretive state institution, if clever and adventurous enough. Judging by secret police records, it is clear that the *Securitate* suspected that Petrescu was up to something. Thanks to the decision to meet and work in total silence, however, Petrescu and Cangeopol finished their manuscript before authorities learned for certain what they were doing.[59] The telephone interview between Petrescu and RFE—the first and only such interview with a Romanian dissident from within the country—represented another reminder that the *Securitate* was not invincible. In Petrescu's own words, the very fact that this telephone conversation could take place in the face of the around-the-clock police surveillance illustrated that, in a country where nothing worked properly, there could never be a single institution that worked perfectly.[60] During this famous interview on 8 October 1989, Petrescu announced a petition that he and ten others supported.[61] This petition, which did not exist materially, opposed Ceaușescu's reelection at the Fourteenth Congress of the RCP in November 1989. This was the first protest that united the two emerging dissident nuclei: the cities of Iași (around Petrescu himself) and Cluj (around Doina Cornea).[62] As Petrescu later admitted, the petition made him think for the first time ever that communism could really be brought down even in Romania.[63] However, the popular revolt of December 1989 occurred before the few Romanian dissidents could organize their own solidarity. Thus, the only organized postcommunist political force to emerge in Romania sprung from the communist party itself,[64] while former dissidents disappeared quickly from politics, before having a real chance to play a significant role.[65]

Conclusions

What remains then to be learned from the rather unique example of a failed tamizdat text produced in a communist country that was in itself atypical enough to make one cautious when generalizing about any Romanian's experiences of the past? Two intellectuals—already known as dissidents after granting interviews to Western journalists—authored this text in extremely unfavorable conditions. The text appeared in uncensored form in a magazine published by the Romanian diaspora in the United

States, after a long and risky travel across many borders. However, its publication occurred only in February 1990, when it could have been published in Romania too. In form of tamizdat, this uncensored text missed its audience. The two authors received neither international recognition nor national fame for their pioneering attempt to diffuse their uncensored thoughts after skillfully surpassing obstacles that others never dared to challenge. Thus, their tamizdat was never canonized as such.

The content of the book remains valuable to this day for students of communism due to its witty insight into Romanians' experiences of muddling through shortages and other adversities of daily life. Besides the authors' perceptive observations, the local oral testimonies used as sources enhance the interest in this essay, unique for the ability of the two insiders to capture the spirit of the time. What is more, the thoughts of these two freethinkers illustrate that Western influences and Central European alternative cultures penetrated even the Romanian borders, despite Ceaușescu's goal of totally isolating his country from any external contacts. Due mostly to Western broadcasting agencies, the transnational flow of ideas reached even the autarchic Romania. This uncensored text epitomizes the uneven stream of influence between the outside world and this country, which flowed always eastward, but rarely in the reverse direction. Romanian nonconformist intellectuals mostly adapted ideas produced westward to the local context, and thus their relevance remains nationally bounded.

Yet, this uncensored text has a meaning beyond its historical content. Petrescu's story illustrates how networks of internal and transnational solidarity made the transmission of texts possible even in the extremely oppressive conditions of communist Romania. It was the delayed publication that obscured the meaning of the adventurous story of its westward travel. Moreover, from today's perspective, when the Internet is able to penetrate even the borders of nondemocratic countries, the problems encountered in the transmission of this essay to its publisher seem indeed ridiculous. Nevertheless, what made this text tamizdat instead of a book "for the drawer" was exactly the transnational dimension contained in the very story of the ludicrous travel to the publisher. Nondemocratic countries are closed societies that isolate their citizens not only from the perils of exposure to democratic ideas, but also from the temptation to share their thoughts freely. Thus, any transnational activity represents an act of nonconformism. The twisted westward travel of this uncensored text highlights not only the impossibility of the communist dream of achieving total control over society, but also the practices associated with forbidden transnational activities. Ultimately, this tamizdat text and its story recuperate the unique experience of two nonconformist intellectuals that lived in communist Romania as if borders did not exist.

Notes

1. See George Schöpflin, *Politics in Eastern Europe, 1945–1992* (Oxford, 1993), 1–36.
2. The interplay between the communist regime and Romanian intellectuals in resurrecting the inter-war nationalist discourse has been analyzed in the already classic book of Katherine Verdery, *National Ideology under Socialism: Identity and Cultural Politics in Ceausescu's Romania* (Berkeley, 1991).
3. Dennis Deletant has analyzed the role of the secret police in his book, *Ceauşescu and the Securitate: Coercion and Dissent in Romania, 1965–1989* (London, 1995). His thesis is that, after succeeding Gheorghe Gheorghiu-Dej, Ceauşescu changed the focus of the secret police from repression to prevention. Romanian authors—who had been not spectators but actors—tried rather to justify than to explain the weakness of dissent in their country. Thus, they tended to always emphasize the alleged omnipotence of the *Securitate*. In fact, the thesis of the all-powerful *Securitate* was so often invoked by Romanian intellectuals after the fall of the regime as an excuse for their compliance that it has become cliché. See, for example, Marius Oprea, ed., *Banalitatea răului: O istorie a Securităţii în documente, 1949–1989* [The Banality of Evil: A History of the *Securitate* in Documents] (Iaşi, 2002). The editor of this volume comprising documents related to the Romanian secret police argues that this institution was one of the most—if not the most—repressive apparatus in the Soviet bloc.
4. One record of the *Securitate* confirms the figure of around 200 signatories from the records of the Radio Free Europe, but also mentions that most of the people who joined writer Paul Goma were only interested in obtaining an emigration passport. From the 430 persons that tried to contact Goma either by phone or directly, the bulk had their applications for emigration rejected or pending. Others, claims the note, had various other personal grievances, mainly related to their jobs, while the rest were people with mental diseases. Also, the *Securitate* discouraged many potential signatories by threatening them or by limiting their access to Goma and his family. Consequently—as *Securitate* records indicate—only 240 people contacted Goma. The final tally reads: "From the above mentioned total, for 184 persons the emigration application was approved; 170 retracted and many of them spoke against Goma's activity; and 76 still have some requests [at the date when the note was issued, that is 12 May 1978], especially related to emigration." See *Cartea Albă a Securităţii: Istorii literare şi artistice, 1969–1989* [The White Book of the *Securitate*: Literary and Artistic Stories, 1969–1989] (Bucharest, 1996), 130. Yet, it should be noted that not all those who requested to emigrate were allowed to. There are also testimonies about cases of people beaten until the request was retracted. See the letter of a German woman from the commune of Giarmata, near Timişoara, in OSA/RFE Archives, Romanian Fond, 300/60/5/Box 6, File Dissidents: Paul Goma.
5. See, in this respect, Andrew Janos's synthesis *East-Central Europe in the Modern World: The Politics of the Borderlands from Pre- to Postcommunism* (Stanford, 2000), 324–25.
6. The trail of Miklós Duray, a leading activist in this committee, was very much advertised in the West by the Czech and Slovak dissidents (especially through VONS), as well as by Hungarian dissidents, mostly by the *Beszélö* group.
7. For more on this, see my study "Who Was the First in Transylvania: On the Origins of the Romanian-Hungarian Controversy over Minority Rights," *Studia Politica* 3, no. 4 (2003): 1119–48.
8. This phenomenon manifested through the activity of several armed groups that withdrew in various mountain areas, escaping for a while from the control of the totalitarian regime. Numerous volumes of documents related to such groups were published after 1989; among them it is worth mentioning that related to the well-organized group

from the Făgăraş Mountains, one of the last to be destroyed by the *Securitate* troups. See *Luptătorii din munţi. Toma Arnăuţoiu. Grupul de la Nucşoara: Documente ale anchetei, procesului, detenţiei* [Fighters from the Mountains. Toma Arnăuţoiu. The Group from Nucşoara: Documents Related to their Interrogation, Trial, and Imprisonment] (Bucharest, 1997). Also, information on such groups is available from the memoirs of the survivors, among whom was Ion Gavrilă-Ogoranu, *Brazii se frîng, dar nu se îndoiesc: Rezistenţa anticomunistă în Munţii Făgăraşului* [Fir Trees Break but Do Not Bend Themselves: Anticommunist Resistance in the Făgăraş Mountains], 6 vols. (Timişoara, 1993–2006). I mention this author as indicative of post-communist Romania, where the dominant public discourse is fiercely anti-communist. While communism is overwhelmingly condemned, nothing is really said about Romanian fascism, which has been implicitly rehabilitated only because it was also an anti-communist movement. In this context, this author is considered a symbol of anti-communist resistance, in spite of the right-wing origins of his convictions, which are disregarded as absolutely insignificant in comparison with the merits of armed resistance in the mountains. Finally, there are oral history testimonies of this phenomenon. The tragic story of Elisabeta Rizea—a woman who was arrested and imprisoned for many years because she had helped the "bandits" in the mountains—represents the most notable example. As a result of brutal treatments during interrogations, she remained handicapped for the rest of her life, but refused to betray anyone. After 1989, Rizea rightly emerged as a heroine of anti-communist resistance, whose moral strength endured the *Securitate*. See Irina Nicolau and Theodor Niţu, eds., *Povestea Elisabetei Rizea din Nucşoara: Mărturia lui Cornel Drăgoi* [The Story of Elisabeta Rizea from Nucşoara: Cornel Drăgoi's Testimony] (Bucharest, 1991).

9. Although figures alone cannot constitute the sole basis for comparing the activity of the two secret police services, the current data could offer a first indication on differences. For instance, the number of the Stasi *inoffizielle Mitarbeiter* in 1989, according to *Die Bundesbeauftragte für die Stasi Unterlagen*, was 174,000 individuals for a population of almost 17 million East Germans. See Klaus Schroeder, *Der SED-Staat: Partei, Staat und Gesellschaft, 1949–1990* (Munich, 2000), 442. This figure is three times smaller than the estimates of the huge network of informers used by the *Securitate*, according to *Consiliul Naţional pentru Studierea Arhivelor Securităţii* [The National Council for the Study of the Securitate Files]. By 1989, the informative network of the Romanian secret police comprised 486,000 individuals who spied on a population of approximately 23 million. See *Arhivele Securităţii* [The Archives of the Securitate], vol. 1 (Bucharest, 2002), 35. According to this calculation, in Romania there was an informer for forty-seven individuals, while in former East Germany one for ninety-seven.

10. In this respect, a typical example is the former dissident Radu Filipescu, a young engineer that was convicted in 1983 and sentenced to ten years in prison for spreading anti-communist manifestos. He was released after three years only because of the huge publicity his case received in the Western media, following intervention by Amnesty International. Filipescu's story is narrated in Herma Köpernik Kennel, *Jogging cu Securitatea: Rezistenţa tînărului Radu Filipescu* [Jogging with the *Securitate*: Young Radu Filipescu's Resistance] (Bucharest, 1998).

11. The political use of psychiatry in order to isolate persons that manifested against the regime is very poorly documented, but it seems to be a common measure taken in the case of individuals unknown abroad, who could have been easily silenced in this way. See the testimony given by Ion Vianu, "La répression psychiatrique: Nous avons les moyens de vous guérir …", and Vasile Paraschiv, "Trois internement psychiatrique: Le témoignage de Vasile Paraschiv," *Roumanie: Crise et répression, 1977–1982. Un dossier de L'Alternative* (Paris), special issue (January 1983): 35–40. See also Oana Ionel and

Dragoș Marcu, eds., *Vasile Paraschiv: Lupta mea pentru sindicate libere în România* [Vasile Paraschiv: My Struggle for Free Trade Unions in Romania] (Iași, 2005).
12. In the letters sent by the late dissident Mihai Botez to the late director of the Romanian desk of RFE Vlad Georgescu, the author bore witness to the fact that during the repeated interrogations by the secret police the officers in charge continuously tried to convince him to give up his open criticism promising to solve any personal problem he had. See Mihai Botez, *Scrisori către Vlad Georgescu* [Letters to Vlad Georgescu] (Bucharest, 2003), 126–40.
13. I use this concept in the sense of Antonin J. Liehm, in his "The New Social Contract and the Parallel Polity," in *Dissent in Eastern Europe*, ed. Jane Leftwich Curry (New York, 1983).
14. Obviously, the policy of co-optation implied a high degree of flexibility since it worked differently, maybe not for each individual, but certainly for each social group. For the trade-off between the communist regime and intellectuals, the social category that makes the subject of this study, see Ileana Vrancea's study broadcast by RFE, "Capcana" [The Trap], OSA/RFE Archives, Romanian Fond, 300/60/6/Box 24, File Intellectual critics: The dissent problem. A more comprehensive analysis on the causes that hampered the Romanian intellectuals to openly criticize the communist regime was authored by dissident Dorin Tudoran, and first published in 1984 in shortened French version in *L'Alternative* (Paris). See the complete version of the essay "Fear or Cold? On the Condition of the Romanian Intellectual Today," in Dorin Tudoran, *Kakistocrația* [Kakistocracy] (Chishinev, 1998), 31–76.
15. Moreover, the case of the engineer Gheorghe Ursu—who was imprisoned in 1985, after his secret diary with critical remarks about the communist regime was disclosed, and savagely beaten to death in prison—deepened the conviction that all those who dared to express any such views would end in the same way. However, this was just an extreme case, and none of the real dissidents of the 1970s and the 1980s—Ursu was, in fact, not an open critic of the regime—died. For the report about Ursu's death, see *Cartea Albă a Securității*, 503.
16. Directions received by this institution regarding the actions to be taken against dissidents can be found in Florica Dobre et al, eds., *Securitatea. Structuri, cadre, obiective și metode: Documente inedite din arhivele secrete ale comunismului* [The Securitate. Structures, Cadres, Objectives, and Methods: Unedited Documents from the Secret Archives of Communism], 2 vols. (Bucharest, 2006).
17. It is interesting to read this period analysis of Romania's turn, which predicted in the mid 1960s, that the country was facing either Albanization or Yugoslavization. See H. Gordon Skilling, *Communism National and International: Eastern Europe after Stalin* (Toronto, 1964), 150–61.
18. The popularity of the regime due to the nationalist policy as well as the role of this factor in inhibiting intellectual dissent was analyzed in Michael Shafir, *Romania. Politics, Economics and Society: Political Stagnation and Simulated Change* (London, 1985).
19. Among those who joined the communist party after Ceaușescu's electrifying "balcony speech" on 21 August 1968 was also the writer Paul Goma, the most known Romanian dissident. Even the famous Polish dissident Adam Michnik confessed that in August 1968, the Poles admired Ceaușescu and envied Romanians for having such a leader. This opinion was expressed in a TV talk show broadcast by a private channel during his visit in Romania in May 1997. At that time very few were able to understand that Ceaușescu's indictment of the WTO invasion in Czechoslovakia was not caused by his approval of the Prague Spring reforms, but by the fear of a similar invasion in Romania. In this respect, the meeting of the Political Executive Committee of the Central Com-

mittee in the morning of 21 August 1968 is extremely relevant. The only preoccupation was the preservation of Romania's national sovereignty. In 1989, when Ceaușescu understood that in Poland the communist system was put under question, he asked for an intervention of the WTO troops. See Mihnea Berindei, "La Position Singulière de la Roumanie en 1968: Ceaușescu et le Printemps de Prague," *Revue Roumaine D'Histoire* 1–4 (January–December 1999): 183–98.

20. A positive appraisal of Romania's policy of independence is to be found in many publications of the 1960s. See, for instance, David Floyd, *Rumania: Russia's Dissident Ally* (New York, 1965). The memoirs of a former American Ambassador to Bucharest reveals how hard it was for him in the mid 1980s to fight against common views of Washington that Ceaușescu was an acceptable partner, in spite of more and more numerous cases of human rights violations. See David B. Funderburk, *Pinstripes and Reds: An American Ambassador Caught Between the State Department and the Romanian Communists, 1981–1985* (Washington, 1987).

21. The so-called Theses of July from 1971 reiterated the crucial role of the communist teachings in guiding all cultural productions in the country, while attacking those who tried to develop the Romanian high culture under the Western influence. See Nicolae Ceaușescu, *Propuneri de măsuri pentru îmbunătățirea activității politico-ideologice, de educare marxist-leninistă a membrilor de partid, a tuturor oamenilor muncii—6 iulie 1971* [Proposals of Actions for the Improvement of the Political-Ideological Activity, for the Education of the Party Members and All the Working People—6 July 1971] (Bucharest, 1971).

22. In negotiating the Helsinki Final Act, the Western countries insisted in linking the issue of security to the issue of human rights by including among the basic principles laid out in the preamble the idea that friendly relations between states can be maintained only if all are committed to respect human rights and fundamental freedoms. The Soviet reply was to diminish the importance of this principle by subordinating it to that stipulating the non-interference in the internal affairs of another state. The Western states, backed by Romania, succeeded in maintaining that all principles should be given the same importance. For more on this, see the introduction to Richard Davy, ed., *European Détente: A Reappraisal* (London, 1992).

23. The only mechanism that worked with Ceaușescu was the renewal of the Most Favored Nation status by the United States. Because he took great pride in being a conduit between the East and the West, he did his best to preserve this status. As long as dissidents were not numerous, the issue could be handled by making concessions related to emigration. When the protests grew in number, the Romanian leader preferred to renounce the MFN status in 1988, rather than respond to external pressure. Thus, the Helsinki process of international cooperation had a limited impact on the improvement of human rights observance in Romania. For more on the MFN as lever of enforcing emigration to the United States, see Vojtech Mastny, ed., *Helsinki, Human Rights and European Security: Analysis and Documentation* (Durham, 1986), and the account given by a former American Ambassador in Bucharest in Roger Kirk and Mircea Răceanu, *Romania versus the United States: Diplomacy of the Absurd, 1985–1989* (New York, 1994).

24. See Timothy Garton Ash, *The Uses of Adversity: Essays on the Fate of Central Europe* (Cambridge, 1989), *The Polish Revolution: Solidarity* (London, 1991), and *The Magic Lantern: The Revolutions of '89 Witnessed in Warsaw, Budapest, Berlin and Prague* (New York, 1993).

25. Traces of individual or collective letters of protest can be found in various archives of communism. This is the case, for instance, of the memorandum against the destruction of historical monuments addressed to Ceaușescu on 21 October 1985 by Dinu C. Giurescu, Grigore Ionescu, Răzvan Teodorescu, Vasile Drăguț, and Virgil Cândea. See

Cartea Albă a Securității, 506–9. See also the personal testimony by Dinu C. Giurescu, *The Razing of Romania's Past* (Washington, 1989).

26. However, this included dissidents and marginalized party officials, but no large organized group. Moreover, a reformist wing within the ruling elite did not emerge until the Revolution of 1989. The dynamics of intra-party struggles that resulted in the elimination of all potential conflicts and opponents within the RCP was analyzed in Pavel Câmpeanu, *Ceaușescu, anii numărătorii inverse* [Ceaușescu, the Countdown Years] (Iași, 2002). On the failure of reformism within the RCP, see also my study "The 'Letter of the Six:' On the Political (Sub)Culture of the Romanian Communist Elite," *Studia Politica* 5, no. 2 (2005): 355–84.

27. Even publications that programmatically promoted the worldwide liberty of expression, such as *Index on Censorship*, included only a few articles on Romania and even fewer authored by Romanian dissidents. Between 1972 and 1990, there were 122 issues of this publication, in which there were around twenty articles tackling different issues related to Romanian developments, amounting to fifty-seven pages. At the same time, Czechoslovakia and Poland were featured in special issues, to say nothing of the almost issue-by-issue presence of dissidents from these countries, as well as Hungary and the Soviet Union, in this publication.

28. Subjected to criticism were the policies of the regime concerning cultural issues, the program of rural systematization, the rationalization of basic goods, etc., and only in some notable cases the very communist system. At the end of the 1980s, the most vocal among dissidents, except for Dan Petrescu in Iași, were Doina Cornea, lecturer at the University of Cluj, the earlier-mentioned Bucharest-based mathematician Mihai Botez, engineer Radu Filipescu, physicist Gabriel Andreescu, and poet Mircea Dinescu. Some others joined them later, on the brink of regime's collapse. For the texts of their protest letters, see OSA/RFE Archives, Romanian Fond, 300/60/3/Box 7, File Dissidents: Doina Cornea; 300/60/3/Box 5, File Dissidents: Mihai Botez; 300/60/3/Box 8, File Dissidents: Radu Filipescu; 300/60/3/Box 6, File Dissidents: Gabriel Andreescu; 300/60/3/Box 7, File Dissidents: Mircea Dinescu. See also Doina Cornea, *Scrisori deschise și alte texte* [Open Letters and Other Texts] (Bucharest, 1991); Gabriel Andreescu, *Spre o filozofie a disidenței* [Towards a Philosophy of Dissent] (Bucharest, 1992); Mihai Botez, *Intelectualii din Europa de Est* [Intellectuals in Eastern Europe] (Bucharest, 1993).

29. See Mark Almond, *Decline Without Fall: Romania under Ceausescu* (London, 1988).

30. The group of Iași was worth assigning a place on Alina Mungiu-Pippidi's map of the Romanian nonconformist intellectual circles under communism. See her "Correspondence from Bucharest: Intellectuals as Political Actors in Eastern Europe, The Romanian Case," *East European Politics and Societies* 10 (Spring 1996): 333–64, republished in a slightly different version as "Romanian Political Intellectuals Before and After the Revolution," in András Bozóki, ed., *Intellectuals and Politics in Central Europe* (Budapest, 1999), 73–100. See also Mihai Șora, "Rădăcina nevăzută a rezistenței române" [The Unseen Origin of the Romanian Resistance], *Transilvania* (Sibiu) 1–2 (1992): 92–96.

31. A particularly funny example is the January 1983 issue, which should have been dedicated to the anniversary of Ceaușescu's birthday (celebrated with great pomp every 26th of January). The front cover reproduced a painting representing the presidential couple admiring a portrait of the medieval ruler, Stephan the Great (1457–1502). Stephan was arguably the most important king of historical Moldova, and a staunch defender of the independence of his lands, for which he fought numerous battles against the invading Turks and Poles, thus a very appropriate personality to compare to Ceaușescu, the alleged defender of Romania's independence from Moscow. The painter, however, was so stupid that he chose to manifest his subservience to Ceaușescu's cult of personality by

depicting Stephan going out of his portrait on the wall to toast glasses with Elena and Nicolae Ceaușescu, who were sitting in front of that painting. Needless to say, such a painting could have been read either as a clumsy attempt to please the painter's leader, or as a very intelligent way of ridiculing Ceaușescu's ambition to present himself as the last in the row in Romania's historical pantheon.

32. For the treatment of publications with "limited public" by the communist regimes, see the volume authored by Kádár's cultural czar György Aczél, *Culture and Socialist Democracy* (London, 1975).

33. In this respect, it is also interesting to make a comparison between *Dialog*, published by the University of Iași, and *Opinia studențească* [The Students' Opinion], published by the local communist youth organization. Although both addressed practically the same public, the former was more critical than the latter.

34. Under Ceaușescu, in 1980 the communist regime celebrated 2050 years since the establishment of the first "Romanian" state. The search for the ancient Tracian and Dacian roots of the Romanian people was part of an entire trend of pushing the origins of the nation as far back in history as possible in order to counterattack the Hungarian view that at their arrival in Transylvania they only found a deserted land there. For more on this controversy with the Hungarians, see the concluding part of my study "Who Was the First in Transylvania," 1145–48.

35. This letter was written by Dan Petrescu to his brother-in-law, Ioan Petru Culianu, and sent abroad via the French lecturer in French from the University of Iași, Romain Réchou, from whom it was confiscated by the border officers. This episode is narrated by Réchou in his "Un Français chez les Roumains," *L'Alternative* (Paris) 27–28 (May–August 1984): 48–51.

36. Dan and Thérèse Petrescu, interview by the author, tape recording, Bucharest, 21 April 2001; Dan Alexe, interview by the author, tape recording, Brussels, 20 July 2002. On the arrest and interrogations, see also Dan Alexe, "Interview with Liviu Cangeopol," *Lupta* (Paris), November 1989, 5–6. See also the list made by the secret police with the items confiscated from Alexandru Călinescu's home reproduced in the second Romanian edition of Dan Petrescu and Liviu Cangeopol, *Ce-ar mai fi de spus: Convorbiri libere într-o țară ocupată* [What Remains to Be Said: Free Conversations in an Occupied Country] (Bucharest, 2000). Alexandru Călinescu was a professor at the University of Iași and a sort of mentor for the group as editor-in-chief of *Dialog* until May 1983, when dismissed from this position with the occasion of the secret police investigation. Later on, in 1989, Călinescu would sign aside other prominent Romanian intellectuals the so-called letter of the seven protesting against Ceaușescu's cultural policy. For the text of this collective open letter, see "Domestic Bloc," no. 560, 21 April 1989, OSA/RFE Archives, Romanian Fond, 300/60/3/Box 18, File Open Letters: The Group of Seven.

37. According to Decree no. 98/1983, which resumed a Stalinist practice, every owner of a typewriter in Romania had to declare it at the police station to get a permit of ownership. This permit needed to be renewed every year, with a sample of standard text typewritten with the authoring typewriter due to the police each time. In this way, the making of typewritten manifestos was made impossible, since the author was easily identifiable by checks against filed samples. For Decree no. 98/1983, see *Buletinul Oficial*, no. 21, 30 March 1983, 29–33.

38. The fundamental text theorizing the so-called resistance through culture as representing the specific way of opposing communism in Ceaușescu's Romania, the only possibility in a country controlled by the *Securitate*, is the introduction to the post-communist edition of Gabriel Liiceanu, *Jurnalul de la Păltiniș: Un model paideic in cultura umanistă* [The Diary From Păltiniș: A Paideic Model in Humanistic Culture] (Bucharest, 1990).

This diary, which was published first in 1983, represented a model of daily "resistance through culture," a repertoire of topics of reflection and a list of canonical readings for all intellectuals that wanted to evade the misery of everyday life under communism. A different, critical view on what represented "resistance through culture" is to be found in Vintilă Mihăilescu, "Ăștia eram noi" [These Were We], in *Cum era? Cam așa: Amintiri din anii comunismului [românesc]* [How Was It? Something Like This: Remembering (Romanian) Communism], ed. Călin-Andrei Mihăilescu (Bucharest, 2006), 18–26.

39. The name Petrescu is probably the third most widespread family name in Romania. This author is not related to the former dissident Dan Petrescu, any more than she is related to Elena Ceaușescu, née Petrescu.
40. For the significance of this strike in the history of worker's revolt in communist Romania, see Dragoș Petrescu, "A Threat From Below? Some Reflections on Workers' Protest in Communist Romania," *Xenopoliana* (Iași), no. 1–2 (1999): 142–68.
41. In June 1987, Dan Petrescu participated in Paris at a conference dedicated to Mircea Eliade. On this occasion, he met Mihnea Berindei, the leader of the League for Defense of Human Rights in Romania, who complained that the Paris-based emigration was forced to turn down all the French journalists constantly asking for names of Romanian intellectuals willing to speak freely about the current situation in the country. In reply, Petrescu promised that from then on he would be ready to speak with any Western journalists. Soon after his return, Gilles Shiller (alias Jean Stern) arrived in Iași and was directed to his house by Alexandru Călinescu. Facing this situation, Dan Petrescu decided on the spot to take this step since somebody must have spoken for all those who did not dare to do it. Dan Petrescu, interview by the author, tape recording, Bucharest, 25 April 1998.
42. The text was later on broadcast by RFE and literary critic Monica Lovinescu commented it on 5 February 1988 in the framework of her series "Teze și antiteze la Paris" [Theses and antitheses in Paris]. See OSA/RFE Archives, Romanian Fond, 300/60/3/Box 6, File Dissidents: Dan Petrescu. A replica on behalf of the Romanian *culturniks*, to use Vlad Georgescu's label for the intellectual obedient to the regime, was given by Mircea Radu Iacoban. See "Minciuna are picioare scurte" [Lie Has Short Legs], *Contemporanul* (Bucharest), 26 February 1988.
43. An excellent synthesis of the "theory and practice" of Central European dissidence, which means Poland, the former Czechoslovakia, and Hungary, is Barbara Falk, *The Dilemmas of Dissidence in East-Central Europe: Citizen Intellectuals and Philosopher Kings* (Budapest, 2003).
44. For more on this, see Cristina Petrescu, "Seven Faces of Dissent: A Micro Perspective on the Study of the Political (Sub)Cultures under Communism," in *Political Culture and Cultural Politics*, ed. Alexandru Zub and Adrian Cioflâncă (Iași, 2005), 305–44.
45. This essay was sent abroad with the French lecturer in Iași at the time, Thomas Bazin. Fragments were published in *Libération* on 15 Febraury 1988. The entire text was broadcast by RFE. For the complete version of the essay, see Petrescu and Cangeopol, *Ce-ar mai fi de spus*, 236–43.
46. It was this belief that motivated him to speak his mind publicly in the name of all those who were afraid or unable to speak up, Petrescu confessed in a later interview to a French press agency. The interview was granted in April 1988 in Iași, but it arrived in Paris only at the beginning of the next year, when it was also broadcast by RFE. See Virgil Ierunca, "Povestea vorbei" [The Story of the Word], no. 662, 8 February 1989, OSA/RFE Archives, Romanian Fond, 300/60/3/Box 6, File Dissidents: Dan Petrescu. See also Petrescu and Cangeopol, *Ce-ar mai fi de spus*, 268–79. In fact, the journalists were fortunate not to take with them the filmed interview because the next day they were

caught by the secret police on the streets of Iași interviewing people, and all filmed materials were immediately confiscated. The interview with Petrescu was sent to Paris later on, when a reliable messenger was found. Parts of this interview were broadcast on 26 January 1989 by TF3 during the program "Résistances" dedicated to the film "The Red Disaster" by Belgian journalist Josy Dubié.

47. The first non-communist president of post-communist Romania, Emil Constantinescu, also contributed to this perception. After four years in power, he decided not to run again for the highest office, publicly announcing that he had been defeated by the *Securitate*. Emil Constantinescu reiterated this argument in a recently published book, which has as its motto: "Un președinte în război cu mafia securisto-comunistă" [A president at war with the communist-secret services Mafia]. See Emil Constantinescu, *Adevărul despre România, 1989–2004* [The Truth About Romania, 1989–2004] (Bucharest, 2004).

48. The letter was broadcast by RFE on 30 August 1989. See OSA/RFE Archives, Romanian Fond, 300/60/3/Box 6, File Dissidents: Dan Petrescu. See also Petrescu and Cangeopol, *Ce-ar mai fi de spus*, 258–67.

49. Made by the Belgian journalist Josy Dubié, "The Red Disaster" showed Western viewers a situation shocking for individuals used to life in a normal world. Only people old enough to have war memories and to recall the food shortages of that period ever underwent similar experiences in their lifetimes. Also, the destruction of Bucharest reminded some of the disasters following earthquakes. Josy Dubié, interview by the author, tape recording, Brussels, 19 July 2002.

50. Acknowledging that the West and the East were equally responsible for the division of Europe, Petrescu pleaded for an alliance across the Iron Curtain, which should have ended the segregation of the continent. Romania, he argued, though in a desperate situation, could have played the role of catalyst. At that time, the reference to the unification of Europe was rather metaphoric; today one can read his text as a prophetic one. The text addressed to the conference was broadcast by RFE with comments by the director Vlad Georgescu himself. See OSA/RFE Archives, Romanian Fond, 300/60/3/Box 6, File Dissidents: Dan Petrescu. See also Petrescu and Cangeopol, *Ce-ar mai fi de spus*, 251–57.

51. A note of the secret police from October 1989 mentioned all the measures taken by this institution in order to put an end to Petrescu's dissent. These measures were extremely diverse, ranging from strict supervision, as described above, to intimidating him into emigration. Also, it is worth mentioning that campaigns to discredit him in the West were launched. A copy of this document from the archives of the *Securitate* is in the possession of the author.

52. Mihnea Berindei, interview by the author, tape recording, Paris, 24 July 2002.

53. The text was published partially in *Libération* on 5 April 1988. The next day, it was broadcast by RFE. See OSA/RFE Archives, Romanian Fond, 300/60/3/Box 6, File Dissidents: Liviu Cangeopol. This text has also an interesting story. When it arrived in Paris, it could not be published immediately, because the League for the Defense of Human Rights in Romania needed more personal data than a simple name in order to protect Cangeopol effectively. In the meantime, some French journalists in search of intellectuals willing to grant interviews were sent to him and the Romanian authorities found his name on their list. Thus, the secret police started to look for Cangeopol as well, forcing him to hide until the publication of his text, which made him a dissident known abroad and implicitly protected. Liviu Cangeopol, interview by the author, tape recording, New York, 17 May 2000.

54. The magazine was established in 1987 by former dissident Dorin Tudoran, together with Vladimir Tismăneanu and Michael Radu, with funds from the National Endowment for Democracy. It reunited great names from the first post-1945 wave of emigration,

such as Eugen Ionescu, Mircea Eliade, Emil Cioran, the most prominent intellectuals of Romanian origin abroad, as well as Monica Lovinescu and Virgil Ierunca, the most popular broadcasters of RFE. Besides them, there were more recent émigrés, such as Matei Călinescu, Virgil Nemoianu, Victor Ieronim Stoichiță, Ioan Petru Culianu, who had never been dissidents at home, aside former dissidents arrived in exile, such as Paul Goma, Ion Negoițescu, Mihai Botez, Géza Szőcs, William Totok. However, the novelty of *Agora* was that it tried as much as possible to publish writers who were still in Romania. A brief look into the collection of this magazine shows that it were only those who were already or would soon become dissidents that dared to publish there. Dan Petrescu published in *Agora* beginning with its second issue of May 1988 and up to the fall of communism, he was present in every issue. Liviu Cangeopol published for the first time in the issue of January 1989, while still in Romania, and continued his collaboration after his departure to the United States. See *Agora* 1, no. 2 (May 1988); *Agora* 2, no. 1 (January 1989); and no. 2 (July 1989).

55. That was, however, their only common enterprise. While Petrescu continued his dissident activity inside Romania, Cangeopol, convinced that communism was still to stay in this country, decided to emigrate and left for the United States in September 1989. Liviu Cangeopol, interview by the author, tape recording, New York, 17 May 2000.
56. The transcription of the text was made by another member of the Iași group, Dan Alexe, who was about to become the third dissident from that city prior to his emigration to Belgium. Dan Alexe, interview by the author, tape recording, Brussels, 20 July 2002. A letter addressed by him to Dan Petrescu was published together with the dialogue in *Agora*, and it was also included in the volume versions published in Romania. See Petrescu and Cangeopol, *Ce-ar mai fi de spus*, 9–10.
57. See Dan Petrescu and Liviu Cangeopol, "Ce-ar mai fi de spus: Convorbiti libere într-o țară ocupată" [What Remains to Be Said: Free Conversations in an Occupied Country), *Agora* 3, no. 1 (February 1990): 45–258.
58. In fact, it is ironic to remark that, by the end of the 1980s, the economic crisis was so deep that it affected the secret police apparatus and collaborators to the same extent as the rest of the citizens. At that time, all basic goods—sugar, edible oil, bread, butter, eggs, meat—were rationed, while other goods could have been bought only in the place of residence. The shadow following Petrescu's wife everywhere stayed together with her in line to catch some hundred grams of salami or a piece of cheese. Dan and Thérèse Petrescu, interview by the author, tape recording, Bucharest, 21 April 2001.
59. Finally, after news that their book had arrived in the West reached Romania through RFE, the secret agents in charge of following them were severely punished. See *Cartea Albă a Securității*, 372–75.
60. This interview was given using the telephone of a friend in Iași, who was not under the surveillance of the secret police. However, the success of the operation relied on Petrescu's ability to ditch his shadowing agent before arriving at his friend's home at the preset hour when Nicolai Constantin Munteanu, the RFE journalist from the Romanian desk in charge of the popular program "Actualitatea românească" [Romanian Actualities], was to call. Dan Petrescu, interview by the author, tape recording, Bucharest, 28 April 1998.
61. News about this petition reached the West via the French journalist Gilles Schiller from *Libération*, the same reporter who interviewed Petrescu the first time.
62. The signatories from Iași were: Dan Petrescu; Luca Pițu, an intellectual from the group around Petrescu, who participated also in the telephone interview; Liviu Antonesei, another intellectual from the group; Filip Răduți, in whose house the interview took place; Eugen Amarandei and Gabriela Iavolschi, Petrescu's neighbors; and Alexan-

dru Tacu, a librarian who visited Petrescu several times. Mariana Marin, a young poet from Bucharest and good friend of the group around Petrescu, also endorsed the petition. The signatories from Cluj were Doina Cornea and her former students Gina and Dan Sîmpălean, who also signed before her open letter to the Pope. This enumeration gives one some idea about the way in which signatures on such protest letters were gathered.

63. An account of the complicated endeavor of collecting signatures around the country, see in Liviu Antonesei, *Jurnal din anii ciumei, 1987–1989: Încercări de sociologie spontană* [Diary From the Years of the Plague, 1987–1989: Attempts at Spontaneous Sociology] (Iași, 1995), 94–116.

64. Although the new ruling elites were considered crypto-communists or neo-communists due to their origin in the party bureaucracy, one has to acknowledge that, after 1989, the rules of the game inevitably changed. There has been a pluralist party system, free elections have been held (although perhaps not entirely fair since the media was controlled by those in power), there has been a developing market economy (although the privatization process was delayed in such a way that those who took advantage of it were the *entrepratchicks*, as Katherine Verdery put it), and, most importantly, freedom of speech has become a reality. In short, the Revolution of 1989 put an end to the closed and monolithic communist system in Romania. On the crucial role of the *entrepratchicks* in the fall of communism and the initiation of the transition processes, which explains the continuities in elite membership between the two systems, see Katherine Verdery, *What Was Socialism, and What Comes Next?* (Princeton, 1996), 19–38.

65. The strange thing is that the complete scarcity of the late 1980s helped raising a wave of sympathy for those who were bold enough to criticize the regime. Although only few cared about such issues as the freedom of speech, while most were only concerned with their daily bread, the economic crisis was so deep that it created by default a feeling of solidarity against hardships. Because of this particular situation, many regarded dissidents as the daring representatives of their own concerns and perceptions, despite the fact that most intellectuals restricted their attacks to cultural issues. Obviously, this situation did not last long after December 1989. A skillfully orchestrated negative propaganda of the first post-communist regime turned the public opinion against the former dissidents. See in this respect Nicolae Manolescu, "Unde ne sînt disidenții" [Where Are Our Dissidents] in his *Dreptul la normalitate: Discursul politic și realitatea* [The Right to Normalcy: Political Discourse and Reality] (Bucharest, 1991), 123–29; and Alina Mungiu, *Românii după '89: Istoria unei neînțelegeri* [Romanians After 1989: The History of a Misunderstanding] (Bucharest, 1995), 96–98.

Chapter 6

THE DANGER OF OVER-INTERPRETING DISSIDENT WRITING IN THE WEST
Communist Terror in Czechoslovakia, 1948–1968

Muriel Blaive

This volume takes as its premise that "the parallel phenomena of samizdat and tamizdat, as well as the much broader circulation of cultural products that was instigated and sustained by these practices, in many ways anticipates what we identify as 'cultural globalization' in Eastern Europe today."[1] Such a novel approach is crucial when discussing the circulation of ideas between the former Eastern and Western blocs. The suggestion that contacts and exchanges did exist between East and West in a mutually influential way, though their importance has been largely underestimated, contributes to a wider and fruitful reevaluation of the Cold War intellectual landscape and heritage taking place today.[2]

In communist Europe, as is well known, a political connotation tended to be ascribed to any unofficial writing, including literature; as such, political meaning was also sought in any "Eastern" text reaching the West. In order to fully account for the literal and figurative reception of samizdat in the West, it is thus necessary to study the politicization of this transmission of information. This chapter will study how the Cold War atmosphere tended in certain circumstances to dictate not just a broad *hunt* for political meaning but also that it was *found*.

If, for obvious reasons, we have approached and received samizdat and other "Eastern" writings with uncritical sympathy—if, in other words, we have not been neutral—it is time to question and reevaluate this past analysis. Many articles in this volume deal with the literary heritage of samizdat and tamizdat; I specifically concentrate on academic writing concerning the history of Stalinism in Czechoslovakia, i.e., in the period between 1948 and 1956.

Notes for this chapter begin on page 152.

Western Reception of Reform Communist Historical Theses

A preliminary remark is necessary: we do not generally speak of samizdat or tamizdat before the end of the 1950s in the context of the Soviet Union. In the case of the "satellite" countries of East-Central Europe, the samizdat movement is generally considered to have begun even later, in the early 1970s. However, as recent, groundbreaking literature has shown, this late start does not preclude the fact that many influent intellectual exchanges were taking place from East to West, from West to East, and within the Eastern bloc at least as far back as 1953.[3] Similarly, this chapter analyzes a corpus of texts and East-West intellectual exchanges, which were not typically considered samizdat or tamizdat at the moment they appeared. Some of those texts were not yet samizdat because they were produced in Czechoslovakia in 1968 and 1969 during the Prague Spring, at a moment when they were legally published and uncensored; only after 1970 did they go underground. Others were produced in the West from 1950 to the 1980s. Before 1969, however, such texts did not influence or initiate a dialogue with "dissident" writers, but rather with official historians and intellectuals who were later expelled from public life after the failure of the Prague Spring. Whichever terms we employ, the fact remains that there were contacts, exchanges, and mutual influences over the Iron Curtain long before the 1970s.

As hinted at above, I concentrate on one example of the "overinterpretation" of history, an overinterpretation that I ascribe to the particular configuration of the Cold War and to its peculiar political reading on both sides of the Iron Curtain: the Western reception of the 1968 debate about the terror of the Stalinist regime in Czechoslovakia.

The historical narrative born in 1968 and carried out by Czech historians and other public figures claimed that Czechoslovakia suffered more than any other People's Democracy from Stalinist terror. These intellectuals based their claims on little or no historical sources and their thesis was taken over and scientifically legitimized by the Western academic community with an equal lack of epistemology. We can see at least five reasons why this could happen:

> (1) The "West" was more than prepared to hear that the Czechoslovak population had been fighting against communism: in fact, it had eagerly expected and awaited as much.

> (2) The reform communist historians who authored this narrative enjoyed a high degree of ideological legitimacy in the eyes of (generally left-wing) Western intellectuals.

> (3) This legitimacy was strengthened by their exclusive access to communist regime archives (they remained until after 1989 the *only historians* who had ever had access to these archives).

(4) This situation was further solidified after the crushing of the Prague Spring, as most of these reform communist historians and intellectuals became dissidents (or exiles), that is, victims.

(5) The "greater Czechoslovak communist terror narrative" came to support an already existing Western anticommunist historical narrative on the Czech culture's democratic heritage.

I will expand on these points after reconstructing the political and historical context of the time, both East and West.

The American Vision of the Cold War in the 1950s

When studying the historical development of Czechoslovakia in the 1950s, the Western interpretation of the information coming from behind the Iron Curtain is a central issue. This information took many different forms: not only academic essays on history but also, and sometimes mainly, eyewitness accounts, documents, letters, exile writings, novels, and underground writings.

In 1968, however, almost everything published in Czechoslovakia was being considered by the West, including the official press, and, between August 1968 and 1969 or 1970, many individual articles. Only then did the real era of the samizdat writing in Czechoslovakia begin, that is, a system of clandestine printing and distribution of dissident, banned literature.

When the Iron Curtain arose around Eastern Europe at the beginning of the 1950s, the most difficult and urgent task was maintaining a mutual exchange of information with the West. Very little was known about what was actually going on inside the communist countries (then refered to in the United States as the "captive nations"), just as those behind the Iron Curtain knew very little about what was happening on the outside. The Americans were instrumental in trying to break through this isolation.

News from Behind the Iron Curtain (NBIC) and Radio Free Europe (RFE) were created for this purpose at the end of the 1940s and in the early 1950s. RFE was mainly intent on broadcasting noncommunist information to countries where political censorship banned independent reporting and the American point of view on world politics, while NBIC tried to relay knowledge about Eastern Europe back to the United States. These American, "free" media had no scientific vocation and could not be put on the same level as academic analyses, but they did constitute an invaluable source of information for scholars—especially in the 1950s.

Indeed, they proved crucial at a time when information was so scarce. In view of both the ideological clash between communism and capitalism and the military balance of terror, this information war was not taken lightly. To collect and report information from and to communist countries was not easy and sometimes dangerous; to correctly interpret them became even more important and difficult. With this purpose in mind, journals of a more analytical nature appeared, like *Preuves* and *Encounter* (both offsprings of the Congress for Cultural Freedom, with direct links to the CIA)[4] and *Problems of Communism* (a journal, as the title suggests, that existed to predict the collapse of the USSR and was published by the United States Information Agency).

NBIC, however, was the most dedicated to sharing information of direct provenance from communist countries. It used official sources (such as the regime newspapers), official state declarations, public speeches, and radio broadcasts, in addition to anything "unofficial" its reporters could lay their hands on (letters, private testimonies, interviews with refugees, and so on).

Editors believed for a long time in the imminent collapse of communism, indeed mirroring the prevailing opinion at that time in the countries under study. The Western media resorted to apocalyptical descriptions of the situation in the Eastern Bloc. The West's wishful thinking is summed up in the following proclamation (broadcast by RFE in 1953): "Czechs and Slovaks, Hear the message which comes to you today from the Free World: The Soviet Union is growing weaker. The people of the captive nations are growing stronger."[5] The post-Stalin thaw was seen as no more than a "desperate attempt to get the most propaganda value from regime concessions."[6]

NBIC frequently quoted the communist press, operating under the assumption that if even Communist officials allowed certain dissatisfied comments to appear in the press, those had to reflect reality. If Communist Youth functionaries, cooperative leaders, or high-ranking personalities denounced certain systemic malfunctions, it was considered sufficient proof of subversive ferment.

With the benefit of hindsight,[7] I contend that taking communist "negative" information for granted amounted in reality to underestimating the fact that regimes closely monitored the media. What Western observers mainly found was what the Communist authorities themselves had decided they should present to the outside world. Extracting meaningful information from the communist press was, of course, possible,[8] but it required a more subtle, time-consuming analysis than a periodical could usually afford. The possibility that the de-Stalinization policy led by the Czechoslovak communist regime between 1953 and 1956 was a shrewd political maneuver on the part of the authorities, rather than the result of a mounting popular pressure, was never really taken into account.[9] And yet, communist propaganda policy left nothing to chance or to alleged "democratic demands" on the part of Czech society, like the West wanted to believe. Ignoring the carefully planned dimension of Czech propraganda does no justice to the party's head intellectual, Zdeněk Nejedlý.

The ideology that sustained the creation of *News from Behind the Iron Curtain*'s mother institution, the National Committee for a Free Europe (NCFE), was virulently anticommunist.[10] The correlation between anticommunist broadcasting and the risks of seeing dissent where there was none becomes obvious when one considers that the NCFE, founded in New York in 1949, created RFE not only to counteract the local propaganda, but also to support, if not fuel, the resistance of the local populations to Moscow through a pioneer "psychological warfare combining the qualities of the written and of the spoken media."[11] The National Committee was secretly financed by the US Congress and the CIA,[12] and its daughter institutions undoubtedly rejoiced at any sign of rebellion in the communist countries, even to the point of confusing reality with wishful thinking, action with activism.

This is how reports in 1953 of a "great, unorganized opposition" among Czechoslovak workers (gathered from unverifiable oral accounts and an anonymous letter addressed to the editor)[13] after a currency reform sparked off two enormous operations called Prospero and Veto (twelve million leaflets balloon-dropped over Czechoslovakia in 1954). The leaders of these operations described coming to the "realization that there was a large, unorganized opposition in Czechoslovakia that was capable of engaging in politically significant actions."[14] RFE called itself the "Voice of the Opposition" and considered itself better informed about local conditions than the inhabitants themselves.[15]

Yet we now know that the "massive 1953 Czechoslovak riots" one read about in NBIC involved in reality a demonstration of five thousand workers in Pilsen (Plzeň) that lasted only a few hours, after which most participants were arrested, and that a massive counterdemonstration was organized that same afternoon, as well a series of strikes across the country that spontaneously petered out the next day. No casualties were reported.[16]

However exhilarating it was for anticommunist warriors to see workers trying to speak freely on the radio and throw Stalin and Gottwald busts out of the window, as did happen briefly in Pilsen, this protest movement remained isolated within Czech society. This fact alone should have raised the question of how to interpret the event, especially in contrast to the East German 17 June 1953 massive protests, where the very existence of the communist regime was threatened (and dozens of protesters were killed). Sympathy and reality are sometimes hard to dissociate. What was more relevant: that a few determined young workers admirably tried to protest and demand some changes, or that all the rest of the population did not dare or refused to join them? Passive onlookers not only refrained from parading with the demonstrators, but many also agreed to take part in the regime's counterdemonstrations, while other workers, militia men, were beating and locking up the protesters. The fact that the Czech official press severely condemned the protests cannot be taken as adequate measurement of their actual scope.

Yet RFE believed and claimed it was in the interest of the captive populations to organize themselves into opposition movements: "Without internal receptivity the efforts of the Free World would indeed become pointless and unnecessary attempts at 'interference,'" whereas its objective was to provide the "external support" that would prevent the "People's Opposition" from "wither[ing] in isolation."[17]

This philosophy incidentally led to sharp criticisms of RFE's policy during the 1956 Hungarian uprising. The radio was reproached for having encouraged an armed assault against the regime and for having encouraged the hope among the Hungarian population that communism would be overcome, despite the fact that the West did not intend to intervene.[18]

The Exiles' Vision of the Cold War in the 1950s and the 1960s

The Cold War ideology led the "West" to select and interpret incoming information in order to find confirmation of what they wanted and expected to hear. But whom do we really mean, when we say "the West"?

As Justine Faure has shown,[19] the main Western consumers and analyzers of information collected from behind the Iron Curtain in the 1950s were (apart from politicians and diplomats) drawn from the American academy, where Czechoslovak studies were largely populated by anticommunist Czech and Slovak exiles, who had fled after the 1948 coup (Eduard Táborský, Ivo Ducháček, Pavel Tigrid, Ferdinand Peroutka, Zdeněk Suda, Vojtěch Mastný, and so on). Some of them even advised the US authorities, for instance the National Security Council, or collaborated with the anticommunist media, like RFE.

These anticommunist exiles' personal backgrounds help us understand why and how the West was prepared, thanks to their mediation, to hear any theory supporting the repressive character of Communist regimes, the hopelessness of any Czechoslovak resistance and the importance of the democratic heritage of the Czech nation.

Democrats in exile were, for the most part, embarrassed, if not traumatized, for having capitulated without any fight to the Communists in 1948. Gottwald's new government was unanimously voted into office in March 1948 by the freely elected 1946 Parliament (230 votes for, 0 against);

not a single Democrat voiced his or her opposition and only nine democratic MPs renounced their political mandate after the coup in February.[20] This guilty feeling[21] was certainly not quelled by the behaviour of two of Czechoslovakia's heralds of democracy: President Beneš signed off on all of Gottwald's demands and remained in office another four months until his death, while the first President Masaryk's son, Jan Masaryk, agreed to stay in the post-February communist government—even if only briefly, as he tragically died in March 1948 after falling from his fourth floor window (it is still unclear today if he was murdered or if he committed suicide). Because their identity was defined as being "democratic" against the "Communists" (not "nationalist" against "pro-Russian," as it happened in Poland and Hungary), the democratic aspect and heritage of Czech culture was greatly emphasized. Last but not least, the "level of Communist repression" was a more comfortable moral and political explanation for the Czechoslovak population's lack of resistance to the communist regime in the 1950s than cowardice or genuine support for the regime.

This historical narrative of Czechoslovakia (especially of the Czech lands) as a country of democratic traditions and culture was characteristic of the exiles' writings. For instance, Ivo Ducháček, a former MP of the Popular Party between 1945 and 1948 in Czechoslovakia, was of the opinion that the Czech democratic culture hindered any violent opposition to the Communist regime, and was a "handicap for revolt."[22] Opponents of the leadership were characterized by a "sophisticated sobriety," "reared in the tradition of democracy and its nonviolent methods of action."[23] He thought the Czechs were so used to casting ballots that they felt powerless when there were no free elections. Yet he considered his countrymen strongly anticommunist: a "bloodless, often more than discreet, but permanent 'civil war'" was allegedly the "order of the day" in 1958 Czechoslovakia.[24] The situation was, in his eyes, best described as one of "evolutionary revolution."[25]

Ducháček's view was representative of the democratic lyricism of the time. The democratic experience of the 1920s, 1930s, and the period from 1945 to 1948 was also understood in Western academia to have left a deep impact on Czechoslovak mentalities.[26] Czechoslovakia's first president, Tomáš Masaryk, was a humanist, a philosopher, and a democrat. As he claimed in 1919: "To be Czech is to be a model man, to be a democrat!"[27] Czech democrats in exile and Western academics alike relentlessly reminded their readers that Czechoslovakia had been the only true democracy in Central Europe during the interwar period; that it was the only country in the region that had not surrendered from the inside to fascism or nazism; and that it was the only country to have held truly free elections in 1946. Democracy was equated to culture and civilization.[28]

What is perhaps more surprising is that, with the passing years and especially after 1956, even Czechoslovak Communists were considered by democrats in exile to be the heirs of this "democratic tradition." For instance, Eduard Táborský, President Beneš's former secretary, saw in Communist leaders between 1948 and 1949 a "comparative hesitancy in refashioning Czechoslovakia's political institutions after the Soviet image"[29] as opposed to the other "satellites"; after the twentieth Congress of the CPSU in 1956, he also saw a "new and surprisingly vigorous inner-Party democracy" reemerge.[30] He did not doubt the "democratic" core of Czechoslovak society:

> This seemingly unruffled surface hides a whole ocean of latent and at times rumbling anti-communism. Although no positive proof is possible, I am convinced that the ratio of genuine believers in Marxism-Leninism per capita of the population is today lower in Czechoslovakia than in most of the other satellite countries, despite the fact that the ratio of Party membership is higher than anywhere else behind the Iron Curtain.[31]

The background was now set for the events of 1968. With reform communism, the Prague Spring, and socialism with a human face, a renewed version of the old historical narrative was about to emerge.

The Historical Narrative on Stalinist Terror

Between 1945 and 1948, Stalin allowed the countries he occupied after World War II, who were to become the "Eastern bloc," so-called national specific paths to socialism. The Czechoslovaks had taken theirs seriously. The Communists had been able to establish a strong basis of popular support on the assumption that the "democratic socialism" they promoted was not far from the "socialist democracy" advocated by democrats. Czech socialism would be very different from what the Soviet Union had experienced. There would be no collectivization of the agriculture, no terrorizing the middle class, and no artificial leveling of the standard of living.[32]

A number of young Czech intellectuals (along with 2.5 million Czechoslovak citizens) enthusiastically joined the Party between 1945 and the end of 1948. They soon found out, however, that communism in practice was far less rosy than they had expected. Klement Gottwald, the historical leader who embodied the national hopes for a regime combining the advantages of democracy *and* socialism, ultimately adopted repressive policies and pursued an all-Stalinist sovietization of the country.

When the Prague Spring came into being in 1968 (a reform having become unavoidable in the long term, not because of a strong democratic spirit but because the economy was structurally collapsing since the beginning of the 1960s), the aforementioned intellectuals, now in leading positions of authority, had to deal with their own Stalinist past. They were eager to repair their mistakes, to rehabilitate the people who had been wrongly sentenced and to return to the alleged democratic roots of Czechoslovak communism. The "errors" of the past were conveniently blamed on the Soviets, whereas Gottwald's destiny rather inspired pity. He, the "Czechoslovak Stalin," was not exonerated from all responsibility but his fate was mainly considered one of personal tragedy, which had led to his alcoholism and premature death.[33] Socialism with a human face was the platform that would restore Czechoslovak communism's democratic face.

One of the crucial challenges in 1968 for the Prague Spring intellectual leaders was to explain how socialist ideals could have been so distorted in the early 1950s. A new historical narrative rapidly took shape. The first steps were taken between June and August 1968, when Czech historian Karel Kaplan wrote a series of three articles entitled "Reflections on Political Trials."[34] The following lines received special attention among the denizen and Western readership: "In Czechoslovakia, the great show-trials began in 1950, at a time when they were already over elsewhere. ... That is why the first judicial sentences already led to almost as many dead as the trials in all the other People's Democracies put together in 1949."[35]

Authors in the East and the West were understandably struck by this statement and quoted it in their own work. However, most of them (as was typical and problematic of "samizdat" reception and circulation of ideas between East and West) rendered this quote in ever-so-slightly modified versions. These multiple cases of minor carelessness must have appeared insignificant at the time, yet, when added up, rapidly gave a whole new dimension to what was meant as a side remark. For instance, where Kaplan wrote that the first judicial sentences passed in Czechoslovakia resulted in *almost* as many dead as in the other communist countries, Antonín Kratochvil quotes him as saying that they provoked *about* as many dead,[36] Jacques Rupnik claimed that they caused *more* dead,[37] and Otto Ulč stated that the number probably exceeded the total in all neighboring countries.[38] When Kaplan wrote that the first sentences *in 1950* brought about as many dead as in the other countries *in 1949*, Antonín Kratochvil leaves out the date of the "first sentences," Jacques Rupnik states that the "first sentences" took place in 1949 and leaves the figures of dead in "other countries" without a date, and Otto Ulč simply omits all dates.

The proportions of Kaplan's original statement got lost as interpretations drifted over time. According to Karel Bartošek, for instance, civil society suffered an "especially violent" repression after February 1948.[39] Václav

Vrabec asserted, "in the 1950s, Czechoslovakia was the country where the Communists were the most persecuted of all the others, where they were most often assassinated."[40] George Feiwel stated that the purges were the most extensive of all the Soviet satellites.[41] Jiří Pelikán alleged, "the numbers of trials and arrests exceeded those of the other Eastern countries."[42] Zdeněk Hejzlar wrote that the witch-hunt for enemies reached a point of hysteria unequalled in the other countries.[43] And Barbara Wolfe Jancar estimated that the range of the purges "rival[ed] the worst excesses of Stalin's great purges of the 1930s"[44] —if it were true, several million Czechoslovaks would have been killed in the 1950s. She wrote, "the number of victims is more than the combined total of those of the purges in all the other East European countries."[45]

"Almost as many," "just as many," "probably more," or "far more" "dead," "victims," or "purges," than "in the other show-trials" or "in the other terror regimes," "put together" or not, "before 1950," "in 1950," "after 1950," "during Stalinism," or without precise dates: the specifics are vague, but the general idea that Czechoslovakia suffered more than the other Eastern countries from communist terror made its way into the historiography; its intellectual appeal was enormous.

"Democratic Traditions" Mobilized Again

Young Stalinist intellectuals at the end of the 1940s like Jiří Pelikán, Antonín Liehm, Karel Kaplan, Eduard Goldstücker, and so on, had become reform communists in the second half of the 1960s, and they supported and sometimes initiated Alexander Dubček's reforms. After Dubček's fall, those who refused to plead allegiance to the Normalization regime were demoted; most emigrated to Western European coutries.

The democrats in exile in the West were thus joined by a new wave of intellectuals, who were now equally opposed to the Czechoslovak government, but who had, for the most part, fervently supported communism after the war and been involved in in the post-1948 regime and state infrastructure

Those who, on the contrary, elected to stay in Czechoslovakia contributed to the emerging "dissident" movement, which brought together people from all walks of life and ideological backgrounds (Václav Havel, Jiří Hájek, Václav Benda, Ludvík Vaculík, Petr Pithart, and many others). Finally, Western scholars of Czechoslovakia, left-wing intellectuals often dazzled by the Prague Spring and its ideals, strengthened the North American academia and contributed to fixing Czechoslovak studies as a lively research sphere for generations to come (for instance, the already well-established Gordon Skilling, Barbara Wolfe Jancar, Jacques Rupnik, Fred Eidlin, and others).

The interaction between these ideologically very different groups turned out to be more harmonious and productive than one might have expected. Already since 1968, despite the Iron Curtain, despite their ideologically antagonistic pasts (Stalinist communists, anticommunist democrats in exile, anticommunist, left-wing Western intellectuals, etc.), in journalistic or academic production officially sanctioned by the Prague Spring regime, in samizdat and tamizdat after 1970 or in Western academic production, they all shared and contributed to this "greater Czechoslovak terror" theory. How is this possible?

We have seen already that the anticommunist community in exile alloted a privileged space to the "democratic culture" argument in the 1950s. In the view of the democrats in exile, there was an inherent democratic component to Czech culture—even in the Communist Party. According to them, this heritage had been momentarily wiped out in the early 1950s due to the Soviet interference. In 1968, the Prague Spring (reform communist) narrative on "greater terror" fit neatly into this background. The post-1968 Western narrative now added the final touch to this historical explanation: it is because the democratic roots of Czechoslovak society had been so deep that the terror level had to be so high, indeed higher than in all the other Popular Democracies put together. Overestimating the level of communist repression hence became both the result and the proof of the "national democratic traditions."

According to George Hodos (himself a victim of a Rajk follow-up trial in Hungary), Gottwald and the rest of the leadership were at first reluctant to "unleash the terror" against their comrades: "The increasing pressure finally swept away the traditional values and moral considerations, and the resulting purge exploded with a ferocity unequalled in neighboring states."[46] Gordon Skilling, Canadian historian and political scientist renowned for his work on Czechoslovakia, wrote: "Stalinism during the fifties represented an even more abrupt and sharp break with the past than in other countries, and assumed a special ruthlessness which was, in a sense, proportionate to the democratic traditions which had to be destroyed."[47] David Rees and František August (the former a journalist, the latter a Czechoslovak Secret Police agent who defected) stated: "For the precise reason of Czechoslovakia's democratic past, its advanced economy, and its many links to the West, it was necessary for the regime to devise a whole series of repressive measures."[48]

These statements, representative of the vast majority of the literature on this topic not only before 1989, but long after, thus point to an unexpected convergence between the reform Communist texts, the samizdat texts written in and after 1968 in Czechoslovakia, the post-1968 tamizdat texts, and the Western understanding of the historical development of this country. They also raise two questions: first of all, was the level of repression in Czechoslovakia really higher than in the other communist countries put together or not? Second, did this terror level really mirror Czechoslovakia's specific democratic past?

Examining the Figures

Before we consider concrete data, I should make clear that it is not my objective here to treat callously the victims of torture and murder as mere statistical figures or to devaluate anyone's suffering. Numbers are important here, however, because they sustain a specific interpretation of Czechoslovak history.

The partial opening of archives after 1989 has allowed us to estimate more precisely the figures of repression, but the data made available in the 1950s would have sufficed to put the "greater Czechoslovak terror" argument to serious doubt. Indeed, the Czechoslovak numbers, although terrible enough, are not in any way worse than in the Polish and Hungarian cases. The available evidence shows that approximately 100,000 people were rehabilitated in 1990 for having been unjustly condemned by Stalinist justice in the period between 1948 and 1956. This figure is to be compared to the stunning 750,000 people amnestied by Imre Nagy in Hungary in 1953 and this, for a slightly smaller population (approximately nine million in Hungary against approximately thirteen million in Czechoslovakia at that time).[49] The number of executions ordered and carried out by court verdicts reached 178 in the years between 1948 and 1954 in Czechoslovakia, but 500 in Hungary in the same period (not including war criminals).[50] As far as democracy was concerned, neither Romania nor Bulgaria could boast about their democratic past, but this did not prevent these countries from experiencing a level of repression akin to a bloodbath under the communist rule.[51]

Although I had a chance in the 1990s to ask Karel Kaplan how he had arrived at his famous statement on the "greater Czechoslovak terror," he told me that he could not remember precisely. After carefully reconstructing his historical theses of the time, my interpretation is that it was the result of a very simple calculation: the Rajk show-trial in Hungary (1949) resulted in three executions, whereas the Dodze (Albania, 1949) and Kostov (Bulgaria, 1949) show-trials resulted in one each, i.e., five in all for this year 1949. Back in Czechoslovakia, the Milada Horáková 1950 show-trial alone almost equalled this "score," since four defendants were hanged.

We can thus read Kaplan's statement again: "In Czechoslovakia, the great show-trials began in 1950, at a time when they were already over elsewhere. ... That is why the first judicial sentences already led to almost as many dead as the trials in all the other People's Democracies put together in 1949." Although technically not wrong, this remark evidently is of little significance for the entire Stalinist terror period, for the whole of East Central Europe. The "great show-trials" might have been "almost over elsewhere," but what about smaller trials? Trials of noncommunists? Repression carried out without trials?

As we have hinted already, both Czechoslovak democrats in exile and reform communists were eager to measure and advertise their share of suffering within the Eastern Bloc out of a sense of moral failure at having misled the country in and after 1948. Presenting a global figure, the reform communists additionally claimed, would accelerate the political rehabilitations. This objective is of course legitimate, but one might argue that other countries joined in on this project of extensive rehabilitations without being so obsessed with computations of a "global," collective figure. In fact, Poland and Hungary had rehabilitated most of their victims of Stalinism, tens of thousands of people, already in 1956, twelve years before the Czechoslovaks. The issue appears to have been moral and political, rather than judicial.

Behind the Figures: Historians' Aims After the 1956 Disaster

I argue here that the hidden purpose of this "terror figures" claim was to justify why no popular revolt of much scope took place in the 1950s in Czechoslovakia, especially not in 1956. Not only did the Czechoslovak population not offer any support to their neighbors in 1956, it acted as a Stalinist buffer between Poland and Hungary, actively preventing the two countries from helping each other. As Czech intellectual Petr Pithart remarked, if all three countries had risen simultaneously against their Communist rulers, history might have taken a different course.[52] In place of a glorious contribution to the 1956 revolutionary wave, the Czechoslovaks were only noticed for their passivity, to the Western observers' dismay and considerable irritation. One journalist even spoke of the "moral treason" of a people "who had made the best of the Soviet domination as it had of the Nazi occupation," concluding that Prague was the "last bastion of Stalinism."[53]

In the United States, the National Security Council was very disappointed. Whereas it had asserted, as late as July 1956, that the Czechoslovak's "relatively long and successful practice of parliamentary democracy between the wars, coupled with a highly conscious cultivation of the late-won right of national self-determination, renders its accomodation to dictatorship and alien institutions psychologically difficult,"[54] the tone had significantly changed by 1958, when a report stated: "Except for a brief period of ferment in the spring of 1956 following the disclosures of the 20th Party Congress in Moscow, Czechoslovakia has been a submissive satellite. The Czech people, although traditionally Western-oriented and anti-communist, have remained largely apathetic under Soviet domination."[55]

The personnel of the US embassy in Prague were equally embittered. Dating back to the early 1950s, they had noted in their "Observations on the Limpness of the Czechoslovak People" [sic] that, "notwithstanding widespread opposition to Communist domination, the citizens of Czechoslovakia do not appear to be stuff from which revolutions are made,"[56] or that "the Czechs seem destined to be kicked around by more aggressive people, and ... are likely to bow their heads and go on working—unwillingly perhaps but nevertheless efficiently and industriously—for any ruthless master who cracks his whip over their heads."[57]

In 1956, after the Hungarian Revolution and the Polish October had proven to leave the Czech population seemingly undisturbed, the American diplomats ironically promoted the return of Santa Claus and the demise of its Soviet version, Father Frost, as the event of the year—or rather as the only event of the year. This symbolic gesture was made by the regime to thank the population for its support during the revolutionary days in Hungary and Poland.[58]

That is why in 1968, it was morally convenient to attribute the passivity of the 1950s to an exceptionally harsh repression, itself allegedly an attack on Czechoslovakia's democratic traditions. The logical circle was now complete and the nation's honor was safe. The absence of resistance in Czechoslovakia in 1956 remained an unsolved mystery for many more decades.

Conclusion: The Legitimization of a Historical Narrative

Czechoslovakia did not suffer from communist terror more than any other People's Democracy, let alone "more than all the other People's Democracies put together." Our contextualized understanding of the facts has given us a new perspective on this historical narrative of communist Czechoslovakia. The script academically sanctioned in the West was designed to fit certain expectations about the Eastern Bloc (the Soviet Union as the "evil empire") and about Czechoslovakia's "democratic heritage," while the story told in Czechoslovakia was meant to preserve (reform) communism's future as a mobilizing ideology, using and instrumentalizing "democracy" as a core value of Czech culture.

State terror and repression (ordered and directed by Moscow) became the main justification for Czechoslovakia's passivity in the 1950s, while there was little to no reflection on local collaboration and responsibilities, or on the extent of Czechoslovak communism's basis of popular support. Samizdat, tamizdat, exile political literature, and Western scholarship all held to the same line concerning Czechoslovak Stalinist history. Such an intellectual convergence greatly relativizes the Iron Curtain's alleged ideological and political impenetrability.

The consensus on the democratic aspect of Czech culture superseded all other ideological differences. But when seeking inspiration from reform communist historians of the Prague Spring, Western (noncommunist) historians critically failed to take into account and analyze the ideological background, education, and motivation of their Czech counterparts. The latter had a distinct tendency to overemphasize the importance of politics, of the Communist Party, and of communist ideology; on the other hand, they dismissed any social approach to history, any reflection on the troubling amount of popular support enjoyed by the communist regime even in its Stalinist phase, and any consideration of the extent of the population's complicity with, or accommodation to, the communist terror regime. Their disregard for the Czech population's share of responsibility is not only symptomatic of a communist worldview in which politics rule everything and society is a passive object (as opposed to a subject), but it also hides the Prague Spring's supporters' guilty feelings about their own involvement in the Stalinist years, at a time when many of them were young, fanatic Stalinists.[59] To designate Stalin and less than a handful of Czech Stalinists as the sole guilty parties for the terror regime was morally, politically, and professionally convenient.

This "ideological heritage" in the historiography of the 1950s has haunted Czechoslovak studies until today, both in the "West" and in the Czech Republic, and remains insufficiently examined and considered. We still know far too little about the social history of Czechoslovakia under communism, although a few historians are at last trying to address the problem.[60] Quite on the contrary, the post-1989 democracy has resorted to a general explanation of the communist past based on a simplistic version of the totalitarianism theory.[61] This latest national script is standing in direct continuation to the "greater terror" narrative, the only difference being that it establishes no difference anymore between the Stalinists and the reform communists: communists of all denominations are now indistinctly considered as the gravediggers of Czech democracy and the sole parties responsible for the nation's depredation under communism.[62] This situation, which is ideologically no less exacerbated than twenty, thirty, or forty years ago has led social historian Michal Pullmann to claim: "Normalization is still not over in the Czech Republic today."[63]

What is relevant for us in the frame of this volume is that this Czech politicization of recent history proves to have been independent from the East-West divide both temporally (it took place before and after 1989) and substantively (it was shared and discussed on both sides of the Iron Curtain.) The Czech historical debate was never isolated from the rest of the world and used "pathways and networks along which information and ideas did circulate across the Iron Curtain."[64] In this respect, it can be considered a case of anticipated "cultural globalization."

Notes

1. Kind-Kovács and Labov, introduction. Many thanks to Jessie Labov and Friederike Kind-Kovács for their invaluable editorial comments. This chapter is dedicated to Eva Hahn.
2. See, for instance, the major exhibit "Cold War Modern: Design 1945–1970," which took place at the Victoria and Albert Museum in London, in 2008–2009. For the monumental catalogue, see David Crowley and Jane Pavitt, eds., *Cold War Modern: Design 1945–1970* (London, 2008).
3. See Michal Kopeček, *Hledání straceného smyslu revoluce. Zrod a počátky marxistického reviozionismu ve střední Evropě 1953–1960* [Searching the Lost Meaning of the Revolution: Birth and Development of Marxist Revisionism in Central Europe 1953–1960] (Prague, 2009).
4. For a masterful analysis of *Preuves*, see Pierre Grémion, *Preuves. Une revue européenne à Paris* (Paris, 1989). See also Frances Stonor Saunders, *The Cultural Cold War: The CIA and the World of Arts and Letters* (New York, 2000).
5. "West Wind Over Prague," *News from Behind the Iron Curtain* 2, no. 8 (August 1953): 22.
6. "The Czechoslovak Course," *News from Behind the Iron Curtain* 3, no. 4 (April 1954): 10.
7. And having wholeheartedly admitted that it is easily said, sixty years later.
8. See, for instance, this excellent analysis of the Slánský trial on the basis of a subtly interpreted communist press: Paul Barton, *Prague à l'heure de Moscou* (Paris, 1954). Barton's real name was Jiří Veltruský, a Czech trade unionist who escaped after 1948.
9. Most of the articles published at that date are pejorative. For instance, "Black Bottleneck," *News from Behind the Iron Curtain* 3, no. 3 (March 1954): 3–7; or "Crisis in the Youth Leagues," *News from Behind the Iron Curtain* 4, no. 6 (June 1955): 32–34. "Czechoslovak Balance Sheet" underlined the persistence of grave economic and political problems, while an "apathetic and resisting" people allegedly refused to give any support to the regime. *News from Behind the Iron Curtain* 4, no. 5 (May 1955): 14.
10. Jacques Semelin, *La liberté au bout des ondes* (Paris, 1997): 43.
11. Ibid., 43–45.
12. Up to 30 million dollars a year. See ibid., 44. See also Sig Mickelson, *America's Other Voices: Radio Free Europe and Radio Liberty* (New York, 1983): 26.

13. See Muriel Blaive, *Une déstalinisation manquée. Tchécoslovaquie 1956* (Brussels, 2005): 179–83.
14. Robert T. Holt, *Radio Free Europe* (Minneapolis, 1958): 154.
15. Ibid., 240.
16. Ibid. See also the testimony of two arrested workers in the documentary film *1956: A Missed Opportunity or the Return of Santa-Claus to Czechoslovakia*, Muriel Blaive (French Center for Research in Social Sciences/Czech Television, 1996).
17. Muriel Blaive, *Une déstalinisation manquée*, 157.
18. See, for instance, Miklós Molnár, *De Béla Kun à János Kádár* (Paris, 1987): 234. Chancellor Adenauer even launched an inquiry into RFE's behavior (which did not conclude, however, that it had acted dishonorably).
19. Justine Faure, *L'ami américain. La Tchécoslovaquie enjeu de la diplomatie américaine* (Paris, 2004).
20. See "Těsnopisecká zpráva o 95. schůzi Národního shromáždění republiky Československé v Praze ve čtvrtek dne 11. března 1948" (shorthand notes on the ninety-fifth meeting of the Czechoslovak National Assembly in Prague, Thursday, 11 March 1948), in *Těsnopisecké zprávy o schůzích Národního shromáždění republiky Československé. Schůze 80-96* (Od 29. října 1947 do 11. března 1948) (Prague, 1948): 2–3.
21. This was apparent, for instance, in the title of Ferdinand Peroutka's pamphlet *Byl Edvard Beneš vinen?* [Was Edvard Beneš guilty?] (Paris, 1950).
22. Ivo Duchacek, "A 'Loyal' Satellite: The Case of Czechoslovakia," in *The Satellites in Eastern Europe*, ed. Henry L. Roberts (Philadelphia, 1958): 116.
23. Ibid., 115.
24. Ibid., 120.
25. Ibid., 119.
26. For lack of space we will not expand this point here. For more on this, see the chapter "The Democratic Heritage: From the KSČ to the Czech Society" in Blaive, *Une déstalinisation manquée*, 69–86.
27. Marie-Élizabeth Ducreux, "Entre catholicisme et protestantisme: l'identité tchèque, " *Le Débat* 59 (March–April 1990): 113.
28. See, for instance, this thick volume (682 pages) with the significant title *The Czechoslovak Contribution to World Culture* (The Hague, 1964). It was edited by Miloslav Rechcígl in precisely the anticommunist spirit that interests us here.
29. Eduard Taborsky, *Communism in Czechoslovakia 1948–1960* (Princeton, 1961), 603.
30. Ibid., 77.
31. Ibid., 606.
32. See Eduard Goldstücker in the film *1956: A Missed Opportunity or the Return of Santa-Claus to Czechoslovakia*.
33. See the accounts of Josef Smrkovský, Karel Kaplan, Jiří Pelikán, and Pierre Daix, in "Klement Gottwald: from personal sympathy to collective forgiveness," in Blaive, *Une destalinisation manquée*, 223–28. This presentation of Gottwald as a "poor devil" still prevails in Czech historiography today. See, for instance, Pavel Kosatík and Karel Kaplan, *Gottwaldovi muži* [Gottwald's Men] (Prague, 2004), 10–77.
34. Karel Kaplan, "Zamyšlení nad politickými procesy," *Nová mysl* no. 6 (1968): 765–94; *Nová mysl* no. 7 (1968): 906–40; *Nová mysl* no. 8 (1968): 1054–78.
35. Karel Kaplan, "Zamyšlení nad politickými procesy," *Nová mysl*, no. 7 (1968): 915.
36. Antonín Kratochvil, *Žaluji I. Stalinská justice v Československu* [I Accuse: Stalinist Justice in Czechoslovakia] (Prague, 1990): 5. First published Munich, 1973.
37. Jacques Rupnik, *Histoire du parti communiste tchécoslovaque* (Paris, 1981), 15.
38. Otto Ulč, *Politics in Czechoslovakia* (San Fransisco, 1974), 85.

39. Karel Bartošek, "Europe centrale et du Sud-Est," in *Le livre noir du communisme*, ed. Stéphane Courtois (Paris, 1997), 444.
40. Václav Vrabec, "Mlýn a mlynáři" (The Mill and the Millers), *Reportér*, no. 3 (24–31 July 1968): ii and vi.
41. George Feiwel, *New Economic Patterns in Czechoslovakia* (New York, 1968), 139.
42. Jiří Pelikán, *S'ils me tuent ...* (Paris, 1975), 82.
43. Zdeněk Hejzlar, *Praha ve stínu Stalina a Brežněva* [Prague in Stalin's and Brejnev's Shadow] (Prague, 1991), 34.
44. Barbara Wolfe Jancar, *Czechoslovakia and the Absolute Monopoly of Power* (New York, 1971): 100.
45. Ibid., 100.
46. George Hodos, *Show Trials* (New York, 1987), 74.
47. Gordon Skilling, *Czechoslovakia's Interrupted Revolution* (Princeton, 1976), 824–25.
48. František August and David Rees, *Red Star Over Prague* (London, 1984): xvii.
49. For a detailed analysis of the available figures, see Blaive, *Une déstalinisation manquée*, 184–206.
50. Jiří Pelikán, ed., *The Czechoslovak Political Trials, 1950–1954* (London, 1971), 56. See also János Rainer and Zoltán Lux, eds., *Hungary 1944–1953: Internet History Book* (Budapest, 2003); and http://www.rev.hu/history_of_45/ora3/index.htm (accessed 19 August 2011).
51. See the chapters on all those countries in Courtois, *Le livre noir du communisme*.
52. Muriel Blaive, "Rok 1956: Proč byli Češi tak hodní? Rozhovor s Petrem Pithartem" [Why Did the Czechs Remain so Quiet? Interview With Petr Pithart], *Listy* 26, no. 6 (1996): 42.
53. Archives of the French Embassy in Prague, Box 353, 20–21, TS 5.3.1, Dépêche de Berne n°3201, "Attitude du peuple tchécoslovaque," 21 December 1956.
54. National Security Archives—Annex to NSC 568—NSC Staff Study on U.S. Policy Toward the Soviet Satellites in Eastern Europe, 6 July 1956, 29.
55. National Security Archives—Presidential Directives on National Security From Truman to Clinton—National Security Council Report, NSC 5811, 9/5/1958, "U.S. Policy Towards the Soviet Dominated Nations in Eastern Europe," 11.
56. National Archives, Declassified E. O. 11652 or E. O. 12356, LM 85 film 1, Report from Prague, 2 May 1950, "Observations on the Limpness of the Czechoslovak People," 1–2.
57. Ibid.
58. Archives of the Department of State, Report from the American Embassy in Prague, 13 December 1956, File 749.00/10-156, Box 3300, General Records of the Department of State, 1955–1959.
59. Karel Kaplan was quite outspoken about his own shame at having participated in a criminal regime, even if in good faith at a time when he knew nothing of the "socialist excesses"—the euphemism later used to refer to the tortures and arbitrary policy of the Secret Police as sanctioned by the Communist Party in the period from 1948 to 1954. See Karel Kaplan, *Dans les archives du Comité Central* (Paris, 1978). This "confession" was not published in Czech before 2004. See Kosatík and Kaplan, *Gottwaldovi muži*, 310–26.
60. Young Czech historians are now slowly turning to social and cultural history. See, for instance, Michal Pullmann, *Konec experimentu. Přestavba a pád komunismu v Československu* [The End of Experimentation: Perestroika and the Fall of Communism in Czechoslovakia] (Prague, 2011); Petr Roubal, "Politics of Gymnastics: Mass gymnastic displays under communism in Central and Eastern Europe," *Body and Society* 9, no. 2 (2003): 1–25; or Martin Franc, *Řasy, nebo knedlíky? Postoje odborníků na výživu k inovacím a tradicím v české stravě v 50. a 60. letech 20. století* [See-weed or Dumplings? The Attitudes of Nu-

trition Experts on Innovation and Tradition in Czech Cuisine in the 1950s and 1960s] (Prague, 2003). The works in progress of Ondřej Matějka on the collaboration of the protestant church with the regime in the 1950s or of Matěj Spurný on the Roma and on the clash between the regime attempts at integration and the popular (racist) rejection of this minority in the 1950s and 1960s should also be mentioned. See the workshop "The 'French School' of Socio-Histoire du Communisme Meets New Czech Historiography of Czechoslovak Communist Dictatorship," Prague, Faculty of Social Sciences at Charles University, 24 September 2010, organized by Ondřej Matějka.

61. Pavel Kolář and Michal Kopeček, "A difficult quest for new paradigms: Czech historiography after 1989," in *Narratives Unbound: Historical Studies in Post-Communist Eastern Europe,* ed. Sorin Antohi, Balázs Trencsényi, and Péter Apor (Budapest, 2007), 173–248.

62. Muriel Blaive, "La question épineuse de la collaboration dans l'appréciation du passé communiste tchèque : quelques réflexions," in *Le passé au présent: gisements mémoriels et politiques publiques en Europe centrale et orientale,* ed. Pascal Bonnard and Georges Mink (Paris, 2010), 217–30.

63. Josef Chuchma, "Normalizace tu ještě neskončila, tvrdí historik Michal Pullmann" (Normalization here is not over yet, claims historian Michal Pullmann), *iDnes.cz* (online edition of the Czech daily Mladá Fronta Dnes), 5 June 2011, http://zpravy.idnes.cz/normalizace-tu-jeste-neskoncila-tvrdi-historik-michal-pullmann-pw7-/kavarna.aspx?c=A110601_183550_kavarna_chu (accessed 19 August 2011).

64. Kind-Kovács and Labov, introduction.

Chapter 7

Renaissance or Reconstruction?
Intellectual Transfer of Civil Society Discourses
Between Eastern and Western Europe

Agnes Arndt

In recent years, few concepts have attracted as much attention as the term *civil society*. Rediscovered in Polish and other East European dissident circles in the course of the 1970s and 1980s, it has become part and parcel of the academic and political discourse in Europe. At the same time, the reasons why this notion has so quickly become a countermodel to authoritarian communist systems in East-Central Europe and Latin America—let alone the relevance of this concept—have rarely been called into question. Only recently and in the light of the mounting political tensions in Poland and Russia have questions about the renaissance and existence of a separate sphere for civil society surfaced anew. In this context, it becomes increasingly obvious that the phenomenon of civil society has been overrated in both the Eastern and the Western European public sphere, particularly in regard to its political potential and its role in the consolidation of democracies. In fact, the notion *civil society* has in many places proven to be a promise yet to be fulfilled.

This chapter aims at taking a fresh look at this promise as well as at possible explanations for the rise and fall of civil society. Its focus is on the development of a trans-European array of debate on civil society that transcended the Iron Curtain. That is, rather than continuing to characterize civil society as a signal of and key to the transformation process in Eastern Europe, I shall examine the function and relevance of the notion and its synonyms for the development of a transnational discussion and action among European intellectuals. The mechanisms and media of spreading the civil society discourse as developed and tested by samizdat, tamizdat, and exile literature between 1968 and 1989 are thus of particular interest.

Notes for this chapter begin on page 168.

By looking at the creation and reception of one of the key texts written by the democratic opposition in Poland, *New Evolutionism* by Adam Michnik, I shall interpret the rediscovery of civil society as part of an important transfer of ideas during the Cold War period, with a view also to exploring the role of this transfer for what was initially the cultural and eventually the political demise of the division of Europe. It is one of my preassumptions that the renaissance of civil society was not an accident, but the result of a gradual reconstruction, consciously pursued by various actors in different parts of Europe and the United States. I set out to delineate the prerequisites and consequences of this process of reconstruction, which occurred within a network of underground and exile literature.

Civil Society and New Evolutionism

Historians usually regard the essay *Nowy Ewolucjonizm* (*New Evolutionism*),[1] written by the then thirty-year-old Adam Michnik, as one of the key texts associated with the beginning of the discourse on civil society.[2] Written in 1976, the text was based on a lecture Michnik had given at a Paris Colloquium in commemoration of the events of 1956 in Poland and Hungary. The original French version was translated into Polish in 1978 and has been published in various other languages ever since. The text is considered to be one of the most prominent and important programmatic essays produced by the Polish opposition—it is, in short, deemed to be the key text for understanding the discourse of civil society in East Central Europe. Michnik, a historian and, since 1989, editor of the Polish *Gazeta Wyborcza*, discusses the possibilities for reforming the political and social system of the People's Republic of Poland.[3] By reviewing the opportunities of 1956 (when de-Stalinization, the rehabilitation of Gomułka, and the liberalization of culture and politics had simultaneously set in in Poland), he dismisses two ideas that had figured prominently in the 1950s. Upon discarding the notions of Revisionism[4] and the so-called Neo-Positivism,[5] Michnik construes a new, evolutionary program of opposition to the communist regime.[6] The quintessence of his idea is his conviction that independent public opinion, not totalitarian rulers, should be the target group of an evolutionary program.[7] The Party is thus no longer regarded to be the bearer of the future. Rather, Polish society assumes responsibility for its political future by also becoming involved in the humanization of the socialist system. Michnik notes that Polish workers should play a prominent role in this context, as "they have already wrested quite some spectacular concessions from the government."[8] By alluding to the strikes that took place in Polish seaports in 1970 and 1976, he characterizes the workers as the "social group the ruling elite fears the most and to whose pressure it has already yielded."⁹ Pressure as exerted by the workers is therefore an indispensable condition for "an evolution of social life towards democratic forms of governance."¹⁰ The creation of independent and permanent workers unions, committed to the protection and defense of the worker, offers, according to Michnik, the best opportunity to turn *New Evolutionism* into a reality.¹¹ "The incessant fight for reforms and an evolution that leads towards an extension of civil liberties while also guaranteeing the protection of human rights" to Michnik "is the only conceivable strategy for dissidents in East Central Europe."¹²

Michnik's evolutionary concept was well placed in an oppositional way of thinking closely connected to the realities of the communist bloc system—a way of thinking, which, by looking back at the intervention of the Warsaw Pact countries in Prague in 1968, had to accept the Brezhnev doctrine. Jadwiga Staniszkis spoke of a "self-limiting revolution" when characterizing the logic of action of the *Solidarność*.¹³ The addressee of Michnik's idea was the *społeczeństwo* (society), that is, those members of society that could read the text in its Polish, English, and French translations after 1976, when the essay was "circulated" for the second time. Rather than continuing to believe in the ability of the political institutions and the legal system to reform, the author placed his idea of a democratic socialism at the center of society, where civil liberties should be restored, democratic procedures and maxims established, and the foundations of a democratic socialism laid. When using the term *evolutionism*, Michnik not only characterized the phenomenon as a process but also sought to coin a counternotion to the form of political battle that was not at the heart of his thinking: not a violent revolution, but a "long march"¹⁴ should shape this evolutionism, thereby denoting "a gradual, step by step, partial transformation and not the forceful overthrow of an established regime."¹⁵ "It is the duty of the opposition," writes Michnik, "to continually and systematically participate in public life, create political realities through collective action and propose alternative solutions."¹⁶

The term *civil society* is not used in Adam Michnik's text. Therefore, from the point of view of discourse theory, neither its history nor its meaning is reflected. Although the text undoubtedly calls for a transformation of the relationship between state and society (by aiming at a partial democratization of the public and social life in the communist system), it nonetheless fails to explore the relationship between this newly "conscious society" and the economic or private sphere.¹⁷ Society is explicitly and exclusively defined in opposition to the state, in a way that resembles the ethical standards of the debates on human and citizens' rights initialized by the Helsinki process. To relate Michnik's vision to the currently prevalent definitions of civil society in Western Europe and the United States is thus hardly possible. At the same time, important overlaps, particularly regarding the logic of action, can be identified between Michnik's view and an understanding of civil society as, for instance, shaped by Jürgen Kocka. Kocka defines civil society as a space in which patterns of action are generated and turned into social practice. These practices are normatively geared toward tolerance, the appreciation of differences, and pluralism, and are aimed at the balancing of diverging interests through compromise.[18] Compared to this, it becomes clear why Michnik's idea of a gradual reform of the political and social system in Poland from within the center of society was very quickly deemed to be the key program of the democratic opposition in Eastern Europe and the discourse on civil society in Western Europe. But how did this text become so popular? Who took part in this popularization? And what, in fact, was so new about the "New Evolutionism"?

Evolutionism and Socialism

In order to answer these questions, it is necessary to detach the reception and proliferation of the text from an exclusively Polish perspective and to place it in the then-existing transnational web of thoughts, ideas, and discussions in Europe. "The protesting intelligentsia," writes Michnik in 1982, "was looking for the way to its own society via London and Paris—successfully so."[19] The attempts of the Eastern European opposition to cooperate and to engage with one another were faced with various limitations and challenges. Information could only be obtained through underground publications in neighboring countries, while personal contacts were often followed by arrests and prison terms on both sides. Against this background, the intellectual opposition in Warsaw Pact countries was concerned more with mutual avowals of solidarity in the face of state repression than with the exchange of ideas (let alone the development of a joint political program).[20] "Leading Polish, Czech and Hungarian intellectuals," writes Timothy Garton Ash, "meet each other more often in Paris or New York than in Prague or Warsaw. They read their books—if they do so—in English, French or German. Besides a few exceptions their works were not translated into any other languages. Even if they have a common basis, they reached it rather independently from each other."[21]

Despite these adverse circumstances, it became the highest concern of the opposition in the People's Republic of Poland to set up such a common ground. As a result, contacts were established between different oppositional circles in East Central Europe, with the aim of reproducing each other's texts as well as each other's calls for solidarity.[22] They focused on informing the Western European audience about the situation in Eastern Europe, and on the creation of a domestic audience receptive to intellectual debates in Western Europe. The publication and proliferation of the Catholic magazine *Więź*, published by Tadeusz Mazowiecki, is the most illustrative example in this regard.[23] The role of mediator was, however, resumed by those magazines and newspapers that, like the Hungarian *Magyar Füzetek* or the Polish *Kultura*, were edited by emigrants. As points of intersection between East and West, they strongly influenced the thinking of intellectuals like Michnik, and became the key link to a communicative network described by Jan Behrends and Friederike Kind-Kovács as the "international market for dissident ideas."[24] In a way, this was the transnational equivalent of the so-called second circulation in Poland, a critical current that had developed in the Polish underground media and literature in the 1970s and spread beyond Polish borders. The structural origins of a Polish counterpublic[25] to real socialism can be found in this very interaction between samizdat and tamizdat, that is, between the oppositional literature published in the underground and abroad.

Important for the development of the Polish tamizdat were above all the monthly *Kultura*, published in Paris by Jerzy Giedroyc, and *Aneks*, published in London by Alexander Smolar. In both editorial staff offices, the rapprochement between East- and West-European literature and politics played a special role. In Adam Michnik's case, it was in 1978 that *Aneks* first published a Polish version of his *New Evolutionism*.[26] And it was *Kultura*, for which Michnik wrote under the pseudonym Andrzej Zagozda, that connected him with a debate that, since the 1950s, dealt with the idea of evolutionism.

The publishers of *Kultura* had first taken up the idea of evolutionism in 1958,[27] referring to the Revisionists' hope of the evolutionary humanization and democratization of communism in Poland. The emigrant, lawyer, and economist Juliusz Mieroszewski was one of the most prominent advocates of this idea. In 1964, he published his book *Ewolucjonizm*, which was groundbreaking for the political influence of Polish literature in exile. In his book, Mieroszewski presented a sample of political essays that contested Poland's social and geopolitical situation, and raised the question of the possibility of an independent development of communism in Poland. The central essay of his book, titled "Model roku 19??" (Model of the year 19??), made clear what Mieroszewski had previously formulated in the following way: "We do not fight with Marxism, but with the current form of its interpretation."[28] The idea of socialism, which, in his opinion, had degenerated to a totalitarian level, had to be humanized by incessant pressure from below[29] and by the de-Stalinization of East Central Europe "towards new forms of socialism."[30] Mieroszewski believed that only "an ideological thaw"[31] could lead to de-Stalinization and to the democratization of communism, and that it would do so by linking socialism to the idea of freedom—beginning with the freedoms of speech and public criticism. He was convinced that even in a one-party system such democratization would be possible, as long as the party would accept the principle of a plurality of opinions. Democracy for Mieroszewski existed not because of the recognition of a huge number of parties but because of the recognition of a huge number of worldviews within a party. "Socialism has a real possibility to become such a party in Poland,"[32] writes Mieroszewski.

How should this plurality be organized in practice? Mieroszewski advocated that clubs within the party should reflect the divergent opinions and points of view of both its members and the general population and should be represented in an adequate way within the party's executive structure. The club that enjoyed the largest support by the population would form the government. The result would be a legally permitted opposition within the party, and thus, "not a democracy for the enemies of socialism, but a democracy for socialists, in contrast to the dictatorship of a clique, which we have today."[33] "If the unity of the socialist movement should not remain a fiction," he continued, "it must be understood dialectically, meaning that it must be pluralistic to the outside and unitaristic inwards."[34] Mieroszewski, who was persuaded that an imitation of West-European constitutional models would be useless in the Polish case (on account of the divergent historical, political, and geographic conditions), supported in 1964—as Adam Michnik did twelve years later—an evolutionistic interpretation of socialism, which should be supplemented but not substituted by democratic elements. For him this idea should mark the beginning "of an evolution from a forced to an accepted socialism"[35] in East Central Europe.[36]

Socialism in Eastern and Western Europe

In the following years, the draft developed by Juliusz Mieroszewski won substantial influence over the editors of *Kultura*. As a result, the magazine opened its publishing to Western intellectuals and started an interesting international debate on the development of socialism in Europe.[37] According to calculations by Giedroyc and Mieroszewski, only the Left in Western Europe could (1) promote the gradual democratization of Polish socialism, (2) help the Eastern European Left in its intellectual development and its renunciation of the totalitarian elements of their ideology, and (3) persuade the Eastern left of the imperialistic character of the socialist internationalism propagated by the Soviet Union.[38] The byproduct that should result from this process, Giedroyc and Mieroszewski believed, would be a new political and programmatic impulse for socialism in Western Europe. Mieroszewski, who accused the Western Left of a lack of initiatives concerning their programmatic development, hoped that the idea of evolutionism would open an international discussion promoting a socialist union between the Left in Western and Eastern Europe. Their purpose would be to develop a new ideology that should connect the best elements of both socialist traditions. The precondition for such a process, thought the publishers of *Kultura,* would be a common language between Eastern and Western intellectuals that had still to be created. Only within a dialectic relationship would the Polish Revisionists get important assistance from their Western colleagues, and only in this way would both sides contribute together to the genesis of a socialism aimed at "a third way," between a much too weak, liberal, and uncontrollably capitalistic Western democracy and an economically steered party dictatorship.[39]

The evolutionistic idea of *Kultura* had a great influence on the oppositional discourses of Polish intellectuals and the ideas of civil society developed by them. This becomes especially clear when one takes into account the efforts that *Kultura* undertook to find political comrades for its program on both sides of the Iron Curtain. In order to convince the West-European Left of the necessity of intellectual and political cooperation with the East European socialists and to contribute to a change in the geopolitical conditions of the Warsaw Pact, *Kultura,* among other publications, referred to the controversial discourses about anticolonialism explored by French intellectuals in the 1960s. *Kultura*'s authors tried to create a structural resemblance between the colonies striving for independence and the East European countries suffering under Soviet hegemony, trying thus to employ the anticolonial debates for its own purposes.[40] *Kultura*'s attempt to find political coalition partners on the other side of the Iron Curtain leads directly to Michnik and his *New Evolutionism.* By the end of the 1960s, Mieroszewski and Giedroyc tried to get into personal contact with Michnik and his revisionist youth group *Komandosy.*[41] Mieroszewski observed "that even those youngsters, who reject not only communism, but also socialism, are still using socialist categories within discussions about constitutional and social questions because they do not know any others."[42] He also assumed that "these youngsters" could possibly form the core of an oppositional movement that would be accepted and supported by Polish émigrés.[43] In 1982, Michnik described Mieroszewski's role as follows: "It is right and, from today's perspective, easy to state that it was particularly Mieroszewski who succeeded in building an intellectual bridge between the subjective maximalism of emigrants and the excessive objective pessimism of people from the country and in shaping a political idea of the evolutionistic system change that later became the practice of the Polish democratic opposition."[44]

Michnik's conclusion and the fact that he wrote, presented, discussed, and published the key text of his political thinking during his 1976 stay in Paris make clear that the ideas launched during the 1960s by the monthly *Kultura* might not have been unknown to him. The paradigmatic change in relation to his addressees, on the one hand, distinguished Michnik's draft of *Evolutionism* from similar drafts developed by emigrants in London or Paris, but, on the other hand, made him feasible for the opposition in Poland. Michnik, who did not believe in an inner-party development of the system, defined the independent intelligentsia, the workers, and the Catholic population of Poland as carrier groups of his evolutionistic idea. The improvement of social reality toward a democratic socialism needed to emanate from society itself. Michnik believed that this would result in a new, equal relationship between society and the state—independent of any change "from above." This was the innovative aspect in Michnik's text, an idea that detached not only from earlier reform efforts (such as *Revisionism* and *Neo-Positivism*), but both perpetuated and transcended Mieroszewski's *Evolutionism* into the realities of Poland by 1970. Unsurprisingly, Michnik's text has since circulated in international research literature as a nucleus of civil society thinking in Eastern Europe. The origin and dissemination of this idea cannot be explained without looking to the networks of samizdat, tamizdat, and exile literature, all of which spread out over Europe between the 1960s and 80s.

Renaissance and Reconstruction of Civil Society in Europe

While Michnik would have placed his text decidedly in the tradition of European civil society thinking, observers of the transformation process in East Central Europe soon credited him with having opened and reanimated exactly this mental map. "Remarkably," writes Andrew Arato,

> the pioneering works of this revival, those of Kołakowski, Mlynar, Vajda and Michnik in the East, of Habermas, Lefort, Bobbio in the West, and Weffort, Cardoso and O'Donnell in the South, were routed in the same or analogous tradi-

tions of Western or Marxist discourse. For them, a knowledge of Hegel, the young Marx and Gramsci represented living links to the usage of the concept of *civil society*, and the state-society dichotomy that was, in various ways, almost universal in the 19th century but which nearly disappeared in 20th century social and political science or philosophy.[45]

Nevertheless, the scant use of the *civil society* concept in the Polish oppositional discourse, and the opinion of one of the best observers of the Polish transformation process cast a rather different light on this interpretation. Polish émigré Aleksander Smolar writes that the notion of *civil society* that became popular in Eastern Europe had "very little in common" with West-European debates about the past and with the "considerations of Locke, Ferguson, Smith, Hegel, Tocqueville, Marx and Gramsci."[46] "The concept of *civil society*," according to Smolar, came "into the language of the developing opposition under the influence of their contacts with western intellectuals. The idea of *civil society* fascinated for different reasons various circles of the Western, post-Marxist Left, as well as neoconservative groups. Both groups searched in the East for an important ally in ideological fights that were discussed in her own world."[47] Which fights does Smolar mean? And which overlaps, connections, and solutions resulted from these fights for Eastern and Western Europe?

As Ansgar Klein has convincingly argued, the self-criticism of Western intellectuals fulfilled an important interpretative function with respect to the events in Eastern Europe.[48] This self-criticism was initialized by debates about Stalinism and the problematic understanding of liberty written into the core of Marxism.[49] It was in this frame of reference that the "normative contours of East European *civil society* concepts, especially its anti-totalitarian commitment"[50] resonated with intellectuals in the West, who in turn read them against the background of their own "revision of the theory of democracy."[51] Influenced and inspired by Antonio Gramsci, whose thinking was rediscovered and reintroduced to an international audience by intellectuals such as Norberto Bobbio, the Western Left revisited its concepts in the course of the 1970s. In the wake of these changes, the Marxist notion of a bourgeois society was disconnected from its negative connotations and a new view on its relationship to the economy and the state emerged.[52] This new understanding of civil society formed the basis of a democratic-socialist civil society discourse, as promoted by authors such as David Held, John Keane, and Jean Cohen in Western Europe. It was at this point that the ever more vociferous critique of the Western European welfare state set in.[53] As summed up by Klein, the preconditions for the reception of Eastern European antitotalitarian interpretations of civil society among the post–Marxist Left in Western Europe were numerous, "regardless of the differing starting points."[54] Among those preconditions, according to Klein, were "a common intellectual background, characterised by the loss of meaning of Marxism, attempts to avoid the notorious juxtaposition of reform and revolution connected therewith as well as an international critique of the operationability of both the authoritarian and the welfare state."[55] In the end, this was how the dialogue between the East and the West was initialized.

Although historical research and social science still uphold the assumption that civil society was rediscovered in East Central Europe, the emergence of this idea can be only fully understood in the general context of a transnational connection between diverging actors, actions, and interests that date back to the early 1960s. In this framework, ideas were intellectually developed and transnationally communicated before they became part of Michnik's key essay of 1976. Therefore, Polish researchers, who ever since the 1990s sought to contextualize the term *civil society*, rightly underline the difficulty of truly revealing the channels and sources of the term's initial usage in the Polish context. In this view, it is even conceivable "that a certain role was played by an increase of the popularity of the term in the West, though Andrew Arato sees the rebirth of the idea of civil society as a gift received by the West from Eastern Europe and America."[56] Western European intellectuals, such as Jacques Rupnik, Arato, and Keane, had been talking about the renaissance of civil society in East Central Europe since 1979.[57] This underscores the fact that a much more prominent role than was earlier assumed was played by those historians and social scientists, who, motivated by either a personal or research interest, turned toward the transformation process in East Central Europe in the early 1980s, constantly trying to describe and explain it with their own terms and concepts.

It was only with the initialization of this process in Western Europe and American scientific writing that the term was more frequently used in the Polish language. It was only in the 1990s the notion of *civil society* entered Polish academic discourse, key dictionaries, and encyclopedias. This late popularization was accompanied by an increase in international conferences and symposia that became more regular especially after the foundation of the Polish *Solidarność*.[58] *Solidarność* advisors Bronisław Geremek and Tadeusz Mazowiecki became then speakers and contemporary witnesses, using the opportunity to present their interpretation of the democratic change in Poland to a Western audience. It was in this context that the term *civil society* proved to be a descriptive-analytical category apt for capturing the transformation in East Central Europe. Geremek, medievalist and future foreign minister of Poland, argued at a 1989 conference in Castel Gandolfo that civil society is an "empirical and political approach very useful for the analysis of East European societies."[59]

Civil society served not only Polish intellectuals, but also West European and North American participants as a point of convergence for a new perspective on the possibilities of civic engagement, as well as a linguistic link to mediating the many different experiences that plagued the East and the West. Two ways of living, whose most important and distinctive attributes were, until 1989, either democracy or authoritarianism, now joined one another, prompted by the common fascination with the phenomenon of civil society. Having emerged in the part of Europe where citizens' rights to actively engage in politics had for decades been blatantly infringed upon, *Solidarność* showed that it was nonetheless possible to develop a civil society organization able to mobilize and unite some ten million people. The civic engagement in Poland reached a level West European academics failed to explain, despite their years of political and academic work on the phenomenon of bourgeois civil society. Most importantly, however, this was a phenomenon that had the potential to change one's view on one's environment, that is, on the political, economic, and social problems of one's country, while simultaneously yielding a desirable impulse as regards the potential for change. Polish intellectuals such as Geremek were well aware of this effect when writing:

> In America, Solidarity aroused enthusiasm and gained wide support as the only mass anticommunist movement and independent trade union behind the Iron Curtain. Europe was fascinated primarily by the spontaneous organizational power, the authenticity of involvement, and the peculiar climate of brotherhood that characterized Solidarity. One might even say that European opinion was transfixed by the vision of a civil society that Solidarity embodied during its heroic period of 1980–81.[60]

Samizdat, Tamizdat, and the Cultural Demise of the Division of Europe

The late emergence of the term *społeczeństwo obywatelskie* (civil society) in the People's Republic of Poland in the 1980s coincided with the appearance of the first academic publications about the renaissance of civil society in East Central Europe, such as the prominent texts of Arato and Keane.[61] A Polish émigré teaching at Oxford, Zbigniew Pełczyński, published *The State and Civil Society*[62] in 1984, drawing in Hegel's famous distinction between the state and bourgeois society to the contemporary discussion about civil society. Between 1986 and 1987, the first academic project, headed by Tadeusz Płużański of the Polish Academy of Sciences, began looking at the renaissance of the term *civil society* from the point of view of the history of ideas, and was able to refer to West European research. By drawing on the work of Pełczyński, Keane, and Bobbio, Hegel's, Marx's, and Gramsci's notions of *civil society* were analyzed and reconceptualized for civil society in the context of Socialism.[63]

As a consequence, the attempt of the Polish dissidents to look at the conflict between an authoritarian state and society (from the point of view of historical continuity) was connected to a debate that had developed in West and East Central Europe, in the course of the 1980s, and raised the frequency of interactions between the two parts of the continent. The term *civil society*, put briefly, enabled Polish intellectuals to get in touch with this transnational discourse, and to establish a common linguistic ground between East and West European politicians. It committed intellectuals to reform and to catch up with what had been impossible to communicate and achieve before 1989.[64] It was only thanks to this international context and by engaging with the political changes taking place in Poland that the term *civil society* was turned into a prominent, if not the predominant, descriptive and analytical category denoting the social utopias that developed between 1968 and 1989.

Concerning Poland, it was mainly the social practice that generated the rediscovery of the term of *civil society*, because, as Michnik explained, "ideas often emerged during the 'march' and there was hardly ever enough time to turn them into a theory worth generalizing."[65] Until 1989, civil society in Poland referred to a model of social action that had been developed as a social practice in the face of circumstances shaped by real socialism. It had neither a theoretical foundation, nor did it need a consistent definition. "It was enough," says Jerzy Szacki, "to believe that it denoted something completely different from the state."[66] It evolved around a highly normative and morally founded social utopia that both reflected and foiled the historical experience of the region. The very vagueness that it retained for years made it all the easier for large parts of the Polish society to relate and subscribe to it. The historical contextualization and theoretization of civil society, as undertaken by some Polish intellectuals, has to be placed in the context of a transnational intellectual discourse on civil society—a process in which a wide range of motives and actors were involved. This discourse was brought about and facilitated by the interplay of samizdat, tamizdat, and exile literature. At a point in time where a détente between East and West was still inconceivable, this interplay created an international debate, where East Central European experiences of authoritarian regimes and West European considerations about the welfare state came together and began influencing one another. In this way, the term *civil society* became the common denominator of an intersection of shared interests and visions for the future in both Eastern and Western Europe. Regardless of how its relevance is assessed from the contemporary perspective, this intersection and the way in which civil society provided a channel for communication between the East and West remains its most remarkable achievement. To refer to this achievement by further exploring it should be the priority of any political or academic public that claims to be interested and committed to working toward unification and cooperation in Europe.

Notes

1. See Adam Michnik, "Nowy Ewolucjonizm," in *Szanse polskiej Demokracji. Artykuły i eseje* (London, 1984), 77–87. The text was written in 1976 and it was first published in French. See Pierre Kende and Krzysztof Pomian, eds., *1956, Varsovie–Budapest. La deuxième révolution d'Octobre* (Paris, 1978), 201–14.
2. See Jean L. Cohen and Andrew Arato, *Civil Society and Political Theory*, 4th ed. (Cambridge, 1994); Winfried Thaa, *Die Wiedergeburt des Politischen. Zivilgesellschaft und Legitimitätskonflikt in den Revolutionen von 1989* (Opladen, 1996); Helmut Fehr, *Unabhängige Öffentlichkeit und soziale Bewegung. Fallstudien über Bürgerbewegungen in Polen und der DDR* (Opladen, 1996).
3. This was the official name of Poland from 1952 to 1989, during its period of rule by the Polish United Workers' Party (Polska Zjednoczona Partia Robotnicza, or PZPR).
4. *Revisionism*—an idea developed by Polish socialists during the ideological thaw after Stalin's death in the 1950s. Polish revisionists like Leszek Kołakowski, Włodzimierz Brus, and Krzysztof Pomian demanded the democratization of the party structure, the reorganization of the trade unions, and the equality of all members of the Soviet bloc, thus hoping to humanize communism in Poland.
5. Positivism was a Polish oppositional movement during the nineteenth century, influenced by the book *Positive Philosophy*, by the French philosopher Auguste Comte. It believed that an end of the Russian predominance in Poland could not be achieved through a military uprising, but through the reinvigoration of Polish tradition and education. The name *Neo-Positivists* was used in the 1950s for those Polish Catholics, who tried to liberalize and to humanize the Polish communist system without directly opposing it.
6. Adam Michnik, "Nowy Ewolucjonizm," 77–87.
7. Ibid., 84. Also, Adam Michnik, *Ginąć odświętnie,* in *Polskie pytania* (Warsaw, 1993), 233.
8. Michnik, "Nowy Ewolucjonizm," 84.
9. Ibid., 84–85.
10. Ibid., 85.
11. Ibid.
12. Ibid., 83.
13. Jadwiga Staniszkis and Jan T. Gross, eds., *Poland's Self–Limiting Revolution* (Princeton, 1984), 73ff.

14. Adam Michnik, "O oporze," in *Szanse polskiej Demokracji*, 93–109. The text has been published first within the Polish samizdat. See Adam Michnik, "O oporze," in *Krytyka* 13–14 (1983): 3–14.
15. Michnik, "Nowy Ewolucjonizm," 83.
16. Ibid., 86–87.
17. See Cohen and Arato, *Civil Society*, 67, 77, and 78; Winfried Thaa, "Zivilgesellschaft – ein schwieriges Erbe aus Ostmitteleuropa," *Osteuropa* 54 (2004): 204; Timothy Garton Ash, *The Uses of Adversity: Essays on the Fate of Central Europe* (London, 1999), 274; Lech Mażewski, *W objęciach utopii. Polityczno–ideowa analiza dziejów Solidarnośći, 1980–2000* (Toruń, 2001), 149–150; and Jerzy Szacki, *Liberalism after Communism* (Budapest, 1995), 99.
18. See Jürgen Kocka, "Zivilgesellschaft. Zum Konzept und seiner sozialgeschichtlichen Verwendung," in *Neues über Zivilgesellschaft. Aus historisch-sozialwissenschaftlichem Blickwinkel*, ed. Jürgen Kocka et al. (WZB Discussion Paper P 01–801, Berlin 2001), 10–11; and Jürgen Kocka, "Civil Society From a Historical Perspective," *European Review* 12 (2004): 68–69. For a slightly other definition of civil society, see John Keane, *Civil Society: Old Images, New Visions* (Stanford, 1998), 6; Wolfgang Merkel and Hans-Joachim Lauth, "Systemwechsel und Zivilgesellschaft: Welche Zivilgesellschaft braucht die Demokratie," *Aus Politik und Zeitgeschichte* 6–7 (1998): 3ff.
19. Adam Michnik, "Dlaczego nie emigrujesz ... List z Białołęki," in *Szanse polskiej Demokracji*, 17. First published under the pseudonym Andrzej Zagozda in *Kultura* 6 (1982).
20. Jan Józef Lipski, *KOR: A History of the Workers' Defense Committee in Poland, 1976–1981* (Berkeley, 1985), 279–85.
21. Timothy Garton Ash, "Mitteleuropa – aber wo liegt es?" in *Ein Jahrhundert wird abgewählt. Aus den Zentren Mitteleuropas, 1980–1990*, ed. Timothy Garton Ash (Munich, 1990), 224.
22. See, for example, Václav Havel, "Siła bezsilnych," *Krytyka* 2 (1980): 5–62; and Václav Benda, "Równoległa polis," *Krytyka* 2 (1980): 63–71.
23. *Więź* published between 1968 and 1989 several texts of Western European authors, among them Hannah Arendt, Timothy Garton Ash, Wolfgang Borchert, Erich Fromm, Jürgen Habermas, Karl Jaspers, George Orwell, Alain Touraine, Volker Rühe, and Richard von Weizsäcker. See the magazine's archive: http://www.wiez.com.pl (accessed 19 August 2011).
24. Jan Behrends and Friederike Kind, "Vom Untergrund in den Westen. Samizdat, Tamizdat und die Neuerfindung Mitteleuropas in den 80er Jahren," *Archiv für Sozialgeschichte* 45 (2005): 427–48.
25. Gábor T. Rittersporn, Malte Rolf, and Jan C. Behrends, "Von Schichten, Räumen und Sphären: Gibt es eine sowjetische Ordnung von Öffentlichkeiten? Einige Überlegungen in komparativer Absicht," in *Sphären von Öffentlichkeit in Gesellschaften sowjetischen Typs. Zwischen partei-staatlicher Selbstinszenierung und kirchlichen Gegenwelten*, ed. Gábor T. Rittersporn, Malte Rolf, and Jan C. Behrends (Frankfurt am Main, 2003), 408ff.
26. Adam Michnik, *1956: W dwadzieścia lat później – z myślą o przyszłości* (London, 1978).
27. Janusz Korek found out that the idea of evolutionism was known to *Kultura* since 1953, when Juliusz Mieroszewski reviewed a book related to this idea, written by the former communist Isaac Deutsch and titled *Russia after Stalin*. See Janusz Korek, *Paradoksy Paryskiej »Kultury«. Ewolucja myśli politycznej w latach 1947–1980*

(Stockholm, 1998), 167. For the subsequent reception of the idea within *Kultura*, see Krzysztof Kopczyński, *Przed przystankiem Niepodległośći*. *Paryska »Kultura« i kraj w latach 1980–1989* (Warsaw, 1990), 7; and Andrzej Friszke, "Jerzego Giedroycia praca u podstaw, 1956–1976," in *Spotkania z paryską Kulturą*, ed. Zdzisław Kudelski (Warsaw, 1995), 14ff.
28. Juliusz Mieroszewski, "Strona bierna," in *Ewolucjonizm* (Paris, 1964), 48.
29. Juliusz Mieroszewski, "Model roku 19??" in *Ewolucjonizm*, 49–57.
30. Ibid., 53.
31. Ibid., 55.
32 Ibid., 56.
33. Ibid.
34. Ibid.
35. Ibid.
36. See Juliusz Mieroszewski, "Refleksje Ćwierćwiecza," in *Ewolucjonizm*, 16.
37. For the reception of Mieroszewski in Poland, see Włodzimierz Mart, "O esejach Juliusza Mieroszewskiego," *Krytyka* 1 (1978): 116; and Rafał Habielski, "Gra możliwości. O pisarstwie Juliusza Mieroszewskiego," in *Myśl polityczna na wygnaniu. Publicyści i politycy polskiej emigracji powojennej*, ed. Andrzej Friszke (Warsaw, 1995), 139, 141, 155.
38. Korek, *Paradoksy*, 167–68.
39. Ibid., 168–69.
40 Ibid., 170.
41. *Komandosy* was a group of young Poles, founded by Adam Michnik and other students in 1964 at the University of Warsaw. The group was oriented toward the humanization of the communist system in Poland and it was mainly influenced by revisionist intellectuals like Leszek Kołakowski. See Stefani Sonntag, "Rola Komandosów w ruchu studentckim 1968 roku," in *Studia i materiały z dziejów opozycji i oporu społecznego*, ed. Łukasz Kamiński (Wrocław, 2000), 54–65.
42. See Juliusz Mieroszewski, *Rozmowy z młodymi*, quoted in Korek, *Paradoksy*, 281.
43. Korek, *Paradoksy*, 279.
44. Michnik, "Dlaczego," 18; and Adam Michnik, "Różne głosy – z dziennika więziennego," in *Diabeł naszego czasu* (Warsaw, 1995), 62–63. First published in *Kultura* 5 (1986) and *Krytyka* 22 (1987).
45. Andrew Arato, "The Rise, Decline and Reconstruction of the Concept of Civil Society, and Directions for Future Research," in *Civil Society, Political Society, Democracy*, ed. Adolf Bibič and Gigi Graziano (Ljubljana, 1994), 3.
46. Aleksander Smolar, "Przygody społeczeństwa obywatelskiego," in *Idee a urządzanie świata społecznego. Księga jubileuszowa dla Jerzego Szackiego*, ed. Ewa Nowicka and Michał Chałubiński (Warsaw, 1999), 387.
47 Ibid.
48. Ansger Klein, *Der Diskurs der Zivilgesellschaft. Politische Hintergründe und demokratietheoretische Folgerungen* (Opladen, 2003), 97ff. See also Cohen and Arato, *Civil Society*, 16 and 71.
49. Klein, *Diskurs*, 254ff.
50. Ibid., 97 and 254ff.
51. Ibid., 19.
52. Norberto Bobbio, "Gramsci and the Concept of Civil Society," in *Civil Society and the State. New European Perspectives*, ed. John Keane (London, 1998), 73–100.
53. See Klein, *Diskurs*, 82; and Cohen and Arato, *Civil Society*, 69ff.

54. Klein, *Diskurs*, 116.
55. See Klein, *Diskurs*, 82; and Cohen and Arato, *Civil Society*, 69ff.
56. Szacki, *Liberalism*, 92.
57. Jacques Rupnik, "Dissent in Poland, 1968–78: The End of Revisionism and the Rebirth of the Civil Society," in *Opposition in Eastern Europe*, ed. Rudolf L. Tökés (London, 1979): 60–112. This was one of the first texts that dealt with the rebirth of civil society in Eastern Europe. Only some months later appeared Andrew Arato's "Civil Society against the State: Poland 1980–1981," *Telos* 47 (1981): 23–47. Michnik's first use of the term *civil society* can be dated to the same time. See Adam Michnik, "Minął rok," in *Szanse polskiej Demokracji*, 69–74.
58. See conferences such as the *Castelgandolfo-Talks* about civil society, organized by Pope Johannes Paul II in Rome, in 1989; the *93. Bergedorfer Gesprächskreis*, organized by the Körber Stiftung between 13 and 14 July 1991 at the Bellevue Castle in Berlin; and the conference titled *The Idea of a Civil Society*, organized at the National Humanities Center in Research Triangle Park, North Carolina from 21 to 23 November 1991. The most important Polish contributions to these conferences were: Bronisław Geremek, "Civil Society and the Present Age," in *The Idea of a Civil Society*, ed. Bronisław Geremek et al. (North Carolina, 1992), 11–18 (it was republished under the title "Civil Society Then and Now," *Journal of Democracy* 3, no. 2 [1992]: 3–12); Bronisław Geremek, "Die Civil Society gegen den Kommunismus: Polens Botschaft," in *Europa und die Civil Society. Castel Gandolfo–Gespräche 1989*, ed. Krzysztof Michalski (Stuttgart, 1991), 257–72; and Tadeusz Mazowiecki, "Einige Thesen über die Schwierigkeiten beim Aufbau der Demokratie," in *93. Bergedorfer Gesprächskreis am 13. und 14. Juli 1991 im Schloss Bellevue* (Berlin, 1991), 10–19.
59. Geremek, "Civil Society," 257.
60. Geremek, "Civil Society Then and Now," 11.
61. See Andrew Arato, "Empire versus Civil Society: Poland 1981–82," *Telos* 50 (1981–82): 19–48; Andrew Arato, "Civil Society against the State: Poland 1980–1981," *Telos* 47 (1981): 23–47; and John Keane, *Democracy and Civil Society* (London, 1998).
62. Zbigniew A. Pełczyński, ed., *The State and Civil Society: Studies in Hegel's Political Philosophy* (Cambridge, 1984).
63. Tadeusz Płużański, "Społeczeństwo obywatelskie sozjalizmu jako przedmot badań," *Studia Filozoficzne* 262 (1987): 3–6.
64. The deficit of a communicative basis between Eastern and Western Europe has been illustrated and analyzed very clearly by John Keane in his text "In the Heart of Europe," in *Democracy and Civil Society*, 194ff.
65. Adam Michnik, *Takie czasy ... Rzecz o kompromisie* (London, 1985), 1.
66. Jerzy Szacki, *Ani książę, ani kupiec – obywatel. Idea społeczeństwa obywatelskiego w myśli współczesnej* (Cracow, 1997), 22.

Section III

Transforming Modes and Practices of Alternative Culture

Chapter 8

THE BARDS OF MAGNITIZDAT
An Aesthetic Political History of Russian Underground Recordings

Brian A. Horne

> *But here we are by choice,*
> *Hey, this is our world!*
> *Have we gone mad,*
> *To come up in a minefield?!*
> *"And now, no more hysterics!*
> *We'll plow into the shore!"*
> *Said the commander.*
>
> *Save our souls!*
> *We're raving from asphyxiation.*
> *Save our souls, hurry to us!*
> *Hear us on dry land -*
> *Our SOS grows fainter, fainter,*
> *And horror cuts our souls in half!*
>
> —Vladimir Vysotsky[1]

In August 2000, the Russian nuclear submarine Kursk sank to the bottom of the Barents Sea with its entire crew of 118 sailors. Those who had survived the accidental torpedo detonation that had crippled the ship had been trapped inside the submarine without light or heat, waiting for rescue as the Kursk slowly flooded. By the time rescue divers finally reached the ship nine days after the accident, the entire crew had drowned.[2] Upon confirmation that none had survived, the Russian television network NTV paid tribute to the crew by listing each of their names and replaying footage of the Kursk going to sea, accompanied by a recording of a 1967 song

---

Notes for this chapter begin on page 187.

entitled "Spasite Nashi Dushi" (Save Our Souls), which tells the story of a doomed submarine crew whose crazed captain has ordered the boat to surface in a minefield. The newspaper *Izvestia* began its editorial on the disaster with a verse from the same song, adding: "The tragedy of the Kursk is the tragedy of our soul. Of our dream. Of our new life. Of our new power. Of the new future of Russia. Once again it's turned out that our life means nothing. How painful, how offensive."[3]

The link between this Soviet era song and this catastrophic example of Russia's post-Soviet "new life" reveals an ironic and paradoxical relationship between experiences of the Russian past, present, and future. "Save Our Souls" is an example of Russian "bardic songs" (*bardovskie pesni*)—or, more generally, of "authorial song" (*avtorskaia pesnya*)"[4]—a musical-poetic art form that emerged in the late 1950s in Moscow and, though officially censored, became phenomenally popular through illegally duplicated and traded home audiotape recordings, known as *magnitizdat* (from the words *magnitofon*, or tape recorder, and *samizdat*, Russian for self-publishing). When "Save Our Souls" was originally performed and illegally published, it was widely regarded as a bitter and thinly veiled indictment of the government, casting the Soviet leadership as a crazed captain leading the Russian soul on a suicidal course.

Today, the bards' songs for which Russians once risked imprisonment have become everyday commodities, mementos of Soviet life, and objects of Russian cultural heritage, sold in hundreds of street kiosks, broadcast on bard-themed radio stations and celebrated at bard festivals. As former contraband of the Soviet era, this music's ubiquitous commercial availability is now a daily reminder of the extreme and pervasive effects of commoditization that have accompanied Russia's economic and political transformations. The controversial bards of the Soviet age are now publicly valorized as Russian heroes with memorials, museums, and annual tribute concerts, as in the case of the most famous bard, Vladimir Vysotsky, who wrote and performed "Save Our Souls."[5] But how did the boldest political protest songs of the past become suitable as tributes to fallen Russian soldiers?

I argue that the history of Russian bards' songs and their transition from illegal underground circulation in the early 1960s to officially sanctioned marketplaces, electronic media, and live venues today cannot—indeed, must not—be reduced to a familiar story of triumphant liberation from Soviet censorship and authority, as many scholars of Russian bardic music and magnitizdat during the Cold War have argued. By relying on an overly simple model of communication and by presuming a stable, repressed dissident message, these accounts fail to recognize the generative effects of the interplay between texts and the unofficial media through which they circulate: effects that manifest themselves not only at the level of explicit political claims, but also at the level of aesthetics.

I propose that an examination of the contemporary cultural and political significance of Russian bards' songs must trace the intricate and historically contingent aesthetic associations of the genre and unofficial media. In short, I want to consider seriously the possibility that the most salient connection between Vysotsky's "Save Our Souls" and the Kursk disaster is not the image of a sinking submarine, but the association between the "sound" of the recorded song itself and a set of specific cultural images, identities, and sociopolitical relationships. In order to understand *bardovskaia pesnia* this way, we need to examine critically the aesthetics of music and politics, as well as the semiotics of audio technologies and underground circulation.

Reexamining the history of Russian bards' songs and their underground circulation allows us to reflect critically upon the Cold War's influence on our studies of media and technology. Throughout this chapter, I will draw upon observations and analyses of magnitizdat and *bardovskaia pesnia* that appeared in Western Europe and the United States during the 1970s and 1980s, both for their insights about this combination of medium and music, and for their value as artifacts of Cold War scholarship and reporting.

A History of Russian Bards, Guitars, and Tape Recorders

Like many musical genres, Russian bardic song has its own origin stories. According to most scholarly and popular accounts published in the United States and Western Europe, the development of *bardovskaia pesnia* as a distinct genre can be traced to a particular time, place, and person: novelist and poet Bulat Okudzhava, performing his poetry to the accompaniment of a Russian seven-stringed guitar (often called a "Gypsy" guitar) in the late 1950s in Moscow. Other poets rapidly adopted the style, singing their poems to small audiences in private apartments.[6]

Beyond the addition of singing and self-accompaniment on guitar, accounts of what formally distinguished this new genre from other poetic and musical art forms vary greatly—so much so that they often contradict one another. Some contend that Russian bardic songs' most identifying and essential trait is their subversive, oppositional, and dissentious lyrics.[7] Others argue that in form and content the bards' poetry "tacitly supports the official [Soviet] line. ... There are no songs that are antipatriotic. ... [A] very noticeable absence of anything that oversteps even narrowly drawn limits of linguistic propriety."[8] For every claim that the music's chord structures and melodies are inherited from so-called criminal songs (*blatnye pesni*), cruel romances (*zhestokie romansy*), or Gypsy songs (*tsyganskie pesni*), another argues that the only stylistic constant among bards' songs is individual artistic freedom and formal diversity.[9]

Despite these diverging and contradictory formal descriptions, there are a few points of general consensus. First, *bardovskaia pesnia* is characterized by narrative poems sung by their authors—the so-called bards (who were, at the time of the genre's emergence, predominantly men). Second, the songs are usually perceived as musically primitive and amateurish. Gerald Stanton Smith, whose 1984 book *Songs to Seven Strings* remains the only English language book devoted entirely to Russian bards' songs, claims that the bards' guitar playing is not so much musical as it is "functional" as a support structure for the author's poems. Smith adds: "Over this primitive rhythmic and harmonic scaffolding stretches the voice. It is manifestly untrained, tonally poor, uncertain in pitch, at times employing crude recitative or ordinary speech—but always enunciating clearly. In guitar poetry[10] the words are always more important than the music."[11]

Finally, central to nearly every account of *bardovskaia pesnia*'s history published outside Russia is a discussion of the official criticism and censorship to which the music was subjected. As early as 1962, the bards and their songs began to draw public and direct censure from Soviet officials such as Leonid Ilyichev, chairman of the Ideological Commission of the Soviet Communist Party's Central Committee. Speaking to a meeting of writers, artists, and cinema professionals, Ilyichev remarked:

> The Soviet people love songs. But side by side with songs with a broad civic motif, songs which sing the spiritual beauty of the Soviet people and reveal the purity of their souls, there are also vulgar songs which are designed to appeal to low and cheap tastes. In particular, the verses and songs of the gifted poet [Bulat] Okudzhava are out of keeping with the entire structure of our life. Their whole intonation—everything about them—does not come from purity of the soul but from spiritual breakdown.[12]

Throughout the 1960s and 1970s, most of the bards' songs were denied official publication in any form, especially as audio recordings.[13] This new form of music would have remained confined to live performances in small, private spaces, according to these accounts, if not for the intervention of a particular technology: the reel-to-reel audiotape recorder, or *magnitofon*.

The first home tape recorders became widely available in the Soviet Union in 1960. Despite their unreliability and poor sound quality, tape recorders were a relatively cheap and effective audio reproduction technology, and were adopted by Russians at a remarkable pace. From 1960 to 1965, the number of tape recorders manufactured per year in the USSR multiplied from 128,000 to almost 500,000. By 1970, the production rate had climbed to more than one million in a single year.[14] Before the tape recorder, the most common way for Russians to obtain bootleg recordings of forbidden jazz music or Gypsy songs had involved carving phonograph tracks into used X-ray plates—a clever technique which became known as music "on ribs" (*na rebrakh*) or "on bones" (*na kostiakh*).[15] With audiotape, sound recordings of every kind could circulate outside the Soviet government's official publishing monopoly and censorial authority. Compared to other types of samizdat publication and duplication technologies, magnitizdat demanded minimal time and labor. Since the process of tape duplication was necessarily automated, each copy's acoustic fidelity was dependent upon the quality of the equipment rather than the attention or skill of a typist.

The guitar bards quickly took advantage of audiotape as a way to share and publish their work. Home recordings of guitar poetry began circulating on a large scale in Moscow and Leningrad, distributed through informal networks, achieving popularity first among university students, academic elites, and the intelligentsia, in particular.[16] Alexei Yurchak observes that "the songs of *bardy* (bards) ... became the first nonofficial cultural objects reproduced in millions of copies and dispersed all over the country by means of home tape-recording."[17] But how do we account for the unprecedented popularity of the bards and the scale of their music's illegal circulation?

To scholars in Western Europe and the United States, the convergence of *bardovskaia pesnia* and magnitizdat seemed no coincidence. Bards' songs appeared formally oriented toward individual expression, and against official Soviet artistic ideals. Likewise, audiotape duplication was perceived as a private, decentralized, and uncensorable medium for transmitting any recordable sound. Thus, guitar-bard music and magnitizdat seemed linked by their common and essential opposition to the structure of Soviet ideology and governance. Rosette C. Lamont, writing in *World Literature Review* in 1979, echoes much of the scholarship to date on the Russian bards' and their relationship to magnitizdat when she concludes that "the poems of the bards are a kind of 'general language,' a universal tongue such as the one envisioned by Pablo Neruda, so that poetic expression and the profound life of the country are made one. The bards have put themselves beyond the reach of censorship and, by doing so, have also triumphed over the mechanisms of self-censorship."[18] Note that Lamont sees the bards themselves escaping censorship entirely—not just censorship of their songs or of audio recordings: the medium and the artistic content combine as matching liberatory instruments for propelling subjects "beyond censorship" at the level of individual psychology and state institutions simultaneously. Gene Sosin, in his essay "Magnitizdat: Uncensored Songs of Dissent," elaborates on how these corresponding technological and artistic innovations provide access to authentic, humanistic values:

> It is not difficult to understand why the singing poets of magnitizdat are so popular with Soviet citizens on many levels of the society. Their songs articulate genuine attitudes, moods, and aspirations, in contrast to the synthetic output of official cultural media. "Authenticity, spontaneity, and human spirit" fill the works of [the most famous guitar bards] Okudzhava, Galich, Vysotsky, and others who, aided by the sophisticated artifacts of the technological-electronic era, are perpetuating the age-old quest for truth and justice so characteristic of Russian folklore, poetry, and song.[19]

I do not deny the phenomenal popularity and cultural significance of *bardovskaia pesnia* and the remarkable scale of its dissemination via magnitizdat. I do, however, wish to critically reexamine these accounts and their assertion that the link between this music and medium was one of anti-Soviet "free speech." After all, censorship and "free speech" are not the universal binary opposites that they appeared to be during the Cold War.[20] Furthermore, most bards' songs (and indeed, most magnitizdat recordings) were not explicitly dissident. These accounts fail to adequately explain *why* the genre was so heavily censored.

For example, Vladimir Frumkin, a musicologist who worked with the Soviet music publisher *Muzyka* before emigrating from the USSR in 1974, provides something of "an insider's story" of how the bards were subjected to Soviet censorship. His account thoroughly complicates the dominant portrayal of *bardovskaia pesnia* as "uncensored songs of dissent" in diametric opposition to the Soviet state. Frumkin had attempted to publish officially a selection of Bulat Okudzhava's songs in the late 1960s and early 1970s with *Muzyka*'s initial agreement, but the collection was never published.[21] According to Frumkin, it was not the overt political content of Okudzhava's lyrics that prevented the project's final approval. "After all," he explains, "most of the lyrics in the collection had already appeared in print, so from an ideological standpoint *Muzyka* was safely insured from risk."[22] The real problem, according to Frumkin, was a more elusive quality of Okudzhava's performances:

> There was something else which alarmed the officials at the music publishing house and the Union of Soviet Composers: the very nature of Okudzhava's music, the way it actually sounded. What was frightening was its simplicity, unpretentiousness and sincerity. To the official Soviet ear it was like some unknown tongue, a strange and alien accent, although Okudzhava's songs are deeply rooted in Russian culture. The poet had found a new voice by turn-

ing to a forgotten (or half-forgotten) old one. His melodies revived the motifs of Russia's once popular waltzes and marches, student songs, love songs and Russian gypsy songs, street ditties, and the tunes of organ grinders—motifs far removed from the conventional sound of Soviet official songs.[23]

What *exactly* is the quality that Frumkin is attempting to describe? What is it about *bardovskaia pesnia*'s *sound*—not the explicit political statements in its lyrics, but the constellations of nonverbal signs in bards' songs that index political claims, relationships, and identities—that provoked such reactions? I propose that we may find clues to the answer if we seriously examine Frumkin's remark about Okudzhava's music being "deeply rooted in Russian culture," the bard's revival of "Russian gypsy songs," as well as the bards' aesthetic sensibility of musical amateurishness and roughness.

Russian Bards and Gypsy Guitars

In their attempts to formally analyze *bardovskaia pesnia* in terms of a finite list of essential poetic and musical features, Cold War–era scholars failed to consider—or more often, dismissed as peripherally significant—the ways in which the genre is *performatively* constituted: that is, how aspects of the very performance of these songs served to reference other kinds of performances and performers, other genres, roles, and identities. Performative qualities often appear to be aesthetic "extras," of secondary importance to a genre's structural and formal characteristics, when in fact they are often essential to the genre's coherence. (For example: "punk rock" is as much defined by its distinctive chord structures as by its performers' dressing and acting as "punks.") Therefore, in order to understand the aesthetics of bards' songs and their mode of circulation, we first need to know more about what it means to assume the role of a "bard."

To begin: why are the Russian guitar-poets called "bards?" The conventional answer is that this title is a reference to medieval or classical bardic traditions.[24] Lamont asserts that the only reason these guitar-playing poets became known as "bards" is because their songs spread by means of audiotape, and thus "allowed for a return to the ancient tradition of oral/aural literature."[25] More specifically, Lamont focuses upon one song by Aleksandr Galich, "We're No Worse than Horace," and interprets this reference to Horace as a claim to an artistic and political lineage from the Roman poet to Galich and his fellow guitar bards. "No flatterer of power, Horace guarded the independence of his views, uncorrupted by imperial Rome. Since the Soviet Union is often compared to the latter both by those within and those outside, the parallel is far from gratuitous," Lamont explains. In short, the connection between Russian bards and Horace is, again, bold individualism and political dissent.

There are, however, other significant cultural associations evoked by the figure of a "bard" singing narrative lyrics while playing a seven-stringed guitar, also known as a "Gypsy guitar." The term *Gypsy guitar* is something of a misnomer, as the instrument's invention is usually attributed to a Russian. Nonetheless, the seven-stringed guitar and its distinctive sound (with all seven strings tuned to an open G major chord) have served as metonyms for *Gypsy* music and culture in Russian art and literature since the nineteenth century.[26]

The figure of the singing Gypsy, in turn, is tied to literary, theatrical, and musical representations of raw, authentic expression, and, notably, to authentic Russianness. Alaina Lemon explains that the popularity of "Gypsy choirs" in the nineteenth and early twentieth centuries in Russia can be attributed in large part to the notion that the Gypsies' "repertoires contained half-forgotten Russian folk songs and ballads embellished in a 'Gypsy style.'"[27] In this way, Gypsies often appear in Russian literature, music, and film as representing a kind of archive for and reflection of authentic Russian culture and history.[28] By taking up the stereotypic instrument and style of Gypsies, the Russian guitar-poets were evoking images of local bardic traditions, and inflecting their music and performances with qualities of "rawness" and "authenticity" associated with Gypsy identity in Russian literature and music.

But it is important to recognize that the Russian bards did not merely play the roles of Gypsy singers, but *played with* that role by creatively adapting and expanding upon its prototypic texts. For example: more than a few bards' songs include in their refrains, "Once more, and again and again (*Eshche raz, eshche mnogo mnogo raz*)," a phrase borrowed from a stereotypic, nineteenth century Gypsy song called "Dve Gitary" (Two Guitars).[29] The seven-stringed guitar, not surprisingly, figures prominently in the song's lyrics, and is even addressed by the singer as a *podruga semistrunnaia* (seven-stringed friend). In other words, these Gypsy-style songs explicitly reference the Gypsy guitars used in their own performance. Building on the work of Michael Silverstein, Richard Bauman, and Charles Briggs have argued that these sorts of "metapragmatic," reflexive references can be powerful devices for linking texts to one another and establishing a sense of continuity within and across genres.[30]

Like Gypsy songs, bards' songs also include frequent references to the seven-stringed guitars used in their performance. The bards, however, took this metapragmatic referencing one step further, and often sang about the tape recorders and their songs' circulation on magnitizdat. For example, the song that Lamont cites, Galich's "We're No Worse than Horace," concludes with just such a reference: "There's no stalls, no boxes, no balcony / No claque going crazy in fits / There's just a 'Iauza' type tape recorder / That's all! But it's enough!"[31] In this way, the bards established the same kind of metapragmatic connection between their songs and magnitizdat as that between Gypsy songs and Gypsy guitars.

This is one manner in which *bardovskaia pesnia* and its illicit circulation became tied to notions of authenticity and Russianness: through verbal and nonverbal performative, metapragmatic references to Gypsiness. I wish to emphasize that this link is not "anti-Soviet"—as posited by previous scholars of bards' songs—so much as it is ante-Soviet, evoking pre-Soviet Russian musical and literary traditions.

It is also worth noting that the very circulation of bards' songs though magnitizdat could easily be regarded as sharing the stereotypic qualities of the Gypsy: the songs are nomadic and uncontrolled. And there is another way in which the "sound" of bards' songs appeared to resemble the qualities of magnitizdat: through the particular meanings ascribed to the "noise" in bards' songs.

The Semiotics of Noise and "Underground" Circulation

In addition to Gypsy song, *bardovskaia pesnia* is usually regarded as closely related to *blatnaia pesnia*, a genre whose name is difficult to translate precisely, but is often rendered in English as "criminal song." These "criminal songs" typically tell stories of betrayal, revenge, and the underworld life. Bards' songs frequently include the uses of *blatnoi zhargon* (criminal slang) and *blatnye khordy* (the so-called criminal chords, A minor, C minor, and D minor, which are most closely associated with *blatnaia pesnia*), which have been interpreted by Western European and American scholars as another way for bards to demonstrate their opposition to the Soviet state and its laws through symbolic association with "criminal songs."[32]

"Criminal song" is, however, not quite adequate as a translation. The difficulty in translating the term *blatnaia pesnia* arises from the stem *blat*, a word of somewhat contested etymology that entered the Russian lexicon sometime before 1917 and denoted petty crime. Beginning in the NEP period—the "New Economic Policy" of limited markets and private enterprise in the Soviet Union from 1921 to 1929—*blat* took on a second meaning: the word came to refer to the everyday, informal, interpersonal exchanges, and favors that people used to cope with Soviet shortages and distribution failures. It is during this same period that *blatnaia pesnia* seems to have flourished.[33] This means that the association between Russian bards' songs and "criminal songs" is not one strictly oriented toward crime and *against* Soviet law, but rather, toward the informal exchanges and underground practices that emerged "in the cracks" of the Soviet system, so to speak. In this case, could there be aesthetic associations between bards' songs and the *blat*-networks of informal exchange through which their audiotape recordings circulated?

As mentioned above, discussions of magnitizdat recordings invariably include the low quality and unreliability of the tape recorders, as well as the background noises that "clutter" most home recordings. For *bardovskaia pesnia*'s listeners, these noises became an "integral part of the ambience of *magnitizdat*."[34] Some authors writing about bards' songs regard such sounds as another aspect of the genre's overall "amateurish" sensibility, but the majority discount these distortions and ambient sounds as an unfortunate side effect of an unreliable recording technology, detracting from the music's quality.

Implicit in such descriptions is a particular model of communication: a given message or signal transmitted from sender to receiver with greater or lesser quality, depending on the medium. From this perspective, an inverse relationship existed between the scale of magnitizdat transmissions and the fidelity with which those messages were transmitted: every new copy extended a song's range, but the quality of that copy was necessarily degraded. But what if we consider a more dialogic model of communication in which medium and message are mutually constitutive? And what if we consider noise as more than just destructive signal interference, and instead examine it as a potentially constructive signal in itself? Noise is not, after all, the absence of signs, as our common sense might predispose us to think.

With this in mind, I want to illustrate how magnitizdat's low sonic fidelity counterintuitively became an index of high political fidelity. As with the typos and blurred edges of paper samizdat carbon copies, the audible distortions of magnitizdat tapes did much more than obscure the transmitted "message": these noises could be recognized as tangible proof of public circulation outside official Soviet channels. Each successive act of copying marked the text with distortions that were readable as artifacts of illicit circulation. At the same time, the background noises—the coughs, the clinking glasses, and creaking chairs regarded as integral to the "sound" of magnitizdat—became signifiers of the informal public spaces and domestic conditions in which the songs were performed and about which the bards sang.[35]

In the terms of C. S. Peirce's semiotic theory, magnitizdat's noises operate for listeners as an "indexical icon," a signifier that represents its signified object simultaneously by likeness and by causality or continuity. Photographs are familiar examples for us of indexical icons and the force of their two modes of signification: the image on my passport photo can serve as a particularly powerful proof of identification because it not only "looks" like me (i.e., shares my visual qualities), but was produced by light reflected from my face onto the surface of the film (i.e., is causally linked to me).[36] In the same way, the noises on magnitizdat recordings of bards' songs are indexically iconic of the music's underground circulation: listeners recognized that the noises were caused by the physical circumstances of their production, duplication, and circulation; and they "sounded" raw, spontaneous, *blatnoi*, and unofficial. Thus, the "sound" of Russian bards' songs—an aesthetic encompassing noise, roughness, and amateurishness—became associated with and reinforced by the medium and informal networks through which it circulated.

The significance of noise and roughness in Russian bards' songs persists today, as does much of the popularity of the guitar bards (especially among Russian émigrés). For example: in a ceremony at Truman College in Chicago on 23 January 2003, a large bas-relief of Vladimir Vysotsky was unveiled in honor of the sixty-fifth anniversary of the bard's birth. The event was attended by dozens of Russian expatriates and local Russian print and television media. Anna Zaigraeva, a Russian emigrant and contributor to the Official Vladimir Vysotsky Foundation website, was asked by Truman College to comment on Vladimir Vysotsky's music and magnitizdat in general. Zaigraeva said, "There are clearer recordings available now, thanks to the advances in digital music and the release of several private studio recordings, but the old static-ridden recordings still hold more appeal for me. In a lot of his songs, static even seems to bring out an extra level of feeling. It's as if Vysotsky is desperately trying to be heard over a howling storm."[37]

Conclusion: Toward an Aesthetic Political History

In this chapter, I have demonstrated that by viewing Russian bards' songs and magnitizdat as corresponding artistic and technological forms of "free speech" opposed to Soviet governance, Western European and American scholars failed to recognize a set of key cultural and political associations that were established and reinforced by the interplay of the genre and medium. This misrecognition has lasting implications for contemporary studies of texts and genres that previously circulated by samizdat. If bards' songs were simply "uncensored songs of dissent," as these authors maintain, then the juxtaposition of Vysotsky's "Save Our Souls" and the Kursk disaster would seem inappropriate, if not perverse. If, however, we understand the song's aesthetic associations to pre-Soviet images of the Russian Soul, and to the unofficial, intimate political and social relationships through which the music circulated during the Soviet era, then we can recognize how "Save Our Souls" resonated with the feelings of loss and injury to the Russian soul evoked by the event.

The fact that so many scholars either failed to observe or discounted the significance of the aesthetic links between *bardovskaia pesnia,* magnitizdat, sociopolitical relationships, and cultural notions of identification raises significant questions about the impact of polarizing Cold War ideologies of absolute "freedom" and "censorship" on the development of theories of media. As I have suggested in this chapter, the claim that "dissident media," by virtue of their inherent properties, allow for the distribution of "free" dissenting messages in structural opposition to dominant media, is based upon an implicit technological determinism and an overly simple and static model of communication in which senders, receivers, messages, and media may be treated as relatively autonomous objects.[38] Such models continue to influence contemporary analyses of mass media and their effects: consider the kinds of popular and scholarly claims made about the democratizing effects of the Internet and its peer-to-peer structure.

As the example of bards' songs and their circulation on magnitizdat illustrates, the meanings and social effects of particular media are not based upon inherent technological properties but upon specific social, cultural, and historical contingencies. The influence of these contingencies is difficult, if not impossible, to detect if one examines only the formal properties of media and the explicit, denotative content of their messages. Thus, we need to pay special attention to the interconnections between nonverbal signs and elaborated political claims and positions over time or, in my own terms, to the aesthetic political history of unofficial media. Furthermore, I have suggested that some of the most salient interconnections of this sort involve signs, which may not even appear as components of the signals people produce and receive. Noises and distortions are simultaneously stealthy and powerful aesthetic components: stealthy because they reside in a kind of aesthetic blind spot, often appearing to be outside of or as interference with intended signals; powerful because they may be experienced as nonarbitrary artifacts of the physical circumstances of their production and circulation.

I wish to emphasize that noises in underground recordings cannot be assumed to have the same associations even when produced under similar historical and cultural conditions. For example, the music and recordings of the Prague rock band, the Plastic People of the Universe (PPU), might seem initially to share the same quality of "noisiness" as that of Russian bards' songs. Like the Russian bards, the Plastic People of the Universe were prominent symbols of unofficial and underground culture beginning in the 1960s and their recordings circulated largely through magnitizdat. And certainly the music of the PPU came to be associated with both the band's underground status and a kind of noise. But as Tony Mitchell points out, the noise of the PPU's performances and audio recordings referenced a set of values quite distinct from those of the Russian bards of the same historical period: The dissonance of the PPU was far more directly related to the aesthetics and political ideals of psychedelic rock bands and "the libertarian hippie music of California of the 1960s."[39]

I offer this brief discussion of the contrasting role of noise in the PPU's music not to discourage the comparative studies of such political aesthetic histories, but rather to highlight the danger of reproducing the same kinds of problems that I have attempted to criticize in previous analyses of underground performances, texts, and circulation. The reason to (re)examine critically and rigorously the politics of noise in samizdat is the same reason they have been dismissed: they appear at first glance (or first audition) as an undifferentiated category of unintentional nonsignals. Even when noises are determined strictly by the material properties of recording technologies and modes of production and circulation, the meanings ascribed to them are always socially and historically contingent. Unless we examine the culturally specific histories of how media and politics "look," "sound," and "feel," we cannot even distinguish signal from noise in our studies of samizdat.

Notes

1. The Russian original:
    Но здесь мы на воле,
    Ведь это наш мир!
    Свихнулись мы, что ли,
    Всплывать в минном поле?!
    "А ну, без истерик!
    Мы врежемся в берег!"
    Сказал командир.

    Спасите наши души!
    Мы бредим от удушья.
    Спасите наши души, спешите к нам!
    Услышьте нас на суше -
    Наш SOS все глуше, глуше,
    И ужас режет души напополам!

    Vladimir Vysotsky, "Spasite Nashi Dushi" [Save Our Souls]. Lyrics from http://kulichki.com/vv/pesni/uxodim-pod-vodu-v.html (accessed 19 August 2011) and translated by

the author, with reference to Nellie Tkach's translation at http://www.kulichki.com/vv/eng/songs/tkach.html#save_our_souls (accessed 19 August 2011).
2. David Filipov, "Rescue drama ends in grief: Russia admits falling short on sub mission, airs names of crew," *Boston Globe,* 22 August 2000, A1.
3. Douglas Herbert, "Kursk fiasco trains spotlight on Russia's soul," *CNN,* 23 August 2000, http://www.cnn.com/2000/WORLD/europe/08/22/russia.suffering/ (accessed 19 August 2011).
4. There is some disagreement about whether the terms *bardovskaia pesnia* and *avtorskaia pesnia* are interchangeable, whether one is a subgenre of the other, or whether these labels apply to completely different kinds of music. I have no desire to enter this debate in this essay, but I have chosen to use the term *bardovskaia pesnia* here because I have found in my ethnographic research that most Russians with whom I discuss my research seem to suggest that this term best reflects my object of study.
5. A yearly concert honoring Vladimir Vysotsky, held in Moscow on the day of his death, 25 July, was titled "Save Our Souls."
6. Vladimir Frumkin, "Liberating the Tone of Russian Speech: Reflections on Soviet Magnitizdat," in *The Soviet Union and the Challenge of the Future. Volume 3: Ideology, Culture, and Nationality,* ed. Alexander Shtromas and Morton A. Kaplan (New York, 1989), 277–98.
7. See Rosette C. Lamont, "Horace's Heirs: Beyond Censorship in the Soviet Songs of the Magnitizdat," *World Literature Today* (Spring 1979): 220–27; and Gene Sosin, "Magnitizdat: Uncensored Songs of Dissent," in *Dissent in the USSR: Politics, Ideology, and People,* ed. Rudolf L. Tökés (Baltimore, 1975), 277–300.
8. Gerald Stanton Smith, *Songs to Seven Strings: Russian Guitar Poetry and Soviet "Mass Song"* (Bloomington, 1984), 110.
9. Ibid., 220. I do not propose to settle in this chapter the question of exactly what *bardovskaia pesnia* is or is not. Rather, I wish to call attention to the manner in which each of these various and divergent descriptions are deployed to the same ends. According to each account published outside Russia, the genre's fundamental qualities (whatever they may be) are described as boldly resistant, cleverly dissident, and ultimately opposed to Soviet oppression.
10. Smith uses the term *guitar poetry* as an English gloss for *avtorskaia pesnia, bardovskaia pesnia,* and *gitarnaia poeziia* in order to emphasize what he regards as the primary significance of poetry over music in the genre.
11. Smith, *Songs to Seven Strings,* 97.
12. Sosin, "Magnitizdat: Uncensored Songs of Dissent," 282.
13. See Frumkin, "Liberating the Tone of Russian Speech."
14. See Smith, *Songs to Seven Strings,* 97; and Alexei Yurchak, "Gagarin and the Rave Kids: Transforming Power, Identity, and Aesthetics in the Post-Soviet Night Life," in *Consuming Russia: Popular Culture, Sex, and Society since Gorbachev,* ed. Adele Marie Barker (Durham, 1999), 83.
15. Sosin, "Magnitizdat: Uncensored Songs of Dissent," 276; Yurchak, "Gagarin and the Rave Kids," 82.
16. See Frumkin, "Liberating the Tone of Russian Speech;" Smith, *Songs to Seven Strings;* and Sosin, "Magnitizdat: Uncensored Songs of Dissent."
17. Yurchak, "Gagarin and the Rave Kids," 83.
18. Lamont, "Horace's Heirs," 226.
19. Sosin, "Magnitizdat: Uncensored Songs of Dissent," 309.
20. Dominic Boyer, "Censorship as a Vocation: The Institutions, Practices, and Cultural Logic of Media Control in the German Democratic Republic," *Comparative Studies in Society and History* 45, no. 3 (2003): 511–45.

21. Frumkin, "Liberating the Tone of Russian Speech."
22. Ibid., 286.
23. Ibid., 287.
24. Ibid., 278.
25. Lamont, "Horace's Heirs," 220–21.
26. Alaina Lemon, *Between Two Fires: Gypsy Performance and Romani Memory from Pushkin to Post-Socialism* (Durham, 2000), 43, 155. Please note that I am using the term *Gypsy* to refer to a Russian stereotypic cultural image, and not to any group of people, such as the Roma, who are often identified in terms of that stereotype.
27. Ibid., 41.
28. Dale Pesman, *Russia and Soul: An Exploration* (Ithaca, 2000), 87.
29. Smith, *Songs to Seven Strings*, 60–63.
30. Richard Briggs and Charles Bauman, "Genre, Intertextuality, and Social Power," *Journal of Linguistic Anthropology* 2, no. 2 (1992): 131–72; Michael Silverstein, "Metapragmatic Discourse and Metapragmatic Function," in *Reflexive Language: Reported Speech and Metapragmatics*, ed. J. A. Lucy (Cambridge, 1992), 33–58.
31. Smith, *Songs to Seven Strings*, 207.
32. Lamont, "Horace's Heirs."
33. Alena Ledeneva, *Russia's Economy of Favours: Blat, Networking and Informal Exchange* (Cambridge, 1998), 12–13; Smith, *Songs to Seven Strings*, 70.
34. Smith, *Songs to Seven Strings*, 98.
35. For an account of the development of such an informal public sphere in Russia in the 1960s and 1970s, see Elena Zdravomyslova, "The Café Saigon *Tusovka*: One Segment of the Informal-public Sphere of Late-Soviet Society," in *Biographical Research in Eastern Europe: Altered Lives and Broken Biographies*, ed. Robin Humphrey, Robert Miller, and Elena Zdravomyslova (Burlington, 2003): 141–77.
36. For a good discussion of how indexical icons serve to establish or reinforce relationships among observers, representations, and things represented, see Michael Silverstein, "Whorfianism and the Linguistic Imagination of Nationality," in *Regimes of language: ideologies, polities, and identities*, ed. P. V. Kroskrity (Santa Fe, 2000): 85–138.
37. Truman College, Truman College honors Vladimir Vysotsky, http://web.archive.org/web/20030202183548/http://www.trumancollege.cc/news/fullstory.php?StoryID=78 (accessed 26 August 2011).
38. Serguei Oushakine argues that scholars of Soviet dissidence have misrecognized samizdat as a covert discursive field in complete and diametric opposition to dominant and official Soviet discourse and politics. Building on Foucauldian theories of power, discourse, and resistance, Oushakine urges us to reconceptualize dissent through samizdat as a process of "mimetic resistance" from within—rather than outside—the dominant symbolic field. See Serguei Oushakine, "The Terrifying Mimicry of Samizdat," *Public Culture* 13, no. 2: 191–214.
39. Tony Mitchel, "Mixing Pop and Politics: Rock Music in Czechoslovakia before and after the Velvet Revolution," *Popular Music* 11, no. 2 (1992): 195.

Chapter 9

WRITING ABOUT APPARENTLY NONEXISTENT ART
The Tamizdat Journal *A-Ja* and Russian Unofficial Arts in the 1970s and 1980s

Valentina Parisi

> When I was a child, I used to look at cows in the fields. One very hot day all the cows were laying on the ground and eating grass, only one of them was standing. When she got tired and lay down on the grass, another one immediately stood up, a little unwillingly, actually. The cattleman explained me that it was a kind of instinct, so as not to be surprised by the wolf. I was the cow who stood up.
>
> —Igor' Shelkovskij[1]

In the second half of the 1970s, tamizdat gradually emerged as the most relevant channel in the cross-cultural exchange of ideas between Eastern and Western Europe, as well as across the Atlantic, and thus considerably redefined the uniqueness of samizdat as the only medium of uncensored intellectual production in the USSR. While in the 1950s and 1960s, the circulation of texts was generally oriented from East toward West (so works that for several reasons could not appear in the Gosizdat were sent abroad in order to be published), during the 1970s, the cultural transfer became less one-sided and implied a West-East axis as well. Uncensored manuscripts often came back to the motherland in a typographical, and therefore less ephemeral shape courtesy of several publishing houses founded by Russian émigrés in the West. Even *Chronicle of Current Events*, possibly the most representative unofficial publication of the late 1960s and early 1970s, circulated in the USSR during the second half of the 1970s more frequently as a Western reprint (by the Alexander Herzen Foundation in

---

Notes for this chapter begin on page 201.

Amsterdam and later by Khronika Press in New York) rather than in its samizdat original shape.

At the same time, the well-established contacts between a part of Soviet *intelligencija* and Western journalists, scholars, and diplomats (who smuggled both samizdat texts abroad and tamizdat or Western publications in the USSR) made possible a reversible circulation of texts and ideas that deeply influenced the development and self-definition of Soviet alternative culture during the second half of the 1970s. Examining the case of the tamizdat art review *A-Ja* and against the predominant interpretation of self-publishing activity in local terms, I will argue that the existence of transnational networks had its consequences on the "compensative role" that samizdat had played from the 1960s in relation to the official cultural industry. Until its disappearing at the end of the 1980s, samizdat had been providing the unofficial author with restricted but highly cooperative groups of readers, thus helping the reaffirmation and perpetuation of neglected cultural heritage. Because the practice of self-publishing acquired in the 1970s an international character, thanks to the Third wave of emigration, tamizdat gradually began to compete with samizdat in the transfer of texts that were unavailable to the reader in a published form. Especially in Moscow, writers preferred to send their works abroad, instead of publishing them in samizdat limited editions, as the Leningrad poet and samizdat editor Viktor Krivulin pointed out already at the beginning of the 1980s, according to Boris Ostanin and Aleksandr Kobak's report:

> A few years ago Viktor Krivulin stated that Samizdat journals were very likely to come soon to an end and based his prediction on what was happening at that time in Moscow, where nobody was interested anymore in such a unfashionable issue like Samizdat, since everyone preferred to send his texts for publication abroad, to Ann Arbor or to "A-Ja". Beside this, according to him, the media on which McLuhan had focused his attention were also on the verge of being replaced by new ones. Following events did not contradict Krivulin's prediction, nor confirmed it. It is a fact that in Moscow just a few short-run journals exist and many authors would rather publish their works abroad.[2]

In Search of a Mirror

An excellent example of the ever increasing role played by tamizdat by the end of the 1970s should be recognized in the already mentioned Russian art review, *A-Ja*, published in Paris from 1979 to 1987, thanks to the efforts of its editor-in-chief, the sculptor Igor' Shelkovskij, who left the Soviet Union in 1976, moved to France, and settled in Elancourt. The seven issues of the dual-language journal (Russian and English) were entirely devoted to the situation of Russian unofficial visual arts[3] and mostly published materials that were smuggled from the USSR by the artists, who enthusiastically met Shelkovskij's proposal to contribute to the new review with articles, texts, and photographs of their own works. *A-Ja* was an autonomous initiative taken by Shelkovskij and the photographer Aleksandr Sidorov, who headed the Moscow editorial board. Furthermore, it is worth noting that *A-Ja* was partly financed by some Western supporters, such as the Paris gallerist Dina Vierny, who in May 1973 had already organized an exhibition of five Soviet artists,[4] and the Swiss businessman Jack Melkonian.[5] In accordance with the intentions of its founders, *A-Ja* helped to spread Soviet unofficial art abroad so as to overcome the complete isolation in which nonconformist artists found themselves at the end of the 1970s. Although the articles published in *A-Ja* were mostly written by art critics and theoreticians (such as Boris Groys, Margarita and Viktor Tupicyn, Vitalij Pacjukov and Evgenij Barabanov), it is unquestionable that such an exhaustive survey on Soviet unofficial visual arts would not have been possible without the contributions of the artists themselves, who sent Shelkovskij a wide array of materials that today represents the largest source of information about the independent cultural milieu in Moscow and Saint Petersburg.[6] As the conceptual artist Igor' Makarevich remarked in a short article about the journal, *A-Ja* was founded by artists who wanted to be critically evaluated.[7]

In fact, between 1977 and 1979, Moscow was, in spite of its heterogeneous and extremely interesting cultural life, without an independent art critic who could appreciate the relevance of these experiments that so unprecedentedly outdistanced socialist realism. Consequently, artists used to turn themselves into theoreticians, describing their own artworks and reflecting on them in order to break the silence that surrounded them. Because of the impossibility of showing their work in public spaces, artists could only rely on the opinions of relatives and friends, as they were denied access to any professional audience. Exhibitions in private apartments and performances organized within circles of friends were the only occasions unofficial artists had to learn how their art impacted the public. Nevertheless, they were perfectly aware of the necessity to have a critical account of their creative practice as compared to the latest tendencies in international contemporary art. In a recent interview, Shelkovskij has conveyed such a desire for a broader resonance recurring to a peculiar, "female" metaphor:

> An artist can't stand to be completely unrecognized. He needs the colleagues' and viewers' opinion, their reaction to his creative work. During those years our journal replaced exhibitions that couldn't take place for political reasons. We didn't know each other, every little group was totally isolated from each

other, an artist didn't know what a colleague living on the next street did. Our journal began to put them together, so that it was possible to compare them. Beside this, an artist seems to consider the reproduction of his own work on a journal as a sort of self-examination, a chance to look at himself from the without. An artist needs publications as much as a woman needs the mirror.[8]

During the seven years of its often troubled existence, *A-Ja* put up with the deficiencies of the situation for artists in the USSR and, at the same time, provided authors with the rare opportunity for a "mirroring effect," which contributed to redefining their status as well as their self-perception. As Igor' Makarevich explained, "before *A-Ja* Russian intellectual art was based on kitchen talks and discussion clubs in ateliers and in private spaces. In the magazine we were confronted with an objective phenomenon: the art process was channelled into a textual space that marked the difference between internal and objective perception. It was a sort of miracle to see your own work printed on glossy paper."[9]

After publication, every artwork enters a new space, detaching itself from the *realia* of its own creation to join the realm of reception and interpretation. Moreover, Soviet unofficial artists could not actually see Western art and were able to form opinions about it only through access to the reproductions of art journals, which scholars, journalists, and diplomats smuggled into the country.[10] Seeing their own work published in *A-Ja*, these Soviet artists began instinctively to associate themselves with the West. As Makarevich pointed out, *A-Ja* represented "a new step in our self-estimation and self-cognition." By reflecting themselves through the tamizdat review's "mirror," Soviet unofficial art began to rethink its status and emerge progressively from apparent nonexistence.

Filling the Gap

In order to achieve this documentary goal, the new journal had to give an account of as many different trends in as lucid and balanced a way as possible and offer a general view of what used to be Soviet unofficial art in Brezhnev's time and thereafter. The all-inclusive title (*a* and *ja* are respectively the first and the last letters of the Russian alphabet) reflects the programmatically pluralistic character of the review. As Shelkovskij pointed out in an interview, "We wanted to cover as many artists as possible. ... *A-Ja* had to be a crossroad, a meeting place of the most different movements and groups."[11] Focusing on widely different phenomena—from conceptual art in Moscow to metaphysical paintings by Mikhail Shvarzman, from the colorful and irreverent "New Wave" of Apt-Art to Francisco Infante's Land Art—Shelkovskij's journal imposed a certain order on the chaotic network of ideas fluttering in the air from the late 1970s to the beginning of Gorbachev's *perestrojka,* leading to the first systematization of Soviet unofficial art.

From the very beginning, all participants agreed with the ethical principles of the journal: to avoid evaluative or glorifying articles, to accent information, and to write less about the artists themselves, and more about the ideas their art developed. In this way, *A-Ja* provided Russian artists, art historians, and critics with a common analytical language—something that already existed in Europe and America, but was still absent in the USSR. In this respect, Shelkovskij's call for linguistic simplicity and inventiveness is significant: "We tried to convince the authors to stop using the unnecessary foreign words, to strive for a clear and transparent language. It is difficult to write simply about complicated things, but that doesn't mean that one should not try."[12] Moreover, Shelkovskij's journal definitely helped to fill a considerable deficit of tamizdat and samizdat periodical issues till that point: "Nobody (except a very few people) wrote about visual arts in the *samizdat*. And, in fact, how it was possible to write about something that nobody saw before? *A-Ja* offered the possibility to express a critical position about unofficial art and to publish it in a real journal."[13] According to a comment by Shelkovskij,[14] the review was published in various print shops in Paris, possibly the cheapest ones, and also had an editorial board in New York, headed by the artist Alexander Kosolapov. Nevertheless, in spite of its classic tamizdat nature, *A-Ja* in many aspects compares to some samizdat journals that, by the end of the1970s, were typed in the Soviet Union. Regarding the journal's style, it tended to enliven the atmosphere of informal, lively conversations, dialogues, and discussions in private apartments that happened to be a main feature of the underground Soviet culture in the 1960s and 1970s. Unlike most tamizdat journals, *A-Ja* did not publish articles that were already circulating within samizdat channels (with the significant exception of Boris Groys's essay "Moscow Romantic Conceptualism").[15] On the contrary, it tried to bring to life new texts that otherwise would probably not have been written at all, thus stimulating artists' awareness and self-criticism. From this viewpoint, *A-Ja,* like many samizdat journals, may be regarded as an attempt to transpose the occurrences of Soviet oral culture into written form, lending them more cohesion and preserving them from oblivion.[16]

A "Sectarian" Edition?

Shocked to realize that the new journal devoted to Russian visual arts edited in Paris offered no place for old masters such as Il'ya Repin or Isaak

Levitan, the Russian emigrant conservative milieu strongly criticized *A-Ja*. Significantly, the tamizdat journal *Kontinent* reproached Shelkovskij's journal from the very start because of its presumed support for all things "new" in the visual arts.[17] To the blameworthy "novatorstvo" pursued by *A-Ja*, *Kontinent* opposed the right-wing, meritocratic approach of the only other tamizdat journal devoted to art, *Tret'ja volna* (The Third Wave), edited by Aleksandr Glezer in Montgeron near Paris from February 1976 until May 1986:

> In general, artists featured by *Tret'ja volna* are mainly concerned with aestetical judgements in terms of "good versus bad" oppositions. In other words, all these artists simply produce paintings or sculptures, they are not interested in using other materials or approaching the viewer in a new way. They do concentrate all energies on figurative art, in the very sense of the word.[18]

The distance of *Tret'ja volna* and *A-Ja* in the view of Russian artistic world becomes clear if we take into account the controversy, which arose between Glezer and Shelkovskij after *A-Ja* had published L. Bekhtereva's essay "Varianty otrazhenija" (Readings of Reflection). From the pages of the New York newspaper *Novaja Gazeta*, Glezer did not hesitate to define *A-Ja* as a "sectarian edition" (сектантское издание), insofar as it was uncritically supporting the new trend of unofficial art that Groys had defined as "Moscow Romantic Conceptualism." In his polemical answer to Glezer, Shelkovskij protested against Glezer's attempt to present himself as the only referent in the West for Soviet unofficial art, therefore claiming his own right to a different approach to the topic:

> Alexander Glezer's sharp reaction is not surprising at all. His complains are always the same, every time an exhibition, whose curator happens not to be him, opens. Just pay attention to what he said after Venice, Turin, Bellinzona, Bochum, Paris…According to him, all these exhibitions provided the viewer with a distorted image of Soviet unofficial art, as such an image could really exist, being all its secrets disclosed to a single person, i. e. A. Glezer. However, art is not crystallized once and for all, even if someone would rather want it to be so; new trends, new ideas are constantly replacing one each other. Art is dynamic and changeable as much as life and I think that Russian journals should reflect such an evolution. Time will tell us who is right.[19]

Glezer's position was shared by "Slavophilic" critics, who regarded Shelkovskij's journal as the elitist organ of the "Westernizer" conceptual movement, indifferent to the holy war waging against the communist enemy and the need to defend traditional spiritual values. In fact, *A-Ja* did not idealize Russia as an eternal, unchangeable "state of soul," and it did not appeal to an impossible return to the pre-revolutionary past. Furthermore, it did not reject Soviet *realia;* on the contrary it tried to analyze them, in order to point out the specificity of Soviet unofficial art in comparison to the Western contemporary framework.

In its pure and simple design, *A-Ja* clearly resembles the Western art journals that Russian unofficial artists occasionally read in their ateliers in the 1970s. Even the otherwise hostile *Kontinent* remarked on the sophisticated accuracy that characterized the new review and its technical finesse:

> And here is the first edition of *A-Ja*. Novel, elegant, custom tailored in a skilful layout, and clearly the work of a consummately professional printer. This journal is free of the crudeness for which Russian publications are commonly reproached. ... One of the unquestionable merits of *A-Ja* are the parallel English translations of their articles. This is, so to speak, an attempt to break through the window to Europe and tell them in their own language about Russian artist-innovators.[20]

Shelkovskij's bilingual edition, in particular, seems to be quite similar to *Art Flash,* the journal edited in Milan by Giancarlo Politi. Between July and August 1977, *Art Flash* devoted a rich survey[21] to Soviet underground art that probably attracted the attention of the Russian sculptor, who at that time already lived in France. On the other hand, *A-Ja* design also references graphic works of Russian avant-garde—a tradition to which Shelkovskij's journal often appealed, in order to demonstrate its own roots in Russian culture. The typeface for the review's cover, for example, was taken from a reprint of Aleksandr Blok's 1921 book *The Last Days of the Tsarist Regime.*[22]

Consider the content of the review's seven issues. The first edition opens with a photograph taken in Moscow, in Beljaevo (on the southern outskirts of Moscow), on 15 September 1974, when the bulldozers completely destroyed what was meant to be the first "Open-Air Exhibition" organized by unofficial artists and afterward referred to as the "Buldozernaja vystavka" (the Bulldozers' Exhibition).[23] By publishing this black-and-white, out-of-focus picture as a visual epigraph to the new journal, Shelkovskij underlined the ties connecting *A-Ja* to the heroic tradition of unofficial Soviet art, which at that moment was first being discovered in Western Europe and United States thanks to several large exhibitions in Washington, London, Paris, and Venice in 1976 and 1977.[24] Beside this picture, there is Boris Groys's aforementioned essay, which should be regarded as a milestone in the conceptualization of aesthetic boundaries that was then emerging in Moscow. "Moscow Romantic Conceptualism" was probably the first attempt to define a Soviet cultural phenomenon and its specificity without polemical overtones toward Western ideological framework. While official Soviet critics continued to attack abstract painting, writing articles with titles like "How Can They Call That a 'Painting?'" and "The Bourgeoisie and Her Avant-Garde,"[25] Groys tried to analyze the most recent experiences of the Moscow underground scene, relating them to such influential Western tendencies as conceptual, minimal, earth, and process art. As he made clear a few years ago, Groys adopted the term *Conceptualism* to help fill the aesthetic gap between Soviet and Western culture: "Actually, I felt for quite a long time a kind of frustration toward Russian art, because I had the impression that Russian artists (it doesn't matter if they were capable or not) were not able to synchronize their creative practice with the international one. They seemed to live in another time, not at all at the same time in which things took place and this got on my nerves."[26] In his article, Groys questioned the extent to which the already-classic categories of Conceptual Art (dematerialization of the art object[27] or de-emphasis on its physical aspect, endless permutation of the piece's parts instead of the presupposition of its uniqueness, accent on linguistic description, withdrawal from demiurgic ambitions) could fit Soviet unofficial art and its "romantic," timeless atmosphere. He therefore succeeded in reconnecting much of the Moscow underground scene to the discourse of international contemporary art, laying the premise for Russian unofficial art's positive evaluation between the late 1980s and the early 1990s.

Between West and East

To provide Western and émigré viewers with otherwise hard to obtain information about Russian "underground, apparently non-existent art"[28] was surely Shelkovskij's main purpose in founding *A-Ja*. The section "Masterskaja" (In the Atelier) offered a comprehensive view of the *terra abscondita* of Soviet unofficial art, pursuing the same self-representational, pseudo-archival goals of many samizdat publications in that period—for instance, the four MANI files, dating from February 1981 to 1982,[29] or the artist book *Po masterskim* (Across the Ateliers), edited in the winter of 1983 by Georgij Kizeval'ter and Vadim Zakharov.[30] Beyond this, *A-Ja* thoroughly documents the existence of Russian artists living in the West during the so-called Third Wave of emigration. In connection to this, we should note Aleksandr Kosolapov's article "A Russian Artist on the Exhibition of Jasper Johns,"[31] based on a questionnaire to Russian unofficial artists who moved to the "Big Apple" (with questions like: "Which artists have you discovered in New York?" and "In which New York gallery would you like to have your exhibition?"),[32] an interview with Joseph Beuys by Bakchanyan and Anatolij Ur in Ronald Feldman's gallery in New York and Rimma,[33] and Valerij Gerlovin's report on Jean Brown's Dada and Fluxus collection in Massachusetts.[34] All these texts reflect an attempt to join the new cultural milieu and to describe it from the "external," independent point of view of a Soviet unofficial artist. The discussion with Beuys especially points out how often misunderstandings arose between Russian emigrants—who suddenly discovered that the Western "Free World of the Arts" was entirely beholden to the rules of the market[35]—and artists like Beuys, who struggled against Capital from *within* capitalistic society and took advantage of its institutions in order to achieve his personal goals. At the same time, of course, the relationship with Western art also contained plenty of aesthetic self-identification and solidarity. A clear example of fruitful interaction with the American context is given by the curatorial activity of the Gerlovins who in 1981 organized the exhibition "Russian Samizdat Art" at the Franklin Furnace in New York.[36] In one of their contributions to *A-Ja,* they underlined how much the "ephemeral and, in consequence of this, not commercial art objects"[37] they had seen in Jean Brown's house had in common with several artifacts connected to samizdat practice, for instance, handmade booklets and experiments in visual poetry. On the other hand, opinions Russian artists generally shared about the native country and its old-fashioned representational strategies were a bit mocking. For example, Vagrich Bakchanyan answered the question "Your attitude toward modern Russian Art?" with the sarcastic triplet: "A lot of past contemporaneity, little of modern contemporaneity, [and] very little of future contemporaneity."[38]

The journal also tried to rediscover and rearticulate its ties to the legacy of the Russian avant-garde of the 1910s and 1920s. Editors devoted particular attention to almost forgotten artists—such as Vasilij Chekrygin and Aleksandr Bogomazon[39]—whose works were still stored in the Russian Museum in Leningrad and the Moscow Tretjakov Gallery and therefore inaccessible to both the audience and to art historians, as Pavel Filonov and Mikhail Matjushin.[40] The name most frequently appearing in the pages of *A-Ja* was undoubtedly Kazimir Severinovich Malevich. From the first issue, Shelkovskij's journal acquainted the reader with several unpublished articles by the father of Suprematism taken from an anthology edited by Jean Claude Marcade in Lausanne[41] (articles like "To the Innovators of the Whole World"[42] and "Concerning the Subjective and the Objective in Art and in General").[43] Additionally, the fifth issue of *A-Ja* questioned Malevich's role in Russian contemporary art, publishing three essays by Moscow unofficial painters (Erik Bulatov, Oleg Vasil'ev, and Il'ja Kabakov).[44] By defining postmodernism as an ironic reaction to the avant-garde claim for "ultimate perfection" (which actually has incarnated itself in the high-flown, bombastic style of soviet realism), Groys pointed out in his preface to the edition how far Soviet unofficial artists were from Malevich's utopism. In comparison with Malevich's attempt to rescue the object from the supremacy of space, they rather tried to emancipate space from the object in their paintings, therefore claiming support for art beyond the limits of the social world—just as Bulatov argued in his short essay "On Malevich's Relationship to Space."[45]

At the same time, it was impossible to ignore Suprematism's problematic heritage, especially after the exhibition "Paris-Moscow" held at the Georges Pompidou Centre in 1979.[46] Both Bulatov and Vasil'ev recognized the importance of this event in bringing Russian avant-garde art to Western and, indirectly, to Soviet viewers.[47] Vasil'ev wrote that "Paris-Moscow" succeeded in providing for the first time an objective "portrait of the age" and acquainted artists who had emigrated to France with works they previously knew of only by reproduction or—as strange as it may sound—by verbal descriptions.[48] Once again Russian artists discovered their own roots abroad, through the mirror Western culture offered. At the same time, they started to legitimize their art in reference to the "first" avant-garde, by expressing in their writings their highly personal, often mythological self-image. Here one should stress the importance of the wonderful essay Il'ja Kabakov wrote for Shelkovskij's journal, "Not Everyone Will Be Taken into the Future," a text that in 2001 inspired the homonymous "total installation" he created for the Venice Biennale.[49] In these pages, Kabakov recalls his first steps in the world of art, when—as a young country boy just landed from Dnepropetrovsk at the Moscow Surikov School of Art—he was apt to consider Malevich the Ultimate Authority, a "source of terror," and "a great boss."[50] In Kabakov's view, Malevich was not only a metaphorical giant, he was the one who unceasingly reminded the young artist he *must* always create something new, if he really wanted to become part of the future and join history. The artist is simply forbidden to give up progression, exactly as the pupil is forbidden to spend the summer at school, even if he has not earned the right to attend Pioneer Camp. "Future" is the only way, and this early 1980s essay clearly reflects Kabakov's (and his collegues') attempt to hop onboard the fabulous train of contemporary art.

A peculiar feature that distinguished *A-Ja* from the other tamizdat journals was the unprecedented interest in conceptualizing socialist realism as the oppressive but inevitable background against which Soviet unofficial art arose and developed. Shelkovskij's review did not demonize socialist realism or consider it unworthy of critical evaluation; on the contrary it tried to explain the nature of this phenomenon and its impact on further developments in Russian art. A telltale of this approach can be seen in the anticipation of the journal's fourth issue in excerpts from the book *Kul'tura dva* (Culture Two) by Vladimir Papernyj, which was currently being in preparation at Ardis.[51] In addition to this epochal event, *A-Ja* became a forum in the 1980s for actively questioning the character of Socialist Realism and describing it from the points of view of internationally known scholars, like Andrej Sinjavskij and Alain Besançon,[52] and Russian artists themselves. On this subject, we should mention the charming, ironic essays of Vitalij Komar and Aleksandr Melamid, notably *The Role of War Department in Soviet Art*,[53] in which they analyzed the problematic interactions between artists and political power in 1920s in the context of a frantic search for employment, on the one hand, and the gradual assessment of state bureaucracy, on the other one. Furthermore, *A-Ja* offered precious insights into contemporary Soviet art politics, branding the last exhibitions held in Moscow, for instance, as a clear example of "hyperconformism,"[54] or, in another example, defining the timeless, self-referential mechanisms that actually ruled the Soviet Academy of Arts.[55]

A-Ja was not "only" an art journal. In 1985, Shelkovskij decided to publish an issue entirely devoted to literature (*Literaturnoe A-Ja*), discussing the close relationship between Soviet unofficial art and literature. The literature *A-Ja* edition included poems by Dmitrij Prigov and Vsevolod Nekrasov, short stories by Eduard Limonov and the prematurely departed Evgenij Kharitonov, an unpublished essay by Varlam Shalamov about writers in the 1920s, and many other texts. Shelkovskij demonstrated how unnatural it would be to split the social and cultural context in which unofficial art and unofficial literature arose. Although Shelkovskij intended to go on publishing similar literature issues beyond the art edition, he soon realized that publishing two reviews simultaneously was almost impossible, given the peculiar conditions of tamizdat editing. Consequently, he decided to sacrifice the former, since by then there were plenty of journals devoted to prose and poetry in the tamizdat, but none—save *A-Ja* and Glezer's *Tret'ja volna*—that wrote about art. Nevertheless, throughout the 1980s, *A-Ja* published several stylish booklets *in octavo*, introducing the Russian émigré audience to new authors like Dmitrij Prigov, who in his *Stichogrammy* created an original genre oscillating between visual art and poetry.

Shelkovskij's initiative marked a significant turning point in Soviet artists' self-perception and, consequently, the circulation of ideas in the theoretical debate about Soviet art and its meaning in the late 1970s. Although *A-Ja* was published in the West, it displays many of the features typical of a samizdat journal, such as its emphasis on oral communication and the peculiarities of cultural exchange in the unofficial circles in Soviet Union, the declared intention to preserve these occurrences and, at the same time, bring nonconformist culture out of the restricted boundaries to which political repression confined it. Shelkovskij's journal's highest achievement was that it proved to be a capable mediator between the almost conspirative and "ascetic" atmosphere of the "underground," on one side, and the international art system, on the other. *A-Ja* sought a balance between elitism and the quest for a broader audience, and the affirmation and preservation of one's own identity in the new context of Western art. In this sense, *A-Ja* cast a positive shadow over the years, and its influence continued into the 1990s, when several periodicals founded in the new sociopolitical context explicitly referred to *A-Ja* as their heroic predecessor. Of these new enterprises, we should mention the eight issues of the thematic journal *Pastor*, which was edited in Cologne by Vadim Zakharov from 1992 until 1999.[56] *Pastor* was devoted to key issues of contemporary art (with special attention to the development of Moscow Conceptualism), art theory, literature, and philosophy. The differences between the two journals are obvious and Zakharov's publication falls more into the tradition of small-time editions, archive collections, and artist books well rooted in the Moscow Conceptual School.[57] *Pastor* is evidence of how the tradition of self-publication survived, outlasting the political and ideological framework, which caused the proliferation of samizdat. Furthermore, *Pastor* inherited from *A-Ja* the keenness with which Russian art has always reflected upon its own achievements in pursuit of a both self-protective and active task.

Notes

1. Natal'ja Nikitina and Igor' Shelkovskij, "Ob *A-Ja*" [About *A-Ja*], *Pastor* 5 (Special issue: "Emigracija i stranniki" [Emigration and Wanderers]) (December 1995): 120.
2. "Несколько лет назад поэт Виктор Кривулин пресказывал скорый закат самиздатских журналов, ссылаясь, во-первых, на опережающий пример Москвы, где такой ерундой давно не занимаются, а просто отсылают тексты в Анн-Арбор и А-Я, во-вторых, на появление пост-маклюэновских средств информации.... Время не подтвердило предсказаний поэта, хотя и не опровергло их. Малотиражные журналы в Москве, действительно, почти не известны, многие московские литераторы печатаются за границей". A. Fomin and T. Chudinovskaja (alias Boris Ostanin and Aleksandr Kobak), "Soobshchenie o *Predloge*. Obzor sbornika perevodov Kluba-81, nn.1–3," *Predlog* 5 (Summer 1985): F. 37 (V. Erl'), Historical Archive of East European Studies at Bremen University. Journal pages are not numbered.
3. On Soviet unofficial art see, for example, J. Chalupesky, "Moscow Diary," *Studio International* (February 1973): 82–96; Igor Golomshtok-Aleksandr Glezer, ed., *Russian Art in Exile* (New York, 1977); "Dall'URSS" [From the USSR], *Flash Art* 76–77 (July–August 1977): 9–19; *Drugoe iskusstvo. Moskva 1956–1976* [The Other Art: Moscow, 1956–1976], (Moscow, 1991); Il'ya Kabakov, "60-e-70-e ... Zapiski o neoficial'noj zhizni v Moskve" [1960s and 1970s: Notes on Unofficial Life in Moscow], *Wiener Slawistischer Almanach, Sonderband* 47 (1997); Viktor Tupicyn, *"Drugoe iskusstvo". Besedy s khudozhnikami, kri-*

tikami i filosofami, 1980–1995 ["The Other Art": Conversations with Artists, Art Critics and Philosophers] (Moscow, 1997); Viktor and Margarita Tupicyn, "Moskva-N'ju Jork" [Moscow-New York], *WAM* 21 (2006).
4. See *Avant-garde russe Moscou 1973*, Galerie Dina Vierny, Paris, 1973. The five Soviet artists represented there were Il'ja Kabakov, Erik Bulatov, Vladimir Jankilevskij, Oskar Rabin, and Mikhail Arkhangelskij.
5. Igor' Shelkovskij and Jack Melkonian met for the first time in 1977 in Venice during the so-called Dissent Biennale. The Swiss businessman remembers: "The exhibition was striking. We watched crowds of Italian journalists passing through the show, discussing their own problems and taking no notice of the art on display. Will they remember it tomorrow? What can be done? … It was then when I had the idea of an art journal as an alternative to a museum." I. Selkovskij, "Al'fa i omega svobodnogo tvorcestva" [The Alfa and Omega of Free Creativity], in *A-Ja, Zhurnal neoficial'nogo russkogo iskusstva 1979–1986*, ed. I. Shelkovskij and A. Obukhova (Moscow, 2004), xx. For an extensive survey on the reception of the Dissent Biennale in Italian media, I refer the reader to my own contribution "Zwischen Unstimmigkeit und Andersdenken. Inoffizielle sowjetische Kunst auf der Biennale di Venezia 1977" [Between Contestation and Dissent. Soviet Unofficial Arts at the Venice Biennale 1977], in *Kursschwankungen. Die russische Kunst im Wertesystem der europäischen Moderne*, ed. Ada Raev and Isabel Wünsche (Berlin, 2007), 166–71.
6. The seven issues of the journal soon became a bibliographical rarity. They (unfortunately with the exception of the only literary issue, *Literaturnoe A-Ja*) have been recently reprinted in an English-Russian edition, together with an essay by Galina El'shevskaja and an interview with Shelkovskij, Sidorov, and Melkonian. See Shelkovskij and Obukhova, *A-Ja, Zhurnal neoficial'nogo russkogo iskusstva*. Here I would like to acknowledge my debt to Elena Romanova, who in 2002 in Moscow generously offered me the opportunity to acquaint myself with her full run of *A-Ja*.
7. See Viktor Misiano's *Moscow Recollections*, edited in collaboration with Daria Beskina, on the Web site http://www.eastartmap.org/text/knowledge/selectors/misiano.pdf (accessed 19 August 2011), 10.
8. Natal'ja Nikitina-Igor' Shelkovskij, "Ob *A-Ja*," 121.
9. Misiano, *Moscow Recollections*, 11,
10. At the beginning of the 1980s, Aleksandr Melamid and Vitalij Komar (who left the Soviet Union respectively in 1977 and 1978) wrote on "Art Forum": "It is with nostalgia that we, the authors of this article, remember Igor Shelkovsky's small studio which could barely hold our friends: Rimma and Valerii Gerlovin, Sasha Kosolapov, and several others. Ivan Cuikov was the only one of us who knew English, and we would gather and listen as he translated for us from the pages of the very magazine which you, dear reader, now hold in your hands." Komar and Melamid, "The Barren Flowers of Evil," *Art Forum* (March 1980): 46. About collective lecture sessions of Western art journals, see also Rimma Gerlovina's recollections in *Russian Samizdat Art: Essays by John E. Bowlt, Szymon Bojko, Rimma and Valery Gerlovin*, ed. Charles Doria (New York, 1988), 89; and Shelkovskij, "Al'fa i omega svobodnogo tvorchestva," ix.
11. "Zhurnal na podookonnike" [A Journal on the Windowsill], *Decorativnoe iskusstvo SSSR* 8 (1990).
12. Shelkovskij, "Al'fa i omega svobodnogo tvorchestva," xxii.
13. Natal'ja Nikitina-Igor' Shelkovskij, "Ob *A-Ja*," 121.
14. Shelkovskij, "Al'fa i omega svobodnogo tvorchestva," xxiv.
15. Boris Groys's famous article was published for the first time in 1977, in the fiftieth issue of the Leningrad samizdat journal *37*. In order to illustrate the fundamental meaning of

this essay in Soviet (and Russian) culture, it will be enough to recall that this very year, Vadim Zakharov took part in the second Moscow Biennale with a peculiar prolegomenon to Groys's article, entitled *Caramel in the Botanical Garden*. See the catalog *2. Moscow Biennale of Contemporary Art: Special Projects* (Moscow, 2007).

16. Compare, for example, the declaration of intent contained in the first issue of the samizdat journal *37*, founded in January 1976 in Leningrad: "Dear readers! We conceive this journal as the logical prosecution of our discussions between friends. Too many ideas fall into oblivion. Important EVENTS in the lively cultural process often remain accessible to little circles. … Therefore our goal is to take everyday cultural exchange in unofficial milieu out of its nonwritten condition (вывести культуру общения из дописьменного состояния)." *37* 1 (January 1976): F 5/1, Historical Archive of East European Studies at Bremen University. Journal pages are not numbered.

17. *Kontinent* felt that *A-Ja* did not take into account the "intrinsic" value of artworks. See, for instance: "Настораживает пока желание пропагандировать одно новое, а не лучшее из неофициального искусства," Vladimir Antonov, "Neoficial'noe iskusstvo: razvitie, sostojanie, perspektivy," *Kontinent* 30 (1981): 392.

18. "В основном, критерий художников, которыми занимается 'Третья волна,' находятся на шкале «хорошо-плохо.» Иначе говоря, это те, кто просто пишет картины, лепит скульптуры, не думая о новых материалах и формах контакта со зрителем. Иначе говоря, заняты изобразительным искусством в истинном понимании этого слова". K. S., "O zhurnalach *Tret'ja volna* i *A-Ja*," *Kontinent* 24 (1980): 395–96.

19. "Резкие протесты А. Глезера — дело не новое. Они возникли после открытия выставок в Венеции, Турине, Белинзоне, Бохуме, Париже, т.е. после каждой экспозиции устроенной не им, Глезером. Мотивы недовольства были всегда одни и те же, искажена подлинная картина развития неофициального искусства. Будто эта подлинная картина — вещь законченная и навсегда решённая и известна она одному лишь человеку А. Глезеру. Но искусство не стоит на месте, как кому-то этого хотелось бы, новые идеи, новые направления, новые имена приходят на смену прежних. Искусство так же переменчиво и динамично, как и жизнь, и дело русских изданий по возможности отразить этот процесс. Окончательная же оценка даст время." Igor' Shelkovskij, unpublished letter to Aleksandr Glezer: F 75 (B. Groys), Historical Archive of East European Studies at Bremen University. About Shelkovskij's relationship to the Russian emigrant milieu see Igor' Shelkovskij, "Moi semidesjatye" [My 1970s], in *Eti strannye semidesjatye, ili poterja nevinnosti* [These Strange 1970s, or the Loss of Innocence], ed. Georgij Kizeval'ter (Moscow, 2010): 346–47.

20. "Вот первый номер «А-Я». Новенький, элегантный, словно английский костюм, с грамотным макетом, сделанным полиграфистом-профессионалом. Он лишен той доморощенности, за которую так часто упрекают русские издания ... Один из неоспоримых достоинств «А-Я» является параллельный перевод статей на английский язык. Это, так сказать, попытка прорубить окно в Европу и рассказать на понятном ей языке о русских художниках-«новаторах»." K. S., "O zhurnalach," 395–96.

21. "Dall'URSS" [From the USSR], *Flash Art* 76–77 (July–August 1977): 9–19. In this reportage we find a few documents that just two years later would reappear in *A-Ja*'s first issue, as for instance some pictures taken in Moscow during the first performances organized by the group "Kollektivnye dejstvija" [Collective Actions] or during the "igry" [plays] by Rimma and Valery Gerlovin.

22. Aleksandr Blok, *Poslednie dni imperatorskoj vlasti* (St. Petersburg, 1921). Recently reprinted in Aleksandr Blok, *Poslednie dni imperatorskoj vlasti* (Moscow, 2005).

23. About the "bulldozers'exhibition," see Aleksandr Glezer, *Iskusstvo pod bul'dozerom. Sinjaja kniga* [Art Under Bulldozers] (London, 1976); Oskar Rabin, *Tri zhizni. Kniga vospominanij* [Three Lives: A Book of Memories] (Paris, 1986); and Aleksandr Glezer, *Chelovek s dvoinym dnom* [A Man with a Secret] (Moscow, 1994). An extensive chronicle of the organization and the influence this famous exhibition had on Brezhnev art politic is to be read in *Drugoe iskusstvo*, 1 (1991): 211–21.
24. See the exhibition catalogues: *La peinture russe contemporaine* (Paris, 1976); Michael Scammel, ed., *Unofficial art from the Soviet Union* (London, 1977); Norton Dodge and Alison Hilton, eds., *New Art from the Soviet Union: The Known und the Unknown* (Washington, 1977); Enrico Crispolti and Gabriella Moncada, eds., *La nuova arte sovietica. Una prospettiva non ufficiale* (Venice, 1977).
25. Both these articles were published after the exhibition at the pavilion "Pchelovodstvo" ("Apiculture") at the VDNX (Exhibition of the People's Economic Achievements), respectively in *Vechernjaja Moskva* [Evening Moscow] (10 March 1975) and in *Moskovskij khudozhnik* [Moscow Painter] (5 June 1975).
26. Quoted from the interview with V. Jaremenko-Tolstoj entitled "Zhesty Groysa" [Groys's actions], *Novyj Mir Iskusstva* [The New World of Art] (22 May 2001): 4.
27. See Lucy R. Lippard, *Six Years: The Dematerialization of Art Object from 1966–1972* (New York, 1973), and Ursula Meyer, *Conceptual Art* (New York, 1972).
28. Natal'ja Nikitina and Igor' Shelkovskij, "Ob *A-Ja*," 122.
29. MANI means "Moskovskij Archiv Novogo Iskusstva" [Moscow Archive of New Art]. Each file was edited in five exemplars. In Europe, the full set of the MANI files is available for viewing at the Historical Archive of East European Studies at Bremen University, Germany. About MANI files and their content, see *Präprintium. Moskauer Bücher aus dem samizdat* (Bremen, 1998), 105–8.
30. About *Po masterskim* see Zakharov's survey in *Präprintium*, 109.
31. See *A-Ja* 1 (1979): 54–55.
32. *A-Ja* 1 (1979): 46.
33. Joseph Beuys, "Iskusstvo i politika" [Art and Politics], in *A-Ja* 2 (1980): 54–55.
34. "Kollekcija Dzhin Braun" [Jean Brown and her collection], *A-Ja*, 3 (1981): 55–57.
35. For example, the Gerlovins remarked: "In the USA everything is censored by the marketplace that permits nothing other than to 'épater le bourgeois,' but at the same time it offers incomparably more opportunities than in Russia" (*Russian samizdat Art*, 177).
36. See Doria, *Russian Samizdat Art*, and the article "Iskusstvo samizdata (Moskovskaja škola)," [Samizdat Art: The Moscow School], *A-Ja* 7 (1986): 10–15.
37. *A-Ja* 3 (1981): 55.
38. *A-Ja* 1 (1979): 46.
39. See "Pis'ma V. Chekrygina k M. Larionovu" [The letters of V. Chekrygin to M. Larionov], *A-Ja* 4 (1982): 40–43; and "Aleksandr Bogomazov (1880–1930)," *A-Ja* 7 (1986): 46–51.
40. See "Mikhail Matjushin (1861–1934)," *A-Ja* 6 (1984): 48–55; and "Pavel Filonov," *A-Ja* 2 (1980): 35–40. This last issue contains Filonov's autobiography as well. Vadim Zakharov recently used this text for his homage project *Monument to Utopia* (for the exhibition *Pavel Filonov: Witness of the Unseen*, shown in St. Peterburg (Russian Museum, 17 July–13 October 2006) and Moscow (Pushkin Museum, 26 December 2006–11 March 2007).
41. K. S. Malevich, *La lumière et la couleur* (Lausanne, 1981).
42. Kazimir Malevich, "Novatoram vsego mira," *A-Ja* 3 (1981): 45–49.
43. Kazimir Malevich, "O sub'ektivnom i ob'jektivnom v iskusstve ili voobshche," *A-Ja* 1 (1979): 42–43.

44. "Moskovskie khudozhniki o Maleviche" [Moscow Artists on Malevich], *A-Ja* 5 (1983): 25–35.
45. *A-Ja* 5 (1983): 26–31.
46. *Paris-Moscou 1900–1930: arts plastiques, arts appliques et objets utilitaires, architecture, urbanisme, agitprop, affiche, théâtre-ballet, littérature, musique, cinéma, photo créative: 31 mai–5 novembre 1979* (Paris, 1979).
47. Bulatov wrote: "Thanks to the exhibition Paris-Moscou, Malevich has finally become visible, both in himself and among his contemporaries" (E. Bulatov, "Ob otnoshenii Malevicha k prostranstvu" [On Malevich's Relationship to Space], *A-Ja* 5 (1983): 26.
48. In his article, Vasil'ev explains that, although he quickly gave a look to Malevich's paintings kept in storage in the basement of a museum (Pushkin Museum?), the idea he had conveyed about them before "Moscou-Paris" was largely influenced by expectations induced by verbal descriptions: "Hearing was stronger than sight." See O. Vasil'ev, *Portret vremeni* [A Portrait of the Age], *A-Ja* 5 (1983): 32.
49. See the catalog, Ilya and Emilia Kabakov, *Not Everyone Will Be Taken into the Future: Materials for the Installation* (Salzburg, 2002). Twenty years after the essay was edited for the first time, Kabakov clearly maintains it is still up to date, since he has reprinted it in the above-mentioned catalog without any alteration.
50. Il'ja Kabakov, "V budushee voz'mut ne vsech" [Not Everyone Will Be Taken into the Future], *A-Ja* 5 (1983): 32.
51. The first chapter of Papernyj's study case on Soviet architecture was published two years before in *37* 20 (August–October 1980): 119–55, probably thanks to Boris Groys, who at that time joined the editorial board of the journal. Ardis published *Kul'tura dva* only in 1985, when Papernyj had already realized that it made no sense to study Russian architecture living more than ten thousand kilometers from the USSR (he moved to the United States in 1981) and therefore began a career as a graphic designer. See the preface to V. Papernyj, *Kul'tura dva* (Moscow, 1996), 9.
52. See, for instance, Andrej Sinjavskij, "Vstrecha v Neapole" [Meeting in Naples], *A-Ja*, 5 (1983): 53–54; and Mikhail Aksenov-Meerson, "Iskusstvo socialisticheskogo realizma," [The Art of Socialist Realism], *A-Ja* 3 (1981): 58–59.
53. V. Komar and A. Melamid, "Rol' vojennogo vedomstva v sovetskom iskusstve,"*A-Ja* 2 (1980): 50–53.
54. Z. M., "V stile giperkonformizma" [New Trends: Hyperconformism], *A-Ja* 4 (1984): 58–59.
55. C. Core, "Akademija Khudozhestv. Jubilejnye razmyshlenija" [Jubilee Reflections on the Academy of Arts], *A-Ja* 7 (1986): 52–58.
56. Recently, Zakharov edited a reprint of materials from *Pastor*'s eight issues. See *Pastor: Sbornik izbrannykh materialov, opublikovannykh v zhurnale "Pastor", 1992–2001* (Vologda, 2009).
57. See the preface Zakharov wrote for the first *Pastor* issue (entitled "Names"): "Ero ["Pastor"] гениалогия доперестроечная и основана на Московской традиции, придерживающейся до сих пор 'слухового' метода общения, приватных коммунальных форм. Журнал продолжает линию сборников МАНИ, маленьких книжечек, уютных бесед. И его тираж в тридцать экземпляров соразмерен традиционно имтимному сосуществованию, несмотря на предыдущие сумасшедшие три-четыре год... ," quoted from Vadim Zakharov, *Erster Titel: Der letzte Spaziergang durch die Elysischen Felder* (Ostfildern: Cantz, 1995), 75. It is interesting that later on, in the fifth issue of *Pastor*, Zakharov published a long interview with the editor of *A-Ja* and several photographs from Shelkokskij's archive. See Nikitina and Shelkovskij, "Ob A-Ja" [About A-Ja], *Pastor* 5, "Emigracija i stranniki" [Emigration and Wanderers]."

Chapter 10

"Video Knows No Borders"
Samizdat Television and the Unofficial Public Sphere in "Normalized" Czechoslovakia

Alice Lovejoy

Tracing the history of alternative film and media practices in socialist Eastern Europe is a daunting project.[1] This is, in part, due to a lack of institutional possibilities for such practices: cinema, Lenin's "most important art," was quickly nationalized throughout the region after World War II, and closely controlled by its constituent states until 1989.[2] Nationalization was possible, effective—and in large part beneficial—in part because of cinema's very nature as a medium. Film, unlike many other arts, typically demands considerable human, financial, and material resources, and nationalization both made these resources more widely available and allowed the state to control their allocation.[3] In fact, throughout state-socialist Eastern Europe, alternatives often emerged *within* state film production systems, as in the cases of the region's modernist "New Waves" of the 1950s to the 1970s.

This essay, however, is concerned with a more obscure object: film and media produced entirely outside nationalized cinema industries. The history of these media is difficult to write not only because of their scarcity, but also because of their often ephemeral nature: precisely because film production was so closely controlled, from the script-writing process to laboratory development, these media often had to be produced in formats, like video or Super 8 film, that were available to everyday consumers—formats that have not, for the most part, found themselves housed in archives and canonized in film histories. It is the former that I discuss in this essay, through the cases of two unofficial video series produced in "normalized" Czechoslovakia: *Videomagazine* (*Videomagazín*), a tamizdat

---

Notes for this chapter begin on page 216.

video periodical produced from 1985 to 1989 in London exile by Czech journalist Karel Kyncl, and *Original Videojournal* (*Originální videojournal*), a samizdat video publication made in Czechoslovakia from 1987 to 1989.[4] Examining the content, aesthetics, and circulation of these videos, and particularly their links to television aesthetics and discourse, I will argue that they were not only the product of Czechoslovakia's alternative (or unofficial) public sphere, but also helped to define this sphere.[5]

I draw in part, here, on two studies of unofficial film in Czechoslovakia: Michal Bregant and Martin Čihák's "Realer than Reality: Alternatives in Czech Film," which traces the history of avant-garde film after 1968; and Alice Růžičková's "Original Videojournal: An Attempt at *Samizdat* Television," a chronicle of *Original Videojournal*'s history. Bregant and Čihák argue that, during Normalization, "the idea of an aesthetic avant-garde ... moved to the sphere of ideological language: the 'avant-garde' became the working class as led by the communist party. And there were no alternatives. Or rather: they were not allowed."[6] Consequently, they write, avant-garde filmmakers, like other artists, moved their work "underground," producing two different kinds of films: documentaries, like *Original Videojournal* and *Videomagazine*, and amateur films. The latter, they argue, became the locus for most of the experimental tendencies in post-1968 Czechoslovak film, thus continuing a tradition of intertwining between amateur and avant-garde film practices that had existed in Czechoslovak cinema since the interwar period, in the work of filmmakers like Alexander Hackenschmied.[7] These two kinds of films were also largely produced in different social spaces: amateur films within the private sphere, and documentary within Czechoslovakia's "parallel culture," which gave birth to Charter 77, The Plastic People of the Universe, the Jazz Section, VONS (The Committee for the Unjustly Persecuted), and other organizations. As Bregant and Čihák write, in this community, "film was usually used as a medium for documentation. ... Here, too, film served as a medium for free expression, but not with the aesthetic and artistic ambitions that we find among amateur filmmakers."[8]

Unofficial activity in communist Czechoslovakia, however, was not as strictly divided as this binary suggests, and encompassed numerous, overlapping spheres: As Josef Alan observes, "borders [between various forms of cultural ... 'otherness'] were slippery and fuzzy, the crossovers between them more or less fluid, mutually crossing over one another and diffusing into one another."[9] Consequently, the domains of amateur and documentary film were also intertwined. *Videomagazine* and *Original Videojournal* illustrated such crossovers not only formally, but also socially, in the way they spanned the private sphere of amateur filmmaking and the unofficial public spheres of dissent or the cultural underground.[10]

Both series originated as amateur productions. *Videomagazine* was, in fact, essentially a home-video production, shot and edited by Kyncl with the technical assistance of his son. *Original Videojournal*, as Růžičková discusses, began in the early 1980s with the work of a group of amateur filmmakers called "Čeněk."[11] In an early phase, the group filmed brief sixteen-millimeter sequences that were sent abroad to Czechoslovak exile groups "for the popularization of contemporary Czechoslovakia and its anticommunist opposition."[12] By 1985, however, Čeněk had begun shooting on Video8, equipment it acquired with the assistance of Václav Havel, who, upon learning of the small, light, and thus inconspicuous video technology, arranged, through the Foundation for Charter 77, to have it sent to the group.[13] Within a few years, Čeněk's activities were closely allied both with political dissent—the Charter, which was the source of its funding—and with the cultural underground.

The content, format, and distribution patterns of *Videomagazine* and *Original Videojournal* also grew out of the productions' location in the "fuzzy" area between the private and unofficial public spheres in communist Czechoslovakia. *Videomagazine* was made up primarily of segments from Western television, spliced into a program that was "hosted" by Kyncl (who played the role of on-screen anchor) and largely followed the format of a news broadcast. As a tamizdat publication, the series' goal was simple: to provide viewers in Czechoslovakia with uncensored access to foreign news, particularly segments with relevance to life at home. In addition to clips from television, *Videomagazine* featured discussions with prominent Czechoslovak dissidents or members of the underground, and reportage segments Kyncl shot himself.

Videomagazine's topics and themes can be divided into three general categories. First, and primary, was news and cultural reporting from Western sources that would not air on Czechoslovak state television. Second was the idea of the border, the West, and escape; and third, Czechoslovak dissidents living domestically and in exile. Into the first category fell Western broadcasts such as one addressing Soviet television's unwillingness to acknowledge the extent of the Chernobyl disaster—information crucial to Czechoslovakia, although it arrived with a considerable delay—and a television program chronicling Andy Warhol's visit to London to promote a new exhibition. The idea of the border was captured in segments such as "Three Escapes to the West," a British television program chronicling escapes from the GDR, "Roll Call of Soviet Jews," a daylong London action in support of Soviet Jews waiting for exit visas, and a section featuring "video postcards" from Rome, Lisbon, and Algiers. Czechoslovak dissidents, finally, were visible in segments such as the "Havel Special," in which the latter reacts to being awarded the Erasmus Prize, and in home-video documentation of a meeting of Czech Catholics in Paris. Kyncl introduced all of the videos' segments, either in voice-over or in person, and his presence, alongside *Videomagazine*'s narratives of exile, travel, and escape, lent an intimate, autobiographical dimension to the program, again emphasizing the links between the private sphere and the unofficial public sphere (visible, here, in interviews with dissidents and discussions of exile).

Where *Videomagazine*, as tamizdat, offered Czechoslovaks reports from abroad and relied heavily on television news footage, *Original Videojournal*'s function was, as samizdat, the opposite: to circulate images and news from the domestic community both internally and to exile and human rights groups abroad. The series thus aimed to become a form of independent television, as Růžičková notes in the title of her essay, and to offer "quality independent journalism that could provide reliable information about alternative goings-on in the cultural sphere, and patch up holes in the official media."[14] As such, *Original Videojournal* was composed primarily of material shot by its team of videographers, with occasional copied segments from tapes such as Kyncl's (the Warhol segment from *Videomagazine*, for example, appears in *Original Videojournal*). And in fact, during the events of November 1989, and for a brief period afterward, *Original Videojournal* transformed into an "official" news source, most notably in a series of tapes that document the protests of November of that year, and observe the fall of the communist government from the theaters and concert halls in which the Velvet Revolution unfolded.

In keeping with its domestic orientation, *Original Videojournal* centered on events in Czechoslovakia. It included, first, segments addressing political issues pertinent to dissident communities at home and in exile: the black-and-white video documentary of the funeral of dissident Pavel Wonka, who died in prison; a demonstration by women (including Olga Havlová, Václav Havel's then-wife and a member of *Original Videojournal*'s editorial board), for basic sanitary supplies. Second, it featured sequences documenting underground or unofficial cultural events in Czechoslovakia, such as openings in unofficial art galleries, or performances such as Fluxus artist Tomáš Ruller's *8.8.88*.[15] Finally, at times, *Original Videojournal* itself performed or *became* a form of underground or unofficial art, in experimental or lyrical segments that hewed more closely to Bregant and Čihák's definition of amateur/avant-garde film. In one such segment, the sound of a police radio was juxtaposed with handheld video images of a nighttime protest; another, a mock documentary, chronicled a fictional expedition by a team of scientists and academics to find the legendary knights of Blaník, who, as the myth holds, will rise from the hillside in which they are buried to protect the Czech nation in a time of need.

Original Videojournal's form and content began to shift in its fifth issue, released in summer 1989 and documenting events of the previous spring. In this issue, political issues are all consuming: the video documents police attacks on protestors at a May Day parade and features footage from a demonstration in Georgia in April of that year. Titles announce *Original Videojournal* number six as the production's "first legal issue," and this and the "Special Editions" that follow it offer a panoramic view of events (demonstrations, political meetings, concerts) occurring throughout Czechoslovakia in the fall of 1989, with little editing and almost no commentary, a format that mirrors the momentum and spontaneous energy of the Velvet Revolution.

Videomagazine and *Original Videojournal*'s circulation patterns resembled those of their print forebears, which relied on social networks for distribution. H. Gordon Skilling writes that samizdat and tamizdat texts were "usually distributed by hand, not by mail, and ... sent abroad through foreign correspondents, foreign embassies, travelers, or by more conspiratorial means," "passed on [from those who supplied the item in the first place] to others who may make copies of their own."[16] "It is impossible to know how many copies are eventually made," he continues, and "the last copies are often almost illegible."[17] As Michal Hybek describes in Růžičková's 1998 documentary *Close-Up on Original Videojournal*, after an edition was edited, its producers created forty-two first-generation VHS cassettes using seven video recorders connected to the same VCR and run repeatedly throughout the night. At least two cassettes from this generation were sent abroad, with the remainder distributed in Czechoslovakia.[18] Domestically, copies of both series were borrowed between friends, dubbed and redubbed, and screened to small audiences in the few homes that had VCRs—a form of public/private exhibition similar to the "living-room theater" (*bytové divadlo*) that emerged in Czechoslovakia during Normalization, in which banned actors or directors would perform plays in private living rooms.[19] International distribution was facilitated in ways similar to those Skilling describes: diplomats transported cassettes abroad during trips or in shipments home, and tourists and other willing travelers smuggled tapes across the border. And as was the case with texts typed on typewriters and carbon paper, the images on these videocassettes became less and less legible as they increased in generations; as tapes were played, dubbed, replayed, and redubbed.

Original Videojournal's circulation was facilitated in part by its links to Charter 77, its funder. The Charter, as Skilling notes, was a major producer of Czechoslovak samizdat: "In 1977 the founding of Charter 77 ... gave birth to a substantial diffusion of typewritten materials, including 'authorized' documents signed by the Charter spokesmen, but also a great volume of uncensored materials written by individuals and groups."[20] Similarly, Růžičková describes Charter 77 as a "fundamental impulse for the intensive growth of samizdat in the 1970s and 1980s," and, more important, as "need[ing] to defend and create its own communication structures."[21] Thus, although it was linked not only to the Charter, but also to underground or parallel cultures in communist Czechoslovakia more broadly, we might read *Original Videojournal* as an alternate "communication structure" for the organization.

The relationship between *Original Videojournal* (and *Videomagazine*) and the Charter had to do not only with funding or with politics, but also with the ways in which the videos "functioned" socially. Indeed, in their writings, Chartists and other Czechoslovak dissidents actively discussed the ways in which the circulation of samizdat and tamizdat texts helped create the country's "unofficial" communities. Philosopher and mathematician Václav Benda, for instance, in his essay "The Parallel *Polis*" (published in samizdat in 1978), envisions the Czechoslovak unofficial public sphere as existing simultaneously with, and alongside, "official" culture. This community, he writes, is made up of "parallel structures that are capable, to a limited degree at least, of supplementing the generally beneficial and necessary functions that are missing in the existing structures."[22] Benda sees the exchange of texts (particularly those published by Charter 77) as crucial to the development and sustenance of this community, writing that "the circulation of information must be considered as important as the actual preparation of the material. ... The informational network so created must be used regularly. ... It is essential to pass information on to places where its further dissemination is assured."[23] Moreover, he argues, "in the future, we will have to consider using other means of reproduction besides the typewriter."[24]

If the exchange of video cassettes thus helped articulate the boundaries of Czechoslovakia's unofficial public sphere, both through creating a common textual reference-point for viewers and through screenings themselves (social events at which community members would gather), the cassettes also represented such a new "means of reproduction," one unique in that it was composed of moving images. And these very properties, in turn—the video series' visual nature and particularly their deliberate adoption of television formats—enhanced their social function. On one hand, in mimicking broadcast news, *Videomagazine* and *Original Videojournal* marked the events that they documented in the unofficial public sphere as "newsworthy." As such, they functioned similarly to various alternative media projects initiated in the United States in the post-1968 period, a comparison to which I will presently return. On the other hand, they elaborated on a central *social* aspect of television, one that

Margaret Morse describes as "the primacy of discourse in television representation."²⁵ Television, according to Morse, "reconstitut[es] a virtual world of face-to-face relationships shared between viewer and television personalities displaced or teleported from elsewhere," thus engaging the viewer and the subject in communication; creating a relationship between them.²⁶

Morse's concept of televisual discourse offers a useful way to read the social dimensions of *Videomagazine* and *Original Videojournal*, for the "television personalities" that appear in these productions were generally members of the same social sphere as their viewers (the Czechoslovak dissident and exile community). The productions thus offered the "virtual world of face-to-face relationships" as a substitute for the *real* face-to-face relationships unavailable to a community fragmented by geographic distance in some cases, and restricted from gathering publicly in others. In this sense, both *Videomagazine* and *Original Videojournal* reinforced the social structures—the private and unofficial public spheres—that made their production and circulation possible.²⁷ Moreover, both provided a virtual forum for *kinds* of dialogue that would not otherwise be publicly permissible, such as Kyncl's interviews with dissidents, and a man-on-the-street poll about life before and after the 1968 Warsaw Pact invasion of Czechoslovakia in a 1988 edition of *Original Videojournal* (timed to coincide with the twentieth anniversary of the invasion).²⁸

In using the recognizable format of television news to posit the importance of such conversations and occurrences, *Original Videojournal* and *Videomagazine* mirrored strategies that US-based alternative media projects (i.e., guerrilla television, public-access television, etc.) undertook in the period after 1968 to challenge mass media's dominant messages and modes. As Dierdre Boyle discusses in her study of guerrilla television, *Subject to Change*, these projects—such as the guerrilla television project TVTV (Top Value Television) and the community television project Paper Tiger Television—combined activist, documentary, and often experimental impulses, shifting not just the content of and communities served by broadcast television, but also its aesthetics, as *Original Videojournal* and *Videomagazine* did.²⁹ While we might, thus, read the Czechoslovak projects as part of a broader, post-1968 alternative media movement, the differences between the Czechoslovak projects and their Western counterparts lay in circulation and distribution. The US series were broadcast on television, primarily on cable or public-access channels. As Boyle writes, "at first, guerrilla television aimed at creating a distinct, parallel system to broadcast TV," but it ultimately transformed into "a reform movement to 'remake' television into something new, vital, peculiarly electronic, and responsive to the needs and expectations of a generation raised on the medium."[30] In Czechoslovakia, however, the state controlled the airwaves as closely as it did film production, and thus series like *Original Videojournal* and *Videomagazine* were never broadcast, circulating instead hand to hand, with the distribution models of samizdat and tamizdat standing in imperfectly for the geographic scope of broadcast transmission. Nevertheless, the notion that such series represented a "distinct, parallel system" to official television was as central in Czechoslovakia as it was in the United States. For as such, *Original Videojournal* and *Videomagazine* not only provided essential news, but also echoed theories like Benda's, which held that such "alternatives" could come to stand in, in a very real way, for "official" institutions.

A crucial factor in the rise of both the US and Czechoslovak series was the advent of consumer video technology, which made the tools of moving-image making more widely accessible. Boyle, for instance, traces the emergence of guerrilla television in the United States to 1968, the year that the Sony video Portapak was commercially released, and when video formats were standardized.[31] Video, however, came considerably later to Czechoslovakia: according to *The Washington Post*, the first consumer VCRs were smuggled into Eastern Europe in 1980–1981.[32] Such Western machines became commercially available in the mid 1980s, but were prohibitively expensive for all but the very wealthiest buyers, and initially available only in hard-currency shops. A 1988 Radio Free Europe report observed that Czechoslovakia had been "assembling small numbers of VCRs from components delivered by the Dutch company, Philips" and that a "joint-stock company was established between two Czechoslovak state enterprises and Philips," with domestic production slated to begin in that year.[33] Nevertheless, VCR ownership was not widespread before 1989, and thus *Original Videojournal* (as well as, of course, *Videomagazine*) relied on Western sources for its technology.

Video's marginalization in Eastern Europe was, in part, a reaction by communist governments to the technology's decentralized nature. Video was not only capable of broadening access to media technology and removing it from state control (unlike film, video does not require a laboratory for processing), it also allowed viewers to watch what they chose (potentially banned films, or pornography), when they chose. This represented a direct challenge to the nationalized system, which monitored not only the sites of production, but also of distribution.[34] The Czechoslovak government, accordingly, reacted to the medium with apprehension: on 10 October 1986, the country's primary daily newspaper, *Rudé právo*, called video a "strong ideological weapon."[35] Radio Free Europe, similarly, noted that "not only is the development of video technology seen as yet another example of communism's failure to keep up technologically with capitalism, but the equipment itself is regarded as a way of getting access to Western culture."[36] More suggestively, in a 1988 article, journalist Martin Novotný articulated a different kind of danger posed by video, writing that the technology threatened not just the ideals, but also the geography of the Czechoslovak state: "Video knows no borders, and we can only defend ourselves from the wave of kitsch and feeblemindedness that is approaching us with our own quality productions."[37]

Novotný's metaphor of an approaching "wave" threatening to wash away the strict geopolitical boundaries of the Cold War was, in fact, prescient. For not only did *Videomagazine* and *Videojournal* articulate the boundaries of Czechoslovakia's unofficial public sphere, they also asserted that this community extended beyond the borders of the state. Video's "borderless" nature was what enabled *Videomagazine* and *Original Videojournal* to be produced: cameras and cassettes were small and easy to transport in and out of the country. But "borderlessness" was also a focus of the productions themselves; for instance, in *Videomagazine*'s coverage of individual escapes, and in Kyncl's "video postcards," which offered a mode of virtual travel. Similarly, *Original Videojournal*'s documentation, in issue two (1988), of a meeting between Czech and Polish dissidents on their common border envisioned a community that extended beyond political frontiers.

Finally, as Novotný and *Rudé právo* feared and Benda and others hoped, the patterns of circulation that individual cassettes took, moving from London to Czechoslovakia, from Czechoslovakia to West Germany and onward, delineated a community that extended beyond the geography of the Cold War. Viewings of videotapes in geographically disparate spaces created, in Morse's terms, "discourse," a sense of shared conversation, between these spaces; a sense not unlike the one engendered by simultaneous viewing of broadcast television. Yet in its transnational dimensions, the community created in these conversations *exceeded* the range of standard broadcasts, and, in its expansive, virtual nature, reflected the dissident idea of "Central Europe," a space that was less geographic than, indeed, discursive. As Svetlana Boym writes, the notion of "Central Europe" was "transgeographical," "a utopia ... pregnant with possibilities."[38]

If Central Europe was a "utopic" space, however, the spaces that *Videomagazine* and *Original Videojournal* traced seemed very real, with their documentary imagery and the shaky immediacy of video. These images presented a starkly different "map" of Czechoslovakia than much "official" media did at various points throughout the postwar period; an alternative to images of state borders as solid and unbreachable (in films about border guards), or discussions of the country's border with West Germany as a "border between worlds." Such an evidentiary charge was, indeed, part of *Original Videojournal*'s mission—as an arm of Charter 77, the series worked, in part, within a human rights discourse. Yet while this dimension to the series was crucial, it is my contention that *Original Videojournal*'s significance, like *Videomagazine*'s, lay equally in its internal social function; in the way it gave shape to the unofficial public sphere. That is, the videos were meaningful less for what they showed and more for how they *moved*.

This question of circulation, in a certain sense, makes the question of "evidence" irrelevant. For by recording and exhibiting events primarily within a single community (in the case of *Original Videojournal*), or by holding an intracommunal dialogue through video (in the case of *Videomagazine*), the two series looked to the unofficial public sphere itself to confirm the veracity of the events they documented. Images, here, were recast from containers of immanent meaning to communally and subjectively understood objects, an idea that corresponds with documentary scholar Brian Winston's assessment of realism in nonfiction film as hinging on reception. As he writes, in an age in which images are understood as representations rather than realities, "grounding the documentary idea in reception rather than in representation ... allows the audience to make the truth claim for the documentary rather than the documentary implicitly making the claim for itself."[39]

In conclusion, however, this idea also returns us to Czechoslovak theories of the unofficial public sphere. Many of these theories conceived of this community as self-sufficient; to repeat Benda's evocative words, as a "parallel *polis*," an independent "city" within the state. As poet and theorist Ivan Martin Jirous, a leading member of the Czechoslovak cultural underground, observes in his 1975 essay "Report on the Third Czech Musical Revival," part of the goal of this parallel culture was to disengage entirely from the standards and values of "official" culture: "The goal of our underground is to create a second culture, a culture completely independent from all official communication media and the conventional hierarchy of value judgments put out by the establishment. It is to be a culture that does not have as its goal the destruction of the establishment, because by attempting this, it would ... mean that we would fall into the trap of playing their game."[40]

This is precisely what these series, as alternative television, did. In the process, however—as the events of November 1989 demonstrate—they created an alternative that was, in the end, viable enough to itself become "official."

Notes

1. For their guidance in the archival and primary-source explorations that were central to my research, I am grateful to Miloš Müller of Libri Prohibiti in Prague; Robert Parnica of the Open Society Archives in Budapest; Michal Bregant; and Alice Růžičková.
2. In Czechoslovakia, cinema was the very first industry to be nationalized (on 11 August 1945), and was taken under state control more than two months before major industries, banks, etc. See Alexej Kusák, *Kultura a politika v Československu, 1945–1956* [Culture and Politics in Czechoslovakia 1945–1956] (Prague, 1998), 188.
3. Antonín Liehm, in his *Closely Watched Films: The Czechoslovak Experience*, and Josef Škvorecký, in *All the Bright Young Men and Women* (28), discuss nationalization as a phenomenon that had both drawbacks and benefits. See Antonín Liehm, *Closely Watched Films: The Czechoslovak Experience* (White Plains, 1974), 3, and Josef Škvorecký, *All the Bright Young Men and Women: A Personal History of the Czech Cinema*, trans. Michael Schonberg (Toronto, 1971), 28.
4. *Normalization* is a term used to describe the years following the August 1968 Warsaw Pact invasion of Czechoslovakia. For a detailed and engaging history of the period and its culture, see Paulina Bren's *The Greengrocer and his TV: The Culture of Communism after the 1968 Prague Spring* (Ithaca, 2010).
5. Similar "samizdat television" projects existed in other East European countries; for instance, a series produced by the Hungarian Black Box collective.
6. Michal Bregant and Martin Čihák, "Skutečnější než realita: Alternativy v českém filmu," in *Alternativní kultura*, ed. Josef Alan (Prague, 2001), 422. All translations in this essay, unless otherwise noted, are my own.
7. Bregant and Čihák in Alan, *Alternativní kultura*, 421. Alexander Hackenschmied (later Hammid), a filmmaker, photographer, and theorist, was a central figure in the Czechoslovak, and later American, cinematic avant-garde.
8. Bregant and Čihák in Alan, *Alternativní kultura*, 424.
9. Josef Alan, "Alternativní kultura jako sociologické téma," in Alan, *Alternativní kultura*, 19.
10. In his essay, Josef Alan describes the cultural underground and dissent as occupying two poles of unofficial culture in communist Czechoslovakia.
11. Alice Růžičková, "Originální Videojournal: Pokus o ‚samizdatovou televizi'," in Alan, *Alternativní kultura*, 476.
12. Ibid.
13. *Zblízka Originální Videojournal* [Close-Up on Original Videojournal], dir. Alice Růžičková, Česká Televize, 1998.
14. Růžičková in Alan, *Alternativní kultura*, 475. Television was widespread in Czechoslovakia in the 1980s. It had first been broadcast in the country in 1953, and as Paulina Bren reports, "by the mid-1970s, nine out of ten families in Czechoslovakia owned a television set." See Bren, *The Greengrocer and his TV*, 113.
15. See http://www.ruller.cz/fotostranky/022.html (accessed 12 November 2012).
16. H. Gordon Skilling, *Samzidat and an Independent Society in Central and Eastern Europe* (Columbus, 1989), 9.
17. Ibid.
18. *Zblízka Originální Videojournal*.
19. Carol Rocamora, *Acts of Courage: Václav Havel's Life in the Theater* (Hanover, 2004), 121.
20. Skilling, *Samizdat and an Independent Society*, 12.
21. Růžičková in Alan, *Alternativní kultura*, 475.

22. Václav Benda, "The Parallel *Polis*," in *Civic Freedom in Central Europe: Voices From Czechoslovakia*, ed. H. Gordon Skilling and Paul Wilson (London, 1991), 36.
23. Benda in Skilling and Wilson, *Civic Freedom*, 38–39. Here, Benda echoes Jürgen Habermas's vision of the public sphere as centered around the discussion of common texts. See Habermas, *The Structural Transformation of the Public Sphere: An Inquiry into a Category of Bourgeois Society*, trans. Thomas Burger (Cambridge, 1991).
24. Benda in Skilling and Wilson, *Civic Freedom*, 38–39.
25. Margaret Morse, "An Ontology of Everyday Distraction: The Freeway, The Mall, and Television," in *Logics of Television*, ed. Patricia Mellencamp (Bloomington, 1990), 200.
26. Ibid., 205.
27. Here again, the notion that *Videomagazine* and *Original Videojournal* existed in the "fuzzy" area between amateur and documentary filmmaking is central, for in the process of "self-documentation," the projects resembled home movies.
28. Similar strategies (interviews, polls, etc.) were, according to Bren, central to television's "explosive popularity during the Prague Spring," and as a consequence, were not used on Czechoslovak state television in the 1970s and 1980s. See Bren, *The Greengrocer and his TV*, 119.
29. Deirdre Boyle, *Subject to Change: Guerrilla Television Revisited* (New York, 1997), xv, 207.
30. Ibid., xiv.
31. Ibid., 4.
32. Jackson Diehl, "VCRs on Fast Forward in Eastern Europe," *The Washington Post*, 17 April 1988 (Special).
33. "Special Report: The Video Revolution in Eastern Europe," *Radio Free Europe/Radio Liberty Soviet East European Report*, V: 12, 20 January 1988, Open Society Archives at Central Europen University, Budapest, Hungary.
34. Exceptions to this existed, such as private film clubs and screening series at foreign embassies.
35. *Rudé právo*, 10 October 1986.
36. "Special Report: The Video Revolution in Eastern Europe."
37. Martin Novotný, "Videokultura: Poslední zvonění?" [source of article unknown], 1988.
38. Svetlana Boym, *The Future of Nostalgia* (New York, 2001), 223. Cross-border viewership was, nevertheless, a major dimension of television culture in Eastern Europe: East German viewers regularly watched West German broadcasts, and large areas of Czechoslovakia's border regions were reached by West German and Austrian broadcasts. See Bren, *The Greengrocer and his TV*, 122 and 120.
39. Brian Winston, *Claiming the Real: The Griersonian Documentary and Its Legitimations* (London, 1995), 253.
40. Ivan Martin Jirous, "A Report on the Third Czech Musical Revival," trans. Erich Dluhosch, *Primary Documents: A Sourcebook for Eastern and Central European Art Since the 1950s*, ed. Laura Hoptman and Tomas Pospiszyl (New York, 2002), 64–65.

Section IV

MOVING FROM SAMIZDAT/TAMIZDAT TO ALTERNATIVE MEDIA TODAY

Chapter 11

POSTPRINTIUM?
Digital Literary Samizdat on the Russian Internet

Henrike Schmidt

> Some day, the historians of samizdat will carefully analyze
> the situation as it has developed in our country in the 1990s.
> The lack of official censorship and the mass implementation
> of computer technology enabled literature lovers to see
> their works published. ... Now, with the development of
> the Internet, the term "samizdat" acquires a new meaning.
> Unchanged remains only the idea of an informal conversation
> among creative people.
>
> —Oleg Novikov[1]

Literary samizdat of the Soviet era developed its own agenda and aesthetics, perhaps best characterized by the term *präprintium*, coined by the literary scholars Georg Witte and Sabine Hänsgen in 1998.[2] Deprived of contemporary printing technologies for political reasons, Soviet samizdat often returned to preprint techniques and, in its handmade aesthetics, set itself in opposition to the high culture of the official sphere.[3]

Digital samizdat[4] differs at first glance from its Soviet predecessor. Though as well excluded, for various political and aesthetical reasons, from the traditional publishing institutions, it nevertheless suffers neither comparable material constraints, nor the lack of a national or even worldwide audience. The media contexts of Soviet and digital samizdat are thus completely different. Contemporary authors publishing their work on the Internet do not find themselves thrown into the anachronistic situation of präprintium, but on the contrary employ the most advanced communication technologies. The unavailability of the official publication channels is not similar to the unavailability of high technology. Far from it, state

---

Notes for this chapter begin on page 238.

media policies are often rather retrograde, especially in the early period of the Internet's rise in Russia in the mid 1990s.

In this chapter, I analyze the changes within the concept of literary samizdat in such a period of postprintium, focusing mainly on the historic phenomenon of Soviet samizdat in the USSR and its reverberations on the Russian / Russian-speaking Internet.[5] What self-identificatory potential has samizdat as a historical legacy for the emerging Internet culture? What is today perceived as censorship, when its official institutions do no longer exist, and what provokes accordingly "new" samizdat practices?[6] How is the historic experience and collective memory of Soviet samizdat integrated into the context of contemporary global media?

Samizdat as a Reference Frame for Russian Internet Culture

> In the phenomenon of samizdat of the 60s–80s, as in a magic crystal, all main principles of life on the web are reflected.
>
> —Sergej Kuznecov[7]

The Internet offers vast possibilities for self-publication that are used actively by millions of people in Russia and around the world. The overwhelming literary activity on the Russian Internet in particular has been noted by participants as well as by researchers.[8] Contemporary observers regard Soviet samizdat to be a likely influence on the level and nature of online self-publication, along with explanations that rely on the recurrent myth that Russian culture is hyper literature-centric.[9] But web resources also refer directly to the historic predecessor. Thus, one of the most popular self-publication forums, based on the server of the "famous" Maksim Moškov library, is named "Samizdat" (http://zhurnal.lib.ru).

Indeed, in the rough and tumble of Perestroika times and the resulting restructuring of the cultural infrastructure, the knowledge of how to use unconventional publishing tools may have largely contributed to the successful extension of the Internet into literary life. The historic circumstances allowed the emerging technology to fill the gaps in the cultural infrastructure, a fact that largely contributed to the significance of the Internet as a cultural sphere in Russia and the Russian-speaking diaspora. Consequentially, the "RuNet," as its users often refer to the Russian or Russian-speaking Internet, is sometimes interpreted as a semantically, sociologically, and culturally distinct sphere within the World Wide Web.[10]

Russian Internet researcher Eugene Gorny considers samizdat even to be one of the main metaphors used to describe the RuNet aside from "kitchen table-talk" and "public sphere" (the latter is, by the way, more a theoretical concept than a metaphor).[11] If the term indeed may be understood as a metaphor describing the RuNet what will be its *tertium comparationis*? What allows us to compare samizdat and publishing activities on the Internet are first of all horizontal patterns of information exchange and the informal character of communication. As a consequence, both are "almost impossible to comprehensively monitor, filter, or suppress,"[12] effectively making complete censorship impossible. In her comparison of samizdat and the Internet, Sharon Balazs adds further similarities (listed in the left column of table 11.1) that may roughly be subsumed under the following categories: technology/infrastructure, content/audience, and "ideology"/agenda (see right column).

Table 11.1. Comparison of historic samizdat and the Internet (based on Sharon Balazs)

Informal communication structures and networks	Technological and communication infrastructure
Collective production and distribution of texts	
Heterogeneity of genres and topics	Content and audiences
Heterogeneity of audiences	
Noncommercial groundings	"Ideology" and agenda
Ideology of free access to information and freedom of expression	
Alternative public sphere	

It is noteworthy, though, that comparisons of historic samizdat and cultural activity on the Internet are inspired less by content or modes of production and distribution, and more by the ideological concept of samizdat as a cultural model with an agenda of free media usage, of an alternative, unrestricted public sphere.

Independent, Collective, Noncommercial: Samizdat as a Positive Cultural Model

Protagonists of samizdat of Soviet times have insisted that their self-publication initiatives and structures were neither illegal, an underground structure, nor even in "opposition" to State institutions,[13] but that samizdat was an independent network of cultural and literary activity, "a refuge for uncensored literature," and a "comparatively free sphere of thought."[14] Aside from the existing structural and technological parallels listed above, this seems to be the most important legacy of historical samizdat for the emerging Russian Internet culture: the agenda of an independent, free, and creative sphere of communication and cultural activity.[15] Such a view is exemplified prototypically by the Russian writer and philosopher Dmitrij Gal'kovskij's concept of "Samizdat-2" (the author himself was a prominent figure of "classical" samizdat in the 1980s). Gal'kovskij wrote a mission statement in 1998 entitled "The Manifesto of New Russian Samizdat," in which he calls on the intelligentsia to take action on the RuNet, in order to withstand the growing monopolization of the new media system, on the one hand, and fight its uncontrolled commercialization, on the other: "By opening my own virtual server, I want to initiate a new cultural, social and, finally, political phenomenon: 'Samizdat-2,' the Russian independent informational sphere. Of course, important steps in this direction have already been taken.... Nevertheless, it seems to me that the birth of the 'Russian internet' as a spiritual phenomenon will take place only now."[16] Dmitrij Gal'kovskij's manifesto is a good example of the attempt to create an independent information sphere in response to the development of the new, postcommunist, "democratic" media system, which is soon experienced as politically corrupt by large parts of the population. The rhetoric of the manifesto is declamatory; it understands samizdat not as a publication "technology," but as a cultural phenomenon leading (back?) to spiritual unity and collective creativity.

The RuNet of early times has indeed repeatedly been interpreted in similar pseudoreligious and mythological terms, stressing especially the aspect of collectivity as a form of "electronic sobornost[17] [conciliarism]."[18] Samizdat and Internet culture thus are both characterized by a strong community feeling—the experience of shared reading. The collective experience of Soviet samizdat led to the feeling of being part of a spiritual unity of "half-mythological" character that carried almost religious connotations.[19] This secular worshiping of the word is tellingly revealed in the description of samizdat manuscripts as relics by Klimontovič.[20]

Sergej Kuznecov also stresses the aspect of collective production and reception of samizdat writings.[21] To Kuznecov, copying a book is like "reading with the finger tips," like "rewriting" a literary work. He describes this as an almost magical process by which the reader incorporates parts of the works, including even bits of the author's personality. The sharing of samizdat copies is likened to the ancient Christians living in the underground or (here he demonstrates a self-ironic approach) to the distribution scheme of Herbalife. Because texts had to be read within a limited time (copies had to be returned), a simultaneity of reading occurred, which led to what Kathleen Parthé called the "one text paradigm,"[22] forming a "huge network whose threads were uniting us all."[23] This, indeed, is an almost exact description of today's Internet.

In a diversifying post-Soviet society and later under the circumstances of market economy, this experience of shared reading was gradually lost. The reference to samizdat gets nostalgic: "Today, in our split culture, there is no such uniting phenomenon any more. I don't know whether this is good or bad. There was a time when, as Andrej Bitov once remarked wittily, 'we all read one and the same book.' Now we read all different books."[24] The RuNet, especially in its early years in the 1990s, has generated a new mode of such simultaneous reading, as digital texts are shared easily (though they are not copies of "one and the same book"), and discussion is encouraged through the interactive possibilities of the medium. Interestingly enough, it is thus the Internet—often accused of depriving writing and reading of its bodily experience—that is attributed a similar intensity, even intimacy, of writing and reading experience. File-sharing, rapid mouth-to-mouth propaganda, the almost instantaneous process of commenting on and interweaving texts with the help of hyperlinks—this is how Internet literature has revived samizdat as a common cultural experience. Präprintium and postprintium, despite of all their differences, both understand literature as a collective practice.[25]

Another important aspect characterizing both Soviet samizdat and "cyberculture" is the decidedly noncommercial ideology of each. Publishing activities are seen as an endeavor of cultural "enlightenment"[26] or as resistance to suppressive forces, be they of a political or economic nature.[27] As Eugene Gorny points out, a significant number of the RuNet's protagonists explain and justify the free-of-charge online circulation of (literary) texts with a specific understanding of private property rights different from the Western concept, inapplicable to the Russian context.[28] This characteristic of contemporary digital samizdat is of course highly relevant to copyright issues.[29]

So-called countercultural resources with a strong "underground" profile (such as the internet magazines *RWCDAX*,[30] *End of the World News*,[31] or *: LENIN:*—most of them not updated any more) vividly demonstrate such an anticommercial impulse, as Saša Šerman points out: "Indeed, 'RWCDAX' turned out to be the only web resource continuing the traditions of samizdat *under the conditions of the triumphant market system* [italics mine]."[32]

Thus, besides the tradition of an intelligentsia as put forward by Gal'kovskij, the underground culture of Soviet times was present at the emergence of the Internet in the 1990s.[33] Briefly summarized, these underground aesthetics may be described as the "aesthetics of ugliness." "Amoral" positions, the "art to be bad," as Šerman writes, result in a topical focus on drugs, pornography, and violence. Satanist, neopagan, and occult sciences are also very popular—characteristics the Russian digital underground shares with its American and worldwide counterparts.

A journal close to the underground tradition mentioned above is *:LENIN: Anti-Cultural Weekly,* founded as a forum for nonconformist artists, writers, and musicians by the mathematician and online writer Michail Verbickij. Besides thematic rubrics about music, literature and politics, literary critics, writers and "politicians" (like the well-known, right-wing philosopher and Eurasian politician Aleksandr Dugin) participated as columnists. Verbickij himself contributed a column dedicated to cyberculture called "Horror and Moral Terror" (Užas i moral'nyj terror).

In one of the last volumes of *:LENIN:* (appearing in 2002), Verbickij promoted the fight against copyright as a national duty and a prolongation of the mission of Soviet samizdat:

> Russians know how to fight against copyright, how to fight the cultural occupation and the dull swinishness of the fat bureaucrats. A way which has been practiced for years. As soon as a written work is taken out of circulation because of "copyright" violations, samizdat steps in and the forbidden text is copied by hand, until it becomes available for everybody who still experiences a vital feeling of patriotism and freedom. The supporters of intellectual property, copyright, the hamburger and Coca Cola can defeat Russia only if they are willing to kill a million people a day, not a year.
>
> As long as Russia is alive, nobody is allowed to speak about copyright on the territory inhabited by Russians.
>
> We do not have any copyright.[34]

Here, the link between the samizdat tradition and copyright issues is actualized in a striking way mixing nationalist and antiglobalist aspects.[35] The paranoid rhetoric of Verbickij's writings shows a typical trait of a certain segment of Russian Internet culture: an eclectic mixture of ideologies from the left (communism) and from the right wing (nationalism, patriotism, and anti-Semitism).

A Danger to Russian Literature?
Samizdat as a Negative Cultural Model

One, of course, finds negative allusions to samizdat and its "reincarnation" on the Web. Russian poet Dmitrij Bykov, for example, sees in both Soviet samizdat and contemporary digital self-publishing what is essentially a battlefield for untalented writers competing for fame they would never acquire if confronted with "real" competition. The very fact of oppression already in Soviet times, to his mind, often became a virtue itself, and questions of aesthetics moved into the background: "In this sense, the literary internet is nothing else than a continuation of samizdat with all its characteristic underground complexes and a tiresome bonfire of the vanities."[36] In Soviet times, belonging to the opposition ennobled authors almost automatically. Their status today is maintained by the idea of belonging at the same time to a technological elite and to a marginal group of outsiders opposing the politics of the current administration, globalized commercialization, and mainstream aesthetics.

One of the most prominent and prolific critics of Internet samizdat is Dmitrij Kuz'min, a Moscow poet and editor of the successful literary site Vavilon.ru.[37] Kuz'min distinguishes *samizdat* from "sam-sebja-izdat," a term introduced in the 1950s by the Russian Soviet poet Nikolaj Glazkov.[38] While the first term describes self-publication (not necessarily of one's own work) forced by reasons of political suppression, the second refers to a "do-it-yourself literature" that avoids, from Kuz'min's point of view, the basic selection process regarding the aesthetic value of the work: "We have Internet samizdat, or more precisely, websites with a free publication, where everybody can publish what he wants. I think that this is an absolutely bad thing, as it blurs the borders between a genius and a hack by putting the whole flow of texts in one row."[39]

Kuz'min does not deny the merits of the Internet as a technological tool helping to distribute "good" or, in his terminology, "professional" literature within the country and among its diasporas. Nevertheless, he states that by circumventing the basic selection processes of traditional legitimizing institutions, Internet publication endangers the qualitative standards and norms of literature as a whole.

From the perspective of the typical graphomaniacs though, who proudly present themselves as the only free writers in today's commercialized media markets, the selection processes provided by the traditional institutions of high culture (literary journals, academies, awards) and the culture industry (publishing houses), represent censorship:

> We graphomaniacs are free like birds. We do not have to embrace the masters of literary circles and we do not have to bow in front of the editors, humbly asking to place our three lines in one of their publications. We, as parachutists, jump deliberately out into the free space, and nothing that happens with us is the result of corrections and guidelines. The ideal of the graphomaniac is not to publish, but to write. Of course, we love to be published ourselves, but as this is not our main function in life, we do not have to go for compromises, the risk of becoming 'sell outs' does not exist for us. As members of a parachutists' club, we fly because our souls demand it, and not because we have to earn money for our "daily bread."[40]

This negation, deliberate or unintentional, of literary quality and professionalism is why the naive, private, and decidedly nonpolitical digital samizdat can be qualified as "dangerous" by the representatives of the cultural elite. This conflict, of course, is not exclusive to the RuNet—it has been discussed worldwide since the 1990s regarding an emerging amateur culture that is seen either as the ultimate liberation of individual creativity or as its apocalypse.[41] In the Russian context, this conflict is rhetorically "nationalized" with regard to the specific tradition of Soviet samizdat and the auratic "nature" of Russian literature. With its millions of authors and texts, the literature-centric RuNet represents both the last refuge and the greatest threat to "Great Russian Literature."

To sum up, (digital) samizdat is understood either as the publication of literary or nonliterary texts that for political reasons cannot be integrated into the institutionalized media sector and thus can be made publicly available only with the help of alternative media. This does not principally contradict mechanisms of qualitative or normative control (such as the monitoring of resources or editorial politics). Samizdat can also be understood merely as self-publication, as a form of unrestricted self-expression not affected by the hierarchies of the social and cultural legitimizing institutions. Typical genres of the latter are personal homepages and, since the late 1990s, standardized publication platforms providing tools for publication as well as a functioning community environment. Samizdat as self-publishing, however, is only at first glance a nonpolitical activity, as it is also a means of attacking commercialization and the canonization of cultural production. In reality, of course, these two types of digital samizdat may overlap.

Digital Samizdat and Censorship

Samizdat—to put it somewhat hyperbolically—needs censorship, or at least a strong institutional force suppressing the freedom of expression. Especially since 1996 and 1997, the RuNet has been obsessed with censorship issues. Users fear censorship by state institutions, despite the fact that there are almost no documented incidents of censorship on the Web.[42] These fears, of course, are grounded in official media policies as well as in corresponding legal initiatives concerning Internet regulation.[43] "Realistic" and "imagined" fear in such a situation can hardly be distinguished— and it is precisely the incoherence of state action that may easily result in self-censorship.[44] It is a rather sad fact that the ominous, almost mythological fear of control and censorship is an experience shared by both Soviet and contemporary digital samizdat: "IT IS VERY DIFFICULT in Russia to delimit an imagined from a real danger," writes Telesin in "Samizdat Inside" in 1973, a diagnosis relevant today as well.

Nevertheless, one should not forget about the striking differences between Soviet and post-Perestroika Russia. Despite the indeed growing control of the media (especially in the fields of television and print), there is no longer a coherent system of censorship.[45] It is often not the suppression and elimination of the written word itself, but the control over the economy of attention in contemporary information society that constitutes governmental information policies today. As a result, the concept of censorship is getting fuzzy, and in consequence I would like to distinguish three major fields of what actually is experienced as censorship by the Russian Internet community: namely, political, ethical, and commercial censorship. The following brief case studies shall illustrate how these facets of real or imagined censorship intermingle, and how the underlying understanding of digital samizdat changes accordingly.

"Is It Acceptable to Sue a Writer?" The Case of Bajan Širjanov

Whereas regarding political issues, there exist observable restrictions in the official print and electronic media in "Putin's Russia," the number of topics that cannot be covered in literary works published in Russia today is comparatively small.[46] Texts that are not admitted to publication usually concern controversial issues like pornography, drug consumption, or violence, including texts expressing fascist, extremist, and nationalist points of view.[47] One prominent example is the scandal surrounding the novel *Nizšij pilotaž* (The Lower Pilotage), published under the pseudonym "Bajan Širjanov" by Kirill Vorob'ev, a successful author of trivial and fantasy novels in his offline life.

The novel *Nizšij pilotaž* explicitly portrays the life of Moscow drug addicts, and includes drastic descriptions of their sexual practices. It was originally published on the Web site "Russian Marginal Culture" (Russkaja Marginal'naja Kul'tura), but in 1997, the provider Glasnet closed down the project for reasons of political correctness. A copy of the manuscript was then made available by the writer and programmer Maksim Kononenko[48] on his personal homepage.

In the same year, the novel was nominated for participation in the online literary contest "Teneta." After ferocious discussions among the jury, the book was awarded first prize in its category.[49] The scandal, as often, functioned as a promotional tool, and the novel finally appeared in print thanks to the publishing houses Gelikon[50] and Ad Marginem,[51] the latter known for its controversial editorial politics mixing postmodern philosophy with right-wing nationalism and literature from the "sexual margins." The publication did not pass unnoticed by the official instances: in 2000, Ad Marginem was served notice by the Ministry of Press, Broadcasting and Mass Communications for the propaganda of drugs: "In Russia, we don't have censorship, and unfortunately we cannot forbid the publication of the book as such, but if there will be another violation registered from the side of the publishing house, we will make a formal record," a representative of the institution explained.[52]

Two years later, Širjanov aka Vorob'ev was accused once again, this time of pornography and for his literary follow-up, the novel *Seredinnyj pilotaž* (The Mid-Level Pilotage),[53] by the pro-Putin youth organization "Walking Together," along with his more prominent colleague, Vladimir Sorokin, regarding his book *Goluboe salo* (Blue Lard). While Sorokin's case got closed within only one year, the Širjanov trial extended over three years, and only in 2005 did the court officially dismiss the charge, concluding, on the basis of different kinds of linguistic expertise, that the novel does not include pornographic passages.

The controversy about limits on the freedom of expression thus affects both online and offline institutions and "communities." As the Širjanov case clearly demonstrates, efforts of censorship are not only displayed by the official institutions, but are an inherent part of the dynamics within the RuNet itself, which is no longer the ultimate refuge for controversial literature. The willingness to tolerate texts violating social norms has changed over time, as a citation by the founder of the literary web award, the "Teneta," Leonid Delicyn, demonstrates:

> We did not mind that, the language [Bajan Širjanov] uses, and the drugs which are described there, and all the stuff. [But] if you would survey people now whether it is acceptable to sue a writer they would say yes—he should go to prison. The more mainstream Russian culture comes to the Internet, the less place for us is there. ... My contest is run by other people now, at least officially there are different directors there. And we have a prosecutor in our jury who inspects all the works for their agreement with the norms of our ethics. *And people believe in that.* They say that it's okay, it's good. It's a different generation now, we serve a different generation of Internet users now. People believe that a literary commission should provide a certain level of ethics accepted in this society, so we say okay: we have a prosecutor who inspects all the works. Some of them understand that that is a joke. Some don't. (interview transcript with author's diction preserved; emphasis mine)[54]

Delicyn's personal observation is validated by sociological surveys: in 2004, about 76 percent of the Russian population voted in favor of politically and ethically censoring of the media (mainly film and television).[55] Censorship on the Internet thus seems to be even more connected to ethical and moral standards than politics in the direct sense.[56] Yet, as the trials against Bajan Širjanov and Vladimir Sorokin demonstrate, the discussions about ethically questionable resources on the Web may easily be politically instrumentalized.

"Unlimited Freedom of Speech?" The Russian Blogosphere

Internet research worldwide interprets blogging as one of the most popular and successful forms of digital samizdat.[57] The significance of electronic diaries offering "other voices" from the margins of society is a main topic and topos of media studies.[58] In Russia, blogging is highly popular, as well. A curious peculiarity of Russian blogging consists in the fact that it is closely affiliated with one specific blogging tool: LiveJournal.com (LJ), a service developed and hosted in the United States. Russian Internet researcher Eugene Gorny argues that LiveJournal, in Russian called ZheZhe (Živoj žurnal), has even turned into a generic term for blogging in general.[59] What makes ZheZhe so specific, according to Gorny, is the fact that LiveJournal, through the integration of individual journals on one server, turns into a network of mutually connected blogs, with a very high identification potential. As a consequence of this high social connectivity, users tend to identify themselves closely with the specific service or platform.

What makes it so especially attractive within the Russian context, though, besides this community-building function, is the exterritorial hosting of the service in the United States, interpreted by many users as protection from the (presumed) intrusive practices of the Russian secret services. Based territorially and juridically in the United States, LiveJournal may be attributed functions of tamizdat, providing a certain level of autonomy and independence. In the years 2005 and 2006, however, the Russian LiveJournal community was hit by two major scandals that seriously affected its status, in the eyes of its users, as a forum for free expression.

The year 2005 in the chronicles of Russian LiveJournal will supposedly be labeled the year of the "Kill-NATO-Campaign." Territorially based in the United States and thus bound to American law, LiveJournal accordingly prohibits the publication of materials calling for violence against other people or against minority rights. An abuse team reacts to violations and has the right to suspend the journals of users who do not follow the rules. In June 2005, a Russian LJ user was suspended for publishing what the LiveJournal abuse team decided was pornographic material. Gorny covered the incident in his analysis of the Russian LiveJournal community:

> The conflict escalated to the next stage ... when Michail Verbickij, a non-conformist writer, announced that one of the journals had been closed for using the slogan, "Kill NATO" (which was considered by the LJ administration as break-

ing the rules of service) and called on others to reproduce the phrase in their journals. The journals of those users who followed the call were also closed by the abuse team. Later on, some of them beat a retreat and removed the controversial phrase. However, the conflict started a wave of discussion about free speech. Several dozens of users, including some popular and respected individuals, declared their ideological disagreement with LJ policy and moved to alternative blogging services such as LJ.Rossia.org in hope of finding *unlimited freedom of speech*. (emphasis mine)[60]

The "unlimited freedom of speech," in the eyes of a significant number of the Russian bloggers, is endangered not only by official Russian media policies, but by the "institution" of American political correctness, as well. Michail Verbickij, the initiator of the "Kill-NATO-campaign" (mentioned above for his radical "Anti-Copyright-Manifesto"), accordingly interprets the fight against copyright and for free publication as a national duty in the legacy of Soviet samizdat. Samizdat, in this interpretation, becomes motivated by an eclectic mix of nationalist, antigovernmental, anticommercial, and antiglobalist attitudes.

In 2006, the next scandal hit the Russian LiveJournal community and seriously damaged what remained of its status as a communication sphere free of censorship and the possible influence from state authorities. In autumn 2006, the owner of LiveJournal, the company Six Apart, concluded a "complex partnership agreement" with Sup Fabric, a Russian media and publishing company partly financed by the "oligarch" Aleksandr Mamut.[61] As a result of this agreement, the management and service rights of the Cyrillic segment of LiveJournal were transferred from the American partners to the Russian company. The following controversial discussions about a "selling-out" of the Russian blogosphere on the eve of presidential elections in 2008 were fueled largely by fears of a possibly increasing control by Russian state authorities. Thus, users feared that personal data could be transferred into the hands of the Federal Security Service of the Russian Federation. A particularly visible reaction to the rumors and fears aroused by the SUP-deal was a post by the creator of LiveJournal, Brad Fitzpatrick, in his Weblog after a visit to Moscow: "I wish I could calm people down, but I realize the political fears/implications of this are way too big for me to make much of a difference."[62]

In the global media environment, samizdat is no longer a phenomenon touching upon the political, juridical, and technological conditions of one nation, state, or territory; it affects media policies and legislative practices on a worldwide scale.[63] Regarding the Russian blogosphere mainly "residing" on the blogging service LiveJournal.com, American legislation is at the same time seen as a danger to free expression when it comes to the implementation of norms of political correctness and as a shelter providing protection from persecution by the Russian state authorities.

Stihi.ru: Efforts to Implement Censorship on the Internet

One should not forget, though, to mention a strong contingent in contemporary Russian society that does not fear censorship, but actively demands it in the media in order to protect the nation from "harmful" ideas and content. This tendency not just to protest, but rather to implement ethical and political censorship on the Internet is illustrated by the very popular literary self-publication platform called Stihi.ru.[64] The Web site created in 1999 by entrepreneur Igor' Sazonov and currently "run" by Dmitrij Kravčuk, was used in 2010 by approximately 261,000 authors who have published more than eight million texts. Publication is free of charge, but additional editing and printing services come at a small fee. Authors comment excessively on each other's writings, producing a strong community feeling and turning the publication platform into a typical postprintium-style communication environment.

It is impossible to give a comprehensive picture of the materials published on this Web site regarding the quantitative amount of texts and the heterogeneity of genres and topics. Nevertheless, the direction of the Web site as a whole, which positions itself as *nacional'nyj server sovremennoj poèzii* (a national server of contemporary poetry), validates the impression that the texts published on Stihi.ru for the most part adhere to ethical and normative standards in literary aesthetics.

Nevertheless, in early 2005, the director and editor-in-chief of Stihi.ru, Dmitrij Kravčuk, published a directive limiting the scope of literary topics admitted for publication on the Web site.[65] According to this directive, any works should be banned from the server that touch upon contemporary political events in Russia (such as war in Chechnya or other armed conflicts). Kravčuk's announcement also forbade any negative references to Russian politicians and political organizations (including the aforementioned pro-Putin youth organization "Walking Together" that sued the writers Širjanov and Sorokin). The authors of Stihi.ru protested, and the initiative had to be dismissed. Nevertheless, the incident clearly illustrates efforts to implement ethics-based norms on the Internet not only top-down, but bottom-up as well.

To summarize: censorship is a key issue on the RuNet. Censorship, nevertheless, is not tied up exclusively or even primarily with politics; it also has an important relationship to ethical and moral norms and values. As censorship became a fuzzy concept with the end of the Soviet regime, it is (re)constructed by the protagonists of Russian Internet culture in very diverse ways. The right of free expression of the Russian Internet community in post-Soviet Russia seems to be endangered by:

(1) the monopoly of the state-controlled media (as well as the monopolies of so-called oligarchs) in the fields of traditional print and television (see Galkovskij's concept of "Samizdat-2");

(2) the "political correctness" of liberal media policies restricting the individual's freedom of expression (see the blogosphere and the "Kill-NATO" scandal); and

(3) the growing commercialization of culture in the capitalist system (sometimes referred to as "corporate fascism"; see Verbickij's paranoid pathos of samizdat as national defense against global consumerism).

Conclusions, Hypotheses, Open Questions

The historic experience and the collective memory of samizdat as (1) an alternative medium for publication and communication and (2) a cultural model for an independent, alternative public sphere have clearly inspired and influenced the development of the RuNet, especially in the literary field but as well in the more general sense of the Web as a means of social and political communication. The question remains, though: How far does the term *samizdat* as an analytical tool adequately describe the processes of political and literary self-publication activities in the changing circumstances of post-Soviet Russia?

Production and communication modes of classical samizdat and nonconformist online culture differ largely. While samizdat publications were officially forbidden and could be accessed only by a very restricted audience, digital samizdat as part of today's transnational online communities is globally accessible. Restrictions, of course, are enforced, but, due to the technological structures of the Web, can only be partially put into practice. Accordingly, the main "filter" regulating participation in literary and public debates is no longer officially enacted censorship, but rather the question of digital empowerment, of access to digital resources of knowledge and communication. Or, as the sinologist Martin Hala puts it with regard to online and digital culture in China: "The Internet has a much broader audience than samizdat ever had, as it does not operate in the underground. The safety and the anonymity which the Internet guarantees do not stem from secrecy and concealment, but at contrary are based on the mere quantitative mass of participants."[66]

In a globally connected world, censorship cannot be enacted anymore as consistently as throughout the times of Soviet informational isolation without endangering economic prospects for the future. Governmental institutions in Russia—as well as worldwide—accordingly react not only by restriction, by blocking or shutting down disagreeable contents and resources. They engage rather in what one could call positive censorship, that is, the manipulation of information and public opinion through new, smart modes of propaganda. Tatjana Gorjaeva, in the conclusion to her study on *Political Censorship in the USSR 1917–1991*, sketches these systematic changes: censorship in post-Soviet Russia may appear in such diverse forms and activities as commercial takeovers, disinformation campaigns, and political PR.[67] Thus, freedom of expression is endangered not only by the suppression of information, but even more by its manipulation and "fabrication." Consequently, the previously distinct space of samizdat erodes. On the Web, nonconformist information coexists with official sources and communiqués. A resolution pledging for a demission of Vladimir Putin as Russian premier is only one click away from the official video blog by President Dmitry Medvedev.

These changes are reflected very well by some of the representatives of the contemporary RuNet community, for example media activist Oleg Kireev. He curated an exhibition in early 2006 called "From Russian Politicized Samizdat to Tactical Media,"[68] a formulation that to my mind expresses very well the emergence of a global culture of resistance within the worldwide media networks and with the RuNet being an integral part of it. The same is valid for the seemingly nonpolitical, graphomaniac samizdat that finds its analogs in the emergence of a worldwide amateur culture. Thus, from my point of view, it seems to be more suitable to restrict the term *samizdat* to the historic period of the Soviet era (or, more precisely, the years between 1956 and 1985), and to analyze current nonconformist media practices on the RuNet in the context of global media usages. To elaborate synchronic similarities within World Wide Web culture might be more productive than to stress diachronic continuities and helps to avoid the danger of uncritically extrapolating traditional stereotypes of Russian culture as, for example, a literature-centric one.

In the diverse disciplinary fields of media theory, cultural studies, and communication studies a range of alternative terms and concepts for the interpretation and analysis of global online cultures has been elaborated, which might as well help to describe more adequately today's digital cultures of resistance in Russia as well as in other postsocialist countries. Thus, Nancy Fraser's feminist re-reading of the Habermasian concept of the public sphere, in which she introduces the concept of "subaltern counter public spheres," has proved to be highly productive for the interpretation of digital mobilization cultures worldwide.[69] The media theoretical approach by scientist and web practitioner Geert Lovink deserves further mention, as he shows in detailed case studies how the digital "carnival of difference" (Karneval der Differenz) interacts with processes of "underlying conformity" (tiefer liegende Konformität), how the "programmatic irrelevance" of graphomaniac and amateur writing, for example in countless blogs, generates their specific potential as a resource for economic and politic strategies of manipulation.[70] The analysis of Russian digital and networked culture might profit from such general theoretical approaches that avoid the prescription of seemingly national characteristics (samizdat, literature-centrism, etc.) and to interpret the RuNet as part of the global cultures of resistance.

Furthermore, when seen from "below," that is, not from an overall theoretical angle, but starting from a practical analysis of what is actually happening on the Russian Internet, its democratic and liberating potential[71] is more and more questionable if not altogether deniable. Thus, Gasan Gusejnov states the discrepancy between Russian online network activities and political apathy in the offline world.[72] Floriana Fossato and John Llyod even more generally propagate the view that the Internet in Russia has not fulfilled its mission as a grass-roots medium.[73] Marcus Alexander and, recently, Evgeny Morozov interpret the RuNet even primarily as an arena for political technologies of all sorts. The subaltern counterpublic spheres, in the sense that Nancy Fraser uses them, are thus transformed into an experimental ground for a new form of digital propaganda.[74] Dmitrij Golynko-Vol'fson subscribes to such a point of view when he argues that the Russian social networks serve rather as soft tools for political propaganda through the encouragement of hedonistic consumerism, instead of mobilizing tools for nonconformist movements. As long as the Russian offline society remains dissociated, according to Golynko-Vol'fson, no digital and network technology will help to promote political participation and nonconformist thinking.[75] From this point of view, the social media revolution, analogous to the so-called social Facebook and Twitter revolutions in the Arab States in spring 2011, should not to be expected in the nearer future.[76]

To sum up: while there obviously exist parallels between Soviet samizdat and nonconformist digital culture in the sense of an agenda of the free word, as illustrated, for example, in a recent thematic issue of the scientific journal *Osteuropa* titled "Look Back Ahead: Samizdat, Internet and the Freedom of the Word," the usage of the term *samizdat* as an analytical tool should be carefully considered and weighed against the given context. At the same time, the metaphorical usage of the term *samizdat* as a self-description by practitioners of the (literary) RuNet is most instructive on the level of discourse analysis. The frequent use of the samizdat metaphor to describe Russian Internet culture in this sense serves a multiplicity of functions:

(1) It ennobles a seemingly banal practice of self-publication by linking itself to a glorious past.

(2) The reference to samizdat helps to reincarnate an auratic understanding of the word and literature, which in a market economy lose their status significantly.

(3) It expresses an understanding of literature not as a private individualistic activity, but as shared experience (postprintium).

(4) It allows the protagonists to reject the basic laws of the economy of attention. In other words: to qualify one's work as belonging among samizdat texts allows the evasion of formal standards (politically, ethically, or aesthetically controversial).

(5) Last but not least, in times of increasing media control since the presidency of Vladimir Putin, the samizdat metaphor articulates fears about the real and imagined threat of restrictions imposed on the Internet.

Postscriptum: The Internet is a communication environment of permanent change. Thus it is impossible to keep track of the dynamics within a book contribution. Nevertheless, this short postscriptum shall highlight the by all means dramatic events of the year 2012. Since this article had been revised for the last time in spring 2011, the protest movement of the so-called 'Russian Winter' demonstrated, how effectively on- and offline mobilization may interact, organizing huge manifestations via blogs and Twitter in Moscow, St. Petersburg and bigger cities in the Russian regions. Some of the cited above critical accounts concerning the supposedly apathetic nature of the Russian society are if not disproved, at least challenged by the events. At the same time, official reactions and legislative initiatives as the law "On Protecting Children from Information Harmful to Their Health and Development" [O zashchite detei ot informacii, prichiniaiushchei vred ikh zdorovij i razvitiu] witness of a possible new, and this is more restrict attitude towards controlling and filtering of the Internet in Russia by official politics. The new law has come into force on November 1, 2012, and aims at protecting children from the dangers of pornography, pedophilia and drug abuse on the Internet, by blacklisting the respective web resources. Critics assume that the law opens up possibilities for misuse in the sense of censoring as well politically disagreeable content. Within the first two weeks, about 180 web resources have been blacklisted and blocked, as for example the parodist encyclopedia, the Russian Lurkmore, which as a result moved to the top-level-domain .to. A phenomenon of emerging digital tamizdat?[77]

Notes

1. Oleg Novikov, "Virtual'nyj samizdat," *Večernyj Peterburg* (12 December 2000). Available online at "(S)negazeta. Literaturnye proizvedenija, raznosti i summy," *Vypusk* 18 (3 March 2001), http://sds.sinor.ru/sn/103/18010314.htm (accessed 19 August 2011): "Когда-нибудь историки самиздата подвергнут тщательному анализу ситуацию, возникшую в нашей стране в 90-х годах XX века. Отсутствие официальной цензуры и массовое распространение компьютерных технологий дали возможность любителям литературы увидеть свои произведения опубликованными. ... Теперь, с развитием Интернета, понятие "самиздат" приобретает новый смысл. Неизменной остается лишь идея неформального общения творческих личностей."
2. Günter Hirt and Sascha Wonders [Pseudonym Georg Witte, Sabine Hänsgen], eds., *Präprintium: Moskauer Bücher aus dem Samizdat* (Bremen, 1998). See also H. Gordon Skilling, "Samizdat: A Return to the Pre-Gutenberg Era?" *Cross Currents* 1 (1982): 64–80.
3. This essay is a shortened version of a chapter on digital samizdat included in my German language monograph *Russische Literatur im Internet. Zwischen digitaler Folklore und politischer Propaganda* (Bielefeld, 2011). See also my contribution "Creative Self Articulation and Censorship: RuNet and the Tradition of Samizdat" [Kreative Selbstartikulation und Verbot. RuNet und die Tradition des Samizdat] as part of the thematic issue of *Osteuropa*, "Look Back Ahead: Samizdat, Internet and the Freedom of the Word" [Blick zurück nach vorn. Samizdat, Internet und die Freiheit des Wortes] 11 (2010): 85–103.
4. Various expressions are used synonymously, such as "digital samizdat" (digital'nyj samizdat), "virtual samizdat" (virtual'nyj samizdat), and "net samizdat" (setevoj samizdat). See Igor' Faramazjan, "Paravozik iz Romaškovo" i ego passažiry (o romane E. Stjažkinoj)," *Intellektual'no-chudožestvennyj žurnal "Dikoe pole. Doneckij proekt"* 1 (2002), http://www.dikoepole.org/numbers_journal.php?id_txt=41 (accessed 19 August 2011); Dmitrij Kuz'min, Ol'ga Zubova, "Nikto ne prosil Puškina byt' prošče, a Pugačevu—složnee. Interv'ju," *Apel'sin. Informacionnoe agenstvo* (4 April 2006), http://apelcin.ru/news/29191-dmitrij-kuzmin-nikto-ne-prosil-pushkina-byt-proshhe-a-pugachevu-slo zhnee.html (accessed 26 August 2011); Novikov "Virtual'nyj samizdat."
5. The Russian Internet, often labeled by its participants as "RuNet," is not synonymous to the Russian-speaking Internet, with the latter one including Web resources and activities in the Russian-speaking diasporas; see Henrike Schmidt, Katy Teubener, and Nils Zurawski,"Virtual (Re)unification? Diasporic Cultures on the Russian Internet," in *Control + Shift: Public and Private Usages of the Russian Internet,* ed. Henrike Schmidt, Katy Teubener, and Natalja Konradova (Norderstedt, 2006), 120–46. Available online at http://www.ruhr-uni-bochum.de/russ-cyb/library/texts/en/control_shift/Schmidt_Teu bener_Zurawski.pdf (accessed 19 August 2011). While there does not exist precise data concerning the number of Russian-speaking users active on the global Internet, the percentage of Internet penetration in the Russian Federation is constantly monitored, for example by Fond Obščestvennoe mnenie (the Public Opinion Foundation). For spring 2011, about 46 percent of the Russian population is reported to use the Internet at least once a month and 33 percent to be online on a daily basis. See "Issledovanija, Internet v Rossii," http://bd.fom.ru/map/projects/internet.
6. It is interesting to see, however, that the Russian word *samizdat* has come to define independent media on a worldwide scale, as illustrated by English-speaking resources devoting themselves to "the American samizdat." See Ernest Partridge, "Amerikanskij samizdat—American samizdat," *The Crisis Papers: An Anthology of the Best Political Opinion and Commentary From the Progressive Internet*, http://www.crisispapers.org/features/samizdat.htm (accessed 19 August 2011): "Today, in what we like to call 'the

Free World,' computers, printers and copiers are abundant. Instead of furtive painstaking hours at the typewriter, 'underground' texts can be duplicated in disks and CDs a few seconds. Accordingly, Soviet-style control of ideas and information by the authorities is no longer possible. Most significantly, perhaps, the computer has given us, via the internet, an 'American Samizdat.'"

7. Sergej Kuznecov, "Pust' poka vsego četyre kopii (Samizdat bez politiki)," *Russkij žurnal. Net-kul'tura* (14 April 1998), http://old.russ.ru/journal/netcult/98-04-14/kuznets.htm (accessed 19 August 2011): "В феномене самиздата 60-80-х, как в магическом кристалле, отразились основные принципы бытования Сети."
8. Ol'ga Černorickaja, "Fenomenologija setevogo avtora," *Topos. Literaturno-filosofskij žurnal* (21 March 2005), http://www.topos.ru/article/3393/printed (accessed 19 August 2011); Robert Hauser, *Technische Kulturen oder kultivierte Technik? Das Internet in Deutschland und Russland* (Berlin, 2010); Natalja Konradova, "The Formation of Identity on the Russian-Speaking Internet: Based on the Literary Website Zagranica," in *Control + Shift*, ed. Schmidt, Teubener, and Konradova, 147–55; Sergej Kuznecov, "Roždenie Igry, smert' Avtora i virtual'noe pis'mo," *Inostrannaja literatura* 10 (1999). Available online in *Setevaja slovesnost'* (17 February 2000), http://www.litera.ru/slova/teoriya/kuznet.html (accessed 19 August 2011); Roman Lejbov, "15 let russkoj literatury v internete: transformacii samizdata," Podcast, *The Future of Russian: Language Culture in the Era of New Technology* (February 2009), http://www.uib.no/filearchive/rl.19.03.09_2.mp3 (accessed 19 August 2011).
9. Vlad Strukov, "Digital (After-)Life of Russian Classical Literature," *Kultura. Russland-Kulturanalysen 1 (2009): Notes from the Virtual Untergrund. Russian Literature on the Internet* (Forschungsstelle Osteuropa an der Universität Bremen, 2009), http://www.kultura-rus.de/kultura_dokumente/artikel/englisch/k1_2009_EN_Strukov.pdf (accessed 19 August 2011), 9–10.
10. Eugene Gorny, *A Creative History of the Russian Internet* (Saarbrücken, 2009). Doctoral dissertation submitted in 2006 to Goldsmiths College, University of London. Available online at http://www.ruhr-uni-bochum.de/russ-cyb/library/texts/en/gorny_creative_history_runet.pdf (accessed 19 August 2011). For a critical review of this concept of the RuNet as being "different," see Ekaterina Kratasjuk, "Construction of 'Reality' in Russian Mass Media: News on Television and on the Internet," in *Control + Shift*, ed. Schmidt, Teubener, and Konradova, 34–50; or Andrei Gornykh and Almira Ousmanova, "Aesthetics of Internet and Visual Consumption. On the RuNet's Essence and Specificity," in *Control + Shift*, ed. Schmidt, Teubener, and Konradova, 156–76.
11. Gorny, *Creative History*, 188–89.
12. Michael Rogers, "Censorship-Resistant Communication over Public Networks," University College of London, Department of Computer Science (2006), http://citeseerx.ist.psu.edu/viewdoc/download?doi=10.1.1.122.7182&rep=rep1&type=pdf (accessed 19 August 2011); Sharon Balazs, "Samizdat and the Internet—A Comparison," University of Alberta (N.d.), http://www.slis.ualberta.ca/issues/sbalazs/samizdat.htm (accessed 14 August 2006).
13. Julius Telesin, "Inside samizdat," *Encounter* 40, no. 2 (1973), 25–33; Balazs, "Samizdat and Internet"; Michael Meerson-Aksenov, "The Dissident Movement and Samizdat," in *The Political, Social and Religious Thought of Russian Samizdat: An Anthology*, ed. Michael Meerson-Aksenov and Boris Shragin (Belmont, 1977).
14. Faramazjan, "Paravozik iz Romaškovo."
15. Gorny, *Creative History*.
16. Dmitrij Gal'kovskij, "Manifest nogovo russkogo samizdata" (17 January 1998). Available online at http://www.guelman.ru/slava/manifest/istochniki/galk.htm (accessed

19 August 2011): "Открывая свой виртуальный сервер, я хочу положить начало новому культурному, социальному и, наконец, политическому явлению: 'Сами-здату-2' — русскому независимому информационному пространству. Разумеется, значительные шаги в этом направлении делались и раньше.... Однако, мне кажется, что рождение 'Русского Интернета' как духовного явления произойдёт только сейчас."

17. A term used in Russian religious philosophy in order to designate the "spiritual community of many jointly living people."
18. Michail Ėpštejn, "SEVERNAJA PAUTINA. Virtual'nye miry russkoj kul'tury," *Žurnal pod redakciej Michaila Epštejna. Vvedenie*, http://old.russ.ru/antolog/intelnet/zh_sever_pautina.html (accessed 26 August 2011).
19. Faramazjan, "Paravozik iz Romaškovo."
20. Nikolaj Klimontovič, "Nostal'gija po samizdatu," *Nezavisimaja gazeta* (4 February 2003), http://www.ng.ru/style/2003-02-04/12_nostalgia.html (accessed 19 August 2011).
21. Kuznecov, "Samizdat bez politiki."
22. Kathleen F. Parthé, *Russia's Dangerous Texts: Politics Between the Lines* (New Haven, 2004), 12–14.
23. Kuznecov, "Samizdat bez politiki."
24. Klimontovič, "Nostal'gija po samizdatu": "Сегодня такого объединяющего явления в нашей раздробленной культуре нет. Не знаю, хорошо это или плохо. То было время, когда, как иронически сострил однажды Андрей Битов, 'мы все читали одну и ту же книгу.' Теперь мы все читаем разные."
25. See Henrike Schmidt, "'Ručkoj skrip-skrip, klaviaturkoj tjuk-tjuk, golovenkoj dum-dum.' O vlijanii sovremennych pis'mennych i kommunikacionnych technologij na russkuju poėziju," *The Russian Language Journal*, Special Issue: "Language Culture in Contemporary Russia," 58 (2008): 19–46.
26. Strukov, "Digital (After-)Life."
27. Various explanations have been proposed in order to historicize the noncommercial agenda of Internet culture, for example through the ethnographic concept of gift culture (see Richard Barbrook, "The Hi-Tech Gift Economy," *First Monday: Peer-reviewed journal on the Internet* 3 (1998), http://www.firstmonday.dk/issues/issue3_12/barbrook/ (accessed 11 November 2004). Commented copy available in First Monday, http://firstmonday.org/htbin/cgiwrap/bin/ojs/index.php/fm/article/view/1517/1432 (accessed 26 August 2011). Within the Russian context, Gorny, *Creative History*, and Anna Bowles, "The Changing Face of the RuNet," in *Control + Shift*, ed. Schmidt, Teubener, and Konradova, 21–33, brought forward the concept of *blat* as an informal network of exchanges and favors (which emerged in the Soviet era) as a possible explanation.
28. Evgenij Gornyj, "Problema kopirajta v russkoj seti: bitva za 'Goluboe salo,'" (September 1999), http://www.zhurnal.ru/staff/gorny/texts/salo.html (accessed 19 August 2011). Of course, not all Russian Internet users oppose Western copyright conventions. As a survey of popular LiveJournal communities shows, copyright legislation is approved by its users to a high extent; see Michail Guzner, "Internetcommunities am Beispiel des russischsprachigen Teils von LiveJournal," Diplomarbeit an der Gerhard-Mercator-Universität Duisburg-Essen (2007).
29. Hauser, *Das Internet in Deutschland und Russland*.
30. *RWCDAX* is a Russian web journal promoting radical views on culture, politics, and literature. See, for instance, "Ėkstremizm: ideologija, kul'tura, ritual," homepage (1996–2000), http://rwcdax.here.ru (accessed 19 August 2011).
31. *End of the World News* homepage, http://imperium.lenin.ru/EOWN (accessed 19 August 2011).

32. Saša Šerman, "I-zin protiv Magazina, ili Iskusstvo byt' plochim," *Russkij žurnal, Netkul'tura* (20 August 1998), http://old.russ.ru:8083/journal/netcult/98-08-20/shermn.htm (accessed 19 August 2011): "На деле 'RWCDAX' стал единственным сетевым продолжателем традиций самиздата в условиях торжествующего рынка."
33. The term *underground*, of course, is problematic, as it cannot be defined sufficiently with regard to scientific criteria. Nevertheless, its usage seems to be justified, as it is applied by protagonists of Russian cyberculture to their own activities.
34. Michail Verbickij, "Antikopirajt," :*Lenin: antikul'turologičeskij eženedel'nik* (January–February 2002), http://imperium.lenin.ru/LENIN/32/C (accessed 19 August 2011): "У русских имеется испытанный десятилетиями способ борьбы с копирайтом, культурной оккупацией и тупым свинством разжиревших бюрократов. Как только то или иное произведение изымается из обращения на основе нарушения 'копирайтов,' вступает в действие самиздат — запрещенный текст копируется из рук в руки, пока он не станет доступен каждому, в ком жив патриотизм и свобода. Сторонники интеллектуальной собственности, копирайтов, гамбургера и кока-колы могут победить Россию, но для этого им нужно убивать по миллиону жителей не в год, а ежедневно. // А пока Россия жива, о копирайте, на территории, населенной русскими, говорить некому — и не с кем. // Копирайта у нас нет."
35. For an analysis of digital file sharing and the concept of samizdat, see, for example, Maria Haigh, "Downloading Communism: File Sharing as Samizdat in Ukraine," *Libri* 57 (2007): 165–78, http://www.tomandmaria.com/maria/publications/LibriDownloadingCommunismMariaHaigh.pdf (accessed 20 August 2011).
36. Dmitrij Bykov, "Detiratura. Nikakoj 'seteratury' ne sučšestvuet," *Literaturnaja gazeta* 28–29 (5797) (12–18 July 2000), http://www.lgz.ru/archives/html_arch/lg28-292000/Literature/art9.htm (accessed 19 August 2011): "В этом смысле литературный Интернет — не что иное, как продолжение самиздата со всеми присущими ему подпольными комплексами и неутомимой, пылкой борьбой самолюбий."
37. See http://www.vavilon.ru (accessed 19 August 2011).
38. Dmitrij Kuz'min, "Kratkij katechizis russkogo literaturnogo Interneta," *Inostrannaja literatura* 10 (1999). Available online in *Setevaja slovesnost'* (17 February 2000), http://www.litera.ru/slova/kuzmin/kuzm-inlit.html (accessed 19 August 2011).
39. Kuz'min and Zubova, "Nikto ne prosil Puškina byt' prošče": "сетевой самиздат, то есть сайты со свободной публикацией, где любой желающий может вывесить все, что угодно. Думаю, вещь это абсолютно вредная. Она размывается представление о том, что такое есть стихи, стирает грани между гением и бездарностью, ставя весь поток текстов через запятую."
40. Graphoman homepage (2003–2006), http://graphoman.com (accessed 19 August 2011): "мы, графоманы — всегда в свободном полете. Нам не надо целовать причинные места руководителей творческих союзов и кланяться редакторам, нижайше испрошая их поместить наши три строчки в какие-либо издания. Мы, подобно парашютистам, сами сознательно выпрыгнули в открытое пространство, и все что происходит с нами там, не подвержено коррекциям и руководствам. Идеальный смысл графоманства — в стремлении писать, а не в жажде публиковаться. Нет, публиковаться мы тоже любим, но так как это не является нашей жизненно-необходимой функцией, то и компромиссов, уступок и риска остаться 'некупленными' у нас не существует. Подобно членам клубов парашютистов, мы парим в пространстве по зову души, а не по необходимости зарабатывать себе этим на 'хлеб наш насущный.'"
41. Nicholas Carr, "The Amorality of Web 2.0," *Rough Type: Nicholas Carr's Blog* (3 October 2005), http://roughtype.com/archives/2005/10/the_amorality_o.php (accessed 19

August 2011); Jaron Lanier, "Digital Maoism: The Hazards of New Online Collectivism," *Edge: The Third Culture* (30 May 2006), http://www.edge.org/3rd_culture/lanier06/lanier06_index.html (accessed 19 August 2011).
42. Gorny, *Creative History;* Lejbov, "Transformacii samizdata."
43. Viktoria Brunmeier, *Das Internet in Russland. Eine Untersuchung zum spannungsreichen Verhältnis von Politik und Runet* (München, 2005).
44. Henrike Schmidt and Katy Teubener, "(Counter)Public Spheres on the Russian Internet," in *Control + Shift,* ed. Schmidt, Teubener, and Konradova, 51–72; Balazs, "Samizdat and the Internet."
45. Tat'jana M. Gorjaeva, *Političeskaja cenzura v SSSR 1917–1991* [Serija «Kul'tura i vlast'» ot Stalina do Gorbačeva. Issledovanija] (Moscow, 2002), 386–93.
46. The situation is different with regard to the field of arts. Since the year 2000 a tendency may be witnessed to censor artworks that critically engage with national and religious symbols. As an example, the trials against curators and participants of art exhibitions may be mentioned; see Michail Ryklin, *With the Law of the Jungle: Russian Culture in the Era of "Guided Democracy"* (Frankfurt a.M., 2006).
47. The label "extremist" is often criticized for being a normative rather than scientifically grounded category. The situation gets even more complicated if we take into account that the terms *extremist* and *fascist* are used within the official Russian political discourse in order to discredit oppositional political agendas. See Aleksandr Verchovskij, "Bor'ba s ėkstremizmom. Russkaja versija," *Prava čeloveka v Rossii,* http://www.hro.org/ngo/discuss/verhovsky2.htm (accessed 26 January 2007).
48. *Sumašedšij dom Mr. Parkera,* http://parker.paragraph.ru/NP (accessed 1 March 2006). Copy available at http://web.archive.org/web/20060210130629/http://parker.paragraph.ru (accessed 26 August 2011). Kononenko is today well known as the author of the popular literary Weblog "Vladimir Vladimirovich.ru," satirizing the former Russian president and now prime minister's daily life.
49. For a comprehensive history of the discussions around "Nizšij pilotaž," see Anatoli Korolev, "Casuistry, Russian Style: Art or Pornography?" *Russian News & Information Agency RIAN* (22 June 2005), http://en.rian.ru/analysis/20050615/40527433.html (accessed 19 August 2011); and the link collection at http://www.gif.ru/themes/culture/basmany (accessed 19 August 2011).
50. Bajan Širjanov [pseudonym Kirill Vorob'ev], *Nizšij pilotaž. Roman v novellach o narkomanach, dlja nich samich i vsech pročich želajuščich* (St. Peterburg, 1998). Available online at http://lib.ru/ZHURNAL/pilotazh.txt (accessed 19 August 2011).
51. Bajan Širjanov [pseudonym Kirill Vorob'ev], *Nizšij pilotaž. Roman v novellach o narkomanach, dlja nich samich i vsech pročich želajuščich* (Moscow, 2000).
52. Cf. Lev Pirogov, "Zagolovok v krasnoj rubašonočke," *Literaturnaja gazeta* (11 July 2001). Online available at http://www.litportal.ru/genre40/author1418/read/page/14/book18880.html (accessed 19 August 2011): "В России цензуры нет, и, к сожалению, нельзя запретить книгу как таковую, но если будет еще одно нарушение со стороны издательства, мы его зафиксируем."
53. Bajan Širjanov [pseudonym Kirill Vorob'ev], *Sredinnyj pilotaž* (St. Peterburg, 2002).
54. Leonid Delicyn, "For us, the Internet was an environment where we were living," interview with Leonid Delicyn, founder of the literary Internet contest "Tenjota" in Moscow (10 March 2004), http://www.ruhr-uni-bochum.de/russ-cyb/survey/interviews/en/moskau_delicyn.htm (accessed 19 August 2011).
55. ROMIR Monitoring, "Den' rossijskoj pečati," *ROMIR Monitoring, Novosti i analitika. Fakty i cifry* (January 2004), http://rmh.ru/news/res_results/87.html (accessed 19 August 2011).

56. Within this context, it should of course be noted that such a control of media content is undertaken in Germany or in the United States as well where age restrictions are put into practice and violent or pornographic materials banned from television. See Roland Seim, *Zwischen Medienfreiheit und Zensureingriffen: eine medien- und rechtssoziologische Untersuchung zensorischer Einflussnahmen auf bundesdeutsche Populärkultur* (Münster, 1998), and Roland Seim, "Eine Zensur findet nicht statt ... oder?" in *Zensur*, ed. Claudius Rosenthal (Sankt Augustin, 2003), 13–39.
57. See Falk, chapter 14.
58. See Gilfillan, chapter 12.
59. Gorny, *Creative History*.
60. Gorny, *Creative History*, 87.
61. Quinn Norton, "Russia growls at LiveJournal Deal," *Wired* (11 November 2006), http://www.wired.com/news/technology/1,72060-1.html (accessed 19 August 2011).
62. Brad Fitzpatrick, "Live Journal, SUP, Russia links," *brad's life: Live Journal* (1 November 2006), http://brad.livejournal.com/2261770.html (accessed 19 August 2011).
63. Gorjaeva, *Političeskaja cenzura*.
64. See http://www.stihi.ru (accessed 19 August 2011).
65. Dmitrij Kravčuk, "Direktiva ob ograničenii tematiki literaturnych proizvedenij, publikuemych na Internet-resursach Rossijskoj Nacional'noj Literaturnoj Seti" (2 February 2005), http://web.archive.org/web/20070126121638/http://www.stihi.ru/about (accessed 26 January 2007). Copy available at http://www.lenizdat.ru/a0/ru/pm1/c-1029658-0.html (accessed 26 August 2011).
66. Martin Hala, "Von der Wandzeitung zum Blog. Meinungs- und Gedankenfreiheit in China heute," *Transit* 34 (2007–2008): 167, http://www.eurozine.com/articles/2008-03-28-hala-de.html (accessed 19 August 2011). "Das Internet hat eine viel größere Reichweite als der Samisdat je hatte, da es nicht wirklich im Untergrund operiert. Die Sicherheit und Anonymität, die das Internet bietet, liegt nicht in Geheimhaltung und Verschwörung, vielmehr im Gegenteil, in der schieren Zahl von Beteiligten."
67. Gorjaeva, *Političeskaja cenzura*, 390–91.
68. Vadim Gur'janov, "Svoe mnenie—svoi media. Ot samizdata k taktičeskim media. Vystavka, posvjaščennaja istorii rossijskogo politizirovannogo samizdata," *Mul'ti media zhurnal Zaart* (28 July 2006), http://mmj.ru/index.php?id=158&article=675 (accessed 19 August 2011).
69. Nancy Fraser, "Rethinking the Public Sphere: A Contribution to the Critique of Actually Existing Democracy," in *Habermas and the Public Sphere*, ed., Craig Calhoun (Cambridge, 1992), 109–42; Nancy Fraser, "Politics, Culture, and the Public Sphere: Toward a Post-Modern Conception," in *Social Postmodernism: Beyond Identity Politics*, ed. Linda Nicholson and Steven Seidman (Cambridge, 1995); Schmidt and Teubener, "(Counter)Public Spheres on the Russian Internet," in *Control + Shift*, ed. Schmidt, Teubener, and Konradova, 51–72, http://www.ruhr-uni-bochum.de/russ-cyb/library/texts/en/control_shift/Schmidt_Teubener_Public.pdf (accessed 19 August 2011).
70. Geert Lovink, *Zero comments: Elemente einer kritischen Internetkultur* (Bielefeld, 2007).
71. See Stephen Kovats, ed., *Ost-West-Internet: elektronische Medien im Transformationsprozess Ost- und Mitteleuropas* (Frankfurt, 1999).
72. Gasan Gusejnov, "Liberty's Autistic Face: Challenges and Frustrations of the Russian Blogosphere," unpublished manuscript, 2008.
73. Floriana Fossato and John Lloyd, with Aleksandr Verchovsky, "The Web that Failed: How Opposition Politics and Independent Initiatives Are Failing on the Internet," *RISJ Challenges*, Oxford: Reuters Institute for the Study of Journalism of the University of Oxford, http://reutersinstitute.politics.ox.ac.uk/fileadmin/documents/Publications/The

_Web_that_Failed.pdf (accessed 19 August 2011); Fossato, "Web as an Adaptation Tool," *The Russian Cyberspace Journal* 1 (2009), http://www.russian-cyberspace.com/issue1/floriana-fossato.php?lng=English (accessed 19 August 2011). That the Internet has as well, in other national contexts, proven to disappoint the hopes set forward for its deliberating, democratizing power, finds no mentioning in this critical accounts of the RuNet. For an insight into the different national cultures of online activism, see, for example, Adrienne Russell, ed., *International Blogging: Identity, Politics and Networked Publics* (New York, 2009).

74. Marcus Alexander, *The Internet in Putin's Russia: Reinventing a Technology of Authoritarianism*, Department of Politics and International Relations, University of Oxford 2003, http://www.psa.ac.uk/cps/2003/marcus percent20alexander.pdf (accessed 19 August 2011); Evgeny Morozov, "The Digital Dictatorship," *The Wall Street Journal*, 20 February 2010, http://online.wsj.com/article/SB10001424052748703983004575073911147404540.html (accessed 19 August 2011); Evgeny Morozov, *The Net Delusion: The Dark Side of Internet Freedom* (London et al., 2011).

75. Dmitrij Golynko, "Social'nye seti v nesetevom sociume," *Digital Icons: Studies in Russian, Eurasian and Central European New Media* 1, no. 2 (2009): 101–13, http://www.digitalicons.org/wp-content/uploads/2009/12/Dmitry-Golynko-DI-2.7.pdf (accessed 19 August 2011).

76. See, for example, the interview with Aleksej Čadaev, leader of the political department of Edinaja Rossija and founder of the Kremlin school of Bloggers, who actively promotes the usage of the Internet for State propaganda and as a tool for the presidential elections in 2012; Aleksej Čadaev, "Twitter-революции — это разводка," *Kommersant online*, 9 March 2011, http://www.kommersant.ru/Doc/1597403 (accessed 19 August 2011).

77. Georgy Bovt. "A harmful law against the Internet," *The Moscow Times* (12 July 2012) http://www.themoscowtimes.com/opinion/article/a-harmful-law-against-the-internet/462234.html (accessed October 31, 2012); Ekho Moskvy, "Runet po novym pravilam. Kogo i otchego zashchishaet gosudarstvo?" http://echo.msk.ru/programs/tochka/909039-echo/#element-text (accessed October, 31, 2012).

Chapter 12

INDEPENDENT MEDIA, TRANSNATIONAL BORDERS, AND NETWORKS OF RESISTANCE
Collaborative Art Radio between
Belgrade (Radio B92) and Vienna (ORF)

Daniel Gilfillan

Radio broadcasting in the context of the Cold War in Europe certainly meant competing transmissions from ideologically stalwart sides of the Iron Curtain, but it also meant frequency seepage, and intermedial support from dissident samizdat networks for stations like Radio Free Europe and Radio Liberty to be able to transmit successfully into the impenetrable frontier of Eastern Europe.[1] In post-1989 Europe, the close relationship between the textual networks of samizdat and the sound broadcast networks of these and other stations underwent significant changes, not only in terms of the technologies of broadcast and transmission, but also in terms of the ever-smaller pockets of space in Eastern Europe that found themselves occupying dissident positions vis-à-vis a totalitarian state. One such pocket developed within the context of the breakup of the Yugoslav state, the Serbian war in Bosnia in the early 1990s, a subsequent war in Kosovo in the late 1990s, and the resulting round of NATO air attacks over Serbia in the spring of 1999. It is within this context of aggression and lack of dissident opinion that an independent radio station began broadcasting in Belgrade and would demonstrate a new phase of samizdat practice combining the distribution of textual accounts via Web-based blogs and the synchronous broadcast of live sound via streaming audio in the form of a radio art broadcast transmitted late one night in April 1999.

On the evening of 29 April 1999, operation "Allied Force," the NATO response to the conflict in Kosovo that spring, began its thirty-seventh day of air operations with "the single most intense period of attacks over

---

Notes for this chapter begin on page 259.

Belgrade" since the operation began.[2] That same evening in Vienna from 10:15 to 11:55 PM, *Kunstradio*, a program on the Ö1 cultural channel of the ORF, broadcast a live mix by Serbian radio artist (and Radio B92 founding member) Gordan Paunović, described as a hundred minutes in support of the free voice of Radio B92. Radio B92 began broadcasting as an independent and experimental youth radio station in Belgrade in May 1989 under the direction of Veran Matić. By 1999, it had established itself as the highest-rated station in Belgrade, and become the primary source of current affairs programming for ANEM, the Asocijacije nezavisnih elektronskih medija (Association of Independent Electronic Media), a consortium of thirty independent broadcasters in Yugoslavia. Under the Milošević government, the station was banned numerous times, culminating in its takeover on 24 March 1999, the day NATO began aerial bombing over Belgrade. The *Kunstradio* project's sponsorship and broadcast of Paunović's live performance supported worldwide efforts in assisting Radio B92 to continue its broadcasts via Internet and other radio channels such as Radio B2-92.[3]

Paunović's live radio broadcast and the ensuing CD remix "Other Voices—echoes from a warzone. Vienna/ Belgrade. April 29, 1999" perform on several levels.[4] They mix and remix audible threads from within the ten-year media landscape that emerged in Serbia between 1989 and 1999. They trace the development of community-based radio and underground artistic practice within the era of Milošević nationalism, and they tease out connections between the creation of alternative media spaces in support of democratic change in Serbia, and the neglect of these media spaces by the global media event, which arose around operation "Allied Force." They document those other voices that get lost or silenced in this folding together of repressive media policy, on the one hand, and the loss of local identity and local response created by an influx of global media conglomerates, on the other hand. They foreground the radio as a multi-layered medium, as a medium in a constant state of flux, and as a medium that, at its core, allows for the same type of circulation and reception practices bound up within the samizdat/tamizdat publishing paradigm. They call attention to the radio's role as a resistant medium within Milošević's Yugoslavia through Radio B92's history of ongoing support of the antiwar and antinationalist movements through on-air performances and protest actions,[5] and its role as a resistant/tactical medium in the context of global media practice given the *Kunstradio* project's support of artistic access to the technologies of broadcast. In view of these very specific resonances with the medial properties of the radio, Paunović's radio piece and CD focus on periods when the radio opens itself to a type of "double underground" moment through its transmission of Yugoslav voices that are themselves caught in a "double bind" landscape of authorized media practice. In this sense, the seamless connections established between radio broadcast and Internet transmission underscore Paunović's performances as demonstrations of the collaborative interplay between the two cities of Vienna and Belgrade, inextricably linked through their common geographical, cultural, economic, and historic ties to the Danube, and now also linked through the intermeshing of their respective soundscapes and electronic networks.[6] Paunović's radio work draws these two cities together through the incorporation of key textual and aural components (essay, live recorded and streamed sound, musical score, personal Internet diaries) that signal both the sense of historical momentum and the atmosphere of atemporality that run headlong into each other in the bombed-out streets of the city. In the performances marked by Paunović's live broadcast and CD remix, the flows of information between Belgrade and Vienna along Internet channels, diary excerpts, email correspondence, and radio waves stand in for the people of Belgrade, as they are caught between a minimized degree of mobility and the impossibility of movement.

Allowing mobility to occur through the flow of information, marketable goods and services, and signals, rather than through the movement of physical bodies across national and international boundaries, points to a set of larger research questions about the links between information as a commodity, network globalization and connectivity, and artistic access to these invariably closed systems. How does the subtraction of the physical body from within an exchange of ideas lead to changes in information reception? That is, how does the removal of the physical body trigger the transformation of intellectual thought into information? In the context of Paunović's radio performance, how are tactical appropriations of these global telecommunications infrastructures providing new modes of interchange within the cross-border region between Vienna and Belgrade? To this end, how is the historical riparian network between Vienna and Belgrade via the Danube being recast in terms of electronic signal flow?

These are questions that seek to unravel the complexity of these telecommunications networks, to engage the radio medium as an agent of networked communication, and to create alternative and experimental points of access to these various networks. It is in this vein that the Austrian *Kunstradio* project, formed in December 1987 under the direction of Heidi Grundmann, strives to connect artists with the often inaccessible technical infrastructure of radio, so that experimental threads can be drawn out from within the standardized infotainment models that characterize much of today's commercial radio. In her essay "Radio as Medium and Metaphor," Grundmann writes: "*Kunstradio* had to do with artists who saw themselves as the initiators of media-based processes and which logically understood its role not as the regulator of access to the radio but as an entry point to the means of production and transmission provided by public radio; as a clearing-point at which strategies were developed in partnership with the artists for avoiding bureaucratic restrictions within the institution itself."[7]

Public access, public domain, public broadcasting, public reception; these are all concepts that uphold a regulatory system and gatekeeper function of haves and have-nots; a structure based on a notion of access that is itself regulated by granting agencies, and systems of content surveillance. Where the *Kunstradio* project builds bridges of access to the means of production symbolized by the ORF broadcasting monopoly, various individual artists or artist groups supported by the project have applied unsanctioned techniques of pirate radio and tactical media in the creation of their radio pieces. Where the semantics of public access and public domain remain lodged within the discursive vocabularies presided over by commercial broadcasting companies and regulatory commissions, the subterranean artistic techniques and media dialogues facilitated by certain radio artists tunnel beneath established notions of radio programming and radio administration to create a new system of radiophonic space—a volatile system of channels unsettling to the dominant telecommunications paradigms representative of the convergent systems of globalization.[8]

It is this actual materiality of the radio, the radio as instrument and the radio as medium, that forms the substance of today's radio art. Contemporary radio artists from around the world have begun to experiment with these traditional notions of radio as a reception device, by cracking it wide open to expose the myriad wavelengths, frequencies, and bandwidths that comprise radio's multiple, yet often inaudible, uses. Grundmann clarifies these types of experiments in the context of the *Kunstradio* program and its institutional support by the ORF in her mid-1990s essay "But is it Radio?":

> The position of *Kunstradio*—however marginalized—inside a public radio institution has made it possible for artists to exploit not only the institution's technical resources but also its mainstream program formats. There have been projects where artists were able to infiltrate other programs and/or channels of the ORF beyond the late-night ghetto, inserting radio-art into Ö3, the pop music channel, or into one or the other of several regional channels. Such interventions outside of the gallery-like space of the weekly national radio-art program are most successful, when they are not announced/perceived as art but are left to be incidents in the public space of everyday radio, anticipating an audience of passers-by who may or may not stop or hesitate for just a brief moment of irritation or even reflection.[9]

Grundmann points to the playfulness involved in the broadcast of radio art. With terms such as *infiltrate* and *intervention* to describe the methods used by *Kunstradio*-supported artists to broaden their audience base beyond the late Sunday evening timeslot provided to the program by ORF, Grundmann's essay highlights what happens when the roles of technician and artist come together in the realm of radio production. Clearly, the types of productions supported by *Kunstradio* (through its provision of artistic access to the technologies of radio) seek to interweave radio's original function as a military relay device, and its consumer function as entertainment device. In this sense, the military's use of the radio for tactical reasons is repurposed through the playfulness of these radio artists, in order to challenge the assumptions set up by the various broadcasting and transmission standards of commercial radio and also to invoke or play out the types of experimentation suggested by Bertolt Brecht in his series of early radio theoretical essays (1926–1932), such as artistic access to broadcasting technologies, listener interactivity, and development of genres specific to the materiality and technique of radio.[10]

Paunović's radio art piece and the *Kunstradio* program's role in its broadcast provide an exceptional example of how artistic experimentation with the radio medium manages to break in to the globalized space of radio transmission and to help reposition and amplify the voices and ideas lost or ignored within these globalized information networks. The live broadcast of *Other Voices* engages these modes of experimentation with the radio device through its performative routing of unique threads of information, each with their own specific spatiotemporal set of source histories and cultural reverberations or echo effects. The intertextual and intermedial play between these individual components of the overall broadcast prompt both the listener and the creator of the broadcast to think more critically about the relationships between each source of information, while also requiring them to delve more deeply into the respective trace histories of each source. In this sense, Paunović never claims ownership to the work, seeing himself instead as a thinking agent, as a stopover within the routing of information, where his own take, his own interpretation of the materials, is added to the mix before sending it back out into the network, or in this case over the radio waves. In total, twenty distinct verbal and artistic sound elements were utilized in the live broadcast. This combination of ambient sound and personal documentary details the quick physical change of Belgrade's skyline, and the slow process of coping with the impending loss of one's home, one's city, and one's identity. Paunović's mixture of tracks from archived music productions, voice overlays, essay commentaries, and live Internet and audio feeds helps to trace these moments of changing experience and displacement of identity.

The live broadcast itself serves as a moment of self-referential tactical media practice, an idea of media that seeks in some way to appropriate the more traditional channels of media as relays of power, and use them as relays for dissent and disruption.[11] The live piece begins with a reading of a short essay by Radio B92 founding editor Veran Matić entitled "Schaffung des Informationsraums: 'Commando Solo.'" As the lead-in component for Paunović's live broadcast mix, Matić's essay introduces themes related to postmodern military practice and telecommunications into the broadcast space of the radio piece. Written during the NATO intervention in April 1999 and sent to the *Kunstradio* studios just two days prior to the live broadcast, the essay takes NATO's use of hybridized weapons combining high-powered bombs and imaging technologies to task, and problematizes the use of captured images and recordings from these hybridized devices by mainstream journalists to provide popular backing for NATO's involvement. Among these themes are discussions about the Commando Solo aircraft to establish an alternative information space through military jamming of civilian radio and television airwaves, as well as the melding together of smart-bomb missiles and cameras to provide logistical and video analysis of targets being bombed: "The only evidence offered to us as the sole truth is from the camera located in the cone of the missile, which hits its target. The day-to-day recurrence of the same or similar photos acquired through these cameras, transforms journalism into a superfluous occupation, since the sole truth originates from the cone of a missile. In this way brutal homicides and destruction become easily tolerated video games."[12] For Matić, the idea that the "truth" behind the success of the NATO intervention resided in a quick media consumption of images captured by smart bombs as they headed toward their targets demonstrates the failure of mainstream journalism to critically engage with the reality of the situation in Serbia and the war in Kosovo, and turns the thirty-plus days of NATO bombing into a video game reminiscent of the first Gulf War. To put it more plainly, the global media event prompted by the NATO response to the Kosovo conflict in spring 1999 overlooks and diminishes the local experience of that event. These ideas about the hybridization of warfare technologies and telecommunications networks, and about the disappearance of any human experience of the NATO bombing in mainstream media coverage serve to emphasize the artistic possibilities inherent in radio as foregrounded by Paunović's radio art piece and by the *Kunstradio* program's role in its broadcast. In June 1999, during production of the CD remix, Paunović writes: "Mainstream media, following guidelines from political establishments on both sides, transformed the reality into a huge propaganda stageset. Beyond the Potemkin villages of the big TV networks, there was another life going on — a life of people who spent years and decades fighting totalitarianism and nationalistic hatred with the power of their expression and creation. Writers, sound artists, radio personalities, media workers, journalists and musicians, suddenly became collateral damage of the war in Yugoslavia."[13] Paunović's motivation for producing this radio performance piece centers on the artists, writers, and media producers who were denied access to the technologies of media production by both the Milošević media state and its broadcasts of the Serbian war and the large television corporations and their broadcasts of the NATO intervention. The function of Matić's essay as epigraph serves as a justification for Paunović's own creation of an alternative information space via the live radio and Internet streaming broadcasts. In this regard, Paunović accomplishes the same type of takeover of radio space that the Commando Solo aircraft has been developed to do militarily. Yet, what Paunović's tactical use of the radio medium adds to the mix are the varying threads from spoken text and sonic elements that evoke the emotive atmosphere of Belgrade in April 1999, as well as traces of the historical, cultural, and political engagement with the post-1989 dissolution of Yugoslavia.

What is missing from the publicly proliferated media landscape surrounding Serbia's war in Kosovo and NATO's intervention are the haunting sounds of air raid sirens, the explosions generated by the aerial bombings, and the rationalized stories from those entrenched in Belgrade's cityscape, all of which arise as elements in Paunović's work. As the website associated with the live version of Paunović's piece points out, the broadcast is structured around three recurrent sound elements: a live audio stream of sounds of the NATO bombing picked up by a microphone hanging outside a window in Belgrade on the evening of 29 April, original recordings of a one-minute air raid alarm from Belgrade sent to the studios in Vienna via an Internet feed, and excerpts from an orchestration by Arsenije Jovanović titled *Concerto grosso balcanico*.[14] Although the broadcast is bounded by the spatiotemporal limitations set up by commercial radio programming timeslots, Paunović's use of these live sound captures and integration of excerpts from topical texts allows the broadcast to transcend its 100-minute time limit, and also transforms the radio from a conduit of transmission and reception into a device that transports its listeners to the streets of Belgrade through a live, point-to-point flow of information. The noise of the bombings captured from the microphone and the air raid alarm taken from the Internet feed evoke the immediacy of Paunović's piece, while the use of Jovanović's earlier sound project invokes a sonic archaeology of the war in the former Yugoslavia. This 1993 soundscape is a disturbing triptych, which blends the sounds of war with the anxious stirrings of animals (sheep, dogs, and wolves) confronted by these very human sounds.

The creation of a CD remix, released in March 2000 to coincide with the anniversary of the beginning of the NATO intervention, emphasizes this function of the live broadcast as archaeological cache or archive, and provides Paunović the creative and reflective time necessary to engage with a particular facet of the longer 100-minute live broadcast. The relationship between the live broadcast and CD remix as one of archive and iteration is one that could continue ad infinitum, and it is one which positions the live broadcast as having the quality of rawness, as a never before heard, never complete, and never deceased sonic snapshot of events occurring in Belgrade in spring 1999.

At the center of the CD are voiced excerpts dated from March and April 1999 from two electronic diaries. One is by Jasmina Tešanović, a 45-year-old writer, filmmaker, and feminist activist, and the other was written by Slobodan Marković, a 21-year-old computer science student at the University of Belgrade, independent media activist, and founder of the online Serbian *Internodium* mailing list, which addresses issues of open access to Yugoslav (.yu) cyberspace.[15] The electronic format of both diaries illustrates two important details. First, it points to the importance of the Internet for the sharing of information from two of Belgrade's citizens during a time of war, which Geert Lovink contextualizes in his essay "Kosovo: War in the Age of the Internet" in terms of the extensive media vacuum that had arisen around the NATO intervention:

> It was hard to grasp that an entire region inside (Southeast) Europe is being turned into an information black hole. ... What the Internet was left with were Serbian witnesses, diaries, personal accounts, mainly from educated urban citizens. Immediately, while the first bomb load was dropped, the Internet diaries started to pop up. Their psycho-geography is limited, by nature, by the very definition of the genre. They did not produce theory or a critical analysis of politics and the war situation. Add to this situation the semi-personal touch of e-mail, and presto, you get an odd, once in a lifetime mixture of paranoia, reflection, pathetic pity, waves of despair, worrisome productions of subjectivity, with here and there valuable pictures of the everyday life under extraordinary circumstances.[16]

Although Lovink's commentary argues that the personal nature of these Internet diaries makes them in some way less valuable theoretically and critically, I want to suggest that it is exactly their personal overtones, their documentary character, that makes them accessible to the Internet medium and transferable to the medium of radio broadcast. In this context of war and atmosphere of despair, the realm of the personal necessarily becomes the locus of knowledge production and the foundation from which more critical and theoretical analyses can take shape. And herein lies the second important aspect of these diaries' respective electronic formats, namely, that they help to illustrate once again the radio's transformation from a device for reception only into a medium that interactively engages its listeners and its source feeds in an intellectual, cultural, and sociopolitical network of idea exchange. In a certain sense, both Tešanović's and Marković's diaries can be viewed as early blogs, or Weblogs, which themselves are types of textual broadcasts of information. The entries used from Marković's email postings originated from his own personal submissions to an Internet-based mailing list known as *The Syndicate Mailing List*, which was formed in January 1996 as a "loose affiliation of artists, curators, networkers, writers and festival organisers, most of them from Eastern Europe, who [were] working in the field of electronic- and media-art."[17] In contrast, Tešanović's diary began its unique life on the Web almost by accident. As the publisher's note to the 2000 American publication of the diary explains, Tešanović did not personally post her diary entries to the web, rather a friend in Sweden took the step of sharing her personal writing with the world Internet community:

> Hours after NATO started bombing Yugoslavia, Jasmina Tešanović received an e-mail from a friend in Sweden, who wanted to know how she was doing. Jasmina didn't have time to write back, so she sent entries from her diary. Her friend, the writer Ana Valdes, posted Jasmina's diary entries on the web site of a magazine she wrote for. Within a week, the diaries had been posted anonymously on fifty web sites, translated into several languages and sent in emails throughout the world. ... The diary of an anonymous woman from Belgrade had become everybody's diary.[18]

Unlike Marković, who knowingly posted his observations on the NATO bombing to the web, Tešanović's diary experienced its anonymous online celebrity through a more grassroots approach to media activism. Both diarists were able to garner a wide audience outside the boundaries of Belgrade and Serbia through utilizing the inherent networks associated with the Internet infrastructure, which facilitated the level of resonance that both achieved in a very short amount of time. With Marković's computer science background and active interest in supporting open artistic and media access to networks in Yugoslav cyberspace, as well as his involvement with media arts groups in Eastern Europe, it is not difficult to understand the reach that his email postings found, nor the types of discussions they informed on several electronic lists in Europe and beyond.[19] In Tešanović's case, the language of her diary entries propelled their movement along Internet streams, and this language, as we will see shortly, was informed by her involvement with feminist activist groups like "Women in Black" and their focus on the situation of women in the various wars in the former Yugoslavia. In much the same way that the live feeds of sounds from Belgrade during the bombing add to the immediacy of the live radio art piece, the echoes of discussion and transmission generated by both of these diaries during the height of NATO activity add a sense of timeliness and urgency to Paunović's piece, as well.

Paunović's implementation of the two electronic diaries for his versions of *Other Voices*–his adaptation of them through translation (into German, in the case of Marković's entries, and into English, in the case of Tešanović's), his staging of them as individual channels for mixing into the live radio broadcast, his enlivening of their written thoughts through dramatic vocal readings, his placing of them into the electronic soundscape that represents the city of Belgrade on this one particular evening in April 1999—reveals the importance of electronic signal flow as a substitution for the physical body, whose movements are restricted or disrupted by both the technologies of war and the technologies of global telecommunications. Both textual documentaries offer eyewitness testimony to the war in Belgrade, providing commentaries on the absurdity of NATO's missile targets and the civilian casualties that resulted from them, and rationalized observations of the developing chaos percolating around them. While Marković's email transmissions recount in emotional detail and sarcastic and ironic tones the nightly destruction wrought by NATO bombs, Tešanović's diary captures the human experience of the war in interstitial terms—of Belgrade's citizens caught between moments of sanity and nervous breakdown, between local compulsive patriotism and global compulsive guilt, and the isolation of staying put and the anonymity of being displaced. In the first voiced excerpt from her diary, listeners to the radio broadcast experienced the paradoxes of this war by hearing Tešanović's rationale for understanding a world that perpetuates war while simultaneously exposing the full range of human relationships and emotions needed for the war's continuation. Dated 26 March 1999 at 5 PM, the entry responds to NATO's first sortie of air strikes against Yugoslavia just two days earlier:

> I hope we all survive this war and the bombs: the Serbs, the Albanians, the bad and the good guys, those who took up the arms, those who deserted, the Kosovo refugees traveling through the woods and the Belgrade refugees traveling through the streets with their children in their arms looking for non-existing shelters when the alarms go off. I hope that NATO pilots don't leave behind the wives and children whom I saw crying on CNN as their husbands were taking off for military targets in Serbia. I hope we all survive, but that the world as it is does not.[20]

Tešanović's remarkable ability to name and empathize with each group of people involved in the Kosovo war, regardless of their ethnic background, refugee status or NATO involvement, points out that the degree of separation between perpetrator and victim (so important in past instances of war) is no longer a distinction that can be made in the age of a telecommunications-based war. Seeing images of their future attackers on CNN, watching the movements of Serb and Albanian troops on state-run television, hearing about the migration of Kosovo refugees from independent broadcasts and seeing the nervous wandering of potential refugees in Belgrade with their own eyes—all this provides a continuum between the insanity of imagined war and the calm concreteness of the real war. Tešanović clarifies this balance in the same entry from 26 March:

> Today is the second aftermath day. The city is silent and paralyzed, but still working, rubbish is taken away, we have water, we have electricity. But where are the people? In houses, in beds, in shelters. I hear several personal stories of nervous breakdowns among my friends, male and female. Those who were in a nervous breakdown for the past year, since the war in Kosovo started, who were very few, now feel better. Real danger is less frightening than fantasies of danger. I couldn't cope with the invisible war as I can cope with concrete needs: bread, water, medicine. And also, very important: I can see an end. Finally we in Belgrade got what all rest of Yugoslavia has had: war on our territory.[21]

Fear of the unknown, of how the war would be played out, is now replaced with the knowledge of how the war would affect their lives. There is a certain spatiality involved in knowing more about how one's life might end. This is a sense of space that becomes progressively smaller, that limits physical movement, and reduces the possibilities of expression. That Paunović places Tešanović's dramatized voice within a surrounding audio stream of air raid alarms, exploding bombs, and chilling cries in the night, expands this sense of spatiality by positioning Tešanović's words as the unspoken thoughts of every citizen of Belgrade in the surrealist buffer of a city experiencing the loss of its most basic infrastructure. Not included in the radio broadcast, but available on the *Kunstradio* website, is her diary entry from 31 March:

> Fear has entered in my mind: I don't know if I dare think what I do, I cannot cope with reality: is it possible that we are all sacrificed for somebody's lack of political judgment, or worse, madness. I am censoring my thoughts afraid to think in personal tones, afraid to be heard, judged and executed. The conflict is escalating, the atrocities are daily happenings. ... My head and language are getting stiff, they have to incorporate all these controversial meanings; I despise getting along in war, no space for feminine language, no free space.[22]

One week into the NATO intervention, the nightly bombing and the daily Serbian war were taking their toll on her sense of self, and her sense of place within the world. Language was undergoing a state of change, transforming as her reality was transformed and not allowing her to write and think as she desired. Tešanović links the ever-decreasing sense of space, freedom of movement, and freedom of thought with equally decreasing possibilities for language. Here, her comment that there is "no space for feminine language, no free space" reminds us of her engagement with feminist-based NGOs, and with the founding of the first women's publishing house in Serbia called "94." However, this comment does not mean she is somehow giving up her feminist perspective. On the contrary, the importance of this feminist work for her sense of self and her sense of well-being was still a factor in her continued existence in the bombed city of Belgrade. This statement underscores, as well, the absurdity of being in a city which is being watched by the whole world, but to whose citizens no one listens. The situational specificity of living in a city that was being attacked by NATO airplanes and barraged by Milošević propaganda made her painfully aware of the lack of a space where such a feminist perspective would be viable or operational as a valid alternative viewpoint to bombs and half-truths. In the entry from 12 April, Tešanović reflects on the prospect of leaving Belgrade, her friends, her streets, her habits, and her language, and becoming Other:

> I couldn't go to sleep last night, finally I took a tranquilizer, there it goes, I started to [sleep]. I postponed all these weeks the use of drugs to stay normal, but I see that no normal person can stay normal without drugs, if you want to stay here. I do not want to go, I do not want to leave my city, my friends, my streets, my habits, my language. I do not believe in Other. I understand those who left, out of fear, out of needs, I could have been one of them too, but I want to stay. Friends from all over the world offer me flats, money, help. But the only thing I need from them and from others all over the world is to try to stop our war.[23]

We hear the resolve in her voice, and again the steadiness of her words places a balance between the two wars in which she and her fellow citizens have to locate themselves: the Serbian war and "compulsive patriotism" during the day, and NATO intervention and "compulsive sense of guilt" at night. In the final three spoken excerpts dated 20 April, 23 April, and 26 April, we come face to face with this interstitial existence, with the impossibility of what Zygmunt Bauman terms the "degree of mobility—the freedom to choose where to be":[24]

> **April 20, 1999.** Now, what is my cross: NATO bombs, Serbian patriotic death. OK, between compulsive patriotism and compulsive sense of guilt, I guess there is no way out. It would take another life to do so [22:25–22:41; 67:09–67:24].
>
> **April 23, 1999.** Just yesterday I thought: now everybody is fighting for our souls, of us Serbs led astray, all these televisions, local and international. We even receive American leaflets from the planes telling us about us. Not even the

Colorado teenaged killers could draw attention from our educational program [23:24–23:47; 68:08–68:30].

April 26, 1999. I do not feel safe with the NATO or any other bombs, NATO being the only ones I know. I do not feel safe without bridges, in a boat, on a horse, on a bicycle, against NATO airplane; I do not feel safe without schools, universities, libraries, against highly technological NATO countries. I am not afraid, not anymore, we are beyond good or evil by now, but my legs simply tremble, when I hear the NATO or any other planes with bombs above my head.[25]

Tešanović's personal diary documents her slow move into war, into isolation, into silence, and then her steady return back to identity, to community, and to expression. These last three excerpts evidence this narrative arc, and also demonstrate Tešanović's realization that her mobility was restricted, in both a physical sense of movement, and in an intellectual sense of sharing ideas and reflections. While the notions of travel, exile, homelessness, and displacement each presume a relocation or dislocation of a physical body, charting this type of movement in the late twentieth century requires an additional investigation into the ways in which information, documentation, and surveillance stand in for the physical body. As Zygmunt Bauman puts it: "In the world we inhabit, distance does not seem to matter much. Sometimes it seems that it exists solely in order to be cancelled; as if space was but a constant invitation to slight it, refute and deny. Space stopped being an obstacle—one needs just a split second to conquer it."[26]

In an epoch of globalized economies, media states, and convergent telecommunications networks, mobility and movement assume characteristics of instantaneity, where the distances of time and space become imaginary, as equally traversable by immobility or staying put, as they are by physical movement. Gordan Paunović's implementation of these diaries into the ethereal flow of radio broadcast and Internet transmission opens a viable network space in which the power of Tešanović's words addresses the hegemonic forces that are keeping her physical body restricted: the nightly NATO bombing, the omnipresent weight of the Milošević regime, and the quelling silence parsed by the constant din of commercial Western media. David Morley, in his study of the media's impact on notions of home, identity, and nationhood, suggests that "traditional ideas of home, homeland and nation have been destabilized, both by new patterns of physical mobility and migration and by new communication technologies which routinely transgress the symbolic boundaries around both the private household and the nation state. The electronic landscapes in which we now dwell are haunted by all manner of cultural anxieties which arise from this destabilizing flux."[27]

Morley's study raises issues concerning the human experience of the intertwining of global economic practice and new communication technologies, and the ways in which these macrolevel structures provoke "the radical intrusion of distant events into the space of domesticity."[28] Here we have to expand on our earlier question concerning the transformation of intellectual thought into information, and ask how this information is subsequently transformed into commodity. How does information for thought become information for sale? In the last of the three diary excerpts presented previously, Jasmina Tešanović links together modes of physical transportation (bridges, bicycles, boats, horses) and intellectual possibility (schools, universities, libraries), seeing both as ineffectual means against the highly technological capabilities of NATO nations. When combined with her previous comments about the depiction of Serbs on international television being led astray, one can easily see how the very politically delicate layers behind the conflict were no longer taken into account, and instead the entire NATO campaign had been conflated as entertainment. In the context of Paunović's live DJ performance vis-à-vis radio broadcast and Web-based networks into the living rooms of Western Europe, we need to take Morley's study to heart in our understanding of how these alternative and subversive modes of media transmission not only draw attention to subjects not commonly covered, but also can assist in repositioning the role and impact of media in the consumer household from one of lulling ambivalence to one of provoking engagement. Here, Caren Kaplan's cautious suggestion in her recent essay "Transporting the Subject" provides a tempering effect by illustrating the very real need to remind ourselves that behind every sound bite or television image exists a set of very real issues, and very real subjects: "The self is believed to have expanded capacities as soon as it is released from the fixed location of the body, built environment, or nation. But the self is always somewhere, always located in some sense in some place, and cannot be totally unhoused. New technologies appear to promise ever-increasing degrees of disembodiment or detachment, yet they are as embedded in material relations as any other practices."[29]

Paunović's radio art piece and the position of Tešanović's diary within the piece demonstrate Kaplan's cautionary approach to the promises of information technologies and the disembodiment of the subject within and through these technologies. The strength of this work of radio art lies in Paunović's ability to amplify the steady, deliberate, and balanced words of Tešanović, to turn the creative impulses of these journalists, musicians, and writers who have been labeled "collateral damage" back into the expressive forms of engagement they were originally intended to be. Her Internet-based diary and its place within Paunović's radio mix allows Tešanović to extend her body beyond its limitations, to circulate her thoughts and knowledge outside the imposed boundaries of war-torn Belgrade, and to take a position as an engaged global citizen. The ability of radio broadcast to affect this extension both echoes and expands upon the Cold War–era paradigm of samizdat/tamizdat. Here the intermedial and compositional nature of broadcast, as well as the transmission/reception networks initiated by a community of listeners, transforms these earlier underground publishing and distribution practices from the realm of textuality into the realm of the aural. The collaboration between Paunović and the Austrian *Kunstradio* project to draw attention to these "other voices" not captured by the global media network also highlights an engaged use of tactical media. Where a culture of fear is readily compounded by the global media event surrounding the conflict in Kosovo, the type of tactical media practice evidenced in Paunović's and *Kunstradio*'s live broadcast allows for a different type[30] of globalized network communication to occur, one that is not founded on easily digestible sound bites and the marketability of information, but rather one that mixes together a multiplicity of knowledge inputs and serves a wide range of outputs. The sounds of displacement—the fear of a disembodied identity that forms the heart of the broadcast's two diaries, the constant air raid sirens that creep into the background of the listener's minds—make the realities of this war audible, recordable, and traceable, and transpose local experience, local identification with the war, onto the European and global imagination.

Notes

1. A version of this article forms a part of chapter 4 of my book, *Pieces of Sound: German Experimental Radio* (Minneapolis, 2009). For a highly interesting history of Radio Free Europe and Radio Liberty, see Arch Puddington's volume *Broadcasting Freedom: The Cold War Triumph of Radio Free Europe and Radio Liberty* (Lexington, 2000); and for a first-hand account, see James Critchlow's *Radio Hole-in-the-Head: Radio Liberty. An Insider's Story of Cold War Broadcasting* (Washington, 1995).
2. Jamie Shea, "NATO Speech: Morning Briefing in Kosovo—30. Apr. 1999," NATO: NATO's role in Kosovo: Background Briefings, http://www.nato.int/kosovo/press/b99 0430b.htm (accessed 19 August 2011). Interestingly, this was the first time since World War II that a European city had been bombed, and, for Belgrade, the fourth time in the twentieth century that it had experienced aerial bombings from an outside military force. The first had been the Austrian bombing of Belgrade in July 1914, the second came with the arrival of the German National Socialists and subsequent occupation in April 1941, and the third with Allied bombings in 1944 to regain the city at the end of the war.
3. Additional information about the history of Radio B92 and a biography of Veran Matić can be accessed at ORF *Kunstradio*, "Veran Matić," http://www.kunstradio.at/BIOS/

maticbio.html (accessed 19 August 2011). Alternately, important background information to the founding and development of Radio B92 can be found in Veran Matić and Drazen Pantic, "War of Words," *Nation*, 29 November 1999, http://www.thenation.com/article/war-words (accessed 19 August 2011).

4. Both the live broadcast and CD remix are available on the *Kunstradio* Web site as streaming audio files: Gordan Paunović, *Other Voices—Echoes from a War Zone*, live broadcast streaming audio, ORF *Kunstradio*, http://www.kunstradio.at/1999A/RA/99_04_29.ram (accessed 19 August 2011); Gordan Paunović, *Other Voices—Echoes from a Warzone*, compact disc streaming audio, ORF *Kunstradio*, http://www.kunstradio.at/2000A/RA/00_04_02.ram (accessed 19 August 2011). The compact disc is also available: Gordan Paunović, *Other Voices—Echoes from a Warzone*, ORF *Kunstradio* (Vienna/Belgrade, 29 April 1999), CD.

5. For a highly charged and highly readable account of Radio B92's role in the antiwar movement during the Bosnian war in the early 1990s, as well as their support of underground music, independent journalism, and various social movements through their use of the radio medium, see Matthew Collin, *This is Serbia Calling: Rock 'n' Roll Radio and Belgrade's Underground Resistance* (London, 2004).

6. Although this essay will not investigate in detail the intricate connections between Vienna and Belgrade as ascertained by their economic and historic ties to the Danube, the natural course of the river across national and international boundaries serves as a telling metaphor for the types of information flow taking place over the airwaves in the production of Gordan Paunović's piece.

7. Heidi Grundmann, "Radio as Medium and Metaphor," in *Net Condition: Art and Global Media*, ed. Peter Weibel and Timothy Druckery (Cambridge, 2001), 239.

8. Although the programmatic components of a radio art piece by any one individual radio artist may seek to subvert or draw attention to the hierarchical nature of commercial or public broadcasting regulations and standards, the institutional relationship between the *Kunstradio* project and the ORF is one that is mutually beneficial. Access to broadcasting technologies and sound studios is extremely important to the radio artists that *Kunstradio* seeks to promote, but ORF also receives a certain cultural capital in return for this support. However skeptical or idealistic one might be about the efficacy of these subversive claims really depends on the level of interactive engagement a listener brings to any individual piece. Certainly one can lament that any artwork (be it a painting, literary text, or sound production) provides no real pathways for social or political change. But it is in the process leading to the artwork's production and in the elements that contribute to the finished product that the real ability of the piece to engage an audience resides. All it takes is the motivation and willingness on the part of the audience to uncover it.

9. Heidi Grundmann, "But is it Radio?" in *Anarchitexts. Voices from the Global Digital Resistance: A Subsol Anthology*, ed. Joanne Richardson (New York, 2003), 158.

10. See, for example, Brecht's essays "Der Rundfunk als Kommunikationsapparat. Rede über die Funktion des Rundfunks," "Vorschläge für den Intendanten des Rundfunks," "Radio—eine vorsintflutliche Erfindung," "Über Verwertungen," and "Erläuterungen zu 'Der Flug der Lindberghs.'" These essays are available in English translation in *Bertolt Brecht on Film and Radio*, ed. Marc Silberman (London, 2000). For additional commentary on Brecht's early radio theory, see chapter 3 of my book *Pieces of Sound: German Experimental Radio*.

11. See Geert Lovink, "An Insider's Guide to Tactical Media," in *Dark Fiber: Tracking Critical Internet Culture* (Cambridge, 2002), 254–74. In this essay, Lovink provides an interesting

discussion of contemporary media activism as it relates to a history of media activism in the United States and Western Europe.
12. Veran Matić, "Schaffung des Informationsraums: 'Commando Solo,'" ORF *Kunstradio*, at http://www.kunstradio.at/WAR/VOICES/matic-commsolo.html (accessed 19 August 2011). "Der einzige Beweis, der uns als die alleinige Wahrheit angeboten wird, [ist] die Kamera im Kopf der Rakete, die ihr Ziel trifft. Die tagtägliche Wiederholung gleicher oder ähnlicher Aufnahmen, die durch diese Kameras gemacht werden, verwandelt den Journalismus in eine überflüssige Berufsgruppe, denn die alleinige Wahrheit stammt aus dem Raketenkopf. Auf diese Art werden brutale Morde und Zerstörungen zu leicht verträglichen Videospielchen."
13. ORF *Kunstradio*, Other Voices CD Release Web site, http://www.kunstradio.at/TAKE/CD/paunovic_cd.html (accessed 19 August 2011). "Die Main Stream-Medien folgten den Richtlinien des politischen Establishments beider Seiten und verwandelten die Realität damit in das riesige Bühnenbild für ein Propagandaschauspiel. Jenseits der Potemkinschen Dörfer der großen Fernsehgesellschaften aber lief ein anderes Leben ab, das Leben von Menschen, die Jahre und Jahrzehnte damit verbracht hatten, mit ihrer Ausdruckskraft und Kreativität gegen Totalitarismus und nationalistischen Hass anzukämpfen. Doch plötzlich waren SchriftstellerInnen, SoundkünstlerInnen, Radiopersönlichkeiten, MedienarbeiterInnen, JournalistInnen und MusikerInnen nichts anderes mehr als 'collateral damage' des Krieges in Jugoslawien."
14. Arsenije Jovanović, *Concerto grosso balcanico*, live broadcast streaming audio, ORF *Kunstradio*, http://www.kunstradio.at/1993A/RA/concerto.ram (accessed 19 August 2011).
15. Excerpts from both Jasmina Tešanović's and Slobodan Marković's diaries used by Gordan Paunović in both the live broadcast and CD remix are reproduced on the *Kunstradio* project's Web site: ORF *Kunstradio*, "WAR DIARIES OF JASMINA TEŠANOVIĆ & SLOBODAN MARKOVIĆ," http://www.kunstradio.at/WAR/DIARY (accessed 19 August 2011). Tešanović's diary and other personal diaries from Belgrade are gathered on the "Help B92" Web site: Jasmina Tešanović, "Personal diaries," "Help B92," http://helpb92.xs4all.nl/diaries/jasmina/jasmina.htm (site now offline). Here they can be read in English and their original Serbo-Croatian. When quoting from the diary entries employed in the live broadcast and CD remix, I will utilize direct transcriptions from the recorded audio, CD version, and provide time settings from both the CD and streaming audio versions to help the reader locate these excerpts. Also, whenever possible, I will provide page numbers for these excerpts from the 2000 Midnight Editions version of Tešanović's diary, published as Jasmina Tešanović, *The Diary of a Political Idiot: Normal Life in Belgrade* (San Francisco, 2000). This will not always be feasible as the American edition has edited some of the passages out that exist in the sound versions of the excerpts. I would like to thank Azerina Began for her help in translating some of the Serbo-Croatian conversations that take place in the live broadcast.
16. Geert Lovink, "Kosovo: War in the Age of Internet (1999)," in *Dark Fiber: Tracking Critical Internet Culture* (Cambridge, 2002), 322–23.
17. "About the Syndicate Network," http://colossus.v2.nl/syndicate/about.html (site now offline).
18. Frédérique Delacoste, note from the publisher for *The Diary of a Political Idiot*, by Tešanović, 10.
19. Marković's posts to *The Syndicate Mailing List* were reposted to several other electronics arts and media activist lists, including nettime.org, and rhizome.org, both of which continue to play primary roles in the world of electronic and digital arts.

20. Tešanović, *The Diary of a Political Idiot*, 72; Paunović, *Echoes from a Warzone*, CD, audio transcript [10:28–11:00]; Paunović, *Echoes from a Warzone*, live broadcast streaming audio, audio transcript [54:59–55:37].
21. Paunović, *Echoes from a Warzone*, CD, audio transcript [11:00–11:48]; Paunović, *Echoes from a Warzone*, live broadcast streaming audio, audio transcript [55:37–56:26].
22. Jasmina Tešanović, "DIARY OF JASMINA TESANOVIĆ," ORF *Kunstradio*, http://www.kunstradio.at/ WAR/DIARY/diary-2.html (accessed 19 August 2011).
23. Tešanović, *The Diary of a Political Idiot*, 89; Paunović, *Echoes from a Warzone*, CD, audio transcript [16:42–17:33]; Paunović, *Echoes from a Warzone*, live broadcast streaming audio, audio transcript [61:26–62:16].
24. Zygmunt Bauman, *Globalization: The Human Consequences* (New York, 1998), 86.
25. Paunović, *Echoes from a Warzone*, CD, audio transcript [25:39–26:12]; Paunović, *Echoes from a Warzone*, live broadcast streaming audio, audio transcript [70:23—70:56].
26. Bauman, *Globalization*, 77.
27. David Morley, *Home Territories: Media, Mobility and Identity* (London, 2000), 3.
28. Morley, *Home Territories*, 9.
29. Caren Kaplan, "Transporting the Subject: Technologies of Mobility and Location in an Era of Globalization," *PMLA* 117 (2002): 34.

Chapter 13

"FROM WALLPAPERS TO BLOGS"
Samizdat and Internet in China

Martin Hala

The exponential growth of the Internet in China since the mid 1990s has attracted much attention internationally, as did the Chinese government's truly Herculean effort to control it, and the cat-and-mouse game that ensued between users and censors.[1] After rather slow and lukewarm beginnings, China has embraced the Internet with a vengeance. Commercial Internet services became available in China in 1996; in the first decade, the online population had grown from an estimated 630,000 users in 1997 to 137 million by the end of 2006, with 90.7 million enjoying broadband connections.[2] After another half a decade, with almost half a billion broadband users, China presently boasts the largest Internet population in the world, ahead even of the United States. In fact, the comparison with the United States no longer makes sense, as China's Internet population is larger than that of all of the Unites States, or any other country save for India.

In the first Internet decade, two forms of online activity established themselves as disproportionately popular in China: the BBS (electronic bulletin boards and online forums) and blogs. The global rise of social media in the last few years led to a proliferation of domestic Chinese substitutes of popular services like YouTube, Twitter, or Facebook, taking advantage of the fact that virtually all of these big international brands are blocked from the Chinese market. Their Chinese look-alikes (Youku, Tudou, Sina Weibo, RenRen, Kaixin001, etc.) may have started as clones, but have meanwhile developed into a distinct local ecosystem that boasts many unique features.

Available surveys suggest that more than half of Chinese Internet users are active in various online forums, about one-third on blogs, and perhaps half on micro-blogs.[3] All these platforms empower users to publish

---

Notes for this chapter begin on page 279.

their views online in a simple way without much technical expertise. Online forums provide more anonymity, while blogs offer more profile for individual writers, who typically go by elaborate pen names, yet whose identity is more often than not quite well known. Real names have been encouraged on micro-blogs, leading to inevitable debates about anonymity, transparency, and security.[4]

The first blogging services were introduced in China in 2002, but for a few more years remained in the shadow of BBS. The steep growth of blogging in China after 2005 is widely attributed to the 2005 crackdown on the most outspoken forums, which drove many users to blogs.[5] The current, ongoing "Olympic" crackdown after 2008[6] has in turn affected all platforms for independent self-expression on the Internet, but long-form blogs arguably suffered more than the more cryptic social media and micro-blogs.

Since the launch of Sina Weibo in 2009, the fastest growing part of the Chinese Internet has been micro-blogging, or weibo, as it is known in Chinese. Weibo is simply a translation of "micro-blog," but the Chinese incarnation of the service is different from its Western counterpart (represented, or dominated, rather, by Twitter) in several important aspects. Like Twitter, most Chinese weibo services are limited in length of postings, but given the difference between the Chinese script and Western alphabets, the weibo's 140 characters can express much more than the Twitter's 180 signs. Secondly, unlike Twitter, weibo users can attach multimedia like photos and videos to their posts, thereby further enriching their messages. With these extra features, weibo micro-blogging in Chinese is closer to traditional blogging than the more constrained tweeting.

If the growth of Chinese Internet in the last decade and a half was impressive, the rise of micro-blogging in the last two years has been mind-boggling. In the first two years since Sina Weibo's release in August 2009, the number of estimated users has grown to some 200 million; it is expected to reach a quarter billion by the end of 2011. Some twenty-million weibo messages are reportedly posted every day.[7]

The full impact of this new phenomenon is only beginning to be felt in incidents like the August 2011 collision of two high-speed trains near Wenzhou in Zhejiang province where immediate weibo reports by survivors broke the official news embargo enforced in mainstream media and eventually forced the authorities to lift their attempted blackout altogether.[8] The new micro-blogging and social media ecosystem has neatly supplemented the already well-developed Chinese blogosphere and helped spawn a new space for comprehensive independent self-expression, constrained as it is but not fully suppressed by official censorship.

Could the Internet, and blogs in particular, play the role that samizdat performed in other communist societies? The answer to such a question, or even the inclination to ask it, probably depends on your understanding of the role and impact of samizdat to begin with. There does not seem to be a straightforward answer to such an inquiry. However, there appear to be at least two distinct areas in which to make meaningful comparison between the two methods of self-publishing: first, samizdat and online publishing as platforms for self-expression, and second, as catalysts for the development of an alternative public sphere.

Even after such narrowing down, any comparisons will necessarily be speculative. Due to the vagaries of history, we can only hypothesize what would have become of samizdat in the age of networked computers. The first laptop and even desktop computers were indeed employed in the late samizdat production in Central and Eastern Europe, but only for graphic design and printing and not for distribution. Their utilization, in any case, was too minimal and last minute to draw any conclusions. The Internet revolution arrived too late for European samizdat to merge with it.

In fact, the very idea of the Internet would have seemed antithetical to samizdat, in the sense that the availability of such a powerful tool for information sharing and cross-border dissemination would have been unthinkable in the kind of closed societies in which samizdat publishing flourished. In other words, the communist regimes in Eastern Europe would never have allowed the Internet in their fiefdoms; were they to have done so, they would have had to transform themselves into entirely different systems. And that is precisely what has happened in China in the last fifteen years or so—the networked China of today is as different from the old Soviet bloc as it is from its former Maoist self. It has undergone a thorough transformation that renders most comparisons with traditional communist societies largely meaningless. Likewise, the Internet has superseded any traditional forms of samizdat just as the current Chinese system has supplanted conventional communism.

With this disclaimer, we can proceed to try some comparisons nevertheless. To do so could be useful in deconstructing some common misconceptions about the Internet's potential social and political impact, as well as the nature of online censorship and self-censorship in China. We need not rely solely on comparisons with eastern European samizdat. China boasts its own proud tradition of underground and unofficial publishing. We should therefore begin with a brief overview of the samizdat tradition in communist China before the Internet.

Papers Printed, Pasted, and Mimeographed: Unofficial Publishing in China before the 1990s

Communist China, at least until the Cultural Revolution, was characterized by a lack of open internal dissent. Most outspoken anticommunists left the mainland in the aftermath of the Civil War (1946–1949); the rest were wiped out—together with many people perfectly loyal to the communist regime—in the violent campaigns of the early 1950s. There was, in fact, so little open dissent that the authorities had to manufacture it by means of another campaign, the Hundred Flowers (1956), which ultimately provided them with an excuse for yet another unnecessary and brutal crackdown.

The monstrous failure of Mao's Great Leap Forward (1958–1959), an economic experiment that resulted in an estimated 20 to 43 million deaths by starvation during the Three Years of Bitterness (1959–1962), finally generated some criticism from within party ranks. This criticism, sometimes thinly veiled, was voiced in the official media, and through regular innerparty channels. It created tensions that eventually burst into open conflict within the party leadership and led to the near breakdown of the whole system during the Cultural Revolution (1966–1969, or 1966–1976, depending on how one counts).

The resultant collapse of state authority unleashed the latent conflict present in society at large, which had built up over the previous seventeen years of communist rule. The post-1949 regime had imposed upon the otherwise fairly homogeneous Chinese society a kind of "class apartheid." All citizens were categorized according to the official "class line" (*jieji luxian*) into clearly defined groups ("classes"); these had nothing to do with citizens' own social and economic standing or political orientation, but rather with that of their family at the time of the revolution in 1949. This static classification governed the social mobility—or lack of it—for everybody, including those born after 1949 into a thoroughly transformed society. The "class line," which during the Cultural Revolution came to be called a "bloodline theory" (*xuetonglun*) by its opponents, in effect created a hereditary hierarchy that divided society into largely antagonistic camps.

The eruption of open conflict set the underprivileged losers within this system against the privileged winners in a bitter struggle that eventually bordered on full-fledged civil war. Despite a clash of interests, both sides claimed to be the true followers of Chairman Mao and employed similar rhetoric, derived from Mao's often obscure quotations, or from his cryptic "latest instructions." Neither side clearly formulated, much less articulated their true interests, and instead resorted to bizarre verbal acrobatics, which only added to the general chaos and confusion.

It was this period of turmoil that finally opened the floodgates for unsanctioned, unofficial opinion, often expressed in forms that could be vaguely designated as samizdat. Initially, arguments, more often merely denunciations or personal attacks, were presented in the form of handmade "big character posters" (*dazibao*), so-called because of the large lettering used, pasted onto walls. Eventually, the polemics became more sophisticated and most moved into semi- or unofficial newspapers published by various Red Guard factions on either side of the "class line." These "small papers" (*xiao bao*) were printed using simple techniques, in relatively small print runs, without prior censorship. Most never rose above primitive ideology full of mechanical rhetoric; nevertheless, a few individuals, and after a while entire groups, did manage to cross the lines (class, blood, or otherwise) and express independent opinion not directly subservient to any of the political dogmas of the time.[9]

Independent opinion was not bound by censorship, but was of course liable to subsequent reprisals. One of the early martyrs of the movement, a nineteen-year-old student named Yu Luoke (1952–1970), is still remembered, though not widely mentioned, in today's China as a pioneer of free expression. He was sentenced to death in 1968 and executed in 1970 for writing and publishing a booklet denouncing the "bloodline theory" as feudal atavism establishing a "new caste system." Ironically, many of his views prevailed shortly afterward among the officially sanctioned "rebel" (*zaofan*) factions of the Red Guards. Some of the "rebel" factions later went on to formulate their own understanding of what was going on in China and published it in the form of political manifestos or theoretical and polemical articles. These wayward groups paid the price when Mao finally authorized a wholesale crackdown on all Red Guard factions, which by now had proven fundamentally ungovernable. Most of their exponents ended up enduring "re-education" through hard labor in poor, remote rural areas, where many stayed for a full decade.

Some of the former Red Guards nevertheless resurfaced during the first real samizdat upsurge, the Democracy Wall Movement (1978–1979), after Mao's death in 1976 and Deng Xiaoping's eventual triumph over Mao's residual satraps in late 1978. Armed with their bitter disillusionment over the Cultural Revolution and their subsequent years in the wilderness, along with practical skills in mimeograph and other printing techniques developed ten years earlier, the former Red Guards embarked on a frenzy of publishing activity that answered Deng Xiaoping's call to "liberate the minds" (*jiefang sixiang*) and "search for truth from facts" (*shishi qiu shi*). After a flood of handwritten dazipaos pasted on the walls of Xidan in central Beijing, the first real samizdat magazines appeared with names like "Beijing Spring" (*Beijing zhi chun*) and 'Today' (*Jintian*). Some (such as the former) were devoted to politics, others (such as the latter) to unofficial literature.[10]

The most remarkable personality to emerge from this movement was a former Red Guard turned electrician named Wei Jingsheng. Wei authored the best-known piece of the time, titled "The fifth modernisation," and also published a samizdat magazine called *Explorations* (*Tansuo*). With his clarity of vision and courage to speak the unspeakable, he transcended the prevalent discourse. Where many still paid lip service to the official policy of the "Four Modernisations" (in agriculture, industry, science and technology, and defense), Wei clearly stated that without a fifth modernization—democratization—the other four lacked purpose. Where others glamorized Deng Xiaoping as a liberator, Wei unequivocally called him a "new dictator."

This finally exceeded the limits of tolerance of the new leadership around Deng Xiaoping. By this time, they had consolidated their newly gained power and felt no more need for expressions of popular support in their struggle with remnant Maoist forces. In March 1979, Deng personally ordered the arrest of Wei Jingsheng and within a year the whole movement was dispersed, together with its magazines. After a show trial, Wei was sentenced to fifteen years in prison. The samizdat magazines disbanded in subsequent crackdown. Some, like Beijing Spring and Today, later reappeared as tamizdat publications in the West.

This crackdown basically ended what can be understood as samizdat publishing in China. The next great popular upsurge, the protest movement focused around Tiananmen Square in April and May 1989, was not accompanied by significant unofficial publishing. During much of the movement, official media operated without censorship, and there was little need for an alternative press. The bloody crackdown on 4 June was followed by a period of brutal repression that made any attempts at samizdat publishing all but impossible. For a while, overseas Chinese student groups used fax machines to send antigovernment materials back to China, but this method proved largely inefficient.

When China finally re-emerged by the mid 1990s from the shadows of Tiananmen, it was a different society. The new market drive initiated by Deng Xiaoping during his legendary 1992 "Southern Inspection Tour" utterly transformed the economy and much of society. China has undergone a metamorphosis that has enabled a nominally communist country not only to join the accelerated process of globalization after the end of Cold War, but to become one of its central motors. China's metamorphosis prepared it for the unfolding Internet revolution and is what makes the Chinese Internet today so different from the previous samizdat publishing in China and Central and Eastern Europe. The society has changed, and so have its forms of self-expression.

Half Full or Half Empty? Freedom, Censorship, Intimidation, and Co-optation on the Chinese Internet

Deng's Southern Tour in effect introduced a New Deal for the Chinese. After the half-hearted attempts of the 1980s, capitalism was finally embraced in full. Chinese people could now unleash their long-dormant economic potential and try to get ahead in material life. To get rich was no longer a taboo; it had suddenly become "glorious." What's more, people could now enjoy the fruits of their (and others') labor without much state meddling in their lifestyles—they could pretty much do whatever they wanted in the private, as long as they did not foolishly venture to challenge the party's monopoly on power. They did not even have to love the party anymore—but please, no swearing in public.

This ideological coup was a huge success. The Communist Party gained a new lease of life and the "masses" discovered a new sense of purpose. China was re-energized and started out on its long march to prosperity. Priorities have changed, as have potential conflicts. The "us and them" mentality began shifting from politics and ideology into the economy. For many ordinary Chinese, harassment by the party and the state was becoming less of a concern than visa and import restrictions imposed by the outside world. Jumping head-on into globalization also led to a new view of the outside world. Countries that had previously been seen as role models have now become competitors trying to "contain" China's ascent.

While the economic and geopolitical rise of China does not benefit everybody, it still makes much of the population proud of the country's achievements. Ordinary Chinese may be cynical about the communist party, but they are quite serious about their country's standing in the world. They have achieved something, and they would like the outside world to acknowledge as much. This new pride and political ambivalence (or, in many cases, indifference) is quite unlike prevailing attitudes in pre-1989 Eastern Europe. China's new freedoms would also have been unheard of during traditional communism. The Chinese travel and do business internationally, send their children to American, Japanese, Australian, and European Universities, shop for luxury items that would have been available only to the top cadres in the *ancien régime*, and so on.

Access to information has changed as well. There are many restrictions on the Chinese media, but not the blanket censorship once imposed on any printed or broadcast material in communist countries. State subsidies for papers and magazines have been cut or abolished altogether, and most publishers now have to sink or swim on the market. Many papers have created popular weekly supplements and daily tabloids with market-friendly content catering to their readers' demands. Their editors navigate carefully between pressures from propaganda departments on one side and readers on the other. Exact boundaries of the permissible are not always clear, and many journalists keep "hitting line balls" (*da cabian qiu*), or constantly testing the limits. Every once in a while, some journalist somewhere gets in trouble for going too far; unlike in the old Soviet or Maoist regimes, however, they do not disappear but resurface in some other paper elsewhere in China, their position and reputation only consolidated by the previous controversy.

It is in this environment, and because of this environment, that the Chinese Internet could gain a foothold at all, and then grow so fast. The old communist regimes would hardly have been able to cope with the Internet and would most likely have forbidden it. While the current Chinese system can live with the Internet, coexistence is not always easy. However, despite many predictions to the contrary,[11] the Internet has not brought about abrupt political change, and is not likely to do so anytime soon. Its significance and implications for Chinese society lie elsewhere.

That is not to say that there is no subversive potential in the Chinese Internet. The government is well aware of it and has been trying its best to preempt it. With the help of many renowned international IT companies, it has introduced a sophisticated system of blocking and filtering, known in China as the "Golden Shield" (*Jin Dun*) and widely described elsewhere as "The Great Firewall of China." The system has been comprehensively analyzed in several studies.[12] It works on several levels. At the level of general infrastructure, it filters out unwanted content and blocks proscribed URLs automatically by keywords on the Internet backbone and at individual Internet Service Providers (ISPs). On the second level, it delegates censorship to the Internet Content Providers (ICPs), who are expected, much like traditional media, to engage in self-censorship or else lose their licenses. Finally, at the third level, the Internet is physically policed for offensive content by departments of the Public Security Bureau. As in most countries, law enforcement agencies have the right to search computers for evidence in criminal cases; but of course, Chinese authorities often criminalize what would constitute political speech anywhere else. Needless to say, constitutional guarantees of freedom of expression are not of much help.

Much has been said about the complicity of foreign Internet companies in this censorship. Apart from passive involvement by companies such as Cisco Systems, which provides routers with a built-in capacity to filter content, there has been active cooperation by Internet giants such as Yahoo, MSN, and Google (until its patience ran out in 2010). There are two aspects worth considering in this issue. First, Internet companies obviously need to comply with Chinese law in their China-based operations, just like any other company based in China. However, given the peculiarities of Chinese law enforcement in handling nonviolent political expression, international ISPs and ICPs should be very careful in deciding what services to host on their China-based computers. Human Rights Watch has documented at least four cases of Chinese government critics (Shi Tao, Li Zhi, Jiang Lijun, and Wang Xiaoning) who have been arrested and sentenced to lengthy prison terms based on evidence obtained from email accounts hosted (and disclosed) by Yahoo in China.[13] Google, on the other hand, has decided, for this very reason, not to provide a Chinese version of its popular email service Gmail. That decision in retrospect looks smart, even if it did not save Google from a series of phishing attacks on Gmail accounts worldwide reportedly initiated from Mainland China.

Second, in aiding censorship, these companies are not always following Chinese law. Search results at google.cn, for example, were filtered when Google still operated in China. While this is arguably less harmful than sending people to prison, it seems to have no basis in Chinese law as such. Naturally, no Chinese legislation proscribes expressions like "democracy" or "Tiananmen." Google.cn admitted as much by adding a tagline to search results for sensitive keywords, saying that some results had been omitted "in accordance with Chinese law and policies." That seems to be stretching the concept of legality. It is one thing to comply with Chinese law, but something else altogether to explicitly accept the controversial policies of Chinese censorship agencies, which themselves may be seen as contradicting China's own constitution.

Thus the usual argument that foreign Internet companies only comply with local law in their China operations would seem to have at least two problematic aspects: (1) Chinese laws may be in direct contradiction with established international practices, and possibly with international legal norms guaranteeing freedom of expression; and (2) in some cases, foreign companies may not be complying with Chinese law, but rather with government policies possibly tampering with the Chinese constitution, and in this manner contributing to a state of lawlessness rather than the rule of law. In July 2011, the *New York Times* indeed called in an editorial for "(legally) enforceable standards of ethical behavior to govern the transfer of digital technologies that could be abused by repressive governments against their citizens, and highlighted China as a glaring example of such abuse."[14]

In January 2010, Google announced it would no longer censor its search results in its Chinese domain (google.cn). The decision may have multilayered reasons, but it was directly prompted by hacking attacks on Google's servers allegedly trying, among other things, to break into Gmail accounts of Chinese human rights activists worldwide. After a protracted standoff, Google left this potentially lucrative market, standing up against censorship and surveillance in China in a manner no other international company and not even most foreign governments would ever dare to attempt.

The Google controversy (and many other similar incidents) also point to another interesting aspect. The Internet is often considered a major tool in undermining the authoritarian Chinese regime. It can, however, cut the other way as well—it can be used for advanced surveillance techniques against the regime's critics. Internet intrusion is in a way a logical extension of Internet censorship—a government that feels entitled to prescribe what information its citizens can or cannot access surely feels entitled to breach their citizens' privacy and tap into their personal communications. In other words, the lack of inhibition to censor implies the lack of inhibition to spy. Censorship and surveillance are just two sides of the same coin.

On the Internet, both censorship and intrusion becomes global. In mid 2011, Google disclosed a campaign of sophisticated "phishing" attacks, allegedly originating from an obscure vocational school in Jinan, prying into Gmail accounts of users worldwide, including those of overseas Chinese activists, China specialists in various countries, and senior US government officials. Many were skillfully personalized "spear-phishing" attacks bordering on identity theft.[15] Hitherto local Chinese practices of "managing" the Internet have in this manner affected individuals far beyond its borders, an entirely new phenomenon that might change the way people think of surveillance and censorship in the Internet age. Traditional censorship and intrusion techniques used to be largely limited to nation-states, or to political blocs at most. Nowadays, these techniques have global impact, with potential, if as yet unclear, consequences for us all.

Internet censorship can in most cases be circumvented by using proxy servers, SSL (secure) connections, and other means. There exist dedicated services designed to help Chinese users get past the Great Firewall. But does the average Chinese Internet user care? For starters, beating Internet censorship is a constant struggle. Proxy servers and anticensorship services usually get blocked after some time and need to change their IP and real-name addresses often. Anybody who has ever used a proxy server knows that it can be a frustrating experience, since it slows the connection considerably. Not everybody has the patience or motivation to spend long hours searching for functioning proxy servers and waiting for the forbidden pages to download.

In real life, very few people seem to bother. According to available surveys, the overwhelming majority (over 70 percent) of Internet users have never used a proxy server. Only 2.5 percent report frequent use of them.[16] These surveys need to be taken with a grain of salt, but anecdotal evidence seems largely to confirm their conclusions. A keen observer of Chinese media writing under the pseudonym Ann Condi posted a piece on the danwei.org blog, describing her experience in discussing anticensorship Web sites with her Chinese students.[17] When informed about the existence of such sites, her students offered a number of predominantly negative responses that Condi categorizes into the following attitudes: "ignorance, apathy, denial, paranoia, downplaying, nationalism, and mild interest." Her post generated intense discussion in the Chinese expat blogosphere, with most writers confirming her observations.

Obviously, many Internet users in China have somewhat different feelings about censorship from their Western counterparts. This is best illustrated by a celebrated hoax performed in 2006 by one of the best-known Chinese bloggers calling himself "Massage Milk" (Anmo Nai). This curious name hides the colorful personality of journalist Wang Xiaofeng, whose day job is with one of the more interesting mainstream magazines, *Life Weekly* (*Shenghuo zhoukan*). Another of his pen names is "Wearing three watches," or Dai sange biao, a pun on (the former president) Jiang Zemin's "theory" of the "Three represents," or Sange Daibiao. Clearly, Wang does not shy from turning his sharp wit and irony on the Chinese government. At the same time, he does not hesitate to turn it against Western media criticizing censorship of Chinese Internet.

On 8 March 2006 (International Women's Day, still celebrated in China), Wang shut down his blog, leaving a message that it was closed "for obvious reasons." The immediate, admittedly knee-jerk reaction of Western observers was that it had been closed down by the authorities, like so many before and after it. The news soon made it to major Western media outlets, including the BBC.[18] Wang then triumphantly reappeared and declared that it was a hoax meant to demonstrate the bias and "peer pressure" exerted by the Western media, which, he claimed, is always ready to jump to conclusions about China. The argument was then repeated, with much satisfaction, in the official Chinese press.

Of course, Wang had a point: the Western media did jump to conclusions without first establishing the facts. On the other hand, the very readiness of the Western media to see censorship everywhere in China is merely a habit born of experience: the BBC's own Web sites are blocked in China, and its broadcast jammed. A number of Wang's colleagues in the Chinese blogosphere were not too happy with his prank, either, arguing that it would diminish future solidarity with Web sites that genuinely are closed. The same point was made by Reporters Without Borders: crying wolf in this way, they argued, will only make it more difficult to defend Wang's less fortunate colleagues whose blogs do get shut down "for obvious reasons." Another blogger, referring to the case of journalist Shi Tao, who was jailed for an email he sent to an overseas publication, commented wryly: "More good news—the journalist Shi Tao has admitted that the story about him being jailed for eight years [for] leaking state secrets was all just an April Fool, too!"[19]

The whole incident probably tells us more about Chinese bloggers, and Internet users in general, than about the Western media. A certain attitude has developed among Chinese netizens, who are certainly not happy with official censorship, but even itchier about Western criticism of it. They feel that the Western focus on censorship somehow diminishes their achievements in working hard to expand, often at some personal risk, the room for free expression on the Chinese Internet.

Typical in this respect would be the stance of journalist Zhao Jing, who blogs under pseudonym Michael Anti. Zhao's site was shut down by Microsoft in December 2005, leading to an outcry in the United States and eventually to congressional hearings over US companies' complicity with Chinese censorship. Not impressed by the hearings, Michael Anti posted a strongly worded comment entitled, "The freedom of Chinese netizens is not up to the Americans." Ironically, his fierce defense of Chinese sovereignty had to be posted on a foreign blogging service blocked for most users in China. The post has since disappeared, so I can only quote it from translation on another blog:

> I am writing to state that I believe that this has nothing to [do] with us whatsoever. This is a purely internal American affair. When we Chinese who love freedom attempt to promote freedom of expression, we never thought that the right to freedom of expression ought to be protected by the US Congress. Every single blog post of mine was written in Chinese, and every sentence was written for my compatriots. I have no interest to cater to the interests of foreign readers.... This is our country.... We must let this generation bring freedom, democracy, security and wealth to China.... When foreigners repeatedly use "totalitarian" to describe China, this is a deep shame for me as a Chinese person. This shame cannot ever be forgotten. These kind of sentiments cannot be understood by foreigners.[20]

Journalist, blogger, and researcher Rebecca McKinnon calls the difference in attitude toward censorship a classic case of "glass half empty, or half full."[21] In other words, it boils down to the question: What is more important, the achievements or the misery of Chinese bloggers? Too much attention to their misery, especially from outsiders, does not go down well with the Chinese bloggers' pride.

Very often, it is professional pride, too. Millions in China blog, but the few influential blogs that draw much of the attention and Internet traffic are, invariably, written by professional journalists with day jobs in official media. Blogger Roland Soong observes that, "In China, the nonmainstream media sector (related to current news and commentary) ... is dominated by the media elite who are continuing to build their authority and reputation, in the manner of American and Hong Kong mainstream opinion columnists."[22]

All of the individual bloggers we have mentioned so far are in this category. They write under elaborate pseudonyms but their identity is no mystery to their readers. Their blogs serve to enhance their professional reputations as cutting-edge journalists, and at the same time help them circumvent one of the biggest hindrances in their work: pervasive self-censorship by responsible editors in the official media. When a story gets killed by an overcautious editor, it often ends up on the writer's blog. Sometimes, journalists post texts on their blogs right away, without even attempting to submit them for official publication. Blogging in China is, more often than not, an extension of the official press, rather than an alternative to it. It pushes the envelope one step further, rather than making a jump out of the mainstream and into the "underground."

That may be one of the starkest differences between the Internet and samizdat in China. The writers of traditional samizdat, in China or elsewhere, took a more or less conscious step out of the system. Chinese bloggers today remain inside the system, although on its cutting edge. Looked at from the other side, we could also say that blogging in China is a testimony to the capacity of the current Chinese system to co-opt potential critics and adversaries. Just like it co-opted the market economy, and later the Internet itself, the remarkably flexible Chinese system has now managed to co-opt blogging, too.[23] It can live with the kind of criticism and ridicule bloggers habitually subject it to, and bloggers can live with the system and its censorship, even if the relationship is often strained and uneasy. This is indeed communism of a different type. It is communism where the party can tolerate the Internet, and the Internet can tolerate party censorship.

The coexistence, indeed symbiosis between the Party and the Internet goes beyond mere co-optation. The regime has been quite successful in manipulating the Internet through proactive agenda setting. The propaganda departments at various levels employ legions of their own "internet commentators," basically freelancers, also known as the "50 cent party" (*wu mao dang*) because of the payments they allegedly collect per post defending the government's position in supposedly independent discussion forums, and in the comments sections on blogs.[24] Such level of infiltration and inside manipulation would of course not have been possible in traditional samizdat.

The Medium Is the Message: Free Minds before Free Speech

The co-optation and manipulation, even more than censorship, is why we cannot really expect the Internet in China to become a platform for radical agitation against the one-party system. That does not mean, however, that it is not ushering in significant change. Bulletin boards and (micro-)blogs may not be changing Chinese politics, but by introducing entirely new forms of self-expression and social interaction, they are gradually transforming society from within. Going back to our original questions about parallels between the Internet and samizdat in China: online forums and blogs have become new forms of self-expression that are perhaps less radical but certainly more widespread than traditional samizdat. They have created a new public space, again less politicized, but larger and more accessible than the samizdat of yesteryear.

During the heated congressional debate about American firms' complicity with online censorship in China, the buzz in the Chinese blogosphere was not about political freedom, or the lack of it, but about an online spoof played by a hitherto unknown prankster named Hu Ge. Hu re-edited one of film director Chen Kaige's less accomplished films into a twenty-minute parody and posted it online. Chen then sued him for intellectual property infringement and made himself the laughing stock of the Chinese Internet.[25] As Rebecca McKinnon points out, it may look as though the Chinese care more about bad movies than bad politics, but the moral of the story goes deeper. The Chinese apparatchiks may still keep a firm grip on politics, but they have all but lost their control over cultural life. Internet cannot bring down the government, but it can ruin the reputation of a famous filmmaker. Anybody who has lived through the decline of communism in Eastern Europe will appreciate what the loss of power over the cultural sphere means for the future of a one-party system.

And it is not just culture, but lifestyle in general that is gradually being transformed by online events. It should be noted that perhaps the personality to be given most credit for the rise in popularity of blogging in China is not an aspiring social or political reformer but a journalist named Li Li, writing under the pseudonym Muzi Mei. Her blog became notorious in 2003 for describing her erotic exploits with a variety of men with a "post-70s attitude to sex (direct and detached)." The propaganda ministry was not amused and Li lost her newspaper job, but was almost immediately hired by the biggest blogging portal, bokee.com. A book of excerpts from her blog diaries was recalled from Chinese bookstores, but sold well in Hong Kong and Taiwan. German and French translations followed.

Soon afterward, another overnight celebrity emerged in the person of Tang Jiali, a former dancer at the State Ballet Troupe who started posting her nude photographs online at www.tangjiali.com. Some of her photos were even reprinted with flattering commentary on the Web site of the official CCP mouthpiece *People's Daily* (*Renmin ribao*)[26]; the only conflict she got into was with her photographer, who sued for proper credits and royalties.[27] The government may still stand firm vis-à-vis the Internet, but all around it old taboos and inhibitions are crumbling. Most people may be careful about what they say online, but there's always somebody somewhere testing the limits. Whether it is in the area of film, sexual mores, or alternative music, the old orthodoxies are eroding fast.

Issac Mao,[28] one of the pioneers and most influential personalities in Chinese blogosphere, and a cofounder in 2002 of the first Chinese blogging service CNblog.org, makes an interesting point.[29] Observing the tendency toward self-censorship in China, he concludes that free speech is difficult, if not impossible, to realize in the absence of free thinking. Freeing people's minds from taboos, layers of propaganda sediments, and other constraints therefore has to precede any serious attempt at introducing free speech. And that is exactly where the Internet, and blogs in particular, are making headway in China. Online expression in China does not exactly equal free speech, but it does work to emancipate people's minds from official ideology still propagated by much of the print and broadcast media. The Internet is not likely to lead to political change, at least not directly, but it is slowly bringing about a profound change in the way people think and communicate. It is this transformation that will render any future political changes possible, and desirable. Political freedoms are only meaningful for people adept in free thinking.

Some Chinese observers have likened the cacophony of voices on the Chinese Internet, and especially blogs, to the chaotic spectacle of "big character posters," or Dazibao, at the beginning of the Cultural Revolution. The famous writer Yu Hua (born 1960), best known in the West for his novel *To Live* (Huozhe), adapted into a Golden Globe nominated movie by Zhang Yimou, recalls his childhood fascination with the "big character posters," which in the absence of real books provided his first literary education:

> I believe my first real literary reading experience began with my reading big character posters during the Cultural Revolution. Big character posters were filled with lies, accusations, denunciations, and attacks. The Cultural Revolution brought out the full potential of Chinese imaginative powers. People invented crimes for each other out of thin air. The crimes were usually made up of a series of stories. I remember carrying my book bag on my way home from school and reading each poster as I walked along. I wasn't interested in the revolutionary slogans. I was interested in the stories.[30]

In an interview with the *New York Times*, Yu Hua summarizes this experience and claimed that in reading the Dazibao, he first realized the power of language: "You could read just about everything in them, even sex. They were like the blogs of today."[27]

The Internet, just like the Dazibao, has provided people with a chance to express themselves free of censorship. Unless they manage to emancipate their minds from the long-term impact of relentless official rhetoric and propaganda, however, this freedom does not automatically translate into free expression, but rather into a caricature of it. This was evident in the early phases of the Cultural Revolution, when people were still under the grip of ideology and only used their new (and rather limited) freedom of expression to abuse each other. Yet the very process of speaking freely is self-cultivating. The medium is the message. By using the tools of free expression, people are learning to liberate their minds. That was eventually the case during the Cultural Revolution, and it is even more so now on the Chinese Internet.

That is where we can make a direct comparison between samizdat and the Internet. Neither could possibly aspire to single-handedly challenge the powers that be by itself. Few people involved in these forms of self-expression would even harbor such ambitions (though some probably do). Much of the unauthorized production in samizdat, like on the Internet, could not be bothered with politics. It was, and still is, more of a lifestyle issue. By engaging in these activities, people change their lives. They step outside of the officially sanctioned discourse into a new public space beyond the (full) control of the State. They liberate themselves, and possibly others.

The Internet enjoys much wider reach than samizdat ever had, since it is not really "underground." The safety and anonymity online does not lie in secrecy and conspiracy, but in the opposite: the sheer numbers of people involved. But the very visibility of online activity makes it more prone to at least partial self-censorship (not to mention manipulation through proactive agenda setting), so the discourse arguably is less blunt and radical than it was in samizdat (at least in the eastern European samizdat; much of the Chinese samizdat, as we have seen, was actually still under the spell of official ideology). But the social effect, to a certain degree, is similar. Both forms of self-expression lead, regardless of what is really being said, to the self-emancipation of the producers, and to lesser extent consumers (readers). Both create an alternative public space beyond direct reach of the State.

Both forms of independent self-expression achieve this in their own peculiar ways. Samizdat may be more outspoken and direct, but it is limited in reach and draws a strict boundary between producers and consumers. The Internet is more vulnerable to censorship and self-censorship, but has much wider reach and is a truly participatory medium with a soft line between writers and readers. Both change the way people live and think. I would argue that in the long run, a certain amount of censorship and self-censorship does not really matter much, however annoying it may be in its daily manifestations. What really matters is the change in attitude and outlook brought about by the experience of articulating one's thoughts and positions freely in a virtual community of peers not bound by social and political hierarchies or regimented discourse.

Notes

1. This is an updated and revised version of an article first published in English in *Eurozine* (25 October 2007), http://www.eurozine.com (accessed 19 August 2011).
2. http://www1.cnnic.cn/IDR/ (accessed 14 November 2012).
3. Markle Foundation and Chinese Academy of Social Sciences survey of Internet use in 5 major cities, http://www.markle.org/downloadable_assets/china_final_11_2005.pdf (accessed 19 August 2011).
4. "China: Radical real name registration campaign," *Global Voices*, 15 June 2010, http://advocacy.globalvoicesonline.org/2010/06/15/china-radical-real-name-registration-campaign (accessed 19 August 2011).
5. Rebecca MacKinnon, "The China Situation: Q&A with Isaac Mao," *Global Voices Online*, 21 March 2005, http://cyber.law.harvard.edu/globalvoices/?p=75 (accessed 19 August 2011).
6. In the words of the London-based author Ma Jian: "This current clampdown began with the Beijing Olympics. The government discovered that they could suppress all forms of dissent, and still receive the approbation of the international community." The *Guardian*, 29 July 2011, http://www.guardian.co.uk/world/2011/jul/29/author-ma-jian-banned-from-china (accessed 19 August 2011).
7. "Micro-blogging War in China," *China Decoded*, 8 April 2011, http://www.chinadecoded.com/2011/04/08/micro-blogging-war-in-china/ (accessed 19 August 2011).
8. Qian Gang, "China's Reporters Push the Boundaries," *The Wall Street Journal*, 3 August 2011, http://online.wsj.com/article/SB10001424053111903520204576484241060215576.html (accessed 19 August 2011).
9. In these observations I rely on my research of the collection of Red Guard publications at the Oriental Institute in Prague.
10. Chen Ruoxi, *Democracy Wall and the Unofficial Journals* (Berkeley, 1982).
11. For one the best known and most reviled in China, see Nicholas D. Kristof, "Death by a Thousand Blogs," *New York Times*, 24 May 2005, http://www.nytimes.com/2005/05/24/opinion/24kristoff.html (accessed 19 August 2011).
12. See, for instance, http://www.hrw.org/reports/2006/china0806 (accessed 19 August 2011), or http://www. opennetinitiative.net/studies/china (accessed 19 August 2011).
13. http://www.hrw.org/reports/2006/china0806/5.htm (accessed 19 August 2011).
14. "Enabling China," *New York Times*, 24 July 2011.
15. "Google Mail Hack Blamed on China," *The Wall Street Journal*, 2 June 2011, http://online.wsj.com/article/SB10001424052702303657404576359770243517568.html (accessed 19 August 2011).
16. Markle Foundation and Chinese Academy of Social Sciences survey of Internet use in five major cities, http://www.markle.org/downloadable_assets/china_final_11_2005.pdf (accessed 19 August 2011).

17. Ann Condi, "Apathy—Glimpses in the Chinese Media," *Danwei*, 1 December 2006, http://www.danwei.org/media_regulation/glimpses_inside_the_chinese_me.php (accessed 19 August 2011).
18. Sebastian Usher, "China shuts down outspoken blog," the *BBC* News, 8 March 2006, http://news.bbc.co.uk/2/hi/asia-pacific/4787302.stm (accessed 19 August 2011).
19. http://blog.bcchinese.net/bingfeng/archive/2006/03/12/59423.aspx (accessed 19 August 2011).
20. http://www.zonaeuropa.com/20060217_1.htm (accessed 19 August 2011).
21. Rebecca McKinnon, personal communication.
22. Roland Soong, "Chinese Bloggers, Podcasters and Webcasters: A Comparison of the Relationship between Mainstream Media versus Blogging Culture in the United States, Hong Kong and China," *EastSouthWestNorth*, 18 September 2005, http://www.zonaeuropa.com/20050918_1.htm (accessed 19 August 2011).
23. It could be argued that it is now trying to co-opt the very notion of democracy, too, or rather to redefine it to suit its own needs. See Joseph Kahn, "Among China's elite, talk of 'democracy,'" *International Herald Tribune*, 20 April 2007.
24. See, for instance, David Bandurski, "China's Guerrilla War for the Web," *Far Eastern Economic Review*, July 2008, http://www.feer.com/essays/2008/august/chinas-guerrilla-war-for-the-web (accessed 19 August 2011).
25. http://www.zonaeuropa.com/culture/c20060108_1.htm (accessed 19 August 2011).
26. http://www.people.com.cn/GB/wenyu/69/20021226/896098.html (accessed 19 August 2011).
27. http://bjyouth.ynet.com/article.jsp?oid=3264667 (accessed 19 August 2011).
28. http://www.isaacmao.com (accessed 19 August 2011).
29. http://ethanzuckerman.com/blog/?p=266 (accessed 19 August 2011).
30. David Barboza, "China's Hit Novel: Tremendous or Trash?" *New York Times*, 3 September 2006, http://www.iht.com/articles/2006/09/03/news/yu.php (accessed 19 August 2011).

Chapter 14

REFLECTIONS ON THE REVOLUTIONS IN EUROPE
Lessons for the Middle East and the Arab Spring

Barbara J. Falk

Where is the Muslim Solidarność? Critics generally pose this question to impugn the democratic possibilities of the Muslim world. The idea of pro-democracy activism arising spontaneously from the shipyards of Gdańsk stands for the hope that in every society, no matter how totalitarian or repressive, there are freedom-loving people who see clearly that democracy is the solution to what ails their country. Yet such popular democracy movements are hard to come by in the contemporary Muslim World.

—Noah Feldman[1]

The lesson of Helsinki is that when demands to uphold human rights are backed by effective action, the cause of freedom and peace can be advanced. The danger today is that the commitment to spread human rights and democracy in the Middle East will remain an empty promise.

That would be most unfortunate. Just as Helsinki helped liberate hundreds of millions of people and defeat an evil empire that threatened the democratic world, the same approach today can transform the Middle East from a region awash in terror and tyranny into a place that provides freedom and opportunity to its own people as well as peace and security for the rest of the world.

—Natan Sharansky[2]

Notes for this chapter begin on page 308.

It is increasingly fashionable to suggest that the Global War on Terror (GWOT)—the rubric under which much counterterrorism activity was subsumed immediately after 9/11—is the "Cold War" of the twenty-first century. As with the Cold War, the War on Terror would be a "long war" without decisive battles, a clash of ideologies, and a battle for "hearts and minds," fought on civilian as well as military terrain, where the enemy cannot be defeated simply through "containment." The GWOT has not been primarily about the conquest of territory, and, although the academic Left delights in its discussion of the "imperial overstretch" of the United States, no one realistically suggested that the Bush Administration or its successor is anxious to establish an empire in any traditional sense. Unlike the Cold War, however, major conflicts have not been fought through local proxies as in Angola, Central America, or Afghanistan. However, assuming the parallel is accurate and relevant, what we have witnessed is an era akin to the early 1950s, the "hot" and "early" phase of the Cold War, when ideological tensions were most dramatic, when American troops were engaged in Korea, and when the tactical battlefield use of nuclear weapons was much discussed. However, following the defeat of McCarthyism, the Cuban Missile Crisis of 1962, and the ignominy of the US withdrawal from Vietnam, it became clearer that the domestic Manichean division of ally and adversary and the foreign demonization of the Soviet threat were both incorrect and counterproductive. It was then important to distinguish between nationalism and communism, in an America with no further appetite for the direct engagement of US troops abroad. In the era of détente and peaceful coexistence, which continued to function even under the "evil empire" rhetoric of Ronald Reagan, successive American administrations promoted new strategies of engagement that were critical to influencing and supporting democratic opposition and civil society movements in Central and Eastern Europe. In exchange for regime recognition and border security, the Helsinki process represented a seismic shift in refocusing the analytical lens from regime change to the more limited and pragmatic aim of human rights protections. We may be on the verge of a similar turning point given the continued foreign policy of the Obama administration and the commencement of the "Arab Spring" in 2011.

I argue that the lessons of the Cold War are found in this later period, when democracy promotion paradoxically worked best because it was not overtly about the instauration of democracy or the establishment of free and fair elections, but it was rather about creating independent space for self-organization and for civil society. Central and East European dissidents worked to extend the authentic existence of uncensored cultural expression and the slow de-monopolization of party-state control over historical truth and contemporary life, via samizdat and the importation of tamizdat, all the while maintaining an overriding commitment to self-limitation and nonviolence. Vacláv Havel famously called this approach "living in truth."[3]

Although much has been written about the ultimate dissident "success" of the creation of viable opposition movements and democratic norms and values, there is a tendency to view the history of the region as retrospectively deterministic—that it was somehow triumphantly inevitable that this would occur, and that the dissidents themselves magically *knew* the careful slow-cook recipe for liberal democracy in advance.[4] In reality, much of this success was owed to the creative, improvisational, and self-limiting nature of dissident activity. Democracy was a happy, but not an entirely foreseen, accident. Moreover, by focusing on the process of alternative institution building, rather than toppling the party-state (the ultimate result), democracy was more successfully brewed. Indeed, critical dissident theoretical and tactical innovations occurred only after the failures of both 1956 and 1968, events that forced a turn away from state capture or reform and decisively toward society.

By exploring theoretical and practical innovation in anticommunist dissent and its potential relevance to the contemporary reality of the Middle East, I am not suggesting that democratization strategies can easily or unproblematically "travel" from one historic moment or geographic place to another and a very high and sensitive degree of "translation" is required. However, I do argue that democracy is not something that is confined by history and human experience to Europe or its largely white settler dominions overseas. Neither is democracy something genetically incompatible with "Islam," when presented as a cultural and religious monolith. Nor is any Islamic religious reformation necessary for democracy to succeed. The best strategy paradoxically is not direct democracy promotion at all, but indirect focus away from the state and toward society. Of course, this is where samizdat and tamizdat reenter the picture, but in a twenty-first century formulation that has been technologically "updated" to take into account the forces of cultural and technological globalization—particularly the Internet, the blogosphere, the creation of virtual communities, mass satellite media, and mobile telephone utilization.

Central and Eastern Europe: Lessons Learned, Theoretical and Practical, and Their Application

One of my central propositions is that, on a fundamental and even causative level, *ideas matter*. Agency does not triumph over structure, nor are ideas solely determinative. Privileging the Hegelian formulation that consciousness precedes being does not preclude a healthy appreciation of the importance of the simultaneous constraints and opportunities presented by structures, institutions, historical legacies, and cultures.[5] This is not just an abstract theoretical proposition—it is key to my argument that, if ideas matter, they are also influential. They impact and indeed transform politics and, most importantly, have the ability to transcend the local and, in the course of their translation and adaptation, are both the source and object of change. No set of ideas is the property of a particular civilization, state, intellectual movement, or language. It is certainly true that the dissidents of Central and Eastern Europe tapped into the centuries-old European Enlightenment tradition (which was, importantly, their own tradition as well), when discussing civil society, the separation of state and society, and politically liberal ideas of freedom of speech and association. However, there was much cultural borrowing as well. The influence of Thoreau, King, and Gandhi can be found in the commitment to nonviolence, creative activism, and civil disobedience. Moreover, the conceptual basis of the Helsinki process—so important in providing a platform for action and debate—had as much to do with transnational, postwar, and postcolonial dialogues about human rights as it did with European nineteenth-century liberalism. In the twenty-first century and the era of cultural, economic, and political globalization, ideas about human rights and democracy are championed by many state and non-state actors, and have become central norms that infuse institutions of global governance, transnational civil society, and international law. Although subject to continual and frustrating "conceptual stretching," it cannot be denied that whatever set of overlapping historical and geographical circumstances gave rise to these ideas, they are now the collective property of humanity (regardless of how local cultures and local "values" continue to influence democratic ideals).

I do not accept the argument that the ideas and actions of anticommunist opposition activists in Central and Eastern Europe have no meaning or relevance in a radically different religious, historical, or geographic context. This approach amounts to intellectual Orientalism, in which the objective and all-knowing gaze of the Westerner both epistemologically and architecturally categorizes, delimits, and authoritatively organizes our "knowledge" of the East.[6] This experience should be familiar to the average "East" European, having been socially and historically constructed as the necessary and mutually constitutive "Other" of the "West."[7] Indeed, one of the major purposes of dissident discourse and activism was breaking down the East-West divide—first, intellectually (recall the Central Europe debate of the 1980s) and then practically (aiming to "return" to Europe). Having made the case for relevance, it is also necessary to delineate the theoretical and practical "lessons learned" that might be applied to the Middle East, particularly with respect to the organization of civil society and the dual commitments of nonviolence and evolutionism.

Civil Society and Nonviolence

In Central Europe, despite the language of antipolitics, civil society was never apolitical or beyond politics. In providing an alternative and noncoercive space for noninstitutional social and cultural activity (neither sanctioned nor censored by the party-state), it was possible to "live in truth," according to Havel's dictum, and openly develop ideas, organizations, and relationships based on respect for human rights, authenticity, morality, and transparency. Such engagement was fundamentally active and creative—through participation, the scope and possibility of further action was enlarged. Self-organization fostered values of reliance, independence, and self-help based on the model of KOR—originally workers persecuted by the Polish authorities as a result of the 1976 Radom/Ursus "riots." There was a strong connection between the mode of organization (civil society) and the style of activism (a principled commitment to nonviolence). This synergy between means and ends was mutually self-reinforcing. The parallel *polis*, to use Václav Benda's terminology, was both a refuge from the "violence" of the party-state, as well as a crucible of nonviolent resistance, where values of pluralism and tolerance—often in the guise of a Bohemian, countercultural lifestyle—were cultivated. A violent uprising was simply not geostrategically viable given two superpowers armed with nuclear weapons. On first analysis, this could have meant paralysis. However, the situation engendered the development of an array of nonviolent tactics aimed at multiple levels: communities of dissent and their respective organizations, broader societies at large, indirectly the party-state, the international community of peace-loving and democratic states, and émigré communities abroad.

By rejecting violence as an acceptable means toward political ends, Central Europeans also refused the transgressive and titillating violence of Georges Sorel, national syndicalism, fascism, and of wartime atrocity. It took almost a century, from the indifference of Russian nihilists to the killing fields in Europe during World Wars I and II, to say "never again" to the zealotry of violence and charismatic leaders bent on remaking humanity. It took a leap of faith to accept that violence was never "purifying." It was a moral as well as a rational choice. Rejecting violence also meant taking human rights at an individual level very seriously. Contrary to the values of both the party-state and fascism, life in the postwar world was held to be a sacred gift, not easily expendable for a larger cause.[8] Jonathan Schell has argued that the nonviolent path chosen by Central and East Europeans was pragmatic, hardheaded, realistic, and undeniably effective.[9] Nonviolent resistance redirected activism toward modest ends and small but sustainable improvements in daily life. Such work was constructive, not destructive, as epitomized by Jacek Kuroń's epithet that workers should not burn down party headquarters but found their own instead. Modesty had its own rewards, not the least of which was the ability to secure small victories, rather than deliver on anything as grandiose as regime change. At no point were Adam Michnik, Jacek Kuroń, Václav Havel, János Kis, or György Konrád counseling their compatriots to engineer the political defeat of authoritarian communism. Michnik was concerned that the use of violence would transform freedom into its opposite; Konrád repeatedly rejected what he called the philosophy of the nuclear *ultima ratio*.

Admittedly, nonviolent resistance may be a greater challenge in the Middle East today than in Central and Eastern Europe. Because the regimes are not ideological, it is impossible to point out the injustice of, for example, attacking workers in a workers' state. The monarchies and despots of the region cling to complex webs of tribal loyalty, cults of personality, and patronage. In the end, this has meant a far more naked and ruthless attachment to power, even if that means detention, torture, and murder of rebelling populations, as the cases of Libya and Syria demonstrate.

New Evolutionism

What Adam Michnik in Poland called "new evolutionism" and János Kis in Hungary called "radical reformism" was a rejection of what was traditionally thought of as revolutionary: a clear-cut break from the past, achieved by violence, ambitiously involving the remaking of society, if not humanity. This deliberate turn away from the state and reform-communist approaches mirrored a similar reversal in thinking about the morality and effectiveness of romantic and futile nineteenth-century-style violence and fiercely patriotic, nationalist outbursts. New evolutionism was premised on a kind of learning-by-doing and careful improvisation, which was neither quick nor easy. This approach, incidentally, is well suited to a region bred on violence, the promise of quick fixes, and the totalizing and seductive vision of political Islam. New evolutionism owes much more to Mohandas K. Gandhi and Martin Luther King Jr. than to John Locke or James Madison.

Finally, ideas about civil society and new evolutionism were not about engineering regime change from below. Capturing the state or reforming the system from above was roundly rejected after the experiences of 1956 and 1968.[10] Only in Poland was a mass movement possible, and its successes and failures both delayed and initiated political reform, ultimately leading (a decade after martial law) to the region's first partially free elections. As Padraic Kenney has cogently argued, it was the carnivalesque younger generation that pushed the envelope from 1988 onward, as it is today in the Middle East and North Africa. The youth took its cue from its intellectual forbears to be sure, but was much more willing to throw caution to the wind with demonstrations, street theater, and spontaneous happenings.[11]

Applicability to the Middle East Today

In comparing the Middle East to Central and Eastern Europe, there is an obvious tendency to focus on two key differences: the oil economy and Europe's Judeo-Christian heritage. Academic literature plays the Islam/Islamism card as overwhelmingly determinative, often in an Orientalist manner. The notion of a "Muslim World" has become popular, despite clear differences between the predominantly Arab states in the Middle East, North Africa, and South East Asia.[12] In a subtler interpretation, the problem is Arab, not Muslim, exceptionalism, in which Arab states are presumed historically and culturally impervious, at worst (or inhospitable, at best), to competitive elections, the rule of law, and transparent and accountable governance.[13] Implicit in the democracy promotion discourse has historically been the equation of Islamic/Arab authoritarianism with terrorism, or the assumption is at least that such authoritarianism provides fertile soil for discontent. Although political parties, candidates, liberal dissidents, social movements, and terrorists may all lay claim to Islam, to brush aside everything as equally "Islamic" or "Islamist" denies important differences.[14] And it denies the possibility of secular activism rooted in culturally and religiously Islamic society—which has profoundly blossomed with the Arab Spring of 2011.

The oil economy of the Middle East, unlike the dilapidated yet diversified economies of Eastern Europe, has guaranteed the ongoing geostrategic importance of the region. Oil wealth has not been evenly distributed, resulting neither in equitable development nor democratization. Central and Eastern Europeans, for all of their complaints about the relative economic advantages enjoyed by the *nomenklatura*, inherited the legacies of communist egalitarianism-collectivization, as state socialism destroyed previous class divisions and forced land reform. As a resource "curse," oil inhibits rather than enlarges the possibilities for democratization. When governments such as Saudi Arabia can fill their coffers with greater revenue from oil than from popular or progressive taxation, there is no incentive to respond to people's needs or aspirations. A "thin" form of illiberal democracy that "elects" leaders but abuses human rights (as in Iran) can also sustain itself on the ever-increasing price of oil. Oil generously allows levels of economic irrationality and arbitrary state control that would otherwise be regulated by open financial, business sectors. Macroeconomic stabilization in petro-states can likewise be safely ignored.

The organization and activism of civil society as a potent factor in democratization has been much discussed, and the contribution of Central and East Europeans has contributed mightily to the literature and practice of democratic theory. In the democracy promotion "business," however, civil society too often becomes part of a step-by-step recipe, in which the creation of a sphere of activity beyond the reach of the authoritarian state is seen primarily as forming an effective counterweight to the repressive exercise of power. Thus, strengthening civil society becomes a project burdened with the weight and expectation of regime change, rather than a grassroots pursuit of its own modest and limited ends. Amy Hawthorne has appropriately cautioned against the wholesale utilization of the civil society mantra as the "magic missing piece of the Arab democracy puzzle."[15] The reality of civil society in the Middle East does not map neatly onto European or North American experience, but civil society has always been about diversity and pluralism—its very messiness and unpredictability is entirely the point.[16] Hawthorne also discusses the unusual success of Middle Eastern states in quashing dissent, political quiescence, and the low level of civic participation, as well as the co-optation of some civil society organizations by states or states' efforts to establish their "own" groups (though this was also true under communism in Central and Eastern Europe). She faults civil society organizations for not developing a "prodemocracy agenda" and Western donors for not contributing enough financially.[17] However, civil society organization, where it has been part of successful democratization efforts in the past, is not primarily about democratization, except in a very local and participative sense. Moreover, one cannot "buy" civil society with Western aid. Indeed, in the Middle East (where the reputation of the United States, in particular, is deeply tarnished by its Cold War policies, uncritical support for Israel, and the invasion of Iraq), external funding is problematic and will continue to be compromising.[18] Europe and North America would be better off negotiating a Helsinki-type process with regional allies, rather than succumbing to authoritarian excuses in place of democratic development in the name of energy security.

More troublesome is the fact that, in the Middle East, civil society organization has not necessarily followed the promotion or practice of liberalization and nonviolence. Particularly in Gaza and Lebanon, civil society organizations have been crucibles of violent rather than nonviolent resistance. This may seem contradictory, for although organizations like Hamas and Hezbollah are best known for their "terrorist" activities, they have also distinguished themselves through the sophisticated and effective provision of local and community services (functioning like KOR in Poland). Because of such activities, these organizations have gained enormous local legitimacy, particularly when official organizations, such as the Palestinian Authority under Yasser Arafat, or the Lebanese government in its previous incarnation as a Syrian puppet, proved to be corrupt and ineffective. The Palestinian Authority has had considerable difficulty in establishing transparent and accountable government, despite its long history as an "opposition in waiting."[19] A transition is more difficult when violence has been a key *modus operandi*, rather than the cultivation of its opposite. Hamas effectively functioned as an opposition-in-waiting, but its uncompromising commitment to violence and nonrecognition of Israel has made negotiated peace a distant possibility. In this respect, one hopes that the Arab Spring portends to be the "game changer" many pundits have prophesized, because if nothing else, it illustrates the profound commitment to nonviolence on the part of the many and varied protest and youth movements whose ranks have populated the street protests.

Moreover, nonviolent strategies rooted in the cultivation of independent civil society have taken root, even prior to the Arab Spring. Embedded in the power of the powerless is the idea that committed actions make others aware of the struggle, show the nakedness of the emperor, and enlarge political possibilities. This is exactly what happened to Tunisian President Zine el-Abidine Ben Ali and Egyptian President Hosni Mubarak. To a limited degree, Palestinians have pursued this strategy in different ways, for example, taking the issue of the Israeli security fence/wall to the International Court of Justice in The Hague.[20] After the 2009 Gaza conflict, nonviolent resistance has become the norm rather than the exception, with weekly protests against the wall, generating a considerable international solidarity movement in the process. Such support was highlighted through international condemnation of the Israeli assault on the Turkish aid flotilla that endeavored to reach Gaza in May 2010.

An obvious lesson from Central Europe is that the tactical choice to eschew violence proved to be both morally superior and more effective. In order to follow the same path, Palestinians have increasingly rejected the explanation—sometimes offered outright as an excuse—that the campaign of suicide terror and the logic of violence is acceptable because of Israel's overwhelming military superiority and the alleged and proven atrocities of the Israeli Defence Force (IDF). In the past, there has been a tendency among intellectuals to privately condemn suicide terrorism while publicly explaining it as resistance to injustice, indicative of the desperation and frustration of endemic poverty, oppression, and voicelessness. If violence reigns in a Gaza ruled by Hamas, it is acceptable in Hobbesian terms to respond with equal violence. The argument that Israeli citizens are fair game, given compulsory military service, must also be rejected as a form of collective punishment. The Right of Return in the Occupied Territories is not morally or pragmatically equivalent to suicide terrorist attacks within Israel's pre-1967 borders.[21] In order to move ahead, such arguments must be defeated on ideological, moral, and practical terrain, as illogical, immoral, and ultimately ineffective. Influential Palestinian scholars such as Rashid Khalidi have already made these arguments, and the 2003 Geneva Initiative championed by Yossi Beilin and Yasser Abed Rabbo strongly rejected violence and terrorism. The National Conciliation Document of the Prisoners (the so-called Prisoners' Document), while infused with the logic and language of resistance and denunciation, condemned the use of weapons in settling internal disputes and promotes dialogue over violence.[22]

At the same time, the symbiotic relationship that exists between terrorism and the media overshadows the point that nonviolent dissent promotes tolerance and liberalization. The operational logic of the media suggests that, the more spectacular the violence, the more newsworthy the story. Nonetheless, de facto pluralism and civil society exist in Palestine, Lebanon, Saudi Arabia, Syria, Yemen, Qatar, the United Arab Emirates, Bahrain, Iran, and Egypt, and the web of organizations and activities is often much richer and varied than is supposed, containing multiple layers, some of which are semiofficial, while others constitute a "grey zone" in Jiřina Šiklová's sense of the term, but they have not been "newsworthy" until the spring of 2011. The ability of groups to operate legally or exist on the margins of state tolerance varies from state to state, and the jury is still out on the extent to which the current protest and democratization movements will result in a widening of permissible activity—which may or may not lead to democratic transition—or violent crackdown. It bears remembering that in Central Europe, this process was neither fast nor smooth. Mass mobilization often marked the end of a process, not the beginning. The story of Solidarity did not begin in the shipyards of Gdańsk; important precursors included the Polish October of 1956, the anti-Semitic crackdown in 1968, the Gdańsk massacre in 1971, and the Radom/Ursus riots (which spread throughout the country) in 1976. As in Central Europe, elites in many of these communities constitute an "intelligentsia," often supported by and in dialogue with concerned and active diaspora communities, particularly in Europe and North America. Though they attract émigré attention and international funding, these individuals did not generally make the nightly news until the winter and spring of 2011, which did much to confirm their existence and confound conventional explanations about the region.

Paradoxically, civil society found richer soil in Eastern Europe because the real achievements of socialism—poverty reduction, literacy, education, health care provision, skilled employment, and (at least on paper) greater equality for women—made it easier. United Nations Human Development reports tell us of structural barriers to both independent societies and the viable democracies in the Middle East, citing high levels of illiteracy, income inegalitarianism, malnutrition, relatively high population growth, property demolition, the repression of women, corruption, and the lack of transparency and good governance.[23] However, these problems are by no means unique to the Arab or Muslim world. The diffusion of ideas from Eastern Europe can be coupled with democratization experiences in developing nations with similar economic, educational, and demographic patterns or with the complicating dynamic of ethnicity and religion, for example, in cases from sub-Saharan Africa or South East Asia. Comparing the Middle East to Central and Eastern Europe is certainly an appropriate comparison but by no means the only possible one. Nonetheless, we find that examples of the modernizing process in the postcolonial regimes in the Middle East (where authorities eliminated feudal and aristocratic economic and landowning structures, founded state institutions, developed administrative capacities and championed economic "growth") were, like in socialist states, examples of modernization.[24]

One of the most hopeful sites of a blossoming of civil society is perhaps also the most paradoxical: Iran. Many groups that made up the opposition to the theocratic regime prior to the Iranian elections of 2009—such as Mellimazhabi and Nehzat Azadi, as well as the various organizations that loosely make up the students' movement, independent labor movement, and women's movement—have thoroughly rejected revolutionary violence, intolerance, and state control. Iran is also the only state in the region where liberalization and democratization might be mutually reinforcing, largely because the "Algeria problem" does not exist.[25] Perhaps because Iran has experienced the forced authoritarian modernization of Reza Shah (1925–1941) and Mohammad Reza Shah (1942–1978) (as well as several decades of Islamist theocracy), many have now eschewed revolutionary violence. The authoritarian result of 1979 has been highly instructive, and revolutionary commitments to human rights, democracy, and freedom have not been forgotten. As a result, Iranian activists are largely self-reflexive, profoundly anti-ideological, and reject totalizing visions and grand theories.[26] Like their counterparts in Central Europe in the 1970s and 1980s, many are liberal in orientation and approach, and see their task as primarily educational—to change and empower society, rather than take over the state. They are seeking smaller yet sustainable changes, while avoiding rigidity and vanguardism. It has not always been clear to Western media and governments that, despite Mahmoud Ahmadinejad's election in 2005 and the ongoing fixation with the nuclear question, the informal opposition was expansive and growing.[27] More than twenty million Iranians had already voted for some kind of reformism in elections prior to 2009, and at the same time were disillusioned with the previous failure of partial reform from above and the stymied efforts of Mohammad Khatami. New alliances emerged, and everyday forms of resistance took on political significance. Blogging was but one measure of such everyday resistance. Prior to the 2009 elections, there were an estimated million-plus bloggers in Iran, creating private virtual communities while skillfully evading regime filters. As the aftermath of the 12 June 2009 "stolen" elections have demonstrated, 21st-century samizdat and social self-organization is powered by the Internet and mobile telephone technology, utilizing social networking applications, e.g., Twitter and Facebook. Nonetheless, claims of direct causality are overblown; social media can no more generate revolutions or the collapse of authoritarian governments than could samizdat and tamizdat alone in Central and Eastern Europe.[28] Both social media and samizdat are better understood as potential enablers, which can have multiplier effects in the dissemination of ideas, a point that gets lost in the never-ending structure versus agency debate at moments of revolution.

The 12 June 2009 elections, the peaceful and mass social mobilization that followed, and the Islamic Republic's violent answer to the protests, confirmed what had already been going on in Iran, not simply what has happened since.[29] The fraudulent and reverse-engineered election outcome was a hastily prepared effort on the part of the authorities to stem the tide of support for opposition candidate Mir Hussein Moussavi, whose campaign support had dramatically increased in the weeks leading up to the ballot. Moreover, the public and colorful display of support beforehand, coupled with the courageous and sustained demonstrations in the face of Revolutionary Guard and Basiji violence afterward, indicated the extent to which cynicism and political acquiescence had been transformed into full-fledged dissent.

The date 12 June 2009 may or may not signal the beginning of the end of the Islamic Republic in the long run, but it most certainly has torn the remaining shreds of the regime's legitimacy. Unfortunately, efforts to produce compliance and quiescence through beatings, arrests, and the sad and gruesome display of forced confessions and show-trials have resulted in anger, derision, and a renewed commitment to change on the ground. Increasingly, there are cracks in the ruling elite, as was evidenced by the support given to the protests by former presidents Mohammad Khatami and Ali Akbar Hashemi Rafsanjani. Indeed, the two opposition leaders going into the election, Moussavi and Mehdi Karroubi, had been members of the political establishment. The Supreme Leader, at one time perceived to be above the political fray and a guarantor of religious and political stability, now has blood on his hands. Furthermore, the brutality of the repression has been ludicrously inept, measured by the explanations provided and confessions extracted. According to the official story, much of what has happened was part of a vast conspiracy in which the United Kingdom was deeply complicit, a charge so laughable that it leads to the rejoinder that the Islamic Republic must be the only existing state to still believe the sun never sets on the British Empire, at least in terms of deep pockets and far-reaching influence.

In many respects, the Iranian experience paved the way for what occurred positively in Tunisia and Egypt in the winter and spring of 2011, and negatively in Libya. The Iranian case ably demonstrated that the Internet and social media have dramatically changed the nature of what we would traditionally call samizdat and tamizdat, much of which now exists virtually as news and monitoring sites, individual blogs, chat groups, and informal email networks. Iranian online debates create a virtual global conversation that unites Iranians in Iran with diaspora communities abroad, and the same has occurred with other Middle Eastern and North African diasporas with respect to ongoing events in Tunisia, Egypt, Libya, Bahrain, Yemen, and Syria. The immediate connectivity and effective range of contemporary samizdat far exceeds what there ever was in Central and Eastern Europe—something that may prove to be a key advantage in the long term.[30] Given globalization and emigration, diasporas are sizeable, connected, and concentrated. In the Iranian case, diasporas in multicultural metropolises such as Toronto and Los Angeles came together despite longstanding internal divisions. The bloody aftermath to 12 June 2009 galvanized and united the previously fractious, politically and generationally divided Iranian diaspora, so much so that it now has the potential to play a powerful role of support for human rights and as a conduit for effective uncensored communication. The Iranian diaspora became an example for other communities, in much the same way as the émigré Poles united in their external support for Solidarity following the introduction of martial law in December 1981.

Many such communities remain economically and politically engaged in their home states. One of the positive legacies of the ill-fated Oslo Accord is that we have seen that, given the opportunity, many members of the Palestinian diaspora were willing to invest their wealth and knowledge into their homelands (and even though much of this fledgling infrastructure had unraveled or been destroyed, the point is that it did and can happen). Lebanese communities abroad underwrote much of the rebuilding of the state following the Civil War, and could do so again if political stability was assured. Moreover, members of these diasporas are increasingly well educated, integrated, invested in multiple, overlapping (and noncontradictory) identities, and are thus more likely to promote solutions rather than violence. Unfortunately, the flip side is the phenomenon of "homegrown terrorism," in which the children of families who, either by choice or circumstances, are often unintegrated and therefore nurture and develop grievances. This generation, righteously self-justified by an ethical denial of common humanity, a means-ends rationality, and a commitment to political Islam, sees themselves as engaging in terrorist activities as a form of collective punishment for the societies in which they find themselves.[31]

New Theses on Hope and Hopelessness

In 1971, Polish maverick intellectual Leszek Kołakowski published his landmark essay "Theses on Hope and Hopelessness," pointing a way forward for the Polish opposition after the events of 1968 in Warsaw and from 1970 to 1971 in Gdańsk. In a time of despair and hopelessness—after tragic losses of life among the workers, supposedly championed by the regime, and after Polish Jews, a historically important segment of Polish society, had been again persecuted in the interest of political expediency—Kołakowski argued against the "ideology of defeatism." He listed all the reasons for pessimism, and then addressed these arguments forcefully and directly. He presciently supposed a greater degree of flexibility in the system than most, rejected an "all or nothing" logic, and proposed exploiting internal contradictions. In short, where others saw problems, he saw opportunities.

The situation in Poland in the late 1960s and early 1970s is similar to the theoretical and practical malaise we find in the Middle East today (or in our mistaken assessment of the region). In order to update Kołakowski's ideas, current theses on hopelessness might include the following: (1) the level of repression is too severe to allow for opposition movements and there are no nonviolent, reform-oriented political liberals to cultivate such movements or civil society, and, even if they do exist, they have no voice, no ability, and no one would listen to them anyway; (2) the discourse is actually between the regional autocrats on the one hand, and those championing a violent interpretation of political Islam on the other; (3) both sides understand only the language of violence; (4) Islam is a "totalizing" faith incompatible with secularism, and the (desirable) separation of religion and state, and is mutually exclusive to both human rights and democracy; (5) secular nationalism as a basis for independent identity and political formation has already been tried and failed miserably; (6) any process of rapid democratization is dangerous because political Islamists will succeed, resulting in a true "clash of civilizations" or sectarian strife between Shia and Sunni; and (7) the United States and the West are not seen as allies of democratization as a result of backing regional autocrats, participating in antidemocratic coups d'état, supporting Israel, intervening in Iraq, and generally exhibiting imperial tendencies.

Yes, There Are Political Liberals

There are growing numbers of writers, journalists, artists, intellectuals, bloggers, students, professionals, and workers who have questioned both the autocracy of their leaders and the better publicized path of the suicide bomber.[32] Moreover, many of these "dissidents," for want of a better term, draw upon rich intellectual lineages of liberal Islamic scholarship and national reform.[33] Many current activists have either flirted with extremism and/or been subject to considerable personal and professional persecution—both of which provide considerable street credibility. Consider Mansour al Nogaidan, former Wahhabi extremist, now a persecuted liberal writer in Saudi Arabia.[34] He once firebombed a video store in Saudi Arabia because it sold Western movies and therefore might lead to the "liberation" of women, but was introduced to liberal Muslim philosophers while in jail for his crimes. Al Nogaidan has since joined an important, if lonely, group of voices calling for tolerance, pluralism, and nonviolence. His hero is Martin Luther as much as Martin Luther King; he has called for an Islamic Reformation that eschews violence. Al Nogaidan would likely enjoy reading Michnik, or maybe he is himself a future Michnik.

In Egypt, the Ibn Khaldun Center for Development Studies has long been a center of liberal thought, free expression, and respected social science. Closed for three years due to the arrest of founder Saad Eddin Ibrahim and several dozen of his colleagues at the behest of the former government, the center long remained an early site of independent analysis. Furthermore, despite the corrupt and clientelist nature of Mubarek's rule, Egyptian activists could lay claim to relative freedom of expression, if only measured by regional norms. Although much has been made of the distributed and leaderless quality of the Tahrir Square protests, activism did not spring forth fully formed and without precedent. The commitment to nonviolence in the face of provocation speak to, in the words of Cairo's American University president Lisa Anderson, Egypt's "culture of deep communal bonds and trust, which manifested itself in the demonstrators' incredible discipline: their refusal to be provoked by thugs and saboteurs, their capacity to police themselves, and co-ordinate their demands, and their ability to organize without any centralized leadership."[35] Tarek Heggy is probably one of the most prolific and well-known liberal intellectuals in Egypt. Having secured the ability to speak and publish relatively freely (thanks in large part to his wealth and his political and business connections), Heggy was often the public face of liberalism throughout the region prior to 2011. His personal Web site documents his background in law and business, his career in natural gas exploration and extraction, his fourteen books published in Arabic, and his more than two hundred essays available in five languages (Arabic, English, French, Russian, and Hebrew). In his "preamble," he states that his work "advances the causes of modernity, democracy, tolerance, and women's rights in the Middle East—advocating them as universal values essential to the region's progress."[36] As a pragmatic and independent-minded secularist well versed in Islam, he rejects the zero-sum mentality that equates compromise with Arab humiliation and defeat.

Noted defense lawyer, human rights activist, and Nobel Peace Prize winner Shirin Ebadi was probably the most internationally well-known and visible opponent of the Iranian regime prior to the June 2009 elections, but she is not alone.[37] Akbar Ganji, Iran's leading investigative journalist and dissident, was arrested in 2000, following his participation in a Heinrich Böll Institute conference, where he spoke on Iranian political and social reform.[38] Human Rights Watch, PEN, and Amnesty International monitored his case throughout his incarceration until his release in March 2006. Ganji has published a Solzhenitsyn-type book entitled *Prison Like Archipelago*. An earlier book, *Dungeon of Ghosts*, implicated former Iranian president Akbar Hashemi Rafsanjani in the "serial murders" of five writers and intellectuals in 1998.[39] Since his release from prison, Ganji toured abroad to galvanize support for detainees, including Mansour Ossanlu, the head of the unrecognized Union of Workers of Tehran and Suburbs Bus Company (Sharekat-e-Vahed), Sayed Ali Akbar Mousavi-Kho-ini, a student leader and former member of the Islamic Consultative Assembly (the *Majlis*, Iran's parliament), and Ramin Jahanbegloo, a prominent intellectual and writer on nonviolence and democracy. Since 12 June 2009, he has led a global intellectual effort to keep the international community focused on the Iranian question, and authored an appeal to UN Secretary-General Ban-Ki Moon.

Jahanbegloo was arrested by Iranian authorities in late April 2006, and was not released until 30 August 2006. Following his release, he spent two years teaching in New Delhi, and in January 2008 returned to the University of Toronto. Before his arrest in Teheran he ran an independent center, the Cultural Research Bureau.[40] The Bureau included a publishing house, gift shop, gallery, and lecture hall—combining aspects of the samizdat boutique of László Rajk and the underground universities of Czechoslovakia and Poland. Like Julius Tomin, Ladislav Hejdánek, and Jiří Müller in Czechoslovakia in the 1980s, Jahanbegloo invited a group of prestigious Western philosophers to give lectures. Before its closure, Richard Rorty, Ágnes Heller, and Michael Ignatieff all visited and lectured at the Bureau. Jahanbegloo has published more than twenty books and articles in English, French, and Farsi, including works on Mohandas Gandhi and Martin Luther King Jr., and interviews with Isaiah Berlin, Paul Ricoeur, and Jürgen Habermas. Jahanbegloo and Ganji demonstrate how liberal intellectuals in Iran have functioned as a bridge between Iranian exiles, universities, intellectual communities abroad and students at home. Coalition building in Iran, much like in Poland in the 1970s and 1980s, will remain a huge challenge, particularly given the success of the potent mixture of Ahmadinejad's working-class, populist, and xenophobic nationalism and the brutal repression following the 2009 elections.[41]

In Syria, novelist and poet Ammar Abdulhamid has long been a thorn in the side of the Bashar al-Assad regime with his surrealist and thickly ironic critiques, reminiscent of Czech novelists Ivan Klíma and Ludvík Vaculík.[42] Like Mansour, he briefly flirted with fundamentalism, which he claims was essential to the formation of his assertive stance: "As a fundamentalist, it was my responsibility to preach and teach, and so I had to live up to this idea I invested in myself. It's why I'm as inquisitive and self-inquisitive as I am today."[43] Having founded the Tharwa Foundation, a leading Syrian human rights and prodemocracy organization, Abdulhamid now lives in exile outside Washington, DC, and is a frequent and well-informed commentator on the civil war in Syria.

It is true that the voices of some of these "liberal dissidents," for want of a better term, are more significant in some states than others. But that they existed long before the Arab Spring of 2011, and were active at great personal risk, is an undeniable reality. That we, in the self-styled "West," have until now paid them little heed is something that should be corrected. Bear in mind it was not until 1989 that many in the Anglo-American world began to read the essays of Havel, Benda, Michnik, Kuroń, Konrád, and Kis. Such activists speak with their own voices and think through their own sets of ideas and tactics, and which reflect their own particular circumstances, constraints, and opportunities. It is clear that they will now be joined by a younger generation of activists, who are more educated than their parents and are not content to accept the shaky premises in which many authoritarian leaders vest their power and authority. If the rules of our mutual engagement are premised on Orientalism, democracy-promotion efforts, or prescriptive policymaking that implies "we" know and "they" need to learn from our experience, any interlocutory experiences will result in stripping such actors of their essential agency, and risks being seen locally as an imperialistic effort. Similarly, falling into the "Good Muslim / Bad Muslim" trap unnecessarily narrows our thinking to a binary construction that admits no grey area, complexity, or fruitful contradiction.

Voices of dissent also find receptive audiences, particularly if the efforts of states to control and regulate the Internet are taken as a measure of dissidents' ability to sway opinion online. The Internet, as the transmission belt of 21st-century samizdat, is a double-edged sword for authoritarian regimes: they wish to promote computer literacy and information technology, yet are unhappy with the inevitable consequences of the free and rapid flow of interpersonal communication and criticism. The Internet, much like the powerful forces of globalization of which it is but one indicator, can facilitate liberation and oppression, communication and censorship, entertainment and surveillance, liberal cosmopolitanism or xenophobic hatred. Internet freedom does not produce human freedom any more than free-market economics does liberal polities—as Russia and China both ably demonstrate. Syria and Saudi Arabia, like most countries in the region, attempt to control information by actively filtering citizens' Internet activity, and Iran has deployed the judiciary (ably assisted by intelligence and security forces) to prosecute bloggers in order to suppress independent opinion.[44] Internet Service Providers (ISPs) frequently block Web sites featuring pornography, gambling, drug use, or homosexuality, but also target sites associated with documenting human rights abuses (such as those of Amnesty International and Human Rights Watch), religious minorities (the Baha'i in Iran and Coptic Christians in Egypt), political criticism, or news sites that publish stories governments do not want told. However, if blogging has been any indication, the ingenuity and technological sophistication of the younger generation of Web-based activists has continually found ways around online censorship and the limited freedom of expression, resulting in a kind of virtual "living in truth."[45] Blogs reveal and track the motivations, awareness, and levels of engagement in repressive societies.[46] And unlike Radio Liberty / Radio Free Europe and the spread of samizdat and tamizdat, the Internet is powerfully immediate and interpersonal, providing multiple webs of communication and commentary that easily transcend the temporal and spatial limitations of earlier activist efforts. One Facebook group in Egypt, formed to protest the 2010 death of businessman and Internet activist Khaled Said, attracted 300,000 members prior to the January 2011 protests. Facebook did not "get" protestors into the streets, but it did generate a usable pool of recruits.[47] Indeed, social media have provided the means to generate news quickly about specific injustices—particularly those that affect the young—that are themselves catalysts or rallying cries for mass mobilization. The self-immolation in Tunisia of 26-year-old fruit vendor Mohamed Bouazizi and the delivery of 13-year-old Hamza al-Khateeb's tortured corpse in Syria are cases in point. Organizations such as Radio Farda and the BBC's Farsi service may prove important in the long run, but equally critical will be the improvisational immediacy of Internet journalists and eyewitness activists who can shape the story as they make it by using social networking applications and cell phones to record and upload videos into YouTube and to feed conventional mainstream news services.[48]

There Is a Middle Ground

The dualistic discourse between regional autocrats and political Islam is premised on violence, the former implementing the repressive violence of state power, and the latter the violence of the oppressed, reinforcing the assumption that both sides will only ever understand violence. However, there is no simple two-sided conflict in any state in the region, and the players include not only ruling autocrats (who can be categorized variously as *dictaduras* or *dictablandas*), but also political Islamists, members of the *ulama* (members of the Islamic clergy, who are better categorized as socially and religiously conservative or traditional, but not uniformly so), as well as liberal dissidents. In the past, autocrats have sought to eliminate all dissent, condemning it as destabilizing. It is important to make distinctions, and understand how one form of repression breeds another in response.

The Saudi state has allied itself historically with Wahhabism, in a mutually recognized implicit contract on the shared monopoly of power, wherein the Saudi royal family controls the state, and Wahhabist clerics enforce religious conservatism, diffusing any demands for change. Somewhat different is Egypt, where repression of political reform historically drove dissent in a radical and insurrectionist direction, first in the post–World War I period against the British and later Israel.[49] In the process, the reform vision of Hassan al-Banna and the original Society of Muslim Brothers was transformed into the extremism of Sayyid Qutb, the intellectual "martyr" of political Islam and pioneer of violent jihad.[50]

In Iran, the repression of former Shah Reza Pahlavi was replaced by the clerical repression of Ayatollah Khomeini. Cold War legacies are important—Iran's Prime Minister Mohammed Mossadegh was overthrown by a CIA-backed coup in 1953, as his efforts to nationalize oil fields were seen as a Soviet-style attempt to destabilize American energy security. History is lived experience as well: the seizure of the US embassy in Tehran in 1979 and the resulting hostage crisis were seen as a kind of revenge for the 1953 coup. Thus, in a state where independence has been associated with anti-Americanism, the possession of nuclear weapons is logically a powerful guarantee of that independence, as well as regional power.

There is no "one" discourse of violence, the players are multiple, and the experiences manifold. Although repression across the region was and is severe, it is not uniformly so. State pressure is subject to continual change, with the ebb and flow of "thaws" and "crackdowns." As in Central and Eastern Europe, such interstices make dissent possible, allowing breathing room for creativity. A 2008 report on Saudi Arabia by the Committee to Protect Journalists commented extensively on the semi-independent press in what we might, in the spirit of Jiřina Šiklová, call a "grey zone."[51] Even the controversial Danish cartoons of the Prophet Muhammad were published, and, in the period of boldness following 9/11, media outlets discussed such topics as crime, unemployment, women's rights, and religious militancy.[52] Progress has been and will continue to be limited and uneven, and the margin of press freedom has been subject to arbitrary and opaque political control. Government officials control editors and issue unpublished yet effective bans that blacklist writers, usually temporarily. While true or mainstream "opposition journalism" does not exist, candid debates occur in discussion groups known as *diwaniyas*—reminiscent of the living-room seminars of Czechoslovakia's parallel *polis*. Critical programs can easily be found on satellite television, particularly Al Jazeera, Al Arabiya, or on the Internet.

Violence Is Neither Enduring Nor Inevitable

Understanding the noninevitability of repetitive cycles of violence and repression means recognizing that such violence is not intrinsic to Islam. Noah Feldman and Mahmood Mamdani are both correct in distinguishing political Islam from the less nuanced categories of Islamism and Islamic fundamentalism. Political Islam is an ideology, not a religion, and was initially generated by political intellectuals—not the religious *ulama*—as a response to colonial oppression. Furthermore, as Mamdani argues, there are similarities between the tenets of political Islam and Marxism-Leninism: both are distinctively modern, "scientifically" based on "prediction," both suggest that using force to realize "freedom" is not contradictory but inevitable, promote the organization of a vanguard, reserve the use of persuasion for friends, promote coercion for enemies, remain preoccupied with political identity, and are obsessed with the capture and remaking of state power, supposedly for the benefit of the community.[53] Both discourage critical thinking and eschew analyses based on facts in deference to ideological purity. Moreover, there is a tendency to discriminate against those who are ascriptively impure (whether infidels, apostates, or class enemies), against whom the teleological project for the betterment of humanity (usually narrowly construed) must be fought.

Combating violence thus means once again facing head-on the familiar dogma that violence is the necessary midwife of revolutionary change. Michnik said it best in his commentary that those who end up storming Bastilles end up building new ones, and this is a key lesson applicable to the region today.[54] Violence, whether conceived by Georges Sorel or Franz Fanon, does not cleanse, purify, wipe the slate clean, or eliminate enemies. Neither political Islam nor autocratic states can be effectively countered internally by dissent that engages in yet another round of senseless violence. In Central Europe, the armed might of the USSR—combined with the military intervention of 1956 and the "fraternal assistance" of 1968—removed the insurrectionary option from the table. In Northern Ireland, South Africa, and now in Spain, a combination of terrorist tactics with national liberationist goals eventually exhausted violence as an effective alternative. Unfortunately, in the Middle East, violence will continue to be a strategy of choice in the short term, and this calculus has not been aided by the United States and its allies in attempting to engineer regime change "from above" in Iraq, or by Israel's efforts to create the conditions for enduring security through military force in Lebanon and Gaza. Liberal dissent may face more violent repression, but its future effectiveness in creating ever-wider circles of space to operate depends upon not taking up arms. Indeed, where liberal dissent and independent civil society were noticeably lacking, as in Libya, recourse to violence and civil war was the immediate result.

Islam Is Not Political Islam

If one separates Islam from "political" or "politicized" Islam, then it is much easier to dispense with the claim that Islam is a totalizing faith incompatible with either human rights or democracy. Islam as a religion cannot be reduced to one narrative or one set of perquisites that can "make" it compatible or not with human rights or democracy anymore than is the case with Christianity or Judaism. Indeed, at its core, Islam is a profoundly interpretative religion that does not countenance any centralized hierarchy or singular doctrinal authority. Moreover, the geographical range and cultural, religious diversity of the world's 1.2 billion Muslims instantly contradicts any effort to essentialize Islam. Defining Islam and the West in concrete, civilizational terms implies both are historically contained and determined comprehensive systems that can be discussed in moral opposition. A more flexible approach is Noah Feldman's suggestion that we look upon both Islam and democracy as "mobile ideas," allowing for engagement with and contestation over meaning.[55] Speaking about democracy and Islam as ideas allows for a more cosmopolitan conversation that searches for common ground, while recognizing that ideas are also articles of faith, contain "self-evident" truth, and are infused with a variety of human practices, rituals, and lived experiences. Both democracy and Islam as ideas are premised on humanity, equality, universality, justice, and notions of rights. Finally, the mobility of ideas necessitates their flexibility, accommodation, and adaptation. They are not simply portable, but translatable. Dialogue and conflict may both result, but contact and engagement in a globalized, cosmopolitan world increasingly result in hybridity.[56] Such hybridity results in mutual alteration, creating a range of new options. Contemporary Turkey, as a model of a democratic "work in progress" is one possibility, post-Suharto Indonesia is another.[57] With its rich interpretations of justice and morality, Islam can be a great source of normative constraints on governance. Recall that Michnik, in the *Church and the Left*, argued that the moderate and critical Catholic intelligentsia ought to make common cause with the anticommunist and secular Left in Poland. Remember that this prescription was not immediately logical—the Church, after all, had allied itself in the past with antidemocratic, nationalist, and obscurantist populism. Islam should not be reduced to political Islam, but explored for its depth of interpretation, speculative theology, and an ethics of corresponding rights and responsibilities. Ideas such as *ijtihad* (independent reasoning, critical and creative adaptation to changing times) and *shura* (consultation, pluralism) are sources for dialogue.

The Secular State Has Not Failed

One of the reasons that political Islam has had such ideological cachet is the historical failure of secular nationalism in the region. Postcolonial governments founded on secular principles were too often belligerent in their nationalism (Gamal Abdel Nasser in Egypt), uncompromising toward religion (Mustafa Kemal Atatürk in Turkey), and, worst of all, rigidly dictatorial (Saddam Hussein in Iraq, Mohammad Reza Shah in Iran). Politics has been marred by corruption, dynastic rule, and the persecution of minorities. Nonetheless, nationalism as a form of secular identity remains high across the region, in many cases superseding religious affinity, and should not be underestimated. Moreover, the 2011 democracy movements across the region provide firm evidence for the continuing validity of the secular state and secular reform, particularly among the "youth bulge" and middle classes that are dominating protesting movements across the region.

Feldman points out that part of political Islam's appeal was that it had few opportunities to govern, and was therefore less tainted.[58] Unfortunately, this leads to another simplistic conclusion—that because secularism and nationalism were discredited, Middle Eastern society is somehow incapable of "rising above" tribal or cultural identities or sectarian religious division. Both the Yugoslav Wars and the Rwandan genocide remind us that supposedly ancient hatred is a socially constructed phenomenon manipulated and reinforced by political elites in their specific struggles for dominance and power.[59] Economic deprivation and poverty provide ample opportunity for scapegoating, and mass media are often deployed to magnify threats and simplistically portray complex social issues in terms of tribalism, ethnic conflict, and sectarian strife. At the same time, in transitional governments the same tendencies that promote moderation in governance given the accountability imperative of elections elsewhere in democratic polities will hopefully take hold.[60] Any societal crucible that contains the elements of authoritarianism, huge economic disparities, violent political ideologies, in addition to both real and perceived historical grievances, is going to be politically unstable, and any process of liberalization or democratization—gradual or otherwise—will be neither smooth nor without conflict. Given the differences between the Middle East and Central Europe outlined above, it was highly unrealistic in 2003 to expect that the toppling of a Saddam Hussein statue would be as relatively unproblematic as breaching the Berlin Wall. Over the last two decades, there has been a journalistic tendency to look upon the fall of the Wall as the climactic moment in the collapse of communism—a short-sighted approach that ignores the decades of opposition activism (and, in a sense, preparation) that occurred before that symbolic moment, not to mention the structural weaknesses in the Soviet system as well as the many exogenous factors that contributed to the demise of communism.

The Middle East Does Not Prove the "Clash of Civilizations" Hypothesis

Those who predict an ongoing clash of civilizations and a continued incompatibility of democracy and Islam have cited the examples of Iraq, Libya, and Syria. However, the two lessons that ought to be drawn from this experience are often conveniently ignored: first, it is highly problematic to engineer regime change from above by means of military invasion or assistance; and, second, real democracy is about a process, not a product, and cannot be instantly generated through the orchestration of free and fair elections. The slow generation of democratic culture cannot occur in a state of war, where the question of human security is paramount, and the provision of such basic needs as electricity and water dwarfs the question of who rules. To speak of "winning hearts and minds" in such an environment is ludicrous. Even among those who supported the March 2003 invasion to depose Saddam Hussein must admit that the United States did not have an effective plan for postwar reconstruction or nation building. Moreover, democratization was a latter-day rationale for the conflict.[61] Iraq does not "prove" the clash thesis, it only reaffirms that tolerance cannot thrive in a conflict zone.

Moreover, the "clash" thesis is belied by the example of contemporary Turkey, which is well positioned to serve as a model for transitioning states in the Middle East and North Africa. Despite Turkish "exceptionalism"—characterized by periods of military rule, political and economic instability, a history of robust secularism, persecution of minorities, and constitutionally entrenched limitations on free expression and religion—the state has emerged in the last decade as a highly successful regional power, and Prime Minister Recep Tayyip Erdogan has both popularity and influence to match. The election of his Justice and Development Party (AKP) in 2001 ushered in a period of parliamentary stability, economic reform, currency stabilization, significant growth, increased trade, and bureaucratic overhaul. The Turks have earned respect for those wary of American influence by not allowing the United States to use their territory to invade Iraq and their increasingly tough stance on Israel—all the while remaining a member of NATO, an emerging power in the G-20, a global voice of moderation and compromise, and a neighborhood player advocating good governance, transparency, and the political participation of women. Turkey's ongoing challenges with youth unemployment, inegalitarian distribution of wealth, and regional disparities also illustrate that the path to democracy and economic stability is neither swift nor easy, but is both desirable and possible.

The Role of the United States Is Complex

Finally, we return to the thorny issue of the role of the United States and the West more generally. Under the presidency of George W. Bush, the United States was not seen as an ally of democratization, despite military and ideological commitments to the contrary. Given past foreign policy decisions in the Middle East, many of which were rooted in the exigencies of the Cold War, the United States cannot easily represent itself as the imagined community of liberation, freedom, wealth, and opportunity that it was for several generations of Europeans following World War II. The United States masterminded the Berlin airlifts, funded Radio Free Europe and Radio Liberty, and was home to tens of thousands of refugees after 1956 and 1968, but it also supported dynastic autocracies (or in the case of Iran, even installed one) when autocratic governments agreed to serve American, not Soviet, interests. Following the 1978 Camp David Accords and the 1979 Egypt-Israel treaty, the United States massively underwrote the Mubarak government with economic and military assistance, support explicitly tied to keeping the peace, and disregarding the distorting political and societal effects long-term. Moreover, the United States and its regional Allies underwrote the largest covert war in history in Afghanistan, unintentionally playing the midwife in the births of political Islam and a closely knit generation of veterans who, confident after their victory over the Soviet Union, believe messianically in their ability to tackle the American superpower.[62] The imposition of sanctions against Bashar al-Assad via the 2003 *Syria Accountabiliy Act*, the covert funding provided for democracy activists (now exposed by Wikileaks), or the cat-and-mouse game the Americans continue to play with respect to engaging Iran while denouncing human rights abuses and the same nuclear ambitions accepted (or at least tolerated) elsewhere demonstrate the fraught and hypocritical nature of American behavior. These interwoven and complicated legacies may shift given NATO intervention in Libya and meaningful economic aid for states in democratic transition, but it is too early to tell.

American support of Israel—perceived as overly generous and uncritical—and its inability to successfully shepherd a road map for peace in Palestine make the United States a complicated supporter of democratization. The future political success and economic stability of Palestine, or even the possibility of the long-trumped "two-state solution," continues to hang in the balance given the disruptive role of Hamas and the disillusionment of Palestinians with the corrupt and ineffective governance of Fatah, and the intransigence of Israel. Israel's current unilateralism—as expressed in its disengagement from Gaza in 2005, its 2006 counterattack on Hezbollah in southern Lebanon, and the war in Gaza from 2008 and 2009—has doomed efforts to secure a durable cessation of hostilities and sustain international, let alone mutual, recognition and negotiation.

President Obama and Secretary of State Clinton have worked in tandem to wade through choppy Mideast waters, aiming less for an overarching doctrinal approach to the region in favor of a strategy of flexible response, depending on a particular state's actions and overall impact on regional and energy stability. Obama's 2009 Cairo speech was a demonstrable beginning, heralded as an effort to reset American relations with the Muslim world. Furthermore, although his 19 May 2011 speech infuriated Prime Minister Benjamin Netanyahu because of his outright endorsement of Israel's 1967 borders "with mutually agreed-upon swaps" as a basis for peace negotiations, the president also strenuously supported Israel's right to defense and called upon Palestinian recognition of its right to exist. Still, Jeffrey Goldberg is correct in highlighting a "core contradiction" in American foreign policy, one it did not have to face in Central and Eastern Europe during the Cold War: "At the same time America is working for permanent and democratic change in certain republics of the Middle East, it has, 235 years after freeing itself from the rule of a despotic king, gone into the monarchy-maintenance business, propping up kings, emirs, and sheikhs who, though they may be as venal as Ben Ali, Qaddafi, and Mubarek, have the oil the West needs, and who serve as a counterbalance to the greatest threat facing the U.S. in the Middle East, the Islamic Republic of Iran."[63] As Kołakowski found in 1971, it is much easier to find reasons for hopelessness than hope. However, hope must be found, ways forward must be debated, and openings discovered. Local actors must be empowered and their voices supported and heard. Events and situations are never as black and white as pundits reductively claim, and politics remains the art of the possible, even in the midst of intractable conflicts. Flourishing civil societies and commitments to human rights, nonviolent social change, liberalization, and dialogues between the ideas of democracy and Islam seem rather idealistic and far off at present, but in the 1970s discussing the fall of communism or the largely peaceful dismantling of Apartheid would have also seemed overly optimistic.

Conclusion: What Is to Be Done?

The GWOT, either in its original form under the Bush presidency, or its tamer and more politically palatable successor under the Obama administration, like the Cold War that preceded it, will continue to be fought on ideological, political, and military terrain. Unfortunately, the indigenous political lessons of Central and Eastern Europe were largely lost in the post-9/11 rhetoric, despite the occasional call by someone of Sharansky's stature for a Middle Eastern Helsinki process, or for the democracy-promotion industry to continue championing the construction of civil society, as if this can be done through the import of money, and a recipe for particular bricks and mortar.

The experience of Central and Eastern Europe has become increasingly relevant with the Arab Spring. Now more than ever, solutions point to the importance of what is happening on the ground, with the people who live and work there, who have been engaged in their own societies, and who are fully cognizant of historical and practical limitations and possibilities. Coalition building, communication, negotiation, and creative resistance will be required. There are no fast fixes. The task is especially monumental for liberal dissidents, for it involves no less than building civil societies and movements of nonviolent resistance in the face of repressive governments cynically willing to do anything to stay in power, avoiding the popular radical ideology of political Islam, and at the same time championing human rights, gender equality, good governance, transparency, tolerance, and compromise.[64] Should the dramatic political change heralded by the Arab Spring continue, states will face a challenge even greater than the "triple transition" faced by the post-Communist governments of Central and Eastern Europe.[65] On top of nation building, economic restructuring, and political consolidation, Middle Eastern states would face problems of much greater poverty, inequality, sectarian tension, and endemic legacies of violence.

In the West, however, closer attention should be turned to where violence is not happening. Spending money to finance liberal-minded groups and individuals has not generated immediate payback, and may cause considerable harm. More helpful are economic assistance, debt relief, direct investment, expertise in democratic governance, scholarly and technical exchanges, information-sharing through conferences, sustained and pragmatic diplomatic engagement, and support for (and listening to) diasporas abroad. A comprehensive and bipartisan approach (not just in the United States, but as a key feature of a revitalized transatlantic partnership) is needed to address both the challenge of terrorism and the requirements for political liberalization. Sharansky may yet prove correct in assessing the need for a Middle Eastern Helsinki, in which liberals such as Mansour al Nogaidan or Akbar Ganji could hold their states accountable to international human rights covenants. Because Helsinki meant that the reputations of the USSR and its satellites were linked to universal human rights norms, dissidents could focus on breaches of norms as a catalyst for change, measuring the gap between intention and reality. Western governments ought to push aggressively for freedom of expression and association, the rule of law, and put broader democratization on the back burner. Perhaps agreement on such a process is contingent upon a two-state solution in Palestine, a complete withdrawal of US troops from Iraq and Afghanistan, or negotiations with Iran over nuclear energy.

Fortunately or not, oil will also guarantee the ongoing meddling of the West in the region. Because of the Yalta agreement and the nuclear stalemate, intervention on the same scale was not possible in Central or Eastern Europe during the Cold War. North American and Western European states have relationships with many states in the Middle East as allies, not enemies. Energy security will continue to rank higher on political agendas compared with liberalization and democratization, as will efforts to secure ongoing cooperation and intelligence assistance from local autocrats in combating violent extremism. These two factors, exploited to the fullest by autocratic regimes, kept the "Algeria problem" front and center in the minds of American foreign policymakers in the first decade post-9/11, powerfully and cynically restraining the United States as an actor, while robbing the world's only superpower of credibility in its democracy promotion efforts abroad.[66] That situation has now fundamentally changed. "Our" fear and "their" repression are not sound bases for regional or global stability. In the same manner European Union membership served as both a "carrot" and "stick" for new democracies in Central and Eastern Europe, so too should incentive structures for reform be built for the Middle East and North Africa.

Moreover, multilateral discussion must look beyond narrow arguments about energy security to the longer-term human and environmental security of the region and the planet. Given that militarily engineered regime-change from above in Iraq has been a dismal failure, and that local populations have taken their discontent to the streets with profound levels of social mobilization, we are at a propitious moment for an examination of alternatives. The capture and death of Al-Qaeda mastermind Osama bin Laden has enlarged and complicated avenues for action. Nonetheless, the Cold War has demonstrated that the early foreclosure of military options does not make political change impossible, but it does make it dependent on many variables, often at odds with one another, necessarily unpredictable, and never straightforward.

Notes

1. Noah Feldman, *After Jihad: America and the Struggle for Islamic Democracy* (New York, 2003), 19.
2. Natan Sharansky, "The Middle East needs its Helsinki," *International Herald Tribune*, 30 March 2004.
3. Václav Havel, "Address to a Joint Session of the United States Congress," in *After the Velvet Revolution: The New Leaders Of Czechoslovakia Speak Out*, ed. Tim Whipple (New York, 1991).
4. See Barbara J. Falk, *The Dilemmas of Dissidence in East-Central Europe: Citizen Intellectuals and Philosopher Kings* (Budapest, 2003); Padraic Kenney, *A Carnival of Revolution: Central Europe 1989* (Princeton, 2003); Andras Bozoki, *Intellectuals and Politics in Central Europe*

(Budapest, 1999); Ralf Dahrendorf, *Reflections on the Revolution in Europe* (New York, 1990); Timothy Garton Ash, *We the People: The Revolution of '89 as Witnessed in Warsaw, Budapest, Berlin, and Prague* (Cambridge, 1990); Grzegorz Ekiert and Jan Kubik, eds., *Rebellious Civil Society: Popular Protest and Democratic Consolidation in Poland, 1989–1993* (Ann Arbor, 2001); Michael Bernhard, *The Origins of Democratization in Poland* (New York, 1993); Rudolf L. Tőkés, *Hungary's Negotiated Revolution: Economic Reform, Social Change and Political Succession* (Cambridge, 1996).

5. Havel, "Address to a Joint Session," 69–80; "Let's Hear it for Hegel!" *Washington Post*, 23 February 1990.
6. See Edward W. Said, *Covering Islam: How the Media and the Experts Determine How We See the Rest of the World* (New York, 1981); Edward W. Said, *Orientalism* (London, 2003).
7. See Larry Wolff, *Inventing Eastern Europe: The Map of Civilization on the Mind of the Enlightenment* (Stanford, 2004), and Maria Todorova, *Imagining the Balkans* (New York, 1997).
8. For example, in the August 1988 protests on the twentieth anniversary of the Soviet invasion of Czechoslovakia, as well as in the autumn of 1989, Charter 77 activists were at first reluctant to support street marches and civil disobedience in the face of riot police. They did not want to put individuals, particularly young people, at risk.
9. In his recent book, *Unconquerable World: Why Peaceful Protest Is Stronger Than War* (New York, 2003, 2004), Jonathan Schell situates the East European experience in the larger context of nonviolent strategies, arguing broadly that the "war system" so eloquently theorized by Clausewitz has exhausted itself as a source of political change, particularly in light of the greater successes of nonviolent movements. See especially chapter 8, "Living in Truth," 186–215.
10. Nor were the dissidents particularly friendly to *perestroika* and *glasnost*, and to the extent Gorbachev's role is celebrated, it is because of his role as a "hero of retreat," to use the language of Hans Magnus Enzenberger.
11. See Kenney, *A Carnival of Revolution*. In *The Dilemmas of Dissidence in East-Central Europe*, I argued that this was fortuitous, because the inherent self-limitation of the dissident approach was helpful in fostering democratic values that would be so critical in the early and middle stages of transformation: a healthy respect for pluralism and debate, combined with a distrust of absolute power, a rejection of universalist or simplistic solutions, recognizing that avoiding confrontation is not the same as avoiding issues, the connection of freedom with responsibility and civic activism, a sense of inclusion, and a preference for mediation and problem solving over the imposition of arbitrary solutions that admit no subtlety, grey area, or room for compromise.
12. Mahmood Mamdani has described "Good Muslims" as those who are secular, peaceful, liberal, and largely integrated into Western democracies and cultures, whereas "Bad Muslims" are those who are doctrinal, antimodern, virulent, and violent. Mamdani cites both Freedom House studies that demonstrate how democracies "lag" in the *"Muslim* world" and the Democracy Project of the Foundation for the Defense of Democracies, which claims that the "roots" of terrorism can be found in Wahhabism, the ideological and doctrinaire underpinning of the Saudi state. See Mahmood Mamdani, *Good Muslim, Bad Muslim: America, the Cold War, and the Roots of Terror* (New York, 2004), 24. It would be more accurate to suggest that democracy has not taken hold in Arab states rather than the *"Muslim* world," but, in any event, much of Europe, Asia, and Africa have also been historically authoritarian. Democracy and liberalism remain new, creative, flexible, and mobile ideas. There is enough evidence to suggest there is no unique affinity for authoritarianism or democracy in any religion or culture. Nonetheless, the American foreign policy community still talks of Arab "exceptionalism" and Freedom House has categorized the Middle East as the least free region on the globe.

13. See also the debate on "Arab Authoritarianism" and "Muslim Exceptionalism" in the *Journal of Democracy* 15, no. 4 (October 2004): 126–46, in reaction to an earlier article by Alfred Stepan in the same journal in 2003. Saad Eddin Ibrahim offered a spirited rebuttal to the Islamic/Arab exceptionalism argument in his lecture, "Toward Islamic Democracies," 2 November 2006, Munk Centre for International Studies.
14. Take, for example, the Justice and Development Party in Turkey (committed to democracy and European integration) and an organization like Hamas. Both have committed themselves to democratic and electoral strategies—but what is "Islamic" about them is actually what is different, not similar.
15. See Amy Hawthorne, "Is Civil Society the Answer?" in *Uncharted Journey: Promoting Democracy in the Middle East*, ed. Thomas Carothers and Marina Ottaway (Washington, 2005). She notes the complexity of the "Arab civil society sector" that comprises Islamic organizations (some of which are more service oriented, others more religious, and some associated with political movements), nongovernmental service organizations (often private charitable organizations), professional associations such as labor unions and professional syndicates, associations designed to foster social solidarity, mutual aid, and business and political conversation, and, finally, prodemocracy associations.
16. See John Keane, *Civil Society: Old Images, New Visions* (Palo Alto, 1999).
17. Financial aid, however, can be problematic. Prominent Iranian dissident journalist Akbar Ganji contends that American aid would be better spent in developing centers for Iranian studies in the US. He claims that, although despotism can be imported, democracy cannot be bought but must be nurtured. See Akbar Ganji, "Money Can't Buy Us Democracy," *New York Times*, 1 August 2006.
18. There is a central paradox inherent to engagement and support, particularly when it comes publicly from the United States. For example, Congress authorized $3 million to support democratic opposition groups inside and outside Iran, but Michael Ignatieff argued that such good intentions have been met with local incredulity, for accepting such aid would be to court arrest as a spy. See Michael Ignatieff, "Iranian Lessons," *New York Times Magazine*, 17 July 2005. Iranian émigré activist Morteza Abdolalian confirmed in an interview with me that American aid is the "kiss of death," branding one with potential CIA connections, in turn providing ammunition for regime propaganda. In 2003, the US State Department brought democracy promotion efforts together under the umbrella of the Middle East Partnership Initiative (MEPI), which was intended to focus initially on respect for the rule of law and greater transparency. Jon Alterman has criticized such efforts as catering to a "client class of Western-educated elites" whom governments will likely tolerate as long as they remain "politically inert." See Jon Alterman, "The false promise of Arab liberals," *Policy Review* 125 (June 2004): 77–86.
19. In the obituaries written about Arafat, many stressed not only his inability to accept Ehud Barak's olive branch at Camp David in 2000, but, underlying this, his ultimate unwillingness to make the personal transition from revolutionary to statesman. In essence, he failed to become the Nelson Mandela of Palestine. Such a comparison may be intrinsically unfair, given that few advocates of targeted violence—deservedly labeled terrorists or not—become statesmen of Mandela's stature.
20. The ICJ process and ruling on 9 July 2004 was reminiscent of the 1971 Namibian precedent (a turning point in international recognition of the illegitimacy of the Apartheid regime in South Africa). The significance of this moment may not yet be appreciated, even though the physical stability of the fence/wall as a border is currently secure.
21. An interesting parallel is that of the ANC in South Africa, which, without renouncing violent resistance, nevertheless did not target white neighborhoods, focusing instead on representatives of the state, such as police and security agencies.

22. See, for example, Rashid I. Khalidi, "Toward a Clear Palestinian Strategy," *Journal of Palestine Studies* XXXI, no. 4 (Summer 2002): 5–12; Yossi Beilin and Yasser Abed Rabbo, "The Geneva Accord," *Tikkun* 19, no. 1 (January–February 2004): 33–52; and the full text of the National Conciliation Document of the Prisoners, 28 June 2006, available on the Web site of the Jerusalem Media and Communication Centre, http://www.jmcc.org (accessed 19 August 2011).
23. See, for example, the publications of the United Nations Development Programme (UNDP), especially the following: *Arab Human Development Report 2004: Towards Freedom in the Arab World*, and *Arab Human Development Report 2009: Challenges to Human Security in the Arab Countries* (2009). Available at http://www.arab-hdr.org (accessed 19 August 2011).
24. Processes of modernization generally undermine social solidarity and cohesion. As states become stronger (especially when development is spearheaded from above) societies are weakened by change, as values erode. State-directed modernization varies according to local histories and cultures, yet one can nevertheless compare path dependencies and patterns.
25. Regional autocrats historically pointed to Algeria in particular as the path to be avoided, wherein antigovernment protests and late 80s–style "people power" succeeded in generating elections and a new constitution. When an Islamic Party, the Front Islamique du Salut (FIS), was poised to win the second round of the elections (despite government efforts to forestall their success by jailing two of their leaders), the voting was summarily canceled, the party banned, and the remaining leaders rounded up. France and the United States, worried about another "Iranian theocracy" that would undermine their own and regional security, tacitly supported Algeria's preventive coup against democracy. Civil war, not security, resulted, and the FIS split, with one faction choosing armed resistance and political Islam. A Faustian bargain for short-term security resulted in a medium-level civil war, with no prospects of long-term security on the horizon. It is difficult to imagine that democratization could have yielded a worse result. The "Algeria problem" represents the "damned if you do, damned if you don't" dilemma and underlines the immense risks involved in political liberalization and potential democratization. The Arab Spring may ultimately undermine this rationale.
26. Akbar Ganji has stressed how the old paradigm of armed struggle, revolution, and utopia had been replaced by a reformist vision that denounced violence and embraced human rights and peaceful gradualism. Akbar Ganji, interview with the author, 31 January 2007.
27. Nazila Fathi, "Iran President Facing Revival of Students' Ire," *International Herald Tribune*, 21 December 2006.
28. There remains considerable controversy on this point. See, in particular, Evgeny Morozov, *The Net Delusion: The Dark Side of Internet Freedom* (New York, 2011). Morozov decries the "cyber utopian" claims of causality regarding the impact of social media, and especially dangerous and factually flawed parallels to 1989.
29. On events pre- and post-June 12, see Roger Cohen, "Iran: The Tragedy and the Future," *New York Review of Books*, 13 August 2009, 7–10. On the crackdown and the trials, a number of excellent anonymously authored pieces have been written in Iran for external dissemination. See, in particular, *New York Review of Books* (2009) and *The New Yorker* (2009).
30. The Iranian government has responded by blocking Web sites, closing down Internet Service Providers (ISPs), and slowing Internet access speeds.
31. This is an ongoing backstory, evident in the 7/7 bombings in London of 2007, the arrest and conviction of the "Crevice 7" in London and Canadian counterpart Momin Kha-

waja, as well as the trials in the remaining "Toronto 18" cases (arrested in the Toronto area in June 2006). The Internet has been a powerful organizing tool for these groups as well.

32. Indeed, the suicide bomber or angry Muslim has become somewhat of a caricature—a familiar Western media trope invested with considerable meaning. Since 9/11, Western and particularly English-speaking readers and viewers have been repeatedly assaulted with the visual imagery of angry young bearded men, either in video clips righteously explaining and taking responsibility as "martyrs" for their jihadist missions, or in crowds of like-minded individuals, with AK-47s hoisted overhead. The stock nature of this imagery is reminiscent of both socialist-realist portrayals of *Homo Sovieticus* or the steely-eyed and unemotional Stakhanovite worker, and Western interpretations of the serious, determined, muscular, automaton-like, Slavic-jawed, boot-wearing, Soviet-era soldier.

33. Many examples are discussed in Barry Rubin, *The Long War for Freedom: The Arab Struggle for Democracy in the Middle East* (Hoboken, 2006). He profiles Egyptian intellectuals such as Qassem Amin, a judge and Islamic scholar who in 1899 published *The Emancipation of Women*, which advocated the integration of women into education and the fight against ignorance; Salama Moussa, a writer and journalist interested in democratic socialism who founded the Egyptian Association of Scientific Culture and advocated Gandhian methods to achieve independence; and Naguib Mahfouz, a prolific novelist who was awarded the Nobel Prize in 1988. Although many intellectuals rejected liberalism in the 1950s and 1960s in favor of Marxism and Arab nationalism, there has been a rebirth of liberalism among those who have been disillusioned by the realities of nationalist autocracy, Marxism, and political Islam.

34. Elizabeth Rudin, "The Jihadi Who Kept Asking Why," *New York Times Magazine*, 7 March 2004; Mansour al-Nogaidan, "Losing my Jihadism," *Washington Post*, 22 July 2007.

35. Lisa Anderson, "Demystifying the Arab Spring: Parsing the Differences Between Tunisia, Egypt, and Libya," *Foreign Affairs* 90, no. 3 (May–June 2011): 6.

36. See Rubin, *The Long War for Freedom*, especially his analysis in chapter 4.

37. Outsiders might be surprised to know how vigorous the human rights movement is throughout pockets of the Middle East. For example, in Iran there is Shirin Ebadi's group called the Center for Defense of Human Rights, the Association of Journalists for Freedom of Press, and the Students Association for Human Rights. For more, see Shirin Ebadi, "The Human Rights Case Against Attacking Iran," *New York Times*, 8 February 2005. Additionally, groups not based in the Middle East, such as the United Kingdom's Article 19, have long taken a strong interest in the Iranian situation. Information on their efforts is available online at: http://www.article19.org (accessed 19 August 2011).

38. In addition to Ganji, four other Iranians were arrested for their involvement with the academic conference. These include: Khalil Rostamkhani, a translator and journalist; Mehrangiz Kar, a writer, editor, and human rights lawyer; Shahla Lahiji, a publisher; and Ezzatollah Sahabi, a journalist. For more information, see Writers in Prison Committee / International Freedom of Expression Exchange (IFEX) Press Release, 16 January 2001. IFEX, a cooperative and joint venture of the most globally significant freedom of expression NGOs and organizations, functions as a clearinghouse for accurate and timely updates and alerts about violations of freedom of expression, is operated by the Canadian Journalists for Freedom of Expression and is located in Toronto.

39. All of Ganji's works are currently banned in Iran, including his most recent, *The Road to Democracy in Iran* (Cambridge, MA 2008).

40. Jahanbegloo had been accused by Intelligence Minister Golam Hossein Mohseni Ejeie of helping to prepare a "Velvet Revolution" in Iran and was held in solitary confinement in Evin prison. More than twenty newspapers were closed from 2006 to 2009, and more than a dozen journalists and bloggers detained without access to visitors or legal counsel—all prior to the post-2009 election crackdown.
41. Ignatieff credits Ahmadinejad's 2005 victory in part to his populist appeals to the poor and the disaffected veterans of the Iran-Iraq war (in which he also served), as well as by tapping into their disillusion with the half-hearted efforts of earlier "reformers," such as Khamtami and Rafsanjani. In the same way that the Warsaw students of 1968 seemed a world away from the 1970 workers of Gdańsk, Iran's liberals and the educated middle-class today were not connected to this constituency, as they largely did not serve, opting for further education or exile. Moreover, the community of dissent is focused more on political liberalization rather than helping the poor, even while acknowledging that the reconstituted economics of import-substitution industrialization and nationalization that passes for official policy will hardly generate the economic growth or, more importantly, guarantee a more equitable distribution of wealth. This shortcoming may change post-June 12, given the broad sociological appeal and participation in the protest movement.
42. Ammar Abdulhamid's 2001 novel *Menstruation* (London) explores the transformation of belief and self-actualization within a repressive and religiously conservative culture. His characters, in the messy complexity of their relationships, sow the seeds of their future dissent.
43. Lee Smith, "A Liberal in Damascus," *New York Times Magazine*, 13 February 2005. It is perhaps not surprising that liberals often begin as radicals—this was the case in Central Europe as well. They were not contrary to the ideals of socialism per se, but the Soviet Union's perverse and authoritarian imposition of socialism on their states and citizens. When "reality" and "facts" contradicted ideology, introspective reflection lead to critical thinking, new ideas, and fresh strategies.
44. For a detailed analysis, see Human Rights Watch, *False Freedom: Online Censorship in the Middle East and North Africa* 17/10(E) (November 2005). The OpenNet Initiative (http://opennet.net, accessed 19 August 2011), a research project of the University of Toronto, Harvard University, and Cambridge University, publishes detailed country-by-country reports on Internet filtering. *Access Denied* was the first global survey of Internet filtering. See Ronald Deibert et al., eds., *Access Denied: The Practice and Policy of Global Internet Filtering* (Cambridge, MA 2008).
45. John Kelley and Bruce Etling from the Berkman Center for Internet and Society have produced a report called *Mapping Iran's Online Public: Politics and Culture in the Persian Blogosphere*. A copy of the report can be found at http://cyber.law.harvard.edu/publications/2008/Mapping_Irans_Online_Public (accessed 19 August 2011).
46. Nasrin Alavi, *We Are Iran: The Persian Blogs* (Brooklyn, 2005).
47. Max Rodenbeck, "Volcano of Rage," *New York Review of Books*, 24 March 2001: 6.
48. These activities often rely on external technological support. For example, the Citizen Lab at the University of Toronto quickly established "right2know" nodes using complex firewall-penetrating and encrypted software to allow Iranian Internet users to access banned Web sites, allowing for mobile phone access and the uploading of streaming video. Citizen Lab founder and brainchild Ron Deibert estimates that more than eighteen thousand Iranians were using services pioneered and made available by the Lab by late June 2009. See Andrew Mitrovica, "New Freedom Fighters," *U of T Magazine* (Autumn 2009): 28–31.

49. Robert Tignor, *Egypt: A Short History* (Princeton, 2010); Tarek Osman, *Egypt on the Brink: from Nasser to Mubarak* (New Haven, 2010).
50. Qutb is increasingly well known and studied as a key theoretician of political Islam, who radically reformulated *jihad*, embraced modernization while rejecting Westernization, and argued that coercion and violence were necessary to achieve "freedom." His resemblance to Lenin is striking. On this point, see extended discussions in both Mamdani, *Good Muslim, Bad Muslim*, and Paul Berman, *Terrorism and Liberalism* (New York, 2004).
51. The publication of Rajaa Al Sanea's *Girls of Riyadh* in 2005 is a case in point. Premised on a series of emails detailing the love lives of four wealthy Saudi teenagers sent by an anonymous character (much like the omniscient narrator in the television series *Gossip Girl*), the book was immediately banned in Saudi Arabia. Nonetheless, as of January 2008, English copies are openly available at major bookstores in Saudi Arabia, and the novel is a bestseller throughout the region.
52. Perhaps most significantly, the CPJ was able to interview over eighty reporters, writers, editors, and intellectuals in Riyadh, Jeddah, Dhahran, Damman, and Qatif, and met with officials from both the Ministries of the Interior and Information, over two fact-finding missions in July 2005 and February 2006. For the complete text of the report, see Joel Campagna's *Princes, Clerics, and Censors: Saudi Arabia Loosens Press Shackles but Religion and Politics Are Still Perilous Topics*, available at http://cpj.org/reports/2006/05/saudi-06.php (accessed 19 August 2011).
53. Mamdani, *Good Muslim, Bad Muslim*, 57–59.
54. Adam Michnik, "Letter from Gdańsk Prison," in *Letters from Prison and other Essays*, trans. M. Latynksi (Berkeley, 1985), 86–87.
55. Feldman is deliberate in his choice of terminology here, and states: "I use the term *ideas* not because the words civilization, culture, world-view, and even ideology are not valuable, but because [the word] *idea* carries fewer implications about the way beliefs and values are bound up with identity." Feldman, *After Jihad*, 31.
56. See Thomas Friedman, *The Lexus and the Olive Tree* (New York, 2000); Kwame Anthony Appiah, *Cosmopolitanism: Ethics in a World of Strangers* (New York, 2006).
57. This hybridity is mutual; thus, the democratic "West" is also influenced and changed by its growing Muslim populations, and not always in the spirit of integration or tolerance. The French experience banning the *hijab* in schools ought to be contrasted, I think, with the Canadian experience of multiculturalism, where the right to wear of religious symbols in schools has been upheld by the Supreme Court of Canada—*Multani v Commission scolaire Marguerite-Bourgeoys* (2006). On Turkey as a model in the current context of the Arab Spring, see Kemal Kirisci, "Turkey's 'Demonstrative Effect' and the Transformation of the Middle East," *Insight Turkey* 13, no. 2 (2011): 33–55; and Alper Y. Dede, "The Arab Uprisings: Debating the 'Turkish Model,'" *Insight Turkey* 13, no. 2 (2011): 23–32.
58. Feldman, *After Jihad*, 20.
59. See Mahmood Mamdani, *When Victims Become Killers: Colonialism, Nativism, and the Genocide in Rwanda* (Princeton, 2011); Samantha Powers, *The Problem from Hell: America and the Age of Genocide* (New York, 2002); Carol Off, *The Lion, The Fox, and the Eagle: A Story of Generals and Justice in Rwanda and Yugoslavia* (Toronto, 2000); Misha Glenny, *The Balkans: Nationalism, War, and the Great Powers, 1804–1999* (New York, 2000); and Mark Mazower, *The Balkans: A Short History* (New York, 2002).
60. Tariq Ramadan, "Democratic Turkey is the Template for Egypt's Muslim Brotherhood," *Huffington Post*, 8 February 2011.

61. Arguably, Hussein's provocative error was not in gassing the Kurds or running a ruthless regime built on the cult of his own personality, but the 1990 invasion of Kuwait. His fate was ultimately decided as a result of his own belligerence and unwillingness in an exaggerated regional power-play to come clean with UN inspectors regarding suspected programs to develop weapons of mass destruction, and the resulting instability he thus represented in an oil-rich region vital to the strategic interests of the United States.
62. See Steve Coll, *Ghost Wars: The Secret History of the CIA, Afghanistan, bin Laden, from the Soviet Invasion to September 10, 2001* (New York, 2004), 23–24; and Mamdani, *Good Muslim, Bad Muslim*, 119–77.
63. Jeffrey Goldberg, "Danger: Falling Tyrants," *The Atlantic*, June 2011, 49.
64. Rubin, *The Long War for Freedom*, 27–36.
65. See Claus Offe, *The Varieties of Transition: The East European and East German Experience* (Cambridge, 1996).
66. Considered by regional autocrats to be a path to be avoided, as discussed in note 25.

Afterword

THE LEGACIES OF DISSENT
Charter 77, the Helsinki Effect, and the Emergence of a European Public Space

Jacques Rupnik

> Though Charter 08 was modeled after Czechoslovakia's Charter '77, the fundamental values it invokes are no more Western than they are Chinese.
> —Václav Havel and Desmond Tutu (2010)[1]

In 1956, Leszek Kołakowski published a famous essay entitled "What is Alive and What is Dead in the Socialist Idea." More than two decades after the fall of communist regimes in East-Central Europe, we can now ask: What is alive and what is dead in the legacy of the human rights movement and, more generally, that of Central European dissent? In what way has it contributed to the overcoming of the partition of Europe in 1989? What does it tell us about the role of public intellectuals in conditions of unfreedom and about intellectuals in the politics of a transition to democracy? What were the implications of the post-1989 marginalisation of the dissident legacy for what can be called "premature democratic fatigue" in East-Central Europe? The questions concerning the legacies of dissent are by no means just of historical or scholarly interest. They became contested issues in the countries concerned and have relevance for those who seek to understand the background to the changes of 1989, the reinvention of democracy in Central Europe and beyond.

Interestingly, the very term *dissent* is a problematic one in at least two ways. It came from the West and was only reluctantly adopted by the protagonists concerning themselves. The opening sentence of Havel's famous essay on "The Power of the Powerless" reads: "A spectre is haunting Eastern Europe: the spectre of what in the West is called 'dissent.'"[2] Secondly,

---

Notes for this chapter begin on page 331.

it suggests misleadingly that we are dealing with dissenting voices within socialism. The term used to be associated with religious heresy and later became transposed to "heretics" in the communist church. That was the meaning Yevgeny Zamyatin had in mind shortly after the Russian revolution: "There should be somebody today to speak heretically of tomorrow. Heretics are the only (bitter-tasting) remedy for entropy of human thought."[3] 1968 is one possible way of establishing a connection between socialist "heretics" and the dissident phenomenon, but that should not obscure the main point: dissent was precisely about breaking with the ideology and political strategies associated with the reform of the socialism. Using the term in this essay as a generalization for a phenomenon that developed in East-Central Europe between the mid 1970s and the late 1980s requires an awareness of the great diversity of meanings, of itineraries—personal and political—it entails.

The perceptions and political instrumentalizations of dissent have not always been congruent there and abroad. It was gradually eclipsed in East-Central Europe in the 1990s just as it became a reference for "democracy promotion" in the US. Charter 77 may be forgotten by the younger generation in Prague today, but is seen thirty years later as an inspiration for the dissidents of "Charter 08" in Beijing.[4] The Chinese Charter, just like its Czechoslovak predecessor, is demanding the implementation of the International Covenant on Civil and Political Rights signed by its government while appealing to universal values and the international public opinion for support. The contrast between benign neglect at home and an inspiration at the other end of the world points to the importance of the variety of receptions of the dissident phenomenon thirty years on in Eastern Europe, in Western democracies, or in emerging nations in other parts of the world. That, too, is now part of the legacy of dissent.

Charter 77 and the "Velvet Revolution" of 1989

Charter 77 provides a good illustration of these changing perceptions of dissent. In Prague, we have moved since 1989 through roughly three phases in the reception of the dissident experience: first came the celebration of former dissidents in the immediate aftermath of the "velvet revolution." They had been propelled to the political center stage in November 1989 through the Civic Forum and the election of its leader Václav Havel as Czechoslovak president a month later, the embodiment of the "velvet revolution" narrative of the successful dissident challenge to the totalitarian system. "Civil society is in power!" claimed Jiří Dienstbier at a press conference in December 1989, when the former stoker became Czechoslovak foreign minister. And indeed the dissidents made their entry into the government while the Civic Forum negotiated the appointment of many of them to the National Assembly, due to prepare the first free elections in June 1990.

The "dissident moment," however, did not last. Within a couple of years the country witnessed the rapid marginalization of former dissidents and their eclipse from political life.[5] A somewhat similar pattern developed in other Central European countries. It was rapid in the Czech case (Civic Movement), and took somewhat longer in Poland: the Citizens' Movement for Democratic Action (ROAD) founded at the beginning of 1990 and disbanded in 1991, was a typical attempt to create a postdissident political party.[6] The list of signatories of ROAD's founding manifesto reads like a "Who's Who" of the Polish independent intelligentsia. The Freedom Union (Unia Wolności), launched a decade later, included some of the same protagonists, but did not last much longer. In Hungary, the Alliance of Free Democrats, a liberal party whose initial core group came from former activists of the Democratic opposition, had a somewhat greater staying power and a more protracted agony, but the pattern was basically the same: the postdissident, center-left liberal parties did not succeed in establishing themselves as lasting components of the new party system in the new democracies that they had helped to bring about.

That eclipse largely corresponds to the transition moving into its second phase dominated by institution building, the privatization of the economy, and other concerns. The political focus and the prevailing discourse in Prague during the 1990s stressed the alleged irrelevance of the dissidents' thinking for the new transition agenda marked by economic reforms, the dismantling of the Czechoslovak state, and the primacy of party politics as prime features of what Václav Klaus called "standard democracy." The Czech prime minister and leader of the conservative ODS party derided the dissidents' notion of "antipolitics" as well as what he curiously called "NGOism" and "humanrightism"—his version of the dissident legacy associated with the name of his main opponent, Václav Havel.

Two decades after 1989, a third phase of this process began with the return of some of the legacies of dissent to public awareness, as if the disenchantment with the state of "standard democracy" allowed for a new, perhaps more sober assessment of the role of dissent and its contribution to alternative approaches of democracy. A second reason for the renewed interest in the dissident experience emerged in recent years in connection with debates about the communist past and the resistance (or lack of) to the Old Regime.

Outside of the Czech lands, however, this post-89 lack of interest in dissent and its relevance for the democratic transition has often baffled observers. It may reveal a difficulty that Czech political elites, the media, and parts of the public at large seem to have with the two major and very different "democratic moments" in postwar Czech society: the Prague Spring of 1968 and the Charter 77 human rights movement. The defeat of the former was associated with the end of an illusion, that of reforming socialism from within. The latter was seen as perhaps relevant under communism, yet ill suited for institutionalized forms of party politics in a parliamentary democracy.

In contrast, we often find the opposite in Western perceptions: a powerful if somewhat simplified narrative of dissent and the Charter 77 human rights movement as both a continuation of the legacies of the Prague Spring of 1968 and a prelude to the democratic revolution of November 1989. The fate of Václav Havel, from dissident to president, embodies the narrative of resistance with a democratic happy ending. Such storytelling, as well as the figure of Václav Havel, himself, helps to account for the widespread international impact of the dissident experience. It is obviously too neat to be true.

It may be useful, therefore, to examine the evidence with hindsight and to try to overcome the simple alternative of debunking vs. myth making that is implicit in the two main theses concerning dissent, and which are also found in different versions in other postcommunist countries. The first saw Charter 77 as a virtuous ghetto of courageous intellectuals who remained largely isolated in a society atomized through a mixture of fear and the lure of an admittedly mediocre version of a consumer society. The second saw the Charter as the tip of the iceberg: the articulation by a dissident minority of the democratic aspirations of the silent majority.

The latter version prevailed in the immediate aftermath of 1989. With the birth of the Civic Forum, Václav Havel and his Chartist friends were propelled to the center stage of the reinvention of democracy: voicing the democratic aspirations of the people but also negotiating a peaceful transition to democracy with the Communist authorities. Even the Czechs thus experienced a brief and condensed version of what the Poles and Hungarians called the "round table," where the dissidents, too, played a major political role.[7]

However, the subsequent eclipse of the dissidents from political life brought back the thesis about the virtuous ghetto: the marginality of the ex-dissidents after 1992 came as the logical extension of their marginal situation under the Communist regime. And this found its translation in the new reading of the "velvet revolution" of November 1989 provided by president Václav Klaus on its fifteenth anniversary. It sounded, in substance, something like this: "It was not the former dissidents who helped to bring down the old regime, but all of you ordinary Czechs, bureaucrats and green grocers, with short working hours and long drinking hours. You in the silent majority have, through a mixture of indifference and *Schlamperei*, turned the old system into an empty shell and thus prepared its demise."

Such an antiheroic version of 1989 may have had quite a resonance at home among the average citizens, especially ODS voters: neither communists nor dissidents, they could more easily identify with the figure of Václav Klaus, the pragmatic economist, than Václav Havel, whose very presence at the Prague Castle was a symbol of pride but also a reminder of the silent majority's bad conscience. In fact, Václav Havel's thirteen-year presidency obscured the political eclipse of the former dissidents. His post-1989 status of president-dissident with an international moral authority gave a somewhat deceptive impression of the continuity of the dissident legacy, while in reality there was a radical breach. But the dissident-president image no doubt also played a part in the Western perception of the significance of Central European dissent in the West (and its relevance for the democracy promotion agenda in other parts of the world).

Dissent and the Birth of a European Public Space

The international dimension of the human rights movements in Eastern and Central Europe was embedded in its very concept. The Charter can be considered as both a new response to the repressive policies that followed the crushing of the Prague Spring of 1968, and as an offspring of the Helsinki Agreement in 1975 that established a new framework for East-West relations in Europe. Among the principles formally subscribed to by the governments involved were: "the respect for human rights and basic freedoms, including freedom of thought, of conscience or faith." In other words, human rights had become part and parcel of East-West relations, which was a major departure from both Brezhnev's and Kissinger's concept of détente on which the 1975 Accord was based. It combined the so-called Brezhnev doctrine of limited sovereignty (the fate of socialism in each country was "guaranteed" by all the members of the block) with what was then known as the "Sonnenfeld doctrine," after Kissinger's main adviser, which argued that East-West détente required stability, even an "organic relationship" between Moscow and its satellites.[8] The critics, including many dissidents, promptly renamed it the "Brezhfeld doctrine," postulating that stability in East-West relations depended on the stability within each bloc. Soviet and American archives have since confirmed that this actually was the underlying assumption on both sides and that the formally included human rights provisions were not actually meant to be implemented.

However, Helsinki also, almost inadvertently, opened the possibility of monitoring human rights provisions at regular review conferences and thus legitimized the attempts by citizens' groups to take their governments at their word and challenge governmental violations of human rights. Simultaneously, it opened the possibility for diplomatic interference in the internal affairs of all signatory states. This interaction between diplomacy and public opinion on both sides of the iron curtain became known as the "Helsinki effect."[9] Charter 77 and other similar rights groups, known as Helsinki committees, used the opportunities opened by the so-called Third Basket of the Helsinki Accords and thus contributed to the derailing of the diplomatic routine of East-West relations. Human rights principles and their violations became part of an increasingly effective interplay in the relations between states, governments, and public opinion, which slowly but surely eroded the status quo that it was meant to preserve, thereby becoming a vector for domestic political change under communism. The human rights component of the Helsinki process will remain a classic case study of unintended consequences in international relations. It is in this sense that dissent and the "Helsinki effect" helped to prepare the ground for the changes of 1989.

Of all the human rights groupings that emerged in the Soviet bloc in the late 1970s (ranging from the KOR in Poland in 1976 to the Helsinki Committee in the Soviet Union) it can be argued that it was the Charter movement that made the most effective use of the "Helsinki effect" and significantly contributed to its transformation. It made explicit references to the international commitments on human rights signed by the Czechoslovak government and contrasted those with their massive violation in the country. The dissidents thus used an external factor to enhance their very limited domestic leverage. This ability to compensate a relative domestic weakness by addressing an international audience was made possible through an institutional framework initially conceived by diplomats, but to which the dissidents and their supporters gave new substance and a momentum that nobody predicted at the time of the signing of the Helsinki Agreement in 1975. The "Third Basket" and its human rights provisions concerning the "free circulation of people and ideas" became the centerpiece of the review conferences held in Belgrade in 1977, in Madrid in 1980, and finally in Vienna in the second half of the 1980s. It surprised communist bloc officials with the unexpected importance of the fine print of Agreements to which they had subscribed, and revealed to governments, East and West, the emergent role of public opinion and non-state actors in the diplomacy of European states.

The human rights challenge to the status quo in a divided Europe was made possible through the convergence of several factors:

- The dissidents altered the concept of détente between states by making it dependent on détente between state and society. You cannot impose, as general Jaruzelski did with his 1981 military coup, the "state of war" on society and promote at the same time disarmament or détente with your Western neighbors.

- West European diplomacy gradually discovered the use of the "Third Basket" and the follow-up conferences in their policy of détente. West European governments started systematically consulting each other about the appropriate position on human rights in the Soviet bloc, which can be considered in retrospect as the first steps toward what is today known as the European Union's "Common European Foreign and Security Policy."[10]

- American diplomacy under President Carter departed from that of its Republican predecessors and put human rights at the heart of its new concept of foreign policy. Jimmy Carter's speech at Notre Dame University in the spring of 1978 ("We must rid ourselves of our inordinate fear of communism") was perhaps the clearest formulation of the new doctrine, suggesting that human rights should not be just a ploy in the Cold War but should concern America's allies as well. The clumsy implementation of that policy in Iran and elsewhere came under severe criticism in the US, but in the European context it certainly strengthened the Third Basket component of the Helsinki process.[11]

- New ties developed among dissident movements in Central and Eastern Europe. The most significant was Charter 77 cooperation with KOR, the Committee for the Defense of Workers founded in 1976 in Poland. The famous meeting of Václav Havel and his associates with Adam Michnik and Jacek Kuron near the Czech-Polish border in August 1978 was the first of a series of meetings throughout the 1980s, and it is obvious that the thinking leading up to Solidarity experiment of 1980 greatly influenced that of the Czech and Hungarian dissidents. Indeed, the crushing of the Prague Spring of 1968 and Jaruzelski's crackdown on Solidarity can be considered as the two founding moments of the Hungarian democratic opposition around János Kis. He released a letter of support of Charter 77 with György Bence and János Kenedi, and then in 1981 launched the first issue of the samizdat journal Beszélő. In contrast to three isolated and defeated attempts to change the system, the dissidents shared the premise that only a concerted movement had a long-term chance of bringing about change. This was a period when personal and political bonds were formed that prepared the ground for the cooperation in the early 1990s of Central European countries (Poland, Hungary, Czechoslovakia) within the Visegrad group and their "return to Europe." The Central Europeans should "approach Western Europe not as poor dissidents or a helpless, amnestied prisoner, but as someone who brings something with him: namely spiritual and moral incentives, bold peace initiatives, untapped creative potential, the ethos of freshly gained freedom."[12]

The dissident idea of "détente from below" caught the imagination of a number of human rights associations and civil society groupings in the West, of which the Helsinki Citizens Assembly was perhaps the best known in the 1980s. Other international organizations such as Amnesty International or Human Rights Watch provided support by publicizing the Soviet bloc regimes' repressive measures.[13] In Paris, an International Committee for the Support of Charter 77 was created and chaired by the poet Pierre Emanuel with members Arthur Miller, Yves Montand, Simone Signoret, Tom Stoppard, and Stephen Spender, among others. Pavel Tigrid, who was editor of a Czech quarterly published in Paris, *Svědectví* (Testimony), was a friend of Pierre Emmanuel, and was active behind the scenes—pointing to the very important and often ignored role of exiles in the so-called Helsinki process. In addition to Tigrid, Jiří Pelikán (the former director of Czechoslovak television during 1968, editor of *Listy* in Rome, and European Parliamentary representative on the slate of the Italian Socialist Party), was effective in addressing left-of-center public opinion, which was traditionally favorable to détente as well as human rights causes (though sometimes with a blind spot for their fate under "real socialism"). The exiles were the middle men who made possible much of the dissemination of information concerning their country of origin and were able to convey the support gathered in the West back to the dissidents in Central Europe. The three major Central European exile journals then published in Paris (*Svedectvi*, edited by Pavel Tigrid in Czech from 1956, *Kultura*, edited by Jerzy Giedroyc in Polish from 1947, and *Magyar Füzetek*, edited by Peter Kende in Hungarian from 1981) found their ways into the samizdat distribution networks in their respective countries. They helped to disseminate samizdat literature, but also, through the contribution of exiles in the West, contributed to broaden the terms of domestic discussion and the political culture, at least among the intellectual elites.

The exiles also played a part in another major dissemination of dissent and unofficial culture, as well as the international response to it, to ordinary citizens in East-Central Europe: Western broadcasting to Eastern Europe. Radio stations such as Radio Free Europe based in Munich (the most "committed" politically, but also the most jammed by the East European regimes), BBC World Service, Voice of America, and others undermined the regimes' claim to a monopoly on information and their censorship of public debate.

Gradually, a loose transnational support network of sympathizers developed. It reflected, in a way, the diversity of the dissidents themselves. It included people of different political persuasions, from leftists and pacifists to conservative "cold-warriors," all committed for a variety of reasons to the support of the dissidents. Through the Western media and public opinion they put pressure on their respective governments, whose diplomacy helped, albeit inadequately, to provide some protection to the human rights campaigners in Central Europe. What started with Charter 77 gained momentum after the December 1981 crackdown on Solidarity in Poland. Communist propaganda became inaudible, human rights concerns gained a new audience with the increasingly postideological turn of the intelligentsia, while many trade unions in Western Europe became involved in support of their Polish counterparts. For a while the "in" thing for students in Paris, London, or Rome was to read Havel's essays and wear a Solidarność badge. This can be considered as the founding moment in the emergence of a European public space.

To be sure, there have been previous such moments of reconnection between the two Europes. 1968 was the most significant one since the end of World War II, with parallel, unfulfilled hopes of change inspired by "sophisticated rebels" in Prague and Paris.[14] There was the simultaneity of student revolts in Paris, Berlin, Warsaw, or Prague (not to mention Berkeley or Mexico) whose common denominator was a challenge to a domestic political order that shook the foundation of the European stalemate. But it also turned out to obscure a misunderstanding. Under the surface of common generational uprisings and "incoherent fraternities," 1968 was also a year of misunderstandings, a tale of two utopias.[15] The 68ers in the West derided "bourgeois freedoms" and legal norms that their Eastern counterparts were reclaiming. Western radicals were turning their attention to the "Third World" (Vietnam, Cuba, China) under the threat of "American imperialism" while their East Europeans were asserting their "Europeanness" threatened by "Soviet imperialism."

Ten years later the political and intellectual landscape in Europe had changed. The radical 68ers in the West discarded Marxism and socialist utopias, became antitotalitarian liberals whose itinerary and concerns converged with those of dissidents in the East. It is in that context that a new nongovernmental dialogue could take place between both halves of Europe. Czech dissent played a significant part in that process. This was made possible thanks to a unique combination of politics and culture, the "Kundera effect" (the rediscovery of Central Europe as the "kidnapped West") combined with the "Havel effect" (the meaning of dissent as "the power of the powerless"). The Charter 77 role in the Helsinki process, along with the capacity of its leading figures to formulate the crisis of communism in their country in broader universal categories, made it possible for people outside the communist bloc to identify with their cause beyond humanitarian sympathy with unjustly persecuted activists.

Charter 77 defined itself as "a free, informal, open community of people of different convictions, different faiths, and different professions united by the will to strive, individually and collectively, for the respect of civic and human rights in our country and throughout the world."[16] This commitment to a culture of pluralism and tolerance was a major source of the Charter's appeal abroad and mirrored the diversity among its external supporters. The Charter represented an attempt to recreate—even on a limited scale—an independent public opinion under a dictatorship. To the extent that it relied on the interplay of domestic and international actors it became part of an emerging European public opinion concerned with fate of democratic politics and the overcoming of the partition of Europe.

However, beyond the Helsinki process, the main reason for the significant impact of Czech dissent in the West concerned its underlying political philosophy. It focused on three major issues:

The first concerned the ethics of responsibility and the crisis of modern civilization. The primacy of ethics over politics implied that under no political circumstances do the ends justify the means. This had been the prevailing idea among East European intellectuals at least since 1956. The dissidents, from Solzhenitsyn to Havel, backed it with a personal commitment that gave it a new sense of urgency and a motto: "living in truth." Jan Patočka, the philosopher best known for his *Heretical Essays*, became one of the first three spokesmen for Charter 77. The police report about his interrogation provides an involuntary homage to his civic courage: "About his role in Charter 77 he declared that he had taken upon himself this civic duty for the simple reason that—had he not done so—'it was unlikely somebody else would find the courage to do it.' He adds that he is aware that this could be a long-term process and that he did not expect to return to normal life." Patočka did not return to normal life; he died of heart attack on 11 March 1977, shortly after his ten-hour police interrogation.

The Kantian moral imperative combined with the Socrates-like determination of the philosopher's readiness "to die for the truth" was part of the "appeal" of the image of the dissident intellectual. Jan Patočka's writings attracted broader readership after he became a "dissident," but did not remain confined to the circumstances of the Charter's birth and the philosopher's death. His message, for those who cared to read him, was that "the care for the soul is not limited to one's own soul, but also to the soul of the City."[17] This notion of responsibility gave its true meaning to rights and therefore to the defense of human rights, which also entails duties. In short: co-responsibility for the fate of rights and the world we live in.

To understand why the writings of Jan Patočka and Václav Havel, the founding fathers of the Charter, had such profound and lasting impact on the Western intellectual milieu one has to go beyond political circumstances or the sympathy for men of courage and take seriously the ideas they profess. Remembering Jan Patočka as a symbol of the defiant power of the intellectual should not discharge us from reading him.[18] Because what we find in his writings is not just a timely denunciation of repression under communism, but also deep insights into its close connection with the crisis of modern Western civilization, or what he called "hypercivilization" ("growth for the sake of growth"). It is also this idea that was at the heart of Václav Havel's writings. For Havel, the totalitarian system was only the extreme form of the crisis of Western or global civilization itself. In his essay "Politics and Conscience" (1984), he goes beyond the simple opposition democracy vs. totalitarianism:

> So, too, the totalitarian systems warn of something far more serious than Western rationalism is willing to admit. They are, most of all, a convex mirror of the inevitable consequences of rationalism, a grotesquely magnified image of its own deep tendencies, an extreme offshoot of its own development and an ominous product of its own expansion. They are a deeply informative reflection of its own crisis. Totalitarian regimes are not merely dangerous neighbors and even less some kind of an avant-garde of world progress. Alas, just the opposite: they are the avant-garde of a global crisis of this civilization, first European, then Euro-American, and ultimately global.[19]

Totalitarianism as a "distorted mirror" of our modern civilization. When Western intellectuals—or students in Paris, at Harvard, or more recently in Beijing—discussed (and still do discuss) Havel's essays such as "The Power of the Powerless," it was not because they were keen to discover new details about the well-known turpitudes of Husák's secret police, but because they also found out something about themselves, about their own societies and about the world we live in.

The second, perhaps most influential feature of the dissident political legacy concerns **the language of rights and civil society** as key ingredients of a democratic polity.[20] Central European dissidents helped to shape the postsocialist liberal ethos of the 1980s by moving away from the ideological utopias of the late 1960s. Liberals on the Right tended to stress the rule of law, liberals on the Left the notions of civil society and social movement. There was undoubtedly a dissident contribution to the rediscovery in Europe of political liberalism (not to be confused with economic liberalism, as has often been the case in Prague in the 1990s). The language of rights was by no means primarily an engagement with the philosophical debates initiated at the time in the West by authors such as John Rawls. It served the dual purpose of providing a common ground for people of very different persuasions, using the already mentioned Helsinki process as an effective opportunity structure. The combination of the moral imperative and the language of rights also became a way of moving beyond politics toward what Havel called "antipolitics"[21] (meaning to avoid politics as a "technology of power" or a "manipulation" by it) but also, by the same token, its classic Right/Left divides that structured debates about the public good in Western democracies.

The third important aspect of the impact of Charter 77 in the West concerns its involvement in the discussions of the 1980s on overcoming the division of Europe. This, too, has several dimensions that are merely sketched out here.

What the Czech (but also Polish and Hungarian) dissident intellectuals did starting in the late 1970s was to put Central Europe back on the map. Europe is not just a "common market," it is based on culture and values to which Central Europe seems all the more attached when it feels that they are under threat. Kundera's thesis about Central Europe as a "kidnapped West,"[22] the idea that the boundaries of civilizations cannot be drawn by tanks, as well as Havel's "power of the powerless," became indispensable companion volumes in the intellectual debate about Europe. The rediscovery of Central Europe through its independent culture, as well as through its dissident movements, as a space distinct from the Soviet East has reinforced the delegitimation of the division of Europe.

This was the intellectual context of the intense political dialogue between Charter dissidents and Western peace movements during the so-called Euromissiles crisis of the early 1980s: the deployment of American cruise missiles in Western Europe in response to the Soviet deployment of SS 20 missiles.

It included several lively exchanges such as the one between Miroslav Bednar (alias "Václav Racek") and the British historian E. P. Thompson in the *New Statesman*. Thompson suggested a link and a symmetry between the dissidents in the East and the pacifists in the West. Both meant to put pressure from below on their respective governments in order to achieve nuclear disarmament in Europe.[23] Racek, independently of the desirability of the goal, questioned the false symmetry between the possibilities available to citizens in democratic societies in the West and those in totalitarian regimes in the Eastern part of the continent. Along similar lines, Václav Havel engaged in a dialogue with the Western peace movements with an essay published in 1985 all over Europe under the title "The Anatomy of a Reticence."[24]

Most participants in the debate on both sides of the Iron Curtain shared the premise that there is a fundamental link between the nature of interstate European order and that of the internal political order of the states concerned. International peace is best guaranteed by peace between state and society; when General Jaruzelski declared the "state of war" inside in December 1981, this also enhanced the risks of confrontation outside.

There was fundamental disagreement, however, on the false symmetry between the political regimes and thus between dissidents in the East and peace activists in the West. The latter enjoyed relatively free expression and means to influence their governments' defense policy, which simply did not exist in the East. Probably the most significant statement on the European stalemate coming from Charter circles was the 1985 "Prague Appeal," which called for a simultaneous dissolution of both NATO and the Warsaw Pact.[25] The dissidents broke a taboo that nobody in Western Europe was then prepared to touch: they saw no objection to the reunification of Germany as a necessary condition for the peaceful and democratic reunification of Europe.

The ethical and philosophical underpinnings of dissent, the rediscovery of liberal values (the language of rights and civil society), and the overcoming of the partition of Europe were the three main elements that became the substance of a remarkable European dialogue across the iron curtain. It helps explain why, since the mid 1970s, dissent acquired an echo so disproportionate with the number of activists involved and why the "velvet revolution" of 1989 captured the Western imagination.

Hence the question: Whatever happened to that European dialogue since then? The short answer is that it has more or less vanished. In the 1980s, direct contact was difficult if not impossible, but the writings of Václav Havel, Adam Michnik, or György Konrád were widely published and discussed in the West. Today, we have easy contact, instant communication, and countless conferences but not much of a transeuropean debate. How to account for this paradox? The first explanation argues that the eclipse of the dissidents and of their message after 1989 is due to the fact that with changed circumstances their message became irrelevant: just as "antipolitics" or the "parallel Polis"(Václav Benda) seemed out of date with the return of pluralism of competing parties and parliamentary institutions,[26] so have the transeuropean networks of intellectuals and human rights activists after the end of the cold war. As if, with the loss of a common problem (the division of the continent) and of a common enemy (Soviet totalitarianism), we no longer had much to say to each other.

A "Kidnapped" Legacy of Dissent?

The second explanation is not so much that the legacy of dissent has become irrelevant as that it has been abandoned. The philosophers Jürgen Habermas and Jacques Derrida jointly published an article casting the February 2003 demonstrations in most European capitals against the American war in Iraq as a founding moment of a European public opinion and the need for a European common foreign policy.[27] The debatable argument (is it plausible, let alone desirable, to build a European public opinion on an opposition to American foreign policy or even on "transatlantic value differences"?) hit a major snag: although public opinion in East-Central Europe overwhelmingly opposed the war in Iraq, most ex-dissidents in the region either supported it or remained silent. First of all, they rejected the very idea of building a European identity in opposition to the United States. Anti-Americanism, as a relic of pre-1989 official ideology, was certainly a nonstarter in postcommunist Eastern Europe and the distinction between the opposition to the Bush administration and to the US was, for different reasons, not made by intellectuals in the "new Europe." More importantly, the "dissident legacy" applied to new circumstances was supposedly that a fall of a dictatorship could not be a bad thing. Hence the ex-dissidents' support for the "war on terror," the struggle of "good vs. evil," and the "politics of values" that may have precedence over international legal constraints and sometimes even the protection of civic freedoms. Trapped by such interpretations of the legacy of their antitotalitarian struggle, many of the ex-dissidents, including Havel, Michnik, and Konrad, found themselves at odds with most of the international human rights community that had supported them in the old days, and closer to the neoconservatives in the United States. In an essay dealing with the American liberal intellectuals' support for the Iraq war (described as the "useful idiots" of the War on Terror), the late historian Tony Judt made a parallel with the stance of the East European dissidents:

> This trend is an unfortunate by-product of the intellectual revolution in the 1980s, especially in the former Communist East, when "human rights" displaced conventional political allegiances as the basis for collective action. The gains wrought by this transformation in the rhetoric of oppositional politics were considerable. But a price was paid all the same. A commitment to the abstract universalism of "rights"—and uncompromising ethical stands taken against malign regimes in their name—can lead all too readily to the habit of casting *every* political choice in binary moral terms."[28]

Twenty years on, such a reading of the dissident legacy is, of course, debatable. But it is legitimate to engage in it to the extent that the dissidents themselves explained their support for regime change in Iraq with references to their own experiences. If the first dissident motto was "to live in truth," then it can hardly be consistent with supporting a war justified with lies. Similarly, the ethos of dissent included the Kantian imperative that "the ends do not justify the means" and the rejection of a revolutionary culture that argues that a better society can be brought about through violent means. Precisely for that reason, the "velvet revolution" of 1989 represented a break with revolutionary culture inherited from the revolutions of the past. How then to account for the silence of ex-dissidents in the face of use of violent regime change or torture at Abu Ghraib?

One of the reasons why the vanishing European dialogue came to a halt was because most of its West European protagonists opposed the Iraq war with its blatant human rights implications (Abu Ghraib, Guantanamo, not to mention curbs on domestic civic freedoms), while many East-Central European ex-dissidents had been "hijacked" by the neoconservatives on the other side of the Atlantic under the umbrella of "democracy promotion." The new narrative celebrated the alliance of dissident values and American power in the defeat of Soviet totalitarianism in the East. It was to become an inspiration for the fight against the menace of "Islamofascism," the other totalitarian threat that came in from the South.

Beyond the debate about the irrelevance, the abandonment or the misinterpretation of the dissident legacy, there is an entirely new predicament of post-1989 Europe. In both halves of the Old continent, we have witnessed the decline of the role of intellectuals in a context shaped by the building of institutions, markets, or meeting the requirements for joining the European Union.

No less important has been the impact of globalized environment. The terms that structured the intellectual and political debates of the post–Cold War period, such as "the end of history," "the clash of civilizations," "the Americans are from Mars, the Europeans from Venus," were established by "great simplificators" in America; Europeans have mainly provided variations on these themes. Paradoxically, just as they reached the aim of the continent's unification through the Eastern enlargement of the EU, they gradually became less interested in each other and, perhaps, in Europe as such.

There are, however, several aspects of the dissident legacy associated with Charter 77 around which the interrupted dialogue may be revived and remain relevant. The first concerns the indivisibility of human rights from Belarus to Burma, beyond diplomatic niceties and double standards. Second, there are new challenges facing the democracies in East Central Europe such as the rise of illiberal nationalism and populism. Just as dissident cooperation in pre-1989 Central Europe prepared the ground for the Visegrad group (Poland, Hungary, Czech Republic, and Slovakia), we now see a human rights agenda resurfacing for domestic reasons. It is also under the influence of the international human rights community (ethnic minorities such as the Roma, death penalty, gender issues, abortion, etc.), but now in the face the new populist and antiliberal backlash in Central European of which the Poland of the Kaczyński twins (2005–2007) and Viktor Orbán's Hungary since 2010 are only the most recent and radical versions.[29] Finally, one of most important legacies of dissent was an attempt to think of Europe not just as a "common market," but as a culture, a civilization, and shared values, without which European institutions risk becoming an empty shell. To address these three issues obliges us to revisit the question of "what is alive and what is dead in the dissident legacy" and to return to the unfinished task of creating a European public space.

Notes

1. Václav Havel and Desmond Tutu, "If China frees Nobel winner, it will show strength", *Washington Post*, 22 October 2010.
2. Václav Havel, "The Power of the Powerless," in *Living in Truth* (London, Boston, 1989), 36.
3. Yevgeny Zamyatin, "Two Manifestoes," in *The Idea of the Modern*, ed. I. Howe (New York, 1977), 174.
4. "China's Charter 08," *New York Review of Books*, 15 January 2009.
5. The would-be successor to the Civic Forum, the Civic Movement, got 4.9 percent of the vote in the June 1992 general election and thus failed to pass the 5 percent threshold to enter Parliament. A similar fate awaited dissident intellectuals in the rest of Central Europe.
6. For a first study of this party, see Katarzyna Chimiak, *ROAD: Politika czasu przełomu, Ruch Obywatelski-Akcja Demokratyczna 1990–1991* (Warsaw, 2010).
7. The negotiations took place between 26 November and 9 December 1989. On 10 December, President Gustáv Husák resigned from office. For the full transcript of the Civic Forum negotiations with the government, see Vladimír Hanzel, ed., *Zrychlený tep dějin* (Prague, 1991) (a new edition was released in 2009).
8. During the 1974 meetings with Kissinger and with Nixon, Soviet Foreign Minister Andrei Gromyko received reassurances to that effect. See Thomas Blanton (National Security Archive, Washington), paper presented at the conference on Charter 77, Prague Charles University, 21–23 March 2007.
9. On the way international norms have affected domestic political change in East-Central Europe, see Daniel C. Thomas, *The Helsinki Effect: International Norms, Human Rights and the Demise of Communism* (Princeton, 2001).
10. For a discussion of the subject by a former French diplomat, see Jacques Andréani, *Le Piège: Helsinki et la Chute du Communisme* [The Trap: Helsinki and the Fall of Communism] (Paris, 2005).
11. The best-known criticism of this policy came from Jean Kirkpatrick in an article that provided the framework for the Reagan administration by drawing a distinction between using the human rights issue in authoritarian regimes and in totalitarian (i.e.) communist regimes ("Traditional authoritarian governments are less repressive than revolutionary autocracies" in "Dictatorships and Double Standards," *Commentary* 68, no. 5 (November 1979): 34–45). By inconsiderately promoting human rights, you may weaken your allies without undermining your enemy.
12. Havel's speech in the Polish Sejm on 21 January 1990 developed the idea of dissident interaction under communism as the basis of the Central European cooperation that

was formally launched by Havel, Wałęsa, and Antál in February 1991 in the town of Visegrad, Hungary. Havel's speech to the Polish Sejm and Senate was published as "The Future of Central Europe" *New York Review of Books*, 29 March 1990.
13. The fact that they addressed human rights violations in the East, West, or in the Third World meant the regime could not simply dismiss them as "anticommunist tools of cold war propaganda" and that the dissidents themselves saw their plight as part of an international endeavor.
14. See chapter 1 of H. Stuart Hughes, *Sophisticated Rebels: The Political Culture of European Dissent, 1968–1987* (Cambridge, 1988).
15. Jacques Rupnik, "Les deux Printemps de 1968," *Études* 152 (May 2008): 585–92; for an attempt to identify the convergence among 68ers East and West, see Paul Berman, *A Tale of Two Utopias* (New York, 1996), and Berman's essay, "Les révoltes de 1968. Une fraternité incohérente," in *Le Printemps tchécoslovaque 1968*, ed. F. Fejtöt and J. Rupnik (Brussels, 1999): 267–71.
16. For the most comprehensive and original study of its origins and, more importantly, of the Czech cultural milieu in which it developed, see Jonathan Bolton, *Worlds of Dissent* (Cambridge, 2012).
17. Jan Patočka, *L'Europe après l'Europe* (Paris, 2007): 213.
18. For two recent volumes on Patočka, see Emilie Tardivel, *La liberté au principe* (Paris, 2011) and the special issue of *Études philosophiques*, "Patočka et la phénoménologie" (Paris, 2011).
19. Václav Havel, "Politics and Conscience," in *Open Letters: Selected Writings, 1965–1990*, selected and ed. Paul Wilson (New York, 1992): 260. The Czech original is in Václav Havel, "Politika a Svědomi," in *Do Různých Stran 1983–89* (Scheinfeld, 1989), 42.
20. On the intellectual and political legacy of dissent, see Tony Judt, "Debating the nature of dissent in Eastern Europe," The Wilson Center, occasional paper no. 9 (Washington, DC, 1988); also Barbara Falk, *The Dilemmas of Dissidence in East-Central Europe* (Budapest, 2003).
21. Havel, "Politics and Conscience," 49.
22. Milan Kundera, "The Tragedy of Central Europe," *New York Review of Books*, 26 April 1984.
23. *New Statesman*, 24 April 1981.
24. Václav Havel, "Anatomie jedné zdrženlivosti," in *Do různých stran 1983–89*, 57–83.
25. Published in *Listy* 15, no. 2 (April 1985): 3–4.
26. See Alan Renwick, "Anti-Political or Just Anti-Communist? Varieties of Dissidence and their Implications for the Development of Political Society," *East European Politics and Society*, 20 no. 2 (2006): 286–318.
27. Jürgen Habermas and Jacques Derrida, "Europe: Plaidoyer pour une politique extérieure commune," *Libération*, 31 May 2003.
28. In "The Silence of the Lambs: On the Strange Death of Liberal America," *London Review of Books* (September 2006); also in *Reappraisals* (New York, 2008): 384–92.
29. Jacques Rupnik, "From Democracy Fatigue to Populist Backlash," *Journal of Democracy* 18, no. 4 (October 2007): 17–26.

APPENDIX
Ardis Facsimile and Reprint Editions

1971

Mandel'shtam, Osip. Kamen' [Stone]. 33 p. 18 cm.// Rpt. of O. Mandel'shtam, Kamen'. Stikhi, S. Peterburg: Akme, 1913. 33 p. 18 cm.

Pil'niak, Boris i Mikhail Zoshchenko. Stat'i i materialy [Articles and Materials]. 117p + 94 p. 20 cm.// Rpt. of Boris Pil'niak, Stat'i i materialy, Leningrad: Academia, 1928, 117 p. + M. Zoshchenko, Stat'i i materialy, Leningrad: Academia, 1928. 94 p. 21 cm.

Tomashevskii, Boris. Teoriia literatury [Theory of Literature]. 239 p. 23 cm.// Rpt. of B. Tomashevskii, Teoriia literatury; poetika, 4 izd., Moskva: Gos. izd-vo. 1928. 239 p. 23 cm.

Shklovskii, Viktor. O teorii prozy [On the Theory of Prose]. 265 p. 20 cm.// Rpt. of Viktor Shklovskii. Teorii prozy. Moskva: Izdatel'stvo "Federatsiia", 1929. 265 p. 20 cm.

1972

Akhmatova, Anna. Chetki [Rosary]. 120 p. 16 cm.// Rpt. of Anna Akhmatova, Chetki. Stikhi. Sankt Peterburg: Giperborei, (n.d.). 120 p. 15 cm.

Babel', Isaak. Bluzhdaiushchie zvezdy [Wandering Stars]. 80 p. 24 cm.// Rpt. of I. Babel', Bluzhdaiushchie zvezdy. Kino-stsenarii, Moskva: Kinopechat', 1926. 80 p. 24 cm.

Blok, Aleksandr. Dvenadtsat' [The Twelve]. 61 p. 32 cm.// Rpt. of Aleksandr Blok, Dvenadtsat'. Risunki Iu. Annenkova. Peterburg: Alkonost, 1918.

Vaginov, Konstantin. Puteshestvie v khaos [Journey into Chaos]. 29 p. 16 cm.// Rpt. of K. Vaginov, Puteshestvie v khaos. Peterburg: Izd. Kol'tsa Poetov, 1921. 29 p.

Kuzmin, Mikhail. Zanaveshennye kartinki [Covered Pictures]. 34 p. 26 cm.// Rpt. of M. A. Kuzmin. Zanaveshennye kartinki. Risunki Vladimira Milashevskago, Amsterdam (Peterburg: Petropolis), 1920.

Mandel'shtam, Osip. Tristia. 75 p. 16 cm.// Rpt. of O. Mandel'shtam. Tristia. Peterburg-Berlin: Petropolis, 1922.

Pasternak, Boris. Temy i variatsii [Themes and Variations]. 125 p. 16 cm.// Rpt. of Boris Pasternak. Temy i variatsii. Chetvertaia kniga stikhov. Moskva-Berlin: Knigoizdatel'stvo Gelikon, 1923. 125 p. 16 cm.

Tsvetaeva, Marina. Versty [Versts]. 121 p. 18 cm.// Rpt. of Marina Tsvetaeva. Versty. Vypusk 1, Moskva: Gosudarstvennoe izdatel'stvo, 1922. 121 p. 18 cm.

1973

Maiakovskii, Vladimir. Pro Eto [About That]. 43 p. 24 cm.// Rpt. of Pro Eto. (Ei i mne). Foto-montazh, oblozhki i illiustratsii konstruktivista Rodchenko, Moskva: Gos. izd-vo, 1923. 43 p. 24 cm.

1974

Nabokov, Vladimir. Mashen'ka [Mary]. 168 p. 19 cm. (Ardis and McGraw Hill).// Rpt. of V. Sirin. Mashen'ka, 168 p., 19 cm. Berlin: Slovo, 1926. 169 p. 19 cm.

Nabokov, Vladimir. Podvig [Glory]. 235 p. 18 cm. (Ardis and McGraw Hill). // Rpt. of V. Sirin. Podvig. Roman. Parizh: Sovremennye zapiski, 1932. 235 p. 20 cm.

1975

Gumilev, Nikolai. Ognennyi stolp [Pillar of Fire]. 73 p., 16 cm. // Rpt. of N. Gumilev, Ognennyi stolp. 2 izd. 73 p. 16 cm. Peterburg-Berlin: Petropolis, 1921. 73 p. 16 cm.

Zabolotskii, Nikolai, Stolbtsy [Scrolls]. 69 p. 19 cm. // Rpt. of N. Zabolotskii. Stolbtsy: stikhotvoreniia. Leningrad: Izd-vo pisatelei v Leningrade, 1929. 69 p. 19 cm.

Nabokov, Vladimir. Dar [The Gift]. 411 p. 23 cm. // Rpt. of V. Sirin. Dar. Roman v piati glavakh. 2-izd. N'iu-Iork: Izdatel'stvo im. Chekhova, 1952. 411 p. 22 cm.

Khodasevich, Vladislav. Tiazhelaia lira [The Heavy Lyre]. 60 p. 19 cm.// Rpt. of V. F. Khodasevich, Tiazhelaia lira: chetvertaia kniga stikhov, 1920-1922. 60 p. 19 cm. Moskva: Gos. izd-vo, 1922. 60 p. 19 cm.

1976

Akhmatova, Anna. Anno Domini MCMXXI. 101 p. 14 cm. // Rpt. of Anna Akhmatova, Anno Domini MCMXXI. Peterburg-Berlin: Petropolis, 1922. 101 p. 14 cm.

Bulgakov, Mikhail. D'iavoliada [Diaboliad]. 160 p. 19cm. // Rpt. of Mikhail Bulgakov. D'iavoliada; rasskazy. Moskva: Nedra, 1925. 160 p. 18 cm.

Zamiatin, Evgenii. Navodnenie [The Flood]. 67 p. 16 cm. // Rpt. of Evg. Zamiatin, Navodnenie. Risunki K. Rudakova, Leningrad: Izdatel'stvo pisatelei v Leningrade, 1930. 67 p. 18 cm.

Mandel'shtam, Osip. Egipetskaia marka [The Egyptian Stamp]. 187 p. 19 cm. // Rpt. of O. Mandel'shtam. Egipetskaia marka. Leningrad: Priboi, 1928. 187 p. 15 cm.

Nabokov, Vladimir. Vozvrashchenie Chorba [The Return of Chorb]. 205 p., 20 cm. // Rpt. of V. Sirin, Vozvrashchenie Chorba. Rasskazy i stikhi. Berlin: Slovo, 1930. 245 p. 21 cm.

Nabokov, Vladimir. Lolita. 304 p. 22 cm. // Rpt. of Vladimir Nabokov. Lolita. Roman. New York: Phaedra Publishers, 1967. 304 p. 22 cm.

Pasternak, Boris. Vozdushnye puti [Aerial Ways]. 139 p. 18 cm.// Rpt. of Boris Pasternak, Vozdushnye puti. Moskva: Gos. izd-vo khudozhestvennoi literatury, 1933. 139 p. 20 cm.

Pasternak, Boris. Sestra moia zhizn' [My Sister - My Life]. 115 p. 18 cm. // Rpt. of Boris Pasternak. Sestra moia zhizn': leto 1917 goda. Berlin-Peterburg-Moskva: Izd-vo Z.I. Grzhebina, 1923. 115 p. 20 cm.

Chukovskii, Kornei. Poet i palach [The Poet and the Hangman]. 48 p. 19 cm. // K. Chukovskii, Poet i palach: Nekrasov i Murav'ev, Peterburg: Epokha, 1922. 48 p. 24 cm.

1977

Akhmatova, Anna. Podorozhnik [Plantain]. 58 p. 12 cm. // Rpt. of Anna Akhmatova, Podorozhnik. Petrograd: Petropolis, 1921. 58 p. 12 cm.

Maiakovskii, Vladimir. Vladimir Maiakovskii. Tragediia [Vladimir Maiakovskii. Tragedy]. 44 p. 19 cm. // Rpt. of Vladimir Maiakovskii. Vladimir Maiakovskii. Tragediia v dvukh deistviiakh s prologom i epilogom. Risunki: Vladimir i David Burliuki, Moskva: Izd-vo Futuristov "Gileia," 1914.

Olesha, Iurii. Zavist' [Envy]. 141 p. 19 cm. // Rpt. of Iurii Olesha. Zavist'. Roman. S risunkami Natana Al'tmana, Moskva: Zemlia i fabrika, 1928. 141 p. 22 cm.

1978

Vaginov, Konstantin. Konstantin Vaginov. 57 p. 14 cm. // Rpt. of Konstantin Vaginov. Konstantin Vaginov. Stikhotvoreniia. Leningrad: Gublit, 1926. 57 p. 15 cm.

Zamiatin, Evgenii. Nechestivye rasskazy [Impious Tales]. 178 p. 18 cm. // Rpt. of Evg. Zamiatin. Nechestivye rasskazy. Moskva: Artel' pisatelei 'Krug', 1927. 178 p. 18 cm.

Kuzmin, Mikhail. Forel' razbivaet led [The Trout Breaks Through the Ice]. 93 p. 18 cm. // Rpt. of M. Kuzmin. Forel' razbivaet led. Stikhi. 1925-1928. Leningrad: Izdatel'stvo Pisatelei v Leningrade, 1929. 93 p. 19 cm.

Nabokov, Vladimir. Vesna v Fial'te [Spring in Fialta]. 313 p. 19 cm. // Rpt. of Vladimir Nabokov, Vesna v Fial'te i drugie rasskazy. N'iu Iork: Izd-vo imeni Chekhova, 1956. 313 p. 22 cm.

Nabokov, Vladimir. Drugie berega [Other Shores]. 268 p. 19 cm. // Rpt. of Vladimir Nabokov. Drugie berega, N'iu Iork, Izd-vo im. Chekhova, 1954. 268 p. 22 cm.

Nabokov, Vladimir, Kamera obskura. [Laughter in the Dark]. 203 p. 18 cm. // Rpt. of Vladimir Nabokov. Kamera obskura. Parizh: Sovremennie zapiski, 1932. 203 p. 20 cm.

Nabokov, Vladimir. Otchaianie [Despair]. 201 p. 18 cm. // Rpt. of V. Sirin, Otchaianie. Roman. Berlin: Petropolis, 1936. 201 p. 21 cm.

Nabokov, Vladimir. Sogliadatai [The Eye]. 252 p. 19 cm. // Rpt. of V. Sirin, Sogliadatai. Rasskazy. Parizh: Russkie zapiski, 1938. 252 p. 20 cm.

Strelets, No. 1 [The Archer]. 216 p. 22 cm. // Rpt. of Strelets. Sbornik pervyi. (Aleksandr Belenson, red.) Petrograd: Izd-vo "Strelets", 1915. 216 p. 25 cm.

Khlebnikov, Velimir. Zangezi. 35 p. 22 cm. // Rpt. of Velimir Khlebnikov, Zangezi, Moskva: Upr. OGES, 1922. 35 p. 25 cm.

Tsekh poetov, No. 1 [The Guild of Poets]. 89 p. 20 cm.// Rpt. of Tsekh poetov, ch. 1, Berlin: Izd-vo. S. Efron, 1922. 114 p. 19 cm.

Shestov, Lev. Nachala i kontsy [Beginnings and Ends]. 197 p. 20 cm. // Rpt. of Lev Shestov. Nachala i kontsy; sbornik statei. 197 p. 20 cm. S.-Peterburg, Tip. M.M. Stasiulevicha, 1908. 197 p. 20 cm.

1979

Akhmatova, Anna. Belaia staia [The White Flock]. 141 p. 16 cm. // Rpt. of Anna Akhmatova, Belaia staia. Stikhotvoreniia. Peterburg: Petropolis, Berlin: Alkonost, 1923. 141 p. 20 cm.

Belyi, Andrei. Serebrianyi golyb' [The Silver Dove]. 2 vols. in one. 299+245 p. 16 cm. // Rpt. of Andrei Belyi. Serebrianyi golub'. Roman, Berlin: Epokha, 1922. 2 vols. 20 cm.

Gazdanov, Gaito. Vecher u Kler [An Evening with Claire]. 188 p. 18 cm. // Rpt. of Gaito Gazdanov. Vecher u Kler. Roman. Parizh : Sovremennye Pisateli, 1930. 188 p. 19 cm.

Gumilev, Nikolai. Koster [Bonfire]. 59 p. 13 cm. // Rpt. of N. Gumilev. Koster. Stikhi. Berlin/Peterburg/Moskva: Izdatel'stvo Z. I. Grzhebina, 1922. 59 p. 15 cm.

Gumilev, Nikolai. K sinei zvezde [To a Blue Star]. 74 p. 14 cm. // Rpt. of N. Gumilev, K sinei zvezde. Neizdannye stikhi 1918 g. Berlin: Petropolis, 1923. 75 p. 14 cm.

Zamiatin, Evgenii. Ostrovitiane [The Islanders]. 260 p. 16 cm. // Rpt. of Evgenii Zamiatin. Ostrovitiane. Povesti i rasskazy. Berlin: Izd – vo Z.I. Grzhebina, 1922. 260 p. 20 cm.

Zoshchenko, Mikhail. Rasskazy [Stories]. 231 p. 16 cm. // Rpt. of Mikhail Zoshchenko, Rasskazy. 1921–1930. Leningrad/Moskva: Gosudarstvennoe izdatel'stvo khudozhestvennoi literatury, 1931. 231 p.

Kuzmin, Mikhail. Vozhatyi [The Guide]. 76 p. 16 cm. // Rpt. of Mikhail Kuzmin, Vozhatyi. Stikhi. Sankt Peterburg : Kn-vo Prometei, 1918. 74 p. 21 cm.

Kuzmin, Mikhail. Kryl'ia [Wings]. 119 p. 16 cm. // Rpt. of Mikhail Kuzmin. Kryl'ia : povest' v trekh chastiakh, Izd. 4. Berlin: Petropolis, 1923. 119 p. 16 cm.

Nabokov, Vladimir. Zashchita Luzhina [Luzhin's Defense]. 266 p. 18 cm. // Rpt. of Vladimir Nabokov (V. Sirin), Zashchita Luzhina. Roman. Paris: Éditions de la Seine, 1930. 266 p. 18 cm.

Nabokov, Vladimir. Korol', dama, valet [King, Queen, Knave]. 259 p. 19 cm. // Rpt. of V. Sirin, Korol', dama, valet. Roman. Berlin: Slovo, 1928. 259 p. 21 cm.

Nabokov, Vladimir. Priglashenie na kazn' [Invitation to a Beheading]. 218 p. 19 cm. // Rpt. of V. Sirin. Priglashenie na kazn'. Roman. 218 p. 19 cm. Parizh, Dom Knigi, 1938. 218 p. 19 cm.

Pil'niak, Boris. Golyi god [The Naked Year]. 155 p. 16 cm. // Rpt. of Boris Pil'niak. Golyi god. Roman, 155 p. 20 cm. Berlin : Izd-vo Z.I. Grzhebina, 1922. 155 p. 20 cm.

Pil'niak, Boris. Krasnoe derevo [Mahogany]. 76 p. 16 cm. // Rpt. of Bor. Pil'niak, Krasnoe derevo, 77 p. 20 cm. Berlin, Petropolis, 1929. 77 p. 20 cm.

Sobol', Andrei. Liubov' na Arbate [Love on the Arbat]. 134 p. 16 cm. // Rpt. of Andrei Sobol', Liubov' na Arbate. Moskva : Zemlia i fabrika, 1926. 134 p.

Sologub, Fedor. Melkii bes [The Petty Demon]. 342 p. 16 cm. // Rpt. of Fedor Sologub. Melkii bes. Roman. Berlin/Peterburg/Moskva: Izdatel'stvo A. I. Grzhebina, 1932. 342 p. 21 cm.

Tsvetaeva, Marina. Proza [Prose]. 410 p. 16 cm. // Rpt. of Marina Tsvetaeva. Proza. 410 p. 22 cm. N'iu-Iork : Izd-vo im. Chekhova, 1953.

1980

Begak, Boris, Nikolai Kravtsov, and Aleksandr Morozov. Russkaia literaturnaia parodiia. 259 p. 21 cm. // Rpt. of B. Begak, N. Kravtsov, A. Morozov, Russkaia literaturnaia pardoiia. Moskva: Gosudarstvennoe izdatel'stvo, 1930.

Evreinov, Nikolai. Samoe glavnoe [The Chief Thing]. 138 p. 21cm. // Rpt. of N. Evreinov, Samoe glavnoe. Dlia kogo komediia, a dlia kogo i drama, v 4 deistviiakh. Peterburg: Gosudarstvennoe izdatel'stvo, 1921. 138 p. 18 cm.

Ermakov, Ivan. Etiudy po psikhologii tvorchestva A. S. Pushkina [Studies in the Psychology of A.S. Pushkin's Creation]. 192 p. 21 cm. // Rpt. of Prof. Ivan Dmitrievich Ermakov, Etiudy po psikhologii tvorchestva A.S. Pushkina (Opyt organicheskogo ponimaniia "Domika v Kolomne," "Proroka" i malen'kikh tragedii). Moskva: Gosudarstvennoe izdatel'stvo, 1923. 192 p. 24 cm.

Ivanov, Viacheslav and Mikhail Gershenzon. Perepiska iz dvukh uglov [Correspondence Across a Room]. 62 p. 22 cm. // Rpt. of Viacheslav Ivanov i M. O. Gershenzon, Perepiska iz dvukh uglov, 62 p. 21 cm. Peterburg: Alkonost, 1921. 62 p. 21 cm.

1981

No reprints in 1981.

SELECTED BIBLIOGRAPHY

Alan, Josef, ed. *Alternativní kultura*. Prague, 2001.
Almond, Mark. *Decline Without Fall: Romania under Ceauşescu*. London, 1988.
Andreescu, Gabriel. *Spre o filozofie a disidenţei* [Towards a Philosophy of Dissent]. Bucharest, 1992.
Appiah, Kwame Anthony. *Cosmopolitanism: Ethics in a World of Strangers*. New York, 2006.
Arato, Andrew. "The Rise, Decline and Reconstruction of the Concept of Civil Society, and Directions for Future Research." In *Civil Society, Political Society, Democracy*, edited by Adolf Bibič and Gigi Graziano, 3–16. Ljubljana, 1994.
Autio-Sarasmo, Sari, and Brendan Humphreys, eds. *Winter Kept Us Warm: Cold War Interactions Reconsidered*. Helsinki, 2010.
Barańczak, Stanisław. "Goodbye, Samizdat." *Wilson Quarterly* 14, no. 2 (1990): 59–66.
Bauman, Zygmunt. *Globalization: The Human Consequences*. New York, 1998.
Behrends, Jan, and Friederike Kind. "Vom Untergrund in den Westen. Samizdat, Tamizdat und die Neuerfindung Mitteleuropas in den 80er Jahren." *Archiv für Sozialgeschichte* 45 (2005): 427–48.
Benda, Václav. "Parallel *Polis*, or An Independent Society in Central and Eastern Europe: An Inquiry." *Social Research* 55, nos. 1–2 (1988): 214–22.
Berman, Paul. *Terrorism and Liberalism*. New York, 2004.
Bernhard, Michael. *The Origins of Democratization in Poland*. New York, 1993.
Beyrau, Dietrich, and Ivo Bock. "Samisdat in Osteuropa Und Tschechische Schreibmaschinen-Kultur," *Bohemia* 29, no. 2 (1988): 280–99.
Bolton, Jonathan. *Worlds of Dissent*. Cambridge, 2012.
Borowska, Maria, and Jakub Święcicki, eds. *Kamp för demokrati. Artiklar och ställningstaganden från den polska demokratiska rörelsen*. Stockholm, 1979.
Boyer, Dominic. "Censorship as a Vocation: The Institutions, Practices, and Cultural Logic of Media Control in the German Democratic Republic." *Comparative Studies in Society and History* 45, no. 3 (2003): 511–45.
Boyle, Deirdre. *Subject to Change: Guerrilla Television Revisited*. New York, 1997.
Boym, Svetlana. *The Future of Nostalgia*. New York, 2001.
Bozoki, Andras. *Intellectuals and Politics in Central Europe*. Budapest, 1999.

Bren, Paulina. *The Greengrocer and his TV: The Culture of Communism after the 1968 Prague Spring.* Ithaca, 2010.
Buell, William A. "Radio Free Europe/Radio Liberty in the Mid 1980s." In *Western Broadcasting Over the Iron Curtain*, edited by K. R. M. Short, 69–97. London, 1986.
Carr, Nicholas. "The Amorality of Web 2.0." *Rough Type: Nicholas Carr's Blog.* 3 October 2005. http://roughtype.com/archives/2005/10/the_amorality_o.php.
Cartea Albă a Securității: Istorii literare si artistice, 1969–1989 [The White Book of the Securitate: Literary and Artistic Stories, 1969–1989]. Bucharest, 1996.
Cohen, Jean L., and Andrew Arato. *Civil Society and Political Theory.* 4th ed. Cambridge, 1994.
Coll, Steve. *Ghost Wars: The Secret History of the CIA, Afghanistan, bin Laden, from the Soviet Invasion to September 10, 2001.* New York, 2004.
Collin, Matthew. *This is Serbia Calling: Rock 'n' Roll Radio and Belgrade's Underground Resistance.* London, 2004.
Critchlow, James. *Radio Hole-in-the-Head: Radio Liberty. An Insider's Story of Cold War Broadcasting.* Washington, 1995.
Deletant, Dennis. *Ceaușescu and the Securitate: Coercion and Dissent in Romania, 1965–1989.* London, 1995.
Diehl, Jackson. "VCRs on Fast Forward in Eastern Europe." *The Washington Post.* 17 April 1988 (Special).
Doria, Charles, ed. *Russian Samizdat Art: Essays by John E. Bowlt, Szymon Bojko, Rimma and Valery Gerlovin.* New York, 1988.
Eisenstein, Elizabeth. *The Printing Press as an Agent of Change: Communication and Cultural Transformations in Early-Modern Europe.* 2 vols. Cambridge, 1979.
Ekiert, Grzegorz, and Jan Kubik, eds. *Rebellious Civil Society: Popular Protest and Democratic Consolidation in Poland, 1989–1993.* Ann Arbor, 2001.
Falk, Barbara J. *The Dilemmas of Dissidence in East-Central Europe: Citizen Intellectuals and Philosopher Kings.* Budapest, 2003.
Feldbrugge, F. J. M. "New Sources of Information on the Soviet Union and their Impact on East-West Relations." *Co-Existence* 13, no. 2 (1976): 209–20.
Feldman, Gayle. "Poland's Underground Publishing Surfaces, Seeks International Help." *Publishers Weekly* 237, no. 2 (1990): 28–29.
The Future of Samizdat: Significance and Prospects, transcript of conference held in London, by Radio Liberty. Committee, April 23, 1971, HIA RFE/RL Corporate Records, 1–47, Sheet 4–5.
Friedman, Thomas. *The Lexus and the Olive Tree.* New York, 2000.
Frumkin, Vladimir. "Liberating the Tone of Russian Speech: Reflections on Soviet Magnitizdat." In *The Soviet Union and the Challenge of the Future. Vol. 3: Ideology, Culture, and Nationality,* edited by Alexander Shtromas and Morton A. Kaplan, 277–98. New York, 1989.
Garton Ash, Timothy. *The Magic Lantern: The Revolution of 1989 Witnessed in Warsaw, Budapest, Berlin, and Prague.* New York, 1990.
———. *The Uses of Adversity: Essays on the Fate of Central Europe.* New York, 1989.
———. *The Polish Revolution: Solidarity, 1980–82.* New York, 1984.
Gilfillan, Daniel. *Pieces of Sound: German Experimental Radio.* Minneapolis, 2009.

Girnius, Kestutis K. "The Opposition Movement in Postwar Lithuania." *Journal of Baltic Studies* 13, no. 1 (1982): 66–73.
Giurescu, Dinu C. *The Razing of Romania's Past*. Washington, 1989.
Glenny, Misha. *The Balkans: Nationalism, War, and the Great Powers, 1804–1999*. New York, 2000.
Goetz-Stankiewicz, Marketa, and Timothy Garton Ash. *Good-Bye, Samizdat: Twenty Years of Czechoslovak Underground Writing*. Evanston, 1992.
Gorny, Eugene. *A Creative History of the Russian Internet: Studies in Internet Creativity*. Saarbrücken, 2009.
Grundmann, Heidi. "But is it Radio?" In *Anarchitexts: Voices from the Global Digital Resistance: A Subsol Anthology*, edited by Joanne Richardson, 157–64. New York, 2003.
Habermas, Jürgen: *The Structural Transformation of the Public Sphere: An Inquiry into a Category of Bourgeois Society*. Translated by Thomas Burger. Cambridge, 1991.
Havel, Václav. "Address to a Joint Session of the United States Congress." In *After the Velvet Revolution: The New Leaders Of Czechoslovakia Speak Out*, edited by Tim Whipple. New York, 1991.
———. *Open Letters: Selected Writings*, 1965–1990, selected and edited by Paul Wilson. Vintage, 1992.
Hawthorne, Amy. "Is Civil Society the Answer?" In *Uncharted Journey: Promoting Democracy in the Middle East*, edited by Thomas Carothers and Marina Ottaway, 81–114. Washington, 2005.
Hill, Cissie Dore. "Voices of Hope: The Story of Radio Free Europe and Radio Liberty." *Hoover Digest* 4 (2001).
Hirt, Günter, and Sascha Wonders, eds. [Pseudonym: Witte, Georg / Hänsgen, Sabine]. *Präprintium: Moskauer Bücher aus dem Samizdat*. Bremen, 1998.
Hoffman, Stefani. "Jewish Samizdat and the Rise of Jewish National Consciousness." In *Jewish Culture and Identity in the Soviet Union*, edited by Yaacov Roi and Avi Beker, 88–111. New York, 1991.
Hughes, H. Stuart. *Sophisticated Rebels: The Political Culture of European Dissent, 1968–1987*. Cambridge, 1988.
Human Rights Watch. *False Freedom: Online Censorship in the Middle East and North Africa*. November 2005, Volume 17, No. 10(E).
Janos, Andrew. *The Politics of the Borderlands from Pre- to Postcommunism*. Stanford, 2000.
Jirous, Ivan. "A Report on the Third Czech Musical Revival." Translated by Erich Dluhosch. In *Primary Documents: A Sourcebook for Eastern and Central European Art Since the 1950s*, edited by Laura Hoptman and Tomas Pospiszyl, 57–65. New York, 2002.
Johnston, Gordon. "What is the History of Samizdat?" *Social History* 24, no. 2 (1999): 115–33.
Kaplan, Caren. "Transporting the Subject: Technologies of Mobility and Location in an Era of Globalization." *PMLA* 117 (2002): 32–42.
Karpiński, Jakub. "The Difficult Return to Normality." *Uncaptive Minds* 3, no. 5 (1990): 24–26.
Keane, John. *Civil Society: Old Images, New Visions*. Stanford, 1998.

Kenney, Padraic. *A Carnival of Revolution: Central Europe 1989*. Princeton, 2003.

Klima, Ivan. "The Unexpected Merits of Oppression." *Nation* 250, no. 22 (1990): 769–73.

Komar, Vitaly, and Alex Melamid. "The Barren Flowers of Evil." *Art Forum* (March 1980): 46.

Komaromi, Ann. "Samizdat and Soviet Dissident Publics." *Slavic Review* 71, no. 1 (2012): 70–90.

———. "Samizdat as Extra-Gutenberg Phenomenon." *Poetics Today* 29, no. 4 (2009): 629–67.

———. "The Material Existence of Soviet Samizdat." *Slavic Review* 63, no. 3 (2004): 597–618.

Kristof, Nicholas D. "Death by a Thousand Blogs." *New York Times*. 24 May 2005.

Kuzio, Taras. "Unofficial Groups and Semi-Official Groups and Samizdat Publications in Ukraine." In *Echoes of Glasnost in Soviet Ukraine*, edited by Romana M. Bahry, 66–101. North York, 1990.

Lamont, Rosette C. "Horace's Heirs: Beyond Censorship in the Soviet Songs of the Magnitizdat." *World Literature Today* (Spring 1979): 220–27.

Ledeneva, Alena. *Russia's Economy of Favours: Blat, Networking and Informal Exchange*. Cambridge, 1998.

Lemon, Alaina. *Between Two Fires: Gypsy Performance and Romani Memory from Pushkin to Post-Socialism*. Durham, 2000.

Liehm, Antonín. *Closely Watched Films: The Czechoslovak Experience*. White Plains, 1974.

Lovink, Geert. *Dark Fiber: Tracking Critical Internet Culture*. Cambridge, MA, 2002.

Major, Patrick, and Rana Mitter, eds. *Across the Blocs: Cold War Cultural and Social History*. London, 2004.

Mamdani, Mahmood. *Good Muslim, Bad Muslim: America, the Cold War, and the Roots of Terror*. New York, 2004.

Matthews, John P. C. "The West's Secret Marshall Plan for the Mind." *The International Journal of Intelligence and CounterIntelligence* 16, no. 3 (2003): 409–27.

Mazower, Mark. *The Balkans: A Short History*. New York, 2002.

Meerson-Aksenov, Alexander, and Boris Shragin, eds. *The Political, Social and Religious Thought of Russian "Samizdat": An Anthology*. Translated by Nicholas Lupinin. Belmont, 1977.

Mianowicz, Tomasz. "Unofficial Publishing Lives on." *Index on Censorship* 12, no. 2 (1983): 24–25.

Michnik, Adam. *Letters from Prison and Other Essays*. Translated by M. Latynksi. Berkeley, 1985.

———. "Nowy Ewolucjonizm." In *Szanse polskiej Demokracji: Artykuły i eseje*, 77–87. London, 1984.

Mitchel, Tony. "Mixing Pop and Politics: Rock Music in Czechoslovakia before and after the Velvet Revolution." *Popular Music* 11, no. 2 (1992): 187–203.

Mitchell, Johnston M. "The Evolution of a Free Press in Hungary: 1986–1990." In *Revolutions for Freedom: The Mass Media in Eastern and Central Europe*, edited by Al Hester and L. Earle Reybold, 131–70. Athens, GA, 1991.

Morley, David. *Home Territories: Media, Mobility and Identity*. London, 2000.

Nichols, Mary Lewallen. "Soviet Literature as a Tool of Education, Gosizdat and tamizdat Writers: 1974–1984." PhD dissertation, Arizona State University, 1986.
Offe, Claus. *Varieties of Transition: The East European and East German Experience.* Cambridge, MA, 1997.
Oushakine, Serguei A. "The Terrifying Mimicry of Samizdat." *Public Culture* 13, no. 2 (2001): 191–214.
Parthé, Kathleen F. *Russia's Dangerous Texts: Politics Between the Lines.* New Haven, 2004.
Petrescu, Cristina. "Seven Faces of Dissent: A Micro Perspective on the Study of the Political (Sub)Cultures of under Communism." In *Political Culture and Cultural Politics*, edited by Alexandru Zub and Adrian Cioflâncă, 305–44. Iași, 2005.
Pilch, Janice T. "U.S. Copyright Relations with Central, East European, and Eurasian Nations in Historical Perspective." *Slavic Review* 65, no. 2 (Summer 2006): 325–48.
Pospielovsky, Dimitry S. "From *Gosizdat* to *samizdat* and *tamizdat*." *Canadian Slavonic Papers* 20 (1978): 44–62.
Powers, Samantha. *The Problem from Hell: America and the Age of Genocide.* New York, 2002.
Puddington, Arch. *Broadcasting Freedom: The Cold War Triumph of Radio Free Europe and Radio Liberty.* Lexington, 2000.
Renwick, Alan. "Anti-Political or Just Anti-Communist? Varieties of Dissidence and their Implications for the Development of Political Society." *East European Politics and Society*, 20, no. 2 (2006): 286–318.
Rocamora, Carol. *Acts of Courage: Vaclav Havel's Life in the Theater.* Hanover, 2004.
Rogers, Michael. "Censorship-Resistant Communication over Public Networks." University College of London, Department of Computer Science (2006). http://www.cs.ucl.ac.uk/staff/M.Rogers/transfer-report.pdf.
Roth, Philip. "A Conversation in Prague." *New York Review of Books* 37, no. 6 (1990): 14.
Ruoxi, Chen. *Democracy Wall and the Unofficial Journals.* Berkeley, 1982.
Rupnik, Jacques. "Les deux Printemps de 1968." *Études* 152 (May 2008): 585–92.
———. "From Democracy Fatigue to Populist Backlash." *Journal of Democracy* 18, no. 4 (October 2007): 17–26.
———. "Dissent in Poland, 1968–78: The End of Revisionism and the Rebirth of the Civil Society." In *Opposition in Eastern Europe*, edited by Rudolf L. Tökés, 60–112. London, 1979.
Said, Edward W. *Orientalism.* London, 2003.
———. *Covering Islam: How the Media and the Experts Determine How We See the Rest of the World.* New York, 1997.
Saunders, Frances Stonor. *The Cultural Cold War: The CIA and the World of Arts and Letters.* New York, 1999.
Scammel, Michael, ed. *Unofficial Art from the Soviet Union.* London, 1977.
Scanlan, James P. "From Samizdat to Perestroika: The Soviet Marxist Critique of Soviet Society." In *The Road to Disillusion: From critical Marxism to Post-Communism in Eastern Europe*, edited by Raymond Taras, 19–40. New York, 1992.

Schell, Jonathan. *Unconquerable World: Why Peaceful Protest is Stronger than War.* New York, 2003.

Schmidt, Henrike, Katy Teubener, and Nils Zurawski. "Virtual (Re)Unification? Diasporic Cultures on the Russian Internet" In *Control + Shift: Public and Private Usages of the Russian Internet,* 120–46. Norderstedt, 2006.

Schöpflin, George. *Politics in Eastern Europe 1945–1992.* Oxford, 1993.

Shafir, Michael. *Romania. Politics, Economics and Society: Political Stagnation and Simulated Change.* London, 1985.

Sharansky, Natan. "The Middle East needs its Helsinki." *International Herald Tribune,* 30 March 2004.

Silverstein, Michael. "Whorfianism and the Linguistic Imagination of Nationality." In *Regimes of Language: Ideologies, Polities, and Identities,* edited by P. V. Kroskrity, 85–138. Santa Fe, 2000.

Skilling, H. Gordon. *Samzidat and an Independent Society in Central and Eastern Europe.* Columbus, 1989.

Skilling, H. Gordon, and Paul Wilson, eds. *Civic Freedom in Central Europe: Voices From Czechoslovakia.* London, 1991.

———. "Samizdat: A Return to the Pre-Gutenberg Era?" *Cross Currents* 1 (1982): 64–80.

Smith, Gerald Stanton. *Songs to Seven Strings: Russian Guitar Poetry and Soviet "Mass Song."* Bloomington, 1984.

Soong, Roland. "Chinese Bloggers, Podcasters and Webcasters: A Comparison of the Relationship between Mainstream Media versus Blogging Culture in the United States, Hong Kong and China." *EastSouthWestNorth.* 18 September 2005.

Sosin, Gene. "Magnitizdat: Uncensored Songs of Dissent." In *Dissent in the USSR: Politics, Ideology, and People,* edited by Rudolf L. Tökés, 277–300. Baltimore, 1975.

Special Report: The Video Revolution in Eastern Europe. Radio Free Europe / Radio Liberty Soviet East European Report V. 2 (20 January 1988).

Staniszkis, Jadwiga, and Jan T. Gross, eds. *Poland's Self-Limiting Revolution.* Princeton, 1984.

Tamás, Gáspár Miklós. "Farewell to the Left." *East European Politics and Societies* 5, no. 1 (1991): 92–112.

Telesin, Julius. "Inside Samizdat." *Encounter* 40, no. 2 (1973): 25–33.

Tešanović, Jasmina. *The Diary of a Political Idiot: Normal Life in Belgrade.* San Francisco, 2000.

Thomas, Daniel C. *The Helsinki Effect: International Norms, Human Rights and the Demise of Communism.* Princeton, 2001.

Todorova, Maria. *Imagining the Balkans.* New York, 1997.

Tőkés, Rudolf L. *Hungary's Negotiated Revolution: Economic Reform, Social Change and Political Succession.* Cambridge, 1996.

———. *Dissent in the USSR: Politics, Ideology and People.* Baltimore, 1975.

Tolstoi, Ivan. *Otmytyi roman Pasternaka. "Doktor Zhivago" mezhdu KGB i TsRU.* [The Laundered Novel: Doctor Zhivago Between the KGB and the CIA.] Moscow, 2009.

Urban, George R. *Radio Free Europe and the Pursuit of Democracy: My War Within the Cold War.* New Haven, 1997.
Verdery, Katherine. *National Ideology Under Socialism: Identity and Cultural Politics in Ceausescu's Romania.* Berkeley, 1991.
———. *What Was Socialism, and What Comes Next?* Princeton, 1996.
Villaume, Poul, and Odd-Arne Westad, eds. *Perforating the Iron Curtain: European Détente, Transatlantic Relations, and the Cold War, 1965–1985.* Copenhagen, 2010.
Wagenleitner, Reinhold. *American Cultural Diplomacy, the Cinema and the Cold War in Central Europe.* Minneapolis, 1992.
Wolff, Larry. *Inventing Eastern Europe: The Map of Civilization on the Mind of the Enlightenment.* Stanford, 2004.
Yurchak, Alexei. "Gagarin and the Rave Kids: Transforming Power, Identity, and Aesthetics in the Post-Soviet Night Life." In *Consuming Russia: Popular Culture, Sex, and Society since Gorbachev,* edited by Adele Marie Barker, 76–109. Durham, 1999.
Zdravomyslova, Elena. "The Café Saigon Tusovka: One Segment of the Informal-public Sphere of Late-Soviet Society." In *Biographical Research in Eastern Europe: Altered Lives and Broken Biographies,* edited by Robin Humphrey, Robert Miller, and Elena Zdravomyslova, 141–77. Burlington, 2003.

Notes on Contributors

AGNES ARNDT (Potsdam) was recently (until Dec. 2011) a visiting fellow at ZZF. From 2004–2005, she was a researcher at the Wissenschaftszentrum Berlin für Sozialforschung. Her research focuses on contemporary European history, in particular on social, political, and discourse history in a transnational perspective. She has published a monograph, entitled *Intellektuelle in der Opposition: Diskurse zur Zivilgesellschaft in der Volksrepublik Polen* (Campus, 2007), and recently coedited the volume *Vergleichen, Verflechten, Verwirren? Europäische Geschichtsschreibung zwischen Theorie und Praxis* (with Joachim Häberlen and Christiane Reinecke; Vandenhoeck & Ruprecht, 2011).

MURIEL BLAIVE (Ludwig Boltzmann Institute, Vienna) is a sociopolitical historian of postwar and postcommunist Central Europe, in particular of Czechoslovakia and the Czech Republic. She is director of the Ludwig Boltzmann Institute for European History and Public Spheres in Vienna, Austria. She has recently coauthored the monograph *Grenzfälle: Österreichische und tschechische Erfahrungen am Eisernen Vorhang* (with Berthold Molden; Weitra, 2009) and coedited the volume *Clashes in European Memory: The Case of the Communist Repression and the Holocaust* (with Christian Gerbel and Thomas Lindenberger; Transaction Publishers, 2010).

BARBARA J. FALK (Canadian Forces College, Toronto) is associate professor in the Department of Defence Studies at the Canadian Forces College in Toronto, Canada, and the author of *Dilemmas of Dissidence* (CEU Press, 2003). She has recently published "From Berlin to Baghdad: Learning the Wrong Lessons from the Collapse of Communism," in *The Global 1989: Continuity and Change in World Politics 1989–2009* (Cambridge University Press, 2010) and an extensive survey of current trends in research on "dissent": "Resistance and Dissent in Central and Eastern Europe: An Emerging Historiography," *East European Politics & Societies* (May 2011). Her current research focuses on postwar political trials across the East-West divide.

DANIEL GILFILLAN (Arizona State University) is associate professor of German Studies at Arizona State University. His research focuses on twentieth-century literature, film, and media studies in the German-speaking sphere, with particular interests in avant-garde/experimental approaches to new forms of media in the past (radio, film) and the influence of these earlier instances of new media on contemporary artistic and cultural practices with telecommunications media. His first book, *Pieces of Sound: German Experimental Radio*, is available from the University of Minnesota Press.

MARTIN HALA (consultant, Prague) is a sinologist based in Prague and Hong Kong. Educated in Prague, Shanghai, Berkley, and Harvard, he has taught at universities in Prague and Bratislava and conducted research in China, Taiwan, and the United States. He was active in publishing both underground (before 1989) and mainstream (after), and worked for several media-assistance organizations in Europe and Asia, before becoming special advisor to the Open Society Institute in Asia. In addition to numerous articles and essays, Hala has coedited the full-length study *Investigative Journalism in China: Eight Cases in Chinese Watchdog Journalism* (with David Bandurski; Hong Kong University Press, 2010).

BRIAN HORNE (University of Chicago) is a doctoral candidate in the Department of Anthropology at the University of Chicago. His dissertation examines post-Soviet generational politics and Russian bardic music in Moscow. His research has been supported by the Wenner Gren Foundation for Anthropological Research and the School of Russian and Asian Studies. In addition to his work on Russian bardic song, Brian's research interests include the politics of affect, audio technologies, and music.

FRIEDERIKE KIND-KOVÁCS (Regensburg University) is assistant professor in the Department of Southeast and East European History at Regensburg University. She recently finished a monograph, entitled "Tamizdat Histories: Out of the Drawer and into the West." She has published articles on literary and cultural transfers during the Cold War, forced migration in post-war Europe and historical conceptions of Central Europe. A recent article on "(Re)joining the Community of Letters? The circulation of uncensored literature in/of Cold War Europe," appeared in *Ideas of/for Europe. An Interdisciplinary Approach to European Identity* (Peter Lang 2012). A forthcoming article deals with "Voices, Letters and Literature through the Iron Curtain: Exiles and the (trans)mission of radio in the Cold War" (*Cold War History* 2013). Currently she is working on her second monograph on child poverty and relief in Hungary between the World Wars.

ANN KOMAROMI (University of Toronto) is assistant professor at the Centre for Comparative Literature, University of Toronto. She has published a number of articles on Soviet samizdat and unofficial culture. Her article "Samizdat and Soviet Dissident Publics" (*Slavic Review,* 2012) analyzed information presented in the database of "Soviet Samizdat Periodicals" (http://samizdat.library.utoronto.ca, launched 2011).

JESSIE LABOV (Ohio State University) is assistant professor in the Department of Slavic and East European Languages and Literatures at The Ohio State University where she teaches classes on Polish literature, comparative Central European culture, and film/media studies. She is currently working on a monograph entitled *Transatlantic Central Europe* about the idea of Central Europe as it was reinvented in the 1980s by émigrés living in the West. Recently published articles include "*Leksikon Yu Mitologije*: Reading Yugoslavia from Abramović to Žmurke" in *Myth and History in Balkan Literature,* ed. Tatjana Aleksić (Cambridge Scholars Press, 2007), and "Genre and Intervention: Reflections on the Reception of *Neighbors* and *Fear* in Germany and Poland" in *Polish-German Post/Memory: Contesting Instrumentalizations of the Past in Contemporary Culture,* ed. Joanna Niżynska and Kristin Kopp (Palgrave McMillan, 2012).

THOMAS LINDENBERGER (Centre for Contemporary History Potsdam) is head of the department "Communism and Society" at the Centre for Contemporary History Potsdam and adjunct professor of history at the University of Potsdam, Germany. From 2009 to 2012 he was director of the Ludwig Boltzmann Institute for European History and Public Spheres in Vienna, Austria. His research interests include the history of the Cold War, police and violence, social and everyday history in the GDR, as well as mass media in contemporary history. His major publications include a number of monographs, edited volumes, and articles in these and other fields of contemporary history. His two most prominent works are *Volkspolizei. Herrschaftspraxis und öffentliche Ordnung im SED-Staat, 1952–1968* (Böhlau, 2003), and *Straßenpolitik. Zur Sozialgeschichte der öffentlichen Ordnung in Berlin, 1900–1914* (Dietz, 1995).

ALICE LOVEJOY (University of Minnesota) is assistant professor in the Department of Cultural Studies and Comparative Literature at the University of Minnesota, and a former editor at *Film Comment*. Her recent publications include "A Military Avant-Garde: Experimentation in the Czechoslovak Army Film Studio, 1967–1969" (*Screen*) and "From Ripples to Waves: Bazin in Eastern Europe" (*Opening Bazin: Postwar Film Theory and its Afterlife*), and she is currently writing a book about the Czechoslovak Army's film studio, 1935–1969.

VALENTINA PARISI received her PhD in the Department of Linguistics, Literature, and Philology at the University of Milan in 2005. In 2009 she was awarded a postdoctoral grant at the Institute of Advanced Studies for the Humanities in Florence. She is currently EURIAS junior fellow at the Central European University in Budapest. Her article "Contro Gutenberg: variazioni samizdat sul tema del libro d'artista" appeared in a special issue of *Progetto Grafico* dedicated to samizdat (November 2007); Parisi's edition of *Das Buch verlassen: Lev Rubinstejns Künstlerbücher* was also published by the Forschungsstelle Osteuropa at the University of Bremen (2007). Her book *The Exceeding Reader: Soviet Samizdat Literary Journals, 1956-1990* is forthcoming in Spring 2013, published by Il Mulino in Bologna.

CRISTINA PETRESCU (University of Bucharest) is lecturer at the Faculty of Political Science at the University of Bucharest. She received her PhD at the Central European University in Budapest, where her thesis was entitled "From Robin Hood to Don Quixote: Resistance and Dissent in Communist Romania." Her publications include articles on the history of communism in Central and Eastern Europe, nationalism, and ethnopolitics. She collaborated on the book project *Nation-Building and Contested Identities: Romanian and Hungarian Case Studies* (Regio Books, 2001). She also contributed to the international research project "Remembering Communism: Methodological and Practical Issues of Approaching the Recent Past in Eastern Europe," which was funded by the Volkswagen foundation.

JACQUES RUPNIK (Sciences Po Paris) is director of research at CERI, Sciences Po, in Paris, and professor at the College of Europe, Bruges, since 1999. Among many other academic honors, he has served as advisor to the president of the Czech Republic, Václav Havel (1990–1992) and advisor to the European Commission (2007–2010). He has published several books since: *Histoire du Parti Communiste Tchécoslovaque* (Fondation nationale des sciences politiques, 1981) and *The Other Europe* (Schocken, 1989); edited (among others) *International Perspectives on the Balkans* (2003), *Les Banlieues de l'Europe, les politiques de voisinage de l'UE* (2007), *The Western Balkans and the EU: The Hour of Europe* (EUISS, 2011), and *The World after 1989* (forthcoming).

HENRIKE SCHMIDT (Freie Universität, Berlin) is private lecturer at the Peter Szondi-Institute for Comparative Literature. Her research interests include theoretical issues of digital and networked culture and their significance for the societies of East and Central Europe, Russian, and Bulgarian literature (with a special focus on intermediality and genre theory). Among her recent publications is the monograph *Russian Literature on the Internet: Between Digital Folklore and Political Propaganda* (in German, Bielefeld, transcript 2011).

LARS FREDRIK STÖCKER (University of Tallinn) is currently working at the Institute of History at the University of Tallinn as a Mobilitas postdoctoral researcher. He received his PhD at the Department of History and Civilization at the European University Institute in Florence, where he defended his dissertation titled "Bridging the Baltic Sea: Networks of Resistance and Opposition during the Cold War Era." In his current research, he focuses on the cooperation between exile and homeland during the late perestroika years in the Estonian SSR. He is the author of "Eine transnationale Geschichte des geteilten Europa? Die Brückenfunktion des polnischen politischen Exils in Schweden 1968–1980," in *"Schleichwege": Inoffizielle Begegnungen sozialistischer Staatsbürger zwischen 1956 und 1989*, edited by Włodzimierz Borodziej et al. (Böhlau Verlag, 2010), and "Bridging the Baltic Sea in the Cold War Era: The Political Struggle of Estonian Émigrés in Sweden as a Case Study," in *The Baltic Sea Region and the Cold War*, edited by Olaf Mertelsmann and Kaarel Piirimäe (Peter Lang, 2012).

KAROLINA ZIOŁO-PUŻUK (Cardinal Stefan Wyszynski University, Warsaw) received her PhD at the Department of Russian and Slavonic Studies at the University of Sheffield. She has been very active in Polish language pedagogy, and has developed an online course for advanced speakers of Polish sponsored by the Centre for East European Language-Based Area Studies. Recent publications include: "From Internationalism to the European Union: An Ideological Change in the Polish Post-Communist Party?" *Communist and Post-Communist Studies* 42 (2009); "Wajda's *Man of Marble's* struggle with censorship" *eSharp* Special Issue: New Waves and New Cinemas (2009); and "The Opposition Movement and Writers—A Difficult Co-Existence: The Polish Writers' Union in the 1970s and 1980s," in *Writing under Socialism*, edited by Meesha Nehru and Sara Jones (Critical, Cultural and Communications Press, Studies in post-conflict cultures, No. 7, 2011); and publications in Polish on the use of new technologies in the second language classroom.

INDEX

A
Abu Ghraib, 330
Acmeism (Acmeist), 36
Ad Marginem, 229
aesthetics, 6, 15, 177, 181, 187, 207, 212, 221, 225–27, 233
Agha-Soltan, Neda, 293
Agora (Romanian tamizdat journal), 13, 124,
Aizenberg, Mikhail, 41,
A-Ja, 15, 190–201,
Akhmatova, Anna, 35, 37–38, 41, 44, 47, 95
Aksenov, Vasilii, 39
Al Arabiya, 300
Al Jazeera, 300
Alexander Herzen Foundation (Amsterdam), 190
Alkonost, 36
Al-Qaeda, 308
alternative culture, 1–2, 4–5, 8, 11, 14, 108–9, 124, 126, 191
alternative media, 11, 15, 206, 211–12, 228, 246
alternative public sphere, 15, 223, 234, 265
Amalrik, Andrei, 85
Amnesty International, 296, 298, 323. *See also* human rights
Anderson, Lisa, 296,
Aneks (Polish tamizdat journal), 56–57, 59–60, 160
Angeli, Claude, 81

Animal Farm, 74
Ann Arbor, 28, 40, 47
anti-Semitism, 226
apartheid, 306, 310n20
Arab Spring ("Arab Spring"), 17, 282, 287, 289, 297, 306–7. *See also* Middle East
Arato, Andrew, 14, 163, 165–66
Ardis Publishing (Ardis publishers), 12, 27–31, 33–47, 199
Arzhak, Nikolai, 93
Ash, Timothy Garton, 92, 115, 159
Asocijacije nezavisnih elektroniskih medija (ANEM), 246
Association of Independent Electronic Media. *See* Asocijacije nezavisnih elektroniskih medija (ANEM)
Atatürk, Mustafa Kemal, 302
Austen, Jane, 33
avtorskaia pesnia, 14, 176

B
Baltic Sea, 54–57, 60–61, 65
Barańczak, Stanisław, 4, 102
bardic song (*bardovskaia pesnia*), (names for bardic song and related genres), 176–81, 183–84, 186
Bauman, Charles, 182
Bauman, Zygmunt, 256, 257
BBC, 70, 79, 81, 115, 273, 299, 323
BBS (electronic bulletin boards and online forums), 263–64, 276

Beatles, 81
Bednar, Miroslav, 327
Beijing Spring (Chinese samizdat journal), 267–68
Beilin, Yossi, 290
Belgrade (bombing of), 245, 254–56, 259
Benatov, Joseph, 7
Bence, György, 322
Benda, Václav, 146, 211, 213–15, 285, 297, 328
Beneš, Edvard, 143–44
Beszélő (Hungarian samizdat journal), 322
Beuys, Joseph, 197–98
biblioteke samizdata, 83
Bin Laden, Osama, 308
Birger, Boris, 34
Bitov, Andrei, 38, 225
blat, 183–84
blog(s), 11, 16, 235–37, 245, 253, 263–64, 272–77, 293, 298. *See also* Twitter
  bloggers, 17, 232, 273–74, 292, 295, 298
  blogosphere, 17, 231–32, 234, 264, 273, 276–77, 283
Blok, Aleksandr, 36, 196
Bobbio, Noberto, 163–64, 167
Boiter, Albert, 80, 83–84
Bosnian War, 245
Brecht, Bertolt, 249
Brezhnev doctrine, 158, 320
Brezhnev, Leonid, 193, 320
Briggs, Charles 182
broadband, 263
broadcasting. *See* radio broadcasting
Brodsky, Joseph, 29, 33–34
Bulatov, Erik, 198–99
Bulgakov, Mikhail, 34, 40
Bulgaria, 71, 74, 148
Bush, George W. (Bush administration), 282, 304, 306, 329
Bykov, Dmitrij, 226

C
Cangeopol, Liviu, 123–25
Carter, Jimmy, 322

Carter, Sebastian, 43
Ceaușescu, Nicolae, 108–14, 120–21, 123, 125
  cult of personality, 109, 116
  cultural policy under, 119
  and nationalism, 113–14, 116
censorship
  anti-censorship, 78, 118–19, 176, 179–80
  and book distribution across the Iron Curtain, 86
  and glasnost, 118
  of information in Poland, 101
  and the internet, 221–23, 230, 233, 270–76, 278, 298
  liberation from, 176
  music and, 176, 178, 179
  and non-communist broadcasting, 139, 323
  policies of, 52, 63
  political narrative about, 31, 180, 186
  post-1989, 11
  in post-1989 China, 264–65, 267–78
  post-Soviet digital samizdat and, 227–30, 232–35
  in Romania, 118
  and samizdat/tamizdat, 3
  self-censorship, 179, 228, 265, 270, 277–78
  in the Soviet Union, 44–45
  and underground media, 15–16
Central (and Eastern) Europe
  boundaries and barriers of, 10, 12
  and civil society, 156–58, 163, 165–67, 282, 285, 288
  and communist regimes and societies, 51, 52, 288, 300
  dissidence/dissidents in, 109–10, 116, 282, 284, 317, 318, 322, 326
  dissident networks in, 160, 322
  and dissidents' nonviolence, 285, 286, 289
  erosion of communism and transformation in, 53, 163, 165, 290, 307, 316, 320
  émigré journals from, 96–97, 102, 323
  exiles from, 53, 323

human rights movement in, 320, 324, 330
idea of, 214, 324, 327
intellectuals in, 290, 327
during interwar period, 143
and the Middle East, 286, 287, 291, 293, 300–1, 303, 306–8, 329, 330
post-1989 relations to Eastern Europe, 87, 92, 93
return to Europe, 322
compared to Romania, 110, 115–17, 120, 122, 124, 126
and samizdat/tamizdat, 4–5, 52, 138, 265, 268, 292, 293
as satellite states, 138, 301
show trials in, 149
and socialism, 161, 287
Western correspondents to, 75
Charter 08, 316–17
Charter 77 (Czechoslovakia), 15, 111, 116, 207–8, 210–11, 215, 316–17, 319, 321–25, 327, 330
China, 11, 17, 53, 234, 263–65, 267–77
dissent in, 265–66
Chinese Civil War (1946–1949), 266
Chojecki, Mirosław, 69n79, 100–1
Chronicle of Current Events (Soviet samizdat journal), 80, 98, 190
CIA, 39, 46, 72–73, 83, 140–41, 293, 300
Citizens' Movement for Democratic Action (ROAD), 318
Civic Forum, 317–19
civil rights, 317
civil society, 7, 14, 17, 120, 145, 156–59, 162–68, 282, 284–86, 288–91, 294, 301, 306, 317, 323, 326, 328
społeczeństwo obywatelskie, 160
Cohen, Jean, 164
Cold War
binary image/narrative/historiography of, 1, 7, 19, 27, 31, 52, 53, 70, 107, 138–39, 180, 186
and censorship, 11, 31, 186
"cold-warriors," 328
collection of materials during, 5
and cross-border contact, 2, 7, 51, 52–53, 64, 73, 137, 142, 157, 180
geography, 214

and globalization, 268
and the Global War on Terror, 282, 305–6
and human rights, 322
lessons/legacy of, 282, 299, 305
magnitizdat during, 176–77
and the Middle East, 288, 305
neutral states, 54
new history of, 53
politics, studies and scholarship, 2, 8, 12, 14, 34, 53, 181
and post-Cold War period, 11, 328, 330
publishing during, 2, 3
radio broadcasting during, 12, 55, 70–72, 245, 259
and samizdat/tamizdat, 4, 7, 14–16, 28, 34, 46, 107
collaboration, 121, 124, 151, 259
collectivization (of agriculture), 144
commercialization, 224, 227–28, 234
Communism
anti-communism, 144
and capitalism, 139, 282
and Charter, 77, 324
Chinese, 265, 269, 175–76
communist authorities, 114, 140, 319
communist Party, 109, 113, 125, 147, 151, 207, 269
criticism of/opposition to, 109, 110, 112, 117, 121–24, 138, 286, 303
erosion/fall of, 53, 92, 109–10, 116, 122, 124, 140, 142, 214, 286, 303, 306, 321
and everyday life, 124, 144
human rights during, 321
internalization of, 123, 162
and internet culture, 226, 275–76
making of, 145–46, 151, 160
Problems of Communism, 140
reforming (belief in reforming), 121, 144, 150–51, 160–61, 319
repression under, 326
in Romania, 107–13, 116–17, 121–25
and samizdat/tamizdat, 109, 117, 121–24
versus "socialism with a human face," 145

and totalitarianism, 7
Western perception of, 322
conceptual art, 8, 192–93, 197
Congress for Cultural Freedom, 140
copyright/copyright violations, 44–45, 65, 225–26, 232
Cornea, Doina, 122, 125
Council for a Free Czechoslovakia, 86
Cuban Missile Crisis, 282
Cultural Cold War, 10, 70
Cultural Revolution, 50, 119, 265–67, 277–78
cultural memory, 5
cyberculture, 226
Czapski, Józef, 95–97, 102
Czechoslovakia
   Charter 77, 15, 111, 116, 207–8, 210–11, 215, 316–17, 319, 321–25, 327, 330
   Council for a Free Czechoslovakia, 86
   Dienstbier, Jiří, 317
   dissidents and dissident activity in, 79, 146, 207–11, 208–9, 211–12, 214
   Dubček, Alexander, 146
   exiles and émigrés from, 208
   Gottwald, Klement, 141–45, 147
   Horáková, Milada (Czechoslovak show trial), 148
   Hungarian minority in, 111
   Klaus, Václav, 318–20
   Klíma, Ivan, 297
   Liehm, Antonín, 146
   Listy, 323
   living-room theater in, 210
   normalization in, 206, 210
   Plastic People of the Universe, 186–87, 207
   Prague Spring, 14, 146
   RFE in Czechoslovakia, 71, 141, 213
   samizdat in. *See* samizdat
   show-trials in, 145, 146, 148, 149
   Socialism with a Human Face Soviet invasion in 1968, 99, 113, 212
   Stalinism in, 137–39, 143–51
   Svědectví, 323
   tamizdat from. *See* tamizdat
   Tigrid, Pavel, 142, 323
   transatlantic relations, 86
   transnational intellectual community in, 115–17, 121, 214
   unofficial film in, 206–11
   Václav Havel, 121, 146, 208–9, 283, 285–86, 297, 316–20, 322, 324–29
   official media in, 213–14
   Vaculík, Ludvík, 146, 297
   Velvet Revolution (Czechoslovakia 1989), 209, 210, 215
   Videomagazín, 15, 206–15

D

Daniel, Yuli, 52, 93
dazibao, 17, 266, 277
de-Stalinization, 140, 157, 161
de Tocqueville, Alexis, 164
Delicyn, Leonid, 230
Democracy Wall Movement, 267
democratic opposition, 51, 61–64, 92, 98, 157, 159, 163, 282, 318, 322
Den Xiaoping, 267–68
Derrida, Jacques, 328
détente, 51, 54–55, 57, 64, 86–87, 167, 282, 320, 322–23
diaspora, 12, 54, 56–57, 62, 94, 107, 120, 125, 222, 227, 290, 293–94, 307
Dienstbier, Jiří, 317
diffusion, 1, 7–9, 108, 115, 210, 291
digital samizdat, 221, 225, 228–29, 231, 234
dissent
   and broadcasting, 80, 141, 250
   Central and Eastern European, 57, 300–1, 316–21
   Chinese, 265–66
   communities of, 285
   concept of, 1, 283
   and filmmaking, 207
   legacy of, 297, 316–21, 323–25, 328–31
   Middle Eastern, 288, 290, 292, 298–301
   non-violent, 290
   political, 208
   in Romania, 13, 107–17, 119, 122–24
   songs of, 180, 182, 185

western perception of, 83
dissidents
  against East-West divide, 284
  broadcasting impact on, 82
  of Charter 08, 317
  contribution to the fall of communism, 117, 321–31
  Czechoslovak, 208–9, 211–12, 214
  dissident movement and community, 98, 110, 114, 209, 283–84
  during the transition, 317–20
  and exiles, 13
  heroic narrative of, 2, 7, 115, 283, 317
  and human rights, 158
  Hungarian dissidents in Romania, 111
  and the internet, 298
  liberal, 287, 297, 299, 307
  Middle Eastern, 287, 295, 296, 297
  networks of, 12, 113
  and opposition, 283
  Polish, 167
  Romanian, 107–8, 112, 113, 116, 120–21, 123
  Russian, 13–15, 98, 176, 180
  samizdat/tamizdat production by, 115, 117, 125
  transatlantic contact to, 33, 113, 114, 115
  transnational meetings of, 214
distortion, 7, 9, 63, 184, 186
Djilas, Milovan, 74, 76
Doctor Zhivago, 46, 74–75
documentary, 15, 116, 193, 207, 209–10, 212, 214, 215, 249, 252
Dodze, Koci (Albanian show trial), 148
drugi obieg, 52, 62
Dubček, Alexander, 146
Ducháček, Ivo, 142–43
Dugin, Aleksandr, 226

E
East Germany, 53, 116
East German Uprising (June 17th 1953), 116, 141

East-West (intellectual exchanges), 77, 115, 138, 284
Eastern Bloc, 3, 39, 70, 74, 81–82, 107, 138, 140, 144, 149, 150
Eastern Europe, 1–2, 16–17, 51–53, 73–76, 96–98, 137, 139, 146, 156, 159–65, 265, 268–69, 276–78, 282–84, 286–88, 291–93, 306–7, 320, 322–24, 327
Ebadi, Shirin, 296
Egypt, 289–90, 293, 295–96, 298–99, 302, 305
Eidlin, Fred, 147
electronic media, 176, 229, 246
émigrés and exiles
  comparison between Britain and Sweden, 56, 62
  and couriers of samizdat, 60
  as cultural translators, 63, 65
  and domestic opposition, 53–54, 63, 64, 65, 74, 78, 162
  and emigration to Paris, 14, 92, 95, 100
  and Helsinki process, 323
  impact of Prague Spring on, 139
  Iranian, 297
  literature, 54, 57, 73, 75–77, 139, 151, 156–57, 160, 163, 167, 323
  and local society, 63, 78, 82
  after Martial Law, 100
  from Poland in Sweden, 51–52, 55
  Polish, 12, 52, 55–56, 59–64, 74, 78, 100, 162
  as recipients of samizdat, 61
  Russian, 13, 185, 190
  and samizdat, 59, 82
  and their vision of the Cold War, 142–44
  and Western broadcasting, 58, 73
Emmanuel, Pierre, 323
Europe, 2, 7, 10, 17, 30, 51, 53–54, 64, 70–72, 86–87, 94, 114, 122, 156–57, 159, 161, 163, 166, 168, 194, 196, 245, 253, 283, 285, 288, 316, 321, 324–31
  Captured Europe, 10
  common market, 327, 331
  return to Europe, 284, 322

exiles. *See* émigrés and exiles
Explorations (Chinese samizdat journal), 267

F
Facebook, 236, 263, 292, 298–99
Fall of Communism (1989), 53, 103, 209–10, 215, 317, 328–30
    path towards 1989, 122, 125, 156–57, 165–71, 206–7, 269, 321
    post-1989 legacy of dissent, 297, 316–21, 328, 330
    post-1989 media, 5, 11–13, 97, 245–46
    post-1989 opening of archives, 138, 147–48, 151–52
    post-1989 political developments, 93, 122
    post-1989 samizdat, 16–17, 245–46
    in Romania, 107–09, 116–117, 119, 122
    Velvet Revolution (Czechoslovakia 1989), 209, 210, 215
Faure, Justine, 142
Feiwel, George, 146
Feldman, Noah, 281, 300, 302–3
Ferguson, Adam, 164
file-sharing, 225
film, 8, 15, 122, 182, 185, 206–9, 213, 215, 230, 276–77. *See also* YouTube
Fluxus, 197, 209
Formalism (Formalist), 36, 71
Fraser, Nancy, 235–36
Free Europe Committee (FEC), 73, 77, 78
Free Europe Press (FEP), 73
Freedom Union (Unia Wolności), 318
Frumkin, Vladimir, 180–81
Futurism, Russian, 30

G
Gal'kovskij, Dmitrij, 224–25
Galich, Aleksandr, 180–82
Garton Ash, Timothy, 92, 115, 159
Gaza, 288–90, 301, 305
Gazeta Wyborcza (Polish daily newspaper), 157
GDR. *See* East Germany

Gelikon, 229
Georges Pompidou Centre, 199
Ghandi, Mahatma (Gandhi), 284, 286, 297
Giedroyc, Jerzy, 13, 57, 59–61, 92–97, 99–103, 160–62, 323
Glazkov, Nikolaj, 227
Glezer, Aleksandr, 195, 200
Global War on Terror (GWOT), 282
globalization, 1, 19n2, 45, 137, 152, 247–48, 268–69, 283–84, 293, 298
Golden Shield (Chinese internet filtering system), 270
Goldstücker, Eduard, 146
Gombrowicz, Witold, 101
Google, 270–72
Gorbachev, Mikhail, 114, 116, 194
Gorbanevskaya, Natalya, 13, 95–102
Gornyj, Evgenij (Gorny, Eugene), 222, 225, 231
Gottwald, Klement, 141–45, 147
Gramsci, Antonio, 164, 167
graphomania, 227, 235–36
Graves, Don, 80
grey zone, 3–4, 290, 300
Groys, Boris, 192, 194–98
Grundmann, Heidi, 247–49
Guantanamo, 330
Gumilev, Nikolai, 35, 38
Gutenberg, 4, 9, 16, 43, 45–46

H
Habermas, Jürgen, 163, 235, 297, 328
Hájek, Jiří, 146
Hamas, 289–90, 305
Havel, Václav, 121, 146, 208–9, 283, 285–86, 297, 316–20, 322, 324–29
Hayward, Max, 81, 85
Hegel, Friedrich, 118, 164, 166–67, 283
Hejdánek, Ladislav, 297
Hejzlar, Zdeněk, 146
Held, David, 164
Helsinki Final Act. *See* human rights
Herling-Grudziński, Gustaw, 96, 101
Hollander, Gayle Durham, 80
Horáková, Milada (Czechoslovak show trial), 148

Hotel Örnsköld (Polish-Swedish tamizdat journal), 65
human rights
 and Charter 77, 111, 215, 319–21, 324–35
 in China, 270–71
 and civil society, 285, 306
 and dissent, 316, 328–30
 and East-West relations, 320–22
 groups and organizations, 4, 113, 209, 323, 330
 and Helsinki Final act, 114, 320–21
 and Helsinki process, 51, 58, 111, 114, 281–82, 284, 320–21
 and "Helsinki Effect," 321
 Human Rights Watch, 270, 296, 298, 323
 Human Rights Watch Shi Tao, 270, 273
 humanrightism, 318
 and internet, 298
 in Iran, 288, 291, 296, 305
 and Iraq War, 330
 League for the Defense of Human Rights (Romania), 123
 and "living in truth," 285
 in Middle East, 295, 301, 307
 and New Evolutionism (Adam Michnik), 158
 and *Original Videojournal*, 209, 215
 in Romania, 111
 and RFE/RL, 70, 80
 Ruch Obrony Praw Człowieka i Obywatela (Movement for Defense of Human and Civic Rights, ROPCiO), 58
 and samizdat, 80
 and "Third Basket" (Belgrade Conference, Madrid, Vienna), 321–22
 and Tharwa Foundation, 297
 violations of, 114
 Western intervention, 114
Hungary
 Beszélő, 322
 Civic Forum, 317–19
 Hungarian Revolution (1956), 111, 116, 142, 149–50, 157
 Hungarian dissidents in Romania, 111
 Kende, Peter, 323
 Kenedi, János, 322
 Kis, János, 286, 297, 322
 Magyar Füzetek, 160, 323
 samizdat in. *See* samizdat
 tamizdat from. *See* tamizdat
 Warsaw Pact invasion in 1956, 10, 71, 73, 77, 79, 115, 116, 117, 121, 143, 147–50, 157, 286, 318, 322, 330
Hussein, Saddam, 302–4

I
Ideological Commission of the Soviet Communist Party's Central Committee, 178
Illovayskaya, Irina, 100
Institut Literacki (The Literary Institute, Paris), 93–94, 97
intellectuals/intelligentsia
 and anti-Americanism, 329
 and book mailing, 75, 77, 78
 and the building of socialism, 144–46
 Catholic, 302
 and Charter 77, 319
 and civil society, 120, 156, 165–66
 contribution to the fall of communism, 316, 330
 discourses of, 77, 85, 86
 and émigrés, 160
 in Israel, 289
 and *Kultura*, 161–62
 and "living in truth," 325
 and magnitizdat, 179
 in the Middle East, 295–96, 300
 and new Russian samizdat, 224
 nonconformist, 108, 117, 123, 125–26, 160–63, 225, 327
 Polish, 14, 55–58, 62, 78, 98–99, 159, 160, 162–63, 166–67, 318, 324, 327
 protests of, 98
 repression of, 113, 115
 Romanian, 113, 115, 116, 123–26
 Russian, 35, 37
 and samizdat/tamizdat, 83–84, 126, 138
 self-criticism of Western, 164

Soviet, 32, 224–25
Stalinist, 145–46
on Stalinist terror in
   Czechoslovakia, 138–39
transnational network of, 72, 97,
   98–99, 159, 164, 290
Western, 3, 14, 62, 63, 86, 146–47,
   161–62, 164–5, 326, 329
and Western radio broadcasting, 73
intelligentsia. *See* intellectuals
Internet, 11, 16–17, 117, 126, 186, 221–37, 246–47, 249, 251–53, 257–58, 263–65, 268, 270–78, 283, 292–93, 298–300
Internet censorship. *See* censorship
Internet Content Providers (ICPs) (China), 270
Internet Samizdat, 227
Iran, 11, 288, 290–93, 296–300, 302, 305–7, 322
Iron Curtain, 1, 6, 10, 12–14, 51–54, 56, 58–65, 70–73, 79, 86–87, 108, 115, 120, 122, 138–39, 141–42, 144, 147, 151–52, 156, 162, 166, 245, 321, 327–28
Islam, 283, 286–87, 291–96, 299–303, 305–7
Islamofacism, 330
Israeli Defence Force (IDF), 289

J
Jaruzelski, Wojciech, 55, 322, 327
jazz music, 88n15, 179
Jirous, Ivan Martin, 215
Journalists, 60, 63, 81–83, 115–16, 119–20, 125, 191, 193, 250–51, 258, 269, 274–75, 295, 299–300
Jovanović, Arsenije (and *Concerto grosso balcanico*), 251
Judt, Tony, 329

K
Keane, John, 14, 164–67
Kende, Peter, 323
Kenedi, János, 322
Kenney, Padraic, 7, 287
KGB, 46, 95
Khalidi, Rashid, 290

Khatami, Mohammad, 292–93
Khodasevich, Vladislav, 40
Khomeini, Ayatollah, 299
Khronika Press (English-language version of *Chronicle of Current Events*), 80, 191
King, Martin Luther Jr., 286, 295, 297
Kireev, Oleg, 235
Kis, János, 286, 297, 322
Klaus, Václav, 318–20
Klein, Ansgar, 164–65
Klíma, Ivan, 297
Kocka, Jürgen (civil society), 159
Kołakowski, Leszek, 17, 163, 294, 306
Komar and Melamid, 202
Komitet Obrony Robotników (Workers' Defense Committee, KOR). *See* KOR
Konrád, György, 286, 297, 328–29
Kontakt (Polish tamizdat journal), 100–2
Kontinent (Russian tamizdat journal), 13, 92–102, 195–96
Kopelev, Lev, 34
KOR (Workers' Defense Committee), 58, 60, 62–63, 98, 102, 116, 285, 289, 321–22
Kostov, Traycho (Bulgarian show trial), 148
Kratochvil, Antonín, 145
Krivulin, Viktor, 191
Kultura (Polish tamizdat journal), 13, 56–57, 92–103, 160–63, 323
Kunstradio (Austrian radio program), 16, 246–50, 255, 259
Kuroń, Jacek, 58, 63, 286, 297, 322
Kuz'min, Dmitrij, 227
Kuznecov, Sergej, 224,
Kyncl, Karel, 15, 207–9

L
Labedz, Leopold, 72, 84–86
Le Nouvel Observateur, 81
Lefort, Claude, 163
Lemon, Alaina, 182
:LENIN: Anti-Cultural Weekly (Russian online "underground" journal), 225–26

Levi-Strauss, Claude, 31
Li Li (pseudonym Muzi Mei), 276
Li Zhi, 270
Libya, 286, 293, 301, 303, 305
Liehm, Antonín, 146
Lijun, Jian, 270
Listeners, 80–81, 83, 87, 184–85, 251, 253–54, 259
Listy (Czechoslovak tamizdat journal), 323
literary underground. *See* underground
lithography, 40, 43, 47
LiveJournal, 11, 232–32
living-room theater, 210
Locke, John, 164, 286
Lovink, Geert, 236, 252

M

magnitizdat, 8, 14–15, 175–77, 179–80, 182–87
Magyar Füzetek, 160, 323
Makarevich, Igor', 192–93
Maksimov, Vladimir, 13, 94–96, 98–102
Maksimovna Litvinova, Tatiana, 99
Malevich, Kazimir Severinovich, 198–99
Mandel'shtam, Nadezhda, 34
Mandel'shtam, Osip, 30, 34–35, 38, 45, 47
Mansour al Nogaidan, 295, 307
Mao Zedong, 266–67
Marković, Slobodan, 252–54
Marx, Karl, 118, 164, 167
Masaryk, Tomáš, 143
Mastný, Vojtěch, 142
Matić, Veran, 246, 250–51
Mauss, Marcel, 32
Maziarski, Wojciech, 102
McKinnon, Rebecca, 274, 276
McClellan, John, 44
media, 79, 82, 115, 120, 123, 140, 257, 273, 292, 323
Medvedev, Dmitrij, 235
memory. *See* cultural memory
Michnik, Adam, 17, 58, 63, 102, 157–63, 165, 167, 286, 295, 297, 301–2, 322, 328–29

Middle East, 17, 281, 283, 285–88, 291, 293–94, 296, 301, 303–4, 306–8
Mieroszewski, Juliusz, 101, 160, 161–63
Mietkowski, Andrzej, 100
Miller, Arthur, 323
Milošević, Slobodan, 16, 246, 251, 256, 257
Miłosz, Czesław, 76
Minden, George, 73
Mitchel, Tony, 187
Mitter, Rana, 7
Mlynar, Zdeněk, 163
Montand, Yves, 323
Morley, David, 257–58
Morozov, Evgenij, 236
Moscow Conceptual School, 201
Moškov, Maksim, 222
Mossadegh, Mohammed, 300
Moussavi, Hussein, 292–93
Mubarak, Hosni, 289, 305
Müller, Jiří, 297
Muslim World, 281, 287, 291, 306

N

Nagy, Imre, 148
National Committee for a Free Europe (NCFE), 73, 141
National Security Council (US), 142, 149
NATO
  and air attacks on Belgrade, 16, 245, 246, 251–57
  and "Commando Solo" aircraft, 250–51
  and operation "Allied Force," 245–46
Nehzat, Azadi, 291
Nejedlý, Zdeněk, 141
Neo-Positivism, 157, 163
Netanyahu, Benjamin, 306
networks, 1, 9–10, 12, 16, 51–52, 56–57, 61–62, 64, 113, 123, 126, 152, 163, 179, 184–85, 191, 210, 223, 235–36, 245, 247, 249–50, 253, 257–59, 293, 323, 328
neutrality, 54, 57, 64
New Evolutionism (Nowy Ewolucjonizm), 14, 17, 157–60, 162, 286

New York Times, 271, 277
News from Behind the Iron Curtain (NBIC), 139–41
NGOism, 318
Niezalezna Oficyna Wydawnicza (Independent Printing House, NOWa), 58, 60–61, 100
Nobel Peace Prize, 296
noise, 6, 183–85, 187, 251
nomenklatura, 287
nonconformist, 2, 8–10, 13, 16, 82, 105, 107–8, 117–18, 126, 192, 200, 226, 234–36
nonviolence, 17, 283–85, 288–89, 295–96
normalization, 146, 152, 206–7, 210
North Africa, 17, 287, 304, 308
NOWa (Independent Publishing House). *See* Niezalezna Oficyna Wydawnicza
NTS (Narodno-Trudovoi Soiuz, the Popular Workers' Union), 35
NTV, 175

O
O'Donnell, Guillermo, 163
ÖESK (Eastern European Solidarity Committee), 60, 62
official press, 12, 139, 142, 275
Okudzhava, Bulat, 177–78, 180–81
Oleszczuk, Thomas, 7
online publishing, 222, 265
opposition, 13, 15, 52, 55, 58, 61–63, 92, 98, 102–3, 157, 164, 294
Orbán, Viktor, 330
ORF, 16, 245–46, 248–49
orientalism, 284, 298
Original Videojournal (Czechoslovak samizdat video journal), 15, 206–15
Orłoś, Kazimierz, 99, 102
Orlova, Raisa, 46–47
Orwell, George, 74, 76
Oslo Accord, 293
Österreichischer Rundfunk (ORF) and *Kunstradio*, 16, 246–50, 255
Ostpolitik, 54
Other Voices—Echoes from a Warzone (radio project), 246–59

P
Pahlavi, Reza Shah, 299
Palme, Olof, 55
parallel polis, 15, 211, 215, 285, 300, 328
Pasternak, Boris, 44, 74, 82
Pastor (Russian tamizdat journal), 201
Patočka, Jan, 325–26
Paunović, Gordan, 16, 246–47, 249–53, 254–55, 257–59
peaceful coexistence, 282
Pełczyński, Zbigniew, 166–67
Pelikán, Jiří, 146, 323
PEN, 296
perestroika, 20, 121, 222, 229
performativity, 181
Peroutka, Ferdinand, 142
Person-To-Person Program, 73–74, 87
Petrescu, Dan, 120–26
phishing, 271–72
Pithart, Petr, 146, 149
Plastic People of the Universe (PPU), 186–87, 207
Płużański, Tadeusz, 166
Poland, 318, 324, 327
 anti-Semitic crackdown, 226
 Barańczak, Stanisław, 4, 102
 censorship of information in Poland, 101
 Chojecki, Mirosław, 100–1
 Czapski, Józef, 95–97, 102
 dissidents in, 167
 émigrés after Martial Law, 100
 émigrés from, 12, 52, 55–56, 59–64, 74, 78, 100, 162
 émigrés in Sweden, 51–52, 55
 Gazeta Wyborcza, 157
 Giedroyc, Jerzy, 13, 57, 59–61, 92–97, 99–103, 160–62, 323
 Herling-Grudziński, Gustaw, 96, 101
 human rights movement and New Evolutionism (Adam Michnik), 158
 Intellectuals in, 14, 55–58, 60, 62, 78, 98–99, 159, 160, 162–63, 166–67
 Kołakowski, Leszek, 17, 163, 294, 306

KOR (Workers' Defense Committee), 58, 60, 62–63, 98, 102, 116, 285, 289, 321–22
Kultura, 13, 56–57, 92–103, 160–63, 323
Kuroń, Jacek, 58, 63, 286, 297, 322
Michnik, Adam, 17, 58, 63, 102, 157–63, 165, 167, 286, 295, 297, 301–2, 322, 328–29
New Evolutionism (*Nowy Ewolucjonizm*), 14, 17, 157–60, 162, 286
Polish emigre journals, 13, 56, 93–94, 96, 98, 100–1
Polish government-in-exile, 55–56, 59
Polish October, 150, 290
Polish political refugees, 12, 55–56, 59
Polish-Russian relations, 92–96, 98
Polonia Book Fund, 73–76
Polonia, 55–56, 60
samizdat in. *See* samizdat
solidarity movement (Solidarność), 52, 60–61, 63–64, 116, 166, 290, 293, 322, 324
strikes in, 98–99, 116, 157
Studencki Komitet Solidarności (Students' Solidarity Committee), 60
tamizdat from. *See* tamizdat
Towarzystwo Przyjaciół "Kultury" (Society of the Friends of *Kultura*), 57
Wałęsa, Lech, 115
political asylum, 55
Polonia (Swedish-Polish tamizdat journal), 55–56, 60
Polonia Book Fund, 73–76
Popa, Ioana, 7
Pospielovsky, Dimitry, 4
Possev (Munich-based Russian tamizdat press), 35
Prague Spring, 113, 138–39, 144–47, 150–51, 319–20, 322
invasion of Czechoslovakia, 113, 116, 212, 301, 305, 319, 320, 322, 324

Pravda, 83
pre-Gutenberg, 4, 9, 16
press freedom, 15, 300
prison, 82, 95, 115, 159, 209, 230, 268, 271, 296
prisoners of war, 98
privacy, 272
Problems of Communism, 140
Proffer, Carl, 12, 17, 28–41, 44–47
Proffer, Ellendea, 12, 17, 28–41, 44–47
propaganda, 140, 225, 230, 235–36, 250, 256, 269, 276–78, 324
protests, 55, 57–58, 62, 98–99, 141–42, 209, 289, 292–93, 295, 299
public space, 184, 192, 248, 276, 278, 316, 320, 324, 331
public sphere, 13, 15, 52, 58, 61, 118–19, 156, 206–9, 211–12, 214–14, 223, 234–36, 265
Putin, Vladimir, 229, 230, 233, 235, 237

Q
Qatar, 290

R
Rabbo, Abed, 290
Rada Uchodźstwa Polskiego (Polish Refugee Council), 56
Radio B92, 16, 245–46, 250
Radio Free Europe (RFE), 10, 12, 55, 58, 70–73, 77, 79–84, 86–87, 115, 121, 123–25, 139–42
Radio Liberty, 10, 12, 70, 79–83, 93, 245, 298, 305
Radio Vatican, 79
radio broadcasting
  and alternative information spaces, 251
  anti-communist Western, 71–87, 115, 119–21, 126, 139, 141, 323
  and B92, 245–62
  and experimental points of access, 247
  and internet transmission, 247, 252
  across Iron Curtain, 70, 71, 115
  and jamming, 71
  as live media practice, 248–62
  and news about captive nations, 16

and pirate radio practices, 248
primary sources for, 140
and radiophonic space, 248
and samizdat/tamizdat practice, 6, 8, 9, 12, 71–87, 246, 259
and secret police, 123
as tactical medium, 246, 250–51
Voice of America (VOA)
Radom/Ursus riots, 285, 290
Rajk, László (Rajk trial), 147–48
Reagan, Ronald, 282
Red Guards, 267
refugees. *See* Poland, Polish Political Refugees
RenRen, 263
repression, (State repression), 112, 145, 147–51, 159, 291, 293, 299–301
reproduction technology, 178
resistance, 5, 9, 11–12, 16, 51–52, 58–59, 111–12, 116, 119, 125, 141–43, 150, 235–36, 245, 247, 285–86, 289–90, 292, 307, 318–19
Reve, Karel van het, 83
revisionism, 109, 157, 163
Ribbentrop-Molotov Pact, 95
Romania
  anti-Sovietism in, 110, 113–14
  censorship in, 118
  communism in, 107–13, 116–17, 121–25
  dissidence in, 115–17
  dissidents in, 107–8, 112, 113, 116, 120–21, 123
  exception in the Soviet bloc, 109
  and the Helsinki Accords, 114
  Hungarian minority in, 111
  and Orthodox influences, 110–12
  resistance in the mountains, 111–12
  resistance through culture, 119
  samizdat in. *See* samizdat
  tamizdat from. *See* tamizdat
  See also Ceaușescu, Nicolae
  See also Securitate
Ruch Obrony Praw Człowieka i Obywatela (ROPCiO, Movement for Defense of Human and Civic Rights), 58
RuNet, 222–25, 228, 230, 233–36

Rupnik, Jacques, 16, 145, 147, 165, 316–31
Russia, 7, 10, 17, 33, 37, 81–83, 85, 92–96, 98–99, 156, 176, 178, 181–82, 195, 222, 226, 228–31, 233–37, 298
Russian unofficial art, 15, 190, 196–97
Russkaya Mysl (Russian tamizdat journal), 100

S

Samizdat Review, 82
samizdat (self-publishing)
  aesthetics of tamizdat and, 6, 9
  as alternative culture, 2, 4, 14, 109, 199, 283
  archival collection of, 5, 18
  biblioteke samizdata, 83
  China: *Explorations*, 267; digital samizdat, 221, 225, 228–29, 231, 234
  as collective memoir, 3, 5
  couriers, courier routes, 57, 60–61
  Czechoslovakia: Charter 77, 15, 111, 116, 207–8, 210–11, 215, 316–17, 319, 321–25, 327, 330; Jiřina Šiklová, 290, 300; *Original Videojournal*, 15, 206–15
  definition of, 1–3, 27, 138
  dissemination/circulation of, 4, 8–9, 12–13, 18, 46, 52, 59, 62–63, 65, 72, 82, 87, 163, 190–91, 211, 265, 292, 323
  historiography of tamizdat and, 4–8, 138
  Hungary: *Beszélő*, 322
  ideas behind/in tamizdat and, 9, 13
  materiality of tamizdat and, 15, 27–28, 41, 43
  and official culture, 3, 14, 124
  Poland: drugi obieg, 52, 62; NOWa, 58, 60–61; Adam Michnik, 17, 58, 63, 102, 157–63, 165, 167, 286, 295, 297, 301–2, 322, 328–29; Mirosław Chojecki, 100–1, 63; Alexander Smolar, 160, 164; Eugeniusz Smolar, 60, 79
  and post-1989 uncensored media, 11, 15–17, 231, 237, 283, 292–3

production of, 1, 4–5, 8–9, 12, 15, 16, 19, 27, 41, 46, 52, 62, 65, 115, 117, 125, 147, 179, 185, 187, 190, 201, 206, 210–13, 222, 223–24, 227–28, 234, 237, 265, 278
and radio broadcasting, 12, 70–91, 259, 298
Romania: Petrescu, Dan, 120–26
Samizdat Review, 82
as social practice, 9, 11, 18, 27, 47, 87
and tamizdat, 1–19, 52, 63, 65, 71–72, 107, 110, 160, 163, 194, 283
tape recorders, 177–79, 182, 184
transnational system and network, 1, 10, 18, 52, 63, 65, 87, 126, 160, 163, 167, 190–91
USSR: *Chronicle of Current Events,* 80, 98, 190
Schapiro, Leonard, 85
Securitate
 methods, 112
 perceptions, 113
 See also Petrescu, Dan
self-censorship. *See* censorship
Serbia, 16, 245–46, 250–56
Sharansky, Natan, 306–307
Shelkovskij, Igor, 15, 190–201
show trials, 145–46, 148–49, 292
Signoret, Simone, 323
Šiklová, Jiřina, 290, 300
Silverstein, Michael, 182
Sina, Weibo, 263–64
Sinyavsky-Daniel trial, 93
Sinyavsky, Andrei, 52, 81, 93
Skilling, H. Gordon, 4, 16, 147, 210
Smith, Gerald Stanton, 178
Smolar, Alexander, 160, 164
Smolar, Eugeniusz, 60, 79
smuggling, 9, 56–57, 59–62, 65, 87
social media, 17, 236, 263, 264, 292–93, 299
Socialist Realism, 9, 192, 199–200
Solidarity movement (Solidarność), 52, 60–61, 63–64, 116, 166, 290, 293, 322, 324
 KOR (Workers' Defense Committee), 58, 60, 62–63, 98, 102, 116, 285, 289, 321–22

Muslim Solidarność, 281
Studencki Komitet Solidarności (Students' Solidarity Committee), 60
Wałęsa, Lech, 115
Solidarność. *See* Solidarity movement
Solzhenitsyn, Alexander, 35, 82–83, 85, 94, 97, 296, 325
Sorel, Georges, 285, 301
Sorokin, Vladimir, 230, 233
Sosin, Gene, 80, 180
Spender, Stephen, 323
Springer, Axel, 97
Stalin, Joseph, 72, 92, 140–41, 144–45, 151
Stalinism (Stalinist Terror), 14, 138, 144, 149
Stihi.ru, 233
Stoppard, Tom, 323
Strikes: Poland, 98–99, 116, 157
Suda, Zdeněk, 142
Süddeutsche Zeitung, 81
Sunday Times, 85
Surveillance, 112, 123–25, 248, 257, 271–72, 298
Svědectví (Testimony, Czech tamizdat journal), 323
Swedish connection, 57, 61–62
Święcicki, Jakub, 59–63
Syria, 286, 290, 293, 297–99, 303, 305
Szulkin, Ryszard, 59–60, 62

T
Táborský, Eduard, 142, 144
Tahrir Square, 295
tamizdat (publishing abroad)
 aesthetics of samizdat and, 6, 9
 and alternative culture, 2, 4, 14, 109, 199, 283
 archival collection of, 5, 18
 China: *Beijing Spring* and *Today* (Chinese tamizdat journals), 268
 circulation of, 6, 14, 18, 52, 63, 65, 71–73, 137, 160, 190–91, 194, 210–13, 246
 as collective memoir, 3, 5, 36
 Czechoslovakia: Videomagazine (*Videomagazín*), 15, 206–215;

Kyncl, Karel, 15, 207–09; Tigrid, Pavel, 142, 323; Pelikán, Jiří, 146, 323
definition of samizdat and, 1–3, 27, 138
and history of Stalinism, 137–55
ideas behind/in samizdat and, 9, 13
historiography of samizdat and, 4–8, 138
Hungary: *Magyar Füzetek,* 160, 323
materiality of samizdat and, 15, 27–28, 41, 43
and official culture, 3, 14, 124
Poland: *Aneks,* 56–57, 59–60, 160; *Kultura,* 13, 56–57, 92–103, 160–63, 323; Smolar, Alexander, 160, 164; Smolar, Eugeniusz, 60, 79; Swedish connection, 57, 61–62; *Hotel Örnsköld* (Polish-Swedish tamizdat journal), 65
and post-1989 uncensored media, 11, 15–17, 231, 237, 283, 292–3
production of, 2, 19, 200
and radio broadcasting, 12, 70–91, 259, 298
Romania: Petrescu, Dan, 120–26
and samizdat, 1–19, 52, 63, 65, 71–72, 107, 110, 160, 163, 194, 283
smuggling, 9, 56–57, 59–62, 65, 87
as social practice, 9, 11, 18. 27, 47, 87
tape recorders, 177–79, 182 , 184
transnational system and network, 1, 10, 18, 52, 63, 65, 87, 126, 160, 163, 167, 190–91
and Universal Copyright Convention, 43–44
USSR: Pasternak, Boris, 44, 74, 82; Orlova, Raisa, 46–47; *Doctor Zhivago,* 46, 74–75; Alexander Herzen Foundation (Amsterdam), 190; *A-Ja,* 15, 190–201; NTS, 35; Possev, 35; Karel van het Reve, 83; *Khronika Press* (New York), 80, 191; *Chronicle of Current Events,* 80, 98, 190; Ardis Publishing (Ardis publishers), 12, 27–31, 33–47, 199; Ann Arbor, 28, 40, 47; Proffer, Carl, 12, 17, 28–41,

44–47; Proffer, Ellendea, 12, 17, 28–41, 44–47; Abram Tertz, 93; Maksimov, Vladimir, 13, 94–96, 98–102; Maksimovna Litvinova, Tatiana, 99
Telesin, Julius, 228, 239
television, 15, 122, 175, 185, 206–9, 211–15, 229–30, 234, 250–51, 255–56, 258, 300, 323
terror, 14, 112, 137–39, 144, 146–51, 199, 226, 281–82, 287, 289, 290, 294, 310, 307, 329
Tertz, Abram, 93
Tešanović, Jasmina, 252–59
thaw, 140, 161, 300
The Last Days of the Tsarist Regime, 196
The Times, 72
Third Wave, 37, 191, 195, 197
Thompson, E. P., 327
Thoreau, Henry David, 284
Tiananmen, 268, 271
Tigrid, Pavel, 142, 323
Today (Jintain, Chinese samizdat journal), 267–68
Tomin, Julius, 297
torture, 148, 286, 299, 330
totalitarianism, 151, 251, 326, 328, 330
Towarzystwo Przyjaciół "Kultury" (Society of the Friends of *Kultura*), 57
trade union, 61, 64, 166, 324
Tret'javolna, 195, 200, 203
Tudou, 263
Tunisia, 289, 293, 299
Twitter, 236–37, 292

U
Ukraine, 11, 92, 94–95, 112
Ulč, Otto, 145
underground, 1, 4–7, 9–11, 14–16, 18, 52, 56, 58–62, 64–65, 72, 76–78, 81, 83–84, 98, 100–103, 108, 138–39, 157, 160, 175–77, 183–87, 194, 196–97, 201, 207–9, 211, 223–27, 246, 259, 265, 275, 278, 297
art, 15–16, 196, 246
circulation in the, 11, 176–77, 183, 185

digital, 225
literary, 5–6, 9–10, 72, 80
United Arab Emirates, 290
United Nations, 291, 296
United States, 29, 37, 44, 59, 72, 77, 86–87, 109, 123–24, 139–40, 149, 157, 159, 177, 179, 196, 211, 213, 231, 263, 274, 282, 288, 295, 301, 304–5, 307–8, 329
unofficial culture, 3, 323
unofficial art, 15, 190, 192–200, 209
unofficial media, 15, 176–77, 186
Unpublished Works of Soviet Authors, 82
US Congress, 73, 141, 274
Union of Soviet Socialist Republics (USSR)
audience/readership in the, 29
avtorskaia pesnia, 14, 176
censorship in, 44–45
Chronicle of Current Events, 80, 98, 190
collapse of, 140
Daniel, Yuli, 52, 93
de-Stalinization, 140, 157, 161
dissidents in, 13–15, 98, 176, 180
Doctor Zhivago, 46, 74–75
Galich, Aleksandr, 180–82
Glazkov, Nikolaj, 227
Gorbachev, Mikhail, 114, 116, 194
Gorbanevskaya, Natalya, 13, 95–102
invasion of Czechoslovakia, 113, 116, 212, 301, 305, 319, 320, 322, 324
invasion of Hungary, 10, 71, 73, 77, 79, 115, 116, 117, 121, 143, 147–50, 157, 286, 318, 322, 330
Khronika Press (New York), 80, 191
Kopelev, Lev, 34
magnitizdat in, 14–15, 175–77, 179–80, 182–87
Mandel'shtam, Nadezhda, 34
Mandel'shtam, Osip, 30, 34–35, 38, 45, 47
and new Russian samizdat, 224
origination of samizdat, 10
Pasternak, Boris, 44, 74 ,82
perestroika, 20, 121, 222, 229
post-perestroika, 229

post-Soviet digital samizdat and, 227–30, 232–35
Pravda, 83
Proffer, Carl, 12, 17, 28–41, 44–47
Proffer, Ellendea, 12, 17, 28–41, 44–47
Putin, Vladimir, 229, 230, 233, 235, 237
radio broadcasting in, 81
samizdat in. *See* samizdat
Sinyavsky-Daniel trial, 93
Sinyavsky, Andrei, 52, 81, 93
Solzhenitsyn, Alexander, 35, 82–83, 85, 94, 97, 296, 325
Stalin, Joseph, 72, 92, 140–41, 144–45, 151
Stalinism (Stalinist Terror), 14, 138, 144, 149
tamizdat from. *See* tamizdat
Tertz, Abram, 93
thaw, 140, 161, 300
transnational networks beyond frontiers of the, 1, 15, 31, 34, 39, 98–99
Universal Copyright Convention, 44
Unpublished Works of Soviet Authors, 82
Vysotsky, Vladimir, 175–77, 180, 185, 187
Zamoyska, Helena, 93

V
Vaculík, Ludvík, 146, 297
Vajda, Mihály, 163
Vasil'ev, Oleg, 198–99
Velvet Revolution (Czechoslovakia 1989), 209–10, 215, 317, 319, 328–29
Venice Biennale, 199
Verbickij, Michail, 226, 231–32, 234
video, 14–15, 206–215, 235, 250, 264, 293, 295, 299
Videomagazine (*Videomagazín*), 15, 206–15
Vietnam, 282, 324
virtual communities, 283, 292
Visegrad countries, 10
Voice of America (VOA), 70, 72, 79, 80, 115, 121, 123

Vorob'ev, Kirill (pseudonym Bajan Širjanov), 229–30
Vysotsky, Vladimir, 175–77, 180, 185, 187

W
Wałęsa, Lech, 115
Wang Xiaoning, 270
War on terror, 282, 329
Warsaw, 54–58, 76, 81, 95, 98–99, 109, 113, 158–59, 162, 212, 294, 324, 328
Weffort, Francisco C., 163
Więź (Polish Catholic weekly), 160
Wolfe Jancar, Barbara, 146–47
World War I, 35, 299
World War II, 57, 94, 144, 206, 305, 324

Y
Yahoo, 270–71
Yearbook of Poles Abroad, 78
Yemen, 290, 293
Youku, 263
YouTube, 263, 299
YuHua, 277
YuLuoke, 267
Yugoslavia, 10–11, 246, 251, 253–55

Z
Żaba, Norbert, 57, 59, 61
Zagozdat, Andrzej, 160
Zakharov, Vadim, 197, 201
Zamoyska, Helena, 93
Zamoyski, August, 93
Zamyatin, Yevgeny, 317
Zhang Yimou, 277
Zhao Jing, 274
Zine el-Abidine Ben Ali, 289

www.ingramcontent.com/pod-product-compliance
Lightning Source LLC
Chambersburg PA
CBHW072142100526
44589CB00015B/2046